300

S0-BRC-131

Bernard C. Baumbach

PURE SOCIOLOGY

PURE SOCIOLOGY

A Treatise

ON THE ORIGIN AND SPONTANEOUS DEVELOPMENT OF SOCIETY

BY

LESTER F. WARD

PROFESSOR OF SOCIOLOGY IN BROWN UNIVERSITY, AUTHOR OF
"DYNAMIC SOCIOLOGY," "THE PSYCHIC FACTORS OF
CIVILIZATION," "OUTLINES OF SOCIOLOGY,"
"APPLIED SOCIOLOGY"

SECOND EDITION

New York
THE MACMILLAN COMPANY
LONDON: MACMILLAN & CO., LTD.
1914

Norwood Press
J. S. Cushing & Co. — Berwick & Smith Co.
Norwood, Mass., U.S.A.

I DEDICATE THIS BOOK

TO

𝕿𝖍𝖊 𝕿𝖜𝖊𝖓𝖙𝖎𝖊𝖙𝖍 𝕮𝖊𝖓𝖙𝖚𝖗𝖞

ON THE FIRST DAY OF WHICH

IT WAS BEGUN

PREFACE TO THE SECOND EDITION

EXACTLY six years ago, to wit, on the first day of the twentieth century, I invited a small company of the *élite* of the National Capital to meet me and lend their valued counsel in considering the scheme which I laid before them for a system of sociology, and especially in advising me as to the proper designation of such a system. The persons thus invited were: Major J. W. Powell, Director of the United States Geological Survey and of the Bureau of American Ethnology; the Hon. David Jayne Hill, Assistant Secretary of State; the Hon. William T. Harris, United States Commissioner of Education; the Hon. Carroll D. Wright, United States Commissioner of Labor and Superintendent of the Tenth Census; Dr. Frank Baker, Superintendent of the National Zoölogical Park; Mr. W. F. Willoughby, now Treasurer of Porto Rico; Mr. Edward T. Peters of the Department of Agriculture; Messrs. David Hutcheson and Roland P. Falkner of the Library of Congress; Mr. Henry F. Blount, manufacturer and banker; and Miss Sarah E. Simons, Head of the English Department of the Washington High Schools. After free discussion and mature deliberation it was decided that the system should consist of two volumes, as far as possible independent of each other, the first to be entitled Pure Sociology and the second Applied Sociology, and the title-pages of these volumes were drawn up.

Slightly more than two years from that date, namely, on February 18, 1903, the first of these volumes appeared, and in a little over three years more, that is to say, on July 2, 1906, the second of the volumes saw the light. To-day the world is calling for a second edition of the first.

Although some of the positions taken in that work were very advanced, and were set forth rather as hypotheses inviting criticism than as established science, and although these questions have been discussed at length by many of the ablest writers of the age, none of the new theories advanced can be said to have been overthrown and many of them have been greatly strengthened. It is therefore too early at least to undertake any extensive revision of the work. Indeed, as I have often said, the works of an author constitute a history of the development of his mind and even of that of the ideas themselves, and any attempt to revise them beyond the correction of positive errors destroys the continuity of those ideas and brings confusion into philosophy. Who, for example, does not regret that Kant was compelled to revise his "Kritik der Reinen Vernunft"? and who could be satisfied with the revised editions alone? The present work must therefore stand for the time being substantially as it was originally penned.

The purpose of this preface must, therefore, chiefly be to draw attention to the fact that the system has been completed as originally outlined, and as the little scrap of its history here introduced was omitted in the preface to the first edition, it seems proper to give it at this time, not only for the sake of the history itself, perhaps of a rather unimportant event, but also as an acknowledgment due from the author to those persons in whom he confided what was at the time, in view of various contingencies, practically a secret. One of those persons whose judgment was most valued has passed off the scene, but his judgment still stands and is embodied in the work, and the author's sense of indebtedness to them all has continued to increase.

If this were the proper place, the phenomenal progress of sociology and of the entire class of ideas and public activities in the field of social science and social progress during the period that has elapsed since the conception of this work might be profitably discussed, but this is known to all, and no claim is made that the system of sociology of which it forms a part is anything more than a product of the *Zeitgeist*, although, like every other such product, it may have exerted its normal reciprocal influence, and may be in some small degree a cause as well as an effect.

L. F. W.

BROWN UNIVERSITY, PROVIDENCE, R.I.,
January 1, 1907.

PREFACE

I MAKE no claim to priority in the use of the term *pure sociology*. It is but natural that those who regard sociology as a science should divide the science, as other sciences are divided, into the two natural departments, pure and applied. But as the term "pure sociology" has been freely used for several years by certain European sociologists, it seems proper to explain that the matter for this work has been accumulating in my hands for many years. I should perhaps rather say that sociological material has been long pouring in upon me, and that the first classification that was made of it was into such as related to the origin, nature, and genetic or spontaneous development of society, and such as related to means and methods for the artificial improvement of social conditions on the part of man and society as conscious and intelligent agents. The first of these classes I naturally called pure sociology, the second, applied sociology.

It was upon my notes as thus classified that in 1897 I delivered two courses of lectures before the Summer School of the University of Chicago, one on Pure Sociology and the other on Applied Sociology. These two courses of lectures under the same titles, but with ever increasing volume of data, I repeated in 1898 at the University of West Virginia, and in 1899 at Leland Stanford Junior University. I think I can therefore justly claim the right, after three years more of research along the same lines, to give to the work in which the first of these classes of materials is systematically elaborated the title of Pure Sociology which I have always applied to that class, and should I succeed in systematically collating the materials of the second class and in reducing them to a suitable form for publication, I shall crave permission to give to them for like reasons the title Applied Sociology.

All the more does it seem advisable to call this work Pure Sociology, because the use that is being made of that term by the sociologists referred to is much narrower than my conception of the science, and practically limited to the application of mathematics to the phenomena of society. I cannot accept such limitations, but must regard all social phenomena as *pure* which are unaffected by the purposeful efforts of man and of society itself. That is, there must be only the two great branches of the science, the pure and the applied, and pure sociology must be made broad enough to embrace everything which cannot be brought under applied sociology, using the term *applied* in strict analogy with its use in other sciences. Hence I have employed a secondary title: The Origin and Spontaneous Development of Society. I wish to lay special emphasis on the word *spontaneous* in this title, as embodying my conception of pure sociology. Whatever is spontaneous *is* pure in this sense. Its two other chief synonyms are "genetic" and "natural" as opposed to "telic" and "artificial." Still, as the telic faculty is itself a genetic product, it cannot be omitted from a treatment of pure sociology, and, as I have shown, its manifestations are in one sense as strictly spontaneous as are those of the dynamic agent.

I will add that the present work is wholly independent of all my previous works, and is in no sense a résumé or condensation of them. While necessarily some of the same ground has been traversed, this is always done for an entirely different purpose and the subjects are viewed from a different angle of vision. But the greater part of all that the work contains is not to be found in my other works nor in any of my previous writings. More vital still is the fact that the purpose and essential character of the work are wholly different from those of any of the others. I am now aiming at a System of Sociology, and should the volume on Applied Sociology be written, the two volumes will practically constitute such a system. This, be it said, is without prejudice to other systems, all of which I recognize and respect, and none of which is at all in conflict with the system which I prefer and adopt.

L. F. W.

WASHINGTON, August 22, 1902.

CONTENTS

PART I. — TAXIS

PART II. — GENESIS

PART III.—TELESIS

PART I

TAXIS

CHAPTER I

GENERAL CHARACTERISTICS OF PURE SOCIOLOGY

THE terms *pure* and *applied* may be used in sociology in the same sense as in other sciences. Pure science is theoretical, applied science practical. The first seeks to establish the principles of the science, the second points out their actual or possible applications. It is in this sense simply that I shall use the terms. Whatever further explanation may be necessary will be due to the special character of sociology as a science.

The titles of the chapters, and especially the names I have given to the three parts into which this work is divided, sufficiently attest the theoretical character of the work. The first part deals with the order or arrangement of sociological data; the remainder of the work deals with their origin and nature, first from the standpoint of nature, and then from the standpoint of intelligent beings.

In view of the flood of sociological literature in our time, notwithstanding the extreme youth of the science, it would be presumptuous to hope to contribute anything absolutely new. Even in the seventeenth century, La Bruyère thought that he had come into the world too late to produce anything new, that nature and life were preoccupied, and that description and sentiment had been long exhausted. And yet, throughout the eighteenth century men continued to thrash literary straw most vigorously. But although the age of literature as an end has passed, and we are living in the age of science, and although in many sciences new truth is being daily brought to light, still, such is the nature of sociology, that this is not true of it unless we understand by truth, as we certainly may, the discovery of new relations. So far as any other meaning of truth is concerned, I have probably already offered the most that I possess, and the chief task that now confronts me is that of endeavoring to organize the facts of sociology, and to bring them together into something like a system. I shall not therefore apologize for the restatement of facts or principles, assuming that the reader will

3

realize that it is done for a different object from any that I have
formerly had in view.

A logically organized system of sociology thus necessarily becomes
a philosophy. Not that it is a speculation, which would imply that
it abandoned the domain of fact, but from the very wealth of facts
which such a highly complex science necessarily inherits from the
entire series of simpler sciences, its proper treatment demands deep
plunges into those domains in order to discover and trace out the
roots of social phenomena. The method of pure science is research,
and its object is knowledge. In pure sociology the essential nature
of society is the object pursued. But nothing can be said to be
known until the antecedent conditions are known, out of which it
has sprung. Existing facts must be interpreted in the light of past
processes, and developed products must be explained through their
embryonic stages and phyletic ancestors. This is as true of social
structures as of organic structures. It is this filiation, this historical development, this progressive evolution, that renders sociology such an all-embracing field, and which makes its proper
treatment so laborious, and at the same time so interesting. It is
this, also, that brings contempt upon it when its treatment is
attempted by those who are not equipped for the task.

By pure sociology, then, is meant a treatment of the phenomena
and laws of society as it is, an explanation of the processes by which
social phenomena take place, a search for the antecedent conditions
by which the observed facts have been brought into existence, and
an ætiological diagnosis that shall reach back as far as the state of
human knowledge will permit into the psychologic, biologic, and
cosmic causes of the existing social state of man. But it must be
a pure diagnosis, and all therapeutic treatment is rigidly excluded.
All ethical considerations, in however wide a sense that expression
may be understood, must be ignored for the time being, and attention concentrated upon the effort to determine what actually is.
Pure sociology has no concern with what society *ought* to be, or
with any social ideals. It confines itself strictly with the present
and the past, allowing the future to take care of itself. It totally
ignores the purpose of the science, and aims at truth wholly for its
own sake.

A fortiori the pure method of treatment keeps aloof from all criticism and all expressions of approval, from all praise or blame, as

wholly inapplicable to that which exists of necessity. Auguste Comte, in one of his early essays, 1822, reflects the true spirit of pure science in the following words : —

Admiration and disapprobation should be banished with equal severity from all positive science, since every preoccupation of this kind has for its direct and inevitable effect to impede or divert examination. Astronomers, physicists, chemists, and physiologists do not admire, neither do they blame, their respective phenomena ; they observe them.[1]

Gumplowicz has put the same thought into the following form : —

Sociology must necessarily abstain from criticising nature. It is only interested in the facts and their regular occurrence. From the sociological point of view there is no ground for asking whether things could not have been other than they are, or whether they could not have been better, for social phenomena are necessarily derived from human nature and the nature of human relations.[2]

This strictly objective treatment also necessitates the looking of facts in the face, however ugly they may be. It is no more the part of pure sociology to apologize for the facts, than to extol or condemn them. Still less can it afford to deny what really exists, or attempt to minimize it or explain it away, merely because it is abhorrent to certain refined perceptions of highly developed races. Such a remark may seem like a truism, but nothing is more certain than that every scientific truth which has at first seemed repugnant to man, has had to be established against powerful opposition, often from eminent men of science in the domain to which it belonged, growing out of nothing but the wholly unscientific aversion to admitting its possibility — the desire to defend the race from the supposed humiliation of such an admission.

Nor does this strict adherence to the facts of nature involve, as certain prominent philosophers seem to suppose, a defense of nature's methods as necessarily the best possible, and their commendation as patterns and models for men to copy and follow. To do this is to violate the canon of pure science : *nil admirari*. This sort of scientific nature-worship, besides not being really scientific in its spirit, is pernicious as promulgating a false doctrine that applied sociology readily disproves, but which, if it becomes current,

[1] "Plan des travaux scientifiques nécessaires pour réorganiser la société." Reprinted as Appendix to Vol. IV of the "Système de Politique Positive," 1853, p. 114.
[2] "Précis de Sociologie," Paris, 1896, p. 222.

as it seemed at one time to be likely to do, takes its place among the erroneous *Weltanschauungen* that have one after another stood in the path of human progress.

We cannot too strongly emphasize the paradox that pure science really rests on *faith*. "Faith," as Dr. Starcke puts it, " that causation is universal." [1] Faith not only that all effects have causes but also that all causes have effects; faith that whatever is is worthy, and that whatever is worth being is worth knowing; and finally faith, since this cannot be wholly suppressed, that some beneficial result will follow the discovery of truth. But this faith need not go so far as to become anthropocentric and optimistic, so as to divert the investigator from the single pursuit of truth and carry him off in a vain search for the supposed necessary uses of facts or for strained analogies and imaginary harmonies.

Another reef to be shunned is the notion that was formerly quite prevalent and which is still continually coming into view, that science consists in the discovery of facts. There is not a single science of which this is true, and a much more nearly correct definition would be that science consists in reasoning about facts. This is perhaps best illustrated in geology, where the facts — rocks — are infinitely older than human history or the human race, and most of them have stared the world in the face throughout all ages, but were never *known* till men began to reason about them and interpret them. But the truth comes nearer home in the more practical sciences like physics and chemistry. The forces of nature and the properties of substances have always existed, but they were of comparatively little use until the age of experimentation which involves the closest reasoning. The electricity that lights our houses and propels our cars was here all the time, and could just as well have been used two thousand or four thousand years ago as now, if any one had thought out and worked out its true nature, as has so recently been done.

The term *pure sociology* has been used considerably of late in the sense of regarding it as an exact science. In this it is usually attempted to reduce its laws to mathematical principles, to deduce equations and draw curves expressing those laws. The best work

---

[1] *Revue Internationale de Sociologie*, janvier, 1898, p. 17. Compare also the address of Andrew D. White at the farewell banquet to Professor Tyndall, *Pop. Sci. Monthly*, Vol. II, April, 1873, pp. 736–739.

of this kind has been done in the domain of economics by men like Cournot, Gossen, Jevons, and Walras, but most of these laws are in a proper sense sociological, and have a far-reaching significance for sociology. I fully recognize the importance of such studies, but I shall only thus briefly mention them in this chapter, deferring the full treatment of so fundamental a subject to the chapter on Methodology (Chapter IV), under which head I class it.

CHAPTER II

ESTABLISHMENT OF THE SCIENCE

I DO not claim that sociology has as yet been established as a science. I only maintain that it is in process of establishment, and this by the same method by which all other sciences are established. Every independent thinker has his system. It is always based on some one leading idea or unitary principle which binds all its parts together, and this principle is the chief matter with the author. The system constitutes a means of thoroughly illustrating his ruling idea. This is not only true of sociology but of all systems of philosophy. This is as it should be, and illustrates the march of ideas and the progress of science in general.

How Science Advances

It will be well to pause a moment and consider this question of how science advances. The progress of science is no even straightforward march. It is in the highest degree irregular and fitful. And yet there is a certain method in it. It is the work of a vast army of workers, and each individual works more or less independently. Scarcely any two are working at exactly the same thing, and when they are their individual peculiarities, their differences of training, and their different environments are certain to render the product different. The history of scientific research in any one of the great fields of investigation is an interesting subject for analysis. Even in astronomy there is great diversity, but especially in laboratory research, as in physics, chemistry, and biology, is this feature made prominent. Whether it relates to the law of gravitation, to the nature of sound, to spectrum analysis, to the different kinds of rays, to the properties of the various substances and gases, to the formation of chemical compounds, including the complex organic compounds, to the study of protoplasm, to the investigation of cells and unicellular organisms, to the origin of tissues and their distribution in the metazoan body, to the phenomena of reproduc-

8

tion, or to the nature and functions of nerves and of the brain, — whatever the field may be, the general method of all earnest scientific research is the same. Every investigator chooses some special line and pushes his researches forward along that line as far as his facilities and his powers will permit. If he is a master, he soon exhausts the resources and appliances of the libraries and laboratories and proceeds to construct a technique of his own for his special purposes. He observes and experiments and records the results. Whenever important results are reached, he publishes them. He not only publishes the results, but he describes his methods. He tells the world not only what he has found, but how he found it.

If the results thus announced are at all novel or startling, others working along similar lines immediately take them up, criticise them, and make every effort to disprove them. Working under somewhat different conditions, with different subjects or specimens and different tools, and possessing different personal peculiarities of mind and character, some of these rivals are certain to bring out something new. Part of the results claimed by the first investigator will be disproved or shown to bear a different interpretation from that given them. Part of them will probably stand the fire and after repeated verification be admitted by all. These represent the permanent advance made in that particular science. But no one investigator can establish anything. Nothing is established until it has passed through this ordeal of general criticism and repeated verification from the most adverse points of view.

Now, each one of the many workers is doing the same thing as the one here considered, only every one chooses a different line and pushes his researches out in a different direction. Thus a thousand lines of research are projected into the unknown from every field of scientific investigation. There is little or no attempt to coördinate the new facts. They have a linear connection with the series of antecedent facts pursued by each, but they do not anastomose, so to speak, with the similar lines run out by others. Nevertheless, ultimately some of the earlier proximal points that have been verified and established will spontaneously become associated and correlated, forming a sort of web between the bases of the lines, which later become the accepted boundary of the established science. Finally the synthetic mind comes forward and performs the work of coördination, to be followed by the text-book writer, who more or less successfully puts the science in the way of social appropriation.

Such is the apparently desultory and haphazard, but really methodical way in which all science advances. True, it is crude and primitive. It is not at all economical, but extremely wasteful in energy and effort. It is a typical method of nature as distinguished from the telic method or method of foresight and intelligence, but it accomplishes its purpose and has given us all the established truth we possess. I have sometimes compared it to the way in which certain shore lines are formed on coasts that are slowly rising, especially in regions where a retreating ice sheet has done its part of the work. If you will glance at a map of the west coast of Scotland, of the east coast of Nova Scotia, or of the south shores of Maine, you will understand this comparison. These shores consist of innumerable tongues of land projecting into the sea, separated by friths or inlets and wider bays. These inlets formerly extended much farther into the land, but the peninsulas had then only begun to form. As the land rose, their bases, which were then much farther inland, gradually coalesced to form the main coast, while the ridges between the furrows plowed by the ice emerged from the water in the form of tongues such as we now see. These may be conceived as being thrust out from the shore something after the analogy of the lines of scientific research that I have described, uniting at their bases to form a permanent domain. Even the islands, of which there are many, have their counterparts in those isolated discoveries of science, like the Röntgen rays, which seem for a time like islands in the sea of the unknown.

Another favorite comparison of mine, and one with the subject of which I am personally more familiar than I am with seacoasts, is with the progress of a prairie fire, such as used to sweep across the mainly treeless grassy plains of northern Iowa. With a front of ten to twenty miles such a fire would advance at the rate of five to ten miles an hour, consuming everything in its way. But the line of flame, which could be distinctly traced, especially in the night, to a great distance by the eye, was never straight, but in consequence of certain checks at one point and specially favorable conditions at another, it would present great irregularities. Long tongues of fire would be seen projecting far in advance of the main line, leaving narrow unburned tracts between them, and every other conceivable form of indentation and irregularity would mark the boundary of the advancing conflagration. In fact this would have a great resemblance to the coasts I have referred to. Occasional sparks carried far in advance by the high wind which the fire alone was capable of generating, would ignite the grass some distance from the point from which it emanated, and temporary islands would be quickly created. But if any one spot be watched, all these separate projections would be seen soon to join and the wider sinuses to be swept along until the whole area in question was completely consumed and the same scene of operations transferred to a point far in advance where the same process was being repeated, and so on indefinitely. The whole country behind these rapidly advancing scenes would be black, the devouring flames not being prevented by any of their erratic performances from ultimately compassing their design. We thus have a kinetographic representation, as it were, of the general method of nature in the march of evolution, the difference between this and the previous illustration being that while this goes on before the eyes almost more rapidly than it can be described, the other is a slow secular process that cannot be observed in operation, but can only be interpreted by the geologist from the facts that he can see and recognize as having themselves recorded their own history.

The progress of discovery, of science, and of knowledge and truth in the world generally, follows this same method, whatever department we may examine. The effect of it is to give the impression during the early stages in the history of any science, that all is chaos, and that no real progress is being made. Every one is making claims for his own results and denying those of all others, so that the mere looker-on and the public at large are led to doubt that anything is being accomplished. They see only the main land of established truth and deny that the sea bottom is rising and that the promontories and islands are being united to the continent. Like the Indians of the Pacific slope who admitted that the grass grew, but denied that the great Sequoias had ever been other than they are, the world perceives the movement of events on the surface of society — political, economic, industrial — but denies that there is a great social movement which is becoming slowly crystallized into a science.

Just at present we are in that initial stage in sociology, in which a great army of really honest and earnest workers is wholly without organization — an army, it might be called, all the members of which are officers having the same rank, and none subject to the commands of any other. Each one is pursuing the one particular line that he has chosen. Nearly every one has some one single thought which he believes to embrace, when seen as he sees it, the whole field of sociology, and he is elaborating that idea to the utmost. Now, it is clear that he will make much more of that idea than any one else could make. He will get all the truth out of it that it contains. It is true that he will carry it too far and weight it down with implications that it will not bear; but these are, like the errors of all scientific investigators, subject to universal criticism and ultimate rejection by putting the real truth in their place.

The notion has always been prevalent that men of one idea are useless or worse than useless. The fact is that they are the most useful of all men. I do not refer to such as are afflicted with the pathological *idée fixe*, but to those who are, as it were, possessed and consumed by some single thought, some favorite hypothesis, some heuristic conception, which grows larger and more all-comprehensive, until it impels them to pursue it untiringly to its last logical conclusion and to work into it great fields of truth that no name that can be given it would even suggest to any one else. Work done under such an inspiration is thoroughly done. The analysis is exhaustive, and it never fails, notwithstanding the necessary error and exaggeration, to constitute a substantial contribution to the general stock of human knowledge and to the true progress of science.

Systems of Sociology

All sciences pass through a long analytic period before reaching the synthetic stage. Sociology is still in its analytic period. There is even a disposition to condemn all attempts at synthesis. No one will recognize anything done by others. There is a spirit of intense individualism. There is no disposition to appropriate the truth that is being produced. The ideas that are put forth seem to have no affinity for one another. On the contrary they are mutually repellent. There is little real controversy because every one regards all other ideas as quite unworthy of attention. There is therefore no discussion, and the necessary prelude to coördination is discussion.

When different writers shall begin to discuss one another's ideas there will be some hope of an ultimate basis being found for agreement, however narrow that basis may be.

In this perfectly independent way a large number of what may be called systems of sociology are being built up, most of which are regarded by their authors as complete, and as superseding all other systems. Any attempt adequately to present all these systems to the reader would require a volume instead of a chapter. This has, however, already been done in great part and ably by Professor Paul Barth[1] in the introduction to a work whose title indicates that he has himself a system, but who differs from most of his contemporaries in not only respecting but also in understanding other systems.

I also undertook an enumeration of the principal systems of sociology from my own special point of view, which was originally intended to be embodied in this chapter, but the treatment of a dozen of these, brief though it had to be, attained so great volume that I decided to publish it separately[2] and content myself with this reference to it, should any desire to consult it. This I can do the better as the present work cannot be historical, and as there is certainly enough to be said in illustration of my own "system" without devoting space to the consideration of those of others. But each of these twelve leading sociological conceptions or unitary principles has been put forward with large claims to being in and of itself the science of sociology. The ones selected for treatment in the papers referred to were considered as embodying in each case the idea entertained by the principal defender or expounder of the principle, or by the group of persons advocating it and thus constituting in each case a sort of school, of what constitutes the science. The principles were therefore preceded by the expression "Sociology as " in analogy to Professor Barth's title: "Sociology as the Philosophy of History." Thus designated, these unitary principles, forming the basis of so many systems or schools of sociology, were the following: —

---

[1] "Die Philosophie der Geschichte als Sociologie." Erster Theil : Einleitung und kritische Uebersicht, Leipzig, 1897.

[2] "Contemporary Sociology." *American Journal of Sociology*, Vol. VII, Chicago, 1902, No. 4, January, pp. 475–500 ; No. 5, March, pp. 629–658; No. 6, May, pp. 749–762. Reprinted as brochure, Chicago, 1902, pp. 70.

Sociology as : —

     I. Philanthropy.
    II. Anthropology.
   III. Biology (the organic theory).
   IV. Political Economy.
    V. Philosophy of History.
   VI. The Special Social Sciences.
  VII. The Description of Social Facts.
VIII. Association.
   IX. The Division of Labor.
    X. Imitation.
   XI. Unconscious Social Constraint.
  XII. The Struggle of Races.

There are of course others, but these may be taken at least as typical examples if not as the principal ones now confronting the student of sociology. Any one of these views might be, and most of them have been, set forth in such a form that, considered alone, it would seem to justify the claim set up. This enumeration is calculated to afford to the unbiased mind something like an adequate conception of the scope of sociology, for no single one of these conceptions is to be rejected. All are legitimate parts of the science, and there are many more equally weighty that remain as yet more or less unperceived. A comprehensive view of them will also illustrate the law set forth at the beginning of this chapter relating to the manner in which not only social science but all science advances. To change the figure there used, all these various lines, together with all others that have been or shall be followed out, may be compared to so many minor streams, all tending in a given direction and converging so as ultimately to unite in one great river that represents the whole science of sociology as it will be finally established.

CHAPTER III

THE SUBJECT-MATTER OF SOCIOLOGY

THE reader will probably say, after reading this chapter, that I have added another to the dozen systems of sociology enumerated in Chapter II. I shall not demur to this. But he will remember that I have not disparaged the multiplications of systems, provided they are based on a real idea. It is the only way in which the science can advance, and the more ideas thus exhaustively worked out, the broader and richer the science will become. The conceptions thus marshaled are sufficiently dissimilar and varied, but I think it will be admitted that the additional one now to be set forth is different still from any of them, and as unlike them as they are unlike one another.

My thesis is that the subject-matter of sociology is human *achievement*. It is not what men are, but what they do. It is not the structure, but the function. Sociologists are nearly all working in the department of social anatomy, when they should turn their attention to social physiology. Most of them have imbibed the false notion that physiology is dynamic, and is in some way connected with social progress. They scarcely dare inquire what social physiology is, for fear that it may involve them in questions of social reform. But physiology is merely function. It is what structures and organs do, what they were made to do, the only purpose they have. Structures and organs are only means. Function is the end. It is therefore easy to see how much more important physiology is than anatomy. The latter is, of course, a necessary study, since functions cannot be performed without organs; but it is in the nature of preparation, and can be relegated to one or other of the special social sciences, which, as I have shown, supply the data for the study of sociology. The principal sources of such data are history, demography, anthropology, psychology, biology, civics, and economics; but all the sciences contribute to that highest science, social physiology.

15

To be less technical, but really repeat the same thing, sociology is concerned with social *activities*. It is a study of action, *i.e.*, of *phenomena*. It is not a descriptive science in the naturalist's sense — a science that describes objects looked upon as finished products. It is rather a study of how the various social products have been created. These products once formed become permanent. They are never lost. They may be slowly modified and perfected, but they constitute the basis for new products, and so on indefinitely. Viewed from the evolutionary standpoint, the highest types of men stand on an elevated platform which man and nature working together have erected in the long course of ages. This is not only true of our time, but it has been true of all times. The most advanced of any age stand on the shoulders, as it were, of those of the preceding age; only with each succeeding age the platform is raised a degree higher. The platforms of previous ages become the steps in the great staircase of civilization, and these steps remain unmoved, and are perpetuated by human history.

Or, to change the figure, the human polyp is perpetually building a coral reef, on the upper surface of which the last generation lives and builds. The generations live and die, but they leave behind them the result of all that they accomplished when living. This result is a permanent part of the great ocean bed of human achievement. As time goes on these successive additions, superimposed the one upon the other, form the bed-rock of civilization. They become lithified, as it were, and constitute the strata of the psychozoic age of the world, through which the true historian, like the geologist, cuts his sections and lays bare in profile the successive stages of human culture.

It is this fact of permanent human achievement that makes the broad distinction between animal and human societies. Just as there is a radical difference between cosmic and organic evolution,[1] so there is a radical difference between organic and social evolution. The formula that expresses this distinction the most clearly is that *the environment transforms the animal, while man transforms the environment.* Now it is exactly this transformation

---

[1] I brought out this distinction as long ago as 1877 in an article on "Cosmic and Organic Evolution," in the *Popular Science Monthly* for October, 1877, Vol. XI, pp. 672–682, in which I showed that even Mr. Spencer had ignored it in his profound analysis of the laws of the redistribution of matter.

of the environment that constitutes achievement. The animal achieves nothing. The organic world is passive. It is acted upon by the environment and adapted to it. And although it is true that in the structural modifications that constitute such adaptation the efforts and activities of the organism play a prominent part, still even this is only a reflex response to the pressure from without, and really constitutes a part of the environment. Man, on the contrary, as a psychically developed being, and in increasing degrees in proportion to his psychic development, is active and assumes the initiative, molding nature to his own use.

There has been no important organic change in man during the historic period. The trifling physical differences which we attribute to differences of environment acting on man during a century or two, would have no diagnostic value in biology. He is no more fleet of foot, keen of vision, or strong in muscle and tendon than he was when Herodotus wrote. Yet his power of vision has been enormously increased by all the applications of the lens, his power of locomotion has been multiplied by the invention of propelling machines, and his strength has become almost unlimited by calling the forces of nature to his assistance. Tools are vastly more effective than teeth or claws. The telescope and the microscope completely dwarf all natural organs of sight. Railroads are fair substitutes for wings, and steamships for fins. In the electric transmission of thought across continents and seas he has developed an organ of which no animal possesses a rudiment. Yet all this is less practically useful than the increased means of production that have resulted from a long series of inventions. It is all the result of man's power to transform the environment. The artificial modification of natural phenomena is the great characteristic fact in human activity. It is what constitutes achievement. No animal is capable of it. Some superficial observers seem to see in the nests of birds, the dams of beavers, the honeycomb of bees, and the various more or less complicated habitations of certain rodents and other animals, an analogy to the achievements of man. But these all lack the essential element of permanence. They cannot be called artificial, and it is their artificial character that distinguishes the results of human activity. The principle here involved will be dealt with in Chapter XVII.

It is necessary to inquire here what in reality constitutes civiliza-

c

tion. We have not in the English language the same distinction
between civilization and culture that exists in the German language.
Certain ethnologists affect to make the distinction, but they are not
understood by the public.   The German expression *Kulturgeschichte*
is nearly equivalent to the English expression history of civilization.
Yet they are not synonymous, since the German term is confined to
the material conditions, while the English expression may and usually
does include psychic, moral, and spiritual phenomena.   To translate
the German *Kultur* we are obliged to say material civilization.
Culture in English has come to mean something entirely different,
corresponding to the humanities.   But *Kultur* also relates to the
arts of savages and barbaric peoples, which are not included in any
use of civilization, since that term in itself denotes a stage of advancement higher than savagery or barbarism.   These stages are even
popularly known as stages of culture, where the word *culture* becomes
nearly synonymous with the German *Kultur*.

To repeat again the definition that I formulated twenty years ago:
*material civilization consists in the utilization of the materials and forces
of nature.*   It is, however, becoming more and more apparent that
the spiritual part of civilization is at least conditioned upon material
civilization.   It does not derogate from its worth to admit that
without a material basis it cannot exist.   But it is also true that the
moment such a basis is supplied, it comes forth in all ages and races
of men.   It may therefore be regarded as innate in man and potential
everywhere, but a flower so delicate that it can only bloom in the
rich soil of material prosperity.   As such it does not need to be
specially fostered.   No amount of care devoted to it alone could
make it flourish in the absence of suitable conditions, and with such
conditions it requires no special attention.   It may therefore be dismissed from our considerations, and our interest may be centered in
the question of material civilization, and this will be understood
without the use of the adjective.

As examples of the forces that are utilized in civilization, stated
in something like the historical order of their use, may be mentioned
heat, light, gravitation, wind, water, steam, and electricity.   The
value of water as a power is in its weight, so that this is only one of
the many applications of gravitation.   More difficult to class, but
perhaps earlier than any other, is the power of inertia in ponderable
matter by which, even in the club, it is made to increase the efficiency

of the unaided hands. Still more subtle, but immensely effective, is the use of the principle of the lever and fulcrum, by which effects are rendered vastly greater than the muscular force exerted. These are only a few of the most obvious of nature's powers which man learned to profit by. Of materials or substances, the simplest were wood, clay, stone, and the metals as fast as means were discovered of separating them from their ores. The reason why bronze (copper) antedates iron is that it more frequently occurs in a pure state, for it is much less abundant. Aluminum, perhaps the most abundant of all metals, was among the last to be utilized, solely because so difficult to obtain in a pure state. After these came the multitudinous chemical substances, elementary and composite, that are now applied to innumerable uses.

The distinction, however, between materials and forces disappears entirely upon analysis. It is no longer metaphysical to say that we know nothing of matter except through its properties. It is only its reactions that affect man's senses, only its properties that are utilized. But no line of demarcation can be drawn between the properties of matter and physical forces. Properties are forces and forces are properties. At bottom, it is simply activities with which we have to do. It is now known that all matter is active, and the only difference between substances is the different ways in which they act. Of course these differences in activity are due to corresponding differences in constitution, but this need not concern us. But if matter is only known by its properties, and the properties of matter are forces, it follows that matter possesses inherent powers. Schopenhauer was right when he said: "Die Materie ist durch und durch Causalität."[1] Matter is causality. Matter is power. Saint Simon had this idea in his apotheosis of industry and the importance of devoting energy to material things. Guyot has attempted to reduce it to a simple formula. In his "Principles of Social Economy" he expresses it in the following form: "Economic progress is in direct ratio to the action of man on things."[2]

In an article of later date he expanded and completed his formula as follows: —

[1] "Die Welt als Wille und Vorstellung," 3d edition, Leipzig, 1859, Vol. II, Table of "Praedicabilia a priori " to p. 55, first page, 3d column.

[2] "Principles of Social Economy," by Yves Guyot. Translated from the French by C. H. d'Eyncourt Leppington. Second edition, London, 1892, p. 298.

Progress is in direct ratio to the action of man on things, and in inverse ratio to the coercive action of man on man.[1]

Matter is dynamic, and every time that man has touched it with the wand of reason it has responded by satisfying a want. This is the true philosophical basis of that "historical materialism" of which we hear so much in these days. Its defenders dimly perceive the principle, but are unable to formulate it, being engrossed by surface considerations. It is this, too, that is meant when it is asserted that material civilization tends in the long run to ameliorate the condition of man. This is denied by some, but most men, I think, feel that it is so, although they might not know how to demonstrate it.

Civilization may be regarded either as an unconscious or as a conscious process, according to the point of view. The efforts and activities that have raised man from round to round of the ladder may be looked upon as the results of the inherent forces of his nature, and hence unconscious and cosmic. Or, the civilizing acts of men may be looked upon as the results of will, ideas, and intelligent aspirations for excellence, and hence conscious and personal. The first of these view-points has been erected into a science, and is sometimes appropriately called *mesology.* Human history thus becomes a simple extension of natural history. This is regarded as the scientific view *par excellence.* It is, however, mainly true that man has risen by dint of his own efforts and activities. The nature of human progress has been the theme of much discussion, and the extreme scientific view seems to negative not only all praise or blame but all hope of success on the part of man himself in trying to accelerate his advancement or improve his condition. The very law of evolution threatens to destroy hope and paralyze effort. Science applied to man becomes a gospel of inaction. But whether we are hero-worshipers or believers in the blind forces of evolution, we must admit that the truly great are the necessary instruments by which human progress is accomplished, and such progress without their intervention is inconceivable. But we are told that these

---

[1] Le progrès est en raison directe de l'action de l'homme sur les choses et en raison inverse de l'action coercitive de l'homme sur l'homme. *Journal des économistes,* 58e année, 5e série, tome XL (Octobre à Décembre 1899), 15 Décembre, 1899, p. 332, being the concluding words of an article entitled; "Le Critérium du Progrès," par Yves Guyot, pp. 321–332.

human instruments of progress are themselves products of antecedent causes which could result in nothing else. *Ergo, laissez faire.*
The fallacy of this reasoning has been hard to point out. I have
finally satisfied myself that it belongs to the class of "fool's puzzles,"
like Zeno's proof of the impossibility of motion, or the feat of the
woman of Ephesus who carried her calf each day from the time of
its birth till it became an ox. I have frequently stated the problem
in my own way, usually giving the argument the name of the
"gospel of action," and Professor Huxley, a short time before his
death, seems to have caught a glimpse of the principle.[1] But perhaps the best statement of the case that has yet been made is that
of Mr. John Morley in his essay on "Compromise." He says : —

It would be odd if the theory which makes progress depend on modification, forbade us to attempt to modify. When it is said that the various
successive changes in thought and institution present and consummate themselves spontaneously, no one means by spontaneity that they come to pass
independently of human effort and volition. On the contrary, this energy
of the members of society is one of the spontaneous elements. It is quite
as indispensable as any other of them, if, indeed, it be not more so. Progress depends upon tendencies and forces in a community. But of these
tendencies and forces the organs and representatives must plainly be found
among the men and women of the community, and cannot possibly be
found anywhere else. Progress is not automatic, in the sense that if we
were all to be cast into a deep slumber for the space of a generation, we
should arouse to find ourselves in a greatly improved social state. The
world only grows better, even in the moderate degree in which it does grow
better, because people wish that it should, and take the right steps to make
it better. Evolution is not a force, but a process; not a cause, but a law.
It explains the source and marks the immovable limitations of social
energy. But social energy can never be superseded either by evolution or
by anything else. [2]

It is human activity that transforms the environment in the interest of man. It is that *interest* [3] which is in the nature of a force,
and which in fact constitutes the social forces, that has accomplished

---

[1] "Prolegomena to Evolution and Ethics," 1894. Collected Essays, Vol. IX.

[2] John Morley, *Fortnightly Review*, Vol. XXII (N. S., Vol. XVI), Aug. 1, 1874,
p. 229; "On Compromise," London, 1874, Chapter V, pp. 160–161.

[3] Ratzenhofer has greatly enriched the terminology of social science by the prominent place he gives to this term (*angeborenes Interesse*) as the precise equivalent of
the social forces, as I have used that expression. See his "Sociologische Erkenntnis,"
pp. 28 ff. *et passim.* M. Espinas used the same term in his "Sociétés animales,"
p. 459, in the same sense, but did not elaborate the thought.

everything in the social world.   It is the social homologue of the
universal *nisus* of nature, the primordial cosmic force (*Urkraft*)
which produces all change.   It is, to use a modern phrase, unilateral,
and hence we find that the activities which have resulted in human
achievement have, when broadly viewed, an orderly method and
a uniform course.   Just as the biotic form of this universal
force pushes life into every crack and cranny, into the frozen tun-
dras and the abysmal depths of the sea, so the generalized social
energy of human interest rears everywhere social structures that
are the same in all ages and races so far as concerns their essential
nature.

But it is time to inquire more specially what the products of achievement are.   The chief failure to understand them is due to the false
and superficial view that they consist in material goods, or wealth.
This is the fallacy upon which chiefly rests the notion that human
society differs from animal society only in degree.   Because
welfare is so largely dependent on wealth, it is natural to suppose
that wealth is the main condition to progress.   There is a sense in
which this is true, but to say that wealth is a product of achievement
involves an ellipsis.   Material goods, as, for example, food, clothing,
and shelter, are, it is true, the ends; but the real products of achievement are means.   They are the means to these ends, and not the
ends themselves.   Involved in the idea of achievement is that of
permanence.   Nothing that is not permanent can be said to have
been achieved, at least in the sense in which that term is here
employed.   Now, material goods are all perishable.   Nothing is
better understood by economists than the instability of wealth.
Says John Stuart Mill : —

When men talk of the ancient wealth of a country, of riches inherited
from ancestors, and similar expressions, the idea suggested is, that the
riches so transmitted were produced long ago, at the time when they are
said to have been first acquired, and that no portion of the capital of a country
was produced this year, except as much as may have been this year added to
the total amount.   The fact is far otherwise.   The greater part, in value, of
the wealth now existing in England has been produced by human hands
within the last twelve months.   A very small proportion indeed of that large
aggregate was in existence ten years ago ; — of the present productive capital
of the country scarcely any part, except farm-houses and factories, and a few
ships and machines ; and even these would not in most cases have survived
so long, if fresh labor had not been employed within that period in putting

them in repair. The land subsists, and the land is almost the only thing that subsists. Everything which is produced perishes, and most things very quickly. . . . Capital is kept in existence from age to age, not by preservation, but by perpetual reproduction.[1]

Mr. Henry George in his " Progress and Poverty," Chapter IV, has further discussed this subject. Most goods of course are consumed at once. These are the most important of all. The real end is consumption, and goods have no value except in consumption. But there are great differences in the degree of perishability of goods corresponding to the different kinds of consumption. A brown stone front on Fifth Avenue requires several generations of occupants to " consume " it, but if not constantly kept in repair it would soon crumble into ruins, and even the stones that face its front would be ultimately buried under accumulations of dust. Wonder is sometimes expressed at the discovery of ruined cities, such as Nineveh, Babylon, Troy, etc., deeply buried under the earth, and it is supposed that it is because the sands of the desert of that region have rapidly entombed them. But in Rome and other ancient cities not in desert regions excavations reveal buildings underneath the sites of the present ones. In the exceptionally clean city of Washington the official files and records stored away in the archives of fireproof buildings are covered with a thick coating of dust in a few years. The deposition of dust in the United States National Museum seems to be about at the rate of one millimeter per annum. It would be many times that out-of-doors, and the National Capital would become a buried Nineveh in a few centuries, if abandoned by man.

Wagons, carriages, and other vehicles only last their owners a certain length of time. Locomotives and railroad rolling stock last only so long, and must be replaced by new, however thoroughly they may be kept in repair. A steamship has a duration of life that is more nearly a fixed quantity than that of a man or an animal, and its mortality is just as certain. It makes very little difference either whether these things are kept in use or not. They disintegrate even more rapidly if lying idle. Machinery rusts and timbers rot more rapidly if always lying in one position than if kept moving. Houses go to pieces faster if unoccupied than if inhabited. Clothing would probably last longer unworn if kept away from moths and moisture

---

[1] "Principles of Political Economy," etc., by John Stuart Mill, Boston, 1848, Vol. I, pp. 93, 94.

than if worn, but sometimes even this does not seem true. I once talked with an aged colored man at the Soldier's Home near Washington, who had been the body servant of General Winfield Scott, and who, since the death of the general, had been assigned the duty of caring for his effects in a room where they were kept. Among these effects were his military clothes, his sashes, etc. The old man said with a sigh of loyal sadness that in spite of all his care they were going to pieces, and with a true touch of superstitious reverence he ascribed their rapid decay to the fact that their owner was no longer alive. But of course he forgot that if he had lived all that time it would probably have been necessary to renew them several times.

If achievement consisted in wealth, the objects of production would have grown more and more durable with the progress of civilization. The fact is precisely the reverse of this. Whatever class of objects we may examine, we find that the farther back we go the more solid and enduring the materials are of which they are constructed. This is perhaps the most strikingly exemplified in architecture. Compare the old with the new part of any city of Europe, or even of America. I once engaged a room in a house on Essex Street, Strand, of which the front door consisted of ponderous planks six inches thick. The enlightened host apologized for it, saying that it was a very old house. Without some such experience, the modern American law student can scarcely understand the phrase he finds in his "Blackstone," that in English law "a man's house is his castle." The clapboarded balloon frames of the Middle West are more like "castles in the air." But any American who has seen Europe, even in the capacity of a tourist, knows that this case was no particular exception. Builders in European cities have unlimited difficulty in trying to introduce into the older buildings such "modern improvements" as water and gas pipes, and electric wires. Such buildings were built to stay, and many of them are still very strong. But to see the perishability of even such structures it is only necessary to visit such castles and châteaus as those of Colchester or Chinon. But there has been a gradual change in the character of architecture, both public and private, in the direction of less and less solidity, durability, and costliness, from the pyramids of Egypt to the cottages of modern summer resorts.

Not less clearly is this tendency illustrated by the history of book-

making since the invention of printing.   Any one who has had occasion to handle books published in the sixteenth or seventeenth
century, does not need to have this point further enforced.   Often
printed on parchment, always with strong, almost indestructible
binding, firmly and securely hand sewed, not to speak of the elaborate ornamentation of the title page and rubrics at the heads of
chapters, these ancient tomes are the embodiments of painstaking
workmanship and durability.   Contrast them with modern books.
Four centuries hence there will scarcely exist a copy of a nineteenth-
century book that anybody reads.   Many an *édition de luxe* even will
go to pieces on the shelves of public libraries.

But to these qualities of durability and expensiveness have succeeded those of ready reproduction and indefinite multiplication.
These are the elements of diffusion and popularization.   It is an
evening up of conditions.   For along with the massive structures,
chiefly for tombs of dead rulers or temples to the gods, there went
great deprivation, even in the means of shelter, for the living men
of the time.   So, too, in the early history of book-making, only
the very few could afford to own a book.   Only the cheap can
become universal, and it is easier to renew a cheap article than
to guard a costly one.   The ages of stone and bronze and iron
have successively passed, and we are living in an age of paper and
caoutchouc.

Achievement does not consist in wealth.   Wealth is fleeting and
ephemeral.   Achievement is permanent and eternal.   And now
mark the paradox.   Wealth, the transient, is material; achievement,
the enduring, is immaterial.   The products of achievement are not
material things at all.   As said before, they are not ends but means.
They are methods, ways, principles, devices, arts, systems, institutions.   In a word, they are *inventions*.   Achievement consists in invention in the Tardean sense.   It is anything and everything that
rises above mere imitation or repetition.   Every such increment to
civilization is a permanent gain, because it is imitated, repeated, perpetuated, and never lost.   It is chiefly mental or psychical, but it may
be physical in the sense of skill.   The earlier developments of civilizing influences consisted mainly in these, and such accounts as we
have consist in descriptions of the physical feats of heroes.   But
mere muscular strength soon yields to cunning and skill.   These do
not achieve until they begin to create.   Language itself was an

achievement of stupendous import, and every one of the steps it has taken — gesture, oral, written, printed forms of language — has marked an epoch in the progress of man. Literature has become one of the great achievements. Art, too, is an achievement upon which we need not dwell. Philosophy and science must be ranked as achievements, vast and far-reaching in their consequences. The invention of tools, instruments, utensils, missiles, traps, snares, and weapons comes under this head, crowned by the era of machino-facture, artificial locomotion, and electric intercommunication.

All these are too obvious and important to have escaped the observation of any one. But I wish to draw attention to a class of products of achievement that are at once typical, important, and little thought of in this connection. They may be called the tools of the mind. Lord Bacon saw the need of instruments or helps to the mind as tools are helps to the hand,[1] but long before his day many such had been invented, and he had used them all his life, and many have been invented since. An arithmetical notation, or mode of expressing numbers by symbols of any kind, is such a tool of the mind, and all leading races have devised something of the kind. Greece had hers, and Rome hers. We still make some use of the latter. But these systems vary greatly in value and usefulness, according to their simplicity and flexibility. It is remarkable that the Greek mind, although so given to mathematics, did not furnish the world with a perfect method of writing numbers. The system that is now universally employed by civilized races is called the Arabic system, but it is probable that the Arabs only somewhat improved it after receiving it from the East. We are told, too, that, like most other things, it has a history and a genesis, but its origin is for the most part lost in obscurity. So far as the decimal system itself is concerned, some form of it (if not decimal, then by fives or twenties) is practically universal, for the simple reason that there are ten fingers on the two hands, and that the fingers (or fingers and toes) are universally used for counting. The origin of the Arabic symbols is a matter of speculation,[2] but these would be evolved very much as were the letters of the alphabet. But the peculiar merit of

[1] "Novum Organum," Aph. II.
[2] An ingenious theory was proposed by Mr. W. Donisthorpe in *Nature* of Sept. 30, 1875, Vol. XII, p. 476, and supplemented by Mr. D. V. T. Qua in the *Popular Science Monthly* for April, 1877, Vol. X, pp. 737–739, and numerous other writers of about that time.

the Arabic system consists in what is called the value of position,[1] and this it is which gives it its wonderful adaptability to business uses.   We need only to figure to ourselves the sorry plight the world would be in if obliged to depend for all the business transactions, engineering calculations, and pedagogic necessities upon, say, the Roman system of numerals, in order to form a just idea of the infinite value to society of the Arabic system.   This illustrates, too, as well as any other case, what is meant by permanence.   The goods whose cost, prices, and values it enables us so readily to calculate, may be produced, transported, exchanged, and consumed a thousand or a million times, but the means of computing all the elements of these processes remain forever, and may be used throughout all future time, as they have been used in the past.   The Arabic system is a typical permanent human achievement.

In like manner we might review all the other kinds of calculus : algebra, which also goes back to India; logarithms, of relatively modern date; analytical geometry, invented by Descartes and now used by all statisticians, by political economists and sociologists; the differential and integral calculus, somewhat independently formulated by Newton, Leibnitz, and Lagrange, and without which astronomy and many other sciences and arts could never have reached their present state of development.   These, too, are among the great permanent achievements of the race.   The three great arts of read-ing, writing, and calculating, viewed from a philosophical standpoint, have raised that part of mankind who possess them high above all those races in which they are unknown, or only rudimentary.   The unreflecting have little idea of the importance of these factors in giving superiority to the advanced races.   I fully agree with Galton, Kidd, and others of their school, that the natural superiority of civilized races as compared with uncivilized ones is greatly exagger-ated, and that it is almost wholly due to this vast mechanical equip-ment of acquired aptitudes, built up along one advancing line of social development, increment upon increment, permanently welded to these races so that they imagine that it is a part of themselves. Mr. Kidd very happily calls the power thus acquired *social efficiency*,

[1] See the learned essay on this subject by Baron von Humboldt, originally published in Crelle's *Journal für die reine und angewandte Mathematik*, Vol. IV, Berlin, 1829, pp. 205–231 (especially pp. 215–227) ; reproduced in part in his "Kosmos," Vol. II (Cotta's edition, Stuttgart, 1870), pp. 288–290.

a term that I gladly adopt and shall freely use. And I fully agree with him when, after illustrating this truth at considerable length, he concludes: —

The true lesson of this, and of the large class of similar experiences commonly supposed to prove the low mental development of uncivilized man, is not that he is so inferior to ourselves, intellectually, as to be almost on a level with Mr. Galton's dog, but that he is almost always the representative of a race of low social efficiency with consequently no social history. On the other hand, the individuals of civilized races with whom he is contrasted are the members of a community with a long record of social stability and continuity, which is, therefore, in possession of a vast accumulated store of knowledge inherited from past generations. That is to say, we are the representatives of peoples necessarily possessing high social qualities, but not by any means and to the same degree these high intellectual qualities we so readily assume.[1]

The industrial arts form a much more obvious, though perhaps not more important, class of human achievements. They are greatly dependent at every step on the tools of the mind, and, properly viewed, they are almost as completely psychic in their nature. For all art is due to invention, and invention is a mental operation. Every tool or implement of industry, however primitive and rude, has cost a large amount, in the aggregate, of thought, although it may be the product of a long series of slight improvements, distributing the mental energy through many different minds acting in different generations. Still it foots up the same quantity of thought applied to the invention. But the increment of improvement is at once materialized in the changed product, and the achievement is thus rendered permanent, and the basis for further improvement. Thought is thus dynamic when applied to matter. The new and better article, if used, will wear out, but the materialized idea lives on in the reproduction of the article as long as it serves its purpose. This part involves what is called labor. The inventor need not make a usable tool or machine at all. He may embody the idea in a model, or even in a drawing, and nowadays the state assumes the duty of registering and preserving these models, and protecting the inventor from having them copied by others who did not invent them.

But the simple reproduction of invented products is not purely physical or muscular. This point has latterly been insisted upon by a number of economists. Says Dr. Gustav Cohn: —

[1] "Social Evolution," by Benjamin Kidd, New York, 1894, p. 272.

Labor, in its economic aspects, whether mental or physical, has its basis, not in nature, but in civilization; it does not depend on physiological but on psychological reasons. Moreover, it is not possible in any case to separate mental from physical labor; for the simplest operation in which the use of the muscles is guided by any trace of thought is a combination of both kinds of labor.[1]

Professor Clark expresses the same truth in the following language : —

In view of the constant presence of these three elements in labor, the physical, the mental, and the moral, any effort, in the supposed interest of the working classes, to depreciate mental labor in comparison with physical is unintelligent. All labor is mental. To a large and controlling extent the mental element is present in the simplest operations. With the laborer who shovels in the gravel pit the directing and controlling influence of the mind predominates, to an indefinite extent, over the simple foot-pounds of mechanical force which he exerts.[2]

This is why human labor and animal activity are generically distinct, and one of the principal reasons why sociology cannot properly include the study of the so-called animal societies, produced and continued by reflex and instinctive forces.

Inventions, in the narrower sense of the word, almost immediately pass into arts. In fact, in most of them there is scarcely any line of demarcation between them. They are preëminently telic, and it is the function that is primarily in the inventor's mind. He knows what he wants done, and merely devises the means of doing it. It is thus that the arts grow up. What the inventor does is to discover the principle by which he can cause the forces of nature, including the properties of the substances that he is acquainted with, to do the work that he wishes to have done and cannot do with his unaided hands. The discovery of this principle and the mode of applying it is what constitutes the achievement. This discovery, and not the resulting material product, is the lasting element in the operation. It can be used thenceforth for all time. It never wears out and is never lost. We hear a great deal about lost arts. I heard a learned lecture once on lost arts, and the thing that chiefly impressed me was the extreme rarity and practical non existence of lost arts. They may be conceived of,

[1] "A History of Political Economy," by Dr. Gustav Cohn. Translated by Joseph Adna Hill, Philadelphia, 1894 (Supplement to the *Ann. Am. Acad. Pol. and Soc. Sci.,* March, 1894), pp. 87-88.

[2] "The Philosophy of Wealth," etc., by John B. Clark, Boston, 1886, p. 21.

but as a matter of fact there are none, at least in the historic (*weltgeschichtliche*) races. The only way in which we can conceive an art to be lost is to suppose several lines of civilization to have developed independently of one another, some of which have for any reason terminated, while others have continued. If inventions and arts had existed in the former that did not exist in the latter, they might thus be lost, and we can imagine that their products, preserved by time and favorable conditions, might subsequently be discovered by surviving races who did not know how they were created. But this is merely hypothetical, and with the increasing intercommunication among nations and consequent cultural anastomosis, the chances of its occurrence are constantly diminishing.

These two great classes of products of achievement, means of handling quantities and means of utilizing forces — calculus and invention — are perhaps the most important, and they have chiefly rendered civilization possible. But others might be enumerated, which, considered alone, might appear to possess still greater weight, and of many of which it can at least be said, that but for them the fruits of the forms of achievement that we have considered could not have been reaped. These are essentially social in their character, and relate to men in a collective capacity. To mention them in something like the probable order of their development, we may enumerate, 1, military systems, 2, political systems, 3, juridical systems, and 4, industrial systems. Whatever views may be entertained relative to the social position of war, the sociologist cannot ignore the rôle it has played in the history of man and society. The subject will be fully dealt with in the tenth chapter, but it may properly be stated here that the earliest of the whole series of means for organizing the social forces were military systems, and that all others grew out of them. The transition from military to political control was natural and gradual, as Gumplowicz and Ratzenhofer have shown. The state was the normal and legitimate outcome of the race struggle, first military, then political. Law, too, began as an economic method of escape from the necessity of constantly exercising military and civil power, and systems of jurisprudence were a natural outgrowth of social conditions under a régime of conquest and subjugation. Lastly, the industrial system, as such, could only arise under the protection of army, state, and law. These may

therefore be called protective or conservative systems or achievements, and neither industry, art, nor science could thrive except
under the protection of law and government having a final appeal
to the military power.

Finally, it may be said in general that all human institutions are
achievements. Even those that we now consider bad, even those
that have been abolished, were useful in the wider sense in their
day and age. The fact that they were developed and actually came
into existence proves to the sociologist that they must have served a
purpose. But there is really no such thing as abolishing an institution. Institutions change their character to adapt them to their time,
and the successive forms may take different names, and be no longer
recognized as the same as the institutions out of which they have developed, but the fundamental principle which underlies them is common to them all, and may usually be traced through the entire series
of changes that an institution may have undergone. The term *institution* is capable of such expansion as to embrace all human achievement, and in this enlarged sense institutions become the chief study
of the sociologist. All achievements are institutions, and there is a
decided gain to the mind in seeking to determine the true subject-
matter of sociology, to regard human institutions and human achievement as synonymous terms, and as constituting, in the broadest sense
of both, the field of research of a great science.

These products of achievement that we have been considering have
one fundamental condition, without which they would have been
impossible. They absolutely require *social continuity*. I have said
that they are permanent, that they are never lost. This is implied
in the term *achievement*. To be lost is not to exist. We may illustrate this from biology. Individuals are short-lived, but the race
persists. Species may become extinct, but genera or families are
carried on. We find certain forms in existence. We know nothing
of other forms. If there have been such, they are the same to us as
if they had not existed. The theory is that the bathmic force is
omnipresent and pushing in every direction, as from the center of a
sphere toward every point on its periphery. We may imagine that,
besides the few lines that succeeded in developing, there were hundreds or even thousands of other lines tested, but found to fail, sooner
or later, leaving only the ones we know. Now a lost art or a lost
institution would correspond to one of these supposed failures of

organic nature.   It would be, to all intents and purposes, non-
existent.   In other words, and it certainly sounds platitudinal,
society consists of existing institutions, just as life consists of existing forms.

But this truth is not quite so simple as it seems when put in this
way.   Social continuity is an important factor, and one that may be
readily thought away.   In fact, and here the biological analogy
seems to fail, it does not apply to all the populations of the globe.
I do not mean to favor any doctrine of polygenism, by doing which
Gumplowicz has so greatly and so unnecessarily weakened his arguments in the eyes of scientific men.   It has nothing to do with the
question of organic descent or with the origin of the human races.
It is a purely sociological fact that all the human races do not
belong to one and the same series of cultural development.   Many
of them are so primitive that even when brought into contact with
the historic races they have nothing to contribute to the general
stream of culture, and become simply subjects for natural history
study, like the flora and fauna of the regions they inhabit.   But
there are others, such as most of the Asiatic races, who have followed
lines of their own, and must have a certain culture history, which,
however, is so unlike that of the European races, that there is very
little in common between them.   Some maintain that Chinese culture,
for example, is equal if not superior to European.   The same claim
is sometimes made for India.   I need not enter into that question
here.   Suffice it to say that Oriental civilization seems to have consisted chiefly in what may be called spiritual culture, largely ignoring
material culture.   But as matter alone is dynamic, they have
acquired very little social energy, or social efficiency.   They have
not called nature to their assistance, and consequently they are
practically powerless when brought into competition with Western
civilization.   I do not refer altogether to their weakness in matters
of war.   They lack in great measure the industrial efficiency of the
West.   They lack chiefly the mechanic arts, and have developed but
little machinofacture, being confined in the main to manufacture in
the literal sense.   They have not employed the two great agencies,
steam and electricity.   Even if their civilization represents a longer
line than that of the Occident, it is certainly immensely behind it in
these respects, which we regard as the most important ones.   They
are beginning to recognize this, and some of the nations of the East,

notably Japan, are rapidly westernizing and working over into the great current of scientific culture.   It is probably safe to predict that all will either do so or be permanently side-tracked.

Sociology, as distinguished from anthropology, deals mainly with historic, or as the Germans call them, *weltgeschichtliche* races, because here alone is social continuity, the *sine qua non* of achievement. Such races may properly be called in analogy to the use of the term in biology, the " favored races."   These alone have built up a civilization.   They have achieved and handed down the products from generation to generation, and from age to age.   It is easy to trace this line back to a state of barbarism.   We can almost see it emerging out of savagery.   At least, we know that it did once so emerge, so that when we say that savages contribute nothing to civilization, we do not mean that a state of savagery is incompatible with historic development; we only mean that in the present state of the world they are contributing nothing to the main existing line of development.   It does not follow that if existing savages could be unmolested for an indefinite period they would not slowly advance along some line of their own.   Letourneau has shown that savages do progress. But it is very difficult now to prove such a point.   If they are near enough to civilized races to be observed, they cannot fail to be affected by them, and it is impossible to say what they would have done if they had never been brought into contact with them.   The study of uncivilized races, therefore, is, and must remain, anthropology and not sociology.   This is true even for the Asiatic civilizations.   They can be used by the sociologist to furnish valuable illustrations and comparisons, but beyond this they form no part of sociology proper.   Should they ever adopt Western methods, acquire the Western spirit, and fall entirely into line with the Western world, the case would be changed.   But except in the case of Japan, and that only quite recently, the fundamental characteristics are so radically different that the sociologist can only study them for comparative purposes.   The widest chasm that separates the East from the West is the lack of individuality in the former contrasted with the exuberant individualism of the latter.   The spirit of resignation, the prevailing philosophy of quietism, the denial or complete subordination of the will to live, that prevail under Buddhism, Brahminism, Shintoism, and other Oriental ' isms,' are fatal to that vigorous push which has wrought Western civilization.   Desire is

D

the social force, and where there is no desire, no will, there is no force, no social energy. Civilization is the product of active social energy. Or, to use Ratzenhofer's terminology, there must be a lively *interest* or there can be no achievement. It is this innate interest (*angeborenes Interesse*) that makes men fight and conquer and struggle. It is the same that makes them undertake voyages of discovery in search of golden fleeces, or El Dorados, or Northwest Passages. Interest impels mankind to explore, to migrate, to invent, to labor, to produce wealth, to seek knowledge, to discover truth, to create objects both of use and beauty — in a word, to achieve. We shall return to this subject in Chapter XI, when it will be time to consider in its full significance the philosophy of effort.

It must be clear from all that has been said that the essential characteristic of all achievement is some form of *knowledge*. But knowledge, unlike capacity, cannot be transmitted through heredity. The germ-plasm can only carry the ancestral strains of parents to their offspring and descendants, and whether " acquired characters " can be thus transmitted or not, it is certain that acquired knowledge is a " character " that does not descend in that way. It has to be acquired anew by every member of society. If it is not thus acquired, it is lost to that member. But as all achievement is knowledge, to be saved it must be transmitted in some way. The process by which achievement is handed down may be aptly called *social heredity.* This social heredity is the same thing that I have otherwise denominated social continuity, and it is the absolute necessity of social continuity that restricts the science of sociology to that great line of social development in which there has been no break in the transmission of achievement. We thus have the continuity of the social germ-plasm, which is as good an analogy as the organicists have discovered. The social germ-plasm is that Promethean fire which has been passed on from age to age, warming the world into life with its glow, and lighting it with its flame through all the long night of the past into the daybreak of the present.

A few rare minds have dimly seen that civilization consists in the cumulative light of knowledge. The most celebrated expression of this truth is that of Pascal in which he says that "the entire series of men during the course of all the ages is to be considered as if it were one and the same man who has always lived and has been constantly learning."[1] Pascal seems to have derived the idea from St. Augustine, of whom he was an admirer and a close student. Bacon has expressed a similar view, and something very close to it occurs frequently in Condorcet's "Esquisse" in connection with his favorite doctrine of the perfectibility of the human race. Herder also entertained similar ideas.

But this conception is only an approach toward the truth. It falls far short of what has actually taken place in the world. It indicates the length but not the breadth of civilization. No one man, however wise, and though immortal, could have accomplished what all men have accomplished. This brings us in full view of one of the most important and at the same time most neglected factors of social evolution, viz., that of individuality in achievement. It is another aspect of the truth we encountered in the last chapter that it is inequality that has broadened and enriched civilization as it has broadened and enriched science. Civilization advances in much the same way that science advances. It is not the work of any one man, but of thousands of men. Each one of these thousands does a somewhat different work from any other. This is due to the natural inequalities of men, chiefly to varied intellectual capacities and attainments which cause them to follow different and almost infinitely varied lines and produce correspondingly varied results. This causes the enormous superiority of all men over any one man. Human achievement may be compared to a great modern city with its buildings of unequal shapes, sizes, and heights, its columns, monuments, domes, towers, and spires differing in all conceivable ways, and yet denoting a still more endless variety of activities and social operations. If we take up the study of any one particular line, it matters not what, we shall find lesser lights and great lights characterizing the history of its development. Different schools of art represented by great masters, each of which has added something to the work of all the rest. Schools of architecture, of sculpture, of painting, of music; types of poetry and prose literature; systems of philosophy; world views and religious systems; qualitative and quantitative powers of perceiving utilities,

[1] "Toute la suite des hommes, pendant le cours de tant de siècles, doit être considérée comme un même homme qui subsiste toujours, et qui apprend continuellement." Pensées de Blaise Pascal suivies d'une Table Analytique, Paris, 1828, p. 28. Saint Augustine ("De Civitate Dei," X, 14; "De Quæstionibus," LXXXIII, Quæst. 18) expressed a similar thought and doubtless Pascal's idea was derived from that source.

resulting in innumerable inventions and arts — all due to natural inequalities in men.   It is thus that civilization acquires its volume and that it becomes that infinitely complex and varied field of study which the sociologist finds before him.

Here come in the diversities of genius and the question of the nature of genius in general. It is necessary to use the word genius, if we use it at all, in a very broad sense. Galton in the prefatory chapter to the edition of 1892 of his "Hereditary Genius" concludes from the criticisms of the term genius as used by him that it would have been better to substitute the word *ability,* but this would have lacked character, and it is much better to retain his original dignified title and simply give to the word genius a greater latitude. This is what all thinkers do when they seek to express a great thought by some one comprehensive term. Kant's *Vernunft,* Schopenhauer's *Wille,* Comte's *positivisme,* are such comprehensive uses of terms much more restricted in common language. I shall use the word genius in this large sense.   Genius is a sort of focalization of psychic power. While there is an immense range to the human mind in general, and enormous differences in the aggregate capacity of different minds, this difference is still further increased by a sort of unconscious or natural concentration of psychic power in special ways in the same mind. That is to say, a mind of only average aggregate capacity may draw off from all but one of its faculties and add on to that one, until it becomes wonderfully keen or able or efficient in that one direction. I believe this to be the case with most typical geniuses in any particular form of achievement.   It is proverbial that artists are very mediocre in all but their art.   There are very few Leonardo da Vincis. It is the same with poets and usually with philosophers.   It is a sort of psychic division of labor that society creates, whereby with a large number of workers it can accomplish the maximum results, just as by the industrial division of labor much greater results are accomplished than could be done if all were doing all kinds of work and only doing them moderately well.

But this process does not stop with producing ordinary genius in all directions by draining other faculties to stock some particular one to the utmost.   It sometimes goes, like everything in nature, to great extremes, and produces what are called prodigies. A prodigy is a person in whom a particular faculty is greatly overdeveloped at the expense of the rest.   Blind Tom, except in music, is very close to an idiot. Zerah Colburn, Vito Mangiamele, Tom Fuller, Jedediah Buxton, Inaudi, Dasah, Zaneboni, were all "lightning calculators," or mathematical prodigies. They varied in respect of other faculties, but are all reported as dull, ignorant, illiterate, or incapable of learning anything. Several of them were defective in some of their senses and more or less physically deformed. There have been many prodigies in other directions, usually deficient in all but the one power. That there is such a power of compensation or substitution of faculties is attested by the history of deaf-mutes and blind persons, in which the remaining senses are usually much sharpened. This concentration of mental power is often very marked in children, and cases of marvelous precocity are recorded without number. Great geniuses are usually precocious, and some men, like John Stuart Mill, Pascal, and Goethe, who were not one-sided in later life, were precocious. But the achievements of prodigies have been comparatively small, and where the specialization runs thus rampant the result is reduced until we reach monomania, the *idée fixe*, or complete insanity, all of which are only further steps in the same direction.

If we expand the meaning of genius to include all that are called great for any reason, we arrive at a crude basis for estimating the proportion of geniuses to population. Galton undertook the computation and concluded that for high grade talent there are in England 250 per million, or one to every 4000 males of fifty years of age and upward. This may perhaps be accepted as approximately the actual state of things in the leading countries of the world. The subject of *potential* genius is much too large to be introduced here, and we can only base our discussion on the observed facts of society and the state of things which social evolution has actually brought about. I do not say that the rest of mankind is socially worthless, but it is mainly devoted to statical work which preserves and perpetuates achievement. It corresponds to heredity in biology, while achievement corresponds to variation. We cannot, therefore, regard the non-achieving classes of society as mere ciphers, nor say with Gracian "that even in the most populous cities not a man was to be met with, but they were all inhabited by lions, tigers, leopards, foxes, apes, cattle, asses, and swine, nowhere a man! but that upon further investigation it was found that the few real men, to avoid seeing how things were, had withdrawn into the solitudes, where one would

expect to find the wild beasts." [1] And yet it cannot be denied that
the paucity of true men in the world makes a true man feel lonesome
unless he has learned to study man objectively as a naturalist studies
animals, and this feeling of contempt for the mass of mankind has
been expressed by many writers, such as Humboldt, Schopenhauer,
and Dean Swift.

The point of view of this chapter furnishes a remedy for this form
of pessimism. It does not really study men or the human race
at all. That belongs to other sciences than sociology, chiefly to
anthropology. It studies activities, results, products, in a word,
achievement. Viewed in this light the contemptible side of humanity vanishes from view, and only what is worthy or grand is presented to the gaze. Even the relatively trifling character of the
contribution of most individuals need not absorb attention, but only
aggregates. Just as the geologist, although no one knows as well
as he that the great ledges and cañon walls were built up by minute accretions through eons of time, need not dwell upon these
aspects, but may study as a whole the miles [2] of stratified rock, so

[1] "El Criticon," Primera Parte, Crisi V. Obras de Lorenzo Gracian, Madrid, 1664,
Vol. I, p. 37.

[2] The Grand Cañon walls are over a mile in vertical thickness from the granite to
the top of the rim (Upper Aubrey), and still we are in primary or Paleozoic (Carboniferous) time. On this are heaped farther eastward the Mesozoic, the Tertiary,
and the Pleistocene.

Haeckel in his " Welträthsel " (pp. 17, 441–443) calls this general view of the world
the "cosmological perspective," and he emphasizes the importance of a clear understanding of the age of the earth as an antidote to the prevailing anthropocentric
world view. He takes up the question of geologic time which has been actively
discussed during the last two decades and gives 100,000,000 as the minimum estimate of the life-bearing period of our globe. Of this he gives 52,000,000 years to
primordial time (Archozoic), ending with the Cambrian, 34,000,000 to the Paleozoic,
11,000,000 to the Mesozoic, and 3,000,000 to the Cenozoic. To this he adds
100,000 years for the Quaternary (Anthropozoic) period. One of his students,
Heinrich Schmidt, brought out these results in a very striking form by conceiving
the whole of this time as a cosmic day (" Schöpfungstag ") of twenty-four equal
parts after the analogy of a solar day, and then assigning to each geological period
its share of this time in hours and minutes. The humiliating conclusion is thus
reached that the traditional 6000 years of human history (" Weltgeschichte ")
occupy five seconds of the cosmic day.

It occurred to me to give to this cosmological perspective a graphic representation
by means of a dial, and I prepared one and have used it in lectures on the geological
history of plants. In the light of all the discussion of the age of the earth I adopted a still
more conservative estimate, placing the total at 72,000,000 years. The Hon. Charles D.
Walcott, Director of the United States Geological Survey, in his address as Vice-
president of the Geological Section of the American Association for the Advancement of Science in 1893, went into a thorough discussion of this question from all

the sociologist may forget the paltry littleness of each increment to civilization and the still more paltry motives that inspired it, and study the monument that the race has thus erected, classifying each stratum, as does the geologist, and working out the stages of human culture. But the sociologist has an advantage over the geologist. The latter finds the world completed, so far as need concern him. The whole period of human occupation counts for nothing in geologic time, and it is idle for him to speculate even as to the future of the life that has been entombed in the rocks or now occupies the earth's surface. But the sociologist deals with a fresh young world. He can see it grow, and he has a perfect right not only to speculate as to the future of society but also to try to accelerate its growth, on what I may call the Morleyan principle above set forth.

points of view (see the Proceedings, Vol. XLII, pp. 129–169), and conceded more to the physicists and astronomers than any other geologist has done, reducing the time scale to 55,000,000 years. He showed that the theories from the cooling of the globe and from the thickness of the strata are in practical harmony both as to the absolute time and also as to the relative lengths of the geological periods. While the former was made much less than geologists generally demand, the latter may be accepted with as much confidence as any of the estimates dealing with this problem. I have substantially adopted them in the following scheme. On the basis of 72,000,000, each hour of the cosmic day represents 3,000,000 years, and we have :

GEOLOGIC PERIODS	YEARS	HOURS
Archean	18,000,000	6
Algonkian	18,000,000	6
Cambrian	6,000,000	2
Silurian	6,000,000	2
Devonian	6,000,000	2
Carboniferous	6,000,000	2
Triassic	3,000,000	1
Jurassic	3,000,000	1
Cretaceous	3,000,000	1
Cenozoic	3,000,000	1
	72,000,000	24

The Cenozoic, including the Pleistocene or Quaternary, may then be further subdivided. The Tertiary need not be divided into Eocene, Miocene, and Pliocene, but it is important to estimate the length of the glacial periods. Haeckel doubtless gives too little time to these events (100,000 years). The minimum estimates exceed twice that, and 300,000 years is about an average. The human period, i.e. the utmost that any one will concede for human history, is not usually considered by geologists, and is left to the ethnologists and archæologists. We may put it at 25,000 years, while 6000 years is generally recognized as covering the entire historic

We see, then, that the results of human effort in bringing about
civilization may all be comprehended under the single word *achievement*, for it is the sum-total of human achievement that we call
civilization. And while achievement is exclusively the work of
individual men, it can only take place in a social state of coöperation on a grand scale, and it is impossible if the series of results
is ever allowed to be interrupted. In the genealogical tree of
social evolution no side branches can persist unless they are kept
constantly nourished by direct contact with the main trunk. The
nature of social evolution as of all organic evolution will be dealt
with in Chapter V, and it is only necessary to say here that it is very
different from the prevailing conception of evolution. But we
cannot regard those leading civilizations that have separated off
territorially from the main trunk and carried with them all the
culture of the mother country, such as the American and Australian
civilizations, as mere branches. They belong to the tree itself

period, or that for which there are any real records. Including these in the
Cenozoic we have : —

Geologic Periods	Years	Hours	Minutes	Seconds
Tertiary	2,675,000		53	30
Pleistocene	300,000		6	
Human	25,000			30
Total Cenozoic	3,000,000	1		
Human History	6,000			7¼

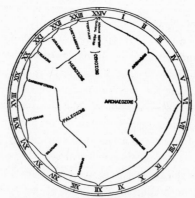

DIAL·OF·THE·COSMIC·DAY
~AGE·OF·THE·EARTH

and are attached to it by every organ and every function essential to the whole.

Although every act must in strict science be recognized as the resultant of all the forces, internal and external, acting upon the agent, still it remains true that achievement is the work of individuals thus acting, and although from this scientific point of view there can be no praise nor blame, no room for criticism and no justification for eulogy, still there are all degrees in the value and meritoriousness of human acts corresponding to the extent to which they contribute to the general result, and such acts therefore become proper subjects for study and analysis. Such study and analysis, sympathetically pursued, tend rather to enhance one's opinion of men's actions and supply a certain corrective to the pessimistic tendencies above pointed out. We find that for the most part those acts which have proved to constitute real contributions to civilization have emanated from motives of a high order, — I do not mean morally, but psychologically. They have as their basis a psychic rather than a physical interest. As soon as men rise to the contemplative stage of development, which occurs very early under a system of caste, which is the first to grow up under the operation of the struggle of races that almost universally prevailed, the psychic or transcendental interest is developed. The brain takes the place of the stomach and loins as a center of feeling, and there arise mental cravings, which constitute as effective social forces as hunger and love. The history of the world bears out this statement, and under these sociogenetic forces (see Chapter XV) art, philosophy, literature, industry, and science came gradually into existence and combined in the work of human achievement.

Under the operation of these forces the chief ambition of all vigorous minds and enlightened spirits became that of contributing something to the great stream of civilization. It is for this to-day and not for pelf, that the student burns the midnight oil, that the genius sweeps the skies of fancy, that the philosopher probes the depths of nature, that the inventor tests the properties of substances and the actions of forces, that the specialist in any branch of science delves deeper than any of his predecessors. It is said that the love of approbation is the principal motive, and this may be admitted to be a less worthy motive than the love of achievement. As from the standpoint of modern psychology all motives are simply functions of the character or *primordium* (*Anlage*)[1] of individuals, worthiness is equivalent to social efficiency or effectiveness, and is here only used in that sense.   Love of approbation is therefore to be welcomed as an aid to other motives in accomplishing the results. But when we look over the history of achievement we shall find that love of approbation plays a less prominent rôle than would seem from an observation of contemporary workers.   The beginnings of all great achievements, which all will admit to be the most important steps, are usually laid in deep obscurity by men impelled by motives difficult to define.   No doubt the idea of utility is a large factor, but not utility to self.   Mere love of activity and pleasure in mental exertion are powerful motives and have caused the most sustained labor often in immensely fertile directions. Originality is difficult to distinguish from love of approbation, because no doubt it has to do with the opinion of others.   The recluse inventor may have motives closely akin to those of the anchoret or the non-religious hermit.   He does not care or expect to have his actions approved, but he may enjoy the sense of having them observed, or even ridiculed.   Let any one, for example, try to analyze the motives that actuated Galvani in his studies of frogs' legs and they will be found complex in the extreme.   Did he even dimly foresee the era of electricity?   Perhaps.   But one thing seems certain. The love of approbation formed no part of his motives.   His work only received disapprobation and contempt.   We might instance other celebrated cases, but this one is typical.

It was much the same way with the older philosophers.   Many wrote without thought even of publication.   The greater part of Leibnitz's works were published posthumously.   Descartes suppressed his most important work, apparently not through fear of persecution, but from doubt as to whether it would be right to publish it.   Many eminent persons write their autobiographies with the condition that they be not published till after their death.   Others write extended treatises in the same way, as, for example, Helvetius's work, "De l'Homme," in two volumes.

[1] Only biologists have thus far, to my knowledge, discussed the question of a proper English equivalent for the German word *Anlage* (see *Nature*, Vol. LVIII, Aug. 25, 1898, p. 390; *Science*, N.S., Vol. VIII, Dec. 2, 1898, p. 793).   The German word is used in a much broader sense than is implied in these discussions.   It applies to mind and society, and may often be rendered *character* or disposition (French *naturel*).   It is here the *intelligibel Charakter* of Kant, or rather its physical basis.

While therefore the love of approbation enters into the motives of men it is usually mingled with the love of achievement, which often includes the idea of doing some good, of benefiting mankind, etc. The desire to be remembered after death, or in remote future ages, must be very strong in many. This seems exactly intermediate between the love of approbation and the love of achievement. It is the love of approbation in the form of ambition to be enrolled after death on the scroll of immortal fame as one of the contributors to the monument erected to the work of the world. And it cannot be doubted that the feeling of being once in the great current of intellectual progress is the highest and most powerful of all incentives.

Thus far only a few have contributed to this stream, but the percentage is probably increasing, and might under improved social conditions be greatly increased, and the time may come when all may at least aspire to the honor of laying some small offering on the altar of civilization. As the ages go by and history records the results of human action it becomes clear to larger numbers that this is the true goal of life and larger numbers seek it. It is seen that only those who have achieved are remembered, that the memory of such grows brighter instead of dimmer with time, and that these names are likely to be kept fresh in the minds of men forever. Achievement, therefore, comes to constitute a form of immortality and has an exceedingly attractive side. This hope of immortality has doubtless formed one of the important motives in all ages, but as the hope of a personal immortality wanes under the glare of scientific truth, especially of biological truth,[1] there is likely to be a still stronger tendency in this direction.

Whatever other forms of immortality may be taught and believed in, the immortality of deeds is not an article of faith but a demonstrated fact. The real immortality is the immortality of achievement. And after all it is a personal immortality. This far it resembles Christian immortality in that only a few attain it. Only the elect are saved. They only are immortal who have achieved. As in Christianity, too, immortality, which is salvation, may be aspired to by all, nay, in some degree, it may be attained by all.

But we may leave the apotheosis of achievement to the rostrum and be content to view it in its strictly scientific aspects as a concep-

---

[1] Cf. Ernst Haeckel, " Die Welträthsel," Bonn, 1899, Chapter XI.

tion of the subject-matter and true end of sociology. Our treatment in this chapter has been much too narrow, and to some it may not seem to be a framework large enough to contain all that the remaining chapters aim to put into it. I can only say that it is so intended, and any apparent failure in this respect will be due to the brevity and imperfection of the presentation of the subject in the present chapter. It is probably in some respects better to have thus made the pattern scant and trust to the reader to fill out the neglected parts as the conception grows.

CHAPTER IV

METHODOLOGY

THE basis of method is logic, and the basis of logic is the sufficient reason or law of causation. The object of method is clearness, and what is logical is usually clear. At least, the same subject, however abstruse or inherently difficult, will be clearer of comprehension if logically presented than if incoherently presented. This principle lies at the foundation of style. I always observed that there was the greatest difference in the ease with which I could read different authors, although all masters in their own field, but it was a long time before I discovered the reason for this. I saw that it had nothing to do with the language I was reading, for it was easier to follow Haeckel's German than Darwin's English. On the other hand, Huxley's English was exceedingly easy while the German of Sachs, for example, was very hard. There was the same difference with French authors. Finally I undertook to investigate the matter, and I soon discovered that aside from all embellishments of style, that which rendered a style easy was the strict logical sequence of ideas. In Huxley or Haeckel, if any one will look into it he will find that every sentence is clearly and causally linked to the sentence that precedes it and so naturally follows from it that it requires no effort of the mind to pass from one to the other. In difficult styles this is not the case. There are either complete breaks in the chain of reasoning, or there are ellipses, digressions, collateral ideas, or neoterisms, which check the flow of thought and impede comprehension. Usually it is simple incoherency or lack of serial order in the arrangement of the ideas expressed, in short, defective method.

What is true of style is true of other things. It is especially true of education, and it is probable that something like double the progress could be made by pupils and students of all grades, if an exact logical method could be adopted in the order of studies, so that every new study would naturally grow out of the one that had preceded it. But every large subject is complex and embraces a great number of component subjects, and if it is carefully looked into, it will be found that most of the subordinate subjects can be arranged in a series of logically connected ideas or facts. The first duty of educationalists should be to arrange all the branches to be taught in their logical, which is their natural order. A glance at the curriculum of any school system or institution of learning will show that this is not only the last thing to be thought of, but that it has probably never been thought of.

A science is a great complex subject composed of many subordinate or component subjects, and these latter may, by the proper effort, be arranged in logical, i.e. causal order, and the science taught in this order. A treatise on any science is easy or hard in proportion as this is done. The work of a methodical investigator can be instantly distinguished by this mark. A large proportion of the scientific specialists in all departments are innocent of the use of method. They plunge into their subject at any point and treat those subjects first that first present themselves, regardless of order or of the relation of parts. Such work, however able, is difficult to use and entails great effort on all who labor in their field. Once, in conversation with Prof. Joseph Le Conte some years before his death, I spoke of his continued fruitful labors and asked him if he was able to accomplish as much as when he was younger. He replied that he could accomplish more, because what he might have lost in strength and endurance was more than made up in method.

The need of method increases with the complexity of a science. Sociology, as the most complex of all the sciences, has the greatest need of it. In the first place it is necessary to recognize that it is a science. Very few seem to treat it as if it was a true science, and the sociologists themselves are largely responsible for the opinion that so widely prevails that sociology is not a science. A true science is a field of phenomena occurring in regular order as the effects of natural or efficient causes, such that a knowledge of the causes renders it possible to predict the effects. The causes are always natural forces that obey the Newtonian laws of motion. The order in which the phenomena occur constitutes the laws that govern the science. These laws must be studied until they are understood the same as the laws of gravitation, heat, light, etc., in physics have been studied. In sociology there is a disposition to deny that there are any such laws, forces, or efficient causes. There are always paradoxers in all sciences, but in social science it is especially common, I had almost said fashionable, to question or deny its claim to the rank of a science. Some, of course, will have nothing of it. Mathematicians and astronomers, who deal with the most exact of all the sciences, usually have no patience with anything that cannot be reduced to mathematical precision. I once heard an eminent astronomer sneer at meteorology because the Weather Bureau often fails to predict the weather for any particular place. Yet it may be questioned which of these two sciences is the more useful to man. There has always been a large number who deny that history is a science. Among these are historians, such as Froude, and historical economists like Dilthey. Some even who believe in sociology and teach it, think that it differs generically in this respect from other sciences. Dr. Ludwig Stein, for example, maintains that we can only arrive at probability or moral certainty, and that there are no laws, only rules.[1]

The favorite standpoint of all who dispute the title of sociology to rank as a science is that of mathematics. The laws of astronomy, of physics, and to a large extent of chemistry, can be reduced to mathematical notation. The assumption is that anything that cannot be so reduced cannot be a science. Comte, who was himself primarily a mathematician, protested against this attitude and called it, as it seems to me, very appropriately "materialism,"[2] because, as he says, "it tends to degrade the noblest conceptions and assimilate them to the grossest," and he characterizes the abuse of mathematics as the initial phase of materialism. But he it was who pointed out that mathematics is not a science but only a standard or criterion. It is a measure of the relative "positivity," i.e. exactness, of all the sciences.

The mathematicians, astronomers, and physicists, who affect to decry sociology because not sufficiently exact for their habit of thinking, usually overlook biology, which they conceive as simply the study of plants and animals, and hence proper enough and quite innocent, and reserve their criticisms for psychology and sociology.

---

[1] "Wesen und Aufgabe der Sociologie," *Archiv f. syst. Philosophie*, Bd. IV, reprint p. 12; *Annales de l'Institut International de Sociologie*, Vol. IV, p. 291.

[2] "Politique Positive," Vol. I, pp. 50, 472.

But all they say of these would be equally true of biology. There has been no greater progress in reducing the phenomena of life to exact mathematical form than there has in so reducing those of mind and society. In fact, in certain departments of both these latter fields there has been more progress in this direction than in any department of biology. In economics, for example, and in statistical researches, much use has been made of mathematics, the only danger being that of abusing this method and making the apparently exact results stand for more than they are really worth. The names of Thünen, Gossen, Cournot, Walras, and Jevons, are intimately associated with the highest order of this class of work. The question, however, whether the broader domain of social activity can be thus reduced to exact notation and the laws of society formulated or stated in equations, has only recently begun to be agitated. Sociologists are duly forewarned of attempting this by the failure of the old-time political economy, which established an "economic man," impelled simply by physical want. This failure was due in part to the fact that there never was such a being, and in part to the fact that the laborer gradually rose in the social and psychic scale until his physical impulses became a less important factor than his social and psychic impulses, for which their formulas were worthless.

It does not always follow that because the phenomena embraced by a science are subject to uniform laws they can always be reduced to mathematical formulas. Only a comparatively small part of physics is of a character to require mathematical treatment. It is still less so in chemistry. Still, the laws of thermology, electrology, and chemistry are just as invariable as those of barology and astronomy. Uniform laws or processes are the essentials of a science. Their mathematical expression is not essential. The sociologist, therefore, need only inquire whether society is a domain of uniform laws. That it should not seem to be to superficial observers is natural enough.

Before proceeding further, I will formulate the principle which, as I see it, underlies the proposition that sociology is a true science. It is that *in the complex sciences the quality of exactness is only perceptible in their higher generalizations.* This is a different thing from the other truth that in the complex sciences safe conclusions can only be drawn from wide inductions. In a field so great as that of human society, a wide induction becomes unmanageable. The number of facts to be dealt with is so great that they bewilder the mind. Something must be done besides accumulating facts, and drawing conclusions from them. A mental process of a higher order must be employed. The attempt to reason from the facts of society directly usually results in error. Conclusions so based are unsafe. The historical school of economists sometimes employ this method, but they do not agree in their results, and often err. They attempt to arrive at truth of too low an order to be established in sociology. It is such attempts and their failures that bring sociology into disrepute. If a sociologist, for example, were to pretend that he could tell from the facts of society how a prospective election would result, he would be making an unwarrantable assumption. This is why sociology can have so little to do with current questions. Their solution depends upon too many minute details and local and personal conditions. All the sociologist can do, even in applied sociology, is to lay down certain general principles as guides to social and political action. A true sociologist will scarcely have an opinion on a current question.

The method in sociology is generalization. Precisely what is meant by this may require some illustration. It is essentially the process of grouping phenomena and using the groups as units. Nature works by this method, for example in chemistry, where it is believed that the higher compounds have as their units compounds of lower orders. The phenomena of society are omnipresent. They obtrude upon the view at every turn. We exist in a social medium. The facts that the sociologist must use are spontaneously supplied to him every moment and everywhere. He need not go in search of them. The ones that are thus hourly thrust upon him are the most important of all. If he travel through all lands he will find the same facts. What he will find additional is only auxiliary and valuable for comparative study. Yet as a rule only the sociologist or true student of society really sees these facts.

The sociologist himself finds them so obvious and natural that it is difficult for him to realize their importance. Their very proximity is a bar to their full comprehension. I have called this "the illusion of the near," and likened it to the difficulty of seeing a city or a forest while in its midst. If we magnify any object sufficiently it loses its character. A tyro with a microscope always uses too high a power and thus fails to obtain the desired results. The relativity

E

of magnitude is interesting to reflect upon, and it was this truth that Dean Swift so forcibly illustrated in his description of the Lilliputians and the Brobdingnagians.

I was once exploring for my own amusement the suburbs of a large city one side of which was flanked by a range of high hills. I climbed over the ridges and was descending one of the slopes toward the town when my attention was arrested by a curious structure that seemed to me without meaning. It inclosed nothing, but presented a crude fabric of large timbers, some upright, some horizontal, some strangely crossing each other and rising twenty feet or more above the ground, in a long row resembling scaffolding, but without obvious purpose. They had been partly painted white, but the paint had mostly disappeared from long exposure to the elements. I pondered over the meaning of this grotesque structure for some time, and started several theories (targets, pyrotechnic frames, etc.), none of which would bear analysis. Finally I resumed the descent of the ridge and ultimately found myself in the back streets of the city half a mile from the spot where I noted the timbers. Being interested to see where I had been and how I had succeeded in getting down, having had to pursue a somewhat winding course on account of obstacles, I turned round and took a prolonged view of the long hillside, noting all the objects that had attracted my attention. I was quite sure of my route, but there was one object standing out in clear lines against the green hillside that caused some doubt, as I had not seen it, and I surely would have noted it had I passed near it. It was a clearly depicted name of a firm that extensively advertised itself in the city. The letters were all perfect and the words stood out with great distinctness. After puzzling awhile it at last occurred to me that this was the strange and awkward collection of timbers whose meaning and purpose I had failed to fathom. A more typical case of the illusion of the near I have never met with, and as I had already formulated that phrase and illustrated it as fully as possible I congratulated myself upon this new and unexpected example.

That which is near seems to lack symmetry and definiteness. It presents a great number of apparently dissimilar and heterogeneous objects. These objects seem to have no other relations than those of coexistence, distance, direction, and position. They do not seem to have any order. To see order in them it is necessary to view them at a distance. We do not apply the term *landscape* to what is close around us. That is only landscape to persons some distance away. Beauty is almost a synonym of order. If objects are far enough off to reveal the order they possess they are usually beautiful. The enchantment that distance lends is the response of our faculties to the order presented, for the mind naturally loves the symmetrical. The development of the human mind is nowhere better illustrated than in the difference between the savage and the civilized man in their ideas of beauty. The savage loves small artificial objects like beads, rings, medallions, trinkets, etc., but he sees no beauty in rivers, groves, mountains, or clouds. This is because his causality is not sufficiently developed to see order or regularity in them. But the developed mind admires landscapes because it can resolve the parts into wholes and grasp the relations that bind them together. A mountain, seen at a distance, is a symmetrical object of rare beauty, but when one is climbing it the rocks and crags, the ridges and gulches, the trees, bushes, briers, and prostrate logs, constitute a disordered mass of obstructions to which the term beauty does not apply. An inverted field glass is a tolerable substitute for distance in bringing order out of chaos and causing near objects to arrange themselves in agreeable form. It simply removes them to the same degree that the same field glass employed in the normal way brings them up to the observer.

The effect of distance, or its equivalent, may be called intensive, as opposed to the extensive effect of proximity. In the latter we only see surface and extension, in the former we see causation. It may be likened to the different wave lengths that cause different colors. It may be illustrated mechanically in the gearing of machinery, where the little wheels, whose surfaces must travel the same distance as those of the large wheels, may describe a thousand revolutions while the latter are describing one. This is the type of intensive motion in general. If the quantity of motion is unchangeable in the universe, as the law of the conservation of energy seems to require us to suppose, the effect of confining motion is necessarily to increase the intensive at the expense of the extensive changes. As the paths are shortened the number of circuits is increased, and motion of translation is finally converted into molecular motion, as it is called. This usually increases the efficiency, or ability to do work. The effects of motion as a cause become apparent. Here again intensity is causation.

The same principle applies in matters of sound as in those of sight. If a string is stretched, as in a stringed instrument, and struck it gives forth a sound corresponding to the amplitude of the vibration of the string, which in turn depends upon its length. If it be shortened by pressing it at any point with the finger, as in fingering, the pitch is raised proportionally, on account of the diminished amplitude of the vibrations. The sound becomes more intense. Any desired tone may thus be produced. As the vibrations become shorter they are more rapid, and we have another illustration of confined motion. The physical laws of all this are of course well known. They were mostly worked out by Pythagoras. I only wish to show that they are merely examples of a general law of universal application.

Besides these examples within the range of the organs of sense there are examples which can only be cognized by the mind. The mind appropriates truth as naturally as the body appropriates nourishment. Its ability to do so depends on two elements, its inherent capacity or power and its equipment. These two together constitute intelligence, as distinguished from intellect on the one hand and knowledge on the other. As intelligence develops the ability to generalize increases and the stage is at length reached at which the mind sees much that the senses cannot apprehend. With the progress of science this power is enormously enhanced and the true interpretation of nature begins. We must be content with a very few illustrations from physical phenomena.

The early pastoral races of the East learned much about the heavens as they lay out under the starry sky tenting their flocks. But their synthetic powers wasted themselves in the fanciful grouping of the stars into constellations that possess no scientific significance. The galaxy or milky way was of course an object of their constant attention, but in their ignorance of the general constitution of the universe they never framed any theory to explain it. It remained for science to propose such a theory, and, so far as I know, only one has been proposed. I do not vouch for it, but, assuming it to be true, I use it as showing the power of the mind in possession of certain facts to bring order out of chaos. This theory is, as the reader doubtless knows, that our solar system belongs to a more or less definitely circumscribed universe or great body of stars; that this stellar aggregate possesses a somewhat lenticular shape; and that our solar system is not located at the center of its shorter axis but some distance to one side of the center. This theory seems to account for the majority of the facts presented by sidereal astronomy, and explains the milky way as simply the effect produced by looking in the direction of the thin edges of the lens where a so much larger number of stars naturally come into view than when looking in the direction of its sides, or, as it were, out into empty space. We thus, by a pure act of the mind, gain an orderly conception of the universe, which may be contrasted with the chaotic conceptions that formerly prevailed, or that must be entertained by any person of reflective habits unacquainted with this theory.

The distribution of land and water on the surface of the earth must appear devoid of order to the child who first sees a map of the world or a globe. It so appears to many persons of mature years who do not reflect or who have never had its relations pointed out. Yet most scientific geographers see in it the operation of a great law. To the geologist, especially one who has given special attention to that modern branch of geology called physiography, this action of law is much more clear still than to those who study only surface phenomena. If with all this is combined a philosophical conception of the origin of the different planets of the solar system and the causes affecting the crust of the earth, the wrinkling due to shrinkage, etc., the epeirogenic and orogenic conditions become clear, and a knowledge of the causes lends a charm to studies of this kind. The oceans and seas, the island groups, the continents, and the mountain chains become systems definitely related to one another, and an orderly method is seen to pervade all the phenomena of the earth's surface and the earth's crust.

Passing over chemistry, which, in its hierarchy of combinations — elements, inorganic compounds, organic compounds, each a subhierarchy in itself — has furnished us with the very principle of generalization ; and biology, where, from the multiplicity of organic forms, no progress can be made without classification, which is generalization, we may enter at once the domain of anthropology and find the same truth exemplified at every point. What Dr. Edward B. Tylor has called " ethnographic parallels," viz., the occurrence of the same or similar customs, practices, ceremonies, arts, beliefs, and even games, symbols, and patterns, in peoples of nearly the same culture at widely separated regions of the globe, proves, except in a few cases of known derivation through migration, that there is a uniform law in the psychic and social development of mankind at all times and under all circumstances. The details will vary with the climate and other physical differences in the environment, but if we continue to rise in the process of generalization we will ultimately reach a plane on which all mankind are alike.

Even in civilized races, including the most enlightened modern peoples, there are certain things absolutely common to all. The great primary wants are everywhere the same and they are supplied in substantially the same way the world over. Forms of government seem to differ immensely, but all governments aim to attain the same end. Political parties are bitterly opposed, but there is much more on which all agree than on which they differ. Creeds, cults, and sects multiply and seem to present the utmost heterogeneity, but there is a common basis even of belief, and on certain occasions all may and sometimes do unite in a common cause.

Not only are the common wants of men the same, but their passions are also the same, and those acts growing out of them which are regarded as destructive of the social order and condemned by law and public opinion are committed in the face of these restraining influences with astonishing regularity. This is not seen by the ordinary observer, and every crime or breach of order is commonly looked upon as exceptional and arouses great local or general interest according to its nature and the circumstances attending it. But when accurate statistics are brought to bear upon this class of social phenomena they prove to be quite as uniform, though not quite so frequent, as the normal operations of life. Even the most extraordinary occurrences, such as the killing of an aged parent by a child or the marriage of brother and sister, actually occur once in about so long, or so as to form a certain percentage of the homicides or marriages. There is a law of deviation from a mean, upon which Galton lays great stress, which explains such cases. In dealing with prodigies in the last chapter we encountered one aspect of this law. Fanatics illustrate another aspect of it. When any question agitates the public mind there is a great central mass of men who take an ordinary enlightened interest in it. Below these there is a body of persons experiencing an interest diminishing in degree until it practically vanishes.   Above the mean there is a certain number with whom the interest is greater, and this rises with diminishing numbers until there is reached a point at which a very few persons are wholly engrossed in the question.   There may be one so completely absorbed as to be capable of committing a terrible crime, such as assassination.   This is probably the true psychological explanation of all three of the presidential assassinations in the United States.   Such acts might be represented geometrically as forming the apex of a curve, or the maximum deviation from the mean.   Even assassinations are regular social phenomena, as any one may see by casting a glance backward through less than half a century.   This does not mean that they cannot and should not be prevented by every power society possesses, nor does it mean that any crime may not be utterly eradicated by appropriate social action.   In fact all history proves that the forces underlying crime, as well as many actions that are not criminal, have been gradually drawn off into other channels, or in scientific phrase, commuted, by civilizing agencies.

The ordinary events of life go unnoticed, but there are certain events that are popularly regarded as extraordinary, notwithstanding the fact that the newspapers every day devote more than half their space to them.   One would suppose that people would sometime learn that fires, and railroad accidents, and mine disasters, and boiler explosions, and robberies, and defalcations, and murders, as well as elopements, *liaisons* in high life, seductions, and rape, were normal social phenomena, after reading of nearly every one of these and hundreds of other similar events every day throughout the whole course of a lifetime.   But this enormous mass of evidence has no effect whatever in dispelling the popular illusion that such events are extraordinary, and the octogenarian whose eyesight will permit still pores over the daily news, as it is called, with the same intense interest as when he was a youth.   There is nothing new in "news" except a difference in the names.   The events are the same.   It was this that Schopenhauer meant when he said that history furnishes nothing new but only the continual repetition of the same thing under different names.   And this is what is meant by generalization.   We have only to carry it far enough in order to arrive at unity.   Society is a domain of law, and sociology is an abstract science in the sense that it does not

attend to details except as aids in arriving at the law that underlies them all.

This has been called the *historical perspective*. It is the discovery
of law in history, whether it be the history of the past or the present, and including under history social as well as political phenomena. There is nothing very new in this. It is really the oldest
of all sociological conceptions. The earliest gropings after a social
science consisted in a recognition of law in human affairs. The
so-called precursors of sociology have been those who have perceived more or less distinctly a method or order in human events.
All who have done this, however dimly, have been set down as the
heralds of the new science. Such adumbrations of the idea of law
in society were frequent in antiquity. They are to be found in
the sayings of Socrates and the writings of Aristotle. Lucretius
sparkles with them. In medieval times they were more rare, and
we scarcely find them in St. Augustine, but Ibn Khaldûn, a Saracen of Tunis, in the fourteenth century gave clear expression
to this conception.[1] His work, however, was lost sight of until
recently, and Vico, who wrote at the close of the seventeenth and
beginning of the eighteenth century, was long regarded as the true
forerunner of Montesquieu. Still, there were many others both
before and after Vico, and passages have been found reflecting this
general truth in the writings of Machiavelli, Bruno, Campanella,
Bacon, Hobbes, Locke, Hume, Adam Smith, Ferguson, Fontenelle,
Buffon, Turgot, Condorcet, Leibnitz, Kant, Oken, etc. Before
Comte had given name and form to sociology Saint-Simon, Bastiat,
Carey, and John Stuart Mill had more or less clearly formulated
the general doctrine of historical determinism, and the philosophy of history had received wide recognition. The theologically
inclined, when this truth was brought home to them, characterized
it by the phrase "God in history," and saw in the order of events
the divine hand guiding the acts of men toward some predestined
goal. This is perhaps the most common view to-day, and the general optimism of mankind furnishes all the faith necessary to harmo-

---

[1] "Prolégomènes historique d'Ibn Khaldoun." Translated from the Arabic by
M. G. de Slane, and published in the Notices et Extraits des Manuscrits de la
Bibliothèque Impériale, publiés par l'Institut de France, Vol. XIX, Pt. I, Paris,
1862, 4°. This includes an autobiography of Ibn Khaldûn and his entire system of
historical science, in which many of the leading questions now under consideration
by sociologists are discussed from an enlightened standpoint.

nize the doctrine with the scientific law of human evolution. But science deals with phenomena and can only deal with phenomena. Sociology, therefore, can only become a science when human events are recognized as phenomena. When we say that they are due to the actions of men there lurks in the word *actions* the ghost of the old doctrine of free will, which in its primitive form asserts that any one may either perform a given action or not, according as he may will. From this point of view it is not supposed that any event in human history needed to have occurred. If the men whose actions caused it had willed otherwise, it would not have occurred. That is, the old form of the doctrine of free will maintained that men might have willed otherwise than they did. It is not merely that they might have acted differently if they had willed to do so, but that they might have willed to act differently. If we substitute wish for will, as of course we may, since it is simply a peculiarity of the English language that there are two words for the same thing which in other languages is expressed by the same word (*volere, wollen, vouloir*, etc.), the doctrine becomes that men might have wished to act otherwise than they did wish to act. This is a violation of the metaphysical axiom of contradiction, or as Sir William Hamilton more correctly calls it, non-contradiction. That axiom is that a thing cannot both be and not be. In other words the old-fashioned doctrine of free will assumes that men may act differently from what they do act irrespective of character and environment. If this were so, there could certainly be no science of action, no philosophy of history, no sociology. There would be no social phenomena but only arbitrary actions due to no true cause, and all power of prevision or prediction would be wanting.[1]

As opposed to this, the scientific view is that human events are phenomena of the same general character as other natural phenomena, only more complex and difficult to study on account of the subtle psychic causes that so largely produce them. It has been seen more or less clearly by the men I have named and by many others that there must be causes, and the philosophy of history that gradually emerged from the chaos of the existing history was simply an attempt to ascertain some of these causes and show how they produced the effects. To those who make the philosophy of

[1] Cf. Gumplowicz, " Actions ou phénomènes," *Revue des Revues* du 15 novembre, 1895.

history coextensive with sociology, this is all that sociology implies.
Certainly it was the first and most essential step in the direction of
establishing a science of society. The tendency at first was strong
to discover in the environment the chief cause of social variation,
and some authors sought to expand the term *climate* to include
all this. This doctrine had its advocates and was of course carried too far, as exemplified in the saying that "mountains make
freemen while lowlands make slaves." It was found that this was
only half of the truth, that it took account only of the objective
environment, while an equally potent factor is the subjective environment, and that the ancient saying, *cœlum non animum mutant
qui trans mare currunt*, is also true. Character, however acquired,
is difficult to change, and must be reckoned with in any attempt
to interpret human events. Thus expanded, the study of society
from this point of view becomes a true science, and recently it has
been given the appropriate name of *mesology*. The great influence of
climate and physical conditions must be fully recognized. It reaches
back into the domain of ethnology and physiology, and doubtless explains the color of the skin, the character of the hair, and the general
physical nature of the different races of men. The psychic effects
of the environment are scarcely less important, and the qualities of
courage, love of liberty, industry and thrift, ingenuity and intelligence, are all developed by contact with restraining influences
adapted to stimulating them and not so severe as to check their
growth. The social effects are still more marked. We first see
them in the phenomena of migration and settlement and the ways
in which men adapt themselves to the conditions, resources, and
general character of the region they may chance to occupy. The
question asked by the traditional boy in the geography class: Why
the large rivers all run past the great cities? illustrates how clearly
everybody sees natural law at work in society. It is the laws of
society that determine the direction and character of migration and
settlement. "Laws," says Montesquieu, "are the necessary relations that are derived from the nature of things,"[1] and this is precisely the sense here implied. In peoples at all advanced the head

---

[1] "Les loix, dans la signification la plus étendue, sont les rapports nécessaires
qui dérivent de la nature des choses." This is the first sentence of Montesquieu's
principal work, "de l'Esprit des Loix." Œuvres de Montesquieu, Nouvelle Édition,
Tome Premier, Paris, 1788, p. 1.

of navigation of rivers is usually the site for the principal towns. A short time ago when water was more used than now as a power, there was usually combined with the advantages offered by the head of navigation (all vessels being then small), the additional advantage of the fall in the stream, which is almost always greatest at the point where the piedmont plateau joins the coastal plain. As streams only reach base level after emerging upon the coastal plain, this sudden fall almost always occurs a short distance above the head of navigation. As this is true of all the streams that drain a continent, a line may be drawn through this point on all the rivers and it will be approximately parallel to the coast. Such a line is called the *fall line* and it is a law of populations that the first settlements of any country take place along the fall line of its rivers.

There are many laws that can be thus illustrated, and careful observation reveals the fact that all social phenomena are the results of laws. But the fundamental law of everything psychic, and especially of everything that is affected by intelligence, is the *law of parsimony*. It has its applications in biology, and even in cosmology, which I need not stop to point out, but it was first clearly grasped by the political economists, and by many it is regarded as only an economic law. Here it is usually called the law of *greatest gain for least effort*, and is the basis of scientific economics. But it is much broader than this, and not only plays an important rôle in psychology, but becomes, in that collective psychology which constitutes so nearly the whole of sociology, the scientific corner-stone of that science also. We have seen that the quality of scientific exactness in sociology can only be clearly perceived in some of its higher generalizations, where, neglecting the smaller unities which make its phenomena so exceedingly complex, and dealing only with the large composite unities that the minor ones combine to create, we are able to handle the subject, as it were, in bulk. Here we can plainly see the relations and can be sure of their absolute uniformity and reliability. When we reach the law of parsimony we seem to have attained the maximum stage of generalization, and here we have a law as exact as any in physics or astronomy. It is, for example, perfectly safe to assume that under any and all conceivable circumstances a sentient, and especially a rational being will always seek the

greatest gain, or the maximum resultant of gain — his "marginal"
advantage.

Those who are shocked by such a proposition take too narrow a
view of the subject. They think that they themselves at least are
exceptions to the law, and that they do not always seek their
greatest gain, and they give illustrations of actions performed that
result in a loss instead of a gain. This is because they understand
by gain only pecuniary gain, or only gain in temporary enjoyment or
immediate satisfaction. If they could analyze their feelings they
would see that they were merely sacrificing a present to a future
advantage, or what they regard as a lower to what they regard as a
higher satisfaction. When Henry Clay said (if he did say it) that
"every man has his price," [1] he may have merely stated this law in a
new form. If we make the important qualification that the "price"
is not necessarily a money price, we may see that the statement contains a truth. Even in the lobby, which he probably had in view,
it is well known that downright bribery is very rarely resorted to.
It is among the least effective of the lobbyist's methods. There are
other far more successful ways of gaining a legislator's vote. Passes
on railroads and other favors of that kind are much more common,
but even these are relatively coarse and transparent, and the great
vested interests of a country know how to accomplish their ends by
much more subtle means. It is only necessary to put those whom
they desire to influence under some form of obligation, and this is
usually easy to do. Among the most effective means to this end are
social amenities and the establishment in apparently the most disinterested ways of a friendly *entente*, which appeals to the sense of
honor, and would make any man ashamed to act contrary to the
known wishes of a friend. Under such powerful sentiments constitu-
encies are forgotten.

But this is by no means the whole meaning of the law. It deals
solely with motives, and worthy motives are as potent as unworthy
ones. It is based, it is true, on interests, but we must give to the
term *interest* all the breadth that Ratzenhofer does. Interest is not
always bad. It is much more frequently good. It was necessarily
good, at least for the individual, in the beginning, since it had the
mission to impel life and race preserving activities. Interest may be

---

[1] In England a similar phrase is commonly ascribed to Sir Robert Walpole. Cf.
Coxe: "Memoirs of Walpole," Vol. IV, p. 369.

perverted, but this is the exception. Men feel an interest in doing good, and moral interest is as real as any other. Ratzenhofer shows that men have been profoundly moved by what he calls "transcendental interests," which he defines as a striving after the infinite, and to this he attributes the great religious movements in society. If therefore we take into account all these different kinds of interest, physical, racial (*Gattungsinteresse*), moral, social, and transcendental, it becomes clear that all action is based on supposed gain of one or another of these orders. Still, the world has never reached a stage where the physical and temporary interests have not been largely in the ascendant, and it is these upon which the economists have established their science. Self-preservation has always been the first law of nature, and that which best insures this is the greatest gain. So unerring is this law that it is easy to create a class of paupers or mendicants by simply letting it be known that food or alms will be given to those who ask. All considerations of pride or self-respect will give way to the imperious law of the greatest gain for the least effort. All notions of justice which would prompt the giving of an equivalent vanish before it, and men will take and use what is proffered without thought of a return or sense of gratitude. In this respect men are like animals. In fact, this is precisely the principle that underlies the domestication of animals and the taming of wild beasts. So soon as the creature learns that it will not be molested and that its wants will be supplied, it submits to the will of man and becomes a parasite. Parasitism, indeed, throughout the organic world is only an application of the law of parsimony.

While therefore no law can be laid down as to how any individual will act under a given set of circumstances, in consequence of the enormous number and variety of causes that combine to determine any single act, we have a law which determines with absolute certainty how all men may be depended upon to act. If there is any apparent exception to this law we may be sure that some element has been overlooked in the calculation. Just as, in the case of a heavenly body which is observed to move in a manner at variance with the established laws of gravitation and planetary motion, the astronomer does not doubt the universality of those laws but attributes the phenomena to some undiscovered body in space of the proper size and in the proper position to cause the perturbation, and proceeds to search for that body ; so in human society, if there are

events that seem at variance with the fundamental sociological law
of parsimony, the sociologist may safely trust the law and proceed
to discover the cause of the social perturbation.

It is the function of methodology in social science to classify
social phenomena in such a manner that the groups may be brought
under uniform laws and treated by exact methods. Sociology then
becomes an exact science. In doing this, too, it will be found that
we have passed from chaos to cosmos. Human history presents a
chaos. The only science that can convert the milky way of history
into a definite social universe is sociology, and this can only be done
by the use of an appropriate method, by using the data furnished
by all the special social sciences, including the great scientific trunks
of psychology, biology, and cosmology, and generalizing and coördi-
nating the facts and groups of facts until unity is attained.

PART II

GENESIS

CHAPTER V

FILIATION

It has become customary to speak of the hierarchy of the sciences and nearly everybody understands what the expression means. For this reason it does no harm to use it and I use it constantly myself. Nevertheless, if we examine it critically we find that it will not bear analysis, and that the relation subsisting among the sciences is a very different one from that expressed by the word *hierarchy*. A hierarchy is a relation of superiority and subordination such as is expressed in the word *rank* as applied, for example, to officers of an army. It is also the same as is involved in all synoptical classification, as in the natural sciences, where the several classific groups (class, order, family, genus, species) are subordinated to one another by the possession of characters of lower and lower classificatory value. This is what may be called *logical* classification. If we examine the relation of the several sciences of the so-called hierarchy (astronomy, physics, chemistry, biology, etc.) we at once perceive that the kind of superiority or subordination is generically different from that subsisting among officers of an army or among classific groups in natural history. As I said, nearly everybody knows just what the nature of this relation is, viz., one of diminishing generality with increasing complexity, and therefore no one stops to consider the appropriateness of the term hierarchy as applied to it. This, however, may be called *serial* classification, and it is important for many reasons to insist upon the complete distinctness of these two kinds of classification. For example, Mr. Spencer dissented from Comte's classification of the sciences and drew up one of his own which, he claimed, conflicted with Comte's. But Mr. Spencer's classification was a logical one while Comte's was a serial one, and it was impossible for them to conflict. In fact they afforded no basis of comparison for the purpose of establishing the truth or falsity of either.[1]

[1] I have several times stated, as have also other writers (De Greef, "Introd. à la Sociologie," I, p. 5, 1886; Dallemagne, "Principes de Sociologie," p. 36, 1886; Hector

Now, what concerns the sociologist is primarily the serial order
of phenomena. The several groups of phenomena constituting the

Denis, "Revue Int. de Sociologie," 8ᵉ année, 1900, p. 778), that notwithstanding Mr.
Spencer's vigorous disclaimer of any indebtedness to Comte, and notwithstanding his
work on the "Classification of the Sciences," he had virtually admitted the correctness
of Comte's serial arrangement by arranging his own subjects in practically the same
order ("First Principles," dealing with inorganic nature, Biology, Psychology, Sociology).   When I repeated this statement in the *American Journal of Sociology* for
July, 1895, p. 18, I received a letter from Mr. Spencer which ought to be made public
because it throws a flood of light upon a number of obscure questions connected
with his views on the classification of the sciences, which he has nowhere made clear
in his works.   This relates especially to his ideas relative to the relations of the simpler sciences dealing with inorganic matter, which he says he was obliged to leave
out of his system because it would so expand it that he could not hope to complete it.

I have felt, too, somewhat keenly, his implied censure for making the statement
referred to, which seemed to me so self-evident that it did not occur to me that it
could give offense, and therefore I am willing to let the world know what the points
are at which Mr. Spencer takes exception, and I therefore give his letter entire, followed by the reply that I made to it after mature reflection: —

                    "64 AVENUE ROAD, REGENT'S PARK, LONDON, N.W.,
                              "Sept. 19, 1895.
"MY DEAR SIR: I have just received a copy of your essay on 'The Place of
Sociology among the Sciences,' and on glancing through it am startled by some of
its statements.
"1. You have not, I presume, read my essay on 'The Genesis of Science'; otherwise you would scarcely say that Comte's classification represents the genetic or
serial order of the sciences.   You would have found that it is in that essay shown
that there is no serial order, and in the second place that Comte's classification does
not at all represent the order of genesis, numerous facts being given to show that the
evolution of the sciences was no such succession as he alleges.
"2. But I am much more amazed by your statement respecting Comte's system
that 'Spencer himself, notwithstanding all his efforts to overthrow it, actually
adopted it in the arrangement of the sciences in his Synthetic Philosophy.'   Now
in the first place, if you will look at my essay on 'The Genesis of Science,' you will
see that the first two great groups of sciences — the abstract, containing logic and
mathematics, the abstract-concrete, containing mechanics, physics, and chemistry
— have no place whatever in the 'Synthetic Philosophy.'   So far from the 'Synthetic
Philosophy' containing them in the order in which Comte places them, they are not
there at all.   The 'Synthetic Philosophy' concerns exclusively those sciences which
I class as concrete sciences — the sciences which have for their subject-matters actual
concrete existences — and treats of each one not in respect of any one set of traits
but in respect of all its traits.
"Setting aside the fact that, as I have pointed out, the sciences which deal with
the forms of phenomena and those which deal with their factors, make no appearance
whatever in the order of sciences forming the 'Synthetic Philosophy,' there is the fact
that even if the sciences as involved in the 'Synthetic Philosophy' are compared with
the system of Comte they are shown to be wholly incongruous with it.   If you will
turn to the original preface to 'First Principles,' in which an outline of the 'Synthetic
Philosophy' is set forth you will see there, between the programme of 'First Principles' and the programme of the 'Biology,' a note in italics pointing out that in logical
order there should come an application of First Principles to inorganic nature, and
that the part of it dealing with inorganic nature is omitted simply because the

true "hierarchy" of the sciences, not only stand in the relation of diminishing generality with increasing complexity, but they stand

scheme, even as it stood, was too extensive. Two volumes were thus omitted — a volume on astronomy and a volume on geology. Had it been possible to write these in addition to those undertaken, the series would have run — astronomy, *geology*, biology, *psychology*, sociology, ethics. Now in this series those marked in italics do not appear in the Comtian classification at all. In the part of the 'Synthetic Philosophy' as it now stands the only correspondence with the Comtian classification is that biology comes before sociology; and surely any one would see that in rational order the phenomena presented by a living individual must come before those presented by an assemblage of such living individuals. It requires no leading of Comte for any one to see this.

"3. But now in the third place, I draw your attention to Table III in my 'Classification of the Sciences.' There you will see that the order of the works already existing in the 'Synthetic Philosophy,' and still better the order in which they would have stood had the thing been complete, corresponds exactly with the order shown in that table, and is an order which evolves necessarily from the mode of organization there insisted upon, and corresponds also to the order of appearance in time, if we set out with the nebular condensation and end with special phenomena. The order of the 'Synthetic Philosophy' does *not* correspond with that of Comte, and it *does* correspond with the order shown in my own 'Classification of the Sciences.' This seems to me undeniable if it is remembered that in the process of evolution there were astronomical phenomena before there were geological; that there were geological phenomena before there were biological; that there were biological before there were psychological; that there were psychological before there were any sociological — that is to say, the order as shown in the table and as followed in the 'Synthetic Philosophy' is the order of actual genesis that has occurred in the course of universal evolution.

"I am
"Faithfully yours
"HERBERT SPENCER.

"LESTER F. WARD, Esq."

After considerable delay I replied to the above letter as follows : —

"1464 R. I. AVE., WASHINGTON, D.C., U. S. AMERICA.
"Jan. 6, 1896.

"MR. HERBERT SPENCER, LONDON.

"My Dear Sir: I received your letter of Sept. 19, 1895, while in the field in California, where it was forwarded to me. I had no facilities for writing at the time and did not reach Washington till well into November. I have been contemplating a reply since that time, but partly from an excess of work of various kinds, and partly from doubts as to what kind of a reply I ought to make, I have procrastinated until now.

"I do not hope that anything I could say would be satisfactory to you, and it seems almost useless to enter into a full discussion of the points involved. Not long ago I received a letter from Mr. Richard Congreve, relative in the main to the same article you criticize, in which he takes me almost as severely to task as you do for not going farther in the same direction in which you think I go too far. Evidently if I had tried to please everybody I should have pleased nobody, and matters would have been no better than they are. But of course I do not want to misquote or in any way misrepresent any one, and have not meant to do so.

"The series of articles that are running through the *American Journal of Sociology* is a course of lectures that I have twice delivered at the Hartford School of Sociology,

in the relation of parent to offspring, *i.e.*, of *filiation*. The more
complex sciences grow out of the simpler ones by a process of differ-

orally in 1894, and in their present form in November last. They were all written
out before I left Washington in August. In this series I have not aimed at much
originality, and only wished to put before the students primarily, but also the numerous teachers of the various social sciences in this country, some general outlines and
fundamental principles, most of which have been stated by me in earlier works. All
the statements you criticise have been made by me before, some of them more than
once. I have taken extra pains to put my writings into your hands, without, however, hoping that you could find time to look them through. Indeed, you have written me how you require to husband your mental strength, and I had long regarded
the sending you my papers as merely a compliment, which I would have been deterred
from making if I had thought you would waste any energy on them.

"I have always maintained that Comte's classification was a true genetic one. I
said all I have to say on this point in 'Dynamic Sociology,' and the only answer I can
make to any of the points in your letter is contained in pages 143 to 149 of the first
volume of that work. There also are to be found all the statements in the article to
which you have taken exception. Having stood there over twelve years unchallenged,
I did not hesitate to repeat them in a more popular form. Although Dr. Youmans
told me you could not read the book, it was to be supposed that you would at least
glance at the first few pages of the chapter that deals especially with your philosophy, and it is these pages on which the statements all occur. Should you care to do
so now you will see that I recognized the omission in your system of the parts relating to inorganic nature, which I have always regarded as unfortunate. But your
'First Principles' partly supply this omission and impressed me with your recognition
of the subordination of astronomical, physical, and chemical, to biological principles.
Exactly in what order you would have treated these departments could not of course
be told, but the extent to which you base biology upon chemical laws in your 'Principles of Biology' seemed to indicate that these were regarded by you as the immediate foundation of biology.

"You will also see by a footnote to page 148 that I had read your 'Classification of
the Sciences,' and some of your strictures on Comte's philosophy, but not until the
matter of that chapter was in type. As soon as I could obtain it I read your 'Genesis
of Science.' In taking down my copy I see that I put an occasional comment in the
margin. At the close of your discussion of Comte I had written: 'Nevertheless
Comte's hierarchy is a grand truth that Spencer recognizes by adopting the same
order in his system.'

"This merely shows how strongly I have always been impressed with this idea,
and the remark made in my footnote to page 146 of 'Dynamic Sociology,' Vol. I, is
just what I should now say to your 'Genesis of Science.' Literally you are right
and Comte wrong, for nothing is clearer than that all science, all knowledge, and all
progress, have been empirical, have come limping along in an irregular, illogical, and
haphazard way, wrong end first, and tumbling over each other, after the wasteful
method of nature in general that some affect so greatly to admire. It was unfortunate that Comte should have blundered as he did in asserting that the historical
order of development conformed to the natural order of genesis, and thus given you
an occasion to take him up on this unessential point, which many no doubt have
mistaken for the essential one. But Comte was always making such blunders, calculated to scare off nearly every one from looking into the merits of his system.

"I am very glad to learn from your letter what your entire system would have
been. So far as the heads are concerned, it is quite as near to Comte's as I supposed.
If your 'geology' could be regarded as the equivalent of his physics and chemistry,
the two series would be identical, for Comte did not ignore psychic phenomena and

entiation. The more general phenomena of the simpler sciences are elaborated into more complex forms. They are the raw material which is worked up into more finished products, much as pig iron is worked up into tools, machinery, cutlery, and watch-springs. The simpler sciences contain all that is in the more complex, but it is more homogeneous, and the process of evolution, as we know, is a

laws, but treated them quite fully and in the same position as you. He only denied that they were distinct from biology. Moreover, in his 'Politique Positive,' he makes ethics the final term, the same as you.

"The difference, then, is not so much in the names or the order of the sciences as in the point of view from which they are contemplated. Here it seems fundamental, and I have never so fully realized this before. You base your classification upon the concrete phenomena or material facts, while Comte based his upon the laws or principles underlying the phenomena. Your geology cannot therefore be reduced to physics and chemistry. Your astronomy is the sun, planets, and stars ; your biology, the animals and plants, and your sociology, associated human beings. But I do not see how you get a concrete basis for psychology, since mind is not concrete. As for ethics, it certainly is not a concrete thing, and I consider it only a department of sociology.

"But is the distinction as fundamental as it seems at first sight? Concrete things are only known by the phenomena they manifest, and philosophy is mainly a process of arriving at the laws and principles underlying phenomena. Each of your treatises avowedly deals with 'principles' — 'the laws of the knowable.' A classification based on the laws of the universe is therefore much more fundamental than one based on the concrete facts, and is, in my judgment, the only one upon which the true 'filiation' of the sciences can proceed.

"Yours with great respect,

"LESTER F. WARD."

In a paper which I read before the Philosophical Society of Washington on Feb. 1, 1896, partly growing out of this correspondence, an abstract of which was published in *Science* for Feb. 21, 1896, I placed the two systems in parallel columns, as follows : —

System of Auguste Comte :	*System of Herbert Spencer :*
1. Astronomy	1. Astronomy
2. Physics ⎱	2. Geology
3. Chemistry ⎰	
4. Biology (including	3. Biology
5. Cerebral biology)	4. Psychology
6. Sociology	5. Sociology
7. Ethics	6. Ethics

The more I reflect upon the use of geology as a coördinate term in this series the more objectionable it appears. In such comprehensive groups as these must necessarily be geology would fall under astronomy, as zoölogy and botany fall under biology. The earth is only one of the planets of the solar system, and only happens to be the one we know most about and can most thoroughly observe, hence it calls for a special science. But there might just as logically be a science of venerology (hesperology), of martiology (areology), of joviology (diology), of saturnology (cronology), or of uranology, as well as of heliology and selenology ; and we already have in common use the terms selenography and areography.

passage from the homogeneous to the heterogeneous. A serial classification is based on this principle of natural differentiation and the resulting filiation. It might be called *tocological.*

In the natural sciences, especially in biology, we have to do with both kinds of classification. Systematic botany, for example, is based on a strict logical classification, as I have described it. But phyto-biology must also deal with genetic relationships, and the terms higher and lower have different meanings when they relate to these two classes of phenomena. Sometimes their meanings may seem to be opposed to each other. Once, when I was obliged to define the two terms *Gymnospermæ* and *Angiospermæ* for a dictionary, I found myself saying that the former were coördinate with the latter, and also that they were lower in the scale of development, and this at first seemed like a contradiction. But a close analysis shows that both statements were true and did not conflict, because, in the one the point of view was systematic, *i.e.*, that of the logical classification, while in the other it was genetic, *i.e.*, that of the serial classification.

The serial order of the sciences is not an optional arrangement in which different authors may differ at will. It is the order of nature, and if all authors do not agree it is because they have not yet fully discovered the true order. As in the progress of establishing truth everywhere, they must ultimately all agree, because the truth is one. We do not accept it on any one's authority, and there is no occasion for trying to be original and saying something else after the truth has been once said. What all right-minded persons want is to discover the true order of nature and the natural arrangement of the sciences.

The filiation of the sciences is also an order of mutual dependence. Just as a child is dependent on its parents, so the complex sciences are dependent upon the general ones. This dependence is specially marked between any one science in the series and the one immediately below it, but in a broader sense all the higher sciences are dependent upon all the lower ones. For the sociologist it is specially important to recognize the dependence of social science on physical science, using these terms in their commonly accepted senses. This might seem to be a truism, but a glance at even modern education is sufficient to justify its emphasis. I think it safe to say that the educational programme or curriculum of none of the leading institu-

tions of learning or popular educational systems makes any pretense
at a serial arrangement of studies in the sense that that term has
here been used — an arrangement by which a knowledge of nature is
acquired in the order in which natural phenomena and natural things
have been developed.

Social science becomes as much more thorough, intelligible, interesting, and useful when based on physical science as is astronomy,
for example, when based on mathematics, or geology and mineralogy
when based on physics and chemistry.   There is no one of the more
general sciences that does not throw light on sociology.   Any one
who looks for them can find "analogies" all through.   There are
almost as many parallels between social and chemical processes as
there are between social and biological.   By extended comparisons
in all fields we find that the operations of nature are the same in all
departments.   We not only discover one great law of evolution
applicable to all the fields covered by the several sciences of the
series, but we can learn something more about the true method of
evolution by observing how it takes place in each of these fields.
Even some of the subordinate sciences falling under the great groups
that we have been considering, are capable of shedding light upon
the method of evolution, and probably any specialist in science, if
he would look carefully for such indications, could supplement the
knowledge we have relative to the essential nature of evolutionary
processes.

As an extreme example of the aid that the higher sciences and the
philosophy of science in general may derive from some of the more
special fields of research I will cite the branch that I have myself
most fully studied, and only for that reason, viz., paleobotany.   Before I had specially pursued that study my ideas of evolution were
similar to those that I observe to prevail among scientific men and
the educated public generally.   But an acquaintance with the extinct
plant life of the globe has wrought a great revolution in my conceptions of the development of life in all its forms and also in the
nature of evolution itself, cosmic, organic, and social.

Sympodial Development

The science of botany in its wide and proper sense — what I call
"the New Botany," the natural history of plants including their geological history — teaches that the prevailing conception of organic

evolution is radically incorrect in one of its essential aspects, and that the true view is as great an improvement upon the current arborescent conception as that is upon the earlier notion of linear development. It shows that plant development at least, and inferentially animal development also, is *sympodial*. This term of course requires definition to all but the botanist, and yet every educated person ought to have learned enough botany at school to understand it. But the botanists, *i.e.*, those who have paid no attention to paleobotany, and the writers of botanical text-books, do not, it must be confessed, clearly explain this term, and having no idea of the importance of the principle involved as bearing upon evolution, they do not lay stress on its essential features. At the risk, therefore, of being elementary I will briefly remark that the vegetable kingdom presents two clearly marked modes of branching known respectively as *monopodial* and *sympodial*. In monopodial branching the stem or main trunk gives off at intervals subordinate stems called branches, containing a comparatively small number of the fibro-vascular bundles of the main stem, which thus continues to diminish in size by the loss of its bundles until all are thus given off and the stem terminates in a slender twig. In sympodial branching, on the other hand, the main stem or trunk rises to a certain height and then gives off a branch into which the majority of the fibro-vascular bundles enter, so that the branch virtually becomes the trunk, and the real trunk or ascending portion is reduced to a mere twig, or may ultimately fail of support altogether and disappear through atrophy. This large branch at length in turn gives off a secondary branch containing as before the bulk of the bundles, and the first branch is sacrificed in the same manner as was the original stem or trunk; and this process is repeated throughout the life of the tree or plant. As might be naturally expected, the resulting series of branches of different orders is zigzag, and in most sympodial herbs this is manifest in the plant. It is somewhat so in vines like the grape vine, but in trees, like the linden, the forces of heliotropism and general upward growth serve to right up these several originally inclined sympodes, the abortive stems of antecedent stages vanish entirely, and the trunk becomes as erect and symmetrical as those of its monopodial companions of the forest. There are other distinctions which may be found set forth in the books, but these are the only ones that concern us here.

Now the monopodial type of branching is of course the one that everybody is familiar with, and this is the type that is alone considered when we speak of the arborescent character of organic development. Its inadequacy in explaining the actual phenomena presented by organic nature has been strongly felt, but no attempt has been made to discover a more correct method of representation. The opponents of evolution have made much use of the facts which, on the current arborescent theory, are in conflict with the doctrine, and even now, after the general truth of evolution has been firmly established, these residual phenomena that refuse to square with hypothesis occasionally obtrude themselves and generate unpleasant doubts. In the earlier pre-Darwinian days of the first half of the nineteenth century, after Lamarck, Goethe, Geoffroy Saint-Hilaire, and Robert Chambers (anonymous author of the "Vestiges of Creation") had filled the air with the idea of evolution, these opposing facts were eagerly seized upon and brought forward as effectually disposing of the doctrine. A class of writers of that time — Dr. William Buckland, Dr. Lindley, Dr. Henry Witham, and Hugh Miller — who were as well acquainted as anybody in their day with the character of the extinct floras of the globe, availed themselves of this scientific knowledge to disprove evolution on scientific grounds, and their arguments are as unanswerable to-day, on the prevailing view of arborescent (monopodial) development, as they were at that time. They never have been answered. On the view here presented that evolution is sympodial and not monopodial, these arguments find their complete answer, and the last objection to the doctrine of evolution is removed.

For example, it was well known to Dr. Lindley, Hugh Miller, and Dr. Buckland, that the great lepidophytes and calamites which formed the forests of the Carboniferous period belonged to the same type of vegetation as our comparatively insignificant club-mosses and horsetails, and they could say with crushing force of argument that there had been no evolution, but degeneration instead. No evolutionist has been able to answer this argument, which is only one of scores that the history of plant development in geologic time presents. As an evolutionist myself, I could not help being impressed with these facts which have been staring me in the face for the past twenty years. Throughout all this time it has been my constant effort to discover a law that would reconcile these

facts with the truth of evolution. Not until the idea had occurred
to me that evolution was sympodial did I find such a law. I then
subjected the new theory to all possible tests, and with each trial
it has grown more solid. There are no facts inconsistent with it,
and the only scientific argument against the general doctrine of
evolution seems to be answered.

I have prepared a course of lectures on Evolution in the Vegetable Kingdom, illustrated by over fifty lantern views, and showing how the law of sympodial development has operated in the
geological history of plants. I cannot even summarize these facts
in this chapter, and will confine myself to giving a few of the
most striking examples. The case of the Lepidodendrales and
the Calamariaceæ has already been mentioned. Neither of these
great phyla crossed the line that divides primary from secondary
time. They reached their maximum development in the Carboniferous epoch, dwindled toward its close, and went down with the
Permian winter to reappear no more forever. These were the
great specialized types that attained such beauty and majesty in
that island world of heat and moisture that prevailed in Carboniferous time. The records do not make it certain what the sympode
was that received the bulk of the fibers and continued these races
of plants, but it is probable that the Coniferæ were the true
descendants of the lepidophytes. The *persistence of unspecialized
types* is a part of the law of sympodial development, and it is these
only that have come down to us from these great lines. The
Calamariaceæ also disappeared at the close of the Paleozoic, but
the large forms of Equisetum of the Mesozoic indicate that the
original phylum did not die out, but persisted down to our time,
gradually dwindling until they are now only represented by our
scouring rushes which are strictly herbaceous. We can only speculate as to what the first great branch of this type was. It may
have been the Gnetaceæ, and the next may have been the Casuari-
naceæ, which most authors regard as dicotyledonous, though Treub
maintains that they are wholly anomalous. The tree-ferns, which
were the true rivals of the lepidophytes in the Carboniferous, have
a history similar to that of the Calamariaceæ. Our ferns of to-day,
including the tree-ferns of the tropics, are doubtless the direct
descendants of the original phylum, which has dwindled slowly
throughout all these ages. It is now almost certain that the first

sympode of that line was the Bennettitales, which reached their
culminating point in the Upper Jurassic or Lower Cretaceous, and
are now extinct, but are represented in our flora, though sparingly,
by the true Cycadaceæ, of which *Cycas revoluta* is the most familiar
example.   The Cordaitales of the Devonian and Carboniferous disappeared in Paleozoic time after playing an important rôle.   The
first sympode of that line was probably Nœggerathia, the second,
Baiera, characteristic of the Mesozoic, and the third, Ginkgo, which
was abundant in the Jurassic, but fell off during the Cretaceous
and Tertiary, and is now represented by a single species, the
maidenhair-tree, native of China, but cultivated throughout all
the warmer temperate parts of the world.   This is without question the most interesting line of descent presented by the vegetable
kingdom.   Whatever may have been the original phylum of which
the Coniferæ constituted a sympode, we at least know that they
first took the form of the Permian genus Walchia, later that of the
Mesozoic genus Palissya, and finally that of the chiefly Cretaceous
and Tertiary genus Sequoia, which, however, much as in the case
of Ginkgo, still persists, although now on the verge of extinction.
Its living representatives are the two great forest monarchs, the
redwood and the mammoth tree of the Coast Range and the Sierras,
respectively, of California.

Space will not permit me to follow out other lines, as I could
easily do, and show that everywhere and always the course of evolution in the plant world has been the same; that the original phylum has at some point reached its maximum development and given
off a sympode that has carried the process of evolution on until it
should in turn give birth to a new sympode, which can only repeat
the same history, and so on indefinitely.   Each successive sympode
possesses attributes which enable it better to resist the environment
and therefore constitutes a form of development or structural advance, so that the entire process is one of true evolution, and has
culminated in the great class of dicotyledonous exogenous plants
which now dominate the vegetable kingdom.   On this view there is
nothing remarkable in our finding extinct forms much superior to
any of the living forms of the same type of structure.   In fact, that
is what we should expect, and it is what we actually find wherever
there is an adequate record of the history of any line.   What we
have in the living flora of the globe to compare with those great

fallen races of the past is merely the persisting unspecialized types, which escaped destruction simply because unspecialized. For the law of the persistence of the unspecialized is only the counterpart of the law of the extinction of the specialized. Specialization is always a preparation for destruction. Although representing adaptation to existing conditions it becomes inadaptation so soon as those conditions change.

From lack of qualifications and opportunity I have not been able to verify the operation of this law in the animal kingdom to the same extent as I have done in the vegetable, but a slight acquaintance with zoölogy, and especially with paleozoölogy, is sufficient to show that it is as true there as in the history of plants. It is only necessary to mention the trilobites of the Cambrian, the molluscan life of the Silurian, the ganoid fishes of the Devonian, the gigantic Neuroptera and cockroaches of the Carboniferous, the enormous lizards (dinosaurs) of the Jurassic, and the mastodons of the Pliocene, in order to suggest at least an almost exact parallel to what I have been sketching for the record of plant life. Any zoölogist who clearly grasps the principle of sympodial dichotomy will doubtless be able to supplement the above enumeration to any required extent.

Passing over, then, with these few hints, the field of zoölogy, let us rise at once to the plane of human history and see whether we cannot find a similar parallel here. We may look upon human races as so many trunks and branches of what may be called the sociological tree. The vast and bewildering multiplicity in the races of men is the result of ages of race development, and it has taken place in a manner very similar to that in which the races of plants and animals have developed. Its origin is lost in the obscurity of ages of unrecorded history, and we can only judge from existing savages and the meager data of archæology and human paleontology, how the process went on. But we know that it did go on, and when at last the light of tradition and written annals opens upon the human races we find them engaged in a great struggle, such as Gumplowicz has so graphically described. But we also find, as both he and Ratzenhofer have ably shown, that out of this struggle new races have sprung, and that these in turn have struggled with other races, and out of these struggles still other races have slowly emerged, until at last, down toward our own times and within the general line of the historic races, the great leading nationalities — French, English,

German, etc. — have been evolved. Now every one of these races of men, from the advanced nationalities last named back to the barbaric tribes that arose from the blending of hostile hordes, is simply an anthropologic sympode, strictly analogous to the biologic sympodes that I have described. And when we concentrate our attention upon those later aspects of this movement which we are fairly well acquainted with, we find a most remarkable parallelism between the phenomena which we popularly characterize as the rise and fall of nations or empires and the rise and fall of the great types of life during the progress of geologic history. As I look back in imagination over the vast stretches of the past I can see the earth peopled, as it were, by these vegetable forms, different in every epoch, and an image presents itself to my mind of the gradual rise, ultimate mastery or hegemony, and final culmination of each of the great types of vegetation, followed by its decline contemporaneously with the rise of the type that is to succeed it. This rhythmic march of evolution has been going on throughout the entire history of the planet, and the path of geologic history is strewn with the ruins of fallen vegetable empires, just as that of human history is strewn with the wreck of political empires and decadent races.

We may distinguish between specialization and evolution. The former consists chiefly in modification of form and size without essential change in the type of structure. The latter depends entirely on modification in the type of structure to adapt it to changes in the environment. At the period of maximum development of any type of structure it must be fairly well adapted to its environment, and it becomes specialized in form and vigorous in growth, usually attaining relatively large size, as in the lepidophytes, calamites, cordaites, and tree-ferns of the Carboniferous, the dinosaurs of the Jura, and the great sequoias. All these must have once been thoroughly adapted to their environment. But as soon as a change begins to take place in the environment the degree of adaptation begins to diminish. The result, however, is not a retracing of any of the steps in specialization that have been taken. It is first diminishing abundance and supremacy of these specialized forms, then their more and more complete subordination to the more vigorous types, *i.e.*, those better adapted to the now changed environment, and finally their extinction. But they go down just as they are, with all their specialization of form and size, and simply perish from inability longer to compete with the rising types of life. It is possible that, if human aid does not prevent it, the last representative of the mammoth trees of the Sierras may be the largest and grandest individual of its race.

Just how specialization entails extinction is an important question. Often, as in most of the cases just cited, the organisms become overgrown, and, as it were, break down by their own weight the moment that perfect adaptation ceases which enabled them to attain such proportions. But there are many other more subtle causes at work in the same direction. I shall not attempt an enumeration of them here, but will instance one case which will give a clear idea of how specialization may work its own destruction. It is well known that some species of Yucca depend for their continuance upon cross fertilization through insect agency, and that their flowers have become specialized so as to permit a certain species of insect, the *Yuccasella pronuba*, to effect this cross fertilization. Now if this plant should be transported by any agency to a habitat where this insect does not exist it must inevitably perish. It cannot wander beyond the range of the insect, and if for any reason the insect should die out the plant must also die. This extreme case vividly illustrates the whole subject of overspecialization and the precarious nature of highly specialized organisms, for there are all degrees of the phenomena and every form of specialization makes the life of the species short and uncertain.

When we say that any once vigorous type has dwindled since the period of maximum development and left only degenerate survivors in our time, the statement is not altogether correct and is misleading. The truth is that the highly specialized forms do not degenerate or retrograde at all, but perish as they were, being simply crowded out of existence. What persists is the unspecialized forms of the same type that were contemporary with the specialized ones, but escaped competition because not specialized. These may come on down and even improve somewhat, but they will appear by comparison to be degenerate. Such are all the long-lived races of both animals and plants that are found, like Lingula, passing on up through many geological formations.

How do all these principles apply to human races? Careful examination reveals a close parallelism. Races and nations become overgrown and disappear. Peoples become overspecialized and fall an easy prey to the more vigorous surrounding ones, and a high state of civilization is always precarious. Races and peoples are always giving off their most highly vitalized elements and being transplanted to new soil, leaving the parent country to decline or be swallowed up. The plot of the " Æneid," though it be a myth, at least illustrates this truth. Troy was swallowed up by Greece, but not until it had been transplanted to Rome, and the *Pergama recidiva* handed on the qualities of Trojan character to later ages. Italy was the vanguard of civilization to the sixteenth century, when she transferred her scepter to Spain, which held it during the seventeenth, and in turn transferred it to France. It passed to England in the nineteenth, and bids fair to cross the Atlantic before the close of the twentieth. Race and national degeneration or decadence means nothing more than this pushing out of the vigorous branches or sympodes at the expense of the parent trunks. The organicists see in colonization the phenomenon of social reproduction. This is at least a half truth. Colonization often means regeneration; it means race development; it means social evolution.

CREATIVE SYNTHESIS

I borrow this expression from Wundt,[1] who gives the central idea of it in the following passage: "There is absolutely no form which in the meaning and value of its content is not something more than the mere sum of its factors or than the mere mechanical resultant of its components " (p. 274).[2] But I shall make of it a still wider application than he does. It seems to me to embody the answer to a large amount of what passes for very wise, but what I have always regarded as not only superficial but also essentially false reasoning. The idea is so far-reaching that I cannot hope to present all its applications in this chapter. The most I can do is to lay down the principle and let the applications come at their proper times and places as we proceed. The conception was not

---

[1] "Logik." Eine Untersuchung der Principien der Erkenntniss und der Methoder wissenschaftlicher Forschung. Von Wilhelm Wundt. Zwei Bände. Zweite umgearbeitete Auflage. Stuttgart, 1895. Zweiter Band. Methodenlehre. Zweite Abtheilung. Logik der Geisteswissenschaften. Zweites Capitel. Die Logik der Psychologie, § 4. Die Principien der Psychologie ; d : Das Princip der Schöpferischen Synthese, pp. 267–281.

[2] " Es gibt absolut kein solches Gebilde, das nicht nach der Bedeutung und dem Werth seines Inhaltes mehr wäre als die blosse Summe seiner Factoren oder die blosse mechanische Resultante seiner Componente," *loc. cit.*, p. 274.

entirely new when I met with the expression in Wundt's "Logik,"
but this expression, I freely confess, had the effect to render it
more definite and clear. As will be seen, it is a composite idea.
The notion embodied in the second component is nothing more
nor less than the fertile truth taught most clearly by chemistry
that a compound of two substances is something more than the
sum of those substances, and is in a proper sense a third and different substance. That its properties are in some way derived
from and due to those of its components is not denied, but the
relation is one that no human insight can fully comprehend. No
one, for example, could predict in advance what kind of a substance would result from even so simple a combination as oxygen
and hydrogen in the proportion of two atoms of the latter to one
of the former. No one could have told till he had tried it whether
the resulting substance would be a gas, like both the components,
or a liquid, as it is at ordinary temperatures, or a solid, as it is at
lower temperatures. Much less could any one have told what its
properties would be.

The common hypothesis on which the substances resulting from
the chemical union of components which are themselves composite
is explained is that the molecules of the components enter into the
new aggregate as units without previous decomposition into their
simpler elements; but it cannot be said that this is known to be
true.

This chemical synthesis has long been believed to typify a large
number of other phenomena in all departments of nature. The
indestructibility of matter requires us to suppose that different
things are nothing but so many combinations of elements that have
always existed, and this truth is apt to generate the idea that there
is really "no new thing under the sun." This idea, although embodying a very general truth, really leads to a false conception of
nature, the conception namely that there are no real differences
in things, and that the universe is a monotonous sameness. The
facts of chemical union resulting in products wholly unlike their
components tend to dispel this illusion, but the law of aggregation
or recompounding is not perceived to be a universal one, applicable
to all departments of nature. Spencer and others have successfully
shown that this is the case, and it is to this truth that Durkheim
appeals in defense of the existence of distinctively social phenomena.

But this universal chemism, or intimate blending of elements with complete loss of individuality and reappearance in new forms, as distinguished from mere mechanical mixture or amalgamation, required to be more deeply studied. The moment we recognize that it is *creative*, although it thereby acquires no quality that it did not possess before, a flood of light is shed on the entire process, and we then see how it can be that an infinite variety may spring from relatively few elements, or, indeed, from an assumed unitary substratum of the universe.

Creation. — The popular conception of creation is vague and confused. The old view, and the theological view generally, is the making of something without materials — creation out of nothing. But the mind cannot conceive this, and in the face of medieval theologism the maxim *ex nihilo nihil fit* has always been constantly repeated and never seriously gainsaid. The only rational or thinkable idea of creation has always been that of putting previously existing things into new forms. If we go outside of metaphysics and confine ourselves wholly to art we find that this is the fundamental conception upon which all art rests. Art erects ideals, and ideals are creations in just this sense. It is common to speak of the perfection of nature and to hear it said that art imitates nature. These are both false conceptions. Nature is everywhere imperfect, and art always aims to improve upon nature. No two natural objects are exactly alike. This is because no natural object is ideally perfect. The differences are due to defects. Let a botanist try to find a perfect specimen of a plant that grows abundantly around him. He will examine dozens or hundreds and then be compelled to take one that he sees to be defective. I have often searched long and faithfully to find a perfect leaf on a tree full of leaves without succeeding. Something is always lacking. The reason why we know our friends and neighbors is because no human face is perfect. Only lovers find each other perfect, and marriage too often quickly dispels the illusion. We think that foreigners all look alike, but among themselves even Chinese and Amerinds know one another. It is said that the Alpine shepherds know their sheep, and I can believe it, because when a boy it was my duty to "tend" my father's sheep, which usually numbered a hundred or more, and I not only knew them all but gave them all names. Now they must have all differed, and these differences

G

were deviations from an ideal, always falling below it, because there is no possibility of rising above it. That would involve a contradiction of terms.

Nature is always imperfect, but the mind, at a certain stage of development, or with a certain amount of cultivation and training, becomes capable of forming ideals of perfection. It acquires the power of seeing the defects in nature and of supplying them in imagination. This is the creative imagination which precedes all art. Creative genius is the next step, which is the capacity for supplying these defects in nature outside of the imagination in some concrete objective way. The fine arts are the ways in which it does this. The history of the formation and execution of ideals is an interesting one. Those strange conventionalized figures that characterize ancient Oriental art and that of barbaric races — obelisks, totem posts, etc. — merely show that the imagination of such peoples was limited to general forms and could not rise to exact representation. Not until we come to Greek art do we find the power of perfect representation coupled with the genius for its complete execution.

It is truly said that imagination cannot exceed observation, that the artist can put nothing into his picture that he has not seen in nature. Creation does not imply this. What the artist does is to take the perfect parts of many imperfect models and combine them in one in which all the parts are perfect. This is the essence of creative genius. The mind cannot make something out of nothing, any more than can the hands. All it can do is to elaborate and rearrange the materials it has previously received through the senses. *Nihil in intellectu quod non prius in sensu.* But with these materials it not only can reconstruct but it can construct. The imagination, as thus understood, is a faculty of the intellect which has developed *pari passu* with its other faculties. The immediate antecedent of imagination is imitation, and there can be no doubt that the former grew out of the latter. Those animals to which we ascribe the highest psychic powers are the most imitative. The reason why the apes are such mimics is that their minds are more highly developed than those of other animals. They are approaching a stage at which the formation of ideals is possible. From the highest degrees of imitativeness to the lowest degrees of imagination is a short step, and it is just here that one of the bridges spans

the chasm between animal and man.　M. Tarde would have laid a
solid psychological foundation for his philosophy if he had recognized
this truth and illustrated it in his customary way.

Social Ideals. — We have seen that the essential condition of all
art is the psychic power of forming ideals.　Their execution is certain to follow their creation.　It has often been remarked that
persons of an artistic turn of mind often become, especially in later
life, social reformers, and the examples of Ruskin, William Morris,
Howells, Bellamy, and others are brought forward.　I once heard a
lecturer on sociology at a university lay great emphasis on this fact
before his class, and he treated it simply as a remarkable and apparently inexplicable coincidence.　This led me to reflect upon it, but
the explanation was not far to seek.　An artist or art critic, like
Ruskin, possesses a mind specially constituted for seeing ideals in
nature.　Such a mind instantly detects the defects in everything
observed and unconsciously supplies the missing parts.　This faculty
is general, and need not be confined to human features, to architectural designs, to statues, portraits, and landscapes.　It may take
any direction.　After a life engaged in the search of ideals in the
world of material things, the mind often grows more serious and is
more and more sympathetic.　It lays more stress on moral defects,
and in the most natural way conceivable, it proceeds to form ethical
and social ideals by the same process that it has always formed
esthetic ideals.　The defectiveness of the social state in permitting
so much suffering is vividly represented, and the image of an ideal
society in which this would be prevented spontaneously arises in
the mind.　Instinctively, too, the born artist, now become a social
artist, proceeds to construct such an ideal society, and we have a
great array of Utopias, and Arcadias, and Altrurias, in which imagination drives out all the hard, stern realities of life, and leaves only
Edens and Paradises.　The highest flights of artistic ingenuity and
creative power are attained, and by looking forward and backward
every shadow that is cast on society is banished leaving only sun-lit
Elysian fields.

To indulge in an apparent hyperbole, the moral and social
reformer, nay, the social and political agitator or even fanatic, provided he be sincere and not a self-seeker, exercises the same faculty
as the poet, the sculptor, and the painter, and out of all these fields
of art, even from that of music, there have been recruited, in this

perfectly natural and legitimate way, philanthropists, humanitarians, socialists, idealists, religious, economic, and social reformers. The list is large, but as representative types, besides those already mentioned, we may properly name Victor Hugo, Tolstoi, Wagner, Millet, Swinburne, and George Eliot.

It may be said that there is a difference between esthetic art and social art, as thus described, in that the first relates to the beautiful while the second relates to the good; but this is rather a distinction than a difference, since there is a recognized moral beauty, and also because, as all true philosophers of art admit, the ultimate object of art is to please, so that both rest on feeling, and thus have a moral basis.   And if the social artist is moved more by pain to be relieved than by pleasure to be enjoyed in his ideal society, this is only a difference of degree, since there can be no doubt that one of the strongest motives to creative art is the pain caused by the defects, maladjustments, discords, jars, and eyesores that the real world constantly inflicts upon the hypersensitive organization of the artist.

Again it may be urged that a work of art is a real and lasting contribution to the world's possessions, not to be set aside as foolish, or trivial, or useless, while a social utopia is an ideal and nothing more, a chimera, an *Unding*, to be set aside as the vaporing of an unbalanced mind. The answer to this objection is that some Utopias do not answer this description, but, independently of all practical considerations, are, in and of themselves, works of art. No one will probably deny this merit to those of Plato and More, and a little later that of Bellamy is likely to become a classic. But be this as it may, it is the psychological nature of these operations that we are considering and not their value. And what is art but exaggeration of nature, a charming unreality, more unrealizable than the wildest utopia? There never was, there never can be an Apollo Belvidere or a Venus of Milo.

The Poetic Idea. — The train of thought that we have been following out naturally leads us to consider the nature of the poetic idea. The close relation or practical identity of poetry and prophecy has been frequently recognized, but an analysis of its psychological character seems to be thus far lacking. This subject furnishes another good illustration of the light that the natural sciences shed on the highest forms of ideation. Already in this chapter it has been shown how difficult it must be for any but a botanist, familiar with the principle of sympodial dichotomy, to seize and firmly grasp one of the most essential characteristics of universal evolution, and now we shall see how a comprehension of the truths of organic development may supply the materials for a clear conception of so different a phenomenon as the unfolding of a poetic or prophetic formula. A true poet, especially one whose mind is stored with the wisdom of the world, is in very truth a prophet, and is the subject of veritable inspirations, which he occasionally formulates as it were unconsciously. He is a seer, *i.e.*, he sees truth that others do not see. He sees it only vaguely and utters it vaguely in forms that may seem meaningless to his contemporaries, but after time has wrought its changes and separated out the elements that were in his mind the meaning of his phrases emerges, and the truth vaguely expressed becomes definite and clear. The faculty is, like imagination, a purely creative one. The truth expressed was never presented to the senses, but only its elements, which he puts together and constructs a new truth which time will ultimately reveal.

Now the objective evolution of nature is parallel to the subjective evolution of mind, and a study of evolution throws light on mental processes. In the organic world we know that the course of evolution is from the homogeneous to the heterogeneous through systematic differentiation. All life has sprung from a homogeneous, undifferentiated plasm, which contained within itself the potency of all the varied forms that have evolved out of this plasm. All through the history of organic development there occur relatively undifferentiated forms which later divide up and take on a number of definite shapes, all of which are suggested by these ancestral forms. Agassiz, who resisted the march of evolutionary ideas to the end of his life, clearly saw this truth, and he it was who called such forms comprehensive or prophetic types. He attributed them to a great preordained plan conceived by the deity and slowly worked out in this way through geologic ages. These comprehensive types occur in all departments of organic nature, and no enumeration of them is called for. But I will mention one that is practically unknown to the world, and which, as I discovered it myself, has brought this truth more closely home to me than any other. As it is quite as good an illustration as could be found anywhere, I feel justified in using it.

In 1883, while operating in the Lower Yellowstone Valley in Montana, I collected in the Laramie Group, in beds underlying the Fort Union deposits, and therefore probably belonging to the extreme Upper Cretaceous, a singular fossil plant, as yet unnamed, but to which I have since devoted considerable study. I described it in a paper read by me before the Geological Section of the American Association for the Advancement of Science at the Cleveland meeting in 1888, and illustrated it by a number of lantern views. I need not repeat the description here, but will quote my conclusions as presented in that paper and published in the Proceedings of the Association for that year (Vol. XXXVII, p. 201) : —

I am disposed to regard it as a " comprehensive type " of vascular cryptogamic life, embodying some of the characters of several well known living types, viz., 1. The large tufted central base is suggestive of that of most species of Isoetes, and the long weak stems of certain of these species are observed to recline and lie prostrate in all directions around this center. 2. The double row of spore-cases at the apex of the stem agrees in all essential respects with that of Ophioglossum, and the elliptic expansion may be regarded as homologues of the larger blade-like fronds of that genus, which may easily be imagined to have the spores borne along its median line instead of on a special fruiting frond. 3. The prostrate sinuous habit is not widely unlike that of certain creeping species of Lycopodium, as, e.g., L. annotinum, and the tooth-like appendages may be the reduced homologues of the scale-like leaves of that genus. 4. A still further approach is seen in Selaginella where the scales have become distichous and the stems flat and closely creeping. This parallel is well-nigh complete in those species, such as S. Douglasii, in which the spores are borne in terminal spikes, like those of most Lycopodiums, except that these are more or less flattened and two-ranked. 5. Finally, ignoring the appendicular organs of Marsilea we see in the fruit-bearing portion a further analogy to our fossil, the fruiting stems radiating from the thickened base and bearing the spores at their apex.

The fossil would thus represent a highly generalized type and may be phylogenetically related to all these more specialized modern forms with each of which it seems to possess some characters in common.

Such facts as these incline me to believe that evolution is not always typically sympodial, although it is probably never typically monopodial. They indicate that there sometimes occurs what may be called polychotomy, in which the main trunk divides up somewhat equally, producing a number of large trunks or branches, each possessing some of the characters of the common ancestor, which subsequently become further differentiated and specialized, resulting in the different existing forms. Thus my prophetic Laramie plant

may have been the common ancestor of Isoetes, Ophioglossum, Lycopodium, Selaginella, and Marsilea. But as some of these genera
have been found to have near relatives at least in still older strata,
it is much more probable that my form is a late, lingering hold-over,
somewhat depauperate, of a much more ancient form.

This case, however, represents at best a somewhat late, and relatively, a highly differentiated type, and far back of it must have
existed more and more homogeneous forms in which these characters
could not be seen, although their elements must have been present in
them. Such are all the earlier ontogenetic stages in the development of even the highest living organisms, whether vegetable or animal, according to Von Baer's law. If these are traced backward we
arrive at last at the egg, the germ cells, and the sperm cells, which
must in some way embody all the *Anlagen* of the mature organism.

These facts now belong to the elementary truths of biology
familiar to all informed persons. But their familiarity does not
detract from their profound significance. It is, however, high time
that the application of all this be made to the poetic idea, although
few readers will probably need to have it made at all, since it must
have already become clear to them. It is that *a poetic idea is a
homogeneous undifferentiated truth* embodying the germs of many distinct truths which in the process of time and of the general development of ideas, are destined to take clear and definite forms. Its
vagueness of both conception and expression belongs to its essential
character as such, as the exact psychologic homologue of the biologic facts above described. It was thus, for example, that Emerson
voiced the great truth of evolution when he said : —

> And, striving to be man, the worm
> Mounts through all the spires of form.[1]

[1] " Nature," by Ralph Waldo Emerson, originally published in September, 1836.
This edition is now very rare but the essay occupies the first place in Emerson's
" Miscellanies," published in 1856. " Nature" is a prose essay, but to it was prefixed
as a motto these lines : —

> A subtle chain of countless rings
> The next unto the farthest brings;
> The eye reads omens where it goes,
> And speaks all languages the rose;
> And, striving to be man, the worm
> Mounts through all the spires of form.

In his work on, " Ralph Waldo Emerson: his Life, Writings, and Philosophy,"
Boston, 1881, Mr. George Willis Cooke states (p. 40) that " Nature " was published

Poesis.[1] — I use this term in the primary sense of the Greek word as used by Herodotus, Thucydides, and other of the older Greek writers, and also sometimes by Plato, and not in the later derivative sense of poesy or poetry. In this sense it is the exact opposite of genesis. It is not, however, to be confounded with telesis, which is the name I give to Part III of this work. That is also the antithesis to genesis, but in a somewhat different sense, and the distinction will be fully pointed out. What it concerns us to emphasize now is that most of what has been said of what is called fine art is true also of practical art. Whichever should stand first, and they were doubtless developed *pari passu*, inventive genius, as well as creative genius, is a faculty for putting together raw materials so as to form new combinations.[2] The product is something different from that which existed before. It is a creation. Poesis is a form of creative synthesis. In esthetic creation the thing made is an ideal freed from the crudities of nature and beautiful to contemplate. In inventive creation the thing made is useful and serves a practical purpose. Here the defects of nature that are specially attended to are the obstructions to existence. Nature is not only crude and uncouth but she is obnoxious and destructive. She is also wasteful and extravagant, and inventive genius works for economy. The special quality to which inventive genius applies itself is *utility*. Here is a new or fourth category to be added to the conventional three — truth, beauty, goodness. The useful is not the same as the good, as used in this formula, but it is even more important because of universal application, while the field of ethics is a restricted one which is constantly contracting. The completed formula should then be: the true, the beautiful, the good, and the useful, in which the useful is not put last because least, but only because the last to be recognized.

But poesis is more than invention and more than art. It is both. It embodies a form of imagination as well as a form of creation. Or

in September, 1836. This poetic adumbration of modern evolutionary doctrine therefore antedates Darwin's "Origin of Species" by twenty-three years. As Emerson was familiar with Goethe's writings it is not surprising that his works should breathe the spirit of evolution. The remarkable thing in this is that he should have mentioned the "worm," since it is through the Vermes that the vertebrate type was derived. If he had said the snail the scientific character of the passage would have been lost.

[1] Gr. ποίησις, a making.

[2] No one has seen or expressed this truth more clearly than Condorcet. See the "Tableau historique des Progrès de l'Esprit humain," Paris, 1900, pp. 327 ff.

rather, as in esthetic art, it first creates an ideal and then creates an object which materializes that ideal. The chief difference is in the nature of that ideal. Instead of an ideal beauty it is an ideal utility. The first step, too, is a form of imagination, for there is little in the raw materials used to suggest that utility, and it requires as high an order of genius to form such an ideal as it does to form an ideal of symmetry and perfection. Not enough has yet been said of this wonderful faculty of imagination.[1] The popular conception of it is far too narrow. We sometimes hear of scientific imagination. There certainly is such. It is that faculty which coördinates the disordered impressions received through the senses and out of them constructs a truth. For truth is also an ideal and thought is a form of creative synthesis. Experience never furnishes truth. Nothing but a creative faculty can bring truth from fact.

Genesis. — Thus far I have only considered the psychological aspect of the subject. Its cosmological aspect is still more important, but can be better understood in the light of these studies in mind. The truth now to be enforced is that nature also creates. The case with which we started of the formation of chemical compounds illustrates this truth, for every new combination is not only a synthesis but a creation. Something is made to exist which did not exist before. It is made of preëxisting materials, but it is different from any of those materials. What we miss is the ideal, but while the creations of mind, being telic, necessarily proceed from ideals, the creations of nature, being genetic, do not proceed from ideals. They are none the less creations. Wherever there is combination, as distinguished from mixture — coalescence as distinguished from coexistence — something new results, and there is creative synthesis. But this is the principal method of nature. All the organized movements in the universe involve combination and coalescence. The word *organic*, in its wider sense, implies this. Relations that are not organic in this sense are merely accidental. They are due to *conjuncture*, which is itself an important factor in the total make-up of things, but does not produce that intimate interlocking of elements necessary to render their union a new unit. The branches of an oak may interlock with those of an elm, but there will be no

---

[1] In the French language *imaginer* is to invent as well as to imagine, and the same is true for most of the romance languages. The distinction between the esthetic and the useful has been differentiated out of the homogeneous idea of creation.

coalescence, no cross fertilization, but two closely related species of oak thus mechanically forced together will hybridize. Entirely different animals, as the cat and the dog, would be sterile *inter se*, but more nearly related ones, as the ass and the horse, are partially fertile. An amalgam or an alloy can scarcely be called a new product, but an acid or a salt is a true creation. There must be a certain degree of resemblance, there must be a mutual affinity, before there can result that organic union which constitutes creation. The synthesis must be natural and not fortuitous.

It is here that we find the application of creative synthesis to the general fact of filiation. The natural order of the sciences is due to the fact that the more complex phenomena of the higher sciences are the creative products of phenomena of a lower order. The former are *generated* by the latter, and all generation, or genesis, is creative. The relation between them is organic. The more complex sciences deal with these new products, which are, indeed, composed of elements constituting the units of the less complex ones, but they are no longer directly recognizable as such, having combined to form units of a higher order, and it is these higher units with which the complex sciences deal. By the laws of motion described in the fourth chapter, under which mechanical motion is converted into molecular motion, physics passes into chemistry. By the recompounding of chemical elements, inorganic compounds, and organic compounds, protoplasm is evolved, and chemistry passes into biology. By a further process of recompounding, to be considered in future chapters, life passes into mind. By a still higher series of creative acts man and society come forth. None of these steps will be neglected, but their full treatment here would be to anticipate.

The order of the dependence of the sciences is thus seen to be something more than the inverse order of generality and complexity. This of itself, as formulated by Comte, is a great truth, but there is a still deeper truth, viz., that each of the higher sciences is a product of the creative synthesis of all the sciences below it in the scale. Each science is thus distinct, though not independent. It is a new and different field of phenomena. Chemistry is not physics, but a science apart. Biology is not chemistry, nor is psychology, as Comte maintained, biology. Sociology is not psychology, still less biology. It is a science, new in two senses, viz., those of being newly created and newly discovered. It is the product of recompounding of the simpler sciences. The sociological units are compounds of psychological units, but differ as much from their components as corrosive sublimate differs from chlorine or mercury. This principle also explains the relation of sociology to the special social sciences. It is not' quite enough to say that it is a synthesis of them all. It is the new compound which their synthesis creates. It is not any of them and it is not all of them. It is that science which they spontaneously generate. It is a genetic product, the last term in the genesis of science. The special social sciences are the units of aggregation that organically combine to create sociology, but they lose their individuality as completely as do chemical units, and the resultant product is wholly unlike any of them and is of a higher order. All this is true of any of the complex sciences, but sociology, standing at the head of the entire series, is enriched by all the truths of nature and embraces all truth. It is the *scientia scientiarum.*

Still another vexed question finds its solution here, to wit, the question of the social consciousness or collective mind. It receives the same answer as the rest. The social mind is a product of spontaneous creative synthesis of all individual minds. In this sense it is real. That it differs widely from any individual mind has been abundantly shown by many writers. In this case the resulting compound, in so far as it can be compared to the component units, somewhat represents their average. It seems to be below the average, but this is partly from the habit of only observing the highest psychic phenomena and disregarding the lowest. The social mind sometimes seems to be embryonic, *i.e.*, to take the form of the more primitive mind of man as we observe it in uncivilized races. This is due to the fact that in manifestations of the social mind the artificial restraints of civilized life are removed. The period of the evolution of civility is very short compared with the precivilized period, and the coat of civility is thin. " Scratch a Russian and you have a Tartar." Scratch a savant and you have a savage. The process of becoming civilized has been one of restraint. The civilized man puts his best foot forward. Civilized life helps to do this. Living in houses, every one concealed from his fellows, favors the process. Witness the restraint that people feel when obliged, even for a brief period, as in certain cottages at the seaside, to live where what they say can be heard by the occupants of adjacent rooms. How the tent life of the earlier ages of European history must have

laid bare human character! That of the army does this now, as I
have had occasion personally to observe. Pioneer life and life
in mining camps has the same effect.[1]

Now, just as in the camp, so in the crowd, the restraints of civilized life are removed. The thin veneering that covers men's acts in
society peels off, and the true character of the civilized man as an
enlightened savage comes to light. The veneering consists of about
half culture and half hypocrisy. The social mind partly lays off
both these garbs and represents men more nearly as they are. The
acts which would be objectionable in private life are shifted to the
broad shoulders of all the rest. No individual holds himself responsible for them. This has been pointed out by various writers and
numerous illustrations given. I will add only one, which relates to
one of the most recently acquired civilized qualities, viz., modesty.
At the Philadelphia Centennial Exposition of 1876 I saw a crowd
of orderly, well-dressed, and evidently genteel people around the
monkey cages, and men, women, boys, and girls alike were laughing
and shouting and gazing at actions of the large apes which probably
not one of those present, if in small companies acquainted with one
another, would have pretended to see. I made a note of the fact at
the time as illustrating how little it requires to rub off the thin wash
of modesty that covers civilized society. And it is much the same
with nearly all distinctively civilized qualities of man. The erratic
and erotic career of Oscar Wilde would furnish another illustration
of the same truth. Remove social restraints and men will act their
natures, and social ideals are so much higher than human nature
that the social mind, which is so much nearer the natural mind than
the individual mind is under these restraints, seems much lower,
cruder, and more primitive than that of individuals. Its qualitative
differences are almost wholly due to the removal of these restraints.
Much more might be said under this head but it would be mainly
a repetition of what has been said by others.

Synthetic Creations of Nature. — We thus see that nature is creative as well as man, that creation is genetic as well as telic, and that
the products of genesis as well as those of telesis are products of
creative synthesis. It is these wide applications of creative synthesis that it chiefly concerns us to note, and we may now briefly review
a few of the most important of them. The fact to be insisted upon

[1] Dr. Ross has emphasized this point. See his "Social Control," pp. 45, 46.

is that evolution is through and through creative. As change after change goes on from the nebular chaos toward universal cosmos, from cosmos to bios, and from bios to logos, long stretches intervene between these several great stadia, during which the creative products have not as yet assumed such definite forms as to constitute turning points or crises in the march of the world's progress. But ever and anon such a stage is reached, and a new creative product is brought forth, so unlike anything that has hitherto existed, and so cardinal in its nature as to give, as it were, a new point of departure to all future evolution. At every such stage the universe seems to change front and thenceforward to march in a new direction. There have been many such cosmical crises, after each of which there has been a new universe.

We know not what the absolutely elementary state of matter may be, but the universal ether is now almost as well proved as the existence of ponderable matter. If out of it there once came those relative condensations which constituted the as yet homogeneous and undifferentiated masses of diffused matter called nebulæ, this must have marked one of the cosmic epochs of which we have spoken, and such a nebula may be regarded as a synthetic creation. That such nebulæ subsequently differentiated into systems of worlds of which our solar system is one is nothing more than a statement of the nebular hypothesis of Kant and Laplace. Every such world system is a cosmic creation. The history of our planet has doubtless been repeated thousands of times in all the countless star systems that we have ocular demonstration of within the limits of our lenticular universe. As we know little of other planets and much of our own, we can only assume that the course of evolution has been similar in all. Confining ourselves to our earth, we practically know that in the course of its history there have been evolved three of the epoch-making properties that we are considering, viz., life, feeling, and thought.

But these properties belong to certain material products that have first been evolved, each of which was a new creation. They have appeared at long intervals in an ascending unilateral series, and each successive product, while possessing all the properties of the one that immediately preceded it, possesses the one additional property by which it is specially distinguished. The activities manifested by these creative products of evolution are either molecular

or molar, and each gives rise to some kind of phenomena which are
capable of classification.   Each product is at once the effect of antecedent causes and the cause of further effects, and the kinds of
causes to which these latter belong may also be classified.   Thus all
activities are either molecular or molar, all phenomena are either
physical, vital, psychic, or social, and all causes are either efficient,
conative, or telic.   Placing these products in a column in the ascending order of their development, and the properties they possess, the
quality of their activities, the phenomena they manifest, and the
nature of the causes through which they work, in parallel columns,
we shall have the following table : —

SYNTHETIC CREATIONS OF NATURE

Products	Differential Attributes			
	Properties	Activities	Phenomena	Causes
Society	Achievement		Social	
Man	Intellect		Psychic	Telic
Animals	Feeling	Molar		Conative
Plants	Life			
Protoplasm	Motility		Vital	
Organic Compounds				Efficient
Inorganic Compounds	Chemism	Molecular		
Chemical Elements			Physical	
Universal Ether	Vibration	Radiant		

Whether we contemplate the products or the properties of this
series, each of these steps in evolution, or synthetic creations of
nature, may be regarded as something new, i.e., as something that
had no existence before.   Although their primary elements always
existed, the combinations resulting in the several products constitute
so many distinct things.   Although the properties are all manifestations of the universal force, still that force never manifested itself
before in anything like the same way.   They are wholly different
modes of motion.   Each new plane of existence thus attained is a
fresh base of operations.   The successive products and properties
are so many discrete degrees in the history of the universe.   Only
his most philosophical disciples know just what Swedenborg meant
by " discrete degrees," but as he was a true poet, this may have been
a poetic idea or prophetic vision of the law of evolution and universal
genesis which I have endeavored to sketch.   He may have dimly

seen the creative power of nature and the principle of creative synthesis, and his discrete degrees may have been an adumbration of the synthetic creations of nature.

I have not introduced worlds into the table because all worlds must consist of chemical elements, inorganic compounds, and organic compounds, and the property of chemism must be common to them all. Protoplasm, though probably the result of some form of recompounding of organic compounds, is unlike any other product of chemism, and marks the transition from spontaneous molecular to spontaneous molar activity, which latter is the fundamental characteristic of vital or biotic phenomena. It came to stay and is, as Huxley says, the physical basis of life. Out of it sprang the plant world and the animal world. But the plant only elaborates inorganic matter, while the animal must re-elaborate the organic matter created by the plant. The chief differential attribute of the animal, however, is what I call feeling — the property of self-awareness. The highest animals, it is true, possess the germs of intelligence, but for convenience of tabular representation, and for all practical purposes, intellect may be made to begin with man. The will belongs to animals and is the kind of force or causation that they employ. At bottom it is a form of the efficient cause, but it is deserving of a special designation. We will call such causes conative. The phenomena presented by protoplasm and by plants are vital. The differential (additional) phenomena presented by animals, including man, are psychic. But intellect is essentially a final cause. Man, with all the attributes of all the lower products and intellect added, generates another and highest product, society. This is also discrete and hitherto unknown. That which chiefly distinguishes it from all other cosmic creations is its capacity for achievement (in the sense in which I use the word, see Chapter III). Social phenomena thus inaugurate another, and thus far the last, new departure in the history of evolution, viz., the movement toward civilization. Many distinct lines of culture have started, but only one promises to possess permanent continuity. The recent rapid westernizing of Japan is probably an earnest of what will be the ultimate result in China, India, and other Oriental civilizations, while the weaker ones will be simply absorbed in the mass of Occidental life that is overflowing and overrunning all the remoter continents and the islands of the sea.

It will not have escaped attention that these broad steps in evolution are closely analogous to the more restricted phenomena of organic development taking place within one of the cosmic periods. The fact is here even more marked that at every one of the culminating points a new direction is given to the whole scheme by the appearance of a new product with its added attributes. The march of cosmic, as of organic evolution is thus zigzag. It resembles the culm of certain grasses that changes its direction at every joint. It is perfectly homologous to the stem of a sympodial plant, which consists of a series of branches each of which has appropriated practically all the energy of the plant. For the differential attribute which each cosmic product possesses in addition to those of all before it immediately becomes paramount and the antecedent ones sink into relative insignificance. Each product with its concomitant attributes is thus a true sympode, and cosmic evolution is also sympodial.

Finally it is to be noted that the series is parallel to that of the sciences of the hierarchy. This follows as a matter of course, it is true, since those sciences simply deal with the phenomena which nature presents. But we saw that the sciences could be arranged in a natural succession and that when so arranged they grew out of one another in such a manner that the term *filiation* could be properly applied to it. But this is because there is a corresponding relation among the phenomena themselves. This corresponding relation is the genetic succession of cosmic products with their differential attributes that we have been considering. The succession is not only genetic but *tocogenetic*. The higher terms are generated by the lower through creative synthesis, and are thus affiliated upon them. The filiation of the sciences is the simple correlate of the filiation of the products and attributes of evolution.

CHAPTER VI

THE DYNAMIC AGENT

GLANCING again at the table of synthetic creations of nature on
p. 94, and giving special attention now to the second column of
"properties," we may note first that it is as true of properties as of
products that they are affiliated upon one another, the lower beget-
ting the higher. It cannot perhaps be said to be known that chemism grows out of ethereal vibrations, though the phenomena of
thermodynamics point that way. But we can almost say that we
know that life emerges in some way from chemism through the
differential attribute of protoplasm, motility. That feeling sprang
from life will be the thesis of the next chapter. The proof that
feeling created intellect will be found in Chapter XVII. That achievement, as defined in Chapter III, is only possible in a rational being,
would seem to require no demonstration.

In the second place it is to be observed that the mode of producing effects, called the "cause" in the last column of the table, is in
feeling conative, and in intellect telic. This distinction is fundamental, and upon it depends the primary subdivision of sociology.
A conative cause is, as was stated in the last chapter, a modality of
the efficient cause, but it is psychic instead of physical, and this distinction, while not generic, is fundamental, and calls for a wholly different method of treatment. The telic or final cause is not a force,
as is every form of efficient cause, but it utilizes efficient causes in
a manner wholly its own, and thus produces effects. It will be both
convenient and correct to regard both the conative and the telic
cause as agencies in sociology, or, still more definitely, as the two
prime *agents* in society. The conative cause, being a true force, is
the *dynamic agent*, the word *dynamic* being here used in its primary
sense denoting force. The final cause is the *directive agent* of
society, the nature of which will be fully set forth in Part III.

There are two somewhat different meanings of the word dynamic
in current use. The primary one, based on the etymology of the

word, simply relates to force. This use of the word is much less common than the other, chiefly because the need of such a term does not often arise. The second or derivative meaning relates to movement and change, and this is the sense in which the word is most frequently used. It is so used in the mathematical science of mechanics, and is opposed to static, which there simply denotes that the forces are in equilibrium. This meaning of the word dynamic has been transferred to other sciences, but so soon as it becomes applicable to real and not hypothetical bodies there is almost necessarily attached to it the notion of change. The more complex the science to which it is applied the more the idea of change becomes prominent until in its biological, psychological, and sociological uses this is the leading idea. It is so often used in connection with the phenomena of evolution that we sometimes find it practically identified with *progressive,* but all careful writers recognize that it may apply as well to catabolic or regressive phenomena as to anabolic or progressive ones. Besides mechanics, astronomy, physics, and geology, in which dynamic phenomena form regular departments, I have, in the course of my reading, observed its application to chemistry, biology, psychology, logic (Tarde), economics (Patten), and sociology.

In all these cases it is in the secondary or derivative sense that the term is used. Certain writers have endeavored to avoid this use of the word dynamic in two senses by substituting *kinetic* for the secondary sense, but this does not accomplish the object, since the notion involved in kinetic is not the same as the one involved in dynamic. Kinetic is essentially a physical term, and signifies actual motion, and the opposite of it is not static, but *potential.* The distinction is clear enough, and almost the same distinction is seen in the two English words *motion* and *movement.* Motion does not imply change, unless it be simple change of position, but movement may and frequently does imply transformation. In all the higher applications of the word dynamic, from geology upward, the idea of transformation is involved. This is the sense in which dynamic, and its substantive form dynamics, will be used in Chapter XI. In the present chapter, and indeed, throughout Part II, as the leading conception embodied in the phrase *dynamic agent,* the term will be used in its primary or etymological sense, as relating to force.

All the cosmic products of creative synthesis — the synthetic creations of nature — have their characteristic properties or modes of acting, and it is through these that they produce effects. Taken together these active properties constitute the forces of nature. These separate and apparently different forces, are, however, only so many modalities of the one universal force, but it is not only convenient but practically correct to treat them as distinct. Each of these products, moreover, may be said to form the basis or subject-matter of a science, and these sciences are distinct in the same sense. They are creations, and represent successively new aspects of cosmic history. Every true science is a domain of forces, and the nature of the forces differs with the science. Indeed this difference in the forces is what constitutes the difference existing among the sciences. Without dwelling on the physical forces, and even passing over the vital forces, we may begin at once the consideration of the psychic forces. For the present, too, we will omit the strictly zoölogical aspect of the subject, and deal only with man. As each product possesses all the properties of the antecedent products with its own peculiar differential attribute added, man possesses feeling in common with the lower animals, and the fact which it is important to note just at this point is that feeling constitutes the dynamic agent, and is therefore the highest attribute that we have to consider so long as we are dealing with the dynamic agent.

Now feeling is a true cosmic force, as will be fully shown, and constitutes the propelling agent in animals and in man. In the associated state of man it is the social force, and with it the sociologist must deal. Under this agency social phenomena take place according to uniform laws which may be studied in the same way that the laws of any other domain of phenomena are studied. Sociology is thus a true science, answering to the definition of a science, viz., a field of phenomena produced by true natural forces and conforming to uniform laws. But feeling as the dynamic agent manifests itself in a variety of ways, and just as it is convenient and practically correct to speak of a plurality of natural forces, the modalities of the universal force, so it is convenient and practically correct to speak of a plurality of social forces, the modalities of the general social force or dynamic agent.

The conservation of energy and correlation of forces are as applicable to psychic and social forces as to physical forces. This truth has been perceived by sociologists, but failure to understand the principle of creative synthesis has led to grave misconceptions.

Some of them, for example, talk as though these higher forces were eternal and could never be added to or subtracted from, but were unchangeable in quantity. The truth is that they are comparatively recent developments. There can be no psychic force where there is no mind, no vital force where there is no life. There can be no mind where there is no brain or nerve ganglia, no life where there is no animal, plant, protist, or protoplasm. The products must first be created in which the forces inhere, but of course the properties appear *pari passu* with the products, and both conform to the process of genesis, or becoming, through infinitesimal increments. This erroneous conception of the uncreatibility and indestructibility of vital and psychic forces tends to keep alive the older and more popular error, which survives from the theological stage of history, that the universe is endowed with life and intelligence. All such erroneous world views rest on a basis of truth. They are simply crude conceptions of the truth. The soul of truth contained in this error is that the universe possesses the potency of life and mind. It has within it all the elements out of which life and mind are constructed. But before life and mind can exist they must first be constructed. To say that they exist in some diffused state in the universe is as false as to say that houses exist in a bank of clay out of which bricks may be made. Vital and psychic forces are new creations, and they can only be brought into existence through the delicate instrumentalities of organic development. They must come through protoplasm, the product of chemism and be elaborated in the alembic of nature. Protoplasm must be concentrated in cytodes and cells, cells must be united into the cormus, the process must be continued until tissues are evolved — ectoderm, endoderm, and mesoderm — and out of these the Metazoan body must be built. The protoplasmic tracts and threads of the Protozoan must be inclosed in sheaths and sent branching and anastomosing through the animal body. Physiological dynamos must be established at convenient points, and from these ganglionic power houses the currents of life and sensibility must be sent round through the animal tissues. Motor and sensor apparatus must be perfectly adjusted. Finally a great central storage battery, the brain, must be devised and put in charge of the whole system. All this must be accomplished before any great development of vital and psychic force can take place. From this point on greater and greater quantities of mind power can be stored for use until the phenomena of intelligence shall at length dimly appear and thenceforward increase until mind reaches the stage at which it can contemplate its own history and development.

The social forces are therefore psychic, and hence sociology must have a psychologic basis. It cannot be based directly upon biology, which only manifests the phenomena of the vital forces. It may be said that animals possess feeling although coming within the domain of biology. This is true, and psychology begins with the animal. It is psychology that rests on biology. Here there is direct filiation, and mind is of biologic origin. The higher terms of the series of modalities are: chemism, bathmism, zoism, and psychism, and there is complete filiation throughout the entire series.

The popular conception of "mind" is wholly inadequate for the sociologist. A race of beings who are capable of thinking on such subjects at all are certain to be so much struck by this thinking power or faculty that they will soon come to regard it as constituting mind, and when they use that word it will only be in the sense of the thinking faculty. When they advance still farther and become philosophers this tendency increases, and we accordingly find most of the works on mind confined to the thinking faculty. The use of the word mind in any other sense is rare, but it is obvious upon the least reflection that it must include much more. It certainly must include the feelings, the emotions, the passions, the will. This is of course recognized by scientific psychologists, who usually divide psychology into two departments, the one (commonly put first) consisting of the senses and the intellect, and the other of the emotions and the will. None of these works, however, draw the clear distinction between these two departments of mind that the sociologist requires. With him it is, or should be fundamental. He must discover the forces that govern social phenomena, and the thinking faculty is not a force. But feeling is a true force and its various manifestations constitute the social forces.

The feelings had, moreover, a much earlier origin than the intellect, so that during a prolonged period they constituted the only psychic manifestations, and do so still throughout practically the entire animal world. The simplest forms of feeling developed out of vitality through motility to irritability and sensibility in a series of very short steps. The sensori-motor apparatus was the first to develop, and for a specific and practical purpose, as will be shown in the next chapter. This great primordial half of mind is sometimes appropriately said to constitute the *affective* side of mind, since it embraces all the *affections* in the broadest sense of that word. It is also, with equal propriety, called the subjective department of mind, the phenomena being wholly subjective or relating to the organism, and never objective or relating to the external world.

Without entering here into other characteristics of feeling, it is essential to our present purpose to point out that one of its inherent qualities is that of seeking an end. That is to say, it is appetitive, and this is popularly recognized by the word *appetite*. All appetites belong to the subjective department of mind. A general term for this quality is *appetition*. Appetition is a motive and impels to action. It is this that constitutes it a force. It is the sensor side of the motor fact, and the force is proportional to the intensity of the feeling. The word *motive* has two meanings. It often means inducement or purpose. This is a telic sense not applicable here. Its primary meaning is that which causes or impels, and this is the one we are using. The French language has a separate word for these two ideas, the first being expressed by *motif* and the second by *mobile*. Appetition is a *mobile*, not a *motif*. It is an efficient cause, not a final cause. In a word, it is conative. It is the psychic motive to action. Action is certain to follow the motive unless prevented by some physical obstacle or by other motives that antagonize it and produce a state of psychic equilibrium. That is, it is similar in all essential respects to all other natural forces. It is further true that no psychically endowed being can move without a motive. Such a thing would be an effect without a cause.

In common parlance, appetition, or psychic motive, is simply desire, and desire of whatever kind is a true natural force. The collective desires of associated men are the social forces. This use of the word desire is, however, very broad. It embraces all wants, volitions, and aspirations. From this point of view feeling is identical with desire. Primarily all feeling is intensive. It not only consists in an awareness of self but in an awareness of some need. Wasting tissues constantly need to be renewed, and feeling consists in a sense of this need. With increased complexity of structure other needs arise, until in man and society the wants are unlimited in number and variety. Man's whole affective nature is composed of them.

All emotions and all passions consist, on final analysis, of appetitions. All cravings, yearnings, and longings, all hopes, anticipations, aspirations, and ambitions, are such. But they may be negative, or forces of repulsion instead of attraction. Such are fear, hate, envy, jealousy. When the desire is beyond all hope of satisfaction they take the form of grief, sorrow, disappointment, and despair. Man is thus a theater of desires, positive, negative, or suppressed, all of which cause some form of action, and which together constitute the dynamic agent.

It is therefore well worth our while to consider for a moment the philosophy of desire. Desire is a psychic condition resulting primarily from restraint, exerted by the impinging environment, to motor activity, and where strong enough it overcomes these barriers and causes activity. It is a sensation, and it must be regarded as an unpleasant sensation. The activity it causes is always expended in removing the restraint. Until this is accomplished the sensation must be a disagreeable one. If it were agreeable the effort would be in the direction of continuing it, not of terminating it. Desire is therefore in the nature of pain. It differs, however, from other forms of pain in containing within it a suggestion of action for relief. A burn, a boil, or any other painful affection, furnishes a sensation which does not embody in the sensation itself any suggestion of action that will relieve the pain. All desire does embody such a suggestion, and the action suggested is certain to be performed unless prevented by some of the causes above specified. The typical form of physical desire is to be found in the phenomenon of itching. Desire is essentially prurient. In cutaneous affections causing this sensation the inclination may become irresistible to produce an alteration in the tissues affected.

There are, it is true, certain sensations which convey a suggestion of the action necessary to relieve them, but which, nevertheless, are not properly itching. There is a sort of disease called mysophobia, a morbid sense of being unclean, which constantly drives the patient to wash himself. The sensation due to being wet, especially that of having wet clothing, is usually disagreeable even when not attended with the sensation of cold, and suggests effort to dry one's self. When the sleeve of an undergarment works up the feeling is very disagreeable and the pulling of it down produces a marked satisfaction. Such sensations and many others, such as that of a bad odor or a bad taste, though disagreeable, are not called pains, any more than is desire, and therefore, as there is no other one word for them, it seems proper to use the word pain in a sense wide enough to include all sensations that are unpleasant or which a sentient being shuns or seeks to remove or relieve. In this sense all desire is pain. As distinguished from the more normal forms of pain, which may be called positive, desire may be called negative pain. It cannot be denied that the greater part of the discomfort experienced by man is due to unsatisfied desire. But the phrase unsatisfied desire is tautological, since the quality of being unsatisfied is implied in the idea of desire. All desire is unsatisfied desire. A satisfied desire would no longer be desire at all. Desire might almost be defined as dissatisfaction. Discontent consists entirely in the desire for things that cannot be attained.

While desire is scarcely ever perceived to be pain, of which it really is a form, it is very commonly regarded as a pleasure, which it is not. This is because in the vague, undisciplined thinking of the mass of mankind desire is so spontaneously and universally associated with its satisfaction that the two wholly distinct things cannot be separated. The fact is that just as the greater part of all unhappiness consists in desires that are not satisfied, so the greater part of all happiness consists in satisfying desires. Relief from any pain, if sufficiently rapid, can scarcely be distinguished from pleasure. It is relative pleasure. If it is arrested before it is complete and a portion of the pain continue, it will soon be recognized as such, although the sudden partial sensation may have seemed to be a pleasure. Desire is a kind of pain which further differs from other kinds in the possibility of more or less rapid relief. As it is always due to something that is withheld the supply of that desideratum satisfies the desire and relieves the pain. In most cases, too, this act of supplying the want and the consequent relief produce a peculiarly agreeable sensation. Desire represents a deprivation, and its satisfaction consists in the supply of the thing of which the subject was deprived. The more intense the desire the more gratifying the satisfaction. Desire differs again from other forms of pain in not generally representing a pathologic state. Other kinds of pain usually result from some derangement of function. There is no essential difference between them and disease. Most diseases are painful, and the pain is due to such derangement. Some pathologists maintain that all disease is due to some lack in the supply of those things needful to perfect health. They may all be reduced to this, because even where extraneous bodies invade the system and derange its functions it may be said that this is equivalent to the want of the proper supply. But the sensation called desire pre-supposes a healthy state of the system. Desire is liable to fail in a diseased state. A strong craving for a natural supply betokens a healthy state. Long deprivation may bring on a diseased state, or the organs may become atrophied by inaction, usually at the expense of other organs. Where the supply is permanently withheld, such is the adjustability of the physical constitution that the desire will ultimately disappear. Usually it takes some other form. This is the principle on which slow habituation to different kinds of diet and different conditions of life become possible.

But supposing that the desire is fresh and healthy its satisfaction is a pleasure, and when we consider the great number and variety of desires to which man is subject and the fact that most of them are actually satisfied sooner or later we may form some idea of the volume of pleasure that is thus yielded. It constitutes the great bulk of all that makes existence tolerable. It is possible to make a rough calculation of the relative amount of satisfied and unsatisfied desire. If the latter prevail over the former we have a social state which Dr. Simon N. Patten has happily characterized as a "pain economy," and if the reverse is the case we have his "pleasure economy." [1] All social progress, in the proper sense of the phrase, is a movement from a pain economy toward a pleasure economy, or at least a movement in the direction of the satisfaction of a greater and greater proportion of the desires of men. It also involves the question of the increase in the number and intensity of desires, but this cannot be entered into here.

In ordinary pains and in diseases from which men recover the lessening of the pain is usually so slow that its character as pain is recognized as long as it endures at all. There is no distinct sense of relief. This is because there is no basis for direct comparison of greater with lesser pains. But if sufficiently rapid for such direct

[1] *The Theory of Social Forces.* Supplement to the *Annals of the Academy of Political and Social Science*, January, 1896, pp. 59, 60, 75.

comparison there is a sense of relief that is a relative pleasure. Most desires are satisfied rapidly enough for such a direct comparison, and the difference between the unsatisfied and the satisfied state is intensely vivid. It amounts to a pleasure commensurate with the intensity of the desire and the completeness of the satisfaction. But it is never instantaneous. Time is always required, and so far as the actual or *presentative* pleasure is concerned, this is all of it. If it was instantaneous there would only be a *representative* pleasure, viz., the comparison of remembered sensations. In the actual case both these elements exist. If only one desire existed and was satisfied this would be all of a man's happiness. But in point of fact all men are always subject to a great number of desires, and if a fair share of them are satisfied at intervals of time there results a general state which is called happiness. Besides the more prominent and intense specific desires of which every one is always conscious, there is constantly present in the healthy organism a stream of minor and chiefly unconscious desires arising out of the normal wants of the system. These are also being perpetually satisfied by the processes of nutrition, assimilation, and metabolism, and the satisfaction, if it cannot be called pleasure, that results constitutes what is called the "enjoyment of health."

Schopenhauer accurately showed that the satisfaction of desire was its termination, but he drew the erroneous conclusion that pleasure was only relief from pain, and had no positive existence — that happiness was an illusion. Hartmann sought to perpetuate this error. They forgot to take into the calculation the time element that we have been considering. This alone can give reality to pleasure, and when we recognize the perpetual stream of desires constantly being satisfied, we see that in a normal human life pleasurable sensations of various kinds practically fill all the intervals of existence. This constitutes human happiness, and is the only object really worth striving for. Even if we admit, as most psychologists maintain, that no part of man's psychic activity is absolutely continuous, but that the stream of feeling really consists in a series of separate shocks rapidly succeeding one another, still the case is virtually unchanged, since the very fact that it required close psychological study to discover this, if it is true, shows that, to all but the psychologist, happiness is a continuous state. The pulse and the beating of the heart must be specially observed to be perceived. Systole, diastole, peristalsis, and even breathing, are practically unconscious, and much more so all the various vibrations of the nervous system, ganglionic, and cerebral transformations that generate feelings and emotions.

Of the stronger, conscious, and often violent desires those of hunger and love of course hold the first place. These are original, *i.e.*, not in any sense derivative, and belong to all creatures above the Protozoa certainly, and perhaps to these also. They are both perfectly typical desires, and all that has been said of desire in general applies to them. They are the chief mainsprings to action, and it may almost be said that all other desires are directly or remotely derived from them. This statement, however, would require qualification. But these forces have not diminished with higher organization and the appearance of other desires. They are quite as strong in man as in animals, and in the higher types of men as in the lower types. In society they become the principal social forces and the foundations of sociology. They impel mankind to the performance of the great bulk of all the operations of society. They are strong and reliable forces and capable of working out spontaneously most of the problems that physical life presents.

This truth has been perceived by philosophers and poets, but the most classical expression of it is that of Schiller in his "Lyrisch-didactische Gedichte":—

> Doch weil, was ein Professor spricht
> Nicht gleich zu allen dringet,
> So übt Natur die Mutter-Pflicht
> Und sorgt, dass nie die Kette bricht,
> Und dass der Reif nie springet.
> Einstweilen, bis den Bau der Welt
> Philosophie zusammenhält,
> Erhält sie das Getriebe
> Durch Hunger und durch Liebe.

Political economists early seized upon it, and it may be regarded as the basis of all economics also. The failure of mathematical economics to meet the modern problems of life and business was not due to any flaw in positing the reliability of human impulses. It correctly grasped the ontogenetic and phylogenetic forces of society, but it grounded on the failure to recognize the sociogenetic and the idea forces. These, as we shall see, were a factor before the era of machinery, and have steadily advanced in importance with civilization, until they have become second only to the primary motives that we are considering.

Ratzenhofer has shown that all interest is derived from satisfactions. If we closely analyze this question we shall see that such is the case. Interest is almost a synonym of desire in the sense here employed. Attention cannot be attracted unless an interest can be aroused, and this can only be done by holding out the prospect of some satisfaction. If some craving of the soul is to be answered by a suggested act that act will be performed. This is all that is involved in inducement or incentive, and when a subject or an action becomes attractive, this simply means that it promises a satisfaction or pleasure. Interest thus involves an ellipsis. The satisfaction of desire is understood. Such elliptical terms are very convenient. They clothe the naked truth, and almost without diminution of clearness, they convey the truth in a delicate way to minds that might be somewhat shocked or pained to view it full in the face. Human interests thus constitute the equivalents of the social forces. They are coextensive with the dynamic agent in society.

Many other elements might be enumerated as entering into so complex a conception as the dynamic agent, and which do not seem at first glance to come strictly under the definitions thus far given, but which in fact may be reduced to them by giving sufficient latitude to the terms. Such, for example, are curiosity and wonder, considered as social stimuli, and no one can deny the influence of ennui in promoting activity. Some of these considerations will recur in the course of the discussion, but they are too much in the nature of details to be dealt with further in this general outline of the dynamic agent. With the development of mankind the derivative forces come more and more into the foreground until a point is at length reached at which they seem at least to be more potent agencies than the original forces. These are also true natural forces and simply swell the volume of social energy. Sociology takes account of them all, and is the science which treats of what the social forces have done and are doing, and of how they accomplish results.

As denoting the position that sociology occupies relatively to the other sciences it is worthy of remark that the attitude of the civilized world toward the social forces is analogous to the attitude of the savage toward the physical forces. All know that this is one of apprehension. Fear and not love of nature is the characteristic of primitive peoples. "It is an inherent attribute of the human mind to experience fear and not hope or joy at the aspect of that which is unexpected and extraordinary."[1] There is something peculiarly awe-inspiring about the phenomena of nature. The fear they arouse is out of all proportion to the real danger. The danger of being run over by a railroad train, of being thrown from a horse or a carriage, or of being killed by any of the common causes of accidents, is much greater than that of being struck by lightning or buried by an earthquake, and yet the fear of these phenomena is scarcely ever experienced, while the others are commonly much feared. Some one sent out a circular to many intelligent persons asking them what of all things they most feared. Few were found to fear those dangers which statistics show to be the really greatest, but many confessed to great fear of natural events, lightning, wind, cyclones, hailstones, etc. A few declared that their greatest dread was that of being struck by meteoric stones! The sensation produced by earthquake shocks has been graphically described by Humboldt[2] and Darwin,[3] who, although rationally assured that there was little real danger, could not suppress that instinctive terror that all men have inherited from the savage state when all nature was regarded as conscious and malignant. It is difficult to reconcile this with the blind foolhardiness with which people are known to crowd up to the foot of volcanoes to be buried under molten lava at the next great eruption. This fact is psychologically a very complex one, and doubtless want and habituation are large elements in it, but at bottom I believe it to rest on a form of superstition akin to that which causes nature to be unduly feared. It is a form of fatalism, a world view characteristic of man before he acquired a scientific conception of the nature of mechanical causation, and under the illusion of which he lost all faith in the efficacy of his own efforts or actions. For it is precisely this sense of personal helplessness that gives rise to those indescrib-

---

[1] Humboldt "Cosmos," Otte's translation, Vol. I, p. 97. This translation scarcely does justice to the original, which is as follows: "Es liegt tief in der trüben Natur des Menschen, in einer ernsterfüllten Ansicht der Dinge, dass das Unerwartete, Ausserordentliche nur Furcht, nicht Freude oder Hoffnung, erregt." "Kosmos," Cotta's edition, 12mo, in 4 vols., Stuttgart, 1870, Vol. I, p. 75.

[2] *Op. cit.*, Vol. I, pp. 137 ff.

[3] "Journal of Researches," New York, 1871, p. 302.

able terrors that natural phenomena inspire. The idea of the possibility of influencing natural events or controlling physical forces
thus manifested is wholly foreign to the primitive man, and the feeling is that if the inscrutable powers of nature really intend his
destruction there is no remedy.

Now, as already remarked, civilized man, although he has learned
not only to avert the dangers of the physical forces but even to subjugate and utilize them, has made no progress with social forces, and
looks upon the passions precisely as the savage looks upon the tor-
nado. Man is only civilized in relation to the lower and simpler
phenomena. Toward the higher and more complex phenomena he
is still a savage. He has no more thought of controlling, much less
utilizing, the social forces than the savage has of controlling or utilizing the thunderbolt. Just as pestilences were formerly regarded
as scourges of God, so the so-called evil propensities of man, which
are nothing but manifestations of social energy, are still looked upon
as necessary inflictions which may be preached against but must be
endured. This difference is wholly due to the fact that while we
now have sciences of physics, chemistry, geology, and bacteriology,
which teach the true nature of storms, electricity, gases, earth-
quakes, and disease germs, we have no science of social psychology
or sociology that teaches the true nature of human motives, desires,
and passions or of social wants and needs and the psychic energy
working for their satisfaction. The sociologist who has a proper
conception of his science as similar in all essential respects to these
other sciences, and as having, like them, a practical purpose and use
for man, looks upon the social forces as everybody looks upon the
physical and vital forces, and sees in them powers of nature now
doing injury, or at least running to waste, and perceives that, as in
the other case, they may, by being first studied and understood, be
rendered harmless and ultimately converted into the servants of
man, and harnessed, as the lightning has been harnessed, to the
on-going chariot of civilization.

CHAPTER VII

BIOLOGIC ORIGIN OF THE SUBJECTIVE FACULTIES

THE supreme importance to sociology of the dynamic agent, the general nature of which was outlined in the last chapter, justifies any amount of effort to acquire a full and fundamental conception of it. The only way in which anything can be completely understood is to learn its history. All of nature's creations are genetic, and therefore their history is always the same as their genesis. As these creations have not always existed, but have come into existence at certain epochs in the course of universal evolution, before which they did not exist, it becomes necessary to learn their origin as an essential part of their genesis. The problem before us, then, is nothing less than the origin and genesis of the dynamic agent. As this includes only part of mind, viz., the subjective faculties, we need not concern ourselves at all with the other part, or the objective faculties, and may refer their treatment to Part III.

All genesis is the result of the operation of efficient causes producing natural effects through the action of the appropriate forces. A study of the genesis of any natural product consists, then, chiefly in a search for the causes that have produced it. The form of research is essentially ætiological. But the principle of creative synthesis furnishes the clue to the pursuit of the causes that have produced the observed results. We know, at least, that the product we are studying has been created out of materials of a lower order that existed anterior to it. It is therefore among these materials and their properties that we must look for the antecedents to the more complex synthetic creations of nature. The small part of the universe that comes within the range of our powers of observation reveals a movement from the lower toward the higher orders of phenomena. Possibly in other parts there may be a corresponding inverse movement, so that progress and regress may upon the whole exactly balance each other, but of this we have only a few suggestive examples. Our earth is now capable of sustaining life over the

111

greater part of its surface.   Paleontology teaches us that there has
been a gradual rise in the type of structure of both plants and animals throughout geologic time.   History, ethnology, archæology,
and what we know of human paleontology, all combine to prove
that the human race has been slowly rising from lower to higher
states.   In neither of these series is there any sign that it is
approaching a culminating point, beyond which it will cease to be
an ascending and become a descending series.

The Object of Nature

While the scientific world does not doubt that all the phenomena
of evolution are strictly genetic and produced by forces from behind
that push things into their observed shapes, still, such unilateral
tendencies as those last mentioned certainly present the appearance
of being directed toward an end, and there is small wonder that
throughout the theological stage of human thought it should have
been believed that they were thus directed.   This stage covered the
entire formative period of language, and the consequence was that
language acquired a teleological form which it is now very difficult
to modify.   It is almost impossible to discuss the phenomena of
nature in any other form of language, and we are practically compelled first to disclaim all teleological leanings and then proceed to
talk in teleological terms.   It certainly brings the idea more vividly
home to the mind to speak of the object of nature in a case like the
present than to speak of the tendencies of things, and when it is
understood that no more is meant by the former than by the latter
form of expression no special harm can result from its use.

We may, then, properly inquire what seems to be the general
object of nature in the creation of the several higher and higher
products that we have been considering.   What is the end toward
which matters seem to be moving in an ascending series of creative
acts such as we observe in our part of the universe at the present
stage of cosmic evolution?   If we go far enough back through the
geologic ages of the earth's history we ultimately arrive at a time
when, if the science of the earth teaches anything, there was nothing
in it or upon it but inorganic matter.   Even at the present time the
amount of inorganic matter is so much greater than that of organic,
or still more of organized and living matter, that it is easy to conceive of this little being blotted out leaving only a dead world.   It

is practically confined to its surface, if we regard the water, like the air, as simply an enveloping medium. After an enormous period following the commencement of the formation of a crust over the molten mass of which the earth was formerly composed, and which is supposed still to constitute the whole of its interior, the simplest forms of life began to appear, the earliest probably consisting of some exceedingly low form of vegetable organism, such as that, whatever it was, which made the graphite beds of the Laurentian. Other forms came slowly on until in the Cambrian we have trilobites and molluscs; in the Silurian, seaweeds and higher molluscs; in the Devonian land plants and fishes; in the Carboniferous, forests of higher land plants, and so on down, the quality and quantity of life both increasing, until the present flora and fauna of the globe were finally produced.

Throughout the entire process it is noteworthy that the increase in the bulk of organized matter was attended with a corresponding increase in the degree of structural development. This might, it is true, be stated the other way, but the lesson would be the same. That lesson seems to be that the increased structural development is the condition to the increased mass of organized matter. It is probable that the quantity of lowly organized matter still largely predominates over that of the highly organized, but among land plants the higher types, such as the coniferous and dicotyledonous forest trees, predominate over the lower types, such as the ferns and mosses. Among animals the herds of ungulates that roamed over vast areas before man commenced their systematic extermination may have constituted the larger part of the animal life of the globe, considered from the sole point of view of mass of organized matter, weight, for example. But man, after all, has done little more than substitute domestic for feral creatures, and there probably never were as many bisons on the western plains of America as there now are cattle on the same area, while the animals that man keeps in existence in thickly peopled countries doubtless greatly exceed in bulk and weight the faunas of those countries before they were settled by man. Even if we consider the subject from the standpoint of brain development, as the highest form of structural organization, we shall find the law to hold good, for it is this that has enabled the human race to increase until the population of the globe has reached about 1,600,000,000, the aggregate mass of whose bodies represents, in

I

addition to an undiminished quantity of animal life, a larger amount of organized matter than could have been produced without the aid of such brain development.

We may therefore probably say with some approach toward the truth that the object of nature, as this phrase has been explained, is to convert as large an amount as possible of inorganic into organic and organized matter. This may be a somewhat unpoetical conclusion, and if we could have things as we want them a more delicate and respectable end might be imagined for nature to pursue. But we are only trying to ascertain what the end really is toward which things tend, and this formula comes nearer to expressing it than any other that has been offered. It may be asked why the end is not rather structural perfection. But this, as we have seen, seems to be a means rather than an end. It obviously accomplishes the end, and it seems to be a more pertinent question how it happened to be hit upon as a means. And here we encounter a curious state of things which we shall find to recur at almost every one of the great cosmic steps. Weismann several times refers to certain peculiar phenomena which he meets with in the course of his biological researches, for which there seems to have been no antecedent preparation, and which in the normal course of things would not be expected. In fact they are usually more or less contrary to the expected result, and seem like mistakes in the economy of nature. For such phenomena he uses the term "unintended." A course or series of events is set on foot generating certain products and properties, when at length some of these latter begin to work at cross purposes to the general movement and tend to antagonize it. They were created for one purpose which they serve, but are found to possess other qualities which develop until they overshadow the original qualities and react against the normal course of things.

Structural development in organic beings sometimes comes partly within this class of occurrences. It serves its purpose admirably at the beginning and for a long period, but when it begins to take the form of extreme specialization it ceases to conduce to the advantage of the race, and, as shown in Chapter V, it prepares for its own destruction. Perfection of structure may be looked upon as a device for securing the end above described. It is simply the means to that end. It therefore seems to be telic. Everywhere in nature genesis simulates telesis. The true scientific explanation of this is that the nisus of nature is in all directions, and the principle of advantage selects the advantageous course. We may imagine every other conceivable method of attaining the end to have been tried and all the rest to have failed because not advantageous. If there is a path to success it is sure to be found because all paths are tried. This secures the same result as if a directive agent had pointed out the only true path, and no other had been tried. We lookers-on, after the success has been achieved, know nothing of the infinite number of failures because they have left no record. This may be taken as the general explanation of the universal belief in teleology during the theological period of intellectual development.

ORIGIN OF LIFE

Planets are formed by the condensation of nebulous matter. As the mass condenses it contracts. The volatilized elements vary greatly in their degrees of volatility and some of them, in the process of cooling through radiation, and from the increasing distance from the central mass (sun), reach their points of liquefaction earlier than others. From the liquid state they finally reach the viscid or molten state, and ultimately the solid state. Thus the different substances become distributed according to their constitutions in the mass of the planet. The heavier substances with high condensing points occupy the center and general mass, while the lighter ones with low condensing points remain at the surface. Some of these, like nitrogen, do not combine with others, and remain elementary. Others, like hydrogen and carbon, combine with part of the oxygen. The first of these combinations resulted primarily in the formation of vast masses of steam, which later partly condensed into vapor and still later into water or even ice. Jupiter seems to consist largely of vapor. The earth doubtless once had an aqueous (steam or vapor) envelope as thick as would be made by converting all the waters of the oceans and seas into vapor. The oxygen also seizes all the carbon and converts it into the dioxide, which is a gas at all ordinary temperatures. After the formation of a crust all round a planet there still remains a large amount of water occupying the cavities of the surface, and an atmosphere of oxygen, nitrogen, carbon dioxide, and aqueous vapor.

These last are the principal materials out of which the biotic products are formed. There is everywhere a universal chemism,

and different substances are constantly being formed through the
contact and elective affinities of matter.   Within a certain somewhat narrow range of temperature, chiefly between the freezing and
the boiling points of water, but increasing in both directions from
these points so as to reach a maximum near the middle of the scale
that separates them (50° C., 122° Fahr.), this chemism may be supposed to pass into zoism during the process of cooling of a planet.
This, however, is of course mere speculation.   What we do practically know is that life did at some time commence on our own
planet.   That this actual beginning of life took place when temperatures were much higher than they are now even in the tropics,
is also practically certain.   Of this *archigonia*, as Haeckel calls it,
we are as sure as we are of the principal facts of geology.   Whether
it is still going on we are not so sure, and it is just possible that it
may have required higher temperatures and different conditions than
now exist to originate the organic world.   We are not so much concerned with this as we are with the products and properties of life.
The products in large measure we know, although we may not
know the absolutely simplest.   The primary differential attributes
are motility and irritability, if there is any difference between these.
The simplest product we know is protoplasm, and this is so simple
when viewed from the biological standpoint that it can scarcely be
called organic, yet when viewed from the chemical standpoint it is
so complex that it cannot be classed among chemical substances.
It occupies the exact middle point between the inorganic and the
organic worlds.   It was perfectly described by Huxley as the
"physical basis of life." [1]

The sea is the mother of all life.   The oceans were formerly
larger and shallower than now, and the waters must have once been
very warm.   Doubtless there was a time when there was no land.
When land first appeared it was in the form of islands and the
continents rose later.   In the warm, almost seething waters that
bathed the shores of these low islands and incipient continents all
the conditions existed for the origination of life.   It came, and its
history from Laurentian times to the present, a period perhaps not
less, possibly much more than one hundred million years, is fairly

---

[1] See Professor Huxley's address with the above title delivered in Edinburgh, Nov.
18, 1868, and first published in the *Fortnightly Review* for February, 1869, many
times reprinted.

well known by the records left in the rocks.   But we are not now considering the forms that life created.   We are concerned at present only with the nature and origin of life itself.   Prior to the appearance of protoplasm all activity had been molecular.   Motion there always was in all bodies and substances, but it was confined to their elements or chemical units.   Masses only moved when impelled by the contact of other moving masses.   To all appearances solid bodies are motionless.   Science only has taught that the particles composing them are in motion.   Even liquids and gases move only when impelled by some force which is usually well understood.   Yet the inherent molecular motions of even the hardest substances are, when properly considered, spontaneous.   But the term *spontaneous* has, from our long ignorance of molecular motion, been applied only to masses that move of themselves.   The bodies capable of doing this are said to be *alive*.   But as all things are endowed with spontaneous molecular motion the only difference between things without life and things alive seems to be that the latter are also capable of spontaneous *molar* motion.   The power of spontaneous molar motion is therefore the differential attribute of life.   It is called *motility*.

Motility first appears in protoplasm.   There is probably no essential resemblance between the movements of protoplasmic masses and those purely physical movements that certain ingenious investigators have succeeded in producing in the laboratory.   The principle underlying the latter, whatever it is, is doubtless wholly different from that of motility.   But motility is so far only an observed fact, not itself a principle.   Its principle cannot be said to be known, and, so far as I am aware, the only hypothesis that has ever been advanced to explain motility is that which I proposed in 1882 and formulated in the following words : —

The primary distinction between these most complex of all known bodies [plasson or protoplasmic bodies] and the less complex ones seems to be, that while in the latter all their activities are molecular, in the former they are to a certain extent molar, and carry with them the whole or a portion of the substances themselves.[1]

I there explained that this might become possible in consequence of the relatively enormous size of the molecules of protoplasm, and showed that the isomeric forms of the next most complex chemical substances, the albuminoid and protein bodies, constitute a certain

---

[1] *American Naturalist*, Vol. XVI, December, 1882, p. 978.

approach toward the property of motility. If protoplasm results from the further recompounding of these highest known true chemical compounds we may well expect that such a substance will possess some remarkable property, and motility is not too remarkable for such an exalted product to reveal. The entire process is one of organization, but until protoplasm was reached the organization was wholly chemical. From that point on we have biotic organization, constantly rising in complexity from the simplest plasson bodies, the amœboid forms, the unicellular organisms, and the Protista, through the Protophyta and Protozoa to the higher types of vegetal and animal life. The life principle was the effect of chemical organization, but it was the cause of biotic organization.

High chemical complexity up to a certain point, as in the alkaloids, shows itself in such properties as astringency, bitterness, corrosiveness, and other intense activities rendering them poisonous to animals and men. But the most complex of all organic compounds, those with the largest molecules and greatest atomic weights, such as the albuminoids, show their complex constitution by such properties as instability and isomerism. But, as we have seen, it is only a step from these properties to that of motility, in which the molecular activities are so strong and so adjusted that they are able to sway the mass. It may be difficult to imagine how this is done. The phenomena presented by the jumping bean may convey a crude idea of such a process. The larva of the moth *Carpocapsa saltitans* finds its way into the seed of the Euphorbiaceous plant *Sebastiania Palmeri* and by its activities causes the seed to seem alive and move and roll about. Intense activities of large compound molecules may produce an effect analogous to this upon the circumscribed bodies which they compose. This at least may pass for a hypothesis of the nature of motility in protoplasm.

But motility in its later stages takes the form of *bathmism*,[1] and

---

[1] A few of Professor Cope's neologisms have proved useful, and I have not hesitated to use this one, for which there is no other exact equivalent. His first use of it seems to have been in his "Review of the Modern Doctrine of Evolution" in the *American Naturalist* for March, 1880, Vol. XIV, p. 176, but it occurs constantly in his later works. See his "Origin of the Fittest," p. 205, and his "Primary Factors of Organic Evolution," pp. 479, 484. It was in the former of these works (p. 430) that he expressed his acceptance of the theory I have been stating, and which, as will be seen by the passage above quoted from my paper on the "Organic Compounds in their Relations to Life," was proposed by me two years earlier than the publication by Loew and Bokorny of their researches leading to a similar result.

becomes the universal growth-force of the organic world. What I wish especially to emphasize here is that motility, with its generalized form, bathmism, is simply a property of protoplasm and of all living organisms, as much so as sweetness is a property of sugar, bitterness of quinine, or isomerism of protein. Zoism is a synthetic creation of chemism.

Origin of Mind

We have now to consider another new property created by the synthetic power of nature, viz., the property of *awareness, consciousness,* or *feeling,* for in their absolute beginnings these three are one. It is the primordial stage of psychism and is a synthetic creation of zoism.[1] As genetic creation is always a becoming there never would be any absolute line of demarcation between any of nature's products or properties if we could know all the terms of the series. Between chemism and zoism there seems to be a great break. We are acquainted with the molecular activities of chemical substances and we have discovered the molar activities of protoplasm. There seems to be a great distance between them, but it is probably due to missing links in the really perfect chain. There may be many kinds of protoplasm possessing the property of motility in varying degrees. But between zoism and psychism — life and mind — there is no such interval, and it becomes almost a metaphysical speculation to discuss the question as to where the latter begins. Do the lowest animals feel ? Do plants feel ? Does protoplasm feel ? That the elements out of which consciousness emerges are present in protoplasm there is no doubt. But may we not say the same of albumen, of any organic compound, of any substance whatever ? Hylozoism cannot be denied, but its true import can only be grasped by the light of creative synthesis. If we are authorized to say that molecular activity is not life, we seem equally authorized to say that motility is not mind. The problem of the origin of feeling still confronts us.

" The proximate components of Mind are of two broadly-con-

---

1 The word *zoism* must be taken in its primary sense from the Greek ζῆν, to live, and not as if derived from ζῶον, an animal. Zoology ought to have had the meaning we give to biology ; the latter, as has been frequently pointed out by Greek scholars, is etymologically inappropriate, since the Greek word βίος was used for life in a moral or conventional sense. It was justified, however, by the special meaning early given to zoology.

trasted kinds — Feelings and the Relations between Feelings." [1]   The
initial and irreducible element of mind is feeling. Feeling must
have had a beginning as well as life. It must have had also a
reason for being. No cosmic step is ever taken without a reason,
which is a little different from saying that no such step is taken
without a cause. The reason for the appearance of a new creative
product is not a final cause, but it is not exactly the same as its
efficient or "occasional" (occasioning) cause. We have seen that
life was a means to an end of nature. It consists of a power that
pushes matter forward and upward into a higher state. The life
force is a new phase of the universal force making for evolution.
It pushes at every point and transfers the largest possible quantity
of inorganic matter to the organized state. But a time comes, and
it came very early, when this process is seriously interfered with
by the nature of the environment. The innumerable trials and
errors that characterize nature's method proved that the most successful form of organized matter was the colloid form in contradistinction to the crystalloid form, which characterizes the formation of
inorganic bodies below the plane of life. This colloid matter must,
too, at least at first, be soft, semi-aqueous, viscid, and gelatinous,
capable of being molded and modified to any required extent.
These plasson or plastic bodies must moreover be so unstable that
they can perpetually renew their constituent particles, exhausted
every moment by the still dominant chemism involved in their
activities.   The problem was to preserve the *form* during this
transformation of the *substance*. The least concussion from without
or disturbance of the medium threatened to destroy the entire
structure thus built up and return its elements to the mineral
kingdom.   These frail structures, thus dependent upon renewal
from the medium, must also possess the power to appropriate fresh
material necessary to supply the losses due to the breaking down
of the complex molecules and their return to the chemical state.
Two great necessities thus arose at the outset, that of supplying
the waste involved in metabolism, and that of escaping the destructive influences of the environment. If an intelligent being were
asked how these two objects might be secured, supposing such
being to know nothing of what actually did occur, such a being
might not be able to think of any adequate means. To a very

[1] Spencer, " Principles of Psychology," Vol. I, New York, 1873, p. 162 (§ 65).

inventive mind the idea might occur. But if such a being were told that this new form of matter acquired in some way the faculty of feeling, this would, at least upon a slight reflection, be seen to satisfy the conditions of the problem. But let us inquire just what is meant by feeling.

In the first place feeling must be something that furnishes an *interest*. It cannot be indifferent and accomplish the end in view. In another place I shall show that feeling may be indifferent and still be feeling, but the form of feeling necessary to secure these two pressing necessities of primordial plastic organisms cannot be indifferent and must be *interested*. But the only conceivable basis of interest is *agreeableness* or its opposite. The only form of feeling that could accomplish the object is agreeable feeling or disagreeable feeling. The appropriation of material needed to supply the waste of metabolism must be attended with some degree of agreeable sensation, and the injurious concussions made by external objects must produce sensations that are not agreeable. Otherwise the property of motility with which these primordial plastic bodies were already endowed would not take the direction necessary to secure these ends. With the faculty of experiencing these sensations it is clear that motility would naturally take that direction, and the creature would have an interest so to move or act as to appropriate the needed supplies and to escape the injury threatened.

Can any one think of any other power, faculty, or property that would secure the same result? Can any one name any other means that would accomplish the end? Nature has not limited herself to this one means. Throughout the vegetable kingdom, at least above its most initial stages, other means are chiefly employed. Firm attachment to the soil, strong tissues protected by a firm covering or bark, and the formation of wood are the chief dependence of plants, while the nourishment is supplied by chemical or even physical action. There is no real proof that plants feel, and as feeling is not necessary to their existence, the principle of advantage does not act in the direction of evolving such a property. In many animals, too, although all are possessed of feeling to some degree, other means of protection, notably shells, are common. But even the Vorticella, instead of moving its cilia in a fortuitous manner, gives them such a vortical motion as to draw the nutrient particles from all sides into its mouth opening. But although certain low forms of life may exist without feeling it is evident that very little of the organic progress that has taken place could have gone on without it. Feeling may then be regarded as a *condition to the existence of plastic organisms.* For this purpose, too, feeling cannot be indifferent or disinterested. It must be *intensive.* In plainer terms, it must involve, in however feeble a degree, a capacity for pleasure and pain. We may then say that pleasure and pain are conditions to the existence of plastic organisms.

I have thus far sought to avoid the use of the word *consciousness,* because psychologists are not agreed as to its meaning. Non-psychological writers are still more at variance on this point. Most of this difference, it is true, is due to the habit of looking at everything from the standpoint of the most highly developed organisms in which there is a great central ganglion or brain which controls the actions of the whole organism. From this point of view nothing is conscious that is not referred to this high court of arbitration. But the history of organic development and of the development of the nervous system of the higher animals and man shows us that this is a superficial view; that there have been all stages in the process of coördination; and that the final subordination of all the lower ganglionic centers to the supreme center was the result of ages of structural progress. It may be compared to the history of the papacy. There was a time when every bishop was a pope, and it took several centuries to invest the bishop of Rome with the supreme power. To deny consciousness to the lower ganglionic centers is to ignore the whole history of animal development. There is no doubt that even in man thousands of pleasures and pains are experienced that are never referred to the brain and of which the man himself as such knows nothing. Such feelings are no more to him than if they were experienced by another person or by the lower animals in the midst of which he moves. These lower centers are conscious units, and in a certain sense exist for themselves. Even the brain, as the phenomena of double and multiple consciousness demonstrate, is not such an indivisible unit as is commonly imagined.

It is due to these and other misconceptions, growing for the most part out of a lack of acquaintance with the history of organic development, that such varied meanings are given to consciousness, and that we meet with such expressions as " unconscious feeling" and " unconscious will." From my own point of view all psychic phenomena are necessarily conscious, and consciousness inheres in all feeling and is its psychic essence. The greater part of the "philosophy of the unconscious," as taught by Schopenhauer and Hartmann, deals with those deep subconscious phenomena that do not rise to the level of the throne of reason, but which, nevertheless, as they show, really give the bent to human action and human history. They represent the *natura naturans*, and are the unseen forces that are at work below the surface, shaping events in apparent opposition to the wishes and intentions of men. They thus appear unconscious or even supernatural, but in and of themselves they as really involve the principle of consciousness as do the often less wise and less successful decrees of the developed brain.

Most psychologists and also the world at large regard consciousness as something that differs *toto cœlo* from all other things. They are scarcely willing to admit that it can be a *natural* thing at all. The testimony on this point is so nearly unanimous that it seems almost presumptuous in any one to attempt to stem such a current. It is not confined to persons of a theological bent, but extends to the most outspoken evolutionists, like Spencer and Huxley. But it is difficult to see why this should be so. It practically amounts to a recognition of discontinuity, and seems to me virtually to give away the whole evolutionary or monistic hypothesis. If at this particular point where psychic phenomena begin there is an absolute break, and something is introduced whose elements are not contained in anything that preceded it, I do not see why we should find any fault with the introduction of any number of such external elements or factors, and there seems to be no reason for stopping short of the most arbitrary theological explanation of all the phenomena of the universe. But there seems to be something particularly objectionable in characterizing consciousness as a property of matter. It is usually asked: How can we conceive of matter being conscious? And often it is declared that consciousness bears no resemblance to the known properties of matter. It might be answered that while we cannot, in one sense, conceive of matter being conscious, still, in the same sense, we cannot conceive of matter being alive, and in the same sense, we cannot conceive of matter being astringent, or caustic, or narcotic. Can we conceive of any property of matter? This question is as legitimate as the other. What we do is to *observe* that certain kinds of matter have certain properties and certain other kinds other properties. And we only observe that some organized beings behave as if they possessed what we know in ourselves as consciousness. So far as the resemblance of consciousness to any known property of matter is concerned, no two properties bear any resemblance whatever to each other. No one could tell anything about them in advance, and no one would have the slightest idea of the nature of the properties of matter who had not had some experience of them. It is purely gratuitous to assert that matter could not have such a property as consciousness. The illogicality of such an assertion is increased when we remember that most of those who are cocksure of it are perfectly willing to believe that not consciousness alone but thought and intelligence are floating about in space independent of all matter and yet capable of directing and creating all the events of the finite world. This seems to most scientific men unthinkable, and why any of them should feel called upon to react against an attempt to explain mind as they themselves explain matter and life can only be accounted for as a last, lingering relic of the theological stage of the development of thought, holding over through the metaphysical and far into the scientific era.[1]

We see then that closely following upon the chemical origin of life we have the biologic origin of mind, for mind in the form of feeling or consciousness was only another step in the direction of attaining nature's great end, the higher organization of matter. And we can see why Comte, who must have had something of the prophet's insight into this subject, declined to regard the phenomena of mind as generically distinct from those of life, and in one of his inspired passages referred to them as the transcendental part of biology.[2] But Comte did not clearly grasp the law of evolution, and he had no idea of creative synthesis, which alone brings out into strong relief the different steps in the evolutionary process.

FEELING IN ITS RELATIONS TO FUNCTION

The same force that pushed life into existence tends to perpetuate and increase it. This is the chief function of organic life, and noth-

---

[1] I have treated this subject more at length in my lecture on the Status of the Mind Problem, published as *Special Papers* No. 1, of the Anthropological Society of Washington, 1894.

[2] Il faut, sous ce dernier point de vue, attribuer surtout cette insuffisante prépondérance actuelle de la philosophie biologique, dans l'ensemble des théories sociales,

ing can be genetically created that does not assist in the performance of it. Such assistance is the test of advantageousness, and nothing is advantageous that does not so assist. Feeling, as we have seen, was the only conceivable means by which plastic organisms could be preserved from destruction and enabled to perpetuate themselves and develop. Plastic organisms are the only ones that are capable of those higher degrees of development that we find in the animal kingdom. They alone, frail as they are, can survive and at the same time advance. Plasticity is a prime element in the fitness to survive, and the " survival of the plastic "[1] is the survival of the fittest. But it was not so much a question of survival as a question of advancement. Rigid organisms, as we have seen, can subsist and perpetuate themselves. If not too rigid they can advance somewhat, but their progress is limited. The endogenous trunk and the crustacean coat of mail circumscribe growth. By such devices as the exogenous structure of stems and the internal skeleton of vertebrates these straitjackets are in whole or in part removed. Flexibility and adaptability are the prerequisites to structural progress. We may gain a homely idea of the superiority of plastic over rigid organisms by comparing the former to a card catalogue and the latter to a blank sheet prepared for the registration of names. Calculate as closely as you may, the latter is sure sooner or later to be congested in some places and blank in others, and ultimately to require to be rewritten, while the card catalogue is perfectly flexible, so that, no matter how anomalous the nature of the entries may be, every card can go into its exact place. Any one who has worked in the library of the British Museum on Great Russell Street, London, has seen an example of a rigid catalogue on a large scale. Card catalogues are to be found in every library. A plastic organism, like a card catalogue, is capable of indefinite expansion in any advantageous direction without danger of being cramped or congested and without hindrance to movement along the lines of least resistance. This means development, and as we know, it is only this class of organisms that have attained a high state of development.

à l'imperfection plus prononcée qui distingue la partie transcendante de la biologie, relative à l'étude générale des phénomènes intellectuels et moraux. "Philosophie Positive," Vol. IV, p. 342.

[1] So far as I can learn this phrase was first used by Mr. Clarence King in an address delivered at the Yale Scientific School in 1877 on Catastrophism and Evolution, variously published. See The American Naturalist, Vol. XI, August, 1877, p. 469.

If the object of nature is that which we have supposed it to be, and function is the performance of those acts necessary to the attainment of that end, and if such acts would not be performed without that interest, incentive, or inducement which feeling supplies, then feeling is a means to function. Considered in themselves feeling and function are two wholly different things. They have no resemblance to each other whatever. And although feeling is a conscious state, still there is no consciousness, at least in the lower stages of development, of the relation of feeling to function. The conscious creature is conscious only of its own states. It is not conscious of the functional effect of its actions in response to those states. This is one of those late derivative forms of consciousness which are so generally present to the mind as to crowd out or obscure the primary conception of consciousness. Feeling came into existence as a means to the performance of function, not through any foresight of the necessity for the action. Not even the simplest nutritive acts are known to be such, much less acts which conduce to higher development. The relation of feeling to function as means to end was brought about through adaptation, and there is a sort of preëstablished harmony between them. Feeling was created as an inducement to functional activity not otherwise attainable. The fact that it furnishes such an inducement alone explains its creation. If a means existed it was certain to be adopted, since all means were tried. Thus is explained the origin of feeling, and, as feeling is the initial step in the creation of mind, it also explains the origin of mind. Since, too, function is the biologic end, feeling is of biologic origin.

Feeling as an End

Thus far we have considered feeling solely as a means, viz., the means to the end of nature, increased life. But it has another aspect, and must also be considered as an end — the end of the creature. This aspect is wholly novel. It has nothing to do with the general scheme of nature. To continue using the convenient teleological language with which we began, it was not contemplated in that plan. It was *unintended*. Preservation, continuation, and augmentation are the three aspects of the cosmic end. These are normal and fully in line with the whole evolutionary movement thus far. No other end can be detected in the scheme. But it merely *happened* that at a certain point it became necessary, in order to secure these ends in the higher organic reaches of evolution, to furnish these later creations with some form of *interest* that should enable them to assist in the prosecution of the plan. Hitherto the products of creative synthesis had been passive. Henceforth they were to become active. Up to that point nature had worked alone, unaided by her creations. From that point on she was to have their coöperation. As, in a family, the parents must for a long time struggle to raise their children, but later, when the children reach the age of usefulness, they begin to contribute to their own support and that of their parents, so the procreative world nursed its infant progeny through the cosmic, physical, chemical, and early biotic periods, until at last, when they had reached the ages of protoplasm, protist, and plant, it became time to intrust them with an interest in the economy of the universe. The form which this interest took was the faculty of feeling, whereby these tocogenetic creations were made to care for themselves. The coöperation of these new factors was a powerful aid and enabled nature to make fresh advances, and, indeed, to execute the grand strides that characterized the higher organic development.

But the creation of this interest involved a series of collateral consequences that had nothing whatever to do with the purpose for which it was called in. As we saw, the creature was only conscious of itself. It was wholly unconscious of the ends it was subserving. Its own interests were its only ends, and it was these and these alone that it pursued. It is true that, at first at least, and to a large extent at all stages, these interests were parallel with the universal interest. The preëstablished harmony was absolute in the beginning and admirably served its purpose. But as the end of nature and that of the creature were totally different it was natural that, with the higher stages of development, and throughout all the vicissitudes of life on the globe during the millions of years of geologic time, there should arise combinations of circumstances in which this parallelism would cease, and even cases in which feeling and function would conflict. Such in fact has been the history of the higher life, and there has ever been a tendency to pursue ends that were opposed to the ends of nature. There has been a perpetual struggle between the individual and the race, and no one will ever know how fierce this struggle was. But the ultimate triumph of function in this struggle is certain, since the existence of the individual depends upon it, and therefore there is a limit beyond which interest cannot go, or beyond which if it does go it is cut off and the record closed. A certain amount of adaptation is therefore always necessary, and the present state of things shows that the degree of inadaptation has never been so great as seriously to interfere with the law of development.

But we are not so much concerned with the struggle between feeling and function as we are with the significance of this new factor thus added to the history of creation. Feeble and accidental as was its origin, it soon proved itself a young giant, and suddenly shot up into enormous importance. It was a true sympode and almost at once assumed the first place in nature. In short, it was nothing less than the dawn of mind in the world. Before its appearance all nature had been mindless and soulless. Henceforth there was to be *animated nature* with all that the phrase carries with it. In it were contained the psychic world and the moral world. With it came pleasure and pain with all their momentous import, and out of it ultimately grew thought and intelligence. Nature cared nothing for any of these. They were unnecessary to her general scheme, and not at all ends of being. Mind was therefore an accident, an incidental consequence of other necessities — an *epiphenomenon*.

The special peculiarity of this new differential attribute is its intense subjectivity. Sir William Hamilton characterized feeling as "subjective subjectivity." [1] It centers entirely in the organism. It is confined to the individual and has no concern for the race. It subserves function, but not for the sake of function. Neither does this property furnish any notion of other properties. To it objects are either agreeable or disagreeable, or else they are as if they were not. In other words it recognizes only *qualities*, not properties. These are psychic phenomena, but they are only subjectively psychic. They belong to the science of psychology, but constitute a department of that science which is properly called subjective psychology. This department of mind is distinct from the other department properly called objective, to be treated in Part III, except in the sense that the latter grew out of the former in precisely the same way that feeling grew out of life and life out of chemism.

[1] " Metaphysics," Lect. 42, Mansel's edition, Edinburgh and London, 1859, Vol. II, p. 432.

Mind is thus divided into the two great branches, which are practically Kant's *Sinnlichkeit* and *Verstand.* Either may be taken up
at its origin and followed out throughout its development without
confusion with the other, but I know of no psychological work in
which this has been done. The two are habitually confounded and
inextricably mixed up until the reader finds himself bewildered.
But the subjective or affective side of mind is the only one in which
the interest in life resides, and in its varied manifestations it constitutes the individual's only object in life. Feeling, which was created as a means, and has remained the most potent of the means to
nature's end, became the sole end of the sentient being and constitutes the moral world.

Philosophy of Pleasure and Pain

We have seen that in its origin all sensation was intensive. It
was created as an aid to function and would have been useless but
for the interest that prompted to action. While nutrition and reproduction are the chief functions to be subserved by it there are many
minor functions, the sum of which is only second in importance to
those primary functions. Every organ has its special function and
its exercise in the performance of this function is physiologically
imperative. Such exercise in every case involves a satisfaction, and
the sum of the satisfactions yielded by the normal exercise of all the
organs is large and increases with structural differentiation which
multiplies organs. In general it may be said that the normal and
healthy exercise of the faculties is attended with pleasure. There
is pleasure in activity, provided the activity be spontaneous and consist in this normal exercise of the faculties. The so-called play
instinct is nothing but this, and is not an instinct in the proper
sense of the word. The idea that pleasure results from ease and
inactivity is doubtless derived from the fact that man has been long
enslaved and compelled to make laborious and painful exertions not
demanded by his faculties. Mill's "paradox of hedonism" is based
on this error. Ennui is one of the most unendurable of pains, and
is the parent of Mr. Veblen's "instinct of sportsmanship" among
the leisure class, impelling them to exertion however useless, while
his "instinct of workmanship" is nothing else than the result of
the satisfaction which all derive from the exercise of their faculties.
The nutritive and reproductive acts are nothing more than special-

K

ized forms of the exercise of the faculties, the degree of satisfaction being as much more intense as the functions are more imperative.

It is common to regard pleasure and pain as opposites, the former as positive and the latter negative, but this is only a convenient conception and is not physiologically true. When we consider their origin and purpose we see that they were both positive attributes created for specific ends. We may call them specializations for these ends or adaptations to these ends, just as instincts and habits, and various psychic attributes, are specialized and adapted. All pleasure is *mandatory* and all pain is *monitory*. In the higher animals the entire nervous system is specialized to lure or to warn. There are pleasure nerves and pain nerves, neither of which is capable of the other sensation. We are told that where the same organ, as the tongue or palate, is capable of yielding both pleasure and pain according to the kind of substance brought into contact with it, the two sensations are furnished by different nerves lying together in the same tissues. Besides these there is usually a third set of nerves that yield the sensation of pain produced by contusion, heat, cold, etc. The entire system is thus elaborately adjusted with reference to function, attracting the nutritive and the fecundative, rejecting the nauseous and the noxious, and sounding the alarm against any form of violence that might threaten injury or destruction. All this is emphasized by the fact that these specialized nerves are not found except where they may be of use, and are confined to the periphery or other exposed surfaces. The great interior of the animal body is feelingless, and the very roots of the great nerve trunks may be severed without producing any sensation whatever. The heart itself may be cut in pieces without pain; obviously because these parts are internal and protected, and are not exposed to the dangers that beset the external parts of the body. These facts help to furnish an idea of the nature of pleasure and pain as means to function and as products of the creative synthesis of nature, and to dispel the popular illusion that they exist in some way as a matter of course. If feeling had not been needed it never would have existed and there would have been nothing above the vegetable.

This conception of monitory pains and mandatory pleasures lies at the foundation of the biologic origin of mind. So long as feeling and function are adapted pleasure means life and health and growth and multiplication, while pain points to danger, injury, waste, destruction, death, and race extinction. Pleasure is anabolic, pain is catabolic. Pleasure and pain do not themselves produce the beneficial or injurious effects ; they only indicate them. Pain itself does not kill, and it usually diminishes or disappears as death approaches. But it marks the danger point and is severest at the time when it is most needed, while there is still time to escape. But for the individual it becomes an end, and it is pain and not danger that it is sought to escape. No animal fears death. It has no conception of death. What makes the bird fly and the antelope run is the fear of pain. Because man knows that danger usually involves life he imagines that animals also fear death, which is entirely a mistake. To the individual pain is evil, and the introduction of pain into the world in the manner I have described, constituted the true origin of evil. Evil therefore was a means of preserving life, and all the evil in the world is, broadly viewed, only premonition.

On the other hand pleasure represents the good. It denotes the performance of function. To the individual it is an end, and so long as the original adaptation of feeling to function exists it also secures the end of nature. As we have already seen, the normal exercise of every organ or faculty is attended with pleasure, and in health the sum total of all these pleasures, moderate and strong, constitutes the state called happiness. This satisfaction lies at the foundation of the economic conception of utility. At bottom all utility consists in satisfaction, *i.e.*, in pleasure. And here again we find a clear contrast arising out of the distinction between feeling and function. It is the contrast between utility and necessity. The standpoint of feeling is utility. The standpoint of function is necessity. The one is the good of the individual, the other is the good of the race, or more broadly, the furtherance of the general scheme of nature. Utility is subjective and relates to feeling; necessity is objective and relates to function. It is on this same distinction that is based the contrast between happiness and virtue. Happiness is subjective while virtue is objective. Virtue relates to function and signifies a course of conduct advantageous to the race and the general scheme. Vice, in the last analysis, is conduct that in some way threatens the race, or that antagonizes the agencies making for the preservation and continuance of life. Its existence emphasizes the fact that the single pursuit of the creature's end led to wide deviations from the

normal path, and this, with the higher and higher development of
organic life, was increasingly accentuated, constituting a perpetual
menace not merely to the continuance of the different species of organisms but to the success of the organic experiment as a whole.
This ever-increasing *waywardness* on the part of sentient beings in
search of pleasure must be checked in the general interest of life.

RESTRAINTS TO FEELING

The origin of feeling was a change of front of the universe.
Through it nature seemed to cut loose from her moorings and to be
drifting out on an unknown sea.   The great problem was to maintain
the relation of harmony that characterized the initial step.   Feeling
was a new power that was called in to supplement the original forces
of matter and life.   The effect was stupendous.   The new power
quickly overshadowed the old and took the reins into its own hands.
But it did not pursue the same end.   At the outset this was immaterial, since the pursuit of its own end exactly accomplished the
primary end.   But this state of things could not always last, and
wayward tendencies set in very early.   Then commenced that remarkable process, *the elimination of the wayward*, which Darwin called
natural selection, and which Spencer, reversing the natural order of
the terms, characterized as the *survival of the fittest*.

To check the growing tendency to deviate from the path of function and thus jeopardize the life of the globe two devices were
adopted, the one for the animal world in general, the other for man
alone.   The first of these was *instinct*.   Nothing has baffled philosophers more than the attempt to explain instinct, and the number
of definitions of instinct is large.   Many of these definitions are
approaches to the truth, and all are agreed that instincts were essential to any high development of animal life.   I need only point out
here that instinct is a means of securing a greater adaptation of
feeling to function, or still better expressed, a means of preventing
too great inadaptation between feeling and function.   What was
needed was a motive to induce animals to perform the functions
necessary to the life of the species.   As no sentient being can perform any spontaneous act whatever without an interest in such act,
without an incentive inhering in its nature sufficient to impel its
performance, it was absolutely essential that acts conducive to self
and race preservation should become attractive, agreeable, pleasur-

able. Through the prolonged operation of the law of the elimination of the wayward and the consequent selection and survival of the least wayward, there were brought about modifications of the brain and nerve structures of most animals such as to make pleasurable many acts which otherwise would have been irksome, but which were acts essential to the rearing of the young and the protection of the species from enemies and from climatal inclemencies. To the looker-on such acts are simply means to functional ends and would require an act of reason or telic process to foresee, but for which no faculty exists in the animal kingdom below man. The same result was accomplished by rendering, in the manner described, these means desirable in themselves. Instinct is the conversion of means into ends. The creature takes pleasure in the performance of the acts that constitute the means to function, and therefore it is the same, so far as the innate interest is concerned, as if it desired the functional ends themselves. Without instinct most animal species would have early succumbed and the higher types would have been impossible. This would have been mainly due to egoistic activity opposed to the performance of functions essential to the preservation and continuance of life.

The second restraint to feeling, which, as stated, was confined to the human species, has somewhat the nature of an instinct, and perhaps might be called social instinct or group instinct, but it usually goes by other names. The advent of reason, which will be fully discussed in Part III, had two effects of the class to be considered here. One was greatly to increase the degree of egoistic activity and waywardness, and the other was to check the development of animal instincts. Both of these effects tended to widen the breach between feeling and function and thus jeopardize the existence of the human race. But while the individual reason tended to destroy the race, there grew up along with it a sort of group reason which was partly instinct, calculated to counteract this tendency. It did not work on the principle of animal instinct, developing new nerve centers, or as they may be called, functional pleasure nerves, but it took the form of counteracting the pursuit of dangerous pleasures by the fear of greater pains. But as in the beginning moral suasion would have been ineffective, this social instinct went further and elaborated a system of social control provided with all the machinery of coercion necessary to hold the refractory and recalcitrant elements in check.

It established an array of sanctions and ultimately a system of regulative edicts, rules, penalties, and conditions, supported by a body of specially appointed persons to whom were intrusted their enforcement. All these were crystallized into customs and surrounded by ceremonies and rites. Although essentially a system of social control for the purpose stated, it early took the form of a religious system based mainly on supernatural sanctions. As most deviations from the path of safety were due to the exuberance of the egoistic reason acting as a guide to dangerous pleasures, this system sought to compel a blind obedience to rules and forms beyond the range of reason and chiefly based on alleged supernatural retributions, the fear of which was a powerful deterrent to the performance of forbidden acts. For want of a better name I have characterized this social instinct, or instinct of race safety, as religion,[1] but not without clearly perceiving that it constitutes the primordial undifferentiated plasm out of which have subsequently developed all the more important human institutions. This "ultra-rational sanction," as Mr. Kidd calls it, if it be not an instinct, is at least the human homologue of animal instinct, and served the same purpose after the instincts had chiefly disappeared and when the egoistic reason would have otherwise rapidly carried the race to destruction in its mad pursuit of pleasure for its own sake.

After reading the article above cited on the "Essential Nature of Religion," Mr. John M. Robertson asked me why I did not say *law* instead of religion, as he did not see why all I said would not be equally applicable to law. I was obliged to admit that this was true, and I may go farther and say that it also applies to government in general. Mr. Spencer has ably shown how all the different classes of institutions treated by him had their origin in what he calls "Ecclesiastical Institutions," which are simply the superstructures, or social structures, that were erected upon the primordial foundation that I have described. I have limited the restraints to feeling to two, instinct and religion, but a third might appropriately be added and called law or government. But as this is so clearly only a further differentiation of the second, it does not seem necessary to regard it as distinct. As regards ethics, it is also wholly embodied in the original homogeneous plasm, and constitutes another

---

[1] "The Essential Nature of Religion," *International Journal of Ethics*, Vol. **VIII**, Philadelphia, January, 1898, pp. 169–192.

ramification in the course of the unfolding of that comprehensive principle. If this were the place it might easily be shown that, just as reason, even in early man, rendered instinct unnecessary, so further intellectual development and wider knowledge and wisdom will ultimately dispense with both religion and ethics as restraints to unsafe conduct, and we may conceive of the final disappearance of all restrictive laws and of government as a controlling agency. But that the world is still far from this ideal state may be realized by reflecting that all that we call vice and crime, and in general all attacks upon the social order, constitute, when we seize their true philosophic import, neither more nor less than so many deviations from the path of function in the interest of feeling.

The considerations set forth in this chapter are sufficient to establish the biologic origin of the subjective faculty. This faculty constitutes the most anomalous of all the differential attributes that have resulted from the creative synthesis of nature, and by it the car of cosmic progress has been shunted off on an entirely new track. Whither does the new route lead? We shall endeavor to answer this question. All that we can note at present is that the new motor is a powerful one, and as we have seen, it is necessary to apply the brakes. But they have been successfully applied, and the train, now for the first time laden with human freight, is safely speeding on.

CHAPTER VIII

THE CONATIVE FACULTY

NATURE is not only a becoming, it is a striving. The universal energy never ceases to act and its ceaseless activity constantly creates. The quantity of matter, mass, and motion in the universe is unchangeable, everything else changes — position, direction, velocity, path, combination, form. To say with Schopenhauer that matter is causality involves an ellipsis. It is not matter but *collision* that constitutes the only *cause*. This eternal pelting of atoms, this driving of the elements, this pressure at every point, this struggle of all created things, this universal nisus of nature, pushing into existence all material forms and storing itself up in them as properties, as life, as feeling, as thought, this is the hylozoism of the philosophers, the self-activity of Hegel, the will of Schopenhauer, the atom-soul of Haeckel; it is the soul of the universe, the spirit of nature, the "First Cause" of both religion and science — it is God.

In the last chapter we traced the history of this creative power to where it took the form of psychic energy, which is only a modality of the universal energy. We found that it constituted the basis of the subjective or affective faculties of mind, and that these were of biologic origin and were created as a condition to the existence of all the higher forms of life. We also saw that this remarkable property, feeling, at first so completely at the service of function, soon became the end of the creature and tended to depart from its normal course, threatening in manifold ways to defeat the very purpose for which it was created, rendering necessary the further creation of powerful checks to this tendency. So long as the functional ends of life were not put in jeopardy these new activities were harmless, and, indeed, since they represented a great increase of life power, they were useful in accelerating the consummation of nature's ends. Feeling added to bathmism or growth force, psychism or mind force, and greatly increased the quantity of force that had been withdrawn from the physical world and converted into organic energy. The conative form of causation now at work was far more potent than the purely mechanical form that had hitherto prevailed.

In defining the dynamic agent in the sixth chapter it was found necessary to enter somewhat fully into the psychological nature of this force and deal with the philosophy of desire. That ground need not be gone over again, but it can now be better seen how desire came to constitute the real psychic force. While feeling, or intensive sensation — pleasure and pain — must be made primary, still the step from this stage to that of desire is very short. Desire presupposes memory, which must therefore be one of the earliest aspects of mind. In fact memory is nothing but the persistent representation of feeling, continued sense vibrations after the stimulus is withdrawn, and involves no mystery. Just as a bell will continue for a time to ring after the clapper ceases to beat upon it, so the nerve fibers, or protoplasmic gelatine, continues to vibrate for a time after the object, agreeable or the reverse, is no longer in contact with it. In case of an agreeable sensation, as the pleasure fades on the withdrawal of the stimulus, a desire arises to renew or continue the more intense presentative pleasure, and this is all that constitutes desire. But though simple in its explanation, it is powerful and far-reaching in its effects. But for this interruption in the agreeable states with faint intermediate mnemonic vibrations there would be no activity directed to the renewal or repetition of those intenser states. The withdrawal of the stimulus is in the nature of a deprivation or want, and this is the true character of all desire.

As the activities thus produced normally led to function and secured the preservation, perpetuation, and increase of life, it was to the interest of these ends that this conative power be increased to the utmost, and consequently we find that in the higher organisms special centers exist in connection with the leading functions for the accumulation of this energy, and the performance of such functions is attended with intense satisfaction, while inability to perform them creates an almost irresistible desire. This is of course best exemplified in the two great primordial functions, nutrition and reproduction, with the corresponding physical imperatives, hunger and love, which are typical desires. But in the higher mammals, and especially in man, many other centers have been developed — storage batteries of psychic energy — which, though in the main more or less connected with the primary ones, are practically distinct. They consist of nerve-plexuses, which are mostly situated within the great sympathetic system and deeply buried within the body, having no connection with the pain and pleasure nerves of the periphery. These latter belong to the cerebro-spinal system which is the seat of most monitory desires and also of many mandatory ones. The great sympathetic contains a vast number of ganglia located in all parts of the body, the functions of many of which are little understood. But it is maintained by many that these plexuses, or at least some of the larger ones, such as the deep cardiac, the semilunar, etc., are the seat of the principal emotions of the human soul. Such sentiments as joy and gladness, enthusiasm, love of the helpless, etc., probably belong here. But painful as well as pleasurable emotions arise, and these are chiefly in the nature of desires. They all represent the deprivation of something once enjoyed. If there is the least chance of regaining the lost object there is scarcely any limit to the amount of exertion that will be put forth for the attainment of that end. This renders them the most powerful forces in society, and next to the efforts put forth for the supply of the primary wants above mentioned, the emotions constitute the chief social stimuli or social forces.

Descartes was the first to treat the emotions from a scientific or even a philosophical standpoint.[1] He really dealt with the subject physiologically, and if there had been more knowledge in the world at the time he wrote his work would have been valuable. But he knew practically nothing of the nervous system, its place being taken by the "animal spirits" then recognized as flowing through the body, and which he described as *un certain air ou vent très subtil*" (Art. 7). But he correctly distinguished the "external senses" from the "internal appetites" (Art. 13). He seems completely to confound the subjective and objective faculties; cognition, perception, thought, and ideas are mixed up with volition, sentiment, emotion, and passion. But this is so commonly done even to-day that we should not too severely judge it in Descartes. The most curious part of his treatment of this subject is his favorite hypothesis "that there is a little gland in the brain in which the soul performs its functions more particularly than in other parts"

[1] " Les Passions de l'Âme."

(Art. 31). He here describes what is now known as the pineal gland, and gives as his reason for regarding it as the special seat of the soul "that the other parts of our brain are all double, as also we have two eyes, two hands, two ears, and finally all the organs of our external senses are double; and that as we have but one sole and simple thought of one same thing at one time, it is necessary that there be some place where the two images that come through the two eyes, or two other impressions that come from one single object through the double organs of the other senses, can combine into one before they arrive at the soul in order that they shall not represent two objects instead of one " (Art. 32).

He proceeds to enumerate, describe, and classify a large number of passions and emotions, and clings constantly to the physiological method of explanation, but modern physiologists would not probably admit that this added to the value of the treatment. For example, understanding pretty well the nature of the circulation of the blood as it had already been explained by Harvey, and believing in animal spirits, he taught that those emotions which caused tears to flow were the ones that generated certain vapors which were carried by the circulation to the eyes and condensed when they reached the surface. *Hinc illæ lacrymæ!* In general it may be said that Descartes' treatment of the passions is disappointing, as have also been to me his metaphysical speculations. But he did admit in a number of passages that the passions are not essentially bad and that they are often useful, and says (Art. 175) that he cannot persuade himself "that nature had given to men any passion that is always vicious and has no good and praiseworthy purpose "; and he concludes (Art. 212) "that it is upon the passions that depend all the good and all the evil of this life."

Spinoza also treated the emotions in a characteristically philosophical way, and it is his special merit to have called the subject ethics. Ethics, as I have shown in the preceding chapter and elsewhere,[1] is based entirely upon feeling, and without the phenomena of pleasure and pain there can be no moral quality. But Spinoza's analyses of the various passions were much more acute than Descartes', and he still more clearly recognized their utility, their importance, and their essential innocence when legitimately exer-

---

[1] *International Journal of Ethics*, Vol. VI, Philadelphia, July, 1896, pp. 441–456. Cf. especially, pp. 443–444.

cised.   His saying (Prop. XLI) that "joy is not essentially bad, but good, while grief is essentially bad," reflects both the asceticism of his time and his own philosophical penetration.

Hume also treated the passions as an essential part of "human nature," making much of sympathy, as was done by Ferguson and Adam Smith, and later by Bentham, each from his own special point of view.   But it was reserved for Schopenhauer to show that the cravings of existence constitute the mainspring of action and the real power of the world.   Comte's spiritual philosophy as set forth in his " Positive Polity " is based on the affective faculties and has altruism for its end.   Other names might be mentioned of those who have contributed to give to the cold, objective, intellectual philosophy that had chiefly prevailed a subjective trend,[1] and to direct attention to the far older and certainly not less important subjective and conative faculties in which alone the psychic and social energy resides.

The Soul

What is the soul?   I do not mean an imaginary thing.   I mean a real thing.   Descartes, as we have seen, used the French word *âme* almost in the sense of the whole mind, the faculties of which he confounded, but he chiefly dealt with those animal spirits that, as it were, *animate* the body.   They produce the passions and the emotions.   Indeed, he makes these two synonymous, and in one place (Art. 28) expresses a preference for the term *emotions*, because, as he says, "not only can this term be applied to all the changes that take place in it [the soul], that is, to all the various impressions (*pensées*) that come to it, but especially because, of all the affections (*pensées*) that it can have there are no others that so strongly agitate and move (*ébranlent*) it as do these passions."   It is therefore evident that he recognized in the passions a moving force, but his *soul* was something more comprehensive.   Our own English word soul is so far given over to religious usage, under the influence of the doctrine of immortality, that it is difficult to separate it from that world view and look upon it as a real scientific fact.   The German word *Seele* seems not to be so trammeled, and expresses the phenomenon of *animation* or conscious spontaneous activity.   This

---

[1] I treated this subject somewhat fully in a paper read before the Institut International de Sociologie in 1897.   See the *Annales*, Vol. IV, pp. 111.-132.

is the central idea in the conception of the soul, and it was possessed by the first and lowest animate beings. The moment an interest to move in a definite way for a definite purpose was planted in them the soul was born, and their continued conscious activities under the spur of that interest is that which has produced the varied forms of animal life.

The soul then is that new-born property that has been engaging our attention through the last two chapters. We have been studying its cosmic and geological development. It was not present when the planets were formed. It does not dwell in rocks. The signs of it in the vegetable kingdom (protoplasmic movements in the utricle, sensitive plants, the behavior of the "tentacles" of Drosera, the closing of the fly-traps of Dionæa, circumnutation, etc.) are few, obscure, and of an ambiguous character, either referable to physical reactions, or else belonging to forms that closely approach the nature of animals, such as the insectivorous plants. Plants *live* but do not *feel.* We are carried back to the famous definition of Linnæus: *Lapides crescunt; vegetabilia crescunt et vivunt; animalia crescunt, vivunt, et sentiunt.* I scarcely need point out the agreement that exists between this and my table of evolutionary products and differential attributes (*supra*, p. 94). The last of the Linnæan attributes, feeling, ushered in the soul.

The soul is well described in Genesis as "the Spirit of God" that "moved upon the face of the waters," for, as we have seen, the sea must have been the cradle of life in which consciousness first dawned. From the standpoint of hylozoism this spirit may be said to "sleep in the stone, dream in the animal, and awake in man," for its elements lay dormant in the inorganic world, and it was only in man, and in a higher type of man, that self-consciousness arose, viz., a consciousness of consciousness. But as more and more inorganic matter was converted into living forms larger and larger quantities of physical and vital energy were converted into psychic energy, and the soul grew and acquired greater power. It became a transforming agency and a potent influence in the transmutation of species and the development of higher and more multiform types of life. It was the chief cause of variation and hence the prime factor in organic evolution. On the human plane the soul has become enriched by the introduction of all the derivative affections, the passions and emotions of which we have spoken, until it has carried its transforming influence beyond the individual organism into the social organism and into the environment, and has become the agent of social evolution.

THE WILL

When we consider all this volume of feeling as essentially a striving we find in it all the elements of the will. It is the conative faculty, and in this lies its immense importance to sociology. Feeling, as we have seen, starts with interest and immediately becomes desire. Using desire in its widest possible acceptation, there is a sense in which it may be identified with will. It is the wish, the vow, the prayer, the yearning of the soul. To clothe this with all the attributes of will we have only to observe it passing into action. Will is the active expression of the soul's meaning. It is inchoate action. If it does not pass into action it at least passes into effort, and it is effort rather than action in which the dynamic quality inheres. The will is that which asserts itself. The interests of life must be subserved, the desires must be satisfied, remembered past pleasures must be renewed, pains experienced or feared must be escaped, life must be preserved and continued, hopes, aspirations, ambitions, goals must be realized. It is will that accomplishes all this. Without it all is lost. This is the meaning of optimism as a principle of nature rather than a world view or tenet of philosophy. There is no balancing of the gains and losses of existence. There is no faltering or hesitation. Existence must be preserved and nature has pointed the way. The will gives the command and the body obeys. The effort is put forth and the result is limited only by the amount of physical power and the amount of resistance encountered. Optimism is the normal attitude of all sentient beings. No other attitude is possible in the animal world or in any type of mankind that has not reached a high degree of intellectual development. Only such a developed intellect when deprived of an adequate knowledge of nature is capable of inventing a quietistic philosophy. The doctrine of the denial of the will, if it could be rigidly enforced, would quickly terminate the course of any race that should practice it. Only the partial failure to enforce such teachings, or their practical reversal and conversion into optimistic teachings among the uninstructed, can have saved the Orient from destruction, and the ease with which European nations can seize, hold, and govern

India, Cochin China, and parts of China, attests the superior social efficiency of optimistic over pessimistic races. And there is no better lesson to teach the superiority of will over reason — of that ancient primordial cosmic power over the newly fledged parvenu intellect — than these odds furnish when the two are brought into conflict.

Natural, spontaneous, or impulsive optimism is true, and is a healthy social influence. It means self-preservation, race continuance, and social progress. But rational optimism is both false and shallow. The moment the light of reason is turned upon it it withers and decays. This is because the condition of mankind from the moral point of view, *i.e.*, from the standpoint of feeling, will not bear analysis. Reason applied to it, if at all thoroughgoing, leads at once to pessimism. It teaches that desire is want, that hunger is pang, that love is pain, that pains are acute and prolonged while pleasures are brief and moderate, that the satisfaction of desire puts an end to feeling, but that no sooner is one desire disposed of than another arises, and so on forever. This is the philosophy that pervades the vast populous regions of southern and eastern Asia, and which has for its universal refrain the injunction : crush the will. This is logical and has been echoed by the wisest seers of optimistic Europe — Goethe, Humboldt, Pascal, Dean Swift, Jeremy Taylor, Huxley [1] — who have simply looked at the world and seen things as they are.

A little reason corrupts and neutralizes the optimistic impulses and produces that false and mongrel optimism that teaches the folding of the arms and the gospel of inaction. More reason penetrates to the dark reality and ends in pessimism or the gospel of despair and nirvana. But it is possible to probe still deeper and to find again the hope that characterizes the first blind subrational or ultra-

---

[1] " Even the best of modern civilization appears to me to exhibit a condition of mankind which neither embodies any worthy ideal nor even possesses the merit of stability. I do not hesitate to express the opinion that, if there is no hope of a large improvement of the condition of the greater part of the human family ; if it is true that the increase of knowledge, the winning of a greater dominion over Nature which is its consequence, and the wealth which follows upon that dominion, are to make no difference in the extent and the intensity of Want, with its concomitant physical and moral degradation, among the masses of the people, I should hail the advent of some kindly comet, which would sweep the whole affair away, as a desirable consummation." Professor Huxley in the *Nineteenth Century*, Vol. XXVII, January–June, 1890, No. 159, May, 1890, pp. 862–863 (in article entitled : " Government: Anarchy or Regimentation," *ibid.*, pp. 843–866).

rational struggle for existence.   Rational optimism and pessimism are products of the naked reason, than which no guide is more unsafe. The true guide, the Moses that is to lead man out of the wilderness, is *science*.   The naked reason must be clothed.   Man must learn to *know*.   He must learn how and why he is subjected to all these woes, and then he may see a way of escaping them.   The only science that can teach this is social science.   This science does teach it, and it gives forth no uncertain sound.   All this belongs to applied sociology and cannot be treated here, but it may at least be remarked that the mental and social state to which social science points is neither optimism nor pessimism, but *meliorism*.   Meliorism means the liberation of the will, so that it may assert itself as freely and as vigorously as it ever did under the rule of blind impulse.   It means the massing and systematic application of all the vastly increased powers of developed man to the perfected machinery of society.   The avenues of action to be cleared and not choked up as at present.   Different social movements to be along appointed paths and not in opposite directions in the same path so as to neutralize each other.   The combined social will may thus be so adjusted as to exert its full force in one harmonious and irresistible effort toward the accomplishment of the supreme social end.

CHAPTER IX

SOCIAL MECHANICS

In the last three chapters the foundations have been laid for a science of social mechanics. The essential condition of such a science is the existence of true natural forces in society that can be depended upon to produce effects with the same certainty and exactness as do physical forces. The dynamic agent, the general character of which was set forth in Chapter VI, and the genesis and full treatment of which have been given in the last two chapters, furnishes the sociologist with all that he requires from this point of view. It is true that the complex phenomena of society necessitate the application of the limiting principle laid down in Chapter IV, that the quality of exactness is difficult to detect except in the relations that subsist among the more highly generalized groups.

MATHEMATICAL SOCIOLOGY

The application of mathematics to sociology is at best precarious, not because the laws of social phenomena are not exact, but because of the multitude and complicated interrelations of the facts. Except for certain minds that are mathematically constituted there is very little advantage in mathematical treatment. It instantly repels the non-mathematical, and however much we may deplore it, the proportion of mathematical minds is very small. Usually a rigidly logical treatment of a subject is quite sufficient even where mathematics might have been used, and when the latter adds nothing to the conception its use is simply pedantic. A number of eminent mathematicians, among whom the names of Cournot, Gossen, Jevons, and Walras are the most frequently heard, have undoubtedly done much to found pure economics on a mathematical basis. At the present time, while there are many mathematical economists, there seems to be but one mathematical sociologist, viz., Dr. Léon Winiarsky of the University of Geneva. In quite a formidable series of papers he has endeavored to lay the foundations of the science of social mechanics as a mathematical science.[1] His claim to being the first to do this seems to be just, but his further claim of priority in conceiving such a science cannot be sustained.[2] The special merit of Dr. Winiarsky's treatment is that it bases the science on the desires and wants of men as the forces with which it deals, and although he scarcely goes beyond the primary impulses of hunger and love, still these are correctly conceived as true natural forces susceptible of the most exact formulation. Moreover, his papers are not overburdened with equations and formulas, and are decidedly readable discussions, abounding in acute observations. They also contain reasonable admissions of the limitations to mathematical treatment.

Comte, although himself a professional mathematician, never tired of condemning the attempt to reduce the complex sciences to the mathematical form. We find in one of his early papers, published in 1822, this remark : —

> The proposition to treat social science as an application of mathematics in order to render it positive had its origin in the metaphysical prejudice that outside of mathematics no real certainty can exist. This prejudice was natural at a time when everything that was positive belonged to the domain of applied mathematics, and when, in consequence, all that this did not embrace was vague and conjectural. But since the formation of the two great positive sciences, chemistry and especially physiology, in which mathematical analysis plays no rôle, and which are recognized as not less certain than the others, such a prejudice would be absolutely inexcusable.[3]

Early in his " Positive Philosophy," and in the volume devoted to mathematics, he further says : —

> Nevertheless we should not cease, as a general philosophical thesis, to conceive phenomena of all orders as necessarily subject in themselves to mathematical laws, which we are simply condemned always to ignore in most cases on account of the too great complication of the phenomena.[4]

[1] *Revue Philosophique*, Vol. XLV, April, 1898, pp. 351–386 ; Vol. XLIX, February, 1900, pp. 113–134; March, 1900, pp. 256–287 ; *Rivista Italiana di Sociologia*, Anno III, Fasc. v, Rome, September, 1899 ; *Premier Congrès de l'Enseignement des Sciences Sociales*, Compte rendu, Paris, 1901, pp. 341–345; *Annales de l'Institut International de Sociologie*, Vol. VII, Paris, 1901, pp. 229–233.

[2] I may have been the first to use the expression "social mechanics." See "Dynamic Sociology," New York, 1883, Vol. I, p. 503 ; cf. *Am. Journ. of Sociology*, Vol. II, September, 1896, pp. 234–254, and " Outlines of Sociology," New York, 1898, Chapter VIII.

[3] " Politique Positive," Vol. IV, Appendix, p. 123.

[4] " Philosophie Positive," Vol. I, p. 117.

In his treatment of chemistry and biology in Vol. III, he encounters the prejudice of which he speaks and characterizes it very severely. The following will serve as a sample of his views in this regard: —

This confusion, difficult to avoid, between acquired instruction and native ability is still more common in the case of mathematical studies on account of the more special and prolonged application which they require and the characteristic hieroglyphic language which they must employ, the imposing aspect of which is so well calculated to mask, to the eyes of the vulgar, a profound intellectual mediocrity.[1]

It was Goethe who said: —

I accept mathematics as the most sublime and useful science so long as it is applied in its proper place; but I cannot commend its misuse in matters which do not belong to its sphere, and in which, noble science as it is, it seems to be mere nonsense; as if, forsooth, things only exist when they can be mathematically demonstrated! It would be foolish in a man not to believe in his sweetheart's love because she could not prove it to him mathematically. She can mathematically prove her dower, but not her love.

And a more modern writer has well said : " No forms of error are so erroneous as those that have the appearance without the reality of mathematical precision." [2]

SOCIAL PHYSICS

I have preferred the name *social mechanics* for this science to that of *social physics*, which Comte first gave to the whole science of sociology, because it is the social forces with which we have to do rather than material bodies with which physics seems more naturally associated, but it is well for us to inquire what Comte meant by social physics. It was in the same early paper from which we have quoted, first published in May, 1822, that he first used this expression. Continuing his remark relative to the use of mathematics, he says: —

It is not as applications of mathematical analysis that astronomy, optics, etc., are positive and exact sciences. This character comes from themselves. It results from the fact that they are founded on observed facts, and it could only result from this, because mathematical analysis separated from the observation of nature, has only a metaphysical character. Only it is certain

---

[1] *Op. cit.*, Vol. III, p. 307.

[2] Dr. George M. Beard in the *Popular Science Monthly*, Vol. XIV, April, 1879, p. 751.

that in the sciences to which mathematics are not applicable close direct observation is the less to be lost sight of; deductions cannot with certainty be carried so far, because the data for reasoning are less perfect. With this exception the certainty is just as complete if kept within proper limits. . . . Such is the final judgment which I believe it is possible to form from attempts made or to be made to apply mathematical analysis to social physics.

After discussing Cabanis's "Rapport du physique et du moral de l'homme," he continues: —

Since the superiority of man over the other animals cannot have, and, in fact, has no other cause than the relative perfection of his organization, all that the human species does, and all that it can do, must evidently be regarded, in the last analysis, as a necessary consequence of his organization, modified in its effects by the environment (*état de l'extérieur*). In this sense, social physics, that is, the study of the collective development of the human species, is really a branch of physiology, that is to say, of the study of man in the broadest sense of the word. In other terms, the history of civilization is nothing else than the succession and necessary completion of the natural history of man.[1]

A little farther on in the same essay, while laying the foundations of the positive philosophy in his well-known classification of the sciences, but before it had taken its final form, he says: —

The four great classes of observations previously established do not comprise, at least explicitly, all the points of view from which existing beings may be considered. There is evidently lacking the social point of view for the beings that are susceptible of it, and especially for man; but we see with the same clearness that this is the only omission (*lacune*). Thus, we possess now a celestial physics, a terrestrial physics, either mechanical or chemical, a vegetal physics, and an animal physics; we still want one more and last one, social physics, in order that the system of our knowledge of nature be complete.[2]

Still more definite and clear is the following statement that follows on the same page with which the passage last quoted closed: —

I understand by *social physics* the science that has for its proper object the study of social phenomena, considered in the same spirit as astronomical, physical, chemical, and physiological phenomena, *i.e.*, as subject to natural invariable laws, the discovery of which is the special object of its investigations. Thus it proposes directly to *explain*, with the greatest possible precision, the great phenomenon of the development of the human species,

[1] " Politique Positive," Vol. IV, Appendix, pp. 123–125.
[2] *Loc. cit.*, pp. 149–150.

considered in all its essential parts; that is, to discover through what fixed series of successive transformations the human race, starting from a state scarcely superior to that of the societies of large apes, gradually led to the point at which civilized Europe finds itself to-day.

At the close of the third volume of the "Positive Philosophy" he says that the next or fourth volume will be devoted to creating the new science of social physics, and early in that (fourth) volume he speaks of instituting what he had already called *social physics*. To the term thus introduced, and which is here italicized, he appends the following foot-note: —

This expression, and that not less indispensable one of *positive philosophy*, were constructed seventeen years ago [this volume appeared in 1839], in my early essays on political philosophy. Although so recent, these two essential terms have already been in some sort spoiled by vicious attempts to appropriate them on the part of various writers who had not at all comprehended their true purpose, although I had, by a scrupulously invariable practice, carefully characterized their fundamental acceptation. I ought specially to point out this abuse, in the case of the first of these terms, by a Belgian savant, who has adopted it in these late years as the title of a book which treats of nothing but simple statistics.[1]

The reference is of course to Quetelet's work entitled: "Sur l'homme et le développement de ses facultés, ou essai de physique sociale," in two volumes, which appeared in 1835. Quetelet also laid stress on the uniformity and regularity of social phenomena, but, as Comte says, from the standpoint of statistics. But there is no more reliable method of proving this than the use of statistics, and no one has done more along this fruitful line than Quetelet. Still it must be admitted that Comte's conception of social physics was vastly broader than this, and as the above passages, and others that might be cited, show, was coextensive with sociology. Indeed, since it was he who gave us the word *sociology* and made it synonymous with social physics as he had defined that term, we must at least agree that his social physics is the same as his sociology. This word, as all sociologists know, was first used by him in the volume from which the passages last quoted occur, but considerably farther along, viz., in the forty-seventh lecture on p. 185. As in the case of *social physics*, he appended a foot-note to the italicized word, and in this he says : —

[1] *"Philosophie Positive,"* Vol. IV, p. 15.

I think I should venture, from now on, to use this new term, exactly equivalent to my expression, already introduced, of *social physics*, in order to designate by a single word that complementary part of natural philosophy which relates to the positive study of the sum total of the fundamental laws governing social phenomena.

We see then that social physics in the Comtian sense is the sociology that he founded, and although, notwithstanding his pains to make it clear, it possesses a certain vagueness due to its comprehensive character, still this combined quality of breadth and vagueness lend to it sufficient elasticity to adapt it to all the unforeseen elements of expansion that have arisen or are likely to arise, and thus make the word sociology an altogether satisfactory name for the whole science. In view of this the term *social physics* has by common consent been dropped out of view. If revived it should be with its original scope, and this, of course, is not what I mean by social mechanics. That is not sociology as a whole, but is a subscience of the science of sociology. It is that branch of sociology which deals with the action of the social forces. It relates to the dynamic agent only, not to the directive agent, and belongs moreover exclusively to pure sociology.

PSYCHICS

As the social forces are psychic social mechanics has to do with psychic forces, and just as the science which treats of the physical forces, of whose positivity mechanics is the mathematical test, is called *physics*, so the science which treats of the psychic forces, of whose exactness social mechanics is the criterion, must be *psychic physics*, which may for the sake of brevity be called *psychics*. Psychics, therefore, is the science or subscience that deals with the exact and invariable laws of mind. The word has found its way into the dictionaries, but is badly defined. Most of them make it a synonym of psychology, which it differs from almost as widely as physics differs from physiology. Others give it a secondary meaning as a synonym of " psychical research." It is well known that the expression " psychical research " has become equivalent to the quasi-scientific attempt to prove the existence of a soul independent of the body, and is simply a prop to spiritualism and occultism. This attempt to prostitute the term psychics may prove fatal to it, as it did to that other etymologically excellent word *phrenology*. There have, however, been some attempts to rescue psychics from this fate. In 1881 Mr. F. Y. Edgeworth published a work entitled : "Mathematical Psychics, an Essay on the Application of Mathematics to the Moral Sciences," London, 1881. He explains the subject of the work to be " the applicability and the application of mathematics to sociology" (p. 1). "Where there are data," he says (p. 2), "which, though not *numerical*, are *quantitative* — for example, that a quantity is *greater* or *less* than another, *increases* or *decreases*, is *positive* or *negative*, a *maximum* or a *minimum*, there mathematical reasoning is possible and may be indispensable." There may have been other uses of the word in a scientific sense prior to the year 1893, when I introduced it [1] in the same sense as that in which I use it now, but I have not met with them. This sense is somewhat broader than that of Edgeworth, and includes data to which mathematics would not apply.

The essential basis of psychics is, of course, that psychic phenomena obey uniform laws. This has been observed and remarked by many writers, some very ancient, and, as we saw in Chapter IV, the recognition of this truth in a collective way, as in human history, is the prime condition to any science of society. But as collective action is made up of individual action, it must also be true of the latter, however contrary it may seem to daily observation. Our failure to perceive it is due to what was there called " the illusion of the near." Herbart is said to have declared that " ideas move in our minds with as much regularity as the stars move in the heavens." [2] Kant said that " if we could probe all the phenomena of volition to the bottom there would not be a single human action which we could not predict and recognize as necessary from its antecedent conditions." [3] Kant is usually regarded as a libertarian, and yet in the only contribution he made to sociology he says : —

Whatsoever difference there may be in our notions of the *freedom of the will* metaphysically considered, — it is evident that the manifestations of this will, viz. human actions, are as much under the control of universal laws of nature as any other physical phenomena. It is the province of history to narrate these manifestations; and let their causes be ever so secret, we know that history, simply by taking its station at a distance and contemplating the agency of the human will upon a large scale, aims at unfolding

---

[1] " Psychic Factors of Civilization," pp. 56, 129.
[2] Professor W. I. Thomas in the *American Journal of Sociology*, Vol. I, p. 441.
[3] " Kritik der reinen Vernunft," ed. Hartenstein, 1868, p. 380.

to our view a regular stream of tendency in the great succession of events;
so that the very course of incidents, which taken separately and individually
would have seemed perplexed, incoherent, and lawless, yet viewed in their
connexion and as the actions of the human *species* and not of independent
beings, never fail to discover a steady and continuous though slow development of certain great predispositions in our nature. Thus for instance
deaths, births, and marriages, considering how much they are separately
dependent on the freedom of the human will, should seem to be subject to
no law according to which any calculation could be made beforehand of
their amount : and yet the yearly registers of these events in great countries
prove that they go on with as much conformity to the laws of nature as the
oscillations of the weather.[1]

Mr. John Watson of Queen's University, a close student of Kant,
and himself a thorough-going libertarian, sums up that part of his
doctrine as follows : —

Take any action you please, and you will find, according to Kant, that its
place in the chain of events is as unalterably determined as the fall of a
stone, or the motion of a projectile through space. Let the action be, say,
the relieving of distress. Setting aside the physical movements which precede the consciousness that a certain person stands in need of relief, and the
physical movements by which the action is carried into effect, there remains
for consideration simply a series of mental events, which will be found to
be connected together in a fixed order of dependence. Following upon the
perception of the object, there arises in the consciousness of the agent a
desire to relieve distress. This desire would not arise at all, did not the
agent possess a peculiar form of susceptibility ; viz., that of pity at the sight
of human suffering. Now, this susceptibility is a part of his sensuous nature,
which he can neither make nor unmake. Not every one is so affected, or
affected in the same degree. Clearly, therefore, the desire to relieve distress
is an event, occurring at a certain moment, and following upon the idea of
another's pain as certainly as any other event that can be named. If the desire is so strong that the agent determines to relieve the other's distress, we
have a further sequence of a certain volition upon a certain desire ; and this,
like all other sequences, is subject to the law of causality. The most rigid
determinist has evidently no reason so far to complain of any want of " vigor
and rigor " in Kant's doctrine.[2]

Archbishop Whately states practically the same case in the
following form : —

Every one is accustomed to anticipate future events, in human affairs, as
well as in the material world, *in proportion* to his *knowledge of the several cir-*

---

[1] " Idea of a Universal History on a Cosmo-political Plan," by Immanuel Kant.
Translated by Thomas De Quincey. *London Magazine*, Vol. X, October, 1824, p. 385.
[2] *Philosophical Review*, Vol. I, January, 1892, p. 11.

cumstances connected with each; however different in amount that knowledge may be, in reference to different occurrences. And in both cases alike, we always attribute the *failure* of any anticipation to our *ignorance* or mistake respecting some of the circumstances. When, *e.g.*, we fully expect, from our supposed knowledge of some person's character, and of the circumstances he is placed in, that he will do something which, eventually, he does not do, we at once and without hesitation conclude that we were *mistaken* either as to his character, or as to his situation, or as to our acquaintance with human nature, generally; and we are accustomed to adduce any such failure as a *proof* of such mistake; saying, " It is plain you *were mistaken in your estimate* of that man's character; *for* he has done so and so: " and this, as unhesitatingly as we should attribute the non-occurrence of an eclipse we had predicted, not to any change in the Laws of Nature, but to some error in our calculations.[1]

This is virtually Kant's position, and is a clear analysis of the meaning of his phrase " intelligible character." John Stuart Mill reëchoed it when he said: " Given the motives which are present to an individual's mind, and given likewise the character and disposition of the individual, the manner in which he will act might unerringly be inferred." [2] But much earlier still than Kant, Hartley had made the following statement: —

By the mechanism of human actions I mean, that each action results from the previous circumstances of body and mind, in the same manner, and with the same certainty, as other effects do from their mechanical causes; so that a person cannot do indifferently either of the actions A, and its contrary *a*, while the previous circumstances are the same; but is under an absolute necessity of doing one of them, and that only. Agreeably to this I suppose, that by free-will is meant a power of doing either the action A, or its contrary *a*; while the previous circumstances remain the same.[3]

Hume, with most of whose writings Kant was acquainted, frequently expressed this same idea in such terms as this: " There is a general course of nature in human actions as well as in the operations of the sun and the climate." [4]

It may be objected that these sayings of philosophers are of no value as lacking proof, and as simply indicating the tendency of the

1 " Elements of Logic," by Richard Whately, reprinted from the 9th (octavo) edition, Louisville, 1854, pp. 236-237.

2 " A System of Logic," by John Stuart Mill, People's edition, London, 1884, p. 547 (Book VI, Chapter II, § 2).

3 " Observations on Man, his Frame, his Duty, and his Expectations," by David Hartley, 5th edition, London, 1810, Vol. I, p. 515.

4 " A Treatise of Human Nature," etc., by David Hume, edited by T. H. Green and T. H. Grose, Vol. II, London, 1898, p. 184.

mind, when untrammeled by facts, to construct a logical scheme. Let us therefore turn to quite the opposite type of mind, viz., that of the practical jurist whose opinions are always derived from the experiences of men in their regular daily operations. Starkie says: —

> Experience and observation show that the conduct of mankind is governed by general laws, which operate, under similar circumstances, with almost as much regularity and uniformity as the mechanical laws of nature themselves. . . . In general, all the affairs and transactions of mankind are as much connected together in one uniform and consistent whole, without chasm or interruption, and with as much mutual dependence on each other, as the phenomena of nature are; they are governed by general laws; all the links stand in the mutual relations of cause and effect. . . .[1]

The use by such writers of such qualifying words as "almost" is not to be construed as indicating that they think there are real exceptions to these natural laws of the mind. It means about the same as it would to say that bodies *almost* always fall to the ground. Because balloons do not fall to the ground does not invalidate the law of gravitation. The mechanical principles of psychic action, instead of losing ground through scientific investigation, are being constantly strengthened, and motives are coming more and more to be recognized as true forces. The reason why so many volitions do not cause action is being explained by various physiological forms of inertia and especially by the great number of simultaneous and conflicting volitions growing out of the more and more complex character of the developing mind. Mr. Spencer states this very well in the following passage: —

> For though when the confusion of a complex impression with some allied one causes a confusion among the nascent motor excitations, there is entailed a certain hesitation; and though this hesitation continues as long as these nascent motor excitations, or ideas of the correlative actions, go on superseding one another; yet, ultimately, some one set of motor excitations will prevail over the rest. As the groups of antagonistic tendencies aroused will scarcely ever be exactly balanced, the strongest group will at length pass into action.[2]

Again he says: —

> The diffused discharge accompanying feeling of every kind produces on the body an effect that is indicative of feeling simply, irrespective of kind

---

[1] "A Practical Treatise on the Law of Evidence," by Thomas Starkie, 9th American from 4th London edition, Philadelphia, 1869, pp. 70, 78.

[2] "Principles of Psychology," New York, 1873, Vol. I, p. 455 (§ 204).

— the effect, namely, of muscular excitement. From the shrinking caused in a sleeping person by a touch, up to the contortions of agony and the caperings of delight, there is a recognized relation between the quantity of feeling, pleasurable or painful, and the amount of motion generated.[1]

Of course this is all much more clearly seen in animals than in man, because the rational faculty, while it does not in the slightest affect the principle, introduces so many incalculable causes of perturbation that the rigidity of the psychic laws cannot always be seen. If this class of obscuring influences can be nearly or quite removed, as it is in the lower animals, the law comes out in great clearness. Action becomes mainly *reflex*, and its physical character can scarcely be distinguished from that of inanimate bodies. As illustrating this Professor Ernst Mach says: —

The ivory snail (*Eburna spirata*) never learns to avoid the carnivorous Actinia, no matter how often it may wince under the latter's shower of needles, having apparently no memory whatever for pain. A spider can be lured forth repeatedly from its hole by touching its web with a tuning-fork. The moth plunges again and again into the flame which has burnt it. The humming-bird hawk-moth dashes repeatedly against the painted roses of the wall-paper, like the unhappy and desperate thinker who never wearies of attacking in the same way the same insoluble chimerical problem. As aimlessly almost as Maxwell's gaseous molecules and in the same unreasoning manner, common flies in their search for light and air stream against the glass pane of a half-opened window and remain there from sheer inability to find their way around the narrow frame. But a pike separated from the minnows of his aquarium by a glass partition, learns after the lapse of a few months, though only after having butted himself half to death, that he cannot attack these fishes with impunity.[2]

Professor James well says that "every instinct is an impulse," and remarks: —

The actions we call instinctive all conform to the general reflex type; they are all called forth by determinate sensory stimuli in contact with the animal's body, or at a distance in his environment. The cat runs after the mouse, runs or shows fight before the dog, avoids falling from walls and trees, shuns fire and water, etc., not because he has any notion either of life or death, or of self, or of preservation. He has probably attained to no one of these conceptions in such a way as to react definitely upon it. He acts in each case separately, and simply because he cannot help it; being so framed that when that particular running thing called a mouse appears in

[1] "Principles of Psychology," Vol. II, p. 541 (§ 496).
[2] *The Monist*, Chicago, Vol. VI, January, 1896, pp. 166–167.

his field of vision he *must* pursue; that when that particular barking and obstreperous thing called a dog appears there he *must* retire, if at a distance, and scratch if close by; that he *must* withdraw his feet from water and his face from flame, etc. His nervous system is to a great extent a preorganized bundle of such reactions — they are as fatal as sneezing, and as exactly cor · related to their special excitants as it is to its own.[1]

Farther on the same author says that " consciousness is *in its very nature impulsive*" (p. 526), and that "*movement is the natural immediate effect of feeling, irrespective of what the quality of the feeling may be. It is so in reflex action, it is so in emotional expression, it is so in the voluntary life*" (p. 527), all of which accords perfectly with the principle under consideration, and is what makes a science of psychics possible.

Professor C. Lloyd Morgan, who of course makes his bow to the traditional world view as to the generic distinctness of matter and mind, has nevertheless introduced a term that may tend somewhat to soften the fall of that conception. He says : —

It is generally admitted that physical phenomena, including those which we call physiological, can be explained (or are explicable) in terms of energy. It is also generally admitted that consciousness is nevertheless in some way closely, if not indissolubly, associated with special manifestations of energy in the nerve-centers of the brain. Now, we call manifestations of energy " kinetic " manifestations, and we use the term "kinesis" for physical manifestations of this order. Similarly, we may call concomitant manifestations of the mental or conscious order "metakinetic," and may use the term " metakinesis " for all manifestations belonging to this phenomenal order. According to the monistic hypothesis, *every mode of kinesis has its concomitant mode of metakinesis, and when the kinetic manifestations assume the form of the molecular processes in the human brain, the metakinetic manifestations assume the form of human consciousness.* . . . All matter is not conscious, because consciousness is the metakinetic concomitant of a highly specialized order of kinesis. But every kinesis has an associated metakinesis; and *parallel to the evolution of organic and neural kinesis there has been an evolution of metakinetic manifestations culminating in conscious thought.* [2]

Morgan's metakinetic energy is therefore the same as my conative energy or form of causation, and the difference between kinesis and metakinesis is the difference between motion produced by physical or ordinary efficient causes and motion produced by psychic or conative causes. The latter are at bottom efficient causes also. All ani-

---

[1] " Principles of Psychology," New York, 1890, Vol. II, p. 384.
[2] " Animal Life and Intelligence," by C. Lloyd Morgan, London, 1890–1891, p. 467.

mals act from these definite forms of causation, call them instincts, impulses, motives, or by any other name. The domestication of animals has only been possible from the knowledge that man has acquired of these uniform and reliable springs of animal action. Cattle, sheep, horses, hogs, etc., can all be depended upon to come where they expect to receive food or whatever satisfies their crav-ings. The owner's call, which they learn to know, brings them in haste and in droves to the crib. They have no sense of pride in thus acting from egoistic motives, but come always. Man knows this, and this knowledge makes him ashamed to act like animals. This sense of shame is the chief additional motive that modifies his action. He has the egoistic motives even more strongly developed than the animal, but he seeks to conceal them, and pretends not to be governed by them. Instead of proceeding directly to the desired object and appropriating it, as animals do, he makes a feint, waits awhile till attention is turned away from him, or starts in a differ-ent direction and follows some circuitous route that ultimately brings him to it. He feigns deliberation and nonchalance, and pretends to care least for that which he most desires. Children early thus become conscious, and, as we say, sophisticated, and begin that life of indi-rection and deception that they are to lead. Here the law of gen-eralization, laid down in Chapter IV, comes in to help us explain the apparent anomalies in human action which the close-range view can only see, and which give rise to the belief that the actions of men are not governed by the same fixed laws as those of animals. For we have only to extend our sphere of observation to an entire community, to a whole people, or to the events of human history, to see that in spite of this pretense of higher motives, or of indepen-dence of motive, the human race really acts in the same way as the animal, pursues the objects of its desires, and secures and appropri-ates them with the same disregard of others as do the more humble creatures. Time, distance, and numbers brush away the thin gauze that obscures the actions of those with whom we are in close con-tact, and lay bare the great psychic law that actuates all sentient creatures alike.

It must not be supposed that even among animals there are not complications that often obscure this law. These are all the result, the same as in man, of conflicting motives. A colt that is " hard to catch " may usually be caught by showing it a lump of salt. It then will stand around and look wistfully at the salt, perhaps approach some distance, and as the person trying to catch it advances, will first for a while evade him and dodge about, but when it finds it cannot have the salt without coming up and taking it from the hand it will usually do this eventually and allow the halter to be put on. But whatever it may do will depend rigidly upon the relative strength of the motives. If it prefers liberty to salt it will decline to come, and *vice versa*. The horse is a very good animal to study from this point of view, for notwithstanding its reputation for intelligence, and the number of fine anecdotes supposed to establish this, having had to do with horses all my life, I have come to about the same conclusion as David Harum, that "hosses don't know but dreadful little, really. Talk about hoss sense — wa'al the' ain't no such thing." [1]

At any rate a horse's motives always seem to stand out more clearly than those of other animals, and they can always be easily read. The wants of horses are few and simple: food, water, home (the stable or place where kept, to which they are strongly wonted), and company, *i.e.*, other horses, for no animal has the "consciousness of kind" more firmly rooted in its nature. Knowing these motives it is easy to predict what a horse will do under given circumstances. It is also easy to understand why horses act thus and so. Conflicting motives in horses are also clearly displayed. In driving or riding a horse away from any of its centers of attraction it will be perfectly apparent that it wants to go in the opposite direction. Its gait and rate will be strongly affected by the fact. It can be compared to rowing a boat against a current. With the same urging the horse will travel much slower away from home than towards home, and the percentage of difference is easily calculated with exactness for the same animal, but will differ with different animals. For the return trip no urging at all is usually required, and it may be necessary to restrain the horse. When the direction is away from the place of wont, if the reins are slackened the speed at first diminishes and would ultimately be reduced to a stop if the road was narrow. But if the course lies across an open plain without a road it will become a case of constrained motion, and if the horse is left wholly to itself it will describe a curve and finally take

[1] "David Harum," A Story of American Life, by Edward Noyes Westcott, New York, 1899, p. 161.

the direction of the stable. If the course is at right angles to that which the horse desires to go it will be necessary to keep one rein tighter than the other to prevent the horse from deviating in the direction of its impulses. This may be compared to the rowing of a boat, or to swimming, across a rapidly running stream. It is necessary to aim at a point considerably one side of the one it is desired to reach, in order to allow for the transverse force. If the point where the horse desires to go is to the right, it is like crossing the stream from the right to the left bank, and *vice versa.*

The conflict of motives may be much more complex than these cases imply, and some of the possible problems might be beyond solution, but most of them might be stated and solved mathematically. Complete inaction among animals, resulting from perfect equilibrium of psychic forces, is probably very rare, because the general law of the " instability of the homogeneous " puts almost infinity to one against it, and this is the true answer to the fool's puzzle of Buridan's ass that starved to death between two stacks of hay because the attraction of one stack was exactly equal to the attraction of the other. It might also be applied to the following amusing rhyme : —

> The centipede was happy quite
> Until a frog, in fun,
> Said, " Pray, which leg comes after which? "
> This raised its mind to such a pitch,
> It lay distracted in the ditch,
> Considering how to run.

But in the case of man, with his vastly greater number of motives, and especially with his reason, by which he is capable of true deliberation, the cases are common in which such a multitude of more or less conflicting, or at least mutually limiting motives, arise and crowd or choke one another in such a way that there is produced, if not an equilibrium, at least a glut and a *chômage* in the mind which renders action impossible during considerable periods. But this state always eventually works itself out, and certain groups of motives gain the ascendant, and action is resumed.

PSYCHOMETRY

Scientific investigation of psychic phenomena does not, however, stop with establishing the qualitative exactness of mental processes. It has attacked the problem of their quantitative relations and has created a science of psychometry. The first truth reached in this direction was the protensive nature of all psychic reactions. In the psychological laboratory the old metaphysical idea of their independence of time and space was quickly dispelled. It was found that sensations occupy time and that the amount of time has a certain relation to the distance they must travel. But the results are greatly modified by the nature of the physiological apparatus through which they are accomplished. Such problems are very complicated. Helmholtz found that sensations travel along the nerves at a rate varying from 84 to 96 feet per second. Since then experiments have been multiplied and considerable variation from these figures has been noted, so that the range may now perhaps be put at from 60 to 150 feet per second. But this does not probably represent the actual velocity of sensation. Much of the time is doubtless lost in a certain process of elaboration in the ganglia and sensory tracts. Between any stimulus and its consequent action a certain interval of time elapses varying from one tenth to three tenths of a second, but the personal equation of different persons varies greatly. It has been found that the act of winking occupies about five one hundredths of a second. The act of vision, however, is almost instantaneous. It has been stated as low as four billionths of a second. The reaction time of various psychic operations has been experimented upon and more or less exact results have been reached. Among the most interesting is that which fixes the time required for a volition at thirty-five thousandths of a second. A great number of instruments have been invented for measuring mental operations, among which is an "algometer" for testing the quantity of pain experienced.

All this has a possible value for sociology, but the most important psychological law, from this point of view, that has been discovered, is the well-known Weber-Fechner law that sensations represent the logarithms of their stimuli. According to this law if a stimulus increases in a geometrical progression the resulting sensation will increase in intensity in an arithmetical progression. This constitutes a sort of psychological law of diminishing returns, and its application to social phenomena is obvious and far-reaching. It is, however, chiefly in applied sociology that its value appears, and therefore this is not the place to enter fully into its discussion. This should also be accompanied with a statement of the qualifications that it has been found necessary to make in the law itself.

THE LAW OF PARSIMONY

We found in the fourth chapter that the law of parsimony was the highest generalization thus far attained in psychic and social phenomena, and that therefore its quality of exactness was the most clearly apparent of all psychic and social laws.　It is therefore one of the most important of the laws of social mechanics.　It is the resultant of the mechanical forces of society, or the algebraic sum of pleasures and pains, and the quantity and quality of human activity depend upon that sum and its sign.　Greatest gain for least effort means, when reduced to these terms: greatest pleasure for least pain.　Pleasure and pain are both motives, and although physiologically they are both positive, sociologically pleasure may be called positive and pain negative.　If the positive terms exceed the negative ones the resultant action will be positive, *i.e.*, it will be in the nature of pursuit.　If the negative terms exceed the positive ones the resultant action will be negative, *i.e.*, it will be in the nature of retreat.　The law is therefore merely the mechanical expression of least action, and is perhaps scarcely more than a case of Maupertius's mechanical theorem of least action, of Lagrange's principle of minimal effort or maximal energy.　Dr. O. Thon has well said: —

> Particular mention should be made of the point of view that differentiation is an effect of effort for conservation of energy.　This thought, which is used in psychology as "the law of minimum effort," and in various ways in the natural sciences, should be made useful in sociology.[1]

Although long regarded as a purely economic law it is found to apply to all human institutions.　M. Tarde calls attention to one of its most striking applications, viz., to language.　He says: —

> The law of least effort explains many irreversibilities.　In virtue of this universal tendency, although unequal and variable, the phonetic softening studied by linguists takes place, that substitution of mild syllables, of a pronunciation easy and rapidly propagated, for strong and harsh syllables; likewise the *attenuation of quantity*, which tends to render the long short, never the short long, as is especially shown by a comparison of the older with the later Latin poets.　Under the influence of this same tendency, symbols, changing so as to propagate themselves farther and more rapidly, are

---

[1] *American Journal of Sociology*, Vol. II, March, 1897, pp. 735–736.

M

simplified, abridged, and polished down, like forms of procedure, business operations, and artistic themes.[1]

It is the same principle that explains that survival of the fittest that goes on among languages whenever several are struggling together for the mastery. No one has so forcibly brought out this point as M. Alphonse de Candolle. " In the conflict of two languages," he says, " other things equal, it is the shortest and simplest that wins. French beats Italian and German, English beats the other languages." As a consequence of this law he concludes that English " will be spoken in half a century by many more civilized men than German and French combined," and that " the Anglo-American tongue is destined by the force of circumstances to become predominant." [2]

The law of parsimony does not always work in the interest of progress. As we saw in Chapter IV, it often causes degeneracy. One of its less serious consequences is its tendency to deter from earnest and fruitful labors. Mr. Spencer says : —

> Nearly all are prone to mental occupations of easy kinds, or kinds which yield pleasurable excitements with small efforts ; and history, biography, fiction, poetry, are, in this respect, more attractive to the majority than science — more attractive than that knowledge of the order of things at large which serves for guidance.[3]

But there is a serious flaw in the statement of this law. The simple form, as the law of *greatest gain,* is perfectly correct. So is the form " greatest satisfaction with least sacrifice," [4] for effort is not always equivalent to sacrifice. The " least effort " part of the formula grew out of the almost universal assumption of economists that labor is always undesirable, unpleasant, irksome, and odious. Mr. Veblen, in his " Theory of the Leisure Class," has admirably shown how, why, and to what extent this is so. Ratzenhofer characterizes it as the " Gesetz der Arbeitsscheu," [5] and sees it in practically the same light as Veblen. Now this *Arbeitsscheu* or *ponophobia,* as it may be called, being purely artificial and due

1 " Logique Sociale," 1895, p. 182.
2 " Histoire des Sciences et des Savants," 2° éd., Genève-Bale, 1885, pp. 368, 454, 543.
3 " Principles of Ethics," Vol. I, New York, 1892, p. 519 (§ 222).
4 Professor Sidney Sherwood in the *Annals of the Am. Acad. of Pol. and Soc. Science,* Vol. X, September, 1897, p. 206.
5 " Die Sociologische Erkenntnis," Leipzig, 1898, p. 142.

either to a stigma of caste or an unnatural excess of compulsory effort, gives the law a different meaning in sociology from that which it has in the rest of the sciences. Effort expended in labor, though it be not arduous, irksome, excessive, or in itself unpleasant, becomes a sacrifice of *pride*.

The true basis of the law of parsimony is utility, and it then becomes little more than another form of expression for the law of marginal utility, which is also a sociological law. But utility itself is ultimately reducible to satisfaction, happiness, pleasure, and we are once more down on psychological bed rock. Condorcet, who was not afraid of words, and who had wonderful penetration into such subjects, uttered about the whole truth in the following passage : —

Man always disposes himself for the action that promises him the greatest happiness. Whether he yields to the attraction of a present pleasure, or whether he resists it in view of a more remote advantage ; whether he allows himself to be drawn on by pleasure, by avarice, by ambition, or whether he sacrifices these to the love of glory, to a feeling for humanity, to tenderness for some individual, to the fear of remorse, to the desire to taste that internal contentment that follows fidelity to the rules of justice and the practice of virtue ; whether he is inclined toward the good by a calculation of interest founded on coarse enjoyments or the noblest and purest pleasures, by the idea of reward and punishment in another life or even by an enthusiasm which unites him to the will of a Supreme Being, he always performs the action from which he expects either a greater pleasure or a lesser pain.[1]

This form of statement of the law of parsimony really requires no qualification, but on account of the prevalent habit of identifying all pleasure with the class that men are pleased to call low or coarse, but which, as I have shown, are not only the most essential to the scheme of nature and the good of mankind, but also the most altruistic, it may require fuller explanation, and this will be given in Chapter XV, where the whole subject will be fully treated.

MECHANICS

Mechanics is that branch of mathematics which treats of the effects of forces as exhibited in the production of motion or rest. In text-books the production of rest is treated before the production of motion, the state of rest being due to an equilibrium of forces.

[1] "Tableau Historique des Progrès de l'Esprit Humain," Paris, 1900, pp. 357–358.

This department is called statics, and the department which treats of forces not in equilibrium, and therefore producing motion, is called dynamics. The principles of mechanics are in their fundamental aspects very simple and the science is one of the most fascinating in the whole range of mathematics. The principle of the composition of forces, susceptible, as it is, to geometrical notation, especially in the parallelogram of forces and its various modifications and derivatives, is one of the most attractive and fertile that have been discovered in any science. It is needless to say that mechanics, applicable, as it is, to the entire domain of physics, has also proved one of the most useful of all sciences. Into all this it would be both profitless and inappropriate to enter here, but it is obvious that the general principles of mechanics apply to any domain of phenomena in which the nature of the underlying forces is clearly understood. In astronomy, in all branches of physics, in geology, to considerable extent in chemistry, and in some restricted departments of biology, these principles have been successfully applied. Their use by political economists has been quite legitimate, and important results have been reached. The only difficulty here has been the ignoring of factors that should have been included, but which were, for the most part, too complex and recondite to be sufficiently understood. In consequence of these same factors, which will be dealt with more fully in Part III, the application of mechanics to sociology is still more difficult, but in some respects the broader aspect of that science gives it a certain advantage over economics proper from this point of view. As I have already said, the use of mathematics in sociology is as yet possible only in a very limited degree. The most that can be done is to insist from the outset and throughout that sociology is a domain of forces and susceptible of such treatment as fast as, and to the extent that, the action of those forces is thoroughly understood.

As pointed out in Chapter IV, it is necessary as yet to confine the attempt to treat sociology as an exact science to its most general aspects, but so long as this limitation is rigidly respected it is possible so to treat it, and the result becomes of the highest value. The laws that have been set forth in this chapter, viz., those of social physics and of psychics, and the law of parsimony or maximum utility, are social generalizations that can be depended upon. Upon them can be established a true science of social mechanics, which, with the proper caution against the neglect of hidden and deranging factors, will include and elucidate the greater part of the vast field of social phenomena.

Social Energy. — The only two absolutely irreducible categories of philosophy are *mass* and *motion*. *Space* and *time* are the essential "forms" that these must be conditioned by. Mechanics deals with these four terms. Velocity is the amount of space (distance) that a body (mass) moves through in a given time. It is represented by the space divided by the time $\left(\dfrac{s}{t} = v\right)$. The quantity of motion (momentum) is the mass into the velocity $\left(\dfrac{ms}{t} = mv\right)$. If a moving mass collides it exerts its *force* on the mass impinged, thus checking the momentum by transferring a part of the motion to the second body. The force thus exerted is expressed by dividing the momentum by the time $\left(\dfrac{ms}{t^2} = \dfrac{mv}{t}\right)$. But the kinetic energy, or *vis viva*, which is what is now understood by physicists by the technical term *energy*, is the product of the mass into the square of the velocity, though if a given force be converted into energy this product must be divided by two. Finally the production or consumption of energy represents the mechanical power, which is to energy what force is to momentum, requiring the energy to be divided by the time.

$$\text{Force} \;=\; \left(\frac{ms}{t^2} = \frac{mv}{t}\right).$$

$$\text{Energy} = \left(\frac{ms^2}{t^2} = mv^2\right).$$

$$\text{Power} \;=\; \left(\frac{ms^2}{t^3} = \frac{mv^2}{t}\right).$$

Sociologists who speak of social forces have been charged with failing to recognize the great advance that was made in physics by the general substitution of energy for force after the discovery of Joule that it is energy that is conserved. Yet Helmholtz's great memoir which laid the foundation for the law of the conservation of energy is entitled "The Conservation of Force" (*Die Erhaltung der Kraft*). The charge against the sociologists is not sustained. Sociology was founded by a mathematician who was thoroughly familiar with the nature of energy. The following passage was first published in 1830 : "The first and most remarkable of them [mechanical theorems], the one that presents the most important advantages in its application, consists in the celebrated theorem of the *conservation of live forces (forces vives)*." And he proceeds to give the history of the discovery of this property by Huyghens, its further application by Jean Bernouilli, who, he says, exaggerated the "famous distinction introduced by Leibnitz between *dead* and *live* forces."[1] I have probably made more of the social forces than any other writer on sociology, and I may not have as fully recognized the distinction between force and energy in my early works as I should have done, but I have constantly used the expression, and in a paper entitled "The Social Forces,"[2] published in 1896, I fully set forth the distinction. Winiarsky is also insisting upon it as altogether applicable to sociology as a mathematical science.

In view of all this, and merely as a sample of much that is being said, let us listen to a modern physicist, who, as in most cases, assumes to be competent to discuss sociological questions : —

It is not only in those departments of science where the uniformity of natural law would seem to be a legitimate deduction that the scientific method has found favor with investigators, for at the present time many of the writers on ethics and sociology and theology are attempting to apply the methods and the laws of physical science in their fields of investigation. It is noticeable, however, that it is not the new physics of energy, but the old physics of forces, which is being thus applied. The physics which has been rendered obsolete by the investigation of the century has been taken up by the sociologist, and we have this mighty organism, man, still struggling with as many forces as were formerly supposed to battle for the control of the physical bodies of his individual members. . . . If there is any spiritual universe, the phenomena of ethics are spiritual phenomena. The assumption of natural law, that is, physical law, in the spiritual universe means that there is no spiritual universe. A universe governed by the laws of physics is a universe in which there is no right or wrong, justice or injustice, reward or punishment : nothing but inevitable consequences. . . . This much, at least, is certain : if there is not a uniformity of nature in social phenomena so that effects follow causes with the same certainty as they do in the physical universe, then is there no science of sociology, and no such thing as a moral or social law. In so far as man is a free, moral agent, capable of determining his own conduct, all attempts at predicting what he will do under given circumstances must fail. Only in so far as man is *governed*, not merely influenced, by laws as unalterable and unvarying as are

[1] Auguste Comte, "Philosophie Positive," Vol. I, pp. 519, 520.
[2] *American Journal of Sociology*, Vol. II, July, 1896, pp. 82–83.

the laws of the physical universe, can his actions furnish the materials of scientific study. If, on the other hand, there are such laws, then all attempts of man at influencing the social order will be as successful as would attempts at revising the law of gravitation.[1]

The last sentence in the above quotation, which, from the point of view of logicality, fairly represents the whole, might be paraphrased as follows : " If there are unalterable and unvarying physical laws, then all attempts of man to utilize physical phenomena will be as successful as would attempts at revising the law of gravitation." For the only object in " influencing " social phenomena must be to utilize them. The idea that sociologists think they are engaged in "revising" social laws is decidedly refreshing. So far as I can see they are simply trying to understand them, just as the physicists tried to understand physical laws, and many of them doubtless have at least a mental reservation that, besides this knowledge for its own sake, some one may some day in some way be benefited by it. Surely this is what the physicists all thought, and the result has abundantly sustained this surmise. The truth is exactly the opposite from his statement, viz., that if there are no " unalterable and unvarying" social laws, then all attempts at " influencing," i.e., improving, the social order would be hopeless.

I am always very chary about using such expressions as " spiritual phenomena," because the word *spiritual* has almost become a synonym of supernatural. Yet the word is a perfectly proper one and ought to be redeemed and freely used, more nearly as a synonym of *psychic* in its widest sense, and I shall not hesitate so to use it. The last three chapters have been devoted to showing that spiritual phenomena are as much natural phenomena as physical phenomena, that spiritual forces are true natural forces, and that there is a spiritual energy, i.e., a psychic and social energy, that is as capable of doing work as any other form of kinetic energy. In fact it is the highest and most effective form of energy or *vis viva*.

There is therefore a true science of social mechanics, and as social energy is only a special mode of manifestation of the universal energy, social mechanics is only a kind of mechanics which deals with this form of energy. The fundamental classification of mechanics,

[1] The Scientific Method and its Limitations. Address at the eighth Annual Commencement, Leland Stanford Junior University, May 24, 1899, by Fernando Sanford, Professor of Physics, Stanford University, 1899, pp. 19–21.

as we saw, is into statics and dynamics, and social statics and social
dynamics are as legitimate branches of mechanics as are hydrostatics
and hydrodynamics, the principles of which are commonly included
in text-books of mechanics.   In fact, Winiarsky has made a direct
application of thermodynamics to social mechanics as essential to its
full treatment.   I shall deal with social statics and social dynamics
in that order, which is the same as that in which mechanics is always
treated, the advantage of which is even greater here than in other
departments, as will be clearly apparent as we proceed.

CHAPTER X

SOCIAL STATICS

THE dynamic agent is a powerful agent. There is no lack of power for propelling the social machinery. Social energy surges through society in all directions, but, like a flood or a storm, it is ruthless The innate interests of men work at cross purposes, often to no purpose. They conflict, collide, and dash against one another, but in such an unorganized, haphazard, and chaotic way that they do not produce equilibrium but mutual ruin. The dynamic agent, like any other cosmic force, is centrifugal, catabolic, destructive. If there was no way of curbing or harnessing the social energy there would be nothing but destruction — no construction. In Chapter VII we considered two modes of natural restraint to feeling, one of which was on the human plane and related to the dynamic agent of society. We must now go much deeper into the general problem of restraining social energy. As, however, the actual process that has gone on in society has done so under the operation of a truly cosmic or universal *principle*, it cannot be adequately understood without first understanding its simpler manifestations in nature at large.

PRINCIPLE VERSUS LAW

I use the word *principle* here instead of law intentionally, because there is an essential difference. Both words are, it is true, often used very loosely and vaguely, so as to render them interchangeable, but the distinction should be insisted upon in any scientific discussion. There is little or no difference between law and *theory*, as the latter term is used by mathematicians and physicists. A law is the general expression of the natural sequence of uniform phenomena. It states the fact that certain phenomena uniformly take place in a certain way. It takes no account of cause, but only of the order of events. A principle, on the contrary, deals wholly with the cause, or, perhaps more correctly, with the *manner*. It is the *modus operandi*. It has to do with the means or instrument by which the

169

effects are produced. It is essentially an ablative conception. As principles deal with causes they must deal with forces. Gravitation, for example, is a force, but it operates in a regular way which we call the law of gravitation. Its various applications are principles or utilize principles. Thus the weight of water is a force, but the different kinds of water-wheels act on so many different principles — overshot, undershot, flutter, turbine, etc. The turbine wheel, for example, acts on the principle of reaction, according to Newton's third law of motion that action and reaction are equal and opposite. Other applications of the law of gravitation are those of weights, the balance, the pendulum, etc., all of which involve different principles. Water and steam expand by heat according to a certain law. This expansion of steam is a force which has been utilized by means of a number of mechanical principles — the piston, the cut-off, the governor, etc.

Again, evolution is a law, or takes place according to a law, the phenomena succeeding each other in a definite order of sequence. We observe the successive phenomena and from them deduce or formulate the law. But natural selection is a principle. It teaches how the effects thus observed are produced. Malthus's great book, the "Principle of Population," was correctly named, and the principle is there fully explained. So the expression which I prefer to others of the same import, viz., the "principle of advantage," conforms to this definition and applies wherever there can be an advantage, i.e., to all sentient things. Creative synthesis is a principle of far-reaching application in both the inorganic and the organic worlds, and each of the synthetic creations of nature passed in review in Chapter V was brought about under the operation of this principle. All the products of natural genesis involve appropriate principles.

A law cannot explain anything, but must itself be explained. Principles alone explain. The law of gravitation is as yet unexplained. No principle has been found that explains it to the satisfaction of physicists. The world is therefore never satisfied with laws. It demands principles. The positivists may affect to dispense with causes and be content with mere observed succession, but the mind will never be at rest until the principle according to which that succession goes on is discovered and the phenomena are thereby really explained.

SYNERGY

That there is a universal principle, operating in every department of nature and at every stage in evolution, which is conservative, creative, and constructive, has been evident to me for many years, but it required long meditation and extensive observation to discover its true nature.   After having fairly grasped it I was still troubled to reduce it to its simplest form, and characterize it by an appropriate name.   I have at last fixed upon the word *synergy* as the term best adapted to express its twofold character of *energy* and *mutuality*, or the systematic and organic *working together* of the antithetical forces of nature.   The third and equally essential and invariable quality of creation or construction is still lacking in the name chosen, unless we assume, as I think we may do, that work implies some product, to distinguish it from simple activity.   Synergy is a synthesis of work, or synthetic work, and this is what is everywhere taking place.   It may be said to begin with the primary atomic collision in which mass, motion, time, and space are involved, and to find its simplest expression in the formula for force $\left(\dfrac{ms}{t^2}\right)$, which implies a plurality of elements, and signifies an interaction of these elements.   Caspari says: —

The notion of force presupposes a relation with another force, the latter a foreign one, which is called resistance.   A force without resistance would be a force without force, *i.e.*, an inconceivable absurdity.   He who speaks of force is therefore obliged to understand by it at the same time the *mechanical resistance* of this force, or else he contradicts himself.   This is why all investigators in philosophy who have become so through the study of the natural sciences and who have studied mechanics, have recognized that it is always necessary to suppose a *primary plurality of separate vehicles of force :* centers of force, atoms of force of Democritus, or monads of Leibnitz, or realities of Herbart, or dynamids of Redtenbacher, etc.[1]

It further seems probable that vortex motion is based on this principle, or is the same principle, and it is through this that some expect the problem of the nature of gravitation to find its solution. The impact theory is taking the place of the old pseudo-conception of attraction.   There can be no such thing as attraction except in the sense in which the little microscopic creature, happily named

---

[1] "Die Philosophie im Bunde mit der Naturforschung." Von Otto Caspari, *Kosmos*, Vol. I, April, 1877, pp. 4–16 (see p. 9).

Vorticella, is said to "attract" the nutrient particles floating in the medium in which it lives into its mouth opening. Any one who will carefully watch this process with a good objective and with the medium properly illuminated will readily see wherein this so-called attraction consists. A circle of cilia surrounds the creature's mouth opening, and these it keeps constantly in motion in such a way as first, to waft all the particles that surround it for some distance outward and forward, and next to produce a true vortex motion which results in the production of a constant stream directly in front toward and into the cavity of its body within the circle of cilia. The separate illuminated particles may be watched as they are first propelled from near the creature's body, then carried forward and made to describe a curve, and finally forced into the in-flowing current, and poured into the animal's body. Certain experiments that have been recently made look in the direction of explaining gravitation on a principle similar to this.

Cosmic Dualism. — It always happens that a great truth receives a name too narrow to comprehend its full scope, and that certain minds in glorifying that truth attach themselves to the name and give currency to something not only less than the truth but also in some degree false. It has been notably thus with the name *monism* which has come into use as the short and economical designation of the great truth that there is a unitary principle running through all nature. Monism has become a sort of philosophic shibboleth, and the term to which it is commonly opposed is *dualism*. It has come about in this way that dualism is used as an epithet which is freely hurled at all who make bold to question even the narrowest and most metaphysical or mystical doctrines into which monism has latterly degenerated. All this has as its natural result to cause other equally important truths, in supposed conflict with monism, to be ignored or fought shy of, whereby a full knowledge of nature's method is prevented and only partial truth or even partial error is propagated and accepted.

Second only in importance, if not of equal importance, to the truth of cosmic unity is the fact of universal polarity. The universe is polarized throughout. Every force meets with resistance, otherwise there could be no energy. Universal conflict reigns. But for this conflict evolution would be impossible. The forces of nature are being perpetually restrained. If centrifugal forces were not constrained by centripetal forces the very orbs of space would fly from their orbits and follow tangents, *i.e.*, straight lines. If there had never been such restraint they would never have been formed. All definite forms of whatever class are due to antagonistic influences restraining, circumscribing, and transforming motion. The conservation of energy results from this law, and all the multiform modes of motion, perpetually being converted one into another, are the products of a ceaseless struggle. Not only do the centrifugal and centripetal forces engage in this struggle, but we also see contending on a gigantic scale the gravitant and radiant forces. We see attraction and repulsion, concentration and dissipation, condensation and dissolution. Though these are all equally modes of manifestation of the universal force, they are nevertheless, by the force of circumstances, pitted against one another in ubiquitous conflict.

We have now to consider some of the effects of this cosmic dualism. Collision produces deflection, constraint, and transfer of motion, resulting in increased intensive activity at the expense of extensive activity, a shortening of paths and circuits with a multiplication of the number of transits or revolutions; motion of translation is converted into vibration, and molar activity into molecular activity. Everywhere we have heightened intensity, increased energy, and more work. It is a process of securing constantly greater and greater cosmic efficiency.

Next as to the form that this concentrated effort of nature assumes. We observe that in the realm of space nebulæ appear. Then these nebulæ condense and assume various definite forms, tending toward and ultimately attaining a close approximation to sphericity. Condensation continues and the central mass becomes a star, *i.e.*, a sun. If, as is usual, smaller masses fail to cohere with the principal mass, these are further condensed and rolled up into balls (planets) that revolve around the contracting and receding central mass. Often still lesser tertiary masses break away from the secondary ones and similarly roll up and revolve about the latter as satellites. The whole now forms a system and clings together under the influence of the same antagonistic forces that presided over its inception and its entire history. There is no department of nature from which the truth comes forth more clearly that the normal and necessary effect of the cosmic struggle is *organization*.

But these great orbs of space consist wholly of the same infinitely minute particles that first existed in a diffused and discrete condition before even the nebulæ were formed. In this molecular world the same law obtains as in the molar universe. Chemistry teaches that there are molecular systems also, and to all appearances these are as symmetrical as world systems and are held together and kept in motion by the interaction of antithetical forces differing scarcely except in degree from planetary forces. Chemical atoms themselves are doubtless such systems, and the more and more complex molecules of inorganic and organic chemistry simply represent so many degrees of chemical organization as the effect of the same law, while aggregations of these atoms and molecules constitute the manifold substances, minerals, rocks, fluids, and gases, that make up the planet. All these substances are theaters of intense internal activity. This molecular activity has resulted from the condensation of formerly free particles flying through space. Forced into relatively contracted portions of space they retained their original quantity of motion. Their mode of motion was changed, their paths, or orbits, or circuits were reduced, and they were compelled to expend the whole of their original, inherent, and unalterable sum of activity within exceedingly minute areas. The whole of this reduction in the space had to be made up by increase in intensity. The quantity of motion was converted into force, the force into energy, and the energy into power. This compromise among the contending forces of nature was effected through organization and the formation of chemical systems, which are so many reservoirs of power, this power being represented by what we call the *properties* of matter. These systems store up energy and expend it in work, but the work is always a collaboration or coöperation of all the competing forces involved. It is synergy.

Passing to the organic world we find new forces that have entered the lists and are participating in the contest. The vital and psychic forces whose genesis we have been studying are now at work, and we have a corresponding change in the character of the products. The kind of systems that result from the struggle on this plane are organic beings, or organisms. These, too, are symmetrical bodies, and the character of the process as one of organization becomes still more apparent. But the bodies of organisms consist of *structures*, and here we see more clearly than in the previous cases that the final result of synergy is *construction*. Solar systems, stars, planets, and satellites are also structures, and so, too, are chemical units of whatever order. The constructive process inheres in all forms of synergy, and the coöperation of antithetical forces in nature always results in making, that is, in *creating* something that did not exist before. But in the organic world this character of structure becomes the leading feature, and we have synthetic products consisting of tissues and organs serving definite purposes, which we call *functions*.

Finally, in the social world, as we shall soon see, we have the same principle at work accomplishing results not generically distinct from those accomplished on the three planes of activity thus far considered. We shall find that it is also a theater of intense activity, and that competing and antagonistic agencies are fiercely contending for the mastery. The complete domination of any one set of these forces would prevent the formation of society. If such a hegemony were to supervene at any given stage it would sweep society out of existence. Here as everywhere any single force, acting without opposition or deflection, would be destructive of all the order attained. Only through the joint action of many forces, each striving for the mastery but checked and constrained by the rest and forced to yield its share in conforming to the general principle, can any structure result. And we shall see that this is what is taking place in society, that society was itself thus created, and that social structures were thus formed which are as real, as definite, and as symmetrical as are biotic, chemic, or cosmic structures.

In the above sketches I have only sought to set forth the true nature of the universal principle of synergy pervading all nature and creating all the different kinds of structure that we observe to exist. While it is the same synthetic creation that was described in Chapter V, we are enabled now to look deeper into it and perceive the principle through which it works. Primarily and essentially it is a process of *equilibration, i.e.,* the several forces are first brought into a state of partial equilibrium. It begins in collision, conflict, antagonism, and opposition, but as no motion can be lost it is transformed, and we have the milder phases of antithesis, competition, and interaction, passing next into a *modus vivendi*, or compromise, and ending in collaboration and coöperation. It is the cosmological expression of the Hegelian trilogy and constitutes the synthesis of all the antinomies at work. Synergy is the principle that explains all organization and creates all structures. These products of cosmic synergy are found in all fields of phenomena. Celestial structures are worlds and world systems, chemical structures are atoms, molecules, and substances, biotic structures are protoplasm, cells, tissues, organs, and organisms. There are also psychic structures — feelings, emotions, passions, volitions, perceptions, cognitions, memory, imagination, reason, thought, and all the acts of consciousness. And then there are social structures, the nature of which it is the principal object of this chapter to explain. These are the products of the social forces acting under the principle of social synergy.

Artificial Structures. — What has been said thus far is scarcely more than a statement of facts. It fails to convey an idea of the exact nature of the principle of synergy. In seeking to do this we may perhaps be aided by an anthropomorphic conception. Just as the primitive man can only understand natural phenomena by analogy with the acts of men, so we may obtain light on this natural principle by examining the analogous artificial principle. A mechanism is something constructed. It may therefore be called a structure. As it is artificial, it is an artificial structure, and we may compare artificial structures with natural structures. The inventor or constructor of any mechanism, no matter how simple, virtually recognizes the law of the conservation of energy. He assumes that the quantity of motion is unchangeable. That is, he acts on the theory that natural forces will continue to act no matter what disposition he may make of his materials. He has no idea of the possibility of increasing or diminishing the sum total of force. But he also recognizes the further truth that the particular manner in which forces act is indefinitely variable, *i.e.*, that the direction, velocity, etc., are matters of indifference, and will depend upon the amount and kind of resistance with which bodies meet. In other words, while he realizes that the quantity of motion is constant, he perceives that the mode of motion is variable. This enables him artificially to modify natural phenomena, to direct and control them. The one universal and generic method of artificially modifying the spontaneous course of natural phenomena is that of offering some kind of resistance. When a man dams a stream he does not expect to stop the stream from flowing on. He knows that the water will continue to rise behind his dam till it overflows it, and will then continue on in its course as before. But if he wants nothing but a pool of water his dam secures that, and the original state of things is altered to that extent. Usually he wants something more. He wants the water to fall perpendicularly as far as it falls by the original inclination of its bed in flowing considerable distance. He therefore constructs above his dam another channel for the water with a very slight incline, and directs the water into it. The desired "head" is thus easily obtained and he causes the same force to act in a different way, far more effective for his purpose. He has controlled a natural force to his own advantage. All mechanisms can be reduced to terms as simple as these. The whole principle is that of interposing barriers to the natural course of phenomena and giving them an artificial course. But what is implied in a barrier, in this resistance? Simply the production of a temporary or a partial equilibrium. A solid material substance placed in the path of a moving body arrests it and there is temporary equilibrium. Open the sluiceway and motion is resumed, but it is less rapid than before because held by a material channel (ditch, trough, tube, etc.) the bed of which is nearly level. If we follow the water to the penstock and see it pour into this until it is full, we only see further barriers to its normal progress. When at last the gate at the bottom of the penstock is opened and the weight of the column forces the water violently against the paddles of a properly constructed wheel, we only see a higher application of the same principle. The most important of these applications is that of *storage*. As already remarked, the inventor does not expect to destroy the force. He wants to utilize it, and in no way can he so effectually utilize it as by storing it until he wants it and using it at will. The flume stores the energy of the water.

Any other use by man of natural forces would have served the purpose as well as the one selected. The steam engine, with its boiler, pipes, cylinders, etc., is a complicated mechanism for confining steam and using it at will. The resistance of the boiler equilibrates the steam till the cocks are opened. The piston produces a partial resistance and brings out the energy of the steam which forces it to move and drive the machinery. Everywhere there are checks and balances. It is an artificially contrived struggle between the force of the steam and the resistance of the apparatus, through

N

which the former is compelled to do work. It is a sort of synergy. Electrical motors would illustrate the subject equally well. But here we have in the storage battery the most complete example of the application of a somewhat permanent equilibrium, capable of being disturbed at will for the utilization of the force. Another important application is that of gearing up machinery. Large wheels are connected by belts or cogs with small ones to secure more rapid rotation. In this way greater intensity is secured. The analogues of all these principles are to be found in the operations of nature unaided by intelligence.

Organic Structures. — While all the synthetic creations of nature and all the products and differential attributes treated in Chapter V are illustrations of the natural storage of energy, and have been evolved under the law of creative synthesis and through the principle of cosmic synergy, organic structures, worked out through the combined action of chemism, zoism, and psychism, furnish more of the elements that the sociologist must use, and are essential to his work. It is here that we see more clearly than on any lower plane the true nature of organization. For here we have true organs, and all the structures more or less fully integrated.

In the organic world the primary contending forces are those of heredity and variation. These correspond to the centripetal and centrifugal forces in astronomy. Heredity may be regarded as that tendency in life to continue in existence whatever has been brought into existence. All forces are essentially alike and the life force or growth force is like any physical force. That is, it obeys the first law of motion and causes motion in a straight line unless deflected by another force. This, if allowed to go on uninfluenced, would simply result in perpetually increasing the quantity of life without affecting its quality. But in the domain of vital force, as in that of physical force, in consequence of the multiplicity of objects in nature, there is necessarily constant collision, constant opposition, constant contact with other forces from all conceivable directions. These constitute the resistance of the environment. Heredity pushes through all this as best it can, striving to pursue the straight path on which it started, but as it is only one of the many forces involved in the contest, it obeys all the other laws of motion and is checked, deflected, shunted, buffeted this way and that, and compelled to pursue a very irregular path. We saw that under the principle of cosmic synergy the primary cosmic force which impels the matter of universal space, similarly colliding and contending, ultimately assumed an organized form and elaborated the matter of space into symmetrical bodies coördinated into systems. In like manner the vital force subjected to all these counter-forces, stresses, and strains, began at the outset to elaborate symmetrical forms and to organize biological systems. The organic world — protists, plants, animals — was the result.

This biological dualism struck the early students of organic nature and has been repeatedly described and abundantly illustrated in all the great philosophical works. The synthetic mind of Goethe clearly grasped it, and he discussed it at length in his "Metamorphosis of Plants" (1790), and earlier in his "Morphology" (1786), but especially in his somewhat later miscellaneous writings. He recognized the analogy of these biologic forces to the centrifugal and centripetal forces in astronomy. In one of his short papers on Natural Science in General which bears date March 17, 1823, he says : —

> The idea of metamorphosis is a most noble, but at the same time very dangerous gift from on high. It leads back to the formless state, destroys and dissipates knowledge. It is like the *vis centrifuga* and would lose itself in the infinite were there not something to counteract it : I mean the specific force, the stubborn power of permanence of whatever has attained reality, a *vis centripeta*, which in its fundamental nature no outside power can affect.[1]

Goethe's metamorphosis is of course what is now called the transmutation of species, and his specific impulse is heredity, which tends to maintain the fixity of species, and was long supposed to do so absolutely. The *vis centrifuga* corresponds to the impinging forces of the environment causing constant deviation from the specific type, *i.e.*, variation. The organism must conform to the mold

---

[1] "Die Idee der Metamorphose ist eine höchst ehrwurdige, aber zugleich höchst gefährliche Gabe von oben. Sie führt ins formlose, zerstört das Wissen, löst es auf. Sie ist gleich der *vis centrifuga* und würde sich ins Unendliche verlieren, wäre ihr nicht ein Gegengewicht zugegeben: ich meine den Specificationstrieb, das zähe Beharrlichkeitsvermögen dessen, was einmal zur Wirklichkeit gekommen, eine *vis centripeta*, welcher in ihrem tiefsten Grunde keine Aeusserlichkeit etwas anhaben kann." Goethes sämmtliche Werke in dreissig Bänden. Vollständig neugeordnete Ausgabe, Stuttgart und Tübingen, Vol. XXIX, pp. 350–351. (This passage occurs under the subtitle "Probleme" of the heading "Problem und Erwiederung," dated "Weimar den 17 März 1823," in the collection of essays entitled "Zur Naturwissenschaft im Allgemeinen," which is put at the end of this volume in the edition cited).

established for it by its environment, which requires modification in the specific type. The process of compelling the organism to undergo these transformations and secure this conformity is what in modern biological language is called *adaptation*. But as the environment is infinitely varied and the number of possible conditions to which organisms may be adapted is infinite, the effect is to differentiate the one original hypothetical form which heredity would perpetuate unchanged into an unlimited number of different forms. The resistance of the environment, therefore, so far from offering an obstacle to life, is of the highest advantage, and has made the existing multiplicity of organic forms possible. All of which brings clearly to view the extraordinary creative and constructive character of organic synergy.

But this is not all of biological statics. Lamarck and Darwin showed that there is going on in the organic world a perpetual struggle for existence. We have here nothing to do with the Lamarckian principle of exercise or the Darwinian principle of natural selection, which are both dynamic principles, but Mr. Herbert Spencer, in his profound analysis of organic phenomena in the first volume of his "Principles of Biology," has shown that there is involved on a vast scale a true process of equilibration, which belongs to biological statics and constitutes its true foundation. In Spencer's direct and indirect equilibration, which are the statical equivalents of the two dynamic principles above named, we have the mechanical philosophy of organic life. Involved in it is the geographical distribution of plants and animals and their adaptation to environment. The ordinary treatment of geographical distribution is very unsatisfactory. The attempt to establish floral and faunal zones is never wholly successful on account of the constant commingling of species. But the study of the habitat of particular species and the causes that circumscribe it leads to exact results. I published such a study in botanical statics in 1876,[1] and since then I have accumulated a large number of additional facts from which a volume might be written.

Structure versus Function. — It is in the organic world that we can best begin the study of function. It is true that every artificial structure also has its function. The function is the end for which

---

[1] "The Local Distribution of Plants and the Theory of Adaptation," *Popular Science Monthly*, New York, Vol. IX, October, 1876, pp. 676–684.

a mechanism is constructed. It is that which it is made to do. The function of a watch is to keep time, of a locomotive to draw trains, of a storage battery to propel machinery, etc. But for the function the structure would be worthless. It is not otherwise with organic structures. The structures are only means. Function is the end. The study of structures is called anatomy, that of function, physiology. But the two are of course intimately bound up together and can only be separated in thought. In fact, all natural structures are developed along with their functions, which may be regarded in a sense as the cause of the structures. The effort of nature to accomplish its ends results in material means capable of accomplishing them, and such means are structures. The function then becomes the particular way in which the structures are utilized in the accomplishment of these ends. In mathematical language, where the word *function* is used in much the same sense, organic function may be regarded as the dependent variable, and organic structure as the independent variable. In biology and all the higher sciences the dependent variable is what the independent variable is for. In mathematics neither can be said to have any purpose.

Such being the relations of structure and function, and all considerations of structure being statical, it is evident that all considerations of function must also be statical. The functions of nutrition and reproduction go on during the entire life of an organism without producing any organic change of structure. All the physiological processes — digestion, assimilation, circulation, secretion, excretion, respiration, sensation, mentation — take place throughout the life of an organism of whatever grade without causing any modification in the tissues and organs by which they are performed. This may go on through hundreds and thousands of generations and through vast geological periods. In fact unless something besides the simple and normal performance of function takes place there will never be any organic change. Function simply as such, has no effect whatever in modifying structure. Plain and self-evident as all this seems, it is astonishing that so many sociologists basing the science of sociology upon biology should have conceived the idea that, while anatomy is a statical science, physiology is dynamic.[1] This confusion of thought

[1] I made a partial enumeration of the sociologists taking this view, in my paper on " La Mécanique Sociale," read at the Congrès de l'Institut International de Sociologie in Paris in 1900. See the *Annales de l'Institut*, Vol. VII, p. 182.

must be ascribed in part to the failure to analyze the phenomena of structure and function, but still more to the utter chaos that reigns among sociologists as to what constitutes statics and dynamics in the concrete sciences.

Not only are nutrition, reproduction, and all the so-called vegetative functions, statical, where they simply preserve the life of the individual and of the species, but they do not cease to be statical when by excess of function they increase the quantity of life through growth and multiplication of the same unaltered types of structure. Size and number do not alter the conditions in this respect. There are some animals whose size seems to depend mainly on age and environment. This is notably the case with certain fishes. When a boy I used to fish around an old mill pond. Among other fishes it contained many pickerels which I learned to catch, although they would not take the hook. They were from six inches to a foot in length, but sometimes, when I would venture some distance into the pond among the drift wood and aquatic vegetation, a huge creature that I had taken for a log would surge out and dart away into the deep water. I finally discovered that these were immense pickerels which, unable to escape from the pond, and well supplied with food (smaller fish), had grown old and attained such a great size. Later, when the pond was drained, a hundred or more of these fishes, many four feet in length and nearly a foot in diameter, were secured. There were also all intermediate sizes, clearly showing that they belonged to the same species that I had been in the habit of spearing. This was simply a case of overgrowth under favorable conditions, and involved no dynamic principle. It is the same when from abundance of food and absence of enemies a species multiplies and attains enormous numbers, as in the swarms of locusts, the clouds of pigeons, or the droves of lemmings that occasionally appear. All this is still within the limits of biological statics.

We may even go further and maintain that simple perfectionment of structure is statical so long as it does not involve the least change in the nature of the structure. Here the distinction becomes fine, but it can be successfully maintained by noting in any given case whether the principle on which the structure works is or is not altered. To illustrate in the case of artificial structures or mechanisms, as, for example, inventions. If a man were to invent a machine and make a rough model, too imperfect to work, he might obtain a patent. In such a case if another man were to present a model of the same machine but much more exactly made, so that the model itself would work, he could not obtain a patent for an improvement simply on the ground that his model was better made. There must be some change in the principle, however slight, to entitle him to a patent for an improvement. It is precisely this distinction that separates the dynamic from the statical, whether in artificial or natural structures.

Social Structures. — Passing over psychic structures which have already been enumerated and the subjective ones fully treated, we come to social structures, for the better understanding of which only, other structures have been considered. But having fully grasped the general principle on which all structures whatever are formed, it is easy to pass from organic to social structures. The principle is the same and the only difference is in the forces. Social structures are the products of social synergy, *i.e.*, of the interaction of different social forces, all of which, in and of themselves, are destructive, but whose combined effect, mutually checking, constraining, and equilibrating one another, is to produce structures. The entire drift is toward economy, conservatism, and the prevention of waste. Still, it must not be supposed that social statics deals with stagnant societies. A static condition is to be sharply distinguished from a stationary condition. Failure to make this distinction is due to what I have called *the fallacy of the stationary.* Social structures are genetic mechanisms for the production of results and the results cannot be secured without them. They are reservoirs of power. A dynamo generates electricity from the electrical conditions that surround it. Those conditions were there before the dynamo was built, but they produced none of the effects that the dynamo produces. They may be described as so much power running to waste. The dynamo simply saves and husbands this power for man's use. It is exactly the same with every true natural structure. Before the dam was built the same quantity of water coursed through the area afterwards occupied by the mill pond. It had the same weight, *i.e.*, power, before as after, but it did no useful work. By means of the dam, the race, the flume, the wheel, the mill, it is utilized and made to do the work required of it. The water in that pond is, as it were, charged with power. The same water occupying a basin without an outlet would soon become stagnant, and instead of doing good would be doing harm by exhaling miasma. The distinction between a mill pond and a stagnant pool is precisely the distinction between a static and a stationary condition in anything whatever — between, for example, an organized and thrifty society and a stagnant society. Social statics deals with social organization.

Social equilibration under the principle of social synergy, while it involves a perpetual and vigorous struggle among the antagonistic social forces, still works out social structures and conserves them, and these structures perform their prescribed functions. Upon the perfection of these structures and the consequent success with which they perform their functions depends the degree of social efficiency. In the organic world the struggle has the appearance of a struggle for existence. The weaker species go to the wall and the stronger persist. There is a constant elimination of the defective and survival of the fittest. On the social plane it is the same, and weak races succumb in the struggle while strong races persist. But in both cases it is the best structures that survive. The struggle is therefore raised above the question of individuals or even of species, races, and societies, and becomes a question of the fittest structures. We may therefore qualify Darwin's severe formula of the struggle for existence and look upon the whole panorama rather as a *struggle for structure*.

The Social Order

The social mechanism taken as a whole constitutes the social order. Order is the product of organization. Social synergy, like all other forms of synergy, is essentially constructive. Social statics may therefore be called constructive sociology. Without structure, organization, order, no efficient work can be performed. Organization as it develops to higher and higher grades simply increases the working efficiency of society. To see how this takes place we have only to contrast the efficiency of an army with that of a mob, assuming that both are striving to accomplish the same object. Social statics is that subdivision of social mechanics, or that branch of sociology, which deals with the social order. The social order, in this respect like an organism, is made up of social structures, and is complete in proportion as those structures are integrated, while it is high in proportion as those structures are differentiated and multiplied and still perfectly integrated, or reduced to a completely subordinated and coördinated system. This branch of sociology will therefore deal chiefly with social structures and their functions, with their origin and nature, their relations of subordination and coördination, and with the final product of the entire process which is society itself. But it is not to be expected that we can constantly adhere to the biological terminology which we have thus far used, nor is it desirable to do so. The object in its use in a strictly genetic treatment like the present is not to lose sight for a moment of the great unity that pervades all science. But sociology should have a terminology of its own, and such, in fact, it already has.

Human Institutions. — The most general and appropriate name for social structures is human institutions. The adjective " human " is really not necessary, however, since it cannot be with propriety said that animal societies (and this itself is a metaphorical expression) consist of, or, indeed, possess institutions. It should be stated at the outset that structures are not necessarily material objects. None of the psychic structures are such, and social structures may or may not be material. Human institutions are all the means that have come into existence for the control and utilization of the social energy. Already in Chapter V, when searching for the true nature and essence of the social energy, we were called upon to deal with that most fundamental of all human institutions, that primordial, homogeneous, undifferentiated social plasma out of which all institutions subsequently developed, and which has been so far overlooked by students of society that it is even without a name. We ventured to call it *the group sentiment of safety,* and showed that its nearest relations to any human institution that has been named are to religion. Out of it have certainly emerged one after another religion, law, morals (in its primitive and proper sense based on *mos,* or custom), and all ceremonial, ecclesiastical, juridical, and political institutions. But there are other human institutions almost as primitive and essential, such as language, art, and industry, that may have a different root, while the phylogeny of thousands of the later derivative institutions may still be difficult to trace. This great phylogenetic study of society will one day become a prominent department of sociology, even as organic phylogeny has so recently become a recognized branch of biology.

A closer examination of human institutions reveals the fact that they are not all quite alike even in their general character. They may be divided into two or three groups or classes. We have already seen that some are material and others immaterial, but even this is not as fundamental or as essential a classification as another which is, indeed, akin to it, but still does not strictly follow the same lines. It is more difficult to define than it is to perceive in the best examples. It might be called the distinction between natural and artificial, or between spontaneous and factitious institutions, although really one class is as natural as the other, and both are partly spontaneous and partly factitious. In many cases, however, there are two cognate institutions, one of which belongs to one class and the other to the other. In such cases the natural or spontaneous one seems older or more primitive, and the artificial or factitious one is in a sense an outgrowth from the first. The one class might therefore be called primary and the other secondary. From still another point of view the secondary institutions may be regraded as products or functions of the primary ones. A few examples will show both the real distinction between these classes and also the difficulty in finding terms capable of clearly characterizing the distinction.

If, for example, we take the institution of marriage, giving the term all the breadth necessary to embrace all stages of human development — the customary relations of the sexes — we perceive that there grows out of it or depends upon it the institution called the family, by which we need not, any more than in the case of marriage, understand any of the developed forms, but simply the customary way of raising children and the relations among kindred generally.

If we consider religion as an institution, even the simple form of it which I have called the group sentiment of safety, we shall see that out of it there grew a system of enforcing conduct conducive to race safety and of punishing conduct opposed to race safety. This is called religion, too, and indeed superficial observers do not see that there is anything behind it and consider it all of religion among primitive peoples. But in reality it is the beginning of both ceremonial and ecclesiastical institutions as defined by Spencer. In its later aspects it becomes the church, and just as Spencer expands the term *ecclesiastical* to cover these early forms, so we may expand the word *church* still farther until it becomes correct and intelligible to say that the church is that secondary or derivative institution which religion, as a primary and original institution, made necessary and virtually created.

Let us next take law, which, as Mr. Robertson suggested (see *supra*, p. 134), is closely allied to religion, or is at least a branch coördinate with the latter of the still earlier and as yet wholly undifferentiated group sentiment of safety or social imperative. Law in its simplest expression is merely a sentiment like religion. It may be called the *sense of order* in society. But out of it grew or developed the whole system of jurisprudence, which is therefore a derivative institution, and law bears the same relation to the court that religion bears to the church.

Morality in its earliest stages was also a branch of the homogeneous social plasm described, and was coördinate with religion and law. At their base all these three are perfectly blended and inseparable. There was very little altruism in primitive morality. There was the parental instinct that exists in animals, and there soon came to be an attachment to kindred generally, which can scarcely be detected below the human plane. Still later, as kindred became the group, the attachment became coextensive with the group, but did not extend to other groups, although these may have been merely offshoots from the same group, broken away when the group grew too large to hold together. Still later when the primitive hordes combined to form clans there was more or less attachment among all the members of the clan, and the sentiment expanded *pari passu* with the expanding group until the end of the primitive peaceful stage of social development. But it was always a *blood bond,* and the sole basis of adhesion was that of real or fictitious kinship. In fact this "ethical dualism," as Dr. Edward A. Ross has so happily styled it,[1] lasted much longer, and will not have entirely disappeared until all race prejudices and national animosities shall cease. But morality within these narrow bounds, the germ of all ethical conceptions, was one of the primordial human institutions. It was essentially social, and had sociability as its central idea. Comte's "morale" is therefore the true scientific and historic morality, and differs widely from the ethics of Spencer and other moralists. Now to what secondary institution, corresponding to the church and the court, did this primary institution give rise? Why, to the moral code, to be sure. The ethical code of all races, peoples, and nations, with the whole mass of rules, precepts, and customs that attend it, constitutes a derivative and factitious institution, growing primarily out of the blood bond.

[1] "Social Control," p. 72.

Political institutions have a later origin, but we may mention as a case in point the institution of government in the abstract as the spontaneous condition which required and ultimately produced the state. As this will soon come up for fuller treatment it need not be more than noted here among the correlative institutions.

Language is among the earliest of human institutions, and was certainly spontaneous. By language I mean the power of rational intercommunication which is an exclusively human institution. The science of language in this sense is the *semantics* of Bréal.[1] It is much broader than oral speech, and includes sign and gesture language. It is probably not true, however, that these latter preceded speech. Most animals communicate feelings at least by means of sounds, and these are not always made by the voice. Voice proper is practically confined to vertebrates and chiefly to mammals. The grammar of animals contains only one part of speech, viz., the interjection. This was probably long true of the animal that finally became man, but the line between animal and man coincides very closely with that which marks the origin of the noun. Speechless man (*Alalus*) is therefore a contradiction of terms. Language was a product of intelligence and has nothing to do with the perfection of the vocal organs. It would be easy to show anatomically that man is by no means the most favored animal in this respect. But without a certain amount of intelligence he would be incapable of language. No animal, no matter how perfect its vocal organs, could possess language without this minimum of rational power. Conversely, any animal endowed with it would inevitably develop language, and this irrespective of its anatomical adaptation. A Houyhnhnm could communicate high-grade ideas with the form of a horse and the mind of a man, while a Yahoo with the form of a man and the mind of a monkey could never do anything but chatter.

To what extent words are suggested by things is one of the insoluble questions of philology, but the general outcome of the voluminous discussion of this question is that this influence is very slight. Most primitive words appear to be wholly arbitrary, but some names of things that consist chiefly in sound or that are usually associated

[1] "Une Science nouvelle, La Sémantique," par Michel Bréal, *Revue des Deux Mondes*, Vol. CXLI, juin, 1897, pp. 807–836. Essai de Sémantique," Paris (Hachette), 1897. "Semantics: Studies in the Science of Meaning," by Michel Bréal, translated by Mrs. Henry Cust, London, 1900.

with sound are undoubtedly onomatopœic. But most of the mimetic words of the culture languages are consciously made by poets and orators who see beauty and force in their use and intentionally introduce them for rhetorical effect. The question remains how particular things got their names, and this is an equally insoluble question. Certain it is that for different linguistic stocks the words for the same thing bear no resemblance to each other. If this were the proper place, it would, however, be possible or even easy, to show how this might have taken place. The imperative necessity for some medium of intercommunication lies at the bottom of the whole problem, and what the words shall be that are to signify particular things is a matter of complete indifference. No word of the most developed language will bear an isolated contemplation. Single out any word, as man, dog, house, and rivet the mind upon its mere sound or its form when written, and it will soon appear absolutely absurd.[1] But things *must* have names, and one is as good as another if it only means some particular thing to all who have to do with it. This being the case the most trifling circumstance is sufficient to associate it with a given sound, and the instant one hears another call it by such and such a name he will imitate him and thus immediately give that name vogue. I can illustrate this from my own experience when a child with my intense desire to know the names of such things as flowers, insects, birds, fish, and other animals, that my companions could not give me names for. If I met any one who would offer a name I would instantly seize upon it and never let it go. I cared absolutely nothing what the name should be if it was only a name. Thus I learned names for many plants that I never forgot, some of which subsequently proved to be wrong, but they served their purpose. I even *coined* names from analogy, resemblance, and association, which my brother and I freely used and by which we were able to talk about such plants. These names, which I never forgot, seemed silly and stupid enough when, as a botanist, I learned the right names of those plants. For example, some one who pretended to know, told me that the painted cup was the sweet-william and I thereafter called it so. A yellow flower that somewhat resembled it except in color and for which no one had ever

---

[1] Cf. James, " Principles of Psychology," Vol. II, pp. 80–81; Tarde, " Lois de l'Imitation," 2e éd., pp. 206–207 (footnote); Gumplowicz, " Der Rassenkampf," pp. 108–109.

suggested a name, we agreed to call the "sweet-john." It proved to be the yellow puccoon. Knowing the lady's-slipper, we named the next handsomest flower the gentleman's-slipper. This was the Dodecatheon. The following case well illustrates the arbitrary character of words and of language in general: A gentleman gave me the name of the wild American cranesbill, *Geranium maculatum,* and I instantly seized upon it and I never forgot it. But a boy does not scrutinize plants. He only cares for showy flowers. I never observed the fruit of the cranesbill. I do not remember having any curiosity to know why it was so called. All I wanted was a name, and the question of the propriety of the name never rose in my mind. The plant as I knew it, flowers and leaves, had nothing about it to suggest a crane's bill, and I was well acquainted with the sandhill crane which my older brothers often brought in and which I frequently saw in flocks high in air. It was not until my botanical days, years afterwards, that I observed the beak-like fruit. There were many other such cases, and it ended by our having a name for every plant and animal in the region where we lived which we mutually understood. But alas! they were for the most part meaningless to others. Later in life I was ashamed of these childish freaks, and not until I began to reflect on the origin of language did they acquire any philosophical significance. I can now see how the primitive savage, in the childhood of the race, must have blundered on the names of things in a manner not widely different from that of a child, filled with curiosity and wonder about the objects of nature that appeal to his senses.

Just as the grammar of animals consists wholly of interjections, so the earliest human speech consisted of interjections and nouns. The other parts of speech, all of which indicate relations, came later, and the verb was one of the latest to appear. It was at first peculiarly the function of gestures and signs to indicate relations, so that gesture language is really a more developed form than speech itself. Relations belong to the stage of ideas, and it was first things that demanded expression. The order of development of the parts of speech was the same as that of the development of the mental faculties. First feelings, then things, then thoughts. There is no more interesting study than that of derivative words. Not only do the roots take on successive modifications to express all manner of relations growing out of the original conceptions of the roots, but the original words themselves acquire more and more complex meanings. I was struck with this in reading Homer and Herodotus, after having read Xenophon and Demosthenes. I soon learned that while in the latter it was among the later derivative meanings that I must look for the one to fit the case, in the former it is always the simplest and most material of all the senses of a word that satisfies the context. And I finally arrived at this generalization, which, I think, will bear analysis, viz., that in the culture languages all words relating to mind originally related to matter.

Language is thus obviously a purely natural product, the result of a struggle on the part of men to understand one another. It is spontaneous and original. We have then to inquire what is the corresponding secondary, derivative, and more or less consciously developed institution which language gave birth to. In the other cases we have considered there was little or no time interval between the original and the derivative institution, the latter being developed *pari passu* with the former. But here there certainly was such a time interval, because the derivative institution was so difficult to create. It consists in any means for broadening the influence of language. Simple language, whether based on sound, or sight, availed only between persons in close proximity with one another and only for present time. The next problem was to communicate at a distance and to make a record for future time. Both these ends were secured by the same general device. We cannot now go into the history of written language through the stages of pictography, hieroglyphics, alphabets, symbolic writing, and printing. It has been written over and over again, and all that remains to do is to point out that literature, giving the term its fullest breadth, is the normal functional outgrowth of language, the institution that was naturally built upon it as its base.

But it may be well to pause at one aspect of the question that is sometimes overlooked by philologists. Written language is mainly a visualization of sound. It is of course secondary, but it is none the less natural on this account. There is a modern school of orthographic reformers who treat it as wholly artificial, and insist that language is based essentially on sound. They are therefore willing to set aside the written forms of words that have grown up with the history of written language, and fall back on a purely phonetic scheme of writing. The principle that they overlook is that language, from the earliest attempts to record it, has constantly tended to become more and more visual, until at the present day in all the culture languages sight is a more important sense than hearing in giving meaning to words. Sound is such a varying factor that the same word may have a wide range of vocal fluctuation, and pronun-ciation differs greatly in different local districts of the same country. The vocal organs of different persons differ, and the powers of articu-lation are as varied as human voices. The written word alone is definite and capable of being made uniform. With this visualization of language there grows up a sense of taste and propriety which is violated by some of the radical changes of orthography proposed. In those languages written in Roman characters[1] this is especially marked. To all esthetic eyes, I think, c and q are more esthetic than k, and, all conventional considerations aside, *culture* and *bouquet* are esthetic while *kulture* and *bookā* are barbaric. I am, however, well aware that such arguments are without weight with "spelling reformers."

This general subject of the dualism of human institutions might be treated much more at length, as almost every original institution sooner or later gives rise to a corresponding derivative one. As the primary ones are the direct products of fundamental wants and de-mands of human nature, and are thus intimately connected with the psychic and social energy, while the secondary ones are much more in the nature of artificial constructions, it might be advantageous at times, and for the sake of distinction, to limit the term *institution* to the former and call the latter *social structures* in the more restricted sense. Not that they are not both structures and also both institu-tions, but this use of the terms may sometimes serve to emphasize what is certainly a real distinction. We might then go on to enum-erate other institutions with their corresponding structures. We should find, for example, that *property* is the institution which has given rise to the *arts* as a social structure, and that out of these roots have grown up all industrial institutions in Herbert Spencer's use of the expression. The division of labor in its widest sense is an institution which underlies all forms of voluntary organization as social structures. These are to be carefully distinguished from

---

[1] The general superiority of the Roman alphabet over all others is brought forcibly home to me by the fact that with the same light I am obliged to wear glasses two numbers stronger to read German, Russian, or Greek text than to read Roman text.

all that pertains to the state on the one hand and to the church on the other. The latter are, in the sociological sense, compulsory organizations into which men are born. It is still so of the state, for if one goes from one country to another one is still under the authority of a state. It seems different in the case of the church, for many belong to no church, and any one is free to unite with any church he pleases. But this is a modern condition of things, and primitive man was as truly subject to the cult of his race as to its government. Over most of the world this is largely the case still, and it was so in Europe until the fifteenth century. As leading up to the developed state matriarchy may be regarded as the institution upon which was founded the clan as a derivative social structure. Patriarchy is similarly related to the gens, while the basis of the more complex groups, such as the tribe, is the blood bond.

This rapid and imperfect sketch of human institutions, or rather of a few of the principal ones, will afford an idea of the nature of social structures. They are all the result of some form of struggle among the social forces whereby the centrifugal and destructive character of each force acting alone is neutralized and each is made to contribute to the constructive work of society. In forming these structures the various forces are equilibrated, conserved, commuted, and converted into energy and power. The structures once created become reservoirs of power, and it is through them alone that all the work of society is performed. All these structures are interrelated and the performance of their functions brings them into contact or even conflict with one another. This mild struggle among social structures has the same effect as other struggles, and leads to general social organization. The final result is the social order, or society itself as an organized whole — a vast magazine of social energy stored for use by human institutions.

SOCIAL ASSIMILATION

The expression social assimilation implies original heterogeneity. However similar primitive races may seem to civilized men, they themselves recognize the greatest dissimilarity. Each race looks upon all others as utterly unlike itself, and usually there exists among different races the most profound mutual contempt. Whenever two races are brought into contact it usually means war. If we go back in thought to a time anterior to all historic records, to a

o

time before any of the early civilizations existed, before the Chinese Indian, Chaldean, Assyrian, Babylonian, or Egyptian periods, and attempt to picture to ourselves the condition of the world of that day, while we may admit that very little is known of it, no one will deny that great areas of the earth's surface were already occupied by men. So far as we can judge from subsequent history and from all that is now known of uncivilized man in the world, there existed at that time a great number of entirely different races, tribes, groups, clans, and hordes, each striving to maintain an existence. Whatever differences of opinion may exist in respect of other matters, all agree as to this primitive multiplicity and heterogeneity of mankind.

It is with regard to the cause of this heterogeneity that opinions chiefly differ. The simplest and most naïve explanation is that all these different races of men represent so many separate and distinct creations, the so-called state of *polygenism*. This of course is a purely theological conception, and belongs to the general doctrine of special creation as opposed to evolution. In the present state of science it would not be worth while to take any notice of it were it not that certain historians, philosophers, and even sociologists, feel compelled to fall back upon it in order to explain the condition of the world. All that can be said in such cases is that such authors cannot be sufficiently imbued with the facts, truths, and spirit of modern biology to weigh exactly the biological evidence on this point. This may look like a serious charge, but when we remember how few even of those who are called highly educated and well-informed persons imbibe enough of real science to be competent to weigh evidence from geology or paleontology, or who have any adequate idea of time limits, we need not so much wonder that historians, or even anthropologists, should fail to see the full meaning of the facts of phylogeny and embryology, not to speak of human paleontology. The theologically educated and all those who have only what is called a "common school education," know absolutely nothing about any of these things, so that between them and the truly scientific mind there is a "great gulf fixed" which keeps their thoughts as completely separated as if they were on opposite sides of the earth. Neither is this deplorable state of things confined to the wholly unscientific. The utterly false idea that prevails relative to the nature of science, according to which any one who can read and write is prepared to take up any scientific specialty and become an astrono mer, a physicist, a chemist, a zoologist, or a botanist, actually places scientific specialists among the least informed members of society. This has been repeatedly exemplified within my own observation by the complete lack of acquaintance on the part of many good botanists with the geological history of plants, and especially with the meaning of geologic time. On one occasion a distinguished botanist, after looking at a collection of fossil plants, perhaps of Cretaceous age, closed the discussion with the remark that he supposed they were all prehistoric! Another, when examining some beautiful Carboniferous ferns, after it had been explained to him that they were of the age of the coal measures, inquired whether that was not before the glacial epoch! The fault is not with these excellent people. The fault is with the educational method, which takes no account of the natural succession of phenomena or the dependence and true filiation of the sciences. But of this enough was said in Chapter V. The hope of the future is not in scientific specialists. A specialty once chosen all interest in general science and the progress of truth ceases. The hope is in the general educated public, who, having no specialties to absorb and narrow them, are interested in all science and all truth.

Such are some of the reflections that naturally grow out of the existence of the false explanation of the original heterogeneity of mankind. The question of polygenism or monogenism is a biological question simply, not a sociological question. It is well for sociologists to recognize it, but only biology can settle it. Most biologists now regard it as settled by the new truths that have, since Darwin, been brought to light, and it is noticeable that the sociologists who suppose that the sociological problems connected with the origin of the human race can only be solved by supposing a plurality of origins cite chiefly those pre-Darwinian biologists, such as Louis Agassiz, who was almost the last of his race. The fact is often mentioned that none of Agassiz's pupils and students accepted his views in this respect, and the number of anti-Darwinian biologists of note can now be counted on the fingers.

But the truth is that the doctrine of polygenism is wholly unnecessary to the sociologist. He has, as sociologist, nothing to do with the origin of man. The heterogeneous condition of the human race as far back as concerns him is easily accounted for without any such violent assumptions. It is fully explained on the simple assumption of the animal origin of man, which is now accepted by the great majority of both biologists and anthropologists. Many of the latter deny that the creature that early inhabited most of Europe, and whose remains are found in certain deposits of the early Pleistocene, or perhaps late Tertiary, was in any proper sense a man, and maintain that it was simply the ancestor of man. There is no doubt that there was such an animal as Pithecanthropus, the remains of which have now been found in the island of Java. This genus was probably widespread during early Pleistocene time. For reasons which we do not understand this genus acquired a relatively high degree of brain development, that is, an advance upon that of other anthropoid apes, which we know possess relatively better brains than other existing animals. The first manifestation of a growing brain is excessive mimicry, *i.e.*, the special faculty of *imitation*. This is not to be confounded with manifestations of cunning relating to the animal's special physical needs and mode of life, which becomes largely a form of instinct. The power of imitation in the apes is independent of their physical needs,[1] is the result of surplus mental energy, and thus represents a higher stage of brain power in general.

As was shown in Chapter V, the next step after this power of imitation is the simplest manifestations of the inventive faculty. While no true apes now known to the fauna of the globe can be said to have reached this stage, it seems probable, and is a reasonable supposition, that Pithecanthropus did really attain to some slight inventive power. This alone would account for almost every fact that reveals itself in the transition from animal to man. The least manifestation of this power would be such an immense advantage in the struggle for existence that natural selection would bring about the rest. Pithecanthropus would almost immediately acquire the ability to expand territorially and occupy great areas. It is not often perceived that the restricted faunal areas of animal species is due to the inability to adapt the environment to their needs. Let any true animal attempt to overstep the bounds of what is called its natural habitat, and it is cut off. The boundaries of faunal regions

[1] Büttikofer relates that the chimpanzees of Western Africa, having seen men bring firewood into camp and build camp fires, will themselves drag together fagots and brush, surround it and blow it, and then hold their hands to it as if warming them, in pure idle imitation of men. "Reisebilder aus Liberia," von J. Büttikofer, Leiden, 1890, Vol. I, p. 230.

are veritable dead lines beyond which an animal cannot go on pain
of death. The Malthusian principle, which is more perfectly applicable to the animal world at large than to man, teaches that the
reproductive power if unchecked would soon make any one being
so numerous as to people the whole world. It is the environment
in its broadest sense that prevents there being ten- a hundred- or a
thousandfold more individuals of any species than can exist in the
actual condition of things. But the least power over the environment, such as a slight development of the inventive faculty would
give, checks the eliminating influence of the environment, and permits the reproductive power to expand to another and much higher
stage. The faunal barriers are broken over and the species expands
territorially, and consequently increases in numbers proportionally
to the area occupied. It was thus, as it would seem, that Pithecanthropus became the master creature and spread over great expanses
of territory in all directions from its original habitat, wherever that
may have been.

If any one should ask why other species did not also acquire this
increased brain power and compete with Pithecanthropus for this
mastery, the sufficient answer would be that in the nature of things
only one master creature could thus arise. The one that first
started on this road would prevent others from doing the same in
a variety of ways. It is not difficult to see that such would be the
case, but if an illustration were needed there is one at hand.
Admitting with Letourneau that native races left undisturbed
naturally tend to progress, let us imagine any of the existing
uncivilized races thus progressing so as to compete with the present
dominant race. The process would be so slow that before any
appreciable advance had been made such a race would certainly be
overwhelmed by the hosts of men going out from civilized centers
in a variety of capacities and occupying the region in question.
Destruction or absorption of the native race would be inevitable
before anything could be done even to indicate that a progressive
tendency existed.

It could scarcely have been otherwise at that early period when a
species of apes acquired the power to modify to any trifling extent the
external conditions of its existence. The difference would be fully as
great between such a species and other species as is that between civilized and uncivilized races to-day. The power to wield a club in

battle, many times increasing the efficiency of the naked hands; any other simple weapon or implement capable of injuring enemies or killing game; the foresight to lay up stores for the future; the art of skinning animals and wrapping the skins around the body for protection; the wit to dig a hole in a bank of clay and crawl in and out; and from this on to the stage of building fire, of making tools and weapons, and of providing more adequate clothing and shelter, and the still higher stage of simplest tillage and the domestication and use of animals — such are some of the early steps by which the inchoate intuitive reason of the creature that was ultimately to dominate the earth must have won its first victories over nature.

These steps once taken, everything else would follow as a matter of course. The faunal boundaries once broken over, the expansion, due to diminished checks to reproduction, would be in all directions. In a very short time the geographical extremes would represent great distances and all contact with the parent stock would cease. Differences in the environment would alone account for all the differences that exist among the races of men. Migration would be along radiating lines, but they would not be straight lines. They would be lines of least resistance. There would also be cross lines and diagonal lines, and curved and crooked lines, and ever and anon at any and all points there would be liability to conjuncture. This might be friendly, but after the different stocks had lost all trace or recollection of one another, this accidental encounter between two hordes or clans would lead to conflict. While between a human horde and the wild animals among which it lived there would be only fear or perhaps affection, between one human horde and another there would be both fear and hatred. Hence collisions, conflicts, and wars would begin even thus early in the history of a race destined to people and transform the earth.

All such questions as those of the "cradle of the race," of the "first pair," and of the origin of races generally, are therefore puerile. As Haeckel aptly says we might as well talk about the first Englishman or the first German as to talk about the first man or the first pair. In nature there is no first, there is only an eternal becoming. Long before there was any record or tradition the human race had spread over the entire Eurasian continent, Africa, and Australia. It had occupied all the Asiatic and Australasian archipelagos and islands. It had pushed northward into Kamtchatka,

crossed Bering Straits into Alaska, swarmed southward and occupied the whole of North America, streamed along the Cordilleras,
over the isthmus of Darien, and followed the Andes to Tierra del
Fuego, peopling the valleys of the Orinoco, of the Amazons, and of
the La Plata, and the plains of Argentina, Bolivia, and Chili. We
have scarcely any adequate idea of the successive dates of this
winning of the world. Long before history dawned man was
everywhere. As Voltaire said of America, we should be no more
surprised to find men there than to find flies.[1]

Social Differentiation. — Taking the animal origin of man and his
monophyletic development as established by the labors of Darwin,
Huxley, Haeckel, and many other biologists of the highest rank, the
problem is to explain the origin and genesis of human society. We
have already seen how the one differential attribute — incipient
reason — removed the chief barrier to indefinite expansion and
enabled that most favored race to overspread the globe. But the
transition from Pithecanthropus to Homo was attended with a
large number of other modifications, some of them physical, others
social. It was during this period that the principal steps toward
the erect posture were taken. I shall not attempt to describe these
steps here.[2] It was also at this time that the transition took place
from a purely herbivorous and frugivorous to a largely carnivorous
life. These were profound anatomical and physiological modifications, but not difficult to account for as the necessary result of
continued brain development. From the sociological point of view
the origin of the family, which also occurred during this period, is
even more significant. Among animals, the mother at least, often
knows her young, and with apes there is probably a somewhat general recognition of the nearest kinship relations. With primitive
man this was carried further and the members of the kinship group
came to be closely cemented together into what may be called
the family. This simply means the parents and children, but as the
children become parents in turn it includes these children of the
second generation, and then of the third, and so on, until the family
or kinship group becomes so large that it cannot longer hold together.

---

[1] " Œuvres complètes," Vol. XVI, 1784, p. 37.

[2] I made my first contribution to this subject in 1881, entitled " Pre-social Man."
Abstract of Transactions of the Anthropological Society of Washington for 1880 and
1881, Washington, 1881, pp. 68–71. This paper was expanded to make Chapter VI
of " Dynamic Sociology." Many others have ably discussed the subject.

It then breaks up in various ways and scatters, resulting in numerous families, or kinship groups. As we have seen, there could be no special first family or first pair because it is one long and slow development out of the animal state, but a primitive family or kinship group, taken in the abstract, may be regarded as a homogeneous and as yet undifferentiated unit. The name *horde* is loosely applied by ethnologists to something similar to this, and Durkheim has not inappropriately called this " social protoplasm." [1]

Complete separation into hordes represents the lowest and simplest form of group life, just above the animal stage, but differing from any form of gregariousness in animals in the more or less rational recognition of consanguineal relationship. At a higher stage, with better reasoning powers the group expanded into the clan, which was the largest group that the men of that stage could recognize as kindred. Thus far kinship was traced to the mother only, as no such fixed relations of the sexes existed as to make it possible to trace it from the father. In fact, parturition and not fecundation, was the test of parentage. Throughout the greater part of this stage the connection of the father with the reproductive function was unknown. There are races now living in which this is the case, the women attributing their pregnancy to some form of sorcery.[2] Reproduction is carried on under the influence of the reproductive forces solely without reference to function. As is well known, the transition to the patriarchal system, which has taken place in nearly all existing races, is effected through a fiction, called the couvade, in which the father feigns the labor of the mother, and is thus assumed to acquire the title to parentage. The astonishing prevalence of this apparently absurd custom only shows how deep-seated has always been the belief among the most primitive peoples in parthenogenesis, of which the numerous later religious myths of an " immaculate conception " are undoubtedly survivals.

It was also during this long maternal, or matriarchal period that language was formed, but as the hordes and clans scattered themselves over vast areas and lost all memory of one another and of their ancestry, each group developed a different language. At the same time customs, ceremonies, and religious rites and practices

---

[1] "De la Division du Travail Social," par Emile Durkheim, Paris, 1893, p. 189.

[2] Letourneau, *Revue de l'École d'Anthropologie de Paris*, Vol. IX, septembre, 1901, p. 280.

grew up, and these, too, would differ widely for each group. The enlargement of the groups was a function of the developing intellect, but there was a limit beyond which it could not go. The sole basis of group adhesion was kinship, and for everything not recognized as akin, there was no attachment, but intense aversion. The tribe was the maximum possible unit, and here exogamy, or the necessity of marrying outside of the narrower kinship group (clan, gens, etc.) was rigidly enforced, doubtless with the twofold object of preserving the vigor of the race and of keeping peace among the clans. The charm of sexual novelty also strongly favored this practice.

Such a state of things can scarcely be called society, and yet it contained all the germs of future society. This was the stage of differentiation. The primitive social protoplasm was beginning to work itself up into multiform shapes and to pervade all lands. It is easy to see that there was no lack of heterogeneity. Although the groups all had the same general pattern, they soon came to differ in all their details. Their languages were different, their customs varied within certain limits, their cults were all different, their fetishes, totems, gods, all bore different names. Only a philosopher looking at them from the highest standpoint could see any similarity among them. They themselves, completely blinded by the illusion of the near, saw nothing common, and regarded one another with the utmost detestation. This great moving, swarming mass of humanity, now become completely heterogeneous, would necessarily from time to time collide. One group would encroach upon the domain of another, and over a large part of the earth hostile tribes of men would find themselves in contact. For we are not limited for time to work out these results. We know that either man, or the animal from which man was directly developed, occupied many parts of the Old World in early Quaternary time. Geologists estimate this time at anywhere from 200,000 to 500,000 years. But 100,000 years would seem to be all the time that the most exacting could demand in which to realize any required transformation. The assumption, therefore, of a polyphyletic origin of man is wholly unnecessary in order to account for the required degree of differentiation and heterogeneity.

This period of social differentiation represents that idyllic stage of comparative peace and comfort to which ethnologists sometimes refer as preceding the era of strife and war between more developed races. In all probability the pre-human animal was a denizen of some tropical clime, and many facts point to Southern Asia as the region which saw the dawn of the human race. Nothing more definite than this can be said with any confidence, and even this is not certain. But that it was somewhere in the tropics of the Old World seems a tolerably safe assumption. Here amid natural abundance and under friendly skies, living like animals, but with sufficient intelligence to outwit and evade the larger carnivores, capable of so far modifying the environment as to escape the fate of other species that overstep the habitat to which they have become adapted, inchoate man could reproduce with great rapidity and a sufficient number of those born could live to the age of maturity to cause an increase of population in a geometrical progression. Collision could be avoided by migration, and peace prolonged during a great period.

The duration of this idyllic period depended principally on position. Those who wandered far could maintain their independence of others much longer than those who clung to the immediate center of dispersion. Certain races that worked off farther and farther into remote regions or even islands, remained wholly unmolested and continued their simple half-animal existence unchanged by contact with other races. Some such exist to-day, and it is from their study that we gain an insight into this truly primitive life of man. But those who did not migrate far came sooner into contact with others on account of the rapidly increasing numbers of men in all the groups. It was therefore in these regions that social differentiation ceased first, and the succeeding stages of human history earliest supervened upon the one described.

Without insisting upon close ethnological distinctions I propose to use chiefly the sufficiently vague and comprehensive term *race* as a general designation for all the different kinds of social groups that were formed during the process of social differentiation. We shall therefore be dealing essentially with the races of men.

Social Integration. — Prolonged as may have been the era of social differentiation with its halcyon days and wild semi-animal freedom, it could not in the nature of things always last, and as already remarked, its close came much earlier in the general region from which the human race originally swarmed forth to people the whole earth. Here the different races, now fully formed, and having lost all trace or tradition of any common origin, and acquired different languages, customs, arts, cults, and religions, first began to encroach upon one another and finally more or less to crowd and jostle together.   Regarding one another as so many totally different orders of beings, every race became the bitter enemy of every other, and therefore on the approach of one race toward another there was no course open but that of war.   The proximity of hostile races was a powerful spur to invention, attention being chiefly turned to the production of the means of offense and defense.   Success in war depended then, as it does to-day, on the mechanical superiority of the instruments of warfare, far more than on personal prowess.   A warlike spirit developed, and ambitious chiefs began to vie with each other for the mastery.

At first sight this might seem to have nothing to do with social integration.   In biology integration is the coördination and sub-ordination of the tissues, structures, and organs of an organism, so that they constitute an integer or whole.   There is here also both differentiation and integration, but in the process of development both these take place together, though of course there must be dif-ferentiation in order that there be integration.   It is so also in society, and our era of differentiation is somewhat of an abstrac-tion, in order clearly to grasp the nature of this process.   The human race began as an undifferentiated group, the horde, con-taining all the elements of the most developed society.   This group first differentiated, somewhat in the manner described.   At length a process of integration began.   We have seen how the former took place.   We are now to inquire by what process and according to what principle the latter was accomplished.   At the very outset it is important to note that this principle is none other than that by which all organization takes place, viz., synergy.   We have the antagonistic forces at work here as everywhere, and we shall see that the entire process is identical with that which formed star sys-tems, chemical systems, and organic forms.   We shall see all the steps in this process, and in many respects social phenomena are not only more clear and patent than are other classes of phenomena, but they actually illuminate the latter, and give us a firmer grasp of the exact workings of this principle on the lower planes.

The Struggle of Races. — Gumplowicz and Ratzenhofer have abun-dantly and admirably proved that the genesis of society as we see it and know it has been through the struggle of races.   I do not hope to add anything to their masterly presentation of this truth, which is without any question the most important contribution thus far made to the science of sociology. We at last have a true key to the solution of the question of the origin of society. It is not all, but it is the foundation of the whole, and while the edifice of sociology must be built upon it, its full recognition and comprehension will demolish all the cheap and worthless rookeries that have occupied the same ground. It is the only scientific explanation that has been offered of the facts and phenomena of human history. It proceeds from a true natural principle which is applicable to man everywhere, and which is in harmony with all the facts of ethnology and anthropology. Finally, this principle proves to be a universal one, and is the one on which are also explained all other natural phenomena. If I succeed in contributing anything to the subject it will consist in pointing out this truth and showing that the struggle of races is simple and typical social synergy and that it is the particular way in which synergy as a cosmic principle operates in the social world.

Conquest and Subjugation. — The first step in the struggle of races is that of the conquest of one race by another. Among races that have pushed their boundaries forward until they meet and begin to overlap war usually results. If one race has devised superior weapons or has greater strategic abilities than the other it will triumph and become a conquering race. The other race drops into the position of a conquered race. The conquering race holds the conquered race down and makes it tributary to itself. At the lowest stages of this process there was practical extermination of the conquered race. The Hebrews were scarcely above this stage in their wars upon the Canaanites but that seems to have been a special outburst of savagery in a considerably advanced race. The lowest savages are mostly cannibals. After the carnivorous habit had been formed the eating of human flesh was a natural consequence of the struggle of races. The most primitive wars were scarcely more than hunts, in which man was the mutual game of both contending parties. But at a later and higher stage head hunting, cannibalism, and the extermination of the conquered race, were gradually replaced by different forms of slavery. Success in conquering weaker races tended to develop predatory or military races, and the art of organizing armies received special attention. Such armies were at length used to make war on remote races, who were thus conquered and held under strong military power. Here the conquered would so greatly outnumber the conquering that extermination would be impracticable. The practice was then to preserve the conquered race and make it tributary to the wealth of the conquering race. Prisoners of war were enslaved, but the mass of the people was allowed to pay tribute.

Social Karyokinesis. — Lilienfeld [1] has likened the process which takes place through conquest to fertilization in biology, comparing the conquering race to the spermatozoa and the conquered race to the ovum, the former active and aggressive, the latter passive and submitting, resulting in a crossing of strains. Similarly Ratzenhofer [2] compares this race amalgamation to conjugation in biology, and says that hordes and clans multiply by division. There certainly is a remarkable " analogy " between the process called karyokinesis in biology and that which goes on in societies formed by the conquest of a weaker by a stronger race. This process has been fully described and illustrated by both Gumplowicz and Ratzenhofer, and they not only agree as to what the successive steps are but also as to the order in which they uniformly take place. I therefore need only enumerate these steps and refer the reader to the works of these authors, especially to Gumplowicz's " Rassenkampf," and Ratzenhofer's " Sociologische Erkenntnis." The following are these steps arranged in their natural order: 1. *Subjugation* of one race by another. 2. Origin of *caste*. 3. Gradual mitigation of this condition, leaving a state of great individual, social, and political *inequality*. 4. Substitution for purely military subjection of a form of *law*, and origin of the idea of legal *right*. 5. Origin of the *state*, under which all classes have both rights and duties. 6. Cementing of the mass of heterogeneous elements into a more or less homogeneous *people*. 7. Rise and development of a sentiment of *patriotism* and formation of a *nation*.

I shall content myself with a few comments on each of these phases and especially on points that do not seem to me to have been adequately brought out.

Caste. — By conquest two different races are brought into close contact, but they are so unlike that no assimilation is possible. None is desired or attempted. The society, if it can be called such,

1 " Zur Vertheidigung der Organischen Methode in der Sociologie," von Paul v. Lilienfeld, Berlin, 1898, p. 50.
2 " Die Sociologische Erkenntnis," Leipzig, 1898, p. 109.

is polarized. The conquering race looks down with contempt upon the conquered race and compels it to serve it in various ways. The conquered race maintains its race hatred, and while sullenly submitting to the inevitable, refuses to recognize anything but the superiority of brute force. This was the origin of caste, and the two mutually antagonistic and defiant races represent the opposite poles of the social spindle. History shows how difficult it is completely to eradicate the spirit of caste.

Inequality. — The inequality of the two races is, however, something more than an inequality of rank. The races were primarily (*i.e.*, before the conquest) thoroughly heterogeneous. They spoke different languages, worshiped different gods, practiced different rites, performed different ceremonies, possessed different customs, habits, and institutions, and the conquered race would die sooner than surrender any of these. The conquering race professed absolute contempt for all these qualities in their subjects, but were powerless to transform them into their own.

Law. — The difficulty, cost, and partial failure attending the constant and unremitting exercise of military power over all the acts of the conquered race, ultimately becomes a serious charge upon the conquering race. For a while, flush with the pride of victory, this race persists in meting out punishments to all offenders against its authority, but sooner or later such personal government grows wearisome, and some change is demanded. It is found that authority may be generalized, and that rules can be adopted for the repression of certain classes of acts, such as are most frequently committed. When this is found to be economical, still larger groups of conduct are made the subject of general regulation. By the continued extension of this economical policy a general system of such rules is ultimately, though gradually, worked out, and the foundation is laid for a government by law. So long as the law is not violated a certain degree of liberty is conceded to the subordinate race, and the performance of acts not in violation of law comes to be recognized as a right.

Origin of the State. — There are always great natural differences in men. In civilized societies everybody knows how immensely individuals differ in ability and character. We naturally assume that with savages and low races this is not the case, but this is certainly a mistake. The natural inequalities of uncivilized races are probably fully as great as among civilized races, and they probably exert a still greater relative influence in all practical affairs. For the complicated machinery of a high civilization makes it possible to cover up mediocrity and to smother talent, so that the places that men hold are very rude indices indeed to their fitness or their true merits. In savage life this is not the case, and a chief is almost certain to be a man of force and relative ability of the grade required at that stage of development.

In a conquered race such individual differences are likely to make themselves felt. The assumption all along is that the races considered are not primarily widely unlike. The issue of battle depends only to a small extent on real differences of mind or character. It may be merely accidental, or due to the neglect of the conquered race to cultivate the arts of war. In all other respects it may be even superior to the conquering race. The latter therefore often has to do with its social equals in everything pertaining to the life of either group. The difficulty of enforcing law in a community constituted as we have described must be apparent. With such an intense internal polarization of interests, the conquering race would find it difficult or impossible to frame laws to suit all cases. It could not understand the conquered race definitely enough to be successful even in securing its own interests. In a word, the conquering race needs the assistance of the conquered race in framing and carrying out measures of public policy. This it is never difficult to secure. A large number of the members of the subject race always sooner or later accept the situation and are willing to help in establishing and maintaining order. The only basis of such order is the creation of correlative rights and duties under the law. This can only be secured through concessions on the part of the master race to the subject race and the enlistment of the best elements of the latter in the work of social reorganization. This, in fact, is what is sooner or later always done. The conquering race may hold out doggedly for a long time in a harsh military policy of repression and oppression, but it is only a question of time when experience alone will dictate a milder policy in its own interest, and the basis of compromise will at last be reached. The two principles involved are both egoistic, but equilibrate each other and contribute jointly to the result. These are economy on the part of the governing class and resignation on the part of the governed class. These produce concessions from the former and assistance from the latter. The result is that form of social organization known as the state.

Formation of a People. — A people is a synthetic creation. It is not a mechanical mixture. It is not either of the antagonistic races and it is not both of them. It is a new product evolved out of these elements through precisely the same process that goes on at every stage in cosmic evolution at which its successive products appear. Only the details of the process are different here from those at any other stage, but this is as true at any other stage as it is here. It is the details only that differ, the process is always the same. But there is no cosmic product in which the detailed operations involved in its formation are as plainly to be seen and traced as they are in the genesis of a people. We have all the elements before us. Two antagonistic races of nearly equal social value, but one of which has by some means succeeded in subjugating the other and is striving to secure the greatest return for the cost involved in so doing. After a long trial of the stern policy of repression the physically superior race tires of the strain and relaxes in the direction of general law, of calling in the aid of the best elements of the weaker race, and at length reaches the stage marked by the formation of a state. At this stage in the process of social karyokinesis the social idants mutually approach the equatorial plate and have already commenced coquetting for a nearer approach. Concession and resignation, compromise and mutual assistance, proceed apace. Animosity abates and toleration increases. A number of potent agencies combine to accelerate the process. The most important of these is *interest*. It is a truth of the deepest significance that *interest unites while principle divides*. What all the theory of race superiority backed by the military power could not accomplish, personal interest and individual advantage secure. The looker-on is apt to concentrate his attention upon the race struggle and the political principles involved and forget that there are other forces at work. These large issues represent the general mass motion of the system and involve only fôrce. But the stage of concentration has now been reached when the most effective activities are molecular, so to speak, and constitute energy. The stage of extensive activity has passed and that of intensive activity has supervened. The individuals of both races have before them the problem of maintaining their existence. If they are of a sufficiently high development they are also interested in the accumulation of wealth. In all this, however bitter their animosities may have once been, each needs the help of the rest. Every man is an aid to every other. Business enterprises are launched and must be supported in order to succeed. When a member of the ruling race establishes a business he must have customers, and the custom of a member of the subject class is as good as one of his own class. He thus becomes dependent upon the lower class, and as that class normally far outnumbers the other, that dependence is increased. In order for the society to flourish and the state to be solvent and strong, arts and industries must spring up everywhere and commercial activity must be fostered and encouraged. The division of labor takes place ramifying in all directions regardless of race lines. Business organizations, corporations, and combinations are formed, based on character and fitness and not on race distinctions.

Propinquity in such matters is a far more potent influence than race. The influence of men upon one another, other things equal, is inversely as the distance. It is those immediately around that interest and assist. Every one, I think, has observed that the particular persons with whom, though it be by mere chance, he is thrown into immediate contact, assume an importance greatly in excess of their actual merits. There is something in the presence of another person that completely alters our attitude towards him. What we might say of some one at a distance we would not venture to say to his face. I call this principle *the sanctity of the second person*. What Dr. Ross calls "the morality of accomplices" [1] is a special case under this broader principle. But we may apply it to the problem before us and we find that it is a leading factor in social karyokinesis. The proud scion of a conquering race meets a bright representative of the race he has regarded as inferior and finds that he may be much his superior in some things, or at least that he can and is willing to be useful to him in the carrying out of cherished objects, and his race prejudice rapidly melts away and he joins with him in some enterprise that contributes to general social development.

But interest is not the only cementing principle. There are many other operations which at a certain stage of development inspire intense activities and possess a powerful socializing influence. Such

[1] "Social Control," p. 348.

P

are many of the ways of pursuing pleasure, knowledge, art, science, and philanthropy, through voluntary organizations. As these are forms of association that are based exclusively on personal qualities — affability, zeal, skill, talent, etc. — and not on race differences, they tend to break down race barriers and unify mankind through the recognition of true personal excellence.

Finally, the time usually comes sooner or later when the state needs the physical and moral support of the lower elements, when outside invaders threaten to overrun and destroy it and plant an alien race over even the race that boasts of its own conquests. At such times the more numerous subject class becomes the main dependence and to it the new state usually owes its preservation. When this is the case two other unifying sentiments arise — a dim sense of gratitude on the part of the ruling classes and a lively sense of pride on the part of the subject race. These work together to the same general end as all the other influences named.

Passing over many other equating and assimilating influences, upon which, like some of those here enumerated, far too little stress has been laid by those who have worked out the law of the struggle of races, I must content myself with the mention of one other, which, though in fact perhaps the most vital of all, has, singularly enough, been almost totally overlooked. This is what I shall call the *social chemistry* of the race struggle, and which begins with the primary conquest itself and continues through the entire assimilative period. In a war of conquest between two savage or barbaric races the women of the conquered race are always appropriated by the conquerors. There is never any such race antipathy as to interfere with the free play of the reproductive forces. Aside from purposes of lust, there exists a certain intuitive sense that the mixture of blood conduces to race vigor. It is an extension of the rule of exogamy and a survival of one of the earliest of human race instincts. Historic examples are numerous, the most celebrated, perhaps, being that of the rape of the Sabines. That this practice was in full force among the Israelites is amply attested by Scriptural passages.[1]

There is another instinct that tends in the same direction, and which may be called the charm of sexual novelty. This is one aspect of a very comprehensive principle which cannot be discussed

[1] See especially Numbers xxxi; Deuteronomy xxi.

here, but which will be treated in its proper place. We only need to note the fact, so vital to the present discussion, that between races that are not too different from each other, when brought into contact from any cause the sexes are strongly attracted to each other. Men are charmed by the women of a different race, and women are not less strongly drawn toward alien men. This sentiment is heightened by war. Whatever may be the degree of race hatred between the contending races, this has no effect to cool the ardor of the sexes. On a low plane of culture the women of the conquered race are systematically appropriated by the men of the conquering race. Nor are the women wholly averse to this. Although they may detest the race that has subjugated their own, there is a glamour attached to the successful military hero that powerfully attracts women under all circumstances. Race miscegenation therefore begins immediately, but it does not cease after the subjugation is complete. Throughout all the stages of social karyokinesis that we have been considering it is constantly going on. All attempts to keep the superior race pure fail utterly, and by the time the state has been established the majority of the inhabitants have in their veins the blood of both races. The formation of a *people*, therefore, is not only a political, civil, and social process, but it is also largely a physiological process.

It is not until after all these steps have been taken, occupying a long period varying in different cases, that a new race is created through the blending of the two, originally hostile and antagonistic races, the active, conquering race having, as it were, fecundated the passive conquered race, introduced the elements that give rise to new processes, and, by a cross fertilization of cultures, created a new social structure. This new social structure is a *people*.

The Nation. — All past animosities are now forgotten and the people thus created have acquired a sense of unity and solidarity. There begins to be formed a national sentiment. A deep-seated affection grows up for both the people and the territory, and individuals come to feel that they have what they call a *country*. This affection is filial from the sense that the country has given them birth, and in most languages the name by which it is known denotes paternity — *patria, patrie, Vaterland.* The sentiment that it inspires receives a name derived from the same root, and is called *patriotism*. This sentiment is popularly regarded as a very high one, but it is **by**

the same logic that places maternal love on such an exalted throne,
when it is only an animal instinct and common to all mammals at
least, also to birds, and probably to many reptiles.   Condorcet loved
the country that persecuted him and drove him to suicide, and in
one passage[1] he very clearly describes the sentiment of patriotism,
giving some of the philosophical grounds on which it rests.   But it
is not a very exalted sentiment and belongs to the same class as that
by which animals become " wonted " to the particular spot where
they.have been raised with no reference to its superiority over other
places.   It may also be called collective egotism, but as Spencer
remarks, " while excess of egotism is everywhere regarded as a fault,
excess of patriotism is nowhere regarded as a fault."[2]   Comte relegated it to the theological stage, its place being taken in the positive
stage by humanitarianism,[3] Bagehot called it "territorial sectarian-
ism," and Dr. Johnson characterized it as "the last refuge of a
scoundrel."

But whatever its rank as a human affection, patriotism plays an
important rôle in the process of social assimilation.   It is the basis
of the national sentiment, or feeling of social solidarity, that is
essential to this last step in the process of social karyokinesis.   It
marks the disappearance of the last vestige of the initial social
dualism.   It means the end of the prolonged race struggle.   It is
the final truce to the bitter animosities that had reigned in the
group.   The antagonistic forces have spent themselves, social
equilibrium is restored, and one more finished product of social
synergy is presented to the world.

Compound Assimilation. — In the above meager sketch I have
described one isolated and typical case of the simplest form of social
assimilation by conquest, struggle, compromise, and equilibration.
It is not of course to be supposed that all cases will conform in all
respects to this norm, but it is not believed that there have been
deviations from it that can be called generic.   But what is specially
to be noted is that such a simple case is theoretical, and that in fact
all the known historic examples are complex or compound.   By this
I mean that social assimilation is a process of social aggregation or
recompounding, and thus conforms in this respect also to the uni-

---

[1] "Tableau historique des Progrès de l'Esprit humain," Paris, 1900, p. 247.
[2] "Study of Sociology," New York, 1880, p. 206.
[3] "Politique Positive," Vol. II, p. 147.

versal process going on in nature. I have assumed two coördinate
social groups as units of aggregation, coming into collision with the
results described. Such cases must occasionally occur and for
them the description given is accurate. But it must be remembered
that these collisions and conjugations of races have been going on
ever since man emerged from the animal stage. None of the groups
of which we have any historical knowledge are thus simple. The
earliest conjugations were doubtless peaceful. Hordes coalesced
into clans and clans into tribes during the early idyllic period. The
struggle did not begin till by the fiction of the couvade the patriarchal system succeeded the age of motherright. Doubtless there
have been numberless cases of the clash of patriarchal tribes as simple as the one described. But the historic cases enumerated by
Gumplowicz, Ratzenhofer, Vaccaro, and De Greef are all later and
between compound races. The process has to be gone through with
over and over again. A nation is fully developed according to this
process, when another more vigorous nation that has been similarly
formed sweeps down upon it and subdues it. Then the entire series
of steps has to be repeated on a higher plane, and all these elements
must be again assimilated by the same slow process. A new state,
a new people, a new nation, have to be created by the same synergetic
principle. But even this is not safe. While it was incubating other
states, peoples, nations, were also slowly coming into being, destined, by further conjuncture, to become the rivals of the other, and
so on forever. Races, states, peoples, nations are always forming,
always aggressing, always clashing and clinching, and struggling
for the mastery, and the long, painful, wasteful, but always fruitful
gestation must be renewed and repeated again and again. Nor need
the social units always be of the same order. Conjuncture is as
likely to take place between races of different orders as between
those of the same order. For example the conquering race may
have resulted from a third or fourth assimilation, while the conquered race may only represent a second assimilation, and have
therefore acquired an inferior degree of social efficiency. An extreme
of this case is where a so-called enlightened nation occupies a region
inhabited by savages. The former may have undergone twenty
assimilations while the latter may be still almost in their idyllic
stage, or Durkheim's stage of simple segmentation. In the case of
the United Kingdom of Great Britain and Ireland, for example, it is

easy to trace five or six assimilations almost within historic time, and yet the last assimilation is so complete that, except in parts of Ireland, loyalty and patriotism are at high water mark. Nearly the same is true of France and Germany, but the case is very different in Austria. Here the process of assimilation is incomplete, but it is progressing appreciably. But the several races that are now undergoing social assimilation in the Austrian empire — Magyars, Czechs, Poles, Styrians, etc. — are for the most part old nations that have each long ago gone through the process, and doubtless, if their entire history could be traced, any one of them would be found to be a social unit of an advanced order.

The objection may be raised that all that has been said does not apply to races so different that they will not mix, and one of which is so inferior to the other that subjugation is very easy. The principal answer to this objection has already been given, viz., that these are cases in which social units of very different orders of assimilation happen to collide. The so-called low races of men have very little social efficiency. Social efficiency, as shown in Chapter III, is the result of achievement. It was impossible in that chapter to explain by what process human achievement is made possible. We can now see that social achievement is only possible through human institutions, and all the higher and more developed institutions are the outcome of social assimilation. Those social units called states, peoples, and nations are of all orders, depending upon the number of assimilations. Every assimilation is a fresh cross fertilization of cultures, and renders the resulting social unit more and more stable and solid. That is, it gives it more and more social efficiency, and it thereby becomes increasingly capable of achievement in the full sense of my definition. The most efficient of all races are those that lie directly in the track of civilization, and which have never had their connection with the past cut off or interrupted. Through this continuity of the social germ plasm, accompanied by repeated crossing of the highest strains, the maximum social efficiency and the maximum achievement are secured. Races that have lived wholly off this line of historic development, that have been, as it were, side-tracked, that have been long undisturbed and never subjugated, have only slightly felt the power of social synergy, and have been left far behind in the race. It is not so much their mental inferiority, though mind obeys the Lamarckian law of exercise, and is strengthened by every fresh effort put forth. But these races possess all the elements of development, and have only lacked the opportunity which comes only through the struggle of races and repeated social assimilations.

The only kind of social assimilation that is increasingly fertile is that between races that occupy substantially the same social position. The case is very similar to that of sexual reproduction. For successful crossing the individuals must belong to the same species and not be too different. With these limitations the more they differ the better. It must be true crossing of stocks and not hybridization, or the crossing of different species. The social groups must, so to speak, belong to the same species. The difference between a modern civilized race and a savage race may be called a specific difference, and while physiologically, the individuals may be perfectly fertile *inter se*, the races as such can only hybridize, with much the same results as attend hybridization in animals.

Pacific Assimilation. — A final question remains. Is this, then, the only possible kind of social assimilation? Is it only through war, conquest, and subjugation that social structures must be formed? The answer is yes and no, according to the point of view. But the only answer needed here is to say that the purpose of this chapter and, indeed, of Part II of this work, as its title denotes, is to study the *genesis* of society. Pure sociology need scarcely go beyond this, although it is not altogether confined to it. The object has not been here to show what man in the social state may and will do. The object has been to show how man entered the social state and what the social state is that he has entered. Whatever may happen in society after it is fully formed, the truth remains that thus far there has been only one way by which society has been formed, and that is through social assimilation by conquest, struggle, caste, inequality, resignation, concession, compromise, equilibration, and final interaction, coöperation, miscegenation, coalescence, unification, consolidation, and solidarization.

But it may as well be said that there are other forms of social assimilation, late derivative, pacific forms, that have already begun to operate in advanced societies, and that may ultimately supersede the original, spontaneous, natural method. It may well be that the one great historic line of social evolution has well-nigh reached its term in the direction of forcible consolidation, and that an era of peaceful rivalry and friendly emulation is about to be inaugurated, but the world has evidently not yet reached the point where war shall cease and where the millennium shall be ushered in. We shall see in the next chapter why this is so, and shall consider certain reasons for thinking, and perhaps for hoping, that it may never reach that point.

Our chapter is already too long. To consider adequately all the supplementary forms of social assimilation would unduly extend it, and in view of the fact that these are the forms commonly treated, while the primary, original, and true natural form has been neglected except by the few authors named, there seems no need of entering into the more detailed internal movements in society, most of which after all are simply the normal and legitimate consequences of the great struggle in its later modified phases.

It is hoped that the considerations set forth in this chapter will be sufficient to furnish a just conception of what constitutes social statics, and that however much sociologists may differ with regard to the classification and terminology of sociology, it need not longer be said that the views of those who recognize a science or subscience of social mechanics, treating of social statics and social dynamics, are vaguely and confusedly entertained. To my own mind it would be impossible to conceive of a more definite branch of science than that of social statics as here presented. It cannot be confounded with any other science or domain of natural law, and we shall see in the next chapter that it is as clearly marked off from social dynamics as from all other sciences, although it is its natural prelude and its study is absolutely essential to the study of social dynamics, which cannot be understood without it as a basis.

Postscript. — This chapter was written as it now stands from Dec. 8 to 29, 1901. On Feb. 11, 1902, I listened to the address of Professor W. H. Holmes as retiring president of the Anthropological Society of Washington on the origin, development, and probable destiny of the races of men. Although working in the same building with him I had never conversed with him on these subjects and had no idea of what his views were. I was therefore both surprised and gratified at the broad philosophical grounds taken in his address, and doubly so as they harmonized so completely with my own views as already expressed in this chapter. The reader of his address and of the chapter, in the absence of this statement, might well infer that we had compared notes and aimed only to present the same truth from our two points of view, the anthropological and the sociological. We have indeed discussed the subject since the delivery of his address, but he has had no more occasion for modifying his views than have I for modifying mine, and neither his address nor my chapter has undergone any change. Notwithstanding this complete harmony, I freely confess that the anthropological view so ably presented by Professor Holmes, greatly illuminates my sociological presentation, and with his courteous sanction I am most happy to be able to embody in this postscript to the chapter so much of his address as bears most directly upon the vital questions involved. His address is now (Aug. 15, 1902) passing through the press, to appear in the forthcoming number (July–September) of the *American Anthropologist,* and he has generously allowed me to make the following extract from the proofs now

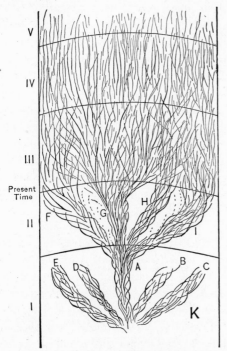

in his hands, including one of the numerous figures, prepared with the skill and finish characteristic of one of America's first artists, as he is also one of America's leading anthropologists, geologists, and men of science — rare combination in these days of scientific specialization.

I wish now to combine in a single diagram (K) a summary of my conception of the development of the species and the races from the period of specialization of the anthropoids up to the present time. The side lines in this diagram stand for the limits of the world within which the branching tree of the *Hominidæ* (A) springs up. The horizontal lines connecting

DIAGRAM K. — Showing origin of the genus *Homo* (A) in Tertiary time, separation into races through isolation in Post-Tertiary time (F, G, H, I), and theoretic blending of all forms in future time. The separate lines in each column represent variant groups parting and again more or less fully coalescing.

across, mark the periods by means of which we separate the stages of development.

The first period (1) is that which witnessed the specialization of the group of creatures (A) from which man sprang. It may be regarded as corresponding somewhat closely to the Tertiary period as formulated by geologists. We know not the exact number of closely related branches at that time, but it is held that the prospective human stem flourished and rose above the others. In the diagram the collateral branches B, C, D, E, are left undeveloped in order that *Homo* (A) may have a clear field — in order that we may illustrate more clearly the manner in which this group, according to our best interpretation, spread from its natal district and occupied the habitable world.

That the home of the human precursor was, at this stage of his development, restricted in area is assumed on reasonable grounds. The apes and monkeys of to-day, which are believed to correspond in grade of development to the human stock of the natal period, are not widely distributed, but occupy very restricted areas and such as are particularly suited to their arboreal habits and their rather delicate constitutions. There is no reason to believe that man at a corresponding stage was more hardy, more enterprising, or more widely scattered.

In the diagram, therefore, the stem A is made narrow below, widening upward, thus suggesting expansion of area with increase in numbers, energy, and intelligence. This expansion was, no doubt, very slow and may or may not have extended to the farthest limits of the land area occupied, but it was prophetic of the greater expansions to be realized in period II. We cannot know in just what part of the world these events took place, just where the prehuman group was transmuted into the human. It may have been in Europe, Asia, Africa, Eurasia, Eurafrica, Lemuria, or America, but this does not matter here. We reach the conclusion that at or near the close of Tertiary time (period I) the change occurred and that upright, self-conscious man took his place permanently in the van of progress. We conceive further that, about this time, the continents assumed approximately their present dimensions and relations and that this creature man, breaking over the barriers that formerly hedged him in, was ready to engage in their conquest. The simple, initial, integrate period of his career had now closed, and a period of marvelous expansion supervened (period II).

Spreading gradually into the various continental areas the incipient human groups, as yet reasonably homogeneous in character, became widely separated. Some were quite completely isolated and went their separate ways, becoming sharply demarcated from the rest. Others less fully isolated continued to intermingle along the margins of the areas occupied, so that gradations of characters occur, and in some cases the resulting hybrid peoples have probably occupied separate areas long enough to become well-established varieties. Three or four groups only became so widely separated and fixed in physical characters that students are agreed to call them separate races, but these comprise the great body of mankind.

The line marking the close of period II stands for the present time, and

F, G, H, and I are the races now in evidence. Let us consider what is happening along this line to-day. The end of the second period — the isolated specializing period — has come for the races, and changes of a momentous kind are being initiated. Man has spread and occupied the world, and the resulting isolations and partial isolations on continent and island of peoples having meager artificial means of transportation, have brought about, directly or indirectly, the variations called races; but the period of group isolation and consequent race specialization is at an end. In the last few hundred years the sea-going ship and the railway have been invented and the extremes of the world are no farther apart than were the opposite shores of a good-sized island when, a little while ago, all men went afoot. The period of differentiation is closed forever and the period of universal integration is upon us. We do not see how rapid these movements are, but contrasted with the changes of earlier days they are as a hurricane compared with the morning zephyr. The continent of America has changed its inhabitants as in the twinkling of an eye, and Asia, Africa, Australia, and the islands of the Pacific are in the throes of race disintegration. To-day each man may go two hundred and forty times around the world in his short lifetime. A single individual may be the parent of progeny in every important land area of the world; and this is only the beginning — the first few hundred years — of a period to which millions must be assigned. Then how shall we project the lines of the diagram into the future? There can be but one answer.

Very briefly we may outline the inevitable course of human history. In period III the races will fade out and disappear as the combined result of miscegenation and the blotting out of the weaker branches. The world will be filled to overflowing with a generalized race in which the dominating blood will be that of the race that to-day has the strongest claim physically and intellectually to take possession of all the resources of the land and the sea. Blood and culture will be cosmopolitan. Man, occupying every available foot of land on the globe, will be a closer unit than he was on the day far back in period I, when, in a limited area hidden away in the broad expanse of some unidentified continent, the agencies of specialization first shaped up the species.[1]

To the fully developed and completely emancipated man of our time the races of men, and even the human race at large, seem coarse, backward, benighted, uninteresting, and repugnant. It is only from that higher ground of the philosopher that they acquire an interest and become an object worthy of thought and attention. This is almost wholly due to the *possibilities* that they embody. When we contemplate the relatively brief time that man has occu-

[1] " Sketch of the Origin, Development, and probable Destiny of the Races of Men." Address of Professor William H. Holmes, delivered Feb. 11, 1902, as Retiring President of the Anthropological Society of Washington. *American Anthropologist*, N. S., Vol. IV, No. 3, July–September, 1902, pp. 369–391 (see pp. 387–390).

pied this planet, as shown by the cosmological perspective (*supra*, pp. 38–40), and connect it with what he has already achieved (see Chapters III, XIX, XX), we have a basis for reflection upon the future. It is common in all such speculations to refer to the evidence in favor of an ultimate decline of life on the globe, due to the gradual withdrawal of the sun's heat and the general conditions of dissolution as the sure sequence of evolution taught by Herbert Spencer. Without questioning the general soundness of this view in the abstract, it is so frequently brought in that it seems proper to point out that certain important truths are usually overlooked. Conscious humanity has occupied about one five hundredth part of the time since the beginning of the Tertiary. There is certainly no probability that the conditions of existence on the globe will begin to decline within a period less than the whole of Tertiary time. The culminating point is at least as remote as three million years from now. But we can scarcely conceive of one million years. That length of time is for all the purposes of a sane philosophy infinite. Any speculation beyond it is utterly devoid of practicality. We may therefore for all practical purposes calculate that physical conditions will *always* be at least as favorable as they are at present.

These reflections have been called forth by the short concluding part of Professor Holmes's address, which indeed was omitted from the address as delivered, but which now appears. It does no harm for the sake of a symmetrical scheme, to look forward to the end, but, for the reasons I have given, this must be regarded as purely theoretical and speculative, and we may concentrate our attention upon that period which is now rapidly approaching, which is no longer a speculation, but is a legitimate and irresistible deduction from all the facts, the period in which the races of men shall have all become assimilated, and when there shall be but one race of men — the human race. That period, as I have said, is likely to last at least a million years, probably as many as three million, the assumed duration of Cenozoic time, and possibly much longer. Let any one attempt to figure to himself the possibilities involved in such a truth!

CHAPTER XI

SOCIAL DYNAMICS

As social statics has to do with the creation of an equilibrium among the forces of human society, so it may be inferred in advance that social dynamics must have to do with some manner of disturbance in the social equilibrium. But surely it cannot relate to the disruption or disintegration of the social structures that have been so slowly and painfully wrought by the rhythmic strife of social synergy. And as we found that neither the growth, the multiplication, nor the perfectionment of social structures involved any dynamic principle, we have yet to learn wherein essentially consists the condition that is truly dynamic. This should be postulated at the outset, as the necessary starting point in the treatment of social dynamics. This postulate may be stated in the following form: *In all departments of nature where the statical condition is represented by structures, the dynamic condition consists in some change in the type of such structures.* To revert to the illustration used in connection with the perfectionment of structures, an " improvement " in an invention must involve some additional principle on which .the apparatus works, so, in order to constitute a dynamic condition, a structure, whether cosmic, organic, or social, must undergo some change in its type, whereby its relations to the environment become different from those previously sustained.

It was pointed out in Chapter VI that the word *dynamic* was used in two senses, a broader and a narrower sense. In the broader sense it relates to force in general according to its etymology, and was there used in this sense in defining the term dynamic agent. In its narrower sense it implies a *movement*. This is the principal sense in which it is used in the concrete sciences. The difference between mere motion in bodies and such a movement consists in the fact that in the latter case it is predicated of structures, and the movement consists in the gradual change taking place in the type of these structures. The term has been so used in its application to chemistry, biology, psychology, economics, and sociology. It is in this sense that it will be used in this chapter. The process by which structures are produced is not a dynamic process. Structures represent a condition of equilibrium and are the normal result of the equilibration of conflicting forces. But no dynamic phenomena can take place until structures are formed. Just here is the fundamental distinction between dynamic and kinetic phenomena, which are so commonly confounded. The motions that take place prior to equilibration, the unrestrained motions in all things in their primitive state, are kinetic. But these produce nothing. They are lost. Unbridled forces running to waste or producing destructive effects upon all structures in their way are kinetic manifestations of force. They construct nothing. Construction is only possible through equilibration. Statics does not imply inactivity or quiescence. On the contrary, it represents increased intensity, and this is what constructs. Dynamic movements are confined to structures already formed and, as stated, consist in changes in the type of these structures. But the important fact to be noted is that not for one moment must the organic nature of the structure be lost or endangered. The change of type must be brought about without destroying or injuring the structure. It is a differential process and takes place by infinitesimal increments or changes. It may be compared to the process of petrifaction, in which every particle of the vegetable substance is replaced by an exactly equivalent particle of mineral substance, so that it is often impossible to distinguish the one from the other, the minutest structures and even the color being exactly reproduced.

This differential process is what characterizes evolution, and the contrast so often popularly made between evolution and revolution is the contrast between a truly dynamic process and a merely kinetic process which breaks up and destroys existing structures in order to make new ones. The structures destroyed by revolution are organic, i.e., genetic structures. It has taken ages to produce them through the secular process of social assimilation described in the last chapter. It is impossible to reproduce them, and all that can be done is to create artificial structures. This, in fact, is what is done in cases of complete revolution; though it may be doubted whether there ever was a complete revolution, and what have been called revolutions have only partially destroyed the previous structures. Very soon after they are over there results an effort to go back and gather

up every remnant of the former order and embody it in the new artificial structure.   After the frenzy is over it is soon seen that human
wisdom is inadequate artificially to replace the time-honored institutions which it has required ages to create, and a reaction usually
sets in, resulting in a return, temporary at least, to conditions as near
as possible to those that existed before the revolution.

SOCIAL PROGRESS

It is common to speak of order and progress as opposites, but an
attempt has been made to show that regressive tendencies are
dynamic as well as progressive ones.   I shall endeavor to show in
how far this is true and also what qualifications it requires.   For
the present it is sufficient to point out the true relation between
order and progress and to show in what the latter really consists.
Assuming that the differential changes that take place in the types
of social structures are advantageous or in the direction of structural advance, a dynamic movement becomes synonymous with
social progress.   The structure represents equilibrium, and as it
must remain intact and still constantly undergo change it represents
a moving equilibrium.   As change in the type of structure presupposes structure to be changed, it is clear that progress presupposes
order.   Order is therefore the necessary basis of progress, its essential condition.   This shows more clearly than any other view point
could do, not only why social statics must be taken into the account,
but also why in the treatment of social mechanics social statics must
precede social dynamics.   When their true relations are perceived it
becomes apparent that the latter cannot be understood until a clear
conception of the former has been gained.   But the literature of
sociology furnishes no clew whatever to these relations or to the
real nature of either.   Comte saw and said that progress is, as he
expressed it, "the development of order," [1] but that he really conceived the principle of social statics as set forth in the last chapter
there is no evidence in his works.   I shall in this chapter also show
that he did not properly conceive the nature of social dynamics,
although he defined it and treated it at great length.   Nor can it be

---

[1] " C'est ainsi que j'ai construit le grand aphorisme sociologique (*le progrès est le
développement de l'ordre*) sur lequel repose tout ce traité."   " Politique Positive,"
Vol. I, pp. 494–495.   In the second volume (p. 41) he repeats this aphorism and says
that he established it "pour lier partout les lois dynamiques aux lois statiques."

denied that his view of social dynamics as historical progress is both
true and vital.. It is not opposed to any other true view and does
not in the least conflict with what will be said in this chapter, but
it can scarcely be said to form a part of social mechanics in a scientific sense. Comte's able treatise on social dynamics, beginning
with the last chapter (51st lecture, p. 442) of Vol. IV of the "Positive Philosophy" and continuing through Vols. V and VI, is a masterly development of the doctrine of Condorcet, earlier formulated
by Leibnitz in the phrase that "the present is pregnant with the
future." But this does not show how social progress takes place,
i.e., the principle or principles through which progressive agencies
work. All these philosophers had a sort of prophetic ken which
enabled them to see in a vague way the truth of social progress, and
Comte's aphorism above quoted is a typical prophetic or poetic idea
as I defined it in Chapter V. It has the requisite vagueness and
will bear the closest analysis, but it explains nothing.

Although sociologists have never formulated the principle of social
statics, still most of their works deal with it because they treat of
social structures. They do not explain how social structures are
formed but they treat them as finished products. Their work is
precisely analogous to that of the systematist in botany or zoölogy
who describes species and regards them as unalterably fixed. In
biology it has now been learned that species are not fixed but variable, and that there has been a perpetual transmutation of species.
This is dynamic, as the other is static biology. And it is not necessary to give up the study of plants and animals, considered as finished products, merely because it has been discovered that they are
undergoing slow changes. It is just as easy and just as important
to describe and classify species as it was before the theory of transmutation was established. It is the same in sociology. Social
statics, like biological statics, is a theoretical science. It assumes
the fixity of human institutions in order to study them, abstracts
for the moment the idea of movement or change, and deals with
society at a given point of time. It takes, as it were, an instantaneous photograph of society, transfers it to the sociological laboratory, and studies it at leisure. That picture at least will not change,
and while the institutions themselves may be transforming, the one
thus stereotyped can be investigated at leisure. Or, reverting again
to biology, the statical sociologist may be compared to the naturalist,

who, although he may be an evolutionist, nevertheless secures his specimens in the traditional way and places them in his cabinet. A dried plant, a stuffed bird, a mounted butterfly or chloroformed beetle, is not going to change in his hands, and he may let the live things go on and change all they may, his specimens at least are fixed. In fact, however, all transformations, social as well as organic, are secular, and their movements can only be seen with the eye of reason, so that human institutions as well as vegetable and animal species are, for all purposes of investigation virtually fixed, and the simple knowledge that they are changing need not disturb their quiet study any more than the knowledge that the earth with all that is on it is swiftly flying through space need disturb the operations of men inhabiting its surface.

Nevertheless, the dynamic condition exists and much of the change is in the direction of progress. I am using the term *progress* here in the same sense that is given it in treating of organic forms. We saw in Chapter V that in nearly all departments of nature at the present stage in the history of this planet evolution is taking place, *i.e.*, things are changing by a series of steps which is an ascending and not a descending series. In general, the movement is in the direction of higher types of structure having greater differentiation and more complete integration of their parts. What is true of the organic world is true of human institutions. We have only to look back over the brief span of human history covered by the written records to see that this has been the case during the past two or three thousand years, but especially so far as regards the historical races. It is probably true only to a less degree of the rest of mankind. It is also a safe inference that what we can thus plainly see at the end of the series has been true for all the earlier terms of it, back entirely through the human into the animal state where we leave it to biology to follow it on through all the phylogenetic stages.

SOCIAL STAGNATION

Social progress, however, is subject to a sort of law of diminishing returns. The progressive forces are themselves subject to equilibration and a rhythmic swing, which gradually diminishes in amplitude and ultimately comes to rest unless some new force is introduced. Imitation preserves what has been gained, but after a change for the better has been adopted and its value recognized it

Q

becomes sacred with time, and the older an institution is the more sacred and inviolate it is. The permanence of social structures from these causes thus becomes the chief obstacle to reform when this is demanded by a changing environment and internal growth. Society is constructed somewhat on the plan of a crustacean.[1] This is especially true of the more backward and somewhat primitive societies, while the later and higher societies have been reconstructed more on the plan of the vertebrate. Mr. Spencer truly says: —

The primitive man is conservative in an extreme degree. Even on contrasting higher races with one another, and even on contrasting different classes in the same society, it is observable that the least developed are the most averse to change. Among the common people an improved method is difficult to introduce; and even a new kind of food is usually disliked. The uncivilized man is thus characterized in a still greater degree. His simpler nervous system, sooner losing its plasticity, is still less able to take on a modified mode of action. Hence both an unconscious adhesion, and an avowed adhesion, to that which is established.[2]

This also accounts for the prevalent idea in civilized nations that progress is the normal condition and always welcome. Says Bagehot: —

Our habitual instructors, our ordinary conversation, our inevitable and ineradicable prejudices, tend to make us think that "Progress" is the normal fact in human society, the fact which we should expect to see, the fact which we should be surprised if we did not see. But history refutes this. The ancients had no conception of progress; they did not so much as reject the idea; they did not even entertain the idea. Oriental nations are just the same now. Since history began they have always been what they are. Savages again, do not improve; they hardly seem to have the basis on which to build, much less the material to put up anything worth having. Only a few nations, and those of European origin, advance; and yet these think — seem irresistibly compelled to think — such advance to be inevitable, natural, and eternal.[3]

Sir Henry Sumner Maine, speaking from a still wider range of observation, fully corroborates these statements when he says: —

Each individual in India is a slave to the customs of the group to which he belongs. . . . The council of village elders does not command anything, it merely declares what has always been. Nor does it generally declare that which it believes some higher power to have commanded; those most entitled to speak on the subject deny that the natives of India necessarily

---

[1] This happy comparison was made by Professor Joseph Le Conte. See the *Monist* for January, 1900, Vol. X, p. 164.

[2] "Principles of Sociology," Vol. I, p. 78 (§ 38).

[3] "Physics and Politics," New York, 1877, pp. 41–42.

require divine or political authority as the basis of their usages; their antiquity is by itself assumed to be a sufficient reason for obeying them.[1]

It is indisputable that much the greatest part of mankind has never shown a particle of desire that its civil institutions should be improved since the moment when external completeness was first given to them by embodiment in some permanent record.[2]

Vast populations, some of them with a civilization considerable but peculiar, detest that which in the language of the West would be called reform. The entire Mohammedan world detests it. The multitudes of colored men who swarm in the great continent of Africa detest it, and it is detested by that large part of mankind which we are accustomed to leave on one side as barbarous or savage. The millions upon millions of men who fill the Chinese Empire loathe it and (what is more) despise it. . . . The enormous mass of the Indian population hates and dreads change. . . . To the fact that the enthusiasm for change is comparatively rare must be added the fact that it is extremely modern. It is known but to a small part of mankind, and to that part but for a short period during a history of incalculable length.[3]

To all of which it may be added that even these few persons in the most enlightened countries desire change or " reform " only in certain institutions and by no means in all. As Dr. Ross fittingly puts it : —

How few there are who honestly believe that improvement is possible anywhere and everywhere! Who expects change in worship or funerals, as he expects it in surgery? Who admits that the marriage institution or the court of justice is improvable as well as the dynamo? Who concedes the relativity of woman's sphere or private property, as he concedes that of the piano or the skyscraper?[4]

All this may seem incompatible with the general law of progress, and may lead some to wonder how there can have been any progress at all. My purpose in introducing it is to clear the ground for the application of the real dynamic principles. But another even more serious fact must also be frankly avowed.

SOCIAL DEGENERATION

The universally recognized fact that social degeneration sometimes occurs has led many to look upon it as the natural antithesis of social progress, and it is said that nations and races have their

[1] "Village Communities in the East and West," by Sir Henry Sumner Maine, New York, 1880, pp. 13–14; 68.

[2] " Ancient Law, its Connection with the Early History of Society, and its Relation to Modern Ideas," by Henry Sumner Maine, with an Introduction by Theodore W. Dwight. Third American from fifth London edition, New York, 1883, pp. 21–22.

[3] " Popular Government," by Henry Sumner Maine, New York, 1886, pp. 132–134.

[4] " Social Control," New York, 1901, p. 195.

regular stages of youth, maturity, and decline as with old age. The basis of truth in all this was pointed out in Chapter V, under the head of Sympodial Development. It was there shown that there is no true opposite to any form of evolution, that development never goes backward, retracing the steps it has taken, and that the loss of any structure that has been acquired can only take place through the crowding out or extinction of the organisms possessing such structure, which is always done by the rise of other more vigorous organisms competing successfully for the means of subsistence. It was also there shown that human races are no exception to this law. There is therefore little to be said here except to point out the place that social degeneration occupies in social mechanics and especially in social dynamics. The chief question is whether degeneracy constitutes a movement in the same sense as progress, so as to make it a factor in the dynamic life of society. It is usually held to be such, but it now becomes clear that this view requires qualification. Degeneration or decadence, if we make these terms synonymous, is not strictly dynamic, but quasi-pathologic. There is only one form of it that seems to constitute an exception to this rule, and this is parasitic degeneracy. This, as was shown in Chapter IV, is always a product of the law of parsimony, and works really to the advantage of the being undergoing it. When a handsome moth, the agile form and gay colors of which were produced by natural and sexual selection, abandons its competitive life and attaches itself to a host from whose stored tissues it directly and far more easily draws an abundant subsistence, its wings become useless and abort under the Lamarckian principle of disuse, its form becomes fleshy, obese, and uncouth, and all its beauty vanishes, because no longer needed in the struggle for existence. To the esthetic looker-on this is degeneracy, and from the standpoint of evolution it is also degeneracy, since it is change in the direction of simplicity of structure, although not in a direction just the reverse of that by which the former more complex structure was acquired. But from the standpoint of the advantage of the organism it is progress, since for the organism the last estate is better than the first. Social parasitism of every kind conforms to the principle of organic parasitism, and therefore does not constitute regression, as the opposite of progression. It is not strictly pathologic, and it may be classed as a form of social progress.

If savage man has come out of an animal state (Homo descended from Pithecanthropus), if barbaric man has come from savage man, if half-civilized man has come from barbaric man, if civilized man has come from half-civilized man, if enlightened man has come from early civilized man, then there has in the long run always been progress in spite of all the forms of degeneracy and all the rhythms to which this series of phenomena has been subjected. The later steps in the series we know to have taken place, because we have a connected historical account of them. The very earliest steps are pretty clearly taught by zoölogy, paleontology, embryology, and phylogeny. The only ones that are not clearly vouched for are the second and third, and even here we are not altogether without evidence, while all theory, all logic, and all scientific analogy support them. Ethnologists have, described certain low races whom they suppose to have degenerated from some higher state, as, for example, the Veddahs, the Akkas, the Fuegians, and even the Ainos and the Esquimaux. From this there are certain to be some who will "jump at the conclusion" that all savages are degenerates. This is but to revive the old doctrine of a "golden age" and the degeneracy of all mankind, or at least Aristotle's doctrine that all savages have degenerated from a civilized state. These doctrines have all been definitely set at rest by Lyell,[1] Tylor,[2] Lubbock,[3] and others, and need not occupy us.

SOCIAL INSTABILITY

Although everything points to social evolution as having always gone on and as still going on, and although there are no indications that there is now or ever has been any true social involution in the sense of retracing the steps that have been taken, still, it must not be inferred that all the modern discussion of the problem of social decadence is to no purpose or based on vain imaginings. The real problem is how to secure social stability. The complicated process by which societies are formed, as set forth in the last chapter, renders them somewhat delicate structures, and although the degree of social efficiency increases directly with the degree of complexity, the

[1] "Antiquity of Man," London, 1863, Chapter XIX, p. 379.
[2] "Primitive Culture," London, 1871, Vol. II, pp. 52 ff.
[3] British Association Report, Dundee Meeting, 1867, London, 1868, Pt. II, Notices and Abstracts, pp. 121 ff.

degree of stability seems to be inversely proportional to the grade
of aggregation. We meet here with a fresh application of the law
that was seen to prevail in the organic world, and which was characterized by the phrase: survival of the plastic. There is a constant
tendency in society to *ossification*, growing out of the intense appreciation that all mankind displays for those social structures that have
served a good purpose. Men perpetually praise the bridge that
took them across the river of life, and continue to praise it and cling
to it after its timbers have decayed and its abutments begin to
crumble. This highly useful conservatism thus becomes a dangerous
misoneism, and the very stability which men thus seek to secure
becomes a source of weakness. Here we encounter the distinction
between the *stable* and the *labile*, or rather the real connection between the two. For only the labile is truly stable, just as in the
domain of living things, only the plastic is enduring. For lability
is not an exact synonym of instability, as the dictionaries teach, but
embodies besides the idea of flexibility and susceptibility to change
without destruction or loss. It is that quality in institutions which
enables them to change and still persist, which converts their equilibrium into a moving equilibrium, and which makes possible their
adaptation to both internal and external modification, to changes in
both individual character and the environment.

As there is no such thing in physics as absolute rest, so there is no
such thing in society as absolute stagnation, so that when a society
makes for itself a procrustean bed it is simply preparing the way
for its own destruction by the on-moving agencies of social dynamics.
The law of the instability of the homogeneous will alone prevent the
continuance of a changeless state, but as structures once formed
never retrace the steps through which they were created, they must
either change organically and move on to higher stages or they must
succumb to the pressure exerted by surrounding dynamic influences.
The case is precisely the same here as that described in Chapter V,
when dealing with the causes of the extinction of species and of
trunk lines of descent under the influence of sympodial development.
It is this that is meant by the instability of society or of civilization.
Social decadence is never universal. If it is going on in one place
a corresponding social progress is going on in others, and thus far
the loss has always been more than made up by the gain. The
causes of social decadence have been so widely, I will not say deeply,

discussed in recent times that I need not dwell upon them. They
are personal, racial, and social.[1] We may therefore admit the force
of the arguments of the school of criminal anthropologists headed
by Lombroso, of the school of anthroposociologists headed by La-
pouge, of the school of individualists headed by Demolins, and
of the statisticians, who have demonstrated the law that the increase of intelligence and of population are inversely proportional;
we may concede with Nietzsche that a high state of morals and
civility is in a certain sense decadent, and with other extremists
that all forms of collective existence are to some extent at the expense of virility; we may recognize all these factors of the problem
without being thereby blinded to the principal fact that in society
and in the human race generally the series has thus far been and
still remains an ascending one, and that social, organic, and cosmic
evolution prevail and have prevailed to the limit of our powers of
fathoming the universe. But, on the other hand, this scientific
optimism should not, and, properly interpreted, does not teach any
laissez faire doctrine, and we cannot afford to close our eyes to the
patent facts of social instability.

　　But I may as well repeat here what was said at the close of the
preceding section, that my purpose in discussing social stagnation,
social degeneration, and social instability has been to prepare the
way for the clear and intelligent discussion of the true principles of
social dynamics. These subjects now so engross public attention
that all proper perspective is destroyed, and the picture presented
of human society has become distorted and obscured.

Dynamic Principles

　　In some respects social dynamics is a more complex branch of
social mechanics than social statics. In the latter we found that all
the phenomena were controlled by a single principle, that of social
synergy, under which social energy is equilibrated and social structures are formed. In social dynamics, on the contrary, several quite
distinct principles must be recognized. We shall endeavor to reduce
these to three, or at least to confine ourselves chiefly to the three
leading dynamic principles. These are, first, *difference of potential*,
manifested chiefly in the crossing of cultures, and by which the

---

[1] See the recent able article on this subject by Miss Sarah E. Simons, *Ann. Acad.
Pol. and Soc. Sci.*, Philadelphia, Vol. XVIII, September, 1901, pp. 251-274.

equilibrium of social structures is disturbed, converting stability into lability; second, *innovation*, due to psychic exuberance, through which the monotonous repetition of social heredity is interrupted, and new vistas are gained; and third, *conation*, or social effort, by which the social energy is applied to material things, resulting in poesis and achievement. All these principles are unconscious social agencies working for social progress.

Difference of Potential. — This expression is of course borrowed from modern physics, and I shall assume that the reader is familiar with the distinction between potential and kinetic energy. It is the broadest of all the dynamic principles, and is, in fact, a cosmic principle like that of synergy. I cannot deal with it in all its bearings upon social science, but must confine myself chiefly to its one great application, the crossing, or cross fertilization of cultures. Although I do not refer here especially to the physiological aspect of the question, still, as this furnishes the clearest illustration of the principle I shall make free use of it, and to render it still more clear I shall begin the discussion with a glance at the nature of sex.

Biologists have only recently discovered the principle of sex. It had always been supposed, and is still popularly supposed, that the purpose of sex is to insure reproduction. But, paradoxical as it may sound, sex has fundamentally nothing whatever to do with reproduction. Not, of course, that in the higher animals reproduction is possible except through the organs of sex, but the great number of organisms now known to science which possess no sex, and which, nevertheless, reproduce asexually in the most prolific manner, clearly shows that sex is not at all necessary to reproduction. What, then, is the purpose of sex ? What office does it perform in organic economy ? The answer that modern biology gives to this question is that *sex is a device for keeping up a difference of potential.*

In asexual reproduction heredity is simple repetition. The structures in existence exactly reproduce themselves. The offspring is in all respects like the parent. Function is fully performed. Growth and multiplication go on at rapid rates. There may be even considerable perfectionment of these same structures. But, as we saw in the last chapter, all these are static operations. The horticulturist well knows that propagation by buds, slips, stolons, grafts, etc., simply continues the stock indefinitely unchanged, while propagation by seed is liable to produce change in the stock in almost any direction. Seedlings frequently will not " come true." This is because seed is the result of sexual fertilization, and embodies elements from two plants, or at least two individuals in the biological sense, according to which a single plant is composed of many individuals.

In native plants the attentive observer can clearly see the effort of nature to avail herself of the advantages of sex. The original and "natural" method of reproduction is asexual, and all sexual differentiation has been a departure from that method. But except in the lowest forms sexuality has been attained throughout the vegetable kingdom. Here, however, it usually goes on along with asexual reproduction. In fact sexual reproduction in plants is almost always an "alternation of generations." This phenomenon when discovered in a few animals was regarded as quite remarkable, and botanists did not have the wit to see that what was an exception in the animal kingdom, was the rule in the vegetable kingdom. But in plants, after true sexuality had been attained there were several steps in the direction of more and more complete dualism in reproduction. There are, for example, the hermaphrodite, the monœcious, and the diœcious states, and the evidence is strong that this is the order in which these states have been developed. But this is not the whole of the story. It is found that among plants that have every outward appearance of being hermaphrodite there are many that are only structurally so, but functionally unisexual. There is a variety of devices for securing this result. The commonest of these is what is called dichogamy, and the two principal forms of dichogamy are proterandry, by which the anthers mature and shed their pollen before the pistils are ready for it, and proterogyny, the reverse of proterandry, in both of which self fertilization is impossible. In other cases, as commonly in the strawberry, although all the flowers have both stamens and pistils, a close inspection shows that in some flowers only the stamens are functional and in others only the pistils. In many monœcious plants, as, for example, in the wild rice (Zizania), the female flowers are above the male, so that the pollen from the latter cannot fall upon the former. But the number of such devices is so great that no enumeration of them is possible here. Everywhere nature is seeking, as Dr. Gray happily expressed it "how not to do it," and the intention, so to speak, is

plainly written over the whole vegetable kingdom to prevent self
fertilization at all hazards.   But when we examine the other more
numerous and obvious class of cases in which it is evidently, and, as
we may say, avowedly sought to secure cross fertilization, we cannot
look amiss of them.   In fact we may almost venture the general
proposition that all irregular flowers are adaptations to insect agency
for this purpose.   Fragrance in flowers seeks the same end, and, in
fact, color, and brilliancy in flowers can have no other object.   But
for the possibility of cross fertilization by insects there would have
been no flowers in the popular sense, and as I have often pointed
out, showy and fragrant flowers came into existence simultaneously
with nectar-seeking insects.

There is a constant tendency in both the vegetable and the animal
kingdoms to escape from asexual reproduction and resort to sexual
reproduction, and in the latter to secure the greatest possible separation of the sexes and difference in the parents.   Although all this is
brought about by natural selection, or the principle of advantage,
and the term *purpose* is a metaphor, still it overwhelmingly demon-
strates that there is an advantage in sexuality.   This advantage is
clear to be seen, since it is nothing less than that of setting up a
difference of potential between organic beings, which may be regarded
in so far as mechanical systems charged with potential energy which
cannot be converted into kinetic energy except through the influence
of other systems foreign to themselves brought into such relations
to them as to act upon them and mutually give and take of their
stored energy.   This sex primarily accomplishes, and it is accomplished in increasing degrees by the wider and wider crossing of
strains.   Thus the object of sex is not reproduction at all but variation.   It is organic differentiation, higher life, progress, evolution.

The crossing of strains is in the highest degree dynamic, and it
applies to all living beings.   It must therefore apply to man, and
before leaving the physiological side of the subject it is well to note
that this is the principle that underlies all the customs and laws of
primitive as well as civilized men looking to the preservation of the
vigor of races.   The most conspicuous and widespread of such customs are those which, in varying forms and degrees, and with varying but usually great severity, enforce the practice of exogamy.
Among higher races the same principle is embodied in laws against
incest, and in codes defining the degrees of consanguinity within

which marriage is forbidden.   Everywhere it is and always has been realized either instinctively, intuitively, or rationally, and now it has been demonstrated experimentally, that close interbreeding is deteriorating and endangers the life of society.   We need not discuss how men so early arrived at this truth.   Personally I am disposed to regard it as in large part a survival of customs so old that they were developed under the biologic principle of natural selection. But be that as it may, from the high standpoint of the sociologist the truth comes forth as one of the clearest exemplifications of the universal principle of social dynamics for which the phrase *difference of potential* seems to be the clearest expression.

But difference of potential is a social as well as a physiological and a physical principle, and perhaps we shall find the easiest transition from the physiological to the social in viewing the deteriorating effects of close interbreeding from the standpoint of the environment instead of from that of the organism.   A long-continued uniform environment is more deteriorating than similarity of blood.   Persons who remain for their whole lives, and their descendants after them, in the same spot, surrounded by precisely the same conditions, and intermarry with others doing the same, and who continue this for a series of generations, deteriorate mentally at least, and probably also physically, although there may not be any mixing of blood.   Their whole lives, physical, mental, and moral, become fixed and monotonous, and the partners chosen for continuing the race have nothing new to add to each other's stock.   There is no variation of the social monotony, and the result is socially the same as close consanguineal interbreeding.   On the other hand, a case in which a man should, without knowing it, marry his own sister, after they had been long separated and living under widely different skies, would probably entail no special deterioration, and their different conditions of life would have produced practically the same effect as if they were not related.

The transition from this semi-physiological aspect of the subject to the wholly sociological one is easy.   The cross fertilization of cultures is to sociology what the cross fertilization of germs is to biology.   A culture is a social structure, a social organism, if any one prefers, and ideas are its germs.   These may be mixed or crossed, and the effect is the same as that of crossing hereditary strains. The process by which the greater part of this has been accomplished, at least in the early history of human society, is the struggle of races. In the last chapter we discussed this phenomenon from one point of view. We saw in it the working of the principle of social synergy, equilibrating antagonistic social forces and constructing human institutions. We kept as completely out of view as possible the other and equally important point, viz., the simultaneous and concomitant working of the principle of the difference of potential. A race of men may be looked upon as a physical system possessing a large amount of potential energy, but often having reached such a complete state of equilibrium that it is incapable of performing any but the normal functions of growth and multiplication. It is reduced by the very principle that constructed it to the power of simple repetition. Under the head of Social Stagnation at the beginning of this chapter it was shown that most savage and barbaric races are actually in this state. They want no change and ask for nothing that does not already exist; nay they detest and consistently oppose all change. If it were left to the initiative of such races there never would be any social progress. We may go further and say that if it were left to the deliberate and conscious action of mankind human progress would be impossible. Fortunately there are great cosmic, unconscious principles that work for progress against the eternal resistance of established social structures.

By sheer force of circumstance, by the exuberant fertility of mankind, by the pushing out of boundaries to avoid overcrowding, by wanderings and migrations, different races, charged with potential energy locked up in varied cults and customs, tongues and tendencies, experience wholly fortuitous encounters and collisions, resulting in conflicts and conquests, whereby all these divergent idea-germs are first hurled promiscuously together and then rudely jostled and stirred into a heterogeneous menstruum that tends to polarize on the social spindle, but ultimately blends in the manner described under the head of Social Karyokinesis. Every one of these social *Anlagen* thus forced into intimate relations is full of energy which can only be released by changing its potential, and this is what is done by the action of dissimilar foreign *Anlagen* brought into contact with them. In the last chapter only the synergetic or constructive effects of the struggle of races were described. But the social equilibrium thus produced is always a moving equilibrium. Without destroying the structures produced by social synergy a molecular or differential change is constantly taking place whereby they are perpetually changing in type and evolving into new and higher types of structure. This is the dynamic movement caused by the change of potential, which is in turn the result of the cross fertilization of cultures.

Progress results from the fusion of unlike elements. This is creative, because from it there results a third something which is neither the one nor the other but different from both and something new and superior to either. But these elements, although they must be unlike, must possess a certain degree of similarity so as not to be incompatible and unassimilable. It must be cross fertilization and not hybridization. All cultures are supposed to be assimilable. Whatever is human must have some points of agreement. Just as all races are fertile *inter se*, so all human institutions may be regarded as belonging to the same species. Still there are some races whose culture differs so widely from that of others that they seem to form an exception to this law. Such differences are, however, usually differences of degree and result, as explained in the last chapter, from differences in the rank or order of the two societies as measured by the number of assimilations which they have undergone. They are theoretically, but not practically assimilable. The one has so little potential energy that it produces no appreciable effect on the other, while the higher civilization immediately overwhelms, engulfs, and absorbs, or destroys the lower.

The distinction between cross fertilization and hybridization may be illustrated by the effect that different ideas sometimes produce. Let a Hegelian, who proceeds from the standpoint of thought or spirit, attempt to discuss any philosophical question with a man of science, who proceeds from the standpoint of concrete facts, and they will make no headway. They cannot understand each other. There is no common ground to stand upon. Their ideas will no more mix than oil and water. They are infertile. But let a zoologist and a botanist discuss some question of general biology, the data for which are found in both the organic kingdoms, and their ideas will instantly attract and supplement each other. Each will adduce fresh illustrations from his own field that will illuminate those of the other and they will harmonize and progress perfectly. In a word, their ideas will cross fertilize each other. It is not otherwise with human societies brought into contact.

Again, anything that increases social activity, especially if it affects the intensity of this activity, is dynamic. Thus increase of population, in and of itself, is not dynamic, but there is such a thing as the "dynamic density" of population, and it may be distinguished from the "material density."[1] By the friction of mind upon mind, especially in a mixed population of a certain density, there is produced a difference of potential among individuals which is in a high degree dynamic.

It is impossible in dealing with this subject to avoid the bearing of war and peace on human progress. All civilized men realize the horrors of war, and if sociology has any utilitarian purposes one of these certainly is to diminish or mitigate these horrors. But pure sociology is simply an inquiry into the social facts and conditions, and has nothing to do with utilitarian purposes. In making this objective inquiry it finds that, as a matter of fact, war has been the chief and leading condition of human progress. This is perfectly obvious to any one who understands the meaning of the struggle of races. When races stop struggling progress ceases. They want no progress and they have none. For all primitive and early, undeveloped races, certainly, the condition of peace is a condition of social stagnation. We may enlarge to our soul's content on the blessings of peace, but the facts remain as stated, and cannot be successfully disproved.

As regards the more civilized races, this much at least must be admitted. The inhabitants of southern, central, and western Europe, call them Aryan, Indo-Germanic, or anything you please, and irrespective of the question whether their history can be traced back and their origin discovered or not, have led the civilization of the world ever since there were any records. They are and have been throughout all this time the repository of the highest culture, they have the largest amount of social efficiency, they have achieved the most, and they represent the longest uninterrupted inheritance and transmission of human achievement. The several nations into which this race is now divided are the products of compound assimilation of a higher order than that of other nations. As a consequence

---

[1] Cf. Émile Durkheim, "Les Règles de la Méthode sociologique," 2e éd., Paris, 1901, pp. 139–140. This question was also ably discussed by M. Adolphe Coste in one of his very last contributions to sociology, "Le Facteur Population dans l'Évolution sociale," *Rev. Int. de Sociologie*, 9e Année, Août–Septembre, 1901, pp. 569–612.

of all this this race has become the dominant race of the globe. As such it has undertaken the work of extending its dominion over other parts of the earth. It has already spread over the whole of South and North America, over Australia, and over Southern Africa. It has gained a firm foothold on Northern Africa, Southern and Eastern Asia, and most of the larger islands and archipelagos of the sea. It is only necessary to understand the modern history of the world and the changes in the map of the world to see this.

Much of this has been peacefully accomplished, but whenever any of the races previously occupying this territory has raised any obstacle to the march of the dominant race the latter has never hesitated to employ force or resort to war. Certain tender-hearted persons have almost always uttered a faint protest against it, but it has been utterly powerless to stem the current. Consider for a moment the settlement of North America by Europeans. It has been almost universally felt that it must be done, and any objection on the ground of the prior occupancy of the native races has been looked upon as mere sentimentality. There have been so-called treaties and purchases and bargains with the savages, but with such odds in intelligence and shrewdness, as well as in advantage, that they amounted to no more than pretense. The white man fixed the terms and if the red man declined them he was simply coerced. If they had all been rejected the result would have been the same. From such transactions the element of justice is wholly excluded. It is only another form of conquest. Indeed, the whole movement by which the master race of the planet has extended its dominion over inferior races differs not the least in principle from the primitive movement described in the last chapter. The effects are different only because of the great disparity in the races engaged, due in turn to the superior social efficiency of the dominant race.

Under the operation of such a cosmical principle it seems a waste of breath to urge peace, justice, humanity, and yet there can be no doubt that these moral forces are gaining strength and slowly mitigating the severity of the law of nature. But mitigation is all that can be hoped for. The movement must go on, and there seems no place for it to stop until, just as man has gained dominion over the animal world, so the highest type of man shall gain dominion over all the lower types of man. The greater part of the peace agitation is characterized by total blindness to all these broader cosmic facts and principles, and this explains its complete impotence. There is a certain kind of over-culture which instead of widening narrows the mental horizon. It is a mark of an effete mind to exaggerate small things while ignoring great things. Maudlin sentimentality and inconsistent sympathy, thinking on problems of the world without discrimination or perspective, incapacity to scent the drift of events or weigh the relative gravity of heterogeneous and unequal facts, are qualities that dominate certain minds which, from culture and advantages, gain the credit of constituting the cream of the most advanced intelligence. Far safer guides are the crude instincts of the general public in the same communities. If the peace missionaries could have made their counsels prevail there might have been universal peace, nay, general contentment, but there would have been no progress. The social pendulum would have swung through a shorter and shorter arc until at last it would have come to rest, the difference of potential would have grown smaller and smaller until it reached the zero point, and all movement in the social equilibrium would have ceased. Whatever may be best for the future when society shall become self-conscious and capable of devising its own means of keeping up the difference of potential, thus far war and struggle with all that they imply have been the blind unconscious means by which nature has secured this result, and by which a dynamic condition has been produced and kept up.

Attention has thus far been confined to those primary social structures called races, nations, etc., which constitute the forms of human association. There are other almost equally important aspects of the subject having their roots in other classes of facts, and to these we may now turn our attention.

Innovation. — The dynamic principle next in importance to that of difference of potential is what I prefer to call innovation. Its biological homologue is the *sport*. This is only possible in sexual reproduction, and is probably to be explained by the fact that the hereditary elements (*Anlagen*) may remain undeveloped during many generations and suddenly appear in offspring whose parents do not possess the given qualities, but in whom they have lain latent as well as in several generations of their ancestors. These then seem to be new elements, and are called sports. This may appear to be only an accidental and subsidiary consideration, but in its broader aspect it takes the form of what I have called *fortuitous variation,* an expression used by Darwin, Spencer, Romanes, Cope, and others, but not always given its full significance. I am free to confess that I studied botany chiefly for the purpose of trying to arrive at the laws and principles of vegetable life, and with little interest in plant forms as such. From the beginning of my botanical investigations I was struck with the manifestations of the principle of fortuitous variation, and I finally undertook to illustrate and formulate the principle. On Dec. 15, 1888, I read a paper before the Biological Society of Washington on: "Fortuitous Variation, as illustrated by the Genus Eupatorium," which I illustrated by a large series of specimens collected by myself, having in each case carefully noted the habitat. This paper, which was not written, should have been published with the illustrations, but I had not the facilities for this, and contented myself with sending a brief abstract of it to *Nature,* which appeared in that journal for July 25, 1889 (Vol. XL, p. 310). I shall not introduce here the technical part even of this note, but as it is now wholly forgotten, I will revive it by quoting a part of the concluding portion in which I attempted to explain the cause of fortuitous variation.

Organized or living matter constantly tends to increase in quantity, which may be regarded as the true end of organic being, to which the perfection of structure, commonly mistaken for such end, is only one of the means. Every organic element may be contemplated as occupying the center of a sphere, toward the periphery of which, in all directions alike, it seeks to expand, and would expand but for physical obstructions which present themselves. The forms which have succeeded in surviving are those, and only those, that were possible under existing conditions; that is, they have been developed along the lines of least resistance, pressure along all other lines having resulted in failure. Now, the various forms of vegetable and animal life represent the latest expression of this law, the many possible, and the only possible, results of this universal *nisus* of organic being. The different forms of Eupatorium, or of any other plant or animal, that are found co-existing under identical conditions merely show that there were many lines along which the resistance was not sufficient to prevent development. They are the successes of nature.

I disclaim any desire to discredit or impair in any way the great law of natural selection. The most important variations, those which lead up to higher types of structure, are the result of that law, which therefore really explains organic evolution; but the comprehension and acceptance of both natural selection and evolution are retarded instead of being advanced by claiming for the former more than it can explain, and it might as well be recognized first as last that a great part — numerically by far the greater

R

part — of the variety and multiplicity, as well as the interest and charm of
Nature, is due to another and quite distinct law, which, with the above
qualifications, may perhaps be appropriately called "the law of fortuitous
variation."

At least one biologist of note, Mr. George J. Romanes, was
attracted by this paper, and urged me to follow the subject up
experimentally, which I was unable to do. He brought it to the
attention of the Biological Section of the British Association for the
Advancement of Science the same year, as in line with his doctrine
of "physiological selection" and what he had called "unuseful" or
"non-utilitarian" characters. I returned to the subject in my address
as president of the Biological Society of Washington in January,
1890, dealing somewhat more at length with the philosophical aspect,
and concluding as follows : —

Here then we have the solution of by far the worst difficulty in the way
of natural selection. The beneficial effect need not be assumed to begin at
the initial stage. It need not be felt until well-formed varieties have been
developed without regard to any advantage in the particular differences
which they present. There seems to be no flaw in this mode of solving this
paramount problem, and if it is objected that it amounts to a new explanation of the origin of species, I am ready to admit it, and I believe that more
species are produced by fortuitous variation than by natural selection.
Natural selection is not primarily the cause of the origin of *species;* its
mission is far higher. It is the cause of the origin of *types of structure.*[1]

It might be supposed that fortuitous variation as thus explained
was something quite apart from the phenomena of sports, but this is
because in these papers I did not attempt to go into the specific
causes of such variations. The chief cause of organic variation, as
already shown in this chapter, is sex. When treating of sex as a
device of nature for producing a difference of potential I did not go
beyond the primary dualism of the parental strains. But it is evident that for any developed organism with a long phylogeny the
number of atavistic stirps must be next to infinite, and as any of
these are liable to lie latent during many generations and crop out
at any time, the possibilities of fortuitous variation are enormous.
This is the inner explanation of fortuitous variation, and is the *way*
in which nature fills every crack, chink, and cranny into which it is
possible for life to be thrust.

[1] Proc. Biol. Soc. Washington, Vol. V, 1890, p. 44.

I am not at this writing acquainted except at second hand with the exhaustive work of Professor Hugo de Vries entitled : "Die Mutationstheorie" (Leipzig, 1901), but from all accounts I have seen of it I infer that he is working at this same problem, and that his theory will not be found to differ widely from my own as above stated, although no one can make extended observations in such a promising field without discovering the necessity of qualifying, and of both restricting and enlarging the attempts of others to formulate the truth that underlies all the phenomena.

It matters not by what name we designate it, whenever the life force breaks over the bounds of simple heredity and goes beyond the process of merely repeating and multiplying the structures that have already been created, it becomes innovation and changes the type of structure. In biologic language this is variation, and all variation is dynamic. Variation due to mere exuberance of life is quite as much so as when due to other causes. These erratic sports, these leaps and bounds of a throbbing, pulsating, exultant nature, under the life-giving power of sunshine and shower, produce a perpetual rejuvenescence and call back into life and activity all the myriad germ-plasms that have been pushed aside in the march of heredity and which line the wayside of evolution. These constitute an inexhaustible source of fresh variations, combining and recombining in an endless series of ever changing forms. Such are the conditions and methods of organic innovation, with which utility, advantage, and fitness to survive have nothing to do.

Social innovation proceeds upon the same principle, and although the immediate conditions and accompanying circumstances may appear very different, we have only to abstract the details and generalize the phenomena to perceive the fundamental unity of process. Social innovation has been called *invention* by Tarde and *impulse* by Patten.[1] Tarde has so fully explained and illustrated the principle that there is no possibility of misunderstanding him. Patten states it so obscurely that in reading his book I missed it entirely, and would never have known what he meant if he had not explained it to me orally. The phenomenon is psychic and involves the whole of mind. Invention unduly emphasizes the intellectual side and impulse the feeling side. Innovation avoids both these extremes. The tendency in social, as in organic structures is simply

---

[1] "Theory of Prosperity," by Simon N. Patten, New York, 1902, pp. 180 ff.

to conserve and reproduce; it is to copy and repeat, grow and multiply, but always to retain the same structures. In both departments the normal process is simple metabolism, and social metabolism would never any more than physiological, produce a new structure. But in society as in organisms there is a surplus of energy that must be worked off. This is not, however, universally diffused. It is a somewhat exceptional product. The great mass have no energy to spare beyond the bare needs of existence. But nature always produces irregularities and inequalities. Its method is utterly devoid of economy. It heaps up in one place and tears away in another. There is a law which Spencer has called the "multiplication of effects." Action begun in a certain direction tends more and more to go in that direction until all homogeneity is destroyed. Advantage creates advantage. The smallest fissure through a dam helps on the work of enlarging that fissure until the dam is undermined and swept away. The least groove on a mountain slope causes this to become the center of erosion and makes a gorge. The more a river bends the more it wears and the bend is cumulatively increased. The same law works in society. Extremes breed extremes, and a state of equality, if it could be conceived to exist, would be ephemeral. A state of inequality would quickly replace it. So that while all the social energy if equally distributed might leave a very small surplus to each member of society, the actual case is: vast numbers in whom the social energy is below the level of healthy activity and small groups in whom it is far above the possibility of ever consuming it. Surplus social energy is confined to these favored groups, and all social innovation emanates from them.

We saw in the last chapter how human association was brought about. We did not, however, penetrate into the inner workings of the principle of social synergy. The great fact of human slavery had to be dismissed with a sentence. A word to the wise was sufficient. The historian has too often told this story. The historian has also fully described the system of caste, but usually without giving any idea of its cause, or else a wrong idea. Nor has he neglected the fact of a leisure class, and often he has correctly portrayed the advantages that have accrued to the world from the leisure class. Our present task is to point out that social innovation has been largely due to this form of social inequality. Not wholly, however, and it is only necessary that the primary wants be supplied without exhausting the social energy for it to crop out in the form of innovation. There is a social bathmism or growth force which ever presses. Physical wants must be supplied, and most of this energy is thus expended, but everything goes to show that the moment this is done this energy overflows in the direction of doing something new. This overflow, too, takes all conceivable forms and by far the greater part of it is utterly wasted, often more than wasted. One only needs to read Professor Veblen's book[1] to see that this is so, but he intentionally left out of view the other side, and he would probably agree that there is another side. It only helps to emphasize two truths: the non-economical character of all of nature's processes, and the small amount of energy that really makes for evolution or social progress. The apparently large gains in this direction are due to the almost unlimited time that there has been in which to realize them.

It is our task to consider the other side and show, not what the leisure class has done for human progress, because others have already done that, but more specifically how it has done it. Mr. Veblen himself has given us the key to the whole process. It is his "instinct of workmanship," which is nothing more nor less than the dynamic principle of innovation. The odium of labor, as he has so ingeniously shown, is something conventional and artificial. If body or mind is not fatigued with the effort required to satisfy the needs of existence, activity in either is pleasurable. As was shown in Chapter V, not only is all normal exercise of the faculties a satisfaction, but at bottom all pleasure, all enjoyment, and all good consist in the normal exercise of the faculties. All want and all pain, and the whole of the so-called *Weltschmerz*, are due to restraints of one kind or another to such exercise. When there is no other form of this pain there remains the form called ennui, which is the most intolerable of all, and which is the chief form in which it is experienced by the leisure class. They *must* work or suffer unendurable torture. Normally they will follow the instinct of workmanship and do something useful. So long as work is respectable, *i.e.*, so long as there is entailed by it no loss of caste, it will be done. The late lamented M. Adolphe Coste has clearly shown[2] that employ-

---

[1] "The Theory of the Leisure Class," by Thorstein Veblen, New York, 1899.

[2] "Les Principes d'une Sociologie Objective," Paris, 1899, pp. 114–115 ; "L'Expérience des Peuples et les Prévisions qu'elle autorise," Paris, 1900. pp. 200–201.

ments which are now exclusively followed by the "working class" and which no "gentleman of leisure" would deign to engage in, were boasted of by the great men of antiquity, many of whom were skilled forgers, masons, carpenters, tanners, and dyers, as well as warriors and hunters. And when we reflect how intimately skilled labor is connected with invention, who can estimate the loss that the world has suffered by that pure conventionality which relegates all skilled labor to the mentally least developed and least equipped classes of society? For labor in and of itself is not dynamic. Most of the labor done in the world is purely static. It simply reproduces after the set pattern. It multiplies exact copies of what has been invented. It is imitation in the Tardean sense. Such is nearly all unskilled labor in all departments of industry. Such is also most so-called skilled labor, for the laborer only learns to make or do one thing over and over again in exactly the same way. Outside of his "trade" he is utterly inefficient, and when a new machine robs him of his trade he is thrown out of employment and has nothing that he can do. Such, too, is all menial service and routine work, most of the work that relates to cleanliness, washing, scrubbing, scouring, dusting, sweeping, brushing; most of the work of women in civilized countries, the eternal round of feeding and caring for mankind. In this there has been degeneracy, for among savages not only the skilled labor but also the invention is done by women as well as by men. Finally most charity and philanthropic work is static, and philanthropists are content to alleviate present suffering by temporary action, when they know that it will have to be done again and again. Many such would disparage a reformer who should suggest a general policy that would if carried out prevent the recurrence of the conditions that call for charity. Statical work has been happily called a web of Penelope. Its usefulness, however, cannot be questioned, since through it alone can the *status quo* be maintained. It is the conservative force of society, preventing the loss of the progress attained, and it must always absorb by far the greater part of all the social energy.

What then is dynamic action? It is that which goes beyond mere repetition. It is heuristic. It discovers new ways. It is Spencer's "fructifying causation." It is alteration, modification, variation. When applied to production it produces according to a geometrical instead of an arithmetical progression. But it need not necessarily be invention. It may be impulse, as Dr. Patten says, exuberance and overflow of spirits, of emotion, of passion even, which will not brook constraint and dashes forward to higher and greater results. Dynamic action is progressive, and, instead of leaving the world in the same condition as before, leaves it in a changed, *i.e.*, in an improved condition. The final criterion of a dynamic action is achievement in the sense in which that term was used in the third and fifth chapters, and every innovation, however slight, constitutes an increment to the world's achievement. It is so much permanently gained, it can never be lost, and does not have to be done again. It constitutes the means of producing something better than could have been produced before, and this product is rendered perpetual by its continual reproduction through imitation or social heredity. This is not innovation, which differs totally from it in the fact that its repetition would be a contradiction of terms. Every innovation is something different from every other. There can be only one innovation in the same sense, although progress consists of many series of innovations in the same direction.

Conation. — We are now prepared to consider the third dynamic principle, which I call conation. These dynamic principles are all related, and the order in which they have been treated is the natural order. Innovation could not be advantageously explained until the general principle of cross fertilization of cultures had been shown to be the essential condition to that unconscious progress which made invention possible. And now, as we shall see, conation or social effort could not be understood without a clear conception of the true nature of a dynamic action, which is the essential condition to innovation. The crossing of cultures is the most fundamental of the dynamic principles. It is a social principle, but it is at the same time organic. It goes to the essence of social structures and works changes in their very type and nature, selecting and preserving all that is best in the different structures thus blended, and creating a new structure which is different from and superior to any of the prior existing structures. It does this, as we have seen, without destroying the structures out of which the new structure is formed. The state of equilibrium established by social synergy in producing the old structures is converted into a moving equilibrium developing higher structures. Innovation is a part of this process, and is not to be considered as a separate movement. It is a partial explanation of how the changes take place. In studying it we simply go deeper into the details of the process and learn to distinguish the strictly dynamic from the wholly static elements of social activity. It consists in dynamic actions. Finally in studying conation we proceed one step further in our analysis and seek to discover what it is that makes an action dynamic. Or, still more accurately stated, we analyze action itself and seek to determine what part of it is dynamic, for in a certain sense no action is wholly dynamic. There are, however, many actions which contain no dynamic element, and therefore we have to do here only with such actions as do contain a dynamic element.

Let us therefore select any action in which a dynamic element resides and subject it to a rigid analysis. It makes no difference what the action is if it is one that leaves society in a state different from that which existed before it was performed, presumably in an improved state, however slight that improvement may be. We have to consider the several effects of such an action, for nearly every action has more than one effect. These effects are the essential things, and the question always is whether any of them are dynamic, and if so which ones. We assume that the action selected for analysis has some dynamic effects as well as some static effects. A close inspection will show that actions are much alike in these respects, and that all dynamic actions have about the same general effects. Leaving out of account all accidental and unessential consequences of such an action we shall find that it always has three necessary and essential effects, viz. : —

1. To satisfy desire.
2. To preserve or continue life.
3. To modify the surroundings.

We will consider each of these effects in and for itself and wholly separate from the rest. This is difficult to do on account of their obvious interrelations and mutual associations, and most of the faulty logic and confusion of ideas, *i.e.*, of the error on this and kindred subjects, is due to the failure to keep these distinct effects separate in the mind. Let us examine the first effect: to satisfy desire. I place this first as it is the condition itself to the action. Every action whatever must have this object, otherwise there is no motive, *i.e.*, no cause. We need not discuss the question whether the action actually satisfies desire. We may assume that it does and proceed, but, as a matter of fact, it must, for the desire, so far as we are concerned here, is simply to act in the direction in which the desire impels, and that is in itself the satisfaction of the desire. Nothing beyond this need be taken into the account. But we will suppose that this part of the action is wholly successful and that the satisfaction sought is attained. The only question that concerns the present discussion is whether this effect of the action is dynamic or not. If we cling strictly to this one fact and keep all its associations wholly out of the way, we can clearly see that the simple satisfaction of the individual's desire contains no dynamic element. It is, in fact, purely physiological. It is also transient. A desire, as we have seen, when satisfied is terminated. Until the satisfaction commences it is a painful sensation, during the period of satisfaction it is a pleasure, enjoyment, happiness, or whatever we may call it. After satisfaction it is nothing. However great the individual good, the social good is purely statical. Permanence can only be attained through indefinite repetition, which is impossible, and if possible would still be statical. We may therefore dismiss this first effect as statical.

Now as to the second effect. If the individual is at all adjusted to his environment his action will contribute in some degree either to the preservation or the continuance of life. At the lower animal stages, as we saw in Chapter V, all desires are adapted to the needs of the creature and their satisfaction conduces to the life of either the individual or the species. Any continuous tendency to the contrary would result in the death of the former or the extinction of the latter. It is not really otherwise with society. We have fully shown how everything in society works for the conservation of the group and the race, and how the wayward tendencies of mankind have been subjected to natural and spontaneous restraints in the interest of social order. This social adaptation is well-nigh as complete as organic adaptation, and it would be impossible for any considerable number of men to persist in anti-social acts for any considerable time without disrupting society altogether. If such has ever been the case such societies have perished and are unknown. Human desires are therefore more or less completely adjusted to individual and social needs, and it is safe to assume that the satisfaction of any normal desire also contributes in some degree to the preservation of the life of the individual or of other individuals (wife, children, family, etc.), or to the maintenance of society, or both. Here again the question for us is whether this effect of the action is or is not dynamic. The answer is that the preservation of life and social order are not dynamic effects. This is too self-evident to require any argument, and we may content ourselves with pointing out that the two effects thus far considered differ in two important respects. The first is conscious, the second unconscious, and while neither can be called direct, the second is clearly indirect, and, as it were, incidental. It is the type of the class of effects that were characterized as "unintended" (see *supra*, p. 114). In fact, it is precisely similar in this respect to the phenomena of nutrition and reproduction in the organic world, and belongs, like them, to the "objects of nature," as distinguished from the object of the individual, which in both cases is the satisfaction of desire.

Finally, let us consider the third effect, viz., that of modifying the surroundings. From one point of view, viz., that of the order of time, this is the first effect of the action, but I put it last as being the most incidental and non-essential of all the effects. It is easy to conceive of an action which should have no such effect. If the desire is for something very easily attainable, something practically in contact with the individual, with no intervening obstacles, or with nothing but simple space between, which can be traversed without moving anything but his own body or limbs, it will be satisfied and have its indirect or functional effect without causing any perceptible modification of the surroundings. The action would then have only the first and second effects, neither of which being dynamic, it would not be a dynamic action at all, which is contrary to our hypothesis. But if there are any obstacles or obstructions in the way of the satisfaction of desire the first part of the action is to remove these, and this modifies the surroundings to that extent. It is obvious that while there may be very simple degrees of this condition, there may be and are also all conceivable degrees of difficulty and complexity in the interval between the desire and its satisfaction. When we consider developed man with some capacity for "looking before and after" we can readily see that most of his actions are thus complex, and that very few of his desires.can be satisfied without first making considerable modification in his surroundings. This quality increases with his general development and with the increasing number and growing complexity of his desires. When at last his desires, like those of most civilized men, become chiefly spiritual and intellectual, usually remote either in space or time, it is necessary both to work and to wait, and this involves prolonged and intense activity. All this activity is expended upon the surroundings, clearing away obstructions and preparing a smooth road to the predestined goal. The satisfaction of every such desire works extensive changes in the immediate environment and a large part of these changes is permanent, contributing somewhat in each case to the sum total of civilizing influences in society. The principal form that all this takes is that of creating means to the end, and such means are permanent contributions to civilization. They do not merely serve the end of the individual who creates them, but remain after he is through with them to serve the ends of other individuals for all time.

This third effect of a dynamic action is therefore chiefly *to transform the environment.* If we examine this principle closely we shall see that, within a legitimate extension of the terms, all social progress consists in transforming the environment. I will not even restrict it to simple material progress, where this is obvious, covering as it does all economic and industrial operations, but will predicate it also of all esthetic, moral, and intellectual operations. It is, indeed, difficult to separate these, as the historical materialists have succeeded in showing, because the latter are to so large a degree dependent upon the former, but even if we succeed in doing this, at least in thought, still these higher spiritual operations, wholly abstracted from their material base, constitute transformations of the environment in a very proper sense. Looked at from a certain point of view, it is these that furnish not only the most important of such transformations but also the most enduring of them. In Chapter III it was shown that civilization consists in human achievement, and also that the great achievements of mankind are not material but spiritual, that material things are fleeting and evanescent, while spiritual things are lasting and indestructible. Still it must not be forgotten that these permanent contributions to civilization are simply the means by which transformations in the material environment in the interest of man can be wrought, and their value consists in the quality of enabling man to work such transformations constantly and for all time. We may therefore say that this third and only dynamic effect of an action consists in the permanent transformation of the environment which constitutes human achievement.

Looking still deeper into the nature of this dynamic effect of action it is perceived that, somewhat as in the second or functional effect, it is not the effect desired or intended by the agent. The only conscious and intentional effect of the action is the one first considered, the satisfaction of desire. This is the only end of the individual, the only one in which he has an *interest*. The second or functional effect, viz., the maintenance of the social order, and the third or dynamic effect, viz., the furtherance of social progress, are not only matters of complete indifference to him, but they are for the most part undesired, unintended, and unknown by him. Except in the most highly developed and most advanced and enlightened of all men, progress, as we have seen, is not only undesirable but odious and detestable, so that the greater part of all progress both in the past and present has taken place and is taking place in opposition to the desires of men and in spite of the universal conservatism and misoneism of mankind. This is true of all progress produced by the cross fertilization of cultures, it is true of progress through innovation, and it is true of progress through conation. All this belongs to the "philosophy of the unconscious," dimly seen by Schopenhauer and Hartmann, by the latter of whom it received this designation, but which at bottom constitutes the essence of all pure science relating to the sentient world. It is the *natura naturans*, the mysterious power of nature working for ends beyond the reach of human wisdom. It is the mission of true science to lift the veil and peer behind it into the workings of this power, and so far as may be to discover the principles and formulate the laws of these unconscious and deep-lying dynamic agencies.

If now we look squarely at this third, dynamic effect of action we shall see that the quantity of the result is measured by the amount of *effort* put forth, so that the essence of the principle is effort. The greater the obstacles to be removed the greater the effort required. The more difficult the end is of attainment the more elaborate will be the means necessary to secure the end. The more remote the end the longer is it necessary to work in order to reach it, and all the work done in this time consists in transforming the environment in the interest of progress. In every case it is effort that produces the effect, and the quantity of the effect will depend upon, and be roughly proportional to the quantity of effort. Of course the quality has also to be taken into the account, and if the effort is chiefly mental, especially if it is inventive, the dynamic effect is far greater, and seems out of proportion to the effort. But here we may apply the dictum of Descartes that all considerations of quality may be reduced to those of quantity, since mind is the result of a vast series of climactic organizations, so that a genial idea represents a prolonged accumulation, a concentration, focalization, and intensification of the simpler forms of energy, and thus really represents an enormously increased quantity of transformed and sublimated muscular effort. Bastiat seems to have. caught a distinct glimpse of the principle under consideration here when he formulated the much quoted phrase, " wants, efforts, satisfactions," [1] which was put forth as the key note to his " Economic Harmonies." He does not, however, work the principle out nor manifest any clear grasp of its sociological importance. As an economist he of course wholly missed the dynamic effect of efforts, and dwelt on the satisfactions, which cannot be logically separated from the wants, which, indeed, constitute the *dynamic agent*, but not the *dynamic principle*. This is effort, and the term *conation* means the same. I use it as a technical term, partly because so important a principle should have a definite name, and partly because not all efforts are necessarily dynamic, and the word is often loosely used. Conation and effort are not therefore strictly synonymous, and the latter would fall short of exactly defining the principle.

The biological homologue of conation is the Lamarckian principle of exercise, which might as well be called the principle of effort. This is a principle of dynamic biology, and coöperates with fortuitous variation, whose sociological equivalent is innovation, to furnish the initial variations upon which natural selection seizes in producing the transmutation of species. The principle is the same in sociology as in biology, but there is an exceedingly important difference in the way in which it works in the two fields. This difference is expressed by the formula that I have so frequently repeated

---

[1] " Besoins, efforts, satisfactions, voilà le fond général de toutes les sciences qui ont l'homme pour objet." *Journal des Economistes*, Vol. XXI, September, 1848, p. 110. The article in which this phrase occurs is entitled : " Harmonies Économiques " (pp. 105–120), which he afterward expanded into a volume (Vol. VI of his complete works, Paris, 1854), the second chapter of which is entitled : " Besoins, Efforts, Satisfactions," which follows the same lines as the preliminary article.

that *in biology the environment transforms the organism, while in sociology man transforms the environment.* The biologists have abundantly shown how the former of these effects is produced, and now I have shown how the latter effect is produced. The one is a physiological effect, the other a sociological effect. The physical nature of man, as was stated in an earlier chapter (see *supra*, p. 17) has undergone very little change since he assumed his completed human form, but in so far as it has changed or is still changing the principle through which the change is produced is the biological and not the sociological principle. With it therefore we have here nothing to do. But it is clear that animals perform dynamic actions as well as men, and any such action may be analyzed as we have analyzed a human dynamic action. The three effects are the same with the above qualification of the third, viz., 1, the satisfaction of desire, 2, the preservation or continuance of life, 3, the modification of the organism. The first alone is conscious, the second is unconscious, unintended, and unknown, but functional and therefore static. The third is unconscious, unintended, and undesired, but as it tends to change the type of structure it is dynamic. All this is too obvious to require anything beyond simple statement, but it furnishes a perfect illustration of the vast cosmic sweep of the fundamental principles here set forth as well as of the true unity of nature in all its departments when we once seize the thread that binds all these departments into one. This is true monism as I understand that term, and reconciles infinite variety with perfect unity.

Society is the beneficiary of all the dynamic principles of sociology. The dynamic effects are social effects, and the general result is achievement and social progress. But we may look still farther into the process. However much mind may enter into it, the effort is expended directly upon the material environment. Its success in causing social progress is conditioned upon the fundamental truth stated in Chapter III that *matter is dynamic.* In the whole history of mankind it is found that effort expended upon matter has yielded advantageous results. Other expenditures of energy have been either statical or fruitless. Expended in coercing men, social energy yields no progressive results (see *supra*, pp. 19–20). Directed to purely spiritual things, it results in a weak, stagnant civilization, like that of India, culminating in caste, oppression, and quietism, hermetically sealed to all dynamic influences. Matter alone possesses the "promise and potency" of progress, and this has been demonstrated by the enormous strides made by the western civilization after it had fairly commenced to concentrate its energies on the material environment.

The dynamic property of matter resides in its susceptibility to change under the influence of external forces. The law of the conservation of energy does not affect this. That law simply predicates the indestructibility of matter and motion. The *quantity* of matter and motion is fixed, but the *form* of matter and the *mode* of motion are indefinitely variable. As Clerk Maxwell expresses it, "The total energy of any material system is a quantity which can neither be increased nor diminished by any action between the parts of the system, though it may be transformed into any of the forms of which energy is susceptible." [1] This establishes the indefinite modifiability of all material things and the possibility of directing all the forces of nature according to the will of the agent. Nature is thus easily "managed" to the extent that her laws are understood, and there is no limit to the extent to which the inexhaustible forces of nature may be brought into the service of man. This is why the material progress of man has so greatly outstripped his moral progress,[2] and this is what I mean by my definition of civilization as "the utilization of the materials and forces of nature," upon which I have so long insisted. Matter is for man, endowed with intelligence and inspired by science, a veritable lamp of Aladdin, which he need but rub, and, as if by magic, all things take on the forms of utility and cast themselves at his feet.

[1] "Matter and Motion," New York, 1892, p. 103.

[2] I drew this contrast in 1885 in a paper entitled, *Moral and Material Progress Contrasted*, read before the Anthropological Society of Washington, Feb. 17, 1885. See Trans. Anthrop. Soc., Washington, Vol. III, Washington, 1885, pp. 121–136.

CHAPTER XII

CLASSIFICATION OF THE SOCIAL FORCES

THERE are many ways of classifying social phenomena. Nearly all the systems considered in Chapter II require classifications of their own, and the different classifications, like the different systems, all have their merits. Our point of view is that of regarding sociology as a true science, and the principal characteristic of a true science is that it is a domain of natural phenomena produced by a special class of forces. The forces producing social phenomena are the social forces, and taken together they constitute the dynamic agent, the nature of which was made the subject of Chapter VI. The five following chapters (VII to XI) have been devoted to working out the principles according to which the dynamic agent operates in human society, and we have at last arrived at the point where we can undertake a classification of the various forces that combine to make up the dynamic agent, and where we can take up the several classes or groups of such forces and treat them in their logical order.

Nothing that has already been said need be repeated and we may proceed at once with the classification. At the outset we encounter the obstacle presented by the choice of terms. Although the dynamic agent consists wholly in feeling, such is the poverty of the language of feeling that it would be difficult or impossible to find the requisite terms in that vocabulary. We might, it is true, designate the two great primordial classes of forces as the hunger forces and the love forces, but we should be troubled for appropriate adjectives and derivatives. And then, this represents only the positive side of individual preservation and race continuance, and in the former at least there would still be lacking terms suitable for designating those negative forms of preservation which consist in defense and escape. With the other classes of forces the difficulty would be still greater, and it seems best to choose most of the terms from the language of function. Here there is comparatively little difficulty. The world has always avoided as far as possible the expression of feeling. It is too personal, too near to the person

256

or the body. It exposes too plainly the bodily and mental states, which are naturally concealed. Under the highest states of feeling indifference is feigned. If the feeling is pleasurable there is either an ascetic sense of its sinfulness or a sense of shame in its avowal, and it is experienced in silence. If it is painful it involves the admission of imperfection or defectiveness, which no one wishes to admit. "Of course," says Schopenhauer, "human life, like any bogus article, is coated on the outside with a false tinsel; whatever is suffered is always concealed; but whatever any one can afford in the way of show and gloss he keeps in full view, and the more unhappy he is the more he tries to make others think he is the happiest of men."[1] This is doubtless due to the sense of imperfection implied in suffering, and the effort to conceal it is heightened by its general recognition in the form of refusing to help any one who lets it be known that he is in need, while willingly showering benefits on those who make it appear that they have need of nothing. This apparently detestable trait in human nature is based on the inevitable association of suffering with worthlessness, and the innate disinclination to waste substance on the worthless.

Everything thus conspires to the suppression of the utterance of feeling and to prevent the possibility of the development of a rich and copious language of feeling. Compare for example the vocabulary of the sense of sight, which is chiefly intellectual, with that of either taste or smell, which are wholly sensual. Think of the number of names of colors and the fine shades that they express, and compare these with the names for odors or tastes. For the latter it is necessary to name some object (flower, perfume, fruit, condiment, etc.) and say it smells or tastes like such and such a thing. Perfumes and flavors, in which the language is most complete, are all so named (violets, ottar of roses, red cedar, incense, vanilla, orange, strawberry, pineapple, etc.). There are no such simple words as red, blue, yellow, green, etc. This is all due to taboo of the sensual and the check thus given to the development of a language of feeling.

But when it comes to function the case is reversed. Here the language is rich and the vocabulary ample. This is because of the supposed dignity and nobility of function. It is instinctively felt that the preservation of the individual and the race, the maintenance of the social order, the furtherance of social progress, and the esthetic

[1] "Die Welt als Wille und Vorstellung," Vol. I, pp. 383–384.

S

moral, and intellectual development of mankind are paramount considerations upon which any amount of effort and energy may be profitably expended. The consequence is that they have from the first been made the subjects of exhaustive treatment and thousands of volumes have been written dealing with them from almost every conceivable point of view. It is this that has rendered the language of function so full and complete.

It has from the first been apparent to me that the foundation of sociology as a true science must be a logical classification of the social forces, and in a paper that I read on Aug. 31, 1880, before the Section of Anthropology of the American Association for the Advancement of Science in Boston, entitled, "Feeling and Function as Factors in Human Development," I proposed the following system, placing it on the blackboard in tabular form:[1] —

Essential Forces
- Preservative Forces
  - Positive, gustatory (pleasurable)
  - Negative, protective (painful)
- Reproductive Forces
  - Direct. The sexual instinct
  - Indirect. Parental and consanguineal affections

Non-essential Forces
- Esthetic
- Emotional
- Intellectual

In "Dynamic Sociology," which appeared in 1883, the table of classification of the social forces occurs on p. 472 of the first volume. As will be seen, it is the same as the above with a few verbal changes: —

The Social Forces are:

Essential Forces
- Preservative Forces
  - Positive, gustatory (seeking pleasure)
  - Negative, protective (avoiding pain)
- Reproductive Forces
  - Direct. The sexual and amative desires
  - Indirect. Parental and consanguineal affections

Non-essential Forces
- Esthetic Forces
- Emotional (moral) Forces
- Intellectual Forces

[1] The paper was published in full in *Science*, original series, Vol. I, Oct. 23, 1880, pp. 210–211, the table occurring on p. 211.

In the "Psychic Factors of Civilization," which appeared in 1893, a chapter (Chapter XVIII) was devoted to the social forces, and the above table was placed at the head of that chapter without change. It was also introduced without change in my article entitled: "The Social Forces," published in the *American Journal of Sociology* for July, 1896, Vol. II, where it occurs on p. 88. This article forms Chapter VII of the "Outlines of Sociology," the table occurring on p. 148. In that article, however, some elective modifications were proposed. For example, it was shown that the Essential Forces may be designated as physical, and the Non-essential Forces as spiritual, the Preservative Forces as forces of individual preservation, and the Reproductive Forces as forces of race continuance. Moreover, it was suggested that the Spiritual Forces are essentially forces of "race elevation," and each of these groups was discussed from the new point of view.

In the present work the point of view is primarily that of the genesis of society, and the classification of the social forces, may, without losing anything of its character as a logical system, be somewhat recast to bring it into harmony with the general treatment. As sociology has not yet acquired a suitable terminology from the standpoint of genesis or evolution, we may conveniently borrow a few appropriate terms from biology, whose evolutional terminology is especially well developed. In discussing the classification of the social forces I have repeatedly shown that the physiological basis of the preservative forces, especially of the positive ones, is nutrition, metabolism, growth, etc., that is to say, the functions that develop and sustain the physical body. From the standpoint of genesis this includes all the phases through which an organism passes during the period of gestation, and this is called its ontogeny. But ontogeny need not, and properly understood, does not end with the birth of the individual, but includes everything that relates to the *being* during its whole existence, excluding only the genetic relations of one being to other beings, *i.e.*, the beings from which derived and the beings generated by the being in question. Consideration of these belongs to phylogeny. But although the forces called preservative in the above tables of classification are desires and wants of individuals and serve primarily to preserve the lives of individuals, it is also true that they are the influences which work for the maintenance of the social order through the principle of social synergy, and they are therefore the forces of social as well as individual preservation. I shall therefore use, as altogether synonymous with the former expression "preservative forces," except as designed to connote also their genetic and evolutionary relations, the expression *ontogenetic forces*.

In like manner the "reproductive forces" of the former classification may be called the *phylogenetic forces*, as the influences that work the perpetuity and continuity of the *phylum*, hereditary stock, or race. From the standpoint of function they take no account of the individual, but in continuing the race they make the life of the individual as it were continuous. In thus continuing the membership of society they continue society itself. This is true social reproduction, but is not what the organicists mean when they use that phrase. If by society we mean associated men in general there is no other social reproduction, but if we regard society as a plurality of social bodies or groups, social reproduction is a sort of gemmation, and is that which was called social differentiation in Chapter X, becoming colonization in advanced societies.

All the social forces that have hitherto been classed as "non-essential" I now propose to call *sociogenetic forces*. These were shown in 1896 to be "spiritual forces," meaning by this that they are psychic in a somewhat different and "higher" or "nobler" sense than the essential forces, which were then designated as "physical," not that they can be other than psychic, but simply that their *functions* are physical, while the functions of the non-essential forces are also psychic. But a step was also there taken in the direction of the present point of view, by treating them as "forces of race elevation." It was then seen that these are the chief civilizing agencies. It remains to be pointed out that they are also the chief socializing agencies. But the difference between civilizing and socializing agencies is not wide. Whatever is socializing either is, or may become, civilizing. Socialization is the first step toward civilization, and all esthetic, moral, and intellectual influences are working for civilization chiefly through socialization. The general subject of socialization and its relations to civilization and human achievement is fully treated in Chapter XX.

The final classification, then, may be given the following form : —

The Social Forces are :	Physical Forces (Function bodily)	Ontogenetic Forces	Positive, attractive (seeking pleasure) Negative, protective (avoiding pain)
		Phylogenetic Forces	Direct, sexual Indirect, consanguineal
	Spiritual Forces (Function psychic)	Sociogenetic Forces	Moral (seeking the safe and good) Esthetic (seeking the beautiful) Intellectual (seeking the useful and true)

Notwithstanding the prominence that the functional has to assume in the terminology of the social forces, the fact must not be lost sight of for a moment that this is not the essence of them, and that the standpoint of the sociologist is not function but feeling. Function is indirect, incidental, and consequential, the result of adaptation and that preëstablished harmony that was considered in Chapter V.   It is biological and not sociological.   The social forces are wants seeking satisfactions through efforts, and are thus social motives or motors inspiring activities which either create social structures through social synergy or modify the structures already created through innovation and conation.   They reside in the individual but become social through interaction, coöperation, and cumulative effects.   They are all primarily physical or physiological, even those classed as spiritual, for the organism is the only source from which they can emanate.   They all have, therefore, their physical seat in the human body, and for most of them this is not difficult to locate.   The ontogenetic forces of the positive or attractive class, which might be called the hunger forces, have their chief seat in the stomach where the principal satisfaction is experienced, but the passageway to the stomach is provided with specialized nerves calculated to attract and convey nutritious substances to the digestive tract.   This office is performed by the sense of taste, located chiefly in the tongue and palate.   The sense of smell is commonly and correctly regarded as ancillary to that of taste, but no one seems to have pointed out that its chief purpose is to enlarge the radius of nutritive attraction by acquainting the individual with the existence of nutrient materials that are not in contact with the organism and may not even be in sight of it. The value of this to the lower organisms is obvious, but it diminishes with structural development until it is scarcely necessary to developed man. The ontogenetic forces of the negative or protective class may be said to have their physical seat in all the specialized pain nerves of the body, wherever these may be located.

The primary or direct phylogenetic forces of course have their physical seat in the loins, but the secondary, indirect, or consanguineal social forces are much more vaguely located and cannot be limited to any definite tract. Philoprogenitiveness, and especially maternal affection, form a true transition from the sexual to the consanguineal, and the latter is more or less restricted to the mammary plexuses. But between this sentiment and the love of the helpless, which some regard as the basis of the moral sentiments, the step is short, and emotions of both these classes can be easily located by any observing person experiencing them in the general region popularly called the "breast."

It might naturally be expected that the spiritual or sociogenetic social forces would be more difficult to locate in the physical system, and some may deny altogether the possibility of doing this. But, while the difficulty may be frankly confessed without humiliation, the task is not hopeless. The fact last noted clearly shows that some at least of the moral sentiments are definitely cantoned in the human breast, as the poets so often tell us, and the anatomist informs us that this chiefly means the large plexuses of the great sympathetic system that are located in this region. It is these and not the great circulative organ or force-pump of the blood, that constitute the "heart" of the emotional literature, whether romantic, moral, or religious. If, therefore, the social forces are to be classified on the basis of their physical organs, the moral forces must undoubtedly follow immediately after the secondary phylogenetic forces out of which they have naturally grown during the historical expansion of the primitive ethical dualism (see *supra*, p. 187). In former classifications I have placed the esthetic before the moral forces without giving any particular reason for doing so, but from a certain sense of the close connection between ideas of beauty and ideas of right, and the extent to which the former grow out of romantic love. But there is perhaps a still closer connection between love and altruistic sentiments, which belong to the moral forces.

The fact is that both moral and esthetic ideas are closely affiliated upon the tender emotion and no linear classification can adequately show this.

It is at least clear that most or all of the moral sentiments, growing as they have out of sympathy, which in turn is a development of the love of kindred, have their seat in the general emotional tracts, *i.e.*, in the great sympathetic plexuses. There are so many of these, and they are so widely distributed throughout the body, that it is impossible in the present state of science to locate these sentiments definitely, and still more so to assign particular sentiments to particular ganglia, even supposing that the system has attained any such degree of specialization. I do not doubt that when experimental psychology shall have advanced much farther than at present the study of what I may call the localization of the emotions will be undertaken somewhat as the localization of the faculties in the brain is now being studied.

The seat of the esthetic forces is still more difficult to determine. The *love* of beauty is clearly a feeling and amounts to an emotion, but it receives its stimulus from the semi-intellectual senses of sight and hearing. The stimuli are propagated from the optic and auditory tracts of the brain to the appropriate emotional centers, which are probably, in part at least, in the brain itself. Any attempt more definitely to locate them would be hopeless, but, as in the case of the moral emotions, they present a problem for the future scientific psychology.

Finally the intellectual forces, usually characterized as the *love* of truth, but also involving the love of knowledge, are clearly centered in the brain and doubtless chiefly reside in the cortical layers. They are therefore affiliated upon the esthetic forces and not on the moral forces, and this is another reason for the order here adopted in the classification of the spiritual forces. But all these sentiments intercross and anastomose. There is an obvious connection between utility and safety, and between both these and the simpler sense of self-preservation. All the social forces represent the innate interests of mankind and whatever interests prompt to action, thus becoming a social motor.

Many other relationships might be pointed out among the social forces. The physical forces may be regarded as original and the spiritual as derivative, and it is practically true that the latter are confined to the human race while the former are common to both men and animals. It is also true that while the former become social by stimulating activities which unconsciously produce social effects, the latter are essentially socializing and tend to race elevation and universal culture. Again, all the physical forces may be regarded in one sense as negative, since they are directed to the prevention of pain rather than the production of pleasure. Hunger, thirst, cold, fear, want of every kind, and also love, are painful states, to escape from which men continually strive, while the satisfactions derived from successful efforts in these directions are for the most part momentary and count for next to nothing as pleasures compared to the gain of having escaped from the pains. On the other hand the spiritual forces may be classed as positive, since to a much less degree are they directed to the relief of pain, and they are almost wholly directed to securing pleasures whose absence is not felt as a pain. Sympathy, it is true, is a secondary or *representative* pain, an echo in self of the pains of others, but most moral action is performed for the pleasure it yields, and not to escape from even this form of pain. The esthetic forces are still more positive in this sense, while the intellectual forces seem to be wholly so.

Among other relations of the social forces we find a class which I will characterize as *paradoxes of the social forces*. There is a wide misconception, not to say ignorance, on the subject, coupled with a large amount of hypocrisy and absurd conventionality, which may be exposed by analysis, although it cannot be dispelled by logic. The facts last stated might be classed among these paradoxes, viz., that the physical impulses are negative while the spiritual ones are positive. But it is also true that the physical forces are altruistic, while the spiritual forces are egoistic. The maintenance of life and of the race are highly altruistic objects, and it is these that the physical forces secure. It need not be maintained that this altruism is conscious, but if this test is to be applied it will compare favorably here with the later and better understood forms of altruism. On the other hand, the spiritual forces are egoistic. This follows from what I have just said that they are not modes of escape from danger to the individual and the race, but ways of pursuing pleasure for its own sake. There is great confusion in the popular ideas of high and low, coarse and refined, worthy and unworthy. The most

worthy and noble of all things are those that preserve and perpetuate the race. This is function and the end of nature. The conception of safety lies at the foundation of all religion. It is the essence
of *salvation*, however far the meaning of that term may have departed from it in the later derivative and distorted cults.   The
physical social forces are therefore those that represent the highest necessity, while the spiritual forces chiefly represent utility,
as I have defined these terms (see *supra*, p. 131).   The fundamental
criterion of utility is the quantity of satisfaction yielded, and,
measured by this standard, it is clear that the spiritual interests far
outweigh the physical interests of developed man.   Physical satisfactions have greater intensity, but spiritual satisfactions have greater
duration.   The former are momentary, and the gain mainly consists in having gotten rid of a pain or a pang or a goad, the gadfly
of eternal passion. The spiritual forces are no such torments, though
aspirations after excellence may constitute a prolonged and uninterrupted incentive to strive and to achieve.   But satisfaction accompanies achievement, and the debt of anticipation is constantly paid
in the coin of participation, so that the satisfaction is to all intents
and purposes continuous.   This gives volume to spiritual pleasures
much more than sufficient to counterbalance the greater intensity of
physical pleasures.   It is only in the sense of being more moderate
and enduring, and thus greater in real volume, that the former can
be said to be higher, more refined, or more worthy than the latter.
But no such comparison of degree is just or logical.   The distinction
is qualitative, not quantitative, and the physical forces are characterized by their necessity, while the spiritual forces are characterized
by their utility.   The former chiefly serve function and secure the
ends of nature, standing thus largely on the biological plane, while
the latter minister to feeling and secure the ends of man, and therefore stand wholly on the sociological plane. The first are ontogenetic
and phylogenetic, while the second are exclusively sociogenetic.

CHAPTER XIII

THE ONTOGENETIC FORCES

We have to consider in this chapter the influence which those human activities that have subsistence and protection for their ends exert on the creation and transformation of social structures. The struggle for existence in the animal world did not cease with the emergence of the human species out of that into the social world, but has always continued. Here it became social synergy and worked for social structure. Just as in the earliest Metazoan life the first organ developed was the stomach, and the first organisms consisted of a stomach only, so in the lowest societies all energy is concentrated on the one supreme function of nutrition or subsistence, and such societies may be not inappropriately characterized as consisting exclusively of a social stomach. But at a very early stage the environment raises opposition and threatens injury, and defensive activities are added to the appetitive activities. The struggle grows more intense and the group sentiment is generated and creates incipient society. The primitive group or horde is the resultant social structure. During the period of social differentiation described in Chapter X great vicissitudes are passed through, during which the multiplied groups grow heterogeneous and ultimately come to differ from one another as widely as coördinate groups of human beings are capable of differing. But thus far the competition is with one another and with the environment (climate, wild beasts, terrestrial obstructions, etc.), and the effect is mainly constructive, intensive, and creative; in a word, it is static. When, however, the time arrives for social integration to begin the competition is one of group with group and wholly new elements enter into the struggle. The stage of race antagonism is reached and the era of war begins. The chase for animal food is converted into a chase for human flesh, and anthropophagous races arise spreading terror in all directions.

EXPLOITATION

All social processes that can be called economic have their origin in exploitation. In entirely primitive social groups, comparable to the Protozoa or unicellular organisms, each individual goes about in the way that animals do, seeking food, shelter, etc., and consumes whatever he finds. There is no social result any more than in the case of animals, certainly no more than in the case of such animals as dig holes, build nests, etc. The efforts thus put forth have only the biological effect of somewhat strengthening the organs thus brought into exercise. The skill acquired in securing animal food strengthens the brain and increases the power of adaptation to varied physical conditions, which was the prime requisite to social differentiation. But early in the stage of social integration, when the various differentiated groups nearest to the center of original radiation began to approach one another and encroach upon territory occupied by other groups, the idea of making some economic use of such proximity was not slow to rise in the minds of those groups that proved themselves superior. The use of the bodies of the weaker races for food was of course the simplest form of exploitation to suggest itself. But this stage was succeeded by that of social assimilation through conquest and subjugation, where the conquered race became something more than a factor in subsistence. Still the conquered race remained an economic element, and the conquering race soon learned to utilize it to far greater advantage than cannibalism could yield. The profound inequality produced by subjugation was turned to account through other forms of exploitation. The women and the warriors were enslaved, and the system of caste that arose converted the conquered race into a virtually servile class, while this service and the exemptions it entailed converted the leaders of the conquering race into a leisure class. There were other influences, especially sacerdotal, that contributed to the same end, but we are concerned here especially with the economic aspects of the problem.

Slavery. — Such was the origin of slavery, an economic institution which is found in the earlier stages of all the histcric races. The moral prejudices of the modern advanced races naturally cause wholly false views to prevail relative to slavery which the sociologist finds it very difficult to contend with. Perhaps his greatest difficulty is not that of conveying true views to others, but that of acquiring them for himself. The danger of seeming to defend an institution which is repugnant to him tends to blind him to much of the real truth. His attitude is liable to become that of the modern advocates of universal peace, discussed in Chapter X. It seems inconsistent to argue against war and slavery in the present while maintaining that they were useful institutions in the past. There are two answers to this charge of inconsistency. The one is the fundamental law that prevails throughout all departments of nature that nothing can come into being that is not demanded by the conditions existing at the time. Nothing that is really useless can by any possibility be developed. *A fortiori* it is a contradiction of terms to speak of the natural genesis of anything injurious or wholly bad. And all this is as true of social as of organic structures. According to the Lamarckian principle it is function that creates structure, and the law of demand and supply is not merely an economic law but a sociologic law, and is nothing more nor less than the economic and sociologic expression of the biologic law of exercise. There never was a human institution that was not called forth in response to a social demand, which from the scientific standpoint, means a social necessity.

The second answer to this charge of inconsistency, of which some sociologists are so much afraid, is that many structures, both organic and social, outlive their usefulness and persist as impediments to the life and health of the organism and of society. In the former case they become " vestiges," and while sometimes quite innocuous except as involving the waste produced in nourishing them, they more frequently become dangerous seats of disease, as in the vermiform appendage, the tonsils, etc. The extreme stability of social structures was noted in Chapter XI as one of the principal obstacles to human progress, and there is no human institution, however necessary it may have been at the time it was created, that will not sooner or later become a burden unless it has the element of lability and is transformed under the influence of some of the dynamic principles that were treated in that chapter. Such transformation may ultimately become so complete as to amount to virtual abolition, but unless it takes place without organic disruption of the original structure it is revolution. Institutions that persist after they have ceased to serve a useful purpose are the exact sociological homologues of vestiges in biology and may be appropriately called *social vestiges*. Major Powell has happily called superstition and folklore vestigial opinion.[1] These too are human institutions and may be classed as social vestiges. In fact social structures are in this respect precisely like organic structures, and exist in all stages from rudiments, or incipient structures, to vestiges, or obsolescent, and also wholly obsolete structures.

Now the proper and scientific attitude toward an institution that is regarded as bad is not wholesale condemnation and denunciation as something that is essentially bad and must have always been bad, but investigation to ascertain what stage of its history it is in, and whether it is in process of transformation, throwing off its outgrown elements and replacing them with elements adapted to existing conditions, and therefore useful. If it is found not to be in this dynamic state, or state of moving equilibrium, it is proper to inquire whether by any human action it can be put into this state. To this end its history and its true nature should be studied, and especially the original conditions which must have developed it and caused it to exist. Until this is done there is no logical ground for attacking it.

With regard to the institution of slavery we have already seen that it was an advance upon the practice of extermination, and still more upon cannibalism. It was universal throughout antiquity and persisted in Europe through the Middle Ages. The causes that conspired to bring about its gradual abolition have been enumerated and discussed by all historians of Europe and need not be entered into here. I will only note how relatively modern is the sentiment condemning it. It is certainly confined, with very rare exceptions, to the last two centuries, and chiefly to the nineteenth century, and it never related to European slavery, but has been almost exclusively confined to that form of slavery which consisted in importing inferior races from their native country, chiefly Africa, and enslaving them in civilized countries. The thing that has been chiefly condemned is the slave trade, but of course the resulting form of slavery became the subject of a general crusade. But as showing how relatively modern was even hostility to the slave trade the fact may be cited that De Foe, when he wrote his " Robinson Crusoe," which appeared

[1] *American Anthropologist*, New Series, Vol. II, January, 1900, p. 1; *The Monist* Vol. X, April, 1900, p. 389.

in 1719, had evidently never heard that there was anything wrong in it, for the shipwrecked vessel was engaged in the slave trade, of which he speaks as one would speak of the cattle trade or of the trade in spices.

Labor. — Economists, socialists, statesmen, and industrial reformers, however widely they may differ on other matters, are agreed that all value in the economic sense is due to labor, but most of them talk as though labor was natural to man, and as though the main question was how to give men work enough to do. However this may be in civilized societies now, nothing is more certain than that the original problem was how to make men work. It does not seem to be seen that the human race has been radically transformed in this respect, and that the modern industrious artisan or laborer is utterly unlike his primitive ancestor. We can gain some little idea of this difference by comparing him with the North American Indian, especially with those tribes that have adhered to their tribal customs and adopted none of the habits of Europeans. Still, only those who have had considerable to do with these races realize how impossible it is for them to do anything that we call work. The total lack of the power of application, especially among the men, is an almost universal characteristic. Not that they do not often follow the chase for sustained periods, and they will also spend hours in fashioning a weapon or a boat, but here the end is immediately before them and the fruition is to be theirs the moment the end is attained. These are elements that are absent from labor proper. The instinct of workmanship is simply the love of, or pleasure in, activities that immediately satisfy desires and which satisfaction is constantly and vividly before the mind. Labor in the conventional sense possesses no such stimulus.

The pursuit of food wherever it can be found by the members of the primitive horde can no more be called labor than can the grazing of a buffalo or the browsing of an antelope. Nor is there any true labor involved in the operations of races at much higher stages of culture, as, for example, the Amerinds already mentioned. Only the work of the women in caring for the men and the children, and in performing the drudgery of the camp approaches the character of labor, and this differs widely from most forms of productive industry. And it may be safely inferred from all that is known of actual savages and primitive peoples that prior to the period of social integration, and at the beginning of the period of conquest, mankind, both the conquered and the conquering races, were utterly incapable of sustained labor and had no conception of it. Men of that type would be perfectly worthless in the industrial world to-day. Their productive power in the economic sense would be nil.

Now contrasting the disciplined laborer of modern society with the undisciplined savage, and admitting that the former has been transformed from the latter, this enormous and all-important change in human character has to be accounted for. How did man learn to work? Did the needs of existence teach him self-denial, tone down his wild unsettled nature, and discipline his mind and body to daily toil? Not at all. It is safe to say that if left wholly to these influences man would have never learned to labor. It required some other influence far more imperative and coercive. In a word, nothing short of slavery could ever have accomplished this. This was the social mission of human slavery — to convert mere activity into true labor. The aim of the conquering race was to gain the maximum advantage from the conquest. The conquered race possessed little that could be seized as booty. This would be soon consumed and gone. The only thing the conquered race possessed that had any permanent or continued value was its power of serving the conqueror. This could not escape the mind of the latter, however low his stage of intelligence, and as a matter of fact and of history, so far as these are known, this has been perceived and generally acted upon. The women and the warriors at least, and as many others as were needed, were enslaved and compelled to serve the conquering race.

The motive to labor is no longer the desire to enjoy the fruits of labor. This, as we have seen, is never sufficient to induce primitive man to perform prolonged and arduous tasks. The motive now is fear of the lash. The slave must work or suffer any punishment his savage master pleases to inflict. If flogging does not suffice he may be tortured, and if torture fails he will be killed. No pen will ever record the brutal history of primitive slavery through generations and even centuries of which mankind was taught to labor. The bitterest scenes of an Uncle Tom's Cabin would be an agreeable relief from the contemplation of the stern realities of this unwritten history. It will never be known how many, unable to adapt themselves to such a great change from their former free, wild, capricious life, failed, faltered, and fainted by the way to have their places taken by stronger, more flexible and more adaptable ones, that could bear their burdens and transmit some small increment of their new-found powers of endurance to their posterity. For the capacity to labor is a typical "acquired character" that has been transmitted in minute additions from parent to offspring and from generation to generation of slaves, until great numbers of men were at last born with a "natural" or constitutional power to apply themselves to monotonous tasks during their whole lives. This truth has been dimly perceived by certain writers, but its immense economic importance has been almost completely overlooked.

The number of conquering races has always been relatively small and the number of conquered races has of course been correspondingly large. This came at length to mean that the "ruling classes" constituted only a small fraction of the population of the world, while the subject classes made up the great bulk of the population. At the time that men began to compile rude statistics of population, which was sparingly done before the beginning of our era, it was found that the slaves far outnumbered the "citizens" of all countries. In Athens there was such a census taken in the year 309 B.C., when there were found to be 21,000 citizens, 10,000 foreigners, and 400,000 slaves! It is not, therefore, a small number of men that have been thus kept in training all these ages, but practically all mankind. It may sound paradoxical to call slavery a civilizing agency, but if industry is civilizing there is no escape from this conclusion, for it is probably no exaggeration to say that but for this severe school of experience continued through thousands of generations, there could have been nothing corresponding to modern industry. And right here is a corollary which Mr. Spencer and other critics of militancy have failed to draw. For slavery, as they admit, is the natural and necessary outcome of war. It is the initial step in the "régime of status." It was therefore in militarism that the foundations of industrialism were laid in social adaptation. There seems to be no other way by which mankind could have been prepared for an industrial era. Or if this is more than we are warranted in saying, it is at least true that this is the particular way in which men were fitted for the rôle that they have been playing in the past two centuries.

Property

An animal can scarcely be said to possess anything. It is true that predatory animals possess their prey after catching it and while devouring it, and dogs will fight over the possession of a bone, but no one would dignify such possession with the name of property. The primitive hordes of men may be said to possess the few things needed for their existence, but here the line is practically drawn at the artificial. Even a club is artificial. The skin of an animal used as a blanket has cost the effort and skill of skinning the animal, and this usually presupposes some kind of instrument, a sharp-edged flint, for example, and such things may be said to "belong" to their "owners." But for most of the possessions of undeveloped races communal or group ownership is the prevalent form. One may call this property, but it is at best only an embryonic form of property in an economic sense. In this respect, as in so many others, the unassimilated races are sharply marked off from the assimilated races. I prefer these sociological terms to biological ones, but there is a certain advantage in having both. In Chapter X, when dealing with the genesis of society, I compared the phenomena of conquest and subjugation with those of fecundation in living organisms. In Chapter XI, when dealing with social evolution, I compared the same phenomena with cross fertilization. Both comparisons were elucidating and altogether appropriate. But this shows that they are not "analogies," for there cannot be two different analogies of the same phenomenon. They are simply comparisons from different points of view that help to render an obscure process clear.

We have now to deal with the same phenomena from still a third point of view, viz., from that of the origin of property. It is clear that neither of the organic operations, fecundation, cross fertilization, previously used will serve here as a term of comparison. There is, however, another still more fundamental biologic fact that will serve as such term not only here but in many other cases. The most important stage in organic development, after the origin of life itself, is unquestionably that which marks the passage from the simple, unicellular condition to the compound multicellular condition, from the protozoic or protophytic to the metazoic or metaphytic type of structure. Now the primitive horde, which has already been

T

called "social protoplasm,"[1] and has even been likened to the independent animal cell, or the Amœba,[2] very exactly represents the first of these two stages, which may therefore be appropriately called the *protosocial stage*, and the horde the *protosocial type* of society, while the whole social fabric which was wrought by social integration and social assimilation may be called the *metasocial type*, the period of conquest, subjugation, fusion, and amalgamation representing the *metasocial stage* of social development. These terms *protosocial* and *metasocial*[3] seem to me every way preferable to Durkheim's terms "unsegmented" and "segmented" which are also intended as biological analogies, but do not correspond to any definite stage in the early development of the metasocial type, such as that of the origin of segmented animals. If the horde is only social protoplasm the unsegmented type must be metasocial, but true social tissues were formed as soon as two societies coalesced. From this time on we may have a science of social histology. And here we might indulge in another analogy and call all tissues formed from or traceable to the conquering race ectodermal, all formed from or traceable to the conquered race, endodermal, and all formed from or traceable to the combined and commingled mass of both races who are neither noble nor slave, mesodermal. These comparisons are certainly better than those of Spencer.

Returning to the subject of property, we may now say that the protosocial form of property is chiefly communal, while the metasocial form is individual possession. But as property is only valuable in so far as it satisfies desire, the first form of metasocial property consisted largely in slaves, *i.e.*, in something that could serve the owner and satisfy his wants. Beginning with women, used both to gratify the lust and also to wait on the person of the military chief, it extended to men, who could surround him with all manner of luxuries and do his general bidding. The other principal form of metasocial property, unknown in the protosocial state, was land. The lower races lay claim to certain regions of country

---

[1] "De la Division du Travail Social," per Émile Durkheim, Paris, 1893, p. 189.

[2] "Die Sociologische Erkenntnis," von Gustav Ratzenhofer, Leipzig, 1898, p. 229.

[3] It is too late to raise the objection of hybrid Græco-Latin etymology, as has been done in the case of the word *sociology*, since there is really no Greek equivalent for the Latin *socius*. It must not, however, be supposed that sociology is the only science in which this etymological sin has been committed. The name of so well established a science as *mineralogy* is open to the same objection.

over which they are accustomed to roam in search of animal and vegetable food, but no one member of the group pretends to an exclusive right to any subdivision of that region. But after the conquest of one race by another the leading warriors of the conquering race lay claim to all the territory occupied by the subject race and proceed to divide it up among themselves, assigning boundaries to the shares of each individual. This assumes more complex forms with successive assimilations, and ultimately creates the latifundia and the feudal fiefs. All the other forms of property grow out of these two general classes, and the ruling classes come into the possession of flocks and herds, castles, vehicles, tools, weapons, and everything that can minister to a life of ease and domination.

But this is only a general view of the economic operations of early society — the social warp, as it may be called. Over it there is everywhere and always woven a social woof, which is not less important to the sociologist. The conception of two antagonistic classes, the conquering and the conquered, falls far short of the real state of things. Both these classes must also be conceived as thoroughly heterogeneous. All this was considered in Chapter X, where the whole process of social karyokinesis was described, resulting in the development of the four great human institutions, law, the state, the people, and the nation. Not all the members of the dominant race are chiefs, rulers, lords, or the immediate protégés of these. A much larger number are simply citizens without special claims upon the rulers and obliged to maintain themselves by their own efforts. Neither are all the members of the subject race slaves. A considerable number are free and in a condition not widely different from the class last mentioned. The two races are virtually equal in natural capacity, and the process of mingling the blood through intermarriage is rapidly obliterating race lines. These two wide margins constantly overlap, interlace, and interpenetrate each other, serving as a sort of leaven for the generation of a common people.

The true economic idea of property is the possession of useful commodities in excess of immediate needs. It is based on the division of labor, which creates all things in excess and secures their mutual exchange. As has been pointed out by many writers, property in this sense is impossible except under the protection of law and under the power of the state. So soon as these institutions are

formed the other coördinate human institution *property* takes form
and henceforth constitutes one of the leading civilizing agents. The
distinction between *meus* and *tuus* does not exist in the mind of
primitive man. Whatever any one has possession of is his by possession, but there is no such notion as its being his by right. If
another can wrest it from him it becomes his, and so indefinitely.
The idea of ownership of anything in possession of another, or of a
thing regardless of where it may be, is a late derivative idea. This
is the idea that lies at the foundation of property, and there could
be no property in any true sense until this idea had taken firm root
in society. But such is human nature, or more properly speaking, the
natural animal constitution of man, that no such idea could arise
in the protosocial state. The substitute for it was communism, which
is in the nature of a *modus vivendi.*

After conquest the possessions of the subjugated race fall for the
most part to the conquerors, or at least the communistic régime terminates. What with sacking and pillaging and sequestering and
portioning, the incipient metasocial society finds itself in a state of
economic chaos, and the process of social karyokinesis affects possessions as it affects persons. The large penumbral mass who are
neither slaves nor rulers constitute the turbulent, unmanageable
element. The races mingle, at first mechanically, but in time
chemically and organically. Interest here as everywhere unites,
and extremes meet on a sort of common ground of struggle for
existence, all demanding concessions from the military power.
Every one seizes whatever he can, defends it by force or hies away
with it to a place of safety. He hides it or buries it, or repairs
to the solitude to enjoy it as best he can. Own it he cannot, and
such a thing as property in any modern or economic sense is
impossible.

No matter how stern and unrelenting the military power may be,
the state of things ultimately becomes intolerable, and the stage of
concession on the one hand and resignation on the other is sooner or
later reached, followed by all the other forms of social equilibration,
until at last the régime of law begins, rights are recognized, and the
state is born. Now for the first time there arises the possibility of
property, and it is at this stage that property as a human institution
begins. When a man can own a camel or a buffalo skin, or a spear,
or a bronze ax, and be secured in its possession without having to

fight for it, or conceal it, it becomes property, and next to personal safety, the first and most important function of the state is to guarantee the security of rightful possession.

Of all the many ways in which the principle of permanent possession, or property, contributed to social development, the principal one was the incentive it furnished to accumulation. Without accumulation property would have very little socializing influence. But when it is seen that any one may own much more of a thing than he can immediately use, can hold it for future consumption, or can barter it for other things that he does not possess, he will begin to acquire as large an amount as possible of that which he can most easily obtain and hold it in store for these and other purposes. Until this was possible the division of labor was useless, and hence we see that the division of labor, which is usually spoken of as a very primitive condition, was impossible until the state was formed. But property in this sense means much more still than this. It was the basis of exchange, of trade, of commerce, and of business in general as well as of industry in the more restricted sense. Property, which is of course only a means to enjoyment, when thus guaranteed and made convertible and flexible, is made an end and is pursued as such. A new desire, a new want, is thus created, which finally develops into the most imperative of all wants. Property assumes the character of wealth, and the pursuit of wealth, wholly irrespective of the power to use it, becomes the supreme passion of mankind. Such a powerful passion is of course sure to have its dark side, but considered as a spur to activity and as an agent in transforming the environment, it must be admitted to be the most powerful of all the motor forces of society.

A large part of the final intensity that this passion acquired was of course due to the adoption at a certain stage of the movement of a symbol or representative of property in the form of a circulating medium, or money. Through this device all forms of property became blended and reduced to one, and the pursuit of wealth was converted into the pursuit of money which stands for wealth. Besides the legitimate effect in giving simplicity and ease to all business transactions, the introduction of money lent an additional charm to the pursuit of wealth and greatly intensified the passion. It gave rise to a universal plutolatry, which took fantastic forms, creating both misers and spendthrifts on the opposite margins of the

social beam, but which had for its main and solid effect to penetrate
and illumine the darkest corners of the material world. To it the
material civilization of the great historic races is chiefly due. As a
factor in human achievement this super-preservative social force,
"the love of money," has had no rival, and still remains the mainspring of economic and industrial activity. If to the moralist it is
"the root of all evil," to the sociologist, studying the causes of social
development, it is the root of all the good there is in material civilization. As shown in Chapter XI, this is the result of efforts
directed toward personal ends but expended on the means to the
attainment of those ends. The pursuit of wealth acquires its highly
dynamic character by virtue of its quality of keeping the end remote
from the means, and of thus rendering the effort indefinitely prolonged and practically continuous.

Production. — Production is the creation of property. This, though
true, is not a definition, since there are forms of property, such as
land, which are not properly produced. But production is only
possible through labor, and is therefore an exclusively metasocial
institution or operation. Economists give a very broad meaning to
production, as anything that creates or increases value. It might
naturally be supposed that under a system of slavery, where the
majority of the population is compelled to labor, production would
be very rapid, but this is not the case. However large the number
of slaves the masters find ways of consuming all they produce. The
non-working classes, though numerically small, are naturally wasteful. Mr. Veblen has shown how the mere maintenance of caste
requires the gratuitous and ostentatious waste of property, and this
is greatly increased by the rivalry in displaying wealth on the part
of the members of the leisure class. The maintenance of the military rule consumes a large share, and another large portion goes to
administration. In all the early societies there exists, besides the
governing class properly so called, a sacerdotal class, which is a
leisure class *par excellence*. This class is habitually the recipient of
large emoluments and costly luxuries. All these expenses are paid
by slave labor and by tribute from the free industrial class. Societies
thus organized produce little in excess of their supposed needs, and
slaveholding nations do not acquire wealth. That modification of
this condition known as feudalism also represents a minimum of
production and of wealth.

The earlier economists laid great stress on agriculture and the production of raw materials, and did not clearly see to how great an extent the value of the latter could be increased by skilled labor expended upon them. They had false ideas of value, and it is only in quite recent times that the truth has gained acceptance that value is measured by the satisfaction yielded. Seen in this light it becomes clear that production does not stop at any stage in the elaboration of the raw materials, but that the utility continues to increase so long as the labor expended adds to the power of the product to satisfy desire. And now it is found that the real wealth of nations consists chiefly in this refinement of the original products. Agricultural nations are never rich, and mining countries do not become rich until provided with extensive manufactories. The great wealth of the leading nations of the world at the present time is almost wholly due to *machinofacture.*

The sociological importance of production as thus understood consists in the power of highly elaborated products to satisfy desire, contribute to ease, comfort, and the enjoyment of life, and in general, to render existence tolerable and desirable. Any one going out of the centers of civilization into regions where "modern conveniences" have not penetrated immediately feels this, and wonders what the inhabitants of such places have to live for. It is curious that such "blessings of civilization" keep in the very van of the advancing races. They are much more universal in America and, I am told, in Australia, than in Europe. An American of moderate means does not find in Britain or on the Continent what he is in the habit of regarding as the ordinary comforts of life. It is a common mistake to suppose that men usually have the means of satisfying all their wants. Aside from the very rich, whose unsatisfied wants consist of things that money will not buy, every one at all times wants unnumbered things that money would buy if he had it. And aside from the abject poor that swarm in the richest countries, there is the great toiling proletariat who not only want many things that they never dare to hope for, but also need much to prevent physical suffering. There is therefore call for a greatly increased production, and there is no danger that too many useful things will be produced. But here we encounter a problem that has thus far baffled economists, sociologists, social reformers, and statesmen. I shall not attempt to solve it, nor even to point out a way to its solution, but if I can succeed in formulating a clear and correct statement of it I shall be more than content.

Social Distribution. — The principles of economic distribution are very simple and have been repeatedly set forth. With them we have nothing to do here. But what may be distinguished as social distribution presents a problem. It may be a question whether it belongs to pure sociology at all. If the social forces do not produce it it does not so belong. But if they do produce it, even to a very limited extent, it comes in for treatment here. Under the exact scientific laws of political economy all surplus production should go to the ruling, owning, employing class. The slave of course owns nothing, any more than does a horse. But neither should the wage worker own anything. The wage, according to the Ricardian law, is fixed at the precise amount that enables him to live and reproduce. If he is able to possess anything beyond these requirements the wage is correspondingly reduced. If he weakens and fails to keep up his numbers the law will spontaneously eke out his wage till he can again keep even. It acts on the same principle as the law of prices, and is at bottom the same law, since it has maximum profits as its basis. Now, the question is, has this law always operated rigidly in society? So far as slavery is concerned we may say that it has, but outside of slavery, has the working man always been obliged to be content with the means of subsistence, including that of a family large enough to insure the rearing of two children for each pair to the age of reproduction, so that the number shall not diminish? If anything beyond this has occurred, then there has been social distribution to that extent.

It can now be seen what I mean by social distribution. It is the socialization of wealth. It is some transgression of the iron law. It is the existence of defects, cracks, pores, and fissures in the economic dam, by which some small part at least of the surplus production seeps through and finds its way into the hands of the wage earner. It is some check to the economic law whereby wages in excess of those required to live and reproduce fail to cause their prompt contraction to that point. No one need of course be told that in the present state of the world, at least, this process is going on. What is supposed to be the final answer to all complaints against the existing industrial system is that the laborer is receiving an increasingly larger share of the wealth produced. This is supposed to dispose of the whole question and relegate all the dissatisfied to the ranks of social agitators, and there is no lack of statistical proof of this fact. As this same argument has been used for about two hundred years we may assume that it has been true during that time, and it is a fair inference that it has always been true to some extent. The flaw in the logic consists in assuming that it is in any sense an answer to the demand for more complete social distribution. As a matter of fact it is an admission of the justice of such a demand. It is never maintained that the laborer gets too large a share of the wealth produced. It is always held that he gets a larger amount now than at some previous period and should therefore be satisfied. But as at any such previous period the same statement was made and is supposed to be true, there is the implied admission that if what he gets now is the just share, what he received then was something less than the just share. And as all this applies to all past periods and will apply to all future ones, the inference is fair that there has never been a time when the laborer received a just share of the wealth produced. But all this belongs to applied sociology, one of the chief problems of which is to formulate the laws and indicate the methods of a perfect social distribution of wealth.

We are content to have discovered that the social forces have spontaneously secured some degree of social distribution, and we may cast a glance at some of the special causes that have produced this result. The principal cause is the heterogeneity of all meta-social groups. It is impossible at the outset for the ruling class to obtain a complete monopoly of labor, and after the establishment of civil law and the formation of the state, whereby rights to property were recognized, the economic laws operating among individuals of all degrees of inequality of mind and character, soon generated a sort of archetypal bourgeoisie with a multiplicity of small owners of varying degrees. The rise of the feudal system interrupted the natural development of this state of things and its gradual transformation into the modern industrial system, but this transformation was ultimately brought about. As all know, the exploiting class then became chiefly the bourgeoisie, and under legal and political protection, especially after the era of machinery began, wealth passed into the hands of industrial leaders, and the great economic struggle began. But industry had now become greatly diversified, the remote regions of the world had been opened up, and there were innumerable outlets for the laborer, dissatisfied with his lot. The great differences in ability and character among workmen produced grades and stimulated ambition. Exceptionally bright hands were called to more lucrative places, compelling employers to raise wages in order to retain their best men. Those who had received the higher grades of salary for considerable time found themselves in position to withdraw and set up business for themselves, thus becoming employers and perhaps "captains of industry." Such are a few of the ways in which the iron law of wages has been gradually mitigated, and social distribution secured. One need not be a panegyrist of natural law in the economic world to recognize the power of the ontogenetic forces to keep up a difference of potential and convert economic structures into systems of moving equilibrium. There has been some social distribution from the earliest times, and it is increasing with increasing production. Under the division of labor, especially in the mechanic arts, production increases as the square of the number employed, reversing the Malthusian law, and the social distribution is a function of the amount of production *per capita*. If for no other purpose, therefore, than to increase the social distribution, increase of production is a social desideratum. The laborer becomes an element in the market, and it is more and more the interest of the proprietor of goods to let him share in their consumption. Increased production means diminished price, and the latter at last comes within the resources of the real producer.

Consumption. — If political economy has nothing to do with consumption, sociology has everything to do with it. Consumption means the satisfaction of desire, which is the ultimate end of conation. In Chapter XI we analyzed a dynamic action and found that the only effect that the individual is conscious of seeking is the satisfaction of desire. The other effects, viz., the preservation of life and the modification of the surroundings, are incidental and indifferent to him. Although the vast importance of these two latter effects makes this first one seem paltry and trivial, nevertheless it must not be forgotten that but for it the action would not be performed at all, and all would be lost. But if we abandon for a moment the high standpoint of nature's end in a scheme of universal evolution, and temporarily ignore the somewhat less exalted standpoint of social progress, we may concentrate attention upon the end, and the only possible end, of the individual, the satisfaction of desire, the enjoyment of life, in short, human happiness, and we shall see that it is not such a trivial object as it at first appeared.

While the particular element in an action which is dynamic is its direct and unintended effect in transforming the environment, the prospect of consumption is the essential condition to the action itself, and therefore, with a slight ellipsis, it may be said, and has been perceived and remarked by several economists (Jevons, Walker, Patten), that consumption is the dynamic element in political economy. Dynamic economics, if any one prefers to call it so, is based on consumption. It may also be called subjective economics. More closely analyzed, it is found to lie at the foundation of the true conception of value, the measure of which is the quantity of pleasure experienced or yielded by the product consumed. But all this, if economics at all, is transcendental economics, and really belongs to the domain of sociology, which starts with consumption, where economics leaves off, and becomes the science of welfare.[1]

Pain and Pleasure Economy. — Sociology is indebted to Dr. Simon N. Patten for the terms "pain economy" and "pleasure economy," [2] and for their justification in the history of the world. Struck with the importance of the truth embodied in these terms, I have on two occasions [3] endeavored to point out applications of them not made by Dr. Patten and to show the deeper psychologic and biologic foundations of the subject. These considerations have been still more fully set forth in this work, especially in Chapter VII, and their relation to the subject of the present chapter is now clear.

The somewhat paradoxical fact was noted in the last chapter that the essential or physical social forces are negative in the sense that they have for their chief purpose to rid mankind of goading and tormenting wants, while the positive satisfactions yielded in so doing, though intense, are so brief as to possess no volume, and that the chief result is therefore relief from pain. Dr.

---

[1] The ablest analysis of this distinction with which I am acquainted is to be found in a series of papers by Professor H. H. Powers, entitled, "Wealth and Welfare," in the *Annals of the American Academy of Political and Social Science*, Vol. XII, November, 1898, pp. 325–357; Vol. XIII, January, 1899, pp. 57–80; March, 1899, pp. 173–211.

[2] "The Theory of Social Forces," Supplement to the *Annals of the American Academy of Political and Social Science*, Vol. VII, No. 1, January, 1896, pp. 75 ff.

[3] "Utilitarian Economics," *American Journal of Sociology*, Vol. III, January, 1898, pp. 520–536; "L'Économie de la Douleur et l'Économie du Plaisir," *Annales de l'Institut International de Sociologie*, Vol. IV, Paris, 1898, pp. 89–132.

Patten states that the animal world represents a pain economy, and the interpretation of this is that all the wants of an animal belong to the physical class. The same is true of primitive man, and the protosocial stage, which is sometimes described as idyllic, is so in the same sense as in the animal. Probably no such positive term as happiness would be applicable to either. If progress means anything more than the objective fact of increasing complexity of organization, if it has any subjective meaning at all, it must consist in an increase in the relative degree to which the end of the organism or the individual is secured. A state in which the end of the creature is completely subordinated to the end of nature, in which function is everything and feeling is nothing, is a typical pain economy, and subjective progress throughout the sentient world consists in an increasing recognition of the claims of feeling.

Animals and the inferior types of men literally "eat to live." The stomach is the main seat of the nutrient attraction. The food is put there as quickly as possible and not allowed to linger on the way to tickle the papillæ of the tongue and palate. Feed a hungry dog bits of meat and watch the process of deglutition. The interval between the time when the morsel touches the animal's jaws till it is safely landed in the stomach is as short as the action of the organs can possibly make it. It is so nearly instantaneous that the eye can scarcely follow the wave that flits along the throat during the act of swallowing. It cannot be said that such an animal takes any pleasure in eating. The demand for nutrition is so imperious that it wholly excludes all other considerations. The satisfaction is no doubt intense, but the enjoyment is nil. I have heard ethnologists describe the manner in which the Chinook Indians eat the shellfish and other sea food that they gather on the shores of Alaska, the refuse of which form the kitchen middens of that region, and it accords with the above description of the way animals eat. It is characterized by excessive gluttony and the quickest possible dispatch of the meal, which receives no preparation except to detach the animal from its shell in the most expeditious manner possible. Mr. Spencer, in support of two very different propositions, has collected a large number of such facts,[1] but they certainly illustrate the principle here under con-

[1] " Principles of Sociology," Vol. I, New York, 1877, pp. 49–52 (§ 26); "Principles of Ethics," Vol. I, New York, 1892, pp. 436–438 (§ 174).

sideration equally well. It might almost be said that the length
of time it requires for food to pass from the lips to the stomach is
a measure of civilization. It typifies the transition from a complete subjection to function to a recognition of feeling as also an
end, from a régime of necessity to a régime of utility, from mere
negative satisfaction to positive enjoyment, from a pain economy
to a pleasure economy.

Such a movement there has been throughout the history of human
development, and it has not been confined to the ontogenetic forces
of society, but it is clearly characterized in them. In connection
with food alone it has consisted in a general improvement in the
palatableness of food. Instead of being eaten in its natural state
nearly all food is now prepared, the most important part of the
preparation consisting in cooking it. This preparation of food,
besides greatly increasing the number of food products, converting
into food many things that previously were not edible, has chiefly
tended to render all kinds of food better, more savory, more palatable and toothsome, and thus to convert the nutritive act from a
mere imperative necessity into a greater and greater source of enjoyment. Along with this, and as a consequence of it, there has
gone an increased inclination to masticate food, and thus to prolong
the period of this enjoyment. The habit of eating slowly, of providing a variety of articles of food, of preparing them in a variety
of ways, of combining them variously, and of seasoning food, and
all the arts of modern cookery — all this represents the same process of seeking to derive the maximum good from the physical
necessity of eating. Busy men, and especially scientific men, often
complain of the time consumed not only in eating but more in the
preparation of food which involves so large an expense, and latterly
we have been hearing of the proposed " synthetic food," prepared
in the chemical laboratory, and consisting of the essence of the most
nutritious substances in a form that can be taken without loss of
time and at such intervals as the system may demand. They should
know that this, instead of a step forward, would be a return not
only to the savage, but to the animal method; but if it represents
the completion of a cycle, we may perhaps be thankful that it cannot be realized.

Not less marked has been the tendency in the same general direction in the satisfaction of the defensive and protective wants of

mankind. If we leave out the means of protection from human enemies in the form of offensive and defensive weapons, these consist chiefly in clothing, shelter, and fuel. To review the progress in all these would be both tedious and unnecessary, but we have only to point to architecture as an esthetic art to show that the movement was toward the realization of ideals, and that the needs of existence soon ceased to be the motive that caused man to build. Here, of course, the problem is complicated by the religious element, which was long the chief spur to architectural progress. In modern times the chief architectural motive is *comfort*, which, after all, is the same as pleasure, enjoyment, happiness. Almost the same might be said of clothing, except that here the field was more open for the extravagances of fashion, and even these are a form of enjoyment for those constituted to prefer them. Upon the whole the evolution of dress has conduced to the fullness of social life.

The relation that the full satisfaction of men's wants bears to the physical and mental development of the race is of the highest interest to the sociologist. Many travelers (Cook, Ellis, Erskine, etc.,) have noted the superior size of the chiefs and rulers of the lower races, and the fact seems to be general. The usual explanation is that the most robust and physically powerful of a tribe are always chosen as leaders. There may be some truth in this, but where the ruling class is hereditary much of it is doubtless to be explained by the better nutrition of that class, always having plenty to eat and being well protected from whatever the unfriendly elements of the environment may be, while the subjects are often insufficiently nourished and are exposed to these unfriendly elements. This state of things, continued through many generations, would bring about all the observed difference in the two classes.

It is also often remarked that civilized men are usually superior to savages physically as well as mentally. On this point Darwin remarks : —

Although civilization thus checks in many ways the action of natural selection, it apparently favors, by means of improved food and the freedom from occasional hardships, the better development of the body. This may be inferred from civilized men having been found, wherever compared, to be physically stronger than savages. They appear also to have equal powers of endurance, as has been proved in many adventurous expeditions. Even the great luxury of the rich can be but little detrimental; for the expectation of life of our aristocracy, at all ages and of both sexes, is very little inferior to that of healthy English lives in the lower classes.[1]

The general physical superiority of great men in all departments, notwithstanding certain marked exceptions which have attracted attention because anomalous, has also been occasionally noted. Galton expresses a feeling I have often experienced, when he says : "A collection of living magnates in various branches of intellectual achievement is always a feast to my eyes; being, as they are, such massive, vigorous, capable-looking animals."[2] A false notion to the contrary of all this prevails, but one has only to look around. Go into any business establishment and you will in nine cases out of ten instantly pick out the proprietor by his superior physique. He is usually the largest man present, and his hale, active, independent mien at once impresses you with his general superiority over all the journeymen, clerks, employees, and even the foremen and chiefs of departments in the business, whatever it may be. This is as true of a store where all the employees are well dressed as of a shop where most of them wear working clothes. And it is pretty generally true not only that a sound mind requires a sound body, but that superior minds, including all the qualities of character that insure success, are associated with superior bodies, usually larger than the mean for the race, and well formed, healthy, active, and strong.

Galton would concede all this, but his conclusion from it is false, or at least only half true. It is that these men are where they are because they are superior. It would probably be more nearly true to say that they are superior because they are where they are. The real truth lies between these two propositions. Galton has emphasized the first. The second should be fully recognized. Life is very flexible. It adapts itself to circumstances. Its preservation is so essential that it cannot be destroyed by reducing the amount of nutrition. In the history of life there have been wide vicissitudes in this respect, and the organism has been adapted and adjusted to these vicissitudes. If food is abundant the organism comes up to that standard and is correspondingly robust. If the supply falls off the standard· is lowered to correspond, but life goes on. Unless too sudden a great diminution of the supply can thus be sustained without destroying life. The creature becomes what is called "stunted,"

---

[1] " Descent of Man," New York, 1871, Vol. I, p. 164.
[2] " Hereditary Genius," London, 1892, p. 321.

but does not perish.   If life is thereby shortened, then, by a curious
law of compensation, fecundity is correspondingly increased.   The
botanist soon learns where to find the plants farthest advanced in
the process of flowering or fruiting.   It is where the soil is poorest.
But the specimens will be depauperate, though bearing an abundance
of precocious fruit.   And the gardener who does not want his plants
to fruit at all has only to make the soil exceedingly rich and they
will bear luxuriant foliage but no flowers.   It is the same with animals.   Reproduction and nutrition are inversely proportional.   The
poorest and most starved and puny are the most prolific.   It is so
with the human race.   The poor and underfed have the largest
families; the low quarters of cities, occupied by laborers and mechanics, swarm with children; the rich have small families, and, as
Kidd says, society is perpetually recruited from the base.[1]

It follows from all this that there is scarcely any such thing as
" over-nutrition "[2] as a social condition, although of course it is
often an individual fact; or rather we should say, over-eating, and
especially the eating of improper things made palatable by the arts
of cookery, is a common occurrence with the leisure class.   This
belongs to the same class of phenomena as other forms of intemper-
ance and relates to social pathology.   Dr. Maurel[3] ascribes to it
a considerable part of the diminished birthrate of France, giving
to the diseases to which it gives rise the general name of arthritism,
which includes, along with infecundity, such maladies as gout, rheu-
matism, gravel, calculus, diabetes, etc.   These are unnatural forms
of living that follow from excessive social inequalities not controlled
by science or good morals, and do not concern us here.

Ample natural nutrition enjoyed by a whole people or by a large
social class will cause a healthy development which will ultimately
show itself through physical and mental superiority.   Thus far,
such has been the history of mankind that it has always been a
special class that has been able to obtain the means thus fully to
nourish the body.   That class has always been superior physically
to the much larger class that has always been inadequately nourished.
Adequate protection from the elements in the way of houses, clothes,

[1] " Social Evolution," New Edition, New York, 1894, p. 263.

[2] " Over-nutrition and its Social Consequences," by Simon N. Patten, *Annals
of the Academy of Political and Social Science*, Philadelphia, Vol. X, pp. 33–53.

[3] " De la Dépopulation de la France, Étude sur la Natalité," par E. Maurel, Paris,
1896.

and fires, tends in the same direction, while improper exposure dwarfs and deforms both body and mind. Leisure, in the proper sense of exemption from the necessity of making painful and prolonged exertion, coupled with such physical and mental exercise as the system demands, or the normal use of all the faculties, coöperates with full nutrition and adequate protection to develop the faculties and perfect the man. On the other hand compulsory exertion in the form of excessive and protracted labor blunts and stunts all the faculties and tends to produce a more or less deformed, stiffened, and distorted race of men. When we remember that in real truth these two opposite influences have been at work in human society ever since its organization, with the intense persistence of caste conditions working to prevent the mixing of the classes, we have abundant cause for all the observed physical and mental inequalities in men. The reason why this explanation is not clearer is that during the past three centuries the original conditions have been disturbed and a great social panmixia has been going on, greatly obscuring the elements of the problem. Still, although slavery has been abolished and the feudal system overthrown, the new industrial system is largely repeating the pristine conditions, and in the Old World especially, and more and more in the New, class distinctions prevail, and differences of nutrition, of protection, and of physical exertion are still keeping up the distinction of a superior and an inferior class. The former has come up to the limit of its possibilities; the latter is arrested on the plane at which it can exist and reproduce. And thus is exemplified the truth that there is in the German calembour of Moleschott: "*man ist was man isst.*" This, too, is the great truth that lies at the bottom of the so-called "historical materialism." Not only does civilization rest upon a material basis in the sense that it consists in the utilization of the materials and forces of nature, but the efficiency of the human race depends absolutely upon food, clothing, shelter, fuel, leisure, and liberty.

U

CHAPTER XIV

THE PHYLOGENETIC FORCES

THE proper subject of this chapter would be the influence exerted by those forces that have reproduction for their functional end in the direction of creating and transforming social structures. Keeping in view, however, the genetic method of treatment, the subject demands, much more than that of the preceding chapter, that deep explorations be made into the remote and obscure beginnings and prehuman course of things leading up to and explaining the facts that lie on the surface of the highly artificial and conventionalized society of to-day. In view, too, of the almost unexplored field in which this must be done, compared with the overdone domain of the economic forces passed over in the last chapter, the apparently uneven and much more extended treatment of the present subject is fully justified. A glance at the number and variety of heads and subheads into which the subject naturally falls, none of which can be wholly ignored, is sufficient to show that it might easily, and should properly, be expanded into a book instead of condensed into a chapter.

REPRODUCTION A FORM OF NUTRITION

The subject may really be regarded as only a continuation of that of the preceding chapter, since no fact in biology is better established than that reproduction represents a specialized mode of nutrition through the renewal of the organism, which, for reasons that we cannot here stop to point out, if indeed they can be said to be fully known, cannot be continued indefinitely. "The process of reproduction," says Haeckel, "is nothing more than a growth of the organism beyond its individual mass."[1] The biological ground for this statement will be set forth a little later, but may now be directly connected with the fact referred to in the last chapter that

[1] Der Vorgang der Fortpflanzung ist weiter Nichts als ein Wachsthum des Organismus über sein individuelles Maass hinaus. "Natürliche Schöpfungsgeschichte," von Ernst Haeckel, achte Auflage, Berlin, 1889, p. 167.

the arrest of nutrition hastens reproduction, while abundant nutrition checks, and may even prevent reproduction. If we recognize only two forms of nutrition, natural selection determines which form shall be employed. Individual nutrition will be continued so long as there is no danger of the individual being cut off. Ultra-individual nutrition will begin as soon as there arises a chance of the individual being cut off, and it will be emphasized by any direct threat to the life of the individual. Hence reproduction is not possible in animals to the young that are growing rapidly, nor to plants that are over-nourished. Trees always die first at the top, but it is also at the top that they first flower and mature their fruit.

This general fact is sufficient reason for treating the ontogenetic before the phylogenetic forces, although from the standpoint of their importance the latter may be given precedence. The race is certainly of more consequence than the individual, and is that for which nature seems chiefly to care, but when the individual is looked upon as being simply prolonged and to merge into a new individual, the individual is seen to be all and to embrace or constitute the race. The race or species becomes an ideal, an abstract conception, and the individual the only thing that is real. The case is analogous to that of "society," in contradistinction to the individual members of society. Society exists only for the members and in preserving the members the society is preserved. So of the race. If the individuals continue to live over into one another, as reproduction provides, the race is conserved. Reproduction is therefore not only ultra-nutrition, in going beyond the individual, but it is *altro-nutrition*, in carrying the process to and into another. It is, as we shall see, the beginning of altruism. As it preserves the race or phylum, it is the condition to phylogenesis, and as connecting these two ideas, it may be called *phylotrophy*, or race nutrition, and stand opposed to *ontotrophy*, or individual nutrition.

THE ANDROCENTRIC THEORY

I propose to present two theories to account for the existing relations between the sexes, between which the reader can choose according to the constitution of his mind, or he can reject both. The first I call the *androcentric theory*, the second the *gynæcocentric theory*. I shall, however, set down the principal facts known to science in support of each of these theories, and these may not be accepted or

rejected at will.   They may be verified, or even proved false, but
unless they are shown to be false and not facts at all, they must
stand on one side or the other of the argument.

The androcentric theory is the view that the male sex is primary
and the female secondary in the organic scheme, that all things
center, as it were, about the male, and that the female, though
necessary in carrying out the scheme, is only the means of continuing
the life of the globe, but is otherwise an unimportant accessory, and
incidental factor in the general result.   This is the general statement
of the androcentric theory as a tenet of biological philosophy, but as
a tenet of sociology or anthropology, it becomes the view that man
is primary and woman secondary, that all things center, as it were,
about man, and that woman, though necessary to the work of reproduction, is only a means of continuing the human race, but is otherwise an unimportant accessory, and incidental factor in the general
result.

The facts in support of the androcentric theory, in both its general
and its special form, are numerous and weighty.   From the former
point of view we have the general fact that in all the principal
animals with which everybody is more or less familiar, including the
classes of mammals and birds at least, the males are usually larger,
stronger, more varied in structure and organs, and more highly ornamented and adorned than the females.   One has only to run over in his
mind the different domestic animals and fowls, and the better known
wild animals, such as the lion, the stag, and the buffalo, and most
of the common song birds of the wood and meadow, to be convinced
of the truth of this proposition.   Among birds the females are not
only smaller and of plain colors, but the male alone possesses the
power of song.   He is often brilliantly colored and far more active
and agile than his mate.   Among animals the male, besides his
greater size and strength, is often endowed with such purely esthetic
accessories as antlers and gracefully curving horns, and such weapons
as tusks.   Some male birds, too, are provided with spurs not possessed by the females.   A comparison of female animals and birds
with the young of the same species shows, as compared to the males,
a marked resemblance, which fact has given rise to the favorite
theory of many zoölogists that the female sex represents a process
of "arrested development" as contrasted with the alleged normal,
and certainly far greater development of the males.   Such are the

main facts which zoölogy furnishes in support of the androcentric theory.

When we narrow the comparison down to the human races we find the same general class of facts somewhat emphasized. The women of all races are smaller than the men. They are less strong in proportion to their size, certainly if size is measured by weight. In the lower races at least the esthetic difference holds, and the male is more perfectly proportioned, and if positive beauty can be predicated of either sex it belongs to the man more than to the woman. In the advanced races female beauty is much vaunted, but women themselves regard men as more beautiful, and in the matter of beard, at least, they have what corresponds to the male decorations of animals. The difference in the brain of man and woman is quite as great as that of the rest of the body. Many measurements have been made of male and female brains both of civilized and uncivilized races, and always with the same general result at least that the female brain is considerably less than the male both in weight and cubic capacity. The average civilized male brain is said to weigh 602 grammes while the average female weighs only 516 grammes, a difference of over fourteen per cent of the former. But there are also qualitative differences showing female inferiority. Some of these are enumerated by Topinard as follows : —

The outlines of the adult female cranium are intermediate between those of the child and the adult man; they are softer, more graceful and delicate, and the apophyses and ridges for the attachment of muscles are less pronounced, . . . the forehead is . . . more perpendicular, to such a degree that in a group of skulls those of the two sexes have been mistaken for different types; the superciliary ridges and the gabella are far less developed, often not at all; the crown is higher and more horizontal; the brain weight and the cranial capacity are less; the mastoid apophyses, the inion, the styloid apophyses, and the condyles of the occipital are of less volume, the zygomatic and alveolar arches are more regular, the orbits higher, etc. [1]

Other parts of the body differ in a similar manner. Professor W. K. Brooks says: "The female is scarcely in any normal case a mere miniature copy of the male. Her proportions differ; the head and the thorax are relatively smaller, the pelvis broader, the bones slighter, and the muscles less powerful.[2]" All these facts are stated over and over again in all the works that treat of the subject,

[1] " Élements d'Anthropologie générale," par Paul Topinard, Paris, 1885, p. 253.
[2] *Popular Science Monthly*, Vol. XIV, p. 202.

with slight variations, it is true, but with substantial agreement, and
they may therefore be safely accepted as true to all intents and
purposes.

But this is only the physical side of the subject. Stress of
course is always laid upon the differences in the male and female
brain, and it is but natural that inferior brain development in
woman should be attended by correspondingly inferior mental
powers. This is found to be the case, and attention is usually
drawn to this as an immediate consequence of the other. In the
first place it is found that women have very little inventive power.
As invention is the great key to civilization, and as the inventive
faculty is the primary advantageous function of the intellect, this
is a fundamental difference and has great weight. If we take the
inventive faculty in a wider sense and include scientific discovery
we shall find woman still more behind man. It is for scientific
discoveries rather than for mechanical inventions that the great
men of history have risen to fame. In the leading countries of
Europe there are scientific academies which from time immemorial
have made it a practice to elect to membership any person who
has made noteworthy scientific discoveries. This of course is not
always done, and there are often narrow prejudices and short-
sighted judgments that have debarred the greatest men for a time
from this honor; but, these aside, membership in such bodies is
prima facie proof of special eminence in one or another department
of science. Professor Alphonse de Candolle, basing his arguments
chiefly on this test, wrote his great work on the "History of
Science and Scientific Men," which has become a recognized
classic, taking rank alongside of the similar works of Francis
Galton, " Hereditary Genius," " English Men of Science," to which
it is in large part an answer. In this work de Candolle devotes two
pages to "Women and Scientific Progress," most of which is so
appropriate to the present discussion that I cannot do better than
to quote it. He says : —

We do not see the name of any woman in the table of scientific associates of the principal academies. This is not wholly due to rules that fail
to provide for their admission, for it is easy to perceive that no person of the
feminine sex has done an original scientific work that has made its mark
in any science and commanded the attention of scientific men. I do not
think that it has ever been proposed to elect a woman a member of any
of the great scientific academies with restricted membership. Madame de

Staël and George Sand might have become members of the French Academy, and Rosa Bonheur of the Academy of Fine Arts, but women who have translated scientific works, those who have taught or compiled elementary works, and even those who have published some good memoir on a special subject, are not elevated so high, although they have not lacked sympathy and support. The persons of whom I have spoken are however exceptions. Very few women interest themselves in scientific questions, at least in a sustained manner and for the sake of the questions and not of persons who are studying them or in order to support some favorite religious theory.

It is not difficult to find the causes of this difference between the two sexes. The development of woman stops sooner than that of man, and every one knows that studies at the age of from 16 to 18 years count for much in the production of a scientist of distinction. Besides, the female mind is superficial (*primesautier*). It takes pleasure in ideas that can be readily seized by a sort of intuition. The slow methods of observation and calculation by which truths are surely arrived at, cannot be pleasing to it. Truths themselves, independent of their nature and possible consequences, are of little moment for most women — especially general truths which do not affect any one in particular. Add to this, small independence of opinion, a reasoning faculty less strong than in man, and finally the horror of doubt, *i.e.*, of the state of mind through which all research in the sciences of observation must begin and often end. [1]

Not only is the inventive genius of woman low as compared to that of man, but so is also her creative genius.[2] The following by a writer in the *Gentleman's Magazine* is fairly representative of what may be found repeated a hundred times in the general literature of the nineteenth century : —

It is notorious that creative genius is essentially of the masculine gender. Women are the imaginative sex, but the work which nature seems to have distinctly allotted to them has been done by men. This strange phenomenon is not due to the fact that women have written comparatively little, because, if it were, the little imaginative work they have done would have been great in quality, and would surpass in quantity the other work they have done. But it has not been great in quality compared with that of men, and, compared with the rest of their own work, has been infinitesimally small. No woman ever wrote a great drama; not one of the world's great poems came from a woman's hand. [3]

---

[1] " Histoire des Sciences et des Savants depuis deux siècles," etc., par Alphonse de Candolle. Deuxième édition considérablement augmentée. Genève-Bale, 1885, pp. 270–271. (This section occurs only in the second edition of the work.)

[2] There is only one art in which women equal and perhaps excel men, and that is the art of acting. Cf. Havelock Ellis, " Man and Woman," p. 324.

[3] " The Physiology of Authorship," by R. E. Francillon, *Gentleman's Magazine*, N. S., Vol. XIV, March, 1875, pp. 334–335.

If we wished to pursue this line further we should find it often asserted that in all the fine arts woman is far behind man. There are very few great women architects, sculptors, painters, or musical composers.

Still less can be said for the female side of speculative genius, the faculty by which the mind deals with abstract truth and rises by a series of ever widening generalizations from multiplicity to unity. Women care very little for truth for its own sake, take very little interest in the abstract, and even concrete facts fail to win their attention unless connected more or less directly with persons and with some personal advantage, not necessarily to self, but to self or others. In short, they lack the power to see things objectively, and require that they be presented subjectively. Innate interests are ever present to their minds, and anything that does not appeal in any way to their interests is beyond their grasp.

A glance at the history and condition of the world in general is sufficient to show how small has been and is the rôle of woman in the most important affairs of life. None of the great business interests of mankind are or ever have been headed by women. In political affairs she has been practically a cipher, except where hereditary descent has chanced to place a crown upon her head. In such cases, however, no one can say that it has not usually rested easily. But from a certain point of view it almost seems as if everything was done by men, and woman was only a means of continuing the race.

The Gynæcocentric Theory

The gynæcocentric theory is the view that the female sex is primary and the male secondary in the organic scheme, that originally and normally all things center, as it were, about the female, and that the male, though not necessary in carrying out the scheme, was developed under the operation of the principle of advantage to secure organic progress through the crossing of strains. The theory further claims that the apparent male superiority in the human race and in certain of the higher animals and birds is the result of specialization in extra-normal directions due to adventitious causes which have nothing to do with the general scheme, but which can be explained on biological and psychological principles; that it only applies to certain characters, and to a relatively small number of genera and families. It accounts for the prevalence of the androcentric theory by the superficial character of human knowledge of such subjects, chiefly influenced by the illusion of the near, but largely, in the case of man at least, by tradition, convention, and prejudice.

History of the Theory. — As this theory is not only new but novel, and perhaps somewhat startling, it seems proper to give a brief account of its inception and history, if it can be said to have such. As the theory, so far as I have ever heard, is wholly my own, no one else having proposed or even defended it, scarcely any one accepting it, and no one certainly coveting it, it would be folly for me to pretend indifference to it.   At the same time it must rest on facts that cannot be disputed, and the question of its acceptance or rejection must become one of interpreting the facts.

In the year 1888 there existed in Washington what was called the Six O'Clock Club, which consisted of a dinner at a hotel followed by speeches by the members of the Club according to a programme.   The Fourteenth Dinner of the Club took place on April 26, 1888, at Willard's Hotel.   It was known to the managers that certain distinguished women would be in Washington on that day, and they were invited to the Club.   Among these were Mrs. Elizabeth Cady Stanton, Miss Phebe Couzins, Mrs. Croly (Jennie June), Mrs. N. P. Willis, and a number of others equally well known.   On their account the subject of Sex Equality was selected for discussion, and I was appointed to open the debate.   Although in a humorous vein, I set forth the greater part of the principles and many of the facts of what I now call the gynæcocentric theory.   Professor C. V. Riley was present and, I think, took part in the discussion.   Many of my facts were drawn from insect life, and especially interested him.   I mention this because a long time afterward he brought me a newspaper clipping from the *Household Companion* for June, 1888, containing a brief report of my remarks copied from the *St. Louis Globe*, but crediting them to him; and he apologized for its appearance saying that he could not explain the mistake.   The reporter had fairly seized the salient points of the theory and presented them in a manner to which I could not object.   This, therefore, was the first time the theory can be said to have been stated in print.   The exact date at which it appeared in the *Globe* I have not yet learned, but presume it was shortly after the meeting of the Club.   Professor Riley did not hesitate to announce himself a convert to the theory, and **we** often discussed it together.

I had long been reflecting along this line, and these events only heightened my interest in the subject. The editor of the *Forum* had solicited an article from me, and I decided to devote it to a popular but serious presentation of the idea. The result was my article entitled, " Our Better Halves." [1]   That article, therefore, constitutes the first authorized statement of the gynæcocentric theory that was published, and as a matter of fact it is almost the only one. Mr. Grant Allen answered my argument on certain points in the same magazine,[2] and I was asked to put in a rejoinder, which I did,[3] but these discussions related chiefly to certain differences between the mind of man and woman and did not deal with the question of origin. I alluded to it in my first presidential address before the Biological Society of Washington,[4] and it came up several times in writing the " Psychic Factors " (Chapters XIV, XXVI).

Such is the exceedingly brief history of the gynæcocentric theory, and if it is entirely personal to myself, this is no fault of mine. Nothing pleases me more than to see in the writings of others any intimation, however vague and obscure, that the principle has been perceived, and I have faithfully searched for such indications and noted all I have seen. The idea has not wholly escaped the human mind, but it is never presented in any systematic way. It is only occasionally shadowed forth in connection with certain specific facts that call forth some passing reflection looking in this general direction. In introducing a few of these adumbrations I omit the facts, which will be considered under the several heads into which the subject will naturally fall, and confine myself for the most part to the reflections to which they have given rise. Many of these latter, however, are of a very general character, and not based on specific facts. In fact thus far the theory has had rather the form of a prophetic idea than of a scientific hypothesis. We may begin as far back as Condorcet, who brushed aside the conventional error that intellect and the power of abstract reasoning are the only marks of superiority and caught a glimpse of the truth that lies below them when he said : —

---

[1] The *Forum*, New York, Vol. VI, November, 1888, pp. 266–275.

[2] "Woman's Place in Nature," by Grant Allen, the *Forum*, Vol. VII, May, 1889, pp. 258–263.

[3] " Genius and Woman's Intuition," the *Forum*, Vol. IX, June, 1890, pp. 401–408.

[4] "The Course of Biologic Evolution," Proc. Biol. Soc., Washington, Vol. V, pp. 23–55. See pp. 49–52.

If we try to compare the moral energy of women with that of men, taking into consideration the necessary effect of the inequality with which the two sexes have been treated by laws, institutions, customs, and prejudices, and fix our attention on the numerous examples that they have furnished of contempt for death and suffering, of constancy in their resolutions and their convictions, of courage and intrepidity, and of greatness of mind, we shall see that we are far from having the proof of their alleged inferiority. Only through new observations can a true light be shed upon the question of the natural inequality of the two sexes.[1]

Comte, as all know, changed his attitude toward women after his experiences with Clotilde de Vaux, but even in his "Positive Philosophy," in which he declared them to be in a state of "perpetual infancy," and of "fundamental inferiority," he admitted that they had a "secondary superiority considered from the social point of view."[2] In his "Positive Polity" he expressed himself much more strongly, saying that the female sex "is certainly superior to ours in the most fundamental attribute of the human species, the tendency to make sociability prevail over personality."[3] He also says that "feminine supremacy becomes evident when we consider the spontaneous disposition of the affectionate sex (*sexe aimant*) always to further morality, the sole end of all our conceptions."[4]

Of all modern writers the one most free from the androcentric bias, so far as I am aware, is Mr. Havelock Ellis. In his excellent book "Man and Woman," he has pointed out many of the fallacies of that Weltanschauung, and without apparent leaning toward anything but the truth has placed woman in a far more favorable light than it is customary to view her. While usually confining himself to the facts, he occasionally indicates that their deeper meaning has not escaped him. Thus he says: "The female is the mother of the new generation, and has a closer and more permanent connection with the care of the young; she is thus of greater importance than the male from Nature's point of view" (pp. 383–384). To him is also due the complete refutation of the "arrested development" theory, above mentioned, by showing that the child, and the young generally, represent the most advanced type of development, while the adult male represents a reversion to an inferior early type, and this in man is a more bestial type.

[1] "Tableau Historique des Progrès de l'Esprit Humain," Paris, 1900, pp. 444–445.
[2] "Philosophie Positive," Vol. IV, Paris, 1839, pp. 405, 406.
[3] "Système de Politique Positive," Vol. I, 1851, p. 210.
[4] *Op. cit.*, Vol. IV, 1854, p. 63.

In the sayings quoted thus far we have little more than opinions, or general philosophical tenets, of which it would be much easier to find passages with the opposite import. In fact statements of the androcentric theory are to be met with everywhere. Not only do philosophers and popular writers never tire of repeating its main propositions, but anthropologists and biologists will go out of their way to defend it while at the same time heaping up facts that really contradict it and strongly support the gynæcocentric theory. This is due entirely to the power of a predominant world view (*Weltanschauung*). The androcentric theory is such a world view that is deeply stamped upon the popular mind, and the history of human thought has demonstrated many times that scarcely any number of facts opposed to such a world view can shake it. It amounts to a social structure and has the attribute of stability in common with other social structures. Only occasionally will a thinking investigator pause to consider the true import of the facts he is himself bringing to light.

Bachofen, McLennan, Morgan, and the other ethnologists who have contributed to our knowledge of the remarkable institution or historic phase called the matriarchate, all stop short of stating the full significance of these phenomena, and the facts of amazonism that are so often referred to as so many singular anomalies and reversals of the natural order of things, are never looked at philosophically as residual facts that must be explained even if they overthrow many current beliefs. Occasionally some one will take such facts seriously and dare to intimate a doubt as to the prevailing theory. Thus I find in Ratzenhofer's work the following remark: —

It is probable that in the horde there existed a certain individual equality between man and woman; the results of our investigation leave it doubtful whether the man always had a superior position. There is much to indicate that the woman was the uniting element in the community; the mode of development of reproduction in the animal world and the latest investigations into the natural differences between man and woman give rise to the assumption that the woman of to-day is the atavistic product of the race, while the man varies more frequently and more widely. This view agrees perfectly with the nature of the social process, for in the horde, as the social form out of which the human race has developed, there existed an individual equality which has only been removed by social disturbances which chiefly concern the man. All the secondary sexual differences in men are undoubtedly explained by the struggle for existence and the position of man in the community as conditioned thereby. Even the security of the horde from predatory animals, and still more the necessity of fighting with other men for the preservation of the group, developed individual superiority in general, both mental and physical, and especially in man. But any individual superiority disturbed the equality existing in the elements of the horde; woman from her sexual nature took only a passive part in these disturbances. The sexual life as well as the mode of subsistence no longer has its former peaceful character. Disturbances due to the demands of superior individuals thrive up to a certain point, beyond which the differentiation of the group into several takes place.[1]

Among biologists the philosophical significance of residual facts opposed to current beliefs is still less frequently reflected upon. I have stated that Professor Riley fully accepted the view that I set forth and admitted that the facts of entomology sustained it, yet, although somewhat of a philosopher himself, and living in the midst of the facts, the idea had not previously occurred to him. Among botanists, Professor Meehan was the only one in whose writings I have found an adumbration of the gynæcocentric theory. He several times called attention to a certain form of female superiority in plants. In describing certain peculiarities in the Early Meadow Rue and comparing the development of the male and female flowers he observed differences due to sex. After describing the female flowers he says: —

By turning to the male flowers (Fig. 2) we see a much greater number of bracts or small leaves scattered through the panicle, and find the pedicels longer than in the female; and this shows a much slighter effort — a less expenditure of force — to be required in forming male than female flowers. A male flower, as we see clearly here, is an intermediate stage between a perfect leaf and a perfect, or we may say, a female flower. It seems as if there might be as much truth as poetry in the expression of Burns, —

> Her 'prentice han' she tried on man,
> An' then she made the lasses, O,

at least in so far as the flowers are concerned, and in the sense of a higher effort of vital power.[2]

It is singular, but suggestive that he should have quoted the lines from Burns in this connection, as they are an undoubted echo of the androcentric world view, a mere variation upon the Biblical myth of the rib. Of course he could find nothing on his side in the classic literature of the world, but wishing to embellish the idea in a popular

---

[1] "Die Sociologische Erkenntnis," von Gustav Ratzenhofer, Leipzig, 1898, p. 127.

[2] "The Native Flowers and Ferns of the United States," by Thomas Meehan, Vol. I, Boston, 1878, p. 47.

work, he tried to make these somewhat ambiguous lines do duty in this capacity. The fact cited is only one of thousands that stand out clearly before the botanist, but not according with the accepted view of the relations of the sexes they are brushed aside as worthless anomalies and "exceptions that prove the rule." In fact in all branches of biology the progress of truth has been greatly impeded by this spirit. All modern anatomists know how the facts that are now regarded as demonstrating the horizontal position of the ancestors of man, and in general those that establish the doctrine of evolution, were treated by the older students of the human body — rejected, ignored, and disliked, as intruders that interfered with their investigations. It is exactly so now with gynæcocentric facts, and we are probably in about the same position and stage with reference to the questions of sex as were the men of the eighteenth century with reference to the question of evolution. Indeed, the androcentric theory may be profitably compared with the geocentric theory, and the gynæcocentric with the heliocentric. The advancement of truth has always been in the direction of supplanting the superficial and apparent by the fundamental and real, and the gynæcocentric truth may be classed among the "paradoxes of nature."[1]

The Biological Imperative. — It is a common belief among the theologically minded that nature is presided over by intelligence and guided toward some predestined goal. Science finds it very difficult to dislodge this belief on account of the number of cases in which really moral ends are worked out by agents unconscious of such ends or even opposed to them. In Chapter XI we saw that most of the progress thus far attained by man has been the result of the several dynamic principles there considered acting quite independently of the human will and unknown to man, in a direction opposite to that which he would have preferred. In the tenth chapter it was shown that the agents in social synergy are wholly unconscious of the social ends they are working for. Gumplowicz says of them : "These founders of states, like all men, never act except in their immediate interest, but social development, above and beyond the egoistic efforts of men, arrives at its end as prescribed by nature."[2] And Spencer somewhat extends this idea when he

[1] "Dynamic Sociology," Vol. I, pp. 47–53.
[2] " Précis de Sociologie," par Louis Gumplowicz. Traduction par Charles Baye, Paris, 1896, p. 196.

says : " While the injustice of conquests and enslavings is not perceived, they are on the whole beneficial; but as soon as they are felt to be at variance with the moral law, the continuance of them retards adaptation in one direction more than it advances in another." [1] All of which is in line with what was set forth in the last chapter in relation to the institution of slavery. Even the general statement of Professor Gerland that " man has developed from his natural animal state in a purely natural and mechanical way," [2] is true, the social forces acting blindly and unconsciously to that end. It is not a malignant force : —

> Ein Theil von jener Kraft
> Die stets das Böse will, und stets das Gute schafft, [3]

but a wholly indifferent amoral or anethical force, a force devoid of all moral quality. The victims who are sacrificed to it have no conception of the rôle they are playing in the grand scheme. The teleological or theological view point assumes that there is an Intelligence that comprehends it all, plans it all, executes it all, but which is raised so far above the capacities of even the wisest of men that they can form no conception of the scheme. Professor James has given the best illustration of this that has thus far been supplied in comparing man to a dog on the vivisection table : —

He lies strapped on a board and shrieking at his executioners, and to his own dark consciousness is literally in a sort of hell. He cannot see a single redeeming ray in the whole business; and yet all these diabolical-seeming events are usually controlled by human intentions with which, if his poor benighted mind could only be made to catch a glimpse of them, all that is heroic in him would religiously acquiesce. Healing truth, relief to future sufferings of beast and man are to be bought by them. It is genuinely a process of redemption. Lying on his back on the board there he is performing a function incalculably higher than any prosperous canine life admits of ; and yet, of the whole performance, this function is the one portion that must remain absolutely beyond his ken. [4]

The main difference is that the dog is incapable of faith, while man, however inscrutable may be the ends that he is serving, is disposed to *believe* that they are good. And right here is a curious paradox, namely, that the most religious, *i.e.*, those who are the most certain that

[1] "Social Statics," abridged and revised, etc., New York, 1892, pp. 240-241.
[2] "Anthropologische Beiträge," von Georg Gerland, Halle a.S, 1875, Vol. I, p. 21.
[3] Goethe: "Faust;" der Tragödie erster Theil, Scene III, Studierzimmer (Mephistopheles).
[4] *International Journal of Ethics*, Vol. VI, October, 1895, pp. 20-21.

they are " pushed by unseen hands," or as Adam Smith expressed it " led by an invisible hand," believe most implicitly in their own individual freedom, and hold the doctrine of free will to be essential to the religious spirit. For whether we take the theological or the scientific view, this sense of a power beyond our control or comprehension is one of the surest indications that we do not control our own acts, and that do what we may by whatever motive, we are contributing to the accomplishment of results of which we do not dream.

But clear as all this may be in the domain of social action, it is in biology that the *natura naturans* works out its most mysterious results. All life is a great illusion, and things are never what they seem. In biology there seems to be a purpose, but this is also an illusion. Yet everything in nature has a meaning, and biology teaches the profounder meaning of things. All of our impulses and instincts possess a deep significance. And there is no department of biology in which these occult principles are more active and potent than in all that relates to reproduction and to sex. The mystery of reproduction is also deepened by social taboo of the subject, and its treatment is delicate and difficult. It is habitually avoided except by special investigators, and the general public is almost completely cut off from all sources of information. But as Bacon said : " Whatever is worth being is worth knowing," [1] and there can be no more vital or fundamental field of truth than that of reproduction upon which depends the existence not merely of the individual but of the species, race, or ethnic group of men.

Reproduction. — In Chapter XI it was shown that reproduction is a very different thing from sexuality, and in the last chapter its practical identity with nutrition was set forth. Both of these truths are wholly contrary to current beliefs, and both will be further elucidated in the attempt to explain in what reproduction really consists. Lamarck came very close to perceiving the latter of these truths. He said : —

When by the aid of circumstances and the proper means nature has succeeded in setting up movements in a body which constitute life, the succession of these movements develops organization and gives rise to *nutrition*, the first of the faculties of life, and from this there arises the second of the

---

[1] " Novum Organum," Lib. I, Aph. cxx, ("Works," Vol. I, New York, 1869, p. 326). " Quicquid essentia dignum est, id etiam scientia dignum, quæ est essentiæ imago."

vital faculties, viz., the growth of the body.   The superabundance of nutrition in giving rise to the growth of this body prepares the materials for a
new being which organization places in position to resemble this same body,
and thereby furnishes it with the means of reproducing itself, whence arise
the third of the faculties of life.[1]

Schopenhauer struck the truth more squarely when he said that
nutrition differs only in degree from reproduction,[2] but this may pass
for a prophetic idea.   It remained for Haeckel in 1866 [3] to give a
clear scientific expression to it in the form that " reproduction is a
nutrition and a growth of the organism beyond its individual mass,
which erects a part of it into a whole."   We may therefore start from
this conception in the further study of reproduction.   Bearing constantly in mind that reproduction and sexuality are two distinct
things we find the word " asexual " superfluous and even misleading,
as tending to confound these two things.   The problem was how to
secure this continuous nutrition and keep the organism growing
beyond the point where the original plastic structure tended to break
down.   This was not always effected in the same way, and there
arose a number of different modes of reproduction.   A careful study
of these has shown that in a general way, with some apparent,
and probably some real exceptions, the different modes of reproduction constitute a sort of ascending series from the point of view of
complexity and adaptation to increasing development of structure —
a series of steps from the more simple to the more complex.
Biologists have worked out these steps from the actual study of
living organisms, and a few authors have attempted to set forth their
logical succession.

The simplest form of reproduction is undoubtedly that by division
or fission, in which the overgrown Amœba, moner, or protist, consisting of an apparently almost homogeneous mass of living protoplasm,
falls apart and resolves itself into two nearly equal portions, each of
which continues to grow as before and again divides, and so on indefinitely.   The growth of any of the higher organisms is a process
very similar to this, only here each cell must be regarded as an
individual.   The cells increase in size and then divide, each half in

---

[1] " Philosophie Zoologique," 1809.   Edition of 1873, Vol. II, pp. 63–64.

[2] " Welt als Wille und Vorstellung," 3d edition, Leipzig, 1859, Vol. I, p. 326.

[3] " Generelle Morphologie der Organismen," von Ernst Haeckel, Berlin, 1866,
Vol. II, p. 16.

x

turn increasing and again dividing, and so on indefinitely, thus constituting the growth of the whole organism.

The second step in the development of the reproductive process is called gemmation, *i.e.*, budding. The unicellular organism, instead of dividing into two practically equal parts, divides, as we may say, into two very unequal parts. A small portion of its substance first protrudes a little and is then separated from the mother-cell by a constriction that grows deeper and deeper until the bud becomes wholly detached. This small bud then grows until it attains the size of the parent cell, and at the proper time it in turn develops a bud that has the same simple life history. This mode of reproduction is not confined to unicellular organisms but takes place in certain bryozoans, worms, and ascidians. In plants, as everybody knows, it is the principal form, the true bud being its type, but through it also are produced rootstocks, runners, stolons, etc.

The third step has been called germinal budding, or polysporogonia. Within an individual composed of many cells a small group of cells separates from the surrounding ones and gradually develops into an independent individual similar to the parent, and sooner or later finds its way out of the mother. This process of reproduction is met with in some zoophytes and worms, and especially in the Trematodes. These young cell groups of course soon attain maturity and go through the same process as the parent group.

The fourth step is strictly intermediate between this last and the simplest forms of bisexuality. It is called germ cell formation or spore formation (monosporogonia, or simply sporogonia). In this a single cell instead of a group of cells becomes detached from the interior of the organism, but does not further develop until it has escaped from the latter. It then increases by division and forms a multicellular organism like its parent. This form of reproduction is common among certain low types of vegetation.

We have to consider still a fifth form of asexual reproduction, which, however, is not usually classed as another step in the series, but rather as a backward step from a more advanced form. This is parthenogenesis or virgin reproduction. Here germ cells similar to all appearances to eggs, are capable of developing into new beings without the aid of any fertilizing agent. The same cells may also be fertilized, and upon the fact of fertilization or non-fertilization usually depends the sex of the resulting creature. Among bees, as is well known, the unfertilized eggs produce only males, while the fertilized eggs produce females. This therefore would not constitute reproduction in the full sense, since without fertilization the race would be quickly cut off. But in certain plant lice the reverse of this has been observed, the unfertilized eggs producing females, capable at maturity of repeating the process. Here then is a form of parthenogenesis which constitutes complete reproduction, although it is not usually depended upon, and might perhaps fail from gradual decline in life energy.

It is not probable that the above are all the steps that have actually been taken by nature in the development of the principle of life renewal to this point. There have probably been intermediate steps between these, perhaps many such, but the forms in which they occur either have not persisted or have not yet been studied. Those that are known, however, are sufficient to show that the reproductive process has been a serial development from simpler to more complicated modes. In fact, as we ought to expect, and as Lamarck said,[1] reproduction at these early stages is nothing but the continuation of the process by which life was originally created, and which could not have been realized as a permanent fact without it. The origination of life (*archigonia, generatio spontanea*), the preservation of life (nutrition, growth), and the continuation of life (*tocogonia, generatio parentalis*, reproduction), are all one fact, and the observed differences are only matters of detail — the different modes corresponding to different conditions.

Fertilization. — Reproduction has for its sole object to perpetuate life. To enable the individual to attain its maximum size, to live out its normal period of existence, to carry itself on into new beings that will do the same, and to produce as large a number as possible of such beings — these are the primary ends of nature in the organic world. The several forms of reproduction above described go

---

[1] "Philosophie Zoologique," Paris, 1873, Vol. II, pp. 76–77. The following passage is particularly suggestive : " Or, ne pouvant donner à ses premières productions la faculté de se multiplier par aucun système d'organes particulier, elle [la nature] parvint à leur donner la même faculté en donnant à celle de s'*accroitre*, qui est commune à tous les corps qui jouissent de la vie, la faculté d'amener des scissions, d'abord du corps entier et ensuite de certaines portions en saillie de ce corps; de là, les gemmes et les differents corps reproductifs qui ne sont que des parties qui s'étendent, se séparent et continuent de vivre après leur séparation, et qui, n'ayant exigé aucune fécondation, ne constituant aucun embryon, se développant sans déchirement d'aucune enveloppe, ressemblent cependant, après leur accroissement, aux individus dont ils proviennent " (pp. 138–139).

no farther than the accomplishment of these ends. Any further steps require a new principle. But this purely quantitative development was not all that the life force accomplished. There was added to it a qualitative development. Here as elsewhere, however, quality is readily reducible to quantity. Quantity remained the end and quality served primarily as a means. We saw in Chapter VII that the end of nature seems to have been the increase of the quantity of matter transferred from the inorganic to the organic state. Anything additional to this is to be classed among the incidental, extra-normal, and "unintended" results. That these became at times highly important does not alter the principle. But this much at least is true, that no collateral process could be inaugurated that did not conduce to the primary end. With the life force pushing in all conceivable directions, as from the center toward every point on the surface of a sphere, every possible process must have been tried. If an advantageous one existed it would prove successful through the operation of the principle of advantage.

It turned out that there was one advantageous process, viz., the process or principle of fertilization. All fertilization is cross fertilization, and we saw in Chapter XI that this was one of the great dynamic principles of nature, calculated to keep up a difference of potential and prevent stagnation. We also saw that mere function — nutrition (assimilation, metabolism, growth), and reproduction (repetition, ultra-nutrition, multiplication) — is essentially static. Simple reproduction by any of the modes thus far described is mere function. It simply continues the type unchanged. To get beyond this and secure any advantageous change in the types of structure a dynamic principle must be introduced. The dynamic principle which in fact was introduced was that of crossing the hereditary strains or stirps through what I prefer to designate fertilization. The various modes by which this was accomplished is what we are next to consider. In any of the advanced stages of this process we have the phenomena of sex, but the use of this term for the earlier stages, if correct at all, is at least misleading. It is so difficult to divest the mind of the idea which the term sex gives rise to, based on the universal familiarity with organisms that have two distinct sexes called male and female, coupled with the almost equally universal lack of acquaintance with organisms that either have no sex at all, such as those considered in the last section, and which, nevertheless, constitute numerically far more than half of all organic beings, or that have this dual character in an exceedingly undeveloped state, such as would not be recognized as the same that is properly known as sex.

Still, it may be advantageous to use the term sex in such a generic sense, and biologists regularly do so, clearly perceiving that out of these mere primordial sketches all the developed forms of sexuality have proceeded by a natural series of ascending steps, much as in the case of asexual reproduction which we have already considered. Taking this view we may say that sex constitutes a dynamic principle in biology, that it arose in this gradual way from the advantage it afforded in securing the commingling of the ancestral elements of heredity, and that its value as a device for maintaining a difference of potential is measured by the degree of completeness that it attains. This is the true meaning of sex, which is not at all that of securing or perfecting reproduction, but the secondary effect of securing variation and through variation the production of better and higher types of organic structure — in a word, organic evolution.

The vitalizing or rejuvenating effect of crossing has always been recognized, but it is usually stated simply as a fact, and just *how* it becomes true is not only not stated, but it has sometimes been put down as among the mysteries, or at least problems of biology. Thus Dr. Gray says: " How and why the union of two organisms, or generally of two very minute portions of them, should reënforce vitality, we do not know, and can hardly conjecture. But this must be the meaning of sexual reproduction."[1] Professor W. K. Brooks has said that "the essential function of the male element is not the vitalization of the germ . . . the male element is the vehicle by which new variations are added."[2] It would be easy to quote a score of competent modern biologists to the same effect, but the best summing up of the subject is perhaps that of Professor Richard Hertwig in an address delivered Nov 7, 1899, before the Gesellschaft für Morphologie und Physiologie in München, and published in its proceedings.[3] Pro-

---

[1] "Darwiniana: Essays and Reviews pertaining to Darwinism," by Asa Gray, New York, 1877, pp. 346–347.

[2] *Popular Science Monthly*, Vol. XV, May, 1879, pp. 149, 150. Cf. *Science*, Vol. IV, Dec. 12, 1884, p. 532.

[3] "Mit welchem Recht unterscheidet man geschlechtliche und ungeschlechtliche Fortpflanzung?" *Sitzb. d. Ges. für Morphologie und Physiologie in München*, Vol. XV, 1899, Heft III, München, 1900, pp. 142–153.

fessor Winterton C. Curtis has done English readers a good service
in summarizing this address and presenting the results in compact
form, and I give a few extracts from his summary: —

> Fertilization and reproduction are phenomena which may be found to-
> gether, but which in their essence have no connection with one another. . . .
>
> If we now attempt an accurate statement of the kinds of reproduction in
> the plant and animal kingdoms, the old conception of sexual and asexual
> reproduction must be given up entirely and replaced by the following
> statement : —
>
> All organisms effect their reproduction in a common way by means of
> single cells which have arisen by cell-division. In single-celled organisms
> every cell-division is an act of reproduction and results in the formation of
> another physiologically self-sustaining individual. In multicellular animals,
> most of the cell-divisions lead to the growth of the multicellular individual,
> and only certain of them serve for reproduction. Fertilization goes on side
> by side with reproduction, because the organism cannot attain its highest
> development without the union of two individualities by nuclear copula-
> tion. Fertilization in its essence has nothing to do with reproduction.[1]

Conjugation. — To the general fact of the union of two elements in
reproduction Haeckel has given the name *amphigonia,* and this is
quite near to Weismann's *amphimixis.* But it begins with conjugation or zygosis. It might almost be said to consist in this, since the
chief difference in this respect between the Protozoa and the Metazoa is that in the latter the conjugating cells are taken from the
bodies of many-celled organisms, while in the former they constitute
two single-celled organisms. To avoid the use of the term "sex" as
inapplicable to the lowest organisms, we may call all forms of reproduction which takes place through the union of two elements *compound reproduction* in contradistinction to the various forms of
simple reproduction that have been described. We may then say
that in all compound reproduction conjugation takes place. In the
Protozoa the whole organism is involved, while in the Metazoa only
the cells specialized and separated off for reproductive purposes are
involved. But in both there are always two cells that unite and
coalesce to form the new being. When conjugation was first observed, and for a long time afterward, it was supposed that the two
conjugating cells simply coalesced and that their entire contents
were converted into a new cell at first to all appearances homogeneous, but later differentiating and forming the rudiments of an

[1] *Science*, N. S., Vol. XII, Dec. 21, 1900, pp. 943, 945.

embryo. In this there was seen an analogy to nutrition, and the cells were sometimes spoken of as mutually devouring each other. The process is now known to be much more complicated than this, but there is no doubt that the extra-nuclear parts of the cells are appropriated as nourishment. But it is the nuclei that contain the hereditary elements, and the fusion of these is a somewhat prolonged process called karyokinesis, which has now been exhaustively studied by a large corps of investigators. Weismann has summed up the results[1] in somewhat convenient form in his biological essays, where references will be found to the original sources.

It would be out of place here to go over this ground, and that was not the purpose of this section, but it is well to emphasize the fact that while conjugation is the universal mode of procuring the union of different hereditary elements in the production of variation and consequent progressive development of living forms, it does not primarily or necessarily imply any such difference in the uniting cells as is implied by the term sex. The biologists sometimes express this by saying that the sexes were originally alike, or that primarily the sexes were not differentiated. The cases are abundant in which no difference is perceptible between the cells that conjugate. They are different only in the sense that they are dual. There must be differences in all cells, but these differences are beyond human power to distinguish with the best appliances. They exist in those primordial hereditary elements that have been called by so many different names — gemmules, biophores, stirps, micellæ, physiological units, etc. — by different investigators; elements so minute as to be practically molecular.

It is true that these conjugating cells, whether constituting the whole of the organism or only germ and sperm cells of many-celled organisms, are, as usually seen, more or less differentiated and unlike, one being commonly larger and motionless, and the other smaller and active, and this differentiation may properly be called sexual. The spontaneous union of two cells must be something more than accidental to become at all general. There must be some reason inherent in the cells themselves for the act of uniting. In other words, there must exist an innate interest in so doing, and

[1] "Essays upon Heredity and Kindred Biological Problems," by August Weismann, Vol. II, Oxford, 1892. See especially the twelfth essay.

this property was developed according to the principles set forth in Chapter V. The law of parsimony would naturally restrict this interest chiefly to one of the cells and leave the other passive. The same causes created the other differences, including those of size. The result is that what is called the male cell or sperm cell is usually a relatively minute cell possessing a form approaching that of a body of least resistance, is provided with locomotive appendages, and endowed with an appetitive faculty by which it actively seeks the female cell and buries itself in its substance. Conjugation thus becomes true sexual union. Needless to say that between the simple mutual coalescence and absorption of two equal cells and the fully developed union of sperm cell and germ cell there are in nature all intermediate conditions.

But if these cells are called sexual, and the latest stages of conjugation are regarded as sexual unions, there may be said to exist two kinds of sexuality, a sexuality of cells and a sexuality of organisms. This, it is true, is very nearly the same as the difference in the sexuality of protozoic and metazoic life, since the sperm cells and germ cells may be regarded as independent unicellular organisms; still the term sex is generally applied to organisms as a whole possessing sex, and when used of the Metazoa and Metaphyta it is the whole organism that is meant and not the reproductive cells. We may therefore now leave the subject of cellular differentiation, which goes no farther than this, and confine our attention to the other aspect of the sex question.

It may be well, however, to note that fertilization, whether as the conjugation of similar cells or as the union of sperm and germ cells, was only gradually resorted to. Asexual generation not only permits no change or development but it also seems ultimately to exhaust itself. It is therefore found as the sole and permanent condition in only a few organisms. Much more frequently is there found that modification of it which is called *alternation of generations,* in which after a long series of asexual reproductions the creature becomes encysted and goes through a resting process followed by conjugation or some other form of fertilization, the resultant progeny again reproducing asexually, and so on. Taking into account the entire history of sexual development, although it varies so widely in different forms, we may say in general that these alternations gradually grow more and more frequent until the period of asexual reproduction is ultimately eliminated entirely. But even then it must be conceived as possible. From this to the stage in which fertilization becomes essential to reproduction is a long step and this stage is only brought about through adaptation. Fertilization, as we have seen, has nothing to do with reproduction, and that it should ever become a necessary condition to it can only be accounted for by the great advantage that it has for the species, first bringing it about that every act of reproduction is in fact preceded by fertilization, and then, through this uniform coupling of the two acts, at last rendering such coupling a prerequisite to reproduction. It is this fact that gave rise to the erroneous view that fertilization is a necessary part of reproduction. This accounts for all the forms of hermaphroditism and parthenogenesis, presently to be considered, which are so many intermediate stages in the process. They may be regarded as temporary and transition forms. Asexual reproduction and the alternation of generations are also comparatively transient stages, although the former is the only mode in some animals and the latter is universal in plants. But complete stability is not attained until the stage not only of sexuality but of unisexuality is reached.

Origin of the Male Sex. — Although reproduction and sex are two distinct things, and although a creature that reproduces without sex cannot properly be called either male or female, still, so completely have these conceptions become blended in the popular mind that a creature which actually brings forth offspring out of its own body is instinctively classed as female. The female is the fertile sex, and whatever is fertile is looked upon as female. Assuredly it would be absurd to look upon an organism propagating asexually as male. Biologists have proceeded from this popular standpoint, and regularly speak of "mother-cells" and "daughter-cells." It therefore does no violence to language or to science to say that life begins with the female organism and is carried on a long distance by means of females alone. In all the different forms of asexual reproduction, from fission to parthenogenesis, the female may in this sense be said to exist alone and perform all the functions of life including reproduction. In a word, life begins as female.

The further development of life serves to strengthen this gynæcocentric point of view. It consists, as we might say, exclusively in the history of the subsequent origin and development of the male sex.   The female sex, which existed from the beginning, continues unchanged, but the male sex, which did not exist at the beginning, makes its appearance at a certain stage, and has a certain history and development, but never became universal, so but that, as already remarked, there are probably many more living beings without it than with it, even in the present life of the globe.   The female is not only the primary and original sex but continues throughout as the main trunk, while to it a male element is afterward added for the purposes above explained.   The male is therefore, as it were, a mere afterthought of nature.   Moreover, the male sex was at first and for a long period, and still throughout many of the lower orders of beings, devoted exclusively to the function for which it was created, viz., that of fertilization.   Among millions of humble creatures the male is simply and solely a fertilizer.

The simplest type of sexuality consists in the normal continuance of the original female form with the addition of an insignificant and inconspicuous male fertilizer, incapable of any other function.   In sexual cells there is no character in which the differentiation goes so far as in that of size.   The female or germ cell is always much larger than the male or sperm cell.   In the human species, for example, an ovum is about 3000 times as large as a spermatozoon. [1] In the parasitic *Sphœrularia Bombi*, the female is a thousand or many thousand times the size of the male. [2]   The Cirripedia present remarkable examples of female superiority, or rather of the existence of minute male fertilizers in connection with normal development in the female.   Darwin was perhaps the first to call attention to this fact in a letter to Sir Charles Lyell, dated Sept. 14, 1849, in which he said : —

The other day I got a curious case of a unisexual, instead of hermaphrodite cirripede, in which the female had the common cirripedial character, and in two valves of her shell had two little pockets, in *each* of which she kept a little husband ; I do not know of any other case where a female invariably has two husbands.   I have one still odder fact, common to several species, namely, that though they are hermaphrodite, they have small additional, or as I shall call them, complemental males, one specimen, itself hermaphrodite, had no less than *seven* of these complemental males attached to it.   Truly the schemes and wonders of Nature are illimitable.[3]

[1] John A. Ryder in *Science*, N. S., Vol. I, May 31, 1895, p. 603.

[2] Herbert Spencer, " Principles of Biology," New York, 1873, Vol. II, p. 417 (§ 332).

[3] " The Life and Letters of Charles Darwin," including an autobiographical chapter, edited by his son Francis Darwin, New York, 1888, Vol. I, p. 345.

Darwin's observations have been abundantly confirmed by later investigators. Huxley asserts the parasitic nature of the male in certain cases, the male being attached to the female and living at her expense.[1] Van Beneden, to practically the same effect, remarks that "the whole family of the Abdominalia [cirripedes] have the sexes separate; and the males, comparatively very small, are attached to the body of each female."[2]

The phenomenon of minute parasitic males is not rare among the lower forms, and that their sole office is fertilization may be clearly seen from the following statement of Milne Edwards: "It is to be noted that in some of these parasites [Ex. *Diplozoon paradoxum*, a nematode] the entire visceral cavity was occupied by the testicles, and that Mr. Darwin could not discover in it any trace of digestive organs."[3] Van Beneden also says that the males are reduced to the rôle of spermatophores: "The male of the Syngami (nematodes) is so far effaced that it is no longer anything but a testicle living on the female."[4] These of course are extreme cases, and the difference is less in most of the animal world, the reason for which will be shown later on. But the examples cited serve to show how sexuality began. Female superiority, however, of a more or less marked degree still prevails throughout the greater part of the invertebrates. It is perhaps greatest among the Arachnidæ or spider family. The courtships of spiders are so often described in popular works that allusion to them almost calls for an apology.[5] They are always regarded as astonishing anomalies in the animal world. While the behavior of the relatively gigantic female in seizing and devouring the tiny male fertilizer when he is only seeking to do the only duty that he exists for, may seem remarkable and even contrary to the interests of nature, the fact of the enormous difference between the female and the male, is, according to the gynæcocentric hypothesis, not anomalous at all, but perfectly natural and normal.[6]

[1] "A Manual of the Anatomy of Invertebrated Animals," by Thomas H. Huxley, New York, 1878, pp. 261–262.

[2] "Animal Parasites and Messmates," by P. J. Van Beneden, second edition, London, 1876, pp. 55–56.

[3] "Leçons sur la Physiologie et l'Anatomie comparée de l'Homme et des Animaux," par H. Milne Edwards, Vol. IX, Paris, 1870, p. 267.

[4] *Op. cit.*, p. 93, of the French edition. This statement does not seem to occur in the English edition.

[5] Cf. Darwin, "Descent of Man," Vol. I, p. 329.

[6] Professors Geddes and Thompson in their useful work on the Evolution of Sex have brought together a large number of examples in various departments of the

In the mantis or praying insect there is much less difference in size than in most spiders, but female superiority shows itself in the ferocity of the female, while the paramount importance of the act of fertilization is clear from the terrible risks that the male takes in securing it, usually resulting in his destruction. I give an example on the authority of one of the best known entomologists : —

A few days since I brought a male of *Mantis carolina* to a friend who had been keeping a solitary female as a pet. Placing them in the same jar, the male, in alarm, endeavored to escape. In a few minutes the female succeeded in grasping him. She first bit off his left front tarsus, and consumed the tibia and femur. Next she gnawed out his left eye. At this the male seemed to realize his proximity to one of the opposite sex, and began vain endeavors to mate. The female next ate up his right front leg, and then entirely decapitated him, devouring his head and gnawing into his thorax. Not until she had eaten all of his thorax except about three millimeters did she stop to rest. All this while the male had continued his vain attempts to obtain entrance at the valvules, and he now succeeded, as she voluntarily spread the parts open, and union took place. She remained quiet for four hours, and the remnant of the male gave occasional signs of life by a movement of one of his remaining tarsi for three hours. The next morning she had entirely rid herself of her spouse, and nothing but his wings remained.

The extraordinary vitality of the species which permits a fragment of the male to perform the act of impregnation is necessary on account of the rapacity of the female, and it seems to be only by accident that a male ever escapes alive from the embraces of his partner.

Riley in his first monthly report, p. 151, says : " The female being the strongest and most voracious, the male, in making his advances, has to risk his life many times, and only succeeds in grasping her by slyly and suddenly surprising her ; and even then he frequently gets remorselessly devoured." [1]

In insects generally the males are smaller than the females, especially in the imago state. It applies to the larvæ to a less extent, but it is often marked even in the cocoons, as, for example, of the silk worm.[2] There are many species, and even genera, belonging to

animal kingdom, many of which have been recorded since Darwin's time. See the edition of 1901, pp. 17 ff., 82. This work is a valuable compilation of facts of all kinds bearing on sex and was much needed. While it is pervaded with the androcentric spirit, the " thesis " of it that the female is anabolic and the male catabolic is a long step in the direction of the gynæcocentric theory, forced or wrested, as it were, from unwilling minds by the mass of evidence. It is correct as far as it goes, but it is only one of the many surface facts resulting from the fundamental principle now under discussion.

[1] Dr. L. O. Howard in a letter to *Science*, dated Sept. 27, 1886. *Science*, Vol. VIII, Oct. 8, 1886, p. 326.

[2] " An Introduction to Entomology: or Elements of the Natural History of Insects," by William Kirby and William Spence, London, 1826, Vol. III, pp. 299 ff.

different orders, in which the male, usually smaller and more slender, is either not provided with any functional organs for eating, or has these so imperfectly developed that it seems improbable that it succeeds in sustaining life beyond the period that the nourishment stored up in the larval state will continue it.   This clearly shows that the sole function of such males is fertilization.   Some of these cases come very close home to us, for example, the mosquito.   Dr. Howard says : —

It is a well-known fact that the adult male mosquito does not necessarily take nourishment and that the adult female does not necessarily rely on the blood of warm-blooded animals.   The mouth parts of the male are so different from those of the female that it is probable that if it feeds at all it obtains its food in a quite different manner from the female.   They are often observed sipping at drops of water, and in one instance a fondness for molasses has been recorded.[1]

Bees constitute another familiar example, the males being what are popularly known as the drones.   Fertilization, as is well known, is almost their only rôle, and if they become at all numerous they are killed off by the workers (neutral females), and the hive is rid of them.   But great differences between the sexes, always involving some form of female superiority, occur also in the Neuroptera, Lepidoptera, Orthoptera, and Coleoptera.   In the other great types of invertebrates this is also true, but only the specialists are acquainted with the facts.   Even in the lower vertebrates there are cases of female superiority.   The smallest known vertebrate, *Heterandria formosa* Agassiz, has the females about twenty-five per cent larger than the males.[2]   Male fishes are commonly smaller than female.   In trout this is well known, and trout fishermen sometimes throw the little males or " studs," as they call them, back into the stream, as not worth taking.   Even in birds, which are the mainstay of the androcentric theory, there are some large families, as, for example, the hawks, in which male superiority is rare, and the female is usually the larger and finer bird.   There are even some mammals in which the sexes do not differ appreciably in size or strength, and very little, or not at all, in coloration and adornment.   Such is the case with nearly all of the great family of rodents.   It is also the

---

[1] " Notes on the Mosquitoes of the United States," by L. O. Howard.   Bulletin No. 25, New Series, U.S. Department of Agriculture, Division of Entomology, Washington, 1900, p. 12.

[2] *Science*, N. S., Vol. XV, Jan. 3, 1902, p. 30.

case with the Erinaceidæ, at least with its typical subfamily of hedgehogs.

All that was said of the Protozoa applies equally to the Protophyta, and indeed in those unicellular forms the distinction between plant and animal is very obscure, Haeckel making a third kingdom of nature, the Protista, which is neither plant nor animal. But the evolution of the male sex in multicellular plants is somewhat different from that of the Metazoa. In dealing with such plants much depends on what we regard as constituting an individual. If we take the growing branch or phyton as the unit of individuality, it may perhaps be truly said that sexual differentiation is universal in the vegetable kingdom. But if we make the individual include all that proceeds from the same root and coheres in one organic system — the whole plant — then we have the following grades of sexuality : 1, hermaphroditism, in which both male and female organs occur in the same flower; 2, monœcism, in which the flowers are either male or female, but both sexes occur on the same plant; and 3, diœcism, in which every plant is either wholly male or wholly female. In the flowerless plants — thallophytes, bryophytes, pteridophytes, formerly known as cryptogams — the sexual cells are borne in a variety of ways, usually separated some distance from each other, often on different plants, but here there occurs in most cases a compound generation, consisting of a short-lived prothallium stage — the true sexual stage — succeeded by a sporebearing stage constituting the principal life of the plant. This peculiarity has no important bearing on the theory under consideration, and being too complicated to be explained without extensive illustration, it need not be dwelt upon here. An acquaintance with it belongs to a proper understanding of botany such as the student of sociology should have.

Confining our attention, then, to the flowering plants, we have to note first that the Cycadaceæ and Ginkgoaceæ form two apparently different transitions from the flowerless to the flowering plants, in that they are both fertilized by means of spermatozoids — active ciliated sperm cells — as in the case of flowerless plants generally, while all the other families of flowering plants, so far as now known, have the entire prothallium stage effaced, abridged, or theoretically condensed into the development of the ovule and pollen grain. The discovery of this important distinction, which has revolutionized the classification of the vegetable kingdom, dates back only to 1896, and was made primarily by two Japanese botanists.[1]

We have next to remark that hermaphroditism in plants is not the anomalous and almost pathologic condition known by that name in the animal world. It seems to have been the common initial state in flowering plants, and deviations from it seem to be the result of the universal struggle of nature to prevent self or close fertilization and to secure the widest possible separation of the sexes. This is, however, nothing but the continuation of the operation of the same principle by which sex itself was introduced. But if the other more scientific and correct view is taken as to what constitutes an individual, this is not hermaphroditism at all. It is simply the bringing of the sexes together in compact and somewhat symmetrically ordered groups, which, before the advent of nectar-loving winged insects, was almost the only way in which fertilization could be brought about. Still, long strides were taken in this direction among the Gymnosperms, in which no showy flowers have ever been developed, and cycads and conifers are either monœcious or diœcious. The maidenhair-tree which has the longest known geological history, is diœcious, and most of the trees whose fossil remains show them to have had a long history are diclinous. Thus the willows and poplars are diœcious and the oaks and plane trees are monœcious. All this points to the law that the longer a type has lived the wider is the separation of the sexes, and as the flowers of plants are rarely preserved in the fossil state we have no warrant for assuming that the ancestral forms that we know were the same in past ages as now in respect of their sexual relations.

We have already had occasion to refer to the fact that showy flowers with nectar glands and nectar-loving insects developed *pari passu* in the history of the world (see *supra*, p. 234). It is now to be noted that the influence of cross fertilization through insect agency is chiefly upon plants with hermaphrodite flowers. On the scientific theory of leaf metamorphosis each stamen and pistil of a flower is a transformed leaf, and therefore a flower is only a cluster of leaves, some of which have been specialized into

[1] " On the Spermatozoid of Ginkgo biloba," by S. Hirase, *Bot. Mag.*, Tokyo, Vol. X, Oct. 20, 1896, p. 325 (Japanese). "The Spermatozoid of Cycas revoluta," by S. Ikeno, *ibid.*, Nov. 20, 1896, p. 367 (Japanese). Other papers in German and French soon followed these preliminary announcements.

stamens, others into pistils, others into petals, and others into seg-
ments of the calyx. The flower may therefore be looked upon as
a little colony. If the ovary is compound it is not the whole pistil
but each lobe or cell of the ovary with its separate style and stigma
that constitutes the individual. In such a colony the conditions
become too uniform for vigorous development, and there has been
an obvious struggle to escape these narrow bonds and secure a wider
separation of the sexes. The mutual interaction of the law of
natural selection and the fact of insect agency has wrought the
most extensive changes in this direction, some of which have been
pointed out.

If we regard stamens and pistils as individuals, it becomes
obvious that in the higher plants generally, and to a much greater
extent than in animals, the male is simply a fertilizer, while the
female goes on and develops and matures the fruit. Stamens always
wither as soon as the anthers have shed their pollen. They have no
other function. If we take the other and more popular view of
individuality, and look upon the whole plant as the vital unit, the
only comparisons between the sexes that can be instituted are those
of dioecious plants. Here of course we usually find the sexes practically equal. This we should expect, since sexual differentiation
has alone brought about this state from a former state of hermaphroditism. If any cases could be found of either male or female
superiority they could only be accounted for either by special over-
development of the superior or by degeneracy of the inferior sex.
In point of fact there are such cases, but only those of female
superiority. An examination of them clearly shows that they are
due to a loss on the part of the male of the powers once possessed.
Again, there are found to be cases in which this decline does not
take place until after the function of fertilization has been performed.

The best known example is that of the hemp plant, *Cannabis
sativa*. It has long been known that when hemp is sown in a field
the sexes cannot at first be distinguished, and this condition of
equality persists until the plants of both sexes reach the period of
fertility. The male plants then shed their pollen and the female
plants are fertilized thereby. Soon thereafter, however, the
male plants cease to grow, begin to turn yellow and sere, and in
a short time they droop, wither, die, and disappear. The fertilized

female plants are then found not to have as yet reached their maximum development. They continue to grow taller and more robust, while at the same time the fruit is forming, swelling, and ripening, which requires the remainder of the season. It is only from these tall, healthy, robust female stalks that the hemp fiber is obtained. It is commonly supposed that this collapse of the male plant only occurs in thickly sown fields, where, after it has performed its function it is only a cumberer of the ground. Certain it is that it amounts to an effective weeding of the field. I have, however, carefully watched the sexes when growing as weeds in waste grounds, and where there were not enough plants to crowd one another in the least, and found that the male plants ceased to grow taller and thicker after shedding their pollen, as did the female plants after being pollenized, but here the males did not perish at once, but continued to live to near the end of the season.

Before I had made any observations on the hemp plant or had heard of the peculiarity above described I had been for a number of years taking notes on a somewhat similar habit in certain native plants of the United States. In my *Guide to the Flora of Washington and Vicinity*, published in 1881, as Bulletin No. 22, U. S. National Museum, which consists chiefly of a catalogue of the plants growing in the region named, and in which I occasionally made a brief note of some special peculiarity in a plant not mentioned in any other work, I find the following note appended to *Ambrosia artemisiæfolia* (p. 90): " Tends to become diœcious, and the fruiting plants crowd out the staminate ones." Subsequently I found this to be even more true of the large species, *A. trifida*, especially farther south where it often covers large areas of abandoned land. At *Antennaria plantaginifolia* (p. 89), this remark occurs : " Female plants much larger than the male, often half a meter in height, and both varying widely." What I regarded as one species has since been found to represent several, and all of them possess this peculiarity. They tend to grow in little patches at a distance from one another, and all the plants in the same patch are of the same sex, either all male or all female, and in these patches the plants are densely crowded together. The male patches form a mat or carpet on the ground, the flowering stems only rising a few inches above the radical leaves. The female patches are less dense, and the flower-bearing stems after fertilization grow a foot or two high. Male infe-

Y

riority was also noted in *Thalictrum dioicum* and many other diœcious herbs.   If carefully looked for it would probably be found to
be general.

All these facts from both kingdoms, and the number that might
be added is unlimited, combine to show that the female constitutes
the main trunk, descending unchanged from the asexual, or presex-
ual, condition; that the male element was added at a certain stage
for the sole purpose of securing a crossing of ancestral strains, and
the consequent variation and higher development; that it began as
a simple fertilizer, assuming a variety of forms; that for reasons
hereafter to be considered, the male in most organisms gradually
assumed more importance, and ultimately came to approach the size
and general nature of the female; but that throughout nearly or
quite the whole of the invertebrates, and to a considerable extent
among the vertebrates, the male has remained an inferior creature,
and has continued to devote its existence chiefly to the one function
for which it was created.   The change, or progress, as it may be
called, has been wholly in the male, the female remaining unchanged.
This is why it is so often said that the female represents heredity
and the male variation.   " The ovum is the material medium through
which the law of heredity manifests itself, while the male element
is the vehicle by which new variations are added. . . .   The greater
variability of the male is also shown by a comparison of the adult
male and female with the immature birds of both sexes." [1]

The last fact is the one usually adduced in support of the theory
that in birds and mammals where the male is superior the female
is an example of " arrested development." Such is, however, probably not the case, and the female simply represents the normal condition, while the condition of the male is abnormal due to his great
powers of variability.   That the female should resemble the young
is quite natural, but the statement is an inverted one, due to the
androcentric bias.   The least unbiased consideration would make it
clear that the colors of such male birds as Professor Brooks had in
mind are not the normal colors of the species, but are due to some
abnormal or supra-normal causes.   The normal color is that of the
young and the female, and the color of the male is the result of his
excessive variability.   Females cannot thus vary.   They represent
the center of gravity of the biological system.   They are that

1 W. K. Brooks in *Popular Science Monthly*, Vol. XV, June, 1879, pp. 150, 152.

"stubborn power of permanency" of which Goethe speaks. The female not only typifies the race but, metaphor aside, she *is* the race.

Sexual Selection.—The fact that requires to be explained is that, as we have seen, the male, primarily and normally an inconspicuous and insignificant afterthought of nature, has in most existing organisms attained a higher stage of development and somewhat approached the form and stature of the primary trunk form which is now called the female. That which might naturally surprise the philosophical observer is not that the female is usually superior to the male, but that the male should have advanced at all beyond its primitive estate as either a fertilizing organ attached to the female, or at most a minute organism detached from her but devoted exclusively to the same purpose. In other words, while female superiority is a perfectly natural condition, male development requires explanation. We have explained the origin of the male as a provision of nature for keeping up the difference of potential among biotic forces. This we found in Chapter XI to be one of the leading dynamic principles. But this principle does not explain the first step nor any subsequent step made by the male toward equality with the female. For this an entirely different principle must be found.

We saw at the outset that in order to fulfill his mission the male must be endowed with an innate interest in performing his work. This was supplied on the principle laid down in Chapter V, viz., appetition. This attribute was absolutely necessary to the success of the scheme, and throughout all nature we find the male always active and eager seeking the female and exerting his utmost powers to infuse into her the new hereditary *Anlagen* that often make up the greater part of his material substance. This intense interest in his work is the *natura naturans*, the voice of nature speaking through him and commanding him, in season and out of season, always and under all circumstances, to do his duty, and never on any pretext to allow an opportunity to escape to infuse into the old hereditary trunk of his species the new life that is in him. This duty he always performed, not only making extraordinary efforts but incurring enormous risks, often actually sacrificing his life and perishing at his post.

The sociological application of this is that the sexual irregularities of human society are chiefly due to this same principle. All attempts on the part of society to regulate the relations of the sexes, necessary though they may be to the maintenance of the social order, interfere with the biologic principle of crossing strains and securing the maximum variation, development, and vigor of the stock. The violation of human laws relating to this class of conduct is usually in obedience to that higher law of nature commanding such conduct. As Havelock Ellis says: —

A cosmic conservatism does not necessarily involve a social conservatism. The wisdom of Man, working through a few centuries or in one corner of the earth, by no means necessarily corresponds to the wisdom of Nature, and may be in flat opposition to it. This is especially the case when the wisdom of Man merely means, as sometimes happens, the experience of our ancestors gained under other conditions, or merely the opinions of one class or one sex. Taking a broad view of the matter, it seems difficult to avoid the conclusion that it is safer to trust to the conservatism of Nature than to the conservatism of Man. We are not at liberty to introduce any artificial sexual barrier into social concerns. [1]

Such violations of the social code are called crimes and are thereby made such, but they are artificial crimes. Those who commit them may even think they are doing "wrong," because they have been taught so; nevertheless they continue to commit them and take the risks of punishment. They obey the biological imperative in the face of all danger in perfect analogy with the action of the male spider or mantis.

This part of the scheme was thus effectively carried out, and so far it was a complete success, and ample variation and consequent diversity and progress were secured in the organic world. The sacrifice of males was a matter of complete indifference, as much so as is the sacrifice of germs, because the supply was inexhaustible, and in fact, throughout the lower orders an excess of males over females is the normal condition, and often the number of males greatly exceeds that of the females. That a hundred males should live and die without once exercising their normal faculty is of less consequence than that one female should go unfecundated. Biologic economy consists in unlimited resources coupled with the multiplication of chances. [2] Success in accomplishing the main purpose is the paramount consideration. The cost in effort, sacrifice, and life is a comparatively unimportant element.

[1] " Man and Woman," 3d edition, London, 1902, p. 397.
[2] " Psychic Factors of Civilization," Boston, 1893, p. 250.

But it is obvious that the interest of the male is wholly unlike the interest of the female. That the female has an interest there is no doubt. She also has to a limited extent the appetent interest of the male, but this is not usually strong enough to cause her even to move from her place, much less to seek the male. From this point of view she is comparatively indifferent, and is, as is so commonly said, the passive sex. But the female has another and wholly different interest and one which is wanting in the male. Through her nature secures another end which is second only to the two great ends thus far considered, viz., reproduction and fertilization. The male element is in a high degree centrifugal. Unlimited variation would be dangerous if not destructive. Mere difference is not all that is required by evolution. Quality is an element as important as degree. The female is the guardian of hereditary qualities. Variation may be retrogressive as well as progressive. It may be excessive and lead to abnormalities. It requires regulation. The female is the balance wheel of the whole machinery. As the primary, ancestral trunk she stands unmoved amid the heated strife of rivals and holds the scales that decide their relative worth to the race. While the voice of nature speaking to the male in the form of an intense appetitive interest, says to him: fecundate! it gives to the female a different command, and says: discriminate! The order to the male is: cross the strains! that to the female is: choose the best! Here the value of a plurality of males is apparent. In such a plurality there are always differences. The female recognizes these differences, and instinctively selects the one that has the highest value for the race. This quality must of course coincide with a subjective feeling of preference, a coincidence which is brought about by the action of the well-known laws of organic adaptation.

This subjective feeling it is which constitutes the distinctive interest of the female. It is clearly quite other than the interest of the male. It is wanting in the plant and in the lowest animals, but nevertheless makes its appearance at a very early stage in the history of sentient beings. In considering it we have to do with a psychic attribute a grade higher than that of pure appetency. In fact it represents the dawn of the esthetic faculty. We have already seen in Chapter VII how the advent of mind gave the world a new dispensation and seemed to reverse the whole policy of nature. We are now about to witness another profound transformation wrought by a special psychic faculty, viz., the faculty of taste. This transformation is nothing less than the work of raising that miniature speck of existence, the primordial fertilizing agent, to the rank of a fully developed animal organism, approaching in varying degrees, and actually reaching in a few instances, the status of the original specific trunk, then called the female.

The foundation of the whole process is the fundamental law of heredity, that offspring inherit the qualities of both their parents. The qualities of the mother, being those of the species in general, are of course inherited and do not concern the transformation. This comes through the qualities of the male. The incipient esthetic tastes of the female cause her to select the qualities from among her suitors that she prefers, and to reject all males that do not come up to her standard. The qualities selected are transmitted to the offspring and the new generation again selects and again transmits. As all females may be supposed to have substantially the same preferences the effect is cumulative, and however slowly the transformation may go on, it is only necessary to multiply the repetitions a sufficient number of times to secure any required result. The particular characters thus selected are called secondary sexual characters; they are chiefly seen in the male because the female already has the normal development. There can be no doubt that in cases, like spiders, where the males are so exceedingly small, one of the preferred qualities is a respectable stature and bulk, and that throughout the lower orders the chief selecting has been that of larger and larger males, until the observed present state of partial sex equality was attained. This is exactly the kind of facts that would be overlooked by the average investigator, attention being concentrated on certain more striking and apparently abnormal facts, such as brilliant coloration, peculiar markings, special ornamental organs, weapons of destruction, etc. These latter, under the joint action of the principle of selection and the law of parsimony, are often not only confined to the male, but do not appear until the age of maturity, at which time they can alone serve the purpose for which they were selected and created, viz., to attract the female and lead to the continued selection of those males in which they are best developed. It is upon these that biological writers chiefly dwell. They point to a certain degree of development in the tastes of the females which lies beyond the simply useful.

To use the language of figure based on fact, it is small wonder that the female should be ashamed of her puny and diminutive suitors and should always choose the largest and finest specimen among them. If her selection were mainly confined to this quality during all the early history of every species the naturalist without the gynæcocentric theory to guide his observations would never discover it. He would simply notice that the difference in the size of the sexes differs widely in different species and families and set it down as a somewhat remarkable fact but without significance. He would be specially attracted by the superficial differences, particularly in the matter of ornamentation in the male. These are certainly remarkable, and a vast array of examples has been marshaled by Darwin and his coadjutors and successors. Darwin found comparatively little evidence of sexual selection among the invertebrates. In the Mollusca hermaphroditism prevails, which means that the fertilizer is simply an organ and not an independent organism; but here, as in hermaphrodite plants, the tendency toward sex separation is general. In the Arthropoda, and especially in the Arachnidæ, there occur those enormous differences in the size of the sexes that we have been considering. But this varies even here in nearly all degrees, which shows that selection in the quality of size has always been going on, and in some species has resulted in something like sex equality. Blackwall, De Geer, Vinson, Westring, and Kirby and Spence had already recorded many facts, and many more have since been added. In insects the equalizing process had gone much farther, and still Darwin was obliged to admit that "with insects of all kinds the males are commonly smaller than the females."[1] In most of them, however, the other more striking characters of the males attract the chief atten- tion. Darwin takes up each class and group of animals in the ascending order of development all the way to man, and makes out an unanswerable case in favor of his principle of sexual selection. Later writers have multiplied facts in its support until it is to-day as firmly established as that of natural selection. Only certain extreme "Neo-Darwinians," as they call themselves, who defend the "all-sufficiency of natural selection," seek to belittle or even deny this principle, but this is done with such an obvious *parti pris* that its scientific value is slight. Even Professor Poulton, who

[1] " Descent of Man," Vol. I., New York, 1871, p. 335.

was the principal translator of Weismann's "Essays," and is an especially competent judge, insists in his lectures, one of which I have heard, upon the undeniable truth of sexual selection, and presents a large mass of fresh and striking evidence in its support.

Jealousy, the "green-eyed monster which doth mock the meat it feeds on," here showed its usefulness, for it coöperated with the esthetic faculty of the female and led to all those intense activities of the rival males that developed the characters that the females preferred. Success in these struggles for favor, due in turn to the qualities that insured success, was the sure passport to favor, and female favor meant parenthood of the race. Size and strength, even more than the accompanying organic weapons, were the elements of success, and in this way the respectable stature and compact build of the males of developed species gradually replaced the diminutiveness and structural frailty of the primitive males. All these influences have been at work in all the types of animal life since the dawn of the psychic faculty, and the effects, as we should naturally expect, have been roughly proportioned to the length of the phylum. There are of course exceptions to this rule, due to other collateral and partially neutralizing influences, often of a very obscure and complex nature, but upon the whole this has been the result, and consequently we find that it is in the birds and mammals, the two latest classes, and the two that possess the longest phylogenetic ancestry, that the effects of sexual selection are the most marked. Here the struggle for size, strength, courage, and beauty reaches its maximum intensity, and begins in a sort of geometrical progression to augment and multiply all the secondary sexual characters of the male and to threaten the overthrow, at least for a time, of the long prevailing gynæcarchy of the animal world.

Male Efflorescence. — We have presided at the birth of the male being, long subsequent to that of the true organism, in the form of a minute sperm-plasm to supplement the much older germ-plasm, not as an aid to reproduction, but simply as a medium of variation and a condition to higher development. We have watched the progress of this accessory element subjected to the esthetic choice of the organism or real animal, until, through the inheritance of the qualities thus chosen it slowly rose in form and volume into somewhat the image of its creator and became a true animal organism resembling the original organism, on account of which naturalists call it the male and the other the female of the same species. Seeing these two somewhat similar forms habitually together, the one still performing the office of fertilizer and the other the work of reproduction, they class them alike, and until recently regarded fertilization as an essential part of reproduction. But the deeper meaning of it all has generally escaped observation.

The esthetic sense of the females has produced many beautiful objects in the form of male decoration in the invertebrate and lower vertebrate classes, but with the advent of bird life this sense became more acute, and having such decorative materials as feathers to work with, it soon surpassed all its previous achievements and wrought gorgeous products on the most ornamental patterns. The following is Wallace's description of the bird of paradise from personal observation in New Guinea, and will serve for a general example, although it is, of course, an extreme one: —

Most celebrated of all are the birds of paradise, forming a distinct family, containing more than twenty-five different species, all confined to this island and the immediately surrounding lands. These singular birds are really allied to our crows and magpies, but are remarkable for their special and varied developments of plumage. In most cases tufts of feathers spring from the sides of the body or breast, forming fans, or shields, or trains of extreme beauty. Others have glossy mantles or arched plumes over the back, strange crests on the head, or long and wire-like tail-feathers. These varied appendages exhibit corresponding varieties of color. The long trains of waving plumes are golden yellow or rich crimson, the breast-shields, mantles, and crests are often of the most intense metallic blue or green, while the general body plumage is either a rich chocolate brown or deep velvety black. All these birds are exceedingly active and vivacious, the males meeting together in rivalry to display their gorgeous plumage, while in every case the female birds are unornamented, and are usually plain or positively dingy in their coloring.[1]

From this we can form some idea of the esthetic tastes of female birds. As was remarked of the tastes of insects in virtually creating the world of flowers (see *supra*, p. 234), so we may now say of birds, the similarity of their tastes to those of men, even of the men of the highest culture, is proved by the universal admiration of mankind for the objects of their esthetic selection and creation. From a certain point of view, therefore the standard of taste is universal among sentient and psychic beings, and the beautiful colors, mark-

[1] " New Guinea and its Inhabitants," by Alfred Russel Wallace, *Contemporary Review*, Vol. XXXIV, February, 1879, p. 424.

ings, and forms of butterflies, moths, and beetles, of ostrich feathers and peacocks' tails, speak for an esthetic unity throughout all the grades and orders of life. It is the same standard of taste, too, that again comes out in the highest class of animals, the mammals, and that produces such universally admired objects as the antlers of the stag, which are the type of a true secondary sexual character. It is through such influences that the males of so many birds and mammals have attained their extraordinary development in the direction of size, strength, activity, courage, beauty, and brilliancy.

The faculty exercised by the female in sexual selection may in a broad sense be called esthetic, but many other qualities than those that are popularly classed as beauty are preferred and created. Some of these may be called moral qualities, such as courage. This is a special element of success, and its development leads to the universal rivalry in the animal world for mates. It is not that the rivals decimate and destroy one another leaving only the final victor. As has been remarked,[1] the battles of the males, however fierce, rarely result fatally, and they often take the form of quasi mock battles in which some do, indeed, "get hurt," but it rarely happens that any get killed. Still less is it true that the strongest and ablest males use their powers to coerce the female into submission. The female, even when greatly surpassed in size and strength by the male, still asserts her supremacy and exercises her prerogative of discrimination as sternly and pitilessly as when she far surpassed the male in these qualities. This is why I reject the usual expression "male superiority" for those relatively few cases in which the male has acquired superior size and strength along with the various ornaments with which the female has decked him out. And nothing is more false than the oft-repeated statement inspired by the androcentric world view, that the so-called "superior" males devote that new-gained strength to the work of protecting and feeding the female and the young. Those birds and mammals in which the process of male differentiation has gone farthest, such as peacocks, pheasants, turkeys, and barnyard fowls, among birds, and lions, buffaloes, stags, and sheep, among mammals, do practically nothing for their families. It is the mother and she alone that cares for the young, feeds them, defends them, and if necessary fights for them. It is she that has the real courage —

[1] Espinas, "Sociétés Animales," 2ᵉ éd., Paris, 1878, pp. 324, 327.

courage to attack the enemies of the species. Many wild animals will flee from man, the only exception being the female with her young. She alone is dangerous. Even the male lion is really somewhat of a coward, but the hunter learns to beware of the lioness. The doe goes off into a lonely spot to bring forth and nurse her fawn. It is the same with the female buffalo and the domestic cow. How much does the bull or the cock care for its mate or its offspring? Approach the brood with hostile intent and it is the old hen that ruffles up her feathers so as to look formidable and dares to attack you. The cock is never with her. His business is with other hens that have no chickens to distract their attention from him.

The formidable weapons of the males of many animals acquired through sexual selection are employed exclusively in fighting other males, and never in the serious work of fighting enemies. The female simply looks on and admires the victorious rival, and selects him to continue the species, thus at each selection emphasizing the qualities selected and causing these qualities to tower up into greater and greater prominence. The whole phenomenon of so-called male superiority bears a certain stamp of spuriousness and sham. It is to natural history what chivalry was to human history. It is pretentious, meretricious, quixotic; a sort of make-believe, play, or sport of nature of an airy unsubstantial character. The male side of nature shot up and blossomed out in an unnatural, fantastic way, cutting loose from the real business of life and attracting a share of attention wholly disproportionate to its real importance. I call it *male efflorescence*. It certainly is not male supremacy, for throughout the animal world below man, in all the serious and essential affairs of life, the female is still supreme. There is no male hegemony or andrarchy. Nevertheless it represents organic evolution of which both sexes have partaken. Its chief value lies in the fact that in lifting the male from nothing to his present estate it has elevated all species and all life and placed the organic world on a higher plane. The apparent male superiority in some birds and mammals instead of indicating arrested development in the female indicates over-development in the male. Male efflorescence is an epiphenomenon. But in all this surplus life infused into the male a certain quantity has found its way into the stock and caused an advance. It has been shown that even the typical secondary sexual characters crop out to a limited extent also in the females. This was perceived by Darwin,[1] and has recently been established on paleontological evidence.[2] But it is especially the more solid and useful characters that have thus advanced.

Primitive Woman. — To the intelligent and sympathetic reader no apology is needed for having dwelt so long on the prehuman stage in the exposition of so unfamiliar a subject as the gynæcocentric theory. It must be perfectly apparent to him that this could be done in no other way. Long before we reach the human stage we find all the alleged evidence of the androcentric theory, and without such a study of origins as we have been making there would be no counter-evidence, and in fact no data for understanding the real meaning of this alleged evidence. We are now in position at least to understand it and to weigh it, and as I said at the outset, there will be differences in the amount of weight given to all the facts depending upon the differences in the constitution of individual minds, and if the facts can be placed before all minds the conclusions drawn from them may be safely left to take care of themselves. But it so happens that while the facts depended upon to support the androcentric theory are patent to all, those that support the gynæcocentric theory are latent and known to very few. But in this it does not differ at all from any of the great truths of science. The facts supposed to prove the apparent are on the surface while those that prove the real, which is usually the reverse of the apparent, lie hidden and only come forth after prolonged investigation and reflection. The androcentric world view will probably be as slow to give way as was the geocentric, or as is still the anthropocentric.

In the larger apes that most resemble man male efflorescence is tolerably well marked, though not so extreme as in some other animals. The comparison is usually with so-called anthropoid or tailless apes, but there are apes with tails that have a physiognomy more like that of man than is that of any of the anthropoids. Certain mandrils that I have seen have strong Hibernian features. The white-nosed seacat, *Cercopithecus petaurista*, has decided African

---

[1] "Descent of Man," New York, 1871, Vol. I, pp. 270, 271.

[2] "On the evidence of the Transference of Secondary Sexual Characters of Mammals from Males to Females," by C. I. Forsyth Major, *Geological Magazine*, N. S., London, Dec. IV, Vol. VIII, No. 6, June, 1901, pp. 241-245.

and even Garibaldian traits, while the nose-ape, *Semnopithecus nasicus*, has an almost English face. This strikingly human appearance in these apes is in part due to the large facial angle, but it is chiefly due to the distribution of the hair on the face, which is practically the same as in a man. The parts above the mouth are hairless as in man while the sides of the face and the chin are provided with much longer hair than that of the rest of the body. In other words these apes have a true beard like that of man. The beard is the most prominent and typical secondary sexual character of man, and we see that it was developed far back in the phylogenetic line. I am not informed how the females differ from the males in these species of ape, but in the orang, gorilla, chimpanzee, and gibbon, the males are much larger and stronger, and the male gorilla at least has much more powerful jaws and teeth, the canines having almost the character of tusks.

Nothing is of course known of the differences in the sexes of Pithecanthropus (ape-man), of which only part of one skeleton has been found, but it is a fair assumption that the males were larger and stronger than the females, and possessed other distinctively male characters. The somewhat hypothetical European Tertiary creature called Homosimius by Gabriel and Adrien de Mortillet[1] would seem to connect the Pithecanthropus of Java with the man of Neanderthal, which King[2] first erected into a distinct species and named *Homo Neanderthalensis* (which view has been accepted by Cope[3] and Schwalbe[4]) and later in the same year[5] declared in favor of its generic distinctness.

Unfortunately Homosimius is thus far known only by his works, no part of his skeleton having been found. Still these authors name three species of this genus, viz., *H. Bourgeoisii*, for the man of

[1] " Le Préhistorique. Origine et Antiquité de l'Homme," par Gabriel et Adrien de Mortillet, 3e éd., Paris, 1900, pp. 96–101.

[2] " On the Neanderthal Skull, or Reasons for believing it belonged to the Clydian Period, and to a species different from that represented by Man," by Professor W. King, British Association Report, 33d meeting, Newcastle-upon-Tyne, 1863, London, 1864, Part II, Notices and Abstracts, pp. 81–82.

[3] " On the Genealogy of Man," by E. D. Cope, *American Naturalist*, Vol. XXVII, April, 1893, pp. 321–335 (see p. 331).

[4] " Ueber die specifischen Merkmale des Neanderthalschädels," von G. Schwalbe, *Anatomischer Anzeiger, Verhandl. d. Anat. Ges.*, XV. Versamml., Bonn, 26–29 Mai, 1901, Jena, 1901, pp. 44–61.

[5] " The Reputed Fossil Man of the Neanderthal," by Professor William King, *Quarterly Journal of Science*, Vol. I, January, 1864, pp. 88–97.

Thenay; *H. Ribeiroi*, for that of Otta; and *H. Ramesii*, for that of Puy-Courny. They claim to have positive proof that the first of these used fire in breaking flints. The other two broke them by percussion. These acts alone would make them men, *i.e.*, rational beings, capable of utilizing the forces of nature to their own advantage. No true animal, as I have successfully maintained, attains to this intellectual stage (see *infra.*, p. 514).

On the evolution theory we are obliged to assume that the transition from the truly animal ancestor of man to the truly human being was by a series of imperceptible steps, and therefore the exact line between animal and man cannot of course be drawn and could not be if all the steps were represented in the paleontological and archæological record. But it is of the greatest interest to discover and trace out in both these sciences as many steps as possible in the series leading up to existing man. From now on we are to deal with man as we actually know him, and to consider the relations between man and woman, physically and socially. In all known human races man is found to be larger and stronger than woman, and to have certain of the typical secondary sexual characters, but these latter differ in different races and have no special value for our subject.

A survey of this field soon shows that we are on a new plane of existence. We have reached another of those turns in the lane of evolution at which a new era begins. It is one of those cosmical crises mentioned in Chapter V, in which a new and at first unperceived and unimportant element suddenly assumes vast proportions and causes a complete change of front in the march of events. We have encountered several such. The rise of the esthetic faculty which led to sexual selection, evolved the male sex, and carried it up to such giddy heights, should have been set down as one of these differential attributes producing unintended effects, which in this sense are, if not abnormal, at least extra-normal, ultra-normal, and supra-normal. On the human plane we encounter another such an element, not indeed one that has been overlooked, but one that produced a large number of deviations from the norm, some of which have been considered, others of which will be considered later on, and one of which now confronts us in our attempts to explain the relations of the sexes. This new element is none other than the presence in man of a rational faculty. We saw in Chapter X how this faculty alone gave man the dominion of the earth. We may now see how the same faculty gave to man in the narrower sense the dominion of woman. We have seen that notwithstanding all the shining qualities with which female taste endowed the males of certain of the higher types of animals, including the immediate ancestors of man, there is not and never can be in any of these types any true male hegemony, and that everywhere and always, regardless of relative size, strength, beauty, or courage, the mothers of the race have held the rein and held the male aspirants to a strict accountability. In a non-rational world there could be no other economy, since to place affairs in the hands of the " fickle and changeable " sex[1] would bring speedy and certain ruin to any animal species.

But the term " rational," as here employed, is misleading to the average mind. The popular idea that it conveys is akin to that implied in the word *reasonable*. A rational being is supposed to be incapable of an irrational act, and from this idea the word is some way connected with right or moral action. But applied to primitive man it should be divested of all these implications. It simply means a being capable of reasoning about the simplest and most material things. The rational faculty began as a purely egoistic servant of the will in better securing the objects of desire. Its chief rôle was to supplant instinct. To do this it must attain a certain strength. It is a preëminently centrifugal faculty, and up to a certain point it must be under the power of instinct. It is instinct which, throughout the animal kingdom below man, maintains female supremacy and prevents the destruction of animal races. But with man reason begins to gain the ascendant over instinct. This means that it is strong enough to break over the restraints of instinct and still avert danger. Until it reaches this point it is self-destructive, since natural selection eliminates the wayward.

Increased brain mass became a secondary sexual character. It has been already noted that the chief stress has been laid on those comparatively unimportant characters, such as horns, spurs, bright colors, and musical powers, as the products of sexual selection, while increased bulk and strength, and the assimilation of form to that of the primary organism or female, are characters rarely mentioned in that connection, although these are by far the most impor-

---

[1] The " varium et mutabile semper femina " of Virgil (Book IV, lines 569–570) is a typical androcentric sentiment, and the precise reverse of the truth.

tant. It is the same with brain development. Because brain is common to both sexes its increase as the result of female preference is not noticed. Yet there can be no doubt that success in rivalry for female favor became more and more dependent upon sagacity, and that this led to brain development. It also seems certain that, as in the case of size of body, so in that of size of brain, a disproportionate share of the increment acquired went to the male. But throughout the later geologic periods, and to some extent in all periods, the brain gained upon the body, as shown by the phenomena of cephalization, whereby the head, and especially the encephalon, has been growing larger in proportion to the body in all the great phylogenetic lines. Natural selection might bring this about to some extent, but the greater part of it is probably attributable to sexual selection, and the male brain has thus gradually gained upon that of the female, until we have the present state of things.

Now this male brain development it is that has brought about the great change, and has constituted man a being apart from the rest of creation, enabling him with increasing safety to violate the restraints of instinct and inaugurate a régime wholly different from that of the animal world out of which he has developed. Having become larger and physically stronger than woman, his egoistic reason, unfettered by any such sentiment as sympathy, and therefore wholly devoid of moral conceptions of any kind, naturally led him to employ his superior strength in exacting from woman whatever satisfaction she could yield him. The first blow that he struck in this direction wrought the whole transformation. The ægis and palladium of the female sex had been from the beginning her power of choice. This rational man early set about wresting from woman, and although, as we shall see, this was not accomplished all at once, still it was accomplished very early, and for the mother of mankind all was lost.

Gynæcocracy. — In a broad general sense the relations of the sexes throughout the animal kingdom, as above described, might be characterized as a gynæcocracy, or female rule, for which the form *gynæcarchy*, already employed (*supra*, p. 328), is perhaps to be preferred. But I propose to restrict the term, as did Bachofen,[1] to the human race,

---

[1] " Das Mutterrecht. Eine Untersuchung über die Gynaikokratie der alten Welt nach ihrer religiösen und rechtlichen Natur," von J. J. Bachofen, Stuttgart, 1861; Zweite unveränderte Auflage, Basel, 1897, 4°, pp. XL, 440.

and to a phase of the early history of man, which, though almost unknown prior to the astonishingly erudite and exhaustive researches
of Bachofen, is now known always to have existed and still to exist
at the proper status of culture or stage of man's history. Making
all due allowance for the unreliability of the accounts of travelers,
and the disposition to exaggerate everything that is opposed to
civilized customs, there still remains far too large a volume of facts
bearing on this state to be passed over as meaningless or worthless.
In fact this tendency to exaggerate them is doubtless more than
counterbalanced by the influence of the androcentric world view in
causing them to be overlooked. Ethnographers constantly lean
toward their rejection or the minimizing of their significance. They
are in their way in working out a complete androcentric system of
ethnology.

It must not be forgotten that the true beginnings of man are not
known in the sense that races exist representing such beginnings.
The lowest races known are relatively far advanced and belong to
old stocks. It is natural to suppose that, at much lower stages than
any of these represent, woman, almost to the same extent as among
the female anthropoids, possessed absolute power of choice and
rejection, and in this most vital respect, was the ruling sex. Sexual
selection may have been still in action, still further modifying the
attributes of men. Mr. Spencer gives one case that points in this
direction even among existing races: "Tuckey, speaking of certain
Congo people who make scars, says that this is 'principally done
with the idea of rendering themselves agreeable to the women:' a
motive which is intelligible if such scars originally passed for scars
got in war, and implying bravery."[1] There are many indications
that woman was slow to surrender her scepter, and that the gradual
loss of her power of rejection and selection took place with all the
irregularity that characterizes all natural phenomena. Circumstances of every kind impeded or favored it, and the scattered
hordes exerted no influence on one another to produce uniformity in
this respect. Nothing is more varied than the relations of the sexes
among existing races of men. Almost every conceivable form of
marriage, or union, has been found. While most persons suppose
that nothing is so certainly fixed by nature, and even by divine
decree, as the particular form of marriage that happens to prevail

---

[1] "Principles of Sociology," Vol. II, New York, 1896, p. 75 (§ 265).

z

in their own country, ethnologists know that nothing is so purely conventional as just this fact of the ways in which men and women arrange or agree to carry on the work of continuing the race.

About the time that the transformation from apehood to manhood took place it is probable that the males were considerably larger and stronger than the females, but that the females compelled the males to conform to their choice, thus keeping up the action of selection and its legitimate effects. With the advent of incipient rationality it could scarcely be otherwise than that this long fixed condition should be somewhat disturbed. As rationality was acquired by both sexes, though perhaps in somewhat unequal degrees, if it was to cause one sex to dominate the other, circumstances must decide, at least at first, which should be the dominant sex. As the female sex had thus far always exercised supremacy in the most vital matters, it might be supposed that woman would prove the dominant sex in primitive hordes. That this was the original tendency and logic of events is abundantly shown by the survivals of it that we find, and by the real condition of the lowest existing races.

The first and most striking form of evidence pointing this way consists in a class of facts that may be roughly grouped under the general head of *amazonism*, although they show not only widely different degrees of this state, but also a great variety of forms of it. These are all described in the numerous standard works in which the facts have been laboriously compiled, and space does not permit me to attempt their enumeration. It is enough to note that phenomena of this class, sufficient to show a greater or less degree of female supremacy, have been observed in at least a score of races. Some of those most frequently referred to are the following: Natives of the Khasi Hills in Assam; Naïars of the Malabar coast; Dyaks of Borneo; Batta people in Sumatra; Dahomans, West Africa; Mombuttus, Central Africa; natives of Madagascar; inhabitants of Imôhagh in the desert of Sahara; natives of New Britain (Neu-Pommern), Australasia; Fuegians; Botocudos of Eastern Brazil; Nicaraguans; Indians of the province of Cueva, Central America. This list covers a large part of the world. That it should consist chiefly of somewhat remote, outlying regions is of course what we should expect. That it was once far more general, however, is proved by records of it even in Europe, notably among the ancient Bretons and Scots. It was probably well-nigh universal, in the sense that each race has passed through that stage, although different races doubtless passed out of it not only at different times, but at different relative points in their history or development.

The other principal group of facts that support the claim for a primitive stage of gynæcocracy is that relating to what is variously called matriarchy, motherright, the matriarchate, and the metronymic family. Bachofen greatly disturbed the smooth androcentric current that had thus far been flowing, when in 1861 he announced that the ancient laws and records, both written and hieroglyphic, indicated a widespread system of descent and inheritance in the female line among both Aryan and Semitic peoples, and from data in his possession he worked out an entirely new theory of the early relations of the sexes. He concluded that the original state was one similar to the hetairism of the early Greeks, and that this passed into a form of female rule which he called " demetric gynæcocracy." [1] Soon after McLennan independently discovered that a large number of existing uncivilized races still reckon through the female line and actually have a more or less complete system of motherright. Morgan in studying the North American Indians found a similar condition of things complicated by a sort of group marriage. Since then ethnologists have studied the marriage relations of large numbers of tribes, finding of course great differences and nearly all gradations from the matriarchal to the patriarchal condition. The literature has become voluminous and is largely controversial, so that it is difficult for one seeking simply the truth to disengage any clear principles. The obvious zeal on the part of many to protect the human race from the supposed disgrace of having ever had sexual relations that their age and country condemns is a large element of untrustworthiness in the discussions.

While the animal origin of man is now almost universally admitted by anthropologists and by well-informed persons generally, there is manifest a very tardy recognition of its full meaning. No blame ever attaches to the sexual relations of animals. They are usually or always such as best subserve the needs of different species; at least they are such as the conditions actually produced. It was the same with man when he emerged from the animal state, and, properly viewed, they have always been such since that date. The multitudinous forms of marriage have all been the products of the con-

[1] " Das Mutterrecht," Introduction, p. XIX.

ditions of existence. A common error tacitly entertained is that animals carry on the process of reproduction and rearing of the young by a conscious attention to this important business. They are supposed to woo and mate for this purpose, and to care for their offspring with an eye to the interests of the species. The fact is that these functional results are the consequences of the law of adaptation, and the agents are wholly unconscious of them as anything to be attained by their actions. They only seek their interests in the form of feelings, which are so regulated by instinct as to secure the results. For example, as has already been said, animals can have no knowledge of the connection between mating and propagating. All they know is that they like to mate. The female brings forth her young with no conception of the part the male has had in it. She cares for her young because she is impelled to do so by an innate interest, in short, because she likes to do so. All this is true of all animal species, and it is not at all probable that the degree of reasoning power that enabled primitive man to perceive that the fertilization of the male was a necessary condition to reproduction was attained until long after the full human estate had been reached and man had advanced far into the protosocial stage. The fact that races still exist incapable of performing such an act of ratiocination proves that the inability to perform it must have once been general.

In such a state it was natural and necessary that everything should be traced to the mother. The father was unknown and unthought of. The idea of paternity did not exist. Maternity was everything. Fertilization and reproduction were as completely separated in thought as they have been shown to be in essence. That under such circumstances mother-rule and mother-right should prevail is among the necessities of existence. Amazonism, matriarchy, and all the forms of gynæcocracy that are found among primitive peoples, instead of being anomalies or curiosities, are simply survivals of this early and probably very long stage in the history of man and society of which no other evidence now exists, but which is the logical and inevitable conclusion that must follow the admission of the animal origin of man.

That the sexual relations of our most remote ancestors under such circumstances should be what would now be called lax, or even promiscuous, is nothing more than we should expect, and notwithstanding the laudable efforts of certain ethnologists to prove the contrary, or at least to palliate the supposed humiliation involved in such a state of things, the facts we have, even among the relatively advanced existing races, abundantly establish inductively the conclusion that can alone be reached deductively. I could easily fill a chapter with the bare enumeration of these facts, but they would be distasteful reading and may all be found in the great storehouses of facts that have been accumulated through the indefatigable labors of ethnographers. Only the general conclusion from all these facts can be stated here, and I prefer to state it in the words of one who labored long and faithfully in this field and who was not afraid of any real truth to which the facts lead: —

In the lower grades of civilization, in the most primitive human hordes, there is nothing yet that deserves the name of marriage. It is by the hazard of necessity that sexual unions, or rather, couplings, take place, and one single law governs them: the law of the strongest.[1]

But even here Letourneau had in mind a later stage than the one we are now considering. This is a stage in which "the law of the strongest" applies only in the sense that the strongest rival wins the prize. It is the strongest man, and has nothing to do with the relative strength of man and woman. So long as woman retains her power to select and reject, relative male strength is an element, but only one element among many. Woman's idea of male beauty still counts in the balance, and such moral qualities as courage, persistence, and powers of persuasion do their share. Finally, already, certain mental qualities begin to tell, especially cunning in outwitting, circumventing, and thereby overcoming rivals.

Androcracy. — At some point quite early in the protosocial stage it began slowly to dawn upon the growing intellect of man that a causal connection existed between these couplings of men and women and the birth of children. It was this simple act of ratiocination that literally reversed the whole social system. For the first time the man began to perceive that he, too, had a part in the continuance of the race, that the children were in part his, and not wholly the woman's. The idea, however, was very slow to take root. The only absolutely certain antecedent to the existence of a child was the parturition of the mother. That the child came from

[1] "La Sociologie d'après l'Ethnographie," par Charles Letourneau, 3e éd., Paris, 1892, p. 375.

her was something about which there could be no doubt. That it came in any manner from him was highly problematical to the primitive mind. In order that a child be born the mother must pass through the throes of child-birth, must suffer pangs, must remain for a greater or less period prostrate and helpless, as if the victim of disease. This temporary illness having always without exception accompanied the birth of a child through the entire history of any horde or race, became indissolubly associated with it, so that the two constituted a single compound conception in the savage mind. It may seem strange to the civilized mind that two such different facts could not be separated in thought, but it is proved that they could not, and I know of no better illustration of the feeble power of abstraction in the dawning intellect than is furnished by this fact. The use of fictions by savages is often referred to as an illustration of their ingenuity. Correctly analyzed it simply proves their incapacity to separate ideas that habitually occur together. Facts that are habitually associated cannot be thought of apart and independently. When their separation is forced upon them they invent some fiction which really avoids the necessity of separating them and still holds them together. Illness and child-birth were two facts that had always been associated, that in fact always had gone together. The existence of a child must presuppose the temporary illness of the person that has the child. If any one should say to a man, that child is partly yours, he may be imagined to reply, How so ? I have not been ill. But when the causal connection finally became generally recognized, and the parental relation of the father admitted, he was naturally disposed to claim his title to the offspring. In complete promiscuity where any one of a large number of men might be the father of a child, no such claim could be set up even if the causal connection referred to was believed to exist. But it may be supposed that even in the most primitive hordes, as among some of the anthropoid apes and many animals less highly developed, a certain amount of monogamic or polygynic pairing would take place, so that the father could be certain that no other man could have had a share in the creation of the children of one or several women with whom he lived. In such cases the claim to paternity would and no doubt did naturally arise. But so firmly did the ideas of temporary illness and child-birth cohere in the mind that it was not considered an adequate claim to any proprietary title to the child until this illness had actually been gone through with. But as the father was not really made ill by the birth of the child it was adjudged essential that he should feign such illness and take to his bed for the prescribed period. Absurd as all this may seem, it is what actually takes place even to-day among a large number of primitive peoples in widely different parts of the world. During these periods the man actually takes the kind of medicine that is given the woman, asafœtida, etc. This is characterized by Tylor as "the world-wide custom of the 'couvade,' where at child-birth the husband undergoes medical treatment, in many cases being put to bed for days."[1] The couvade has been so generally treated by ethnographers and writers on uncivilized races that it need not be discussed here further than to point out its social significance. Bachofen[2] came quite as near its correct interpretation as have his critics and later writers. Sir John Lubbock[3] (Lord Avebury) gives the views of a number of authors, most of which are highly improbable, inclining himself to connect it in some way with the doctrine of signatures. It certainly represents one of Tylor's "ethnographic parallels," but he denies that he regards it as "evidence that the races by whom it is practised belong to one variety of the human species,"[4] and finally admits that "it may have come to serve in something like the way suggested by Bachofen, as a symbol belonging to the rule of male kinship."[5] The fact is that wherever now met with it exists chiefly as a survival from a remote and forgotten past, and like everything else it has during this long history surrounded itself with a mass of absurd practices, gross superstitions, and extraneous associations, and these have come to take the first place in the savage mind, while the real reason for the existence of such a custom has been wholly lost from view. Those who practice it are therefore the last persons in the world from whom to expect a correct explanation of it. Letourneau, who went carefully over the whole field of the status of primitive woman, said in his concluding lecture: —

For a long time it was not suspected that the man had anything to do with the pregnancy of the woman. When it began to be suspected the

---

[1] "Primitive Culture," by Edward B. Tylor, London, 1871, Vol. I, p. 76.
[2] "Das Mutterrecht," Stuttgart, 1861, pp. 17, 255, 256.
[3] "Origin of Civilization," New York 1871, p. 12.
[4] "Researches into the Early History of Mankind," New York, 1878, p. 305 (footnote).   [5] *Ibid.*, p. 298.

ridiculous ceremonies of the couvade were invented by which the man, in recognizing his paternity, sought also to draw upon himself, in part at least, the malevolence of the evil spirits who watched the mother during and after the labor of parturition. The couvade has been discovered in a sufficient number of races and sufficiently often to justify the belief that the state of mind that it reveals was common to all peoples at a certain stage of their evolution.[1]

He had previously said that in Africa "the husband sometimes submits to the ceremony of the couvade in order to reënforce the bonds of parentage with the children of his wife. . . . In many [South American] tribes the practice of the couvade is observed, which seems to be an effort to create paternal filiation."[2]

One of the objections to this interpretation of the meaning of the couvade was that a certain tribe, the Mancusis, who practice it, "so far from reckoning the parentage as having been transferred to the father by the couvade, are actually among the tribes who do not reckon kinship on the father's side, the child belonging to the mother's clan."[3] It is not to be supposed that the couvade would produce a sudden reversal of what had been the order of nature throughout all past time. It is not probable that the father expected by it to demonstrate his exclusive right to the ownership of the child. It is forgotten that prior to the couvade the father had not suspected that he had contributed in the least to the creation of the child. The object of the couvade was solely to establish by a fiction the fact of paternity or joint action with the mother in bringing the child into existence. The question of domination or supremacy was an after consideration. The couvade was the first step toward fatherright and the patriarchate. Certain it was that the latter could never have been attained so long as children were believed to be the exclusive creation of women. So long as that view obtained gynæcocracy was the only condition possible.

But the idea once firmly established that the family was a joint product of the woman and the man, it is easy to see the important results that would naturally follow. The same strengthening of the

---

[1] "La femme à travers les âges. Leçon de clôture d'un cours sur la condition des femmes dans les diverses races," par Charles Letourneau, *Revue de l'École d'Anthropologie de Paris*, onzième année, Vol. IX, septembre, 1901, pp. 273–290. See p. 280.

[2] "La Sociologie d'après l'Ethnographie," 3e éd., Paris, 1892, pp. 384, 385.

[3] Tylor, *loc. cit.*, p. 298.

reasoning powers that made the discovery of paternity possible worked in all other directions. Paternity implied power over the child, which was now exercised by the father as well as by the mother. But it went much farther. Equal authority with the mother soon lead to a comparison of physical strength between the sexes, which had never been made before for precisely the same reason that the lion never compares strength with the lioness, the hart with the hind, the bull with the cow, or the cock with the hen. Physical strength never comes in question in the gynæcocratic state. The female dispenses her favors according to her choice, and the males acquiesce after venting their jealousy on one another. The idea of coercing the female or extorting her favor never so much as occurs to the male mind. The virtue of the female animal is absolute, for virtue does not consist, as many suppose, in refusal, but in selection. It is refusal of the unfit and of all at improper times and places. This definition of virtue applies to human beings, even the most civilized, as well as to animals. The female animal or the human female in the gynæcocratic state would perish before she would surrender her virtue.

The passage from the gynæcocratic to the androcratic state was characterized on the part of man by the loss of his normal chivalry and respect for the preferences of woman, and on the part of woman by the loss of her virtue. Both the time-honored assertion of authority by woman and submission to it by man were abrogated. In discovering his paternity and accompanying authority man also discovered his power, which at that stage meant simply physical strength. He began to learn the economic value of woman and to exert his superior power in the direction of exacting not only favors but service from her. The gynæcocratic régime once broken over the steps were short and rapid to complete androcracy. The patriarchate or patriarchal system, in which the man assumed complete supremacy, was the natural sequel to the process that had begun. It was all the product of the strengthening intellect which refused longer to be bound by the bonds of animal instinct and broke away from the functional restraints that adaptation had imposed upon the sexes. The man saw that he was the master creature, that woman was smaller, weaker, less shrewd and cunning than he, and at the same time could be made to contribute to his pleasure and his wants, and he proceeded to appropriate her accordingly.

The Subjection of Woman. — When John Stuart Mill used this expression as the title for his book he had only the philosopher's penetration into a great truth. He had comparatively little light from anthropology and scarcely any from biology. Its true meaning, therefore, as a phase of the history of man, as something impossible to the so-called "brute creation," and as a pure product of human reason untempered by altruistic sentiments, was for the most part lost to him. The most unfortunate fact in the history of human development is the fact that the rational faculty so far outstripped the moral sentiments. This is really because moral sentiments require such a high degree of reasoning power. The intuitive reason, which is purely egoistic, is almost the earliest manifestation of the directive agent and requires only a low degree of the faculty of reasoning. But sympathy requires a power of putting one's self in the place of another, of representing to self the pains of others. When this power is acquired it causes a reflex of the represented pain to self, and this reflected pain felt by the person representing it becomes more and more acute and unendurable as the representation becomes more vivid and as the general organization becomes more delicate and refined. This high degree was far from being attained by man at the early stage with which we are now dealing. Vast ages must elapse before it is reached even in its simplest form. And yet the men of that time knew their own wants and possessed much intelligence of ways of satisfying them. We need not go back to savage times to find this difference between egoistic and altruistic reason. We see it constantly in members of civilized society who are capable of murdering innocent persons for a few dollars with which they expect to gratify a passion or satisfy some personal want. It is true in this sense that the criminal is a survival from savagery. Civilization may, indeed, be measured by the capacity of men for suffering representative pain and their efforts to relieve it.

In our long and somewhat dreary journey down the stream of time we have now reached the darkest spot, and fain would I omit its description were this not to leave a blank in the story and to drop out an essential link in the chain of evidence for the gynæcocentric theory. But in recording this history I prefer in the main to let others speak. And first let us hear Herbert Spencer. This is what he says : —

In the history of humanity as written, the saddest part concerns the treatment of women; and had we before us its unwritten history we should find this part still sadder. I say the saddest part because, though there have been many things more conspicuously dreadful — cannabalism, the torturings of prisoners, the sacrificings of victims to ghosts and gods — these have been but occasional; whereas the brutal treatment of woman has been universal and constant. If, looking first at their state of subjection among the semi-civilized, we pass to the uncivilized, and observe the lives of hardship borne by nearly all of them — if we then think what must have gone on among those still ruder peoples who, for so many thousands of years, roamed over the uncultivated Earth; we shall infer that the amount of suffering which has been, and is, borne by women, is utterly beyond imagination. . . . Utter absence of sympathy made it inevitable that women should suffer from the egoism of men, without any limit save their ability to bear the entailed hardships. Passing this limit, the ill-treatment, by rendering the women incapable of rearing a due number of children, brought about disappearance of the tribe ; and we may safely assume that multitudes of tribes disappeared from this cause: leaving behind those in which the ill-treatment was less extreme.[1]

The general fidelity of this picture cannot be questioned, but, in the light of all that has been said thus far, I must protest against the term "brutal" as characterizing the treatment of woman by man. Far too many human sins are attributed to the brute that still lurks in man, but in this case it is flagrantly unjust to do this, since, as has been seen, no male brute maltreats the female, and the abuse of females by males is an exclusively human virtue.

In the second place, I think Spencer's picture a little too dark in assuming that this state of things must have been progressively worse as we recede from the present toward the past. It may have been worse in some races at an earlier date, and no doubt in all it has been bad for a very long period, but if any race could be traced back far enough we should find it in its gynæcocratic stage when the women were not only well treated, but themselves meted out justice to the men. All the cases enumerated in the last section are more or less modified survivals of that stage.

That the abuse of women by men is due in the main to the feeble development of sympathy is well stated by Spencer in an earlier work: —

The status of women among any people, and the habitual behavior to them, indicate with approximate truth, the *average* power of the altruistic sentiments; and the indication thus yielded tells against the character of the primitive man. Often the actions of the stronger sex to the weaker

[1] "Principles of Ethics," New York, 1893, Vol. II, pp. 335, 336 (§ 428).

among the uncivilized are brutal; generally the weaker are treated as mere
belongings, without any regard for their personal claims; and even at best
the conduct towards them is unsympathetic. That this slavery, often
joined with cruelty, and always with indignity, should be the normal condition among savages, accepted as right not by men only but by women themselves, proves that whatever occasional displays of altruism there may be,
the ordinary flow of altruistic feeling is small.[1]

To practically the same effect Letourneau remarks : —

In the human brain ideas of right and justice, the sentiment of respect
for the weak, are fruits of a high culture, unknown to primitive civilizations
in which man, realizing certain conceptions of Greek mythology, is still more
than half beast. Now, throughout the world woman has the misfortune to
be less strong than her companion; we must then expect to find her lot
harder in proportion as the society of which she forms a part is more rudimentary. The condition of women may even furnish a good criterion of the
degree of development of a people.[2]

The great length that this chapter is assuming will almost compel
me to limit myself to giving a few of these general statements, but
they are found either at the beginning or the end of long recitals of
facts observed and recorded of great numbers of tribes in all parts
of the world. Any attempt to enumerate these facts would carry
me much too far. I will, therefore, offer only a few of the briefer
accounts, which may be taken as illustrating the subjection of
woman in the stage of androcracy, which is that in which we now
find most of the lower savages. Thus Lubbock says, quoting in
part from Eyre : —

In Australia "little real affection exists between husbands and wives, and
young men value a wife principally for her services as a slave ; in fact, when
asked why they are anxious to obtain wives, their usual reply is, that they
may get wood, water, and food for them, and carry whatever property they
possess." The position of women in Australia seems indeed to be wretched
in the extreme. They are treated with the utmost brutality, beaten and
speared in the limbs on the most trivial provocation. " Few women," says
Eyre, " will be found, upon examination, to be free from frightful scars upon
the head, or the marks of spear-wounds about the body. I have seen a
young woman who, from the number of these marks, appeared to have been
almost riddled with spear wounds." If at all good-looking their position is,
if possible, even worse than otherwise.[3]

1 "Principles of Sociology," Vol. I, New York, 1877, p. 78 (§ 37).
2 "La Sociologie d'après l'Ethnographie," 3e éd., Paris, 1892, p. 168.
3 "Origin of Civilization," New York, 1871, p. 52. Cf. Edward John Eyre, "Journals of Expeditions of Discovery into Central Australia and Overland from Adelaide
to King George's Sound, in the Years 1840-1." London, 1845. Two volumes, 8°.
Vol. II, pp. 321, 322.

Du Chaillu describes two distressing cases of the apparently wanton torture of women in Central Africa,[1] one of which he succeeded in relieving. He intimates that this practice of torturing women was connected with some detestable superstition among the natives by which women were suspected of sorcery and witchcraft. But how much better were the people of Europe, and even of America, in this respect, down to the end of the seventeenth century ?

"Among the Kaffirs," says Spencer, quoting Shooter, "besides her domestic duties, the woman has to perform all the hard work ; she is her husband's ox, as a Kaffir once said to me, — she had been bought, he argued, and must therefore labor." [2]

The complete slavery of woman to man is shown by the following : "Of a Malagasy chief Drury says — 'he had scarcely seated himself at his door, when his wife came out crawling on her hands and knees till she came to him, and then licked his feet . . . all the women in the town saluted their husbands in the same manner.' " [3]

"Almost everywhere in Africa," says Letourneau, "woman is the property (*chose*) of her husband, who has the right to use her as a beast of burden, and almost always makes her work as he does his oxen." [4]   "In certain Himalayan regions near the sources of the Djemnah in Nepaul, etc., the Aryan Hindoos have adopted Thibetan polyandry. The women are for them a veritable merchandise which they buy and sell. At the time of which Fraser writes a woman among the peasants cost from 10 to 12 rupees, a sum which it was pleasant to receive but painful to expend. They also freely sold their daughters, and the brothers of each family bought a common wife, whom they rented without hesitation to strangers." [5]

That the subjection of woman was due entirely to her physical inferiority to man, or rather to that superior size and strength which men had acquired in common with most of the other higher animals through female selection, seems beyond controversy, the tendency to deny and escape it being inspired wholly by shame at admitting it. I find the following noble sentiment in the fragments of Condorcet :

[1] "Adventures in the Great Forest of Equatorial Africa and the Country of the Dwarfs," by Paul Du Chaillu, London, 1861, Chapter X, p. 122 ; Chapter XII, pp. 157-158.

[2] "Principles of Sociology," Vol. I, p. 687 (§ 305).

[3] *Op. cit.* Vol. II, pp. 124-125 (§ 386).

[4] "La Sociologie d'après l'Ethnographie," p. 336.

[5] *Op. cit.*, p. 366.

Among the advances of the human mind most important for the general welfare, we should number the entire destruction of the prejudices which have produced between the sexes an inequality of rights injurious even to the favored sex. In vain is it sought to justify it by differences in their physical organization, in the strength of their intellects, in their moral sensibilities. This inequality has had no other origin than the abuse of power, and it is in vain that men have since sought to excuse it by sophisms.[1]

Darwin says: "Man is more powerful in body and mind than woman, and in the savage state he keeps her in a far more abject state of bondage than does the male of any other animal;"[2] and Spencer remarks: "Without implying that savage men are morally inferior to savage women (the last show just as much cruelty as the first where opportunity allows), it is clear that among people who are selfish in extreme degrees the stronger will ill-treat the weaker; and that besides other forms of ill-treatment will be that of imposing on them all the disagreeable tasks they are able to perform."[3]   In New Zealand, according to Moerenhaut, a father or brother, in giving his daughter or his sister to her future husband, would say, "If you are not satisfied with her, sell her, kill her, eat her, you are absolute master of her."[4]   "Almost at the origin of human society woman was subjugated by her companion; we have seen her become in succession, beast of burden, slave, minor, subject, held aloof from a free and active life, often maltreated, oppressed, punished with fury for acts that her male owner would commit with impunity before her eyes."[5]

The whole difficulty in understanding these abuses lies in the fact that civilized men cannot conceive of a state in which no moral sentiments exist, no sympathy for pain, no sense of justice. And yet every day, in every civilized country of the world, the public press informs us of wife beatings that are scarcely less horrid than those of savages, and these would of course be far more common and shocking but for the restraints of law and police regulation. At the stage in the history of any race at which the transition from gynæ-

---

[1] "Tableau Historique des Progrès de l'Esprit Humain," Bibliothèque Positiviste, Paris, 1900, pp. 180–181.

[2] "Descent of Man," Vol. II, p. 355.

[3] "Principles of Sociology," Vol. III, p. 343 (§ 730).

[4] "Voyages aux Îsles du Grand Océan," par J. A. Moerenhaut, Paris, 1837, Vol. II, p. 69. These are the closing words of a set speech delivering the woman to the man, which may not be varied, and which corresponds to that of a modern marriage ceremony.

[5] Letourneau, Rev. Ecole d'Anthrop. de Paris, Vol. IX, p. 288.

cocracy to androcracy took place, and for a long period afterward, all men were morally below the level of the basest wife-beater of modern society, at a state in which the first spark of sympathy for suffering in others had not yet been kindled. It was this manner of man, just coming to consciousness through the dawn of a purely egoistic intellect, who, suddenly as it were, discovered that the physically inferior being who had, without his knowledge, endowed him with his superiority, was in his power and could be made to serve him. Hence the subjection of woman.

The Family. — It is customary to speak of the family with the most unreserved respect. Comte, who knew scarce anything of primitive man, and whose own family affairs were wretched in the extreme, made it the unit and the bulwark of society. In this he has been followed by many sociologists, and most of those who prefer some other social unit still hold the family to be an essential if not a sacred institution. But Comte was aware that the word *family* originally meant the servants or slaves.[1] The philologists have traced it back to the Oscan word *famel* from which the Latin *famulus, slave,* also proceeds, but whether all these terms have the same root as *fames,* hunger, signifying dependence for subsistence, is not certain. It is true, however, that *familia* was only rarely and not classically used by the Romans in the sense of the modern word family, *i.e.,* as including parents and children. For this *domus* was usually employed. But perhaps etymology signifies little in the present case.

The important thing is to gain something like a just conception of what the primitive family was. Under the régime of gynæcocracy there could of course be no proper family. The father was unknown and the mother cared for her children in obedience to an instinct common certainly to all mammals and birds and probably to many lower vertebrates. With the beginning of the régime of androcracy the women were enslaved and both women and children became the chattels of the men. The men still continued to fight for the women, but instead of thereby seeking to secure their favor and to become the chosen ones, they fought for their possession and seized each as many women as possible. The weaker men were, as before, condemned to celibacy, and the women were subject to a monopoly of the strong. This polygamous life made paternity practi-

---

[1] " Politique Positive," Vol. II, p. 201.

cally certain, and led direct to the patriarchate or patriarchal family. Brain development, among its other effects, led to the invention of artifices and devices for catching game and fish, and of weapons for more effectually combating rivals, who were now often killed and eaten, the distinction between war and the chase having as yet scarcely arisen. The primitive androcratic society was thus formed of patriarchal polygamous families and celibate men, the weaker of whom may have been also made slaves. All women were abject slaves, and the children were compelled to do any service of which they were capable. The patriarchs had absolute power over the persons of all within their families. Lippert[1] holds that the invention of the first implements and weapons produced a true revolution. The chase becomes possible, but only for man; woman, embarrassed by her child, cannot take part in it. Man begins to have need of her to carry his simple baggage; he must therefore maintain her and the children. Marriage is from the beginning an association dictated by economic needs. Man, devoting himself to the chase, becomes little by little physically superior to woman, and so becomes her master. Of course Lippert had no idea of the real causes that produced man's physical superiority to woman, but this passage is as clear a picture of the actual transition as I find in the writings of anthropologists, most of whom, strange to say, have scarcely any biological equipment for their work.

Ratzenhofer portrays the primitive family in the following terms:

> The need of authority in this group makes the father its head, and from this arises a new social phenomenon, the *family*, as the union of both sexes with their children under the leadership of one part, with the moral duty of mutual protection and sustentation. The headship of the father (exceptionally in a few peoples of the mother) is the fundamental condition of the family. Although in the horde with peaceful relations between man and wife a sort of marital relation may have existed, still this only acquired permanence through dominion and subjection in the family; only through these was an indissoluble marriage made to conform to the innate interests of men. But as the family bond of the community has an economic basis (*Veranlassung*) it lowers (*verschlechtert*) in general the position of women and children, sometimes also that of the parents; the stronger father reduces wife and children to the condition of workers for him, while he is supported and eventually devotes himself only to the chase or to combating wild animals. It may be said that this condition of wife and children is the most

---

[1] " Kulturgeschichte der Menschheit in ihrem organischen Aufbau," von Julius Lippert, Stuttgart, 1887. Zwei Bände, Band I, pp. 64 ff.

widespread of social phenomena. Not only do all culture peoples who have developed the family from the community or the tribe show from that time to the present this economic state of things, but primitive tribes have gradually brought about the enslavement of woman, and without the aid of other social influences, have transferred the labor to the wife. Not only the wife of the negro, the Hindu, and the Kirghis, but also the wife of the present Slav of the Balkan peninsula and of Russia, is the misused slave of her husband, and as the result of the effort to escape labor, we see the unwholesome interchange of wife and child labor in the West European factories, which would make greater gains from the laborer at the expense of wife and child, while at the same time they lower their wages.[1]

And in another place he remarks : —

Whether a man subjects one or several women to himself and treats the children as an addition to their working capacity, or whether a patriarchal community under the leadership of the oldest father devotes itself to similar economic ends, or whether several men appropriate one woman with a common economic object, or whether finally the monogamic family prevails through the honored relation of one man to one woman — it remains the same, the family is in all its forms an economic arrangement on the basis of the sex relation.[2]

It thus appears that, whatever the family may be to-day in civilized lands, in its origin it was simply an institution for the more complete subjugation and enslavement of women and children, for the subversion of nature's method in which the mother is the queen, dictates who shall be fathers, and guards her offspring by the instinct of maternal affection planted in her for that express purpose. The primitive family was an unnatural androcratic excrescence upon society.

Marriage. — We have now to invade another " sanctuary " only to find it, like the last, a " whited sepulcher." It may look like a strange inversion of the natural order of things to place marriage after the family, but if the promiscuous intercourse of the sexes that characterized the gynæcocratic stage cannot be properly called marriage, scarcely more can that stage be so called in which the men forcibly seize the women and make them their slaves and concubines without ceremony or pretence of consulting their will. The original patriarchal family implies marriage only in the sense that it is implied in a harem of seals on a rookery under the dominion of an old bull. Less so, in fact, for, although we are told that the bull does sometimes gently bite his refractory cows, he never abuses or

---

[1] " Die Sociologische Erkenntnis," pp. 142–143.
[2] *Ibid.*, pp. 230–231.

2 A

injures them, much less kills and eats them. That function is reserved for the "lord of creation," the only being endowed with a
"moral sense," made "in the image of his Creator," and often after
his death erected by his descendants into a god. Indeed, most gods
are themselves accredited with these sublime attributes !

The word *marriage* in the English language has three meanings, viz. : 1, the mutual voluntary union of a man and a woman;
2, the act of union of a man to a woman, or of a woman to a man;
3, the causing of a woman to unite with a man. The first of these
is a neuter or "middle" sense, and the corresponding verb is reflective in most other languages. The other two meanings are active,
the second having an entirely different verb in the Romance languages (*épouser*, etc.). The third is active and transitive, and is
little used, being more commonly expressed by the phrase "giving
in marriage." Even this is now more or less a matter of form.
These uses of the word marriage represent an evolution, and the first
meaning was the last to be developed, and represents the greatest
mutuality and equality of the marrying parties that has been attained. The second at first chiefly applied to the man who married
the woman without implying her consent, and has only in comparatively recent times carried with it the idea of a woman marrying a
man. The third, and now nearly obsolete meaning, was the only one
that the word possessed throughout all the early ages of human
development. The patriarch who owned all the women disposed
of them as he saw fit. They were looked upon by him as so much
value, and if the oxen, spears, boats, or other merchandise offered
for a woman were worth more to him than the woman, he sold
her for a price, and marriage consisted in nothing more than the
ratification, by whatever ceremony might prevail, of the bargain
thus made. In selling a woman to a man her owner is said to marry
her to him, and such was primitive marriage. In later stages and
in different tribes of course variations arose in the nature of the
ceremonies, and a great variety of so-called forms of marriage has
been described, but all of them wholly ignore the wishes of the
woman and constitute so many different ways of transferring and
holding property in women.

When the protosocial stage was passed and wars, conquests, and
social assimilation had begun, the women of the conquered races became the slaves of the conquerors, and ultimately the warriors also

and many of the other men.   Then commenced the period of universal slavery with the qualifications set forth in Chapter X.   The
system of caste was no doubt favorable to woman, since those of the
noble classes, whatever their relations to the men of those classes,
were on a higher plane than those of the lower classes.   The patriarchal system was strengthened rather than weakened by social
assimilation, and the principal effect it had upon marriage was
to diversify forms and, along with its other socializing influences,
somewhat to mitigate the rigor of woman slavery.   Polygamy prevailed, and with the establishment of a leisure class it was greatly
strengthened, the nobility and ruling class being secured in the possession of as many wives as they desired.   The enslavement of men
was some relief to women from drudgery, and harems were established in which the handsomest women were kept without labor and
always fresh for breeding purposes and to satisfy men's lusts.

Among the lower classes, and especially in the large middle class
that were neither slaves nor nobles, which carried on the principal
industrial operations of the now developing state and people, marriage took more rational forms, becoming, from considerations of
enforced justice, more frequently monogamic, and, as was shown,
resulting in the complete mixture of the blood of the two races.
With the origin of the state and the establishment of more and more
complete codes of law, marriage was legalized and regulated and
became more and more a human institution.   But when we see how
little advanced marriage was in Greece and Rome during what we
call "antiquity," we may easily imagine what it must have been at
an earlier date and among more backward races.   In Homer's day
the distinction between the first or real wife, presumably the one
who belonged to the noble caste, and the concubines, probably for the
most part from the lower caste, was clearly drawn.

The characteristic feature of Homeric marriage-preliminaries, in perfect
consonance with the patriarchal mode, is wife-purchase.   "Women," i.e.,
concubines, had values set upon them, were given as prizes and bought like
cattle; they were mere slaves and treated as such.   A wife, on the other
hand, was regularly sought with gifts, that is, was bought in a more formal
and distinctive way. . . .   The father's power was very great; to him the
daughter belonged, and he promised and married her with no thought of her
own feeling in the matter.[1]

[1] "Homeric Society. A Sociological Study of the Iliad and Odyssey," by Albert
Galloway Keller, New York, 1902, pp. 212, 214.

Letourneau says : —

In the first ages of Rome the wife formed part of the family of her husband only in the quality of a slave. . . .   She was owned like any chattel, for the virtuous Cato lent his wife Marcia to his friend Hortensius and took her back on the death of that friend.   The Roman husband had the right to beat his wife ; for, according to the expression of Monica, Saint Augustine's mother, Roman marriage was only a "contract of servitude."   The wife was for a long time purchased, and marriage *per coemptionem* always existed.   If the betrothed was of patrician race, the sale was disguised by the ceremony of *confarreatio*, consisting in partaking with the future husband, before ten witnesses, of a cake given by the priest of Jupiter.   For at Rome marriage, the *justes noces*, long the sole privilege of patricians, required religious consecration.   But once married by coemption or confarreation, the woman belonged to her husband, body and goods ; she was "in his hands." [1]

It would be hopeless to attempt to enumerate all the multitudinous forms of marriage, but down to comparatively modern times they all have one thing in common, viz., the proprietorship of the husband in the wife.   So slow has the idea of the wife being a slave of her husband been in disappearing that the word "obey" still remains in the marriage ceremony of all countries, and is only stricken out by a few emancipated people or liberal sects.

Almost from the beginning there existed a sort of "ceremonial government," growing more and more "ecclesiastical," *i.e.*, acquiring more and more a religious character, and by this the relations of the sexes were greatly modified.   This was what I have called *the group sentiment of safety*.   Its action was not moral in the sense of mitigating the abuse of women by men ; it was moral only in the sense of imposing restraints upon tendencies injurious or destructive to the race.   Among other such influences the ones that chiefly concern us here were those that worked for the maintenance of race vigor and the prevention of degeneracy.   Nature, as has been seen, constantly strives to keep up the difference of potential, and the origin of sex was one of the most effective of all devices for this purpose.   Nothing further seemed to be required in the animal world except to avoid hermaphroditism and secure bisexuality.   But among men forming themselves into kinship groups, the tendency to interbreed too closely was strong, and required to be checked.   The collective wisdom, or instinct, if any one prefers, perceived this, and offset it in a

---

[1] Letourneau, " La Sociologie d'après l'Ethnographie, " p. 371. Cf. De Greef, " Introduction à la Sociologie," Pt. II, 1889, pp. 136–140.

number of ways. In the protosocial stage this was accomplished chiefly through exogamy, which, as is well known, widely prevails, and although showing considerable variation, consists essentially in the crossing of clans. In many tribes marriage within the clan is severely punished, often with death. The era of war, conquest, and race amalgamation inaugurated a system of cross fertilization on a large scale, and this was adequately treated in Chapter XI. But one of the principal consequences that followed was the introduction of a system of marriage by rape, in which whole races engaged, and women were sought in war as trophies, and were captured for wives, thus effectively crossing the different stocks, and greatly strengthening the physical and mental constitution of the races involved. Marriage by capture thus became a system and was real for ages and over large parts of the earth. But with the increase and spread of population and the formation of states and peoples it gradually lost its serious character and was reduced to a mass of fictions and conventional symbolizations. Survivals of it persisted far down into the historic period, and some still exist. There seems no doubt that the "wedding tour" is a survival of the marriage flight following wife-capture, made to escape the fury of the wife's relatives, while the charivari or "horning" typifies the attack of the members of the wife's clan upon the pair, who seek to conceal themselves.

Ethnographers and historians all tell us that polygamy, meaning polygyny, or a plurality of wives, prevails and has prevailed in nearly all parts of the world and throughout all time. No doubt it has been the accepted form, but the substantial numerical equality of the sexes requires the assumption of a large amount of accompanying male celibacy. Wherever the facts have been ascertained no prevalent form of marriage has been able to prevent the coexistence with it of a widespread system of promiscuity. In civilized countries this is called prostitution, and by making it illegal without being able to suppress it, it has been rendered base and dangerous to the public health. But if all countries are studied it is found that from this quasi-criminal character it shades off more and more into a recognized form, if not of marriage at least of sexual union, and that it becomes natural and harmless in proportion as it is more fully tolerated and recognized. It is certain that monogamy does not lead to its abolition, and polygamists insist that their system is less favorable to it than monogamy.[1] As in civilized countries this form of marriage is not allowed to result in propagation it becomes a case of the complete triumph of feeling over function, and in which feeling is the sole end, and is sought for its own sake. The high group morality, expressing itself largely through religion, therefore condemns it. If function were the sole end, and feeling had no right to exist as an end, this condemnation would be altogether just. But even this sterile form of marriage may, from a wider standpoint, be compared with the wholesale destruction of germs going on in nature. The phylogenetic forces as such are irrepressible, but there must be a limit to multiplication, and this may be looked upon as one of the ways of preventing undue multiplication while at the same time permitting the action of the reproductive forces.

Upon the whole, however, marriage has accomplished its purpose, which, as we have seen, is not exclusively the producing and protecting of offspring and consequent continuation of the race, although this of course is its chief function, but which is also, to a large extent qualitative, and secures a degree of variation, crossing, and mixing, compatible with the prevention of stagnation and degeneracy and with the maintenance and increase of race vigor and of those physical and psychic qualities that have contributed to make the human race what we find it at its best.

We have seen that at a certain stage rape was a form of marriage, and that it was based on the unconscious but universal sense of the advantage of crossing strains, which is reënforced by the charm of sexual novelty, both of which motives are equally products of the biological imperative. It will be interesting to trace the influence of these early principles into later stages of society where rape has become a crime. The philosophy of rape as an ethnological phenomenon may be briefly summed up under the following heads : —

---

[1] In Utah it is exclusively confined to the "gentiles." In all countries it is almost wholly due to the economic dependence of women. Winiarsky justly remarks (*Revue Philosophique*, 25e Année, mars, 1900, p. 276) that " in regard to prostitution we have to do with a regular market, recognized for the most part by states, in which the supply of and demand for virtue exist and in which prices fix themselves according to the laws of economic mechanics." What would happen if women should acquire economic independence it may be difficult to predict, but it is easy to see that prostitution would practically cease. It would seem that there would then exist a demand without a supply, but in practice there would only remain the general fact that the sexes demand each other, and there can be no doubt that they would find ways of supplying this mutual demand. It could scarcely fail to produce a profound revolution in marriage institutions.

1. The women of any race will freely accept the men of a race which they regard as higher than their own.

2. The women of any race will vehemently reject the men of a race which they regard as lower than their own.

3. The men of any race will greatly prefer the women of a race which they regard as higher than their own.

These are fundamental and universal principles of ethnology, and when closely analyzed they will be seen to be all the result of the more general principle which makes for race improvement. When a woman of an inferior race yields to a man of a superior race there is a subconscious motive probably more powerful than physical passion, which is, indeed, the inspirer of the physical passion itself — the command of nature to elevate her race. When a woman of a superior race rejects and spurns the man of an inferior race it is from a profound though unreasoned feeling that to accept him would do something more than to disgrace her, that it would to that extent lower the race to which she belongs. And when the man of an inferior race strives to perpetuate his existence through a woman of a superior race, it is something more than mere bestial lust that drives him to such a dangerous act. It is the same unheard but imperious voice of nature commanding him at the risk of "lynch law" to raise his race to a little higher level.

In this last case, therefore, the philosophical student of races, however much he may deplore anything that tends to lower a higher race, sees reasons for partially excusing the "crime," since, although the perpetrator does not know it, it is committed in large measure under the influence of the biological imperative. It may be compared to the brave conduct of the male mantis or male spider in his zeal to perpetuate his race. On the other hand, the indignation and fury of the community in which such an act is performed is to be excused in a measure for the same reason. Although the enraged citizens who pursue, capture, and "lynch" the offender do not know any more than their victim that they are impelled to do so by the biological law of race preservation, still it is this unconscious imperative, far more than the supposed sense of outraged decency, that impels them to the performance of a much greater and more savage "crime" than the poor wretch has committed.

The terrible penalty attached to the attempt to raise a lower race by lowering a higher one renders this form of race mixture very

rare.   Fortunately perhaps for the human species at large, there is
a fourth law, which may be stated as follows : —

4. The men of any race, in default of women of a higher race,
will be content with women of a lower race.

The necessary corollary to all these laws is that in the mixture of
races the fathers of the mixed race almost always belong to the
higher and the mothers to the lower component race.   What the
effect of this is upon mankind at large is matter for speculation.
Whether the opposite would produce a better or a poorer mixture is
not known.   That it would be a very different one there is little
doubt.   The difference might be compared to that between a mule
and a hinny.   At all events the process of race mixture that has
always gone on and is still going on through the union of men of
superior with women of inferior races is at least in the nature of a
leveling *up*, and not a leveling *down*.

Male Sexual Selection. — With the earliest forms of social assimilation through conquest the lowest point seems to have been reached
in the moral degradation of man.   From this point on the ethical as
well as the intellectual curve gradually rises, and the horrors of
savagery become by degrees mitigated.   The esthetic sense through
which the female mind had created the male being, including man
as we find him, was not extinguished, it was simply overwhelmed
by the power of the new-born egoistic reason of man, using the
strength acquired through female selection in the subjugation and
domination of the innocent and unconscious authoress of these gifts.
Nor was this esthetic sense an exclusively female attribute.   It is
an invariable concomitant of brain development.   Beauty is that
which is agreeable to sense, and its effect is measured by the development of the senses and sensory tracts of the brain.   But the esthetic
sense is not intense.   It constitutes an interest of mild type.   By
the side of the sexual interest of the male in animals and earliest
man it is so feeble as scarcely to make itself felt.   The male therefore did not select or exercise any choice.   All females were alike
for the male animal and savage.   The only selection that took place
down to the close of the protosocial stage was female selection.   The
females alone were sufficiently free from the violence of passion to
compare, deliberate, and discriminate.   This they did, and we have
seen the result.

But with the advent of the metasocial stage due to conquest and subjugation, inaugurating the system of caste and establishing a leisure class, brain development was greatly accelerated by cross fertilization, and for the higher classes the primary sexual wants were more than satisfied by universal polygamy in those classes. It is a sociological law that as the lower, more physical wants are satisfied the higher spiritual wants arise. With an unlimited supply of women men began to compare them, and their esthetic sense was sharpened to stimulate their sated physical sense. Female sexual selection, which for the sake of brevity and precision may be called *gyneclexis*, had long ceased. The advent of androcracy and the subjection of woman had terminated its long and fruitful reign, and throughout the entire protosocial stage of man physical passion was supreme. But now there comes a calm in the long stormy career of man, and a small number are placed in a position to allow the spiritual forces free play. In this way male sexual selection, which may be called *andreclexis*,[1] arose, and this has since played a considerable rôle in the history of the human race.

Darwin did not overlook the phenomenon of male sexual selection. He even observed cases in the higher animals, and called special attention to the case of man. The following is his principal allusion to the subject: —

There are, however, exceptional cases in which the males, instead of having been the selected, have been the selectors. We recognize such cases by the females having been rendered more highly ornamented than the males — their ornamental characters having been transmitted exclusively or chiefly to their female offspring. One such case has been described in the order to which man belongs, namely, with the Rhesus monkey. Man is more powerful in body and mind than woman, . . . therefore it is not surprising that he should have gained the power of selection. Women are everywhere conscious of the value of their beauty; and when they have the means, they

---

[1] The various kinds of selection play such an important rôle in modern dynamic biology that they seem to demand a special terminology. The phrases "natural selection," "artificial selection," "sexual selection," etc., besides being too long for convenient use, are not all free from ambiguity. For example, sexual selection does not indicate which sex does the selecting, but it is generally understood that by it only female selection is meant. To express the opposite it is necessary to say, male sexual selection. It should be possible to designate each different kind of selection by a single word, and I therefore propose the following terms derived from the Greek word ἔκλεξις, selection, and an appropriate first component expressing the kind of selection: —

Geneclexis, natural selection; *teleclexis*, artificial (intentional) selection; *gyneclexis*, female sexual selection; *andreclexis*, male sexual selection; *ampheclexis*, mutual sexual selection, as explained below (p. 396).

take more delight in decorating themselves with all sorts of ornaments than do men.   They borrow the plumes of male birds, with which nature decked this sex in order to charm the females.   As women have long been selected for beauty, it is not surprising that some of the successive variations should have been transmitted in a limited manner ; and consequently that women should have transmitted their beauty in a somewhat higher degree to their female than to their male offspring.   Hence women have become more beautiful, as most persons will admit, than men.   Women, however, certainly transmit most of their characters, including beauty, to their offspring of both sexes ; so that the continued preference by the men of each race of the more attractive women, according to their standard of taste, would tend to modify in the same manner all the individuals of both sexes belonging to the race.[1]

In the undeveloped state of male tastes the qualities preferred by men are apt to be mere monstrosities, as in the steatopygy of the Hottentot women,[2] but even here it proves the possibility of producing secondary sexual characters in the female as well as in the male by sexual selection. ʻDe Candolle is the only author I have noted who has signalized the value of polygyny in securing female beauty. He says : —

Polygamy — which should be called polygyny — is a natural consequence of the abuse of power.   Along with many bad effects it has this advantage that the population of the wealthy class is physically improved by a continual choice of women endowed with beauty and with health.[3]

Although this effect is chiefly confined to the leisure class, the nobility, and the priesthood where this last is not celibate, and in more advanced and somewhat industrial societies, to the wealthy classes generally, still in polygamous countries it must be very great. Especially the large seraglios of Oriental Semitic and Aryan peoples were and still are stirpicultural nurseries of female beauty.   Kings and high dignitaries canvass the surrounding countries for the most perfectly developed women to stock these seraglios.   Circassian and Caucasian girls having the pure white complexion, small hands, feet, and limbs, and perfect pelvic and thoracic development, are among those of whom we read as constituting the favored inmates of these establishments.   If we reflect that this process had been going on for untold ages, before the time of Greek sculpture, we can readily understand how the models for the most celebrated statues may

---

[1] " Descent of Man and Selection in Relation to Sex," New York, 1871, Vol. II, p. 355.

[2] *Ibid.*, p. 329.

[3] " Histoire des Sciences et des Savants," 2ᵉ éd., 1885, p. 129.

have actually existed in that epoch, requiring scarcely any exercise of the sculptor's imagination to reproduce them in marble.

The fact that this andreclexis was so long confined to a numerically small class of mankind accounts for the great differences in the beauty of women; and the fact that this beauty is a secondary sexual character renders it somewhat ephemeral, so that the same women who were beautiful during their reproductive period are apt to become ugly during the latter part of their lives. As it is purely physical, and mind plays no part in its production, this element of durability is also wanting, and the quality is in a high degree superficial. In fact there is some resemblance between the effects of male and of female sexual selection, as the former was described a few pages back. There is a certain unreality, artificiality, and spuriousness about female as well as about male secondary sexual characters. The two processes differ, however, in many respects. Man, for example, does not desire women to be larger and stronger, but prefers frailty and a certain diminutiveness. He does not want cunning nor courage, nor any sterling mental or moral qualities, and therefore woman does not advance in these directions. Even fecundity and the physical development necessary to render it successful are not specially selected, and under this influence woman grows more sterile rather than more fertile. In short, almost the only quality selected is bodily symmetry with the color and complexion that best conform to it. The result is that if this were to go on a sufficient length of time without the neutralizing and compensating effect of other more normal influences, woman might ultimately be reduced to a helpless parasite upon society, comparable to the condition of the primitive male element, and the cycle might be completed by the production of complemental females corresponding to Darwin's complemental males in the cirripeds. There are certain women now in what is regarded as high society who are even less useful, since they contribute nothing to the quantity or quality of the human species. They represent what Mr. Veblen calls "vicarious leisure" and "vicarious consumption," devoting their lives to "reputable futility." In fact most leisure class ideas tend in the direction of making the women of that class as useless as possible. In China, as is well known, the ideal of female beauty consists in small feet, and not satisfied with the slow processes of selection and heredity, artificial clamps are put on at an early age to prevent the feet from growing, and so far is this carried that we are told that many women are unable to walk.

Notwithstanding all these capricious and unnatural tendencies, male sexual selection has been perhaps upon the whole beneficial in securing increased physical perfection of the race, primarily of women, a sort of female efflorescence, but also in some degree of men.

Woman in History. — The series of influences which we have been describing had the effect to fasten upon the human mind the habit of thought which I call the androcentric world view, and this has persistently clung to the race until it forms to-day the substratum of all thought and action. So universal is this attitude that a presentation of the real and fundamental relation of the sexes is something new to those who are able to see it, and something preposterous to those who are not. The idea that the female is naturally and really the superior sex seems incredible, and only the most liberal and emancipated minds, possessed of a large store of biological information, are capable of realizing it. At the beginning of the historical period woman was under complete subjection to man. She had so long been a mere slave and drudge that she had lost all the higher attributes that she originally possessed, and in order to furnish an excuse for degrading and abusing her men had imputed to her a great array of false evil qualities that tended to make her despise herself. All Oriental literature, all the ancient sacred books and books of law, all the traditional epics, all the literature of Greek and Roman antiquity, and in fact all that was written during the middle ages, and much of the literature of the fifteenth, sixteenth, and seventeenth centuries, teem with epithets, slurs, flings, and open condemnations of women as beings in some manner vile and hateful, often malicious and evil disposed, and usually endowed with some superstitious power for evil. The horrors of witchcraft were nothing but the normal fruit of this prevailing spirit in the hands of superstitious priests of a miracle-based cult. Near the end of the fifteenth century a certain book appeared entitled, "The Witch Hammer," which received the sanction of Pope Innocent VIII, and formed the companion to a bull against witches issued by him. The following is a sample passage from this book: —

The holy fathers have often said that there are three things that have no moderation in good or evil — the *tongue*, a *priest*, and a *woman*. Concerning woman this is evident. All ages have made complaints against her. The wise Solomon, who was himself tempted to idolatry by woman, has often in his writings given the feminine sex a sad but true testimonial; and the holy Chrysostom says: "What is woman but an enemy of friendship, an un-avoidable punishment, a necessary evil, a natural temptation, a desirable affliction, a constantly flowing source of tears, a wicked work of nature covered with a shining varnish?" Already had the first woman entered into a sort of compact with the devil; should not, then, her daughters do it also? The very word *femina* (woman) means *one wanting in faith;* for *fe* means "faith" and *minus* "less." Since she was formed of a crooked rib, her entire spiritual nature has been distorted and inclined more toward sin than virtue. If we here compare the words of Seneca, "Woman either loves or hates; there is no third possibility," it is easy to see that when she does not love God she must resort to the opposite extreme and hate him. It is thus clear why women especially are addicted to the practice of sorcery. The crime of witches exceeds all others. They are worse than the devil, for he has fallen once for all, and Christ has not suffered for him. The devil sins, therefore, only against the Creator, but the witch both against the Creator and Redeemer.[1]

The Hebrew Bible myth of the rib has been made a potent instrument for the subjection of woman. Bossuet in his "Élévations sur les Mystères," uttered the following classical note which has since been hurled at woman on every possible occasion: —

Let women consider their origin and not boast too much of their delicacy; let them remember that they are after all only a supernumerary bone, in which there is no beauty but that which God wished to put into it.[2]

Among these characteristic fables we give the first place to the one that has been preserved for us by the Bible, and according to which woman was a secondary creation of God: she was formed out of a rib of man which justifies her domination by him. That is probably one of the most ancient examples proving that a *de facto* domination is never embarrassed in proving its "right."[3]

[1] The only copy of this work that I have seen is as old as 1487, and although it has no title page, place or date of publication, it bears the name "Malleus Maleficarum" on the back of the cover, and properly begins with the heading : "Apologia auctoris in malleum maleficarum." This is preceded by the text of the bull of Pope Innocent VIII, "adversus heresim." The pages are not numbered and passages can only be cited by the signature marks at the bottom, which consist of letters in alphabetical order accompanied by Arabic numbers for the general heads or rubrics. The above passage occurs under the rubric : "Sequitur quo ad ipsas maleficas demonibus se subjicientibus," which is in signature C and is No. 4. It need not be quoted in full in the Latin text, but the part relating to the etymology of the word *femina*, woman, reads thus : "Dicitur enim femina fe, et minus, quia semper minorem habet et seruat fidem." The authorship of the work is ascribed to Heinrich Institor and Jacob Sprenger.

[2] "Élévations sur les Mystères," Vᵉ Semaine, IIᵉ Élévation. La Création du second sexe. Œuvres de Bossuet, Tome quatrième, Paris, 1841, p. 653.

[3] Gumplowicz, "Précis de Sociologie," p. 182.

The literature and thought of India is thoroughly hostile to woman. A large number of proverbs attest this widespread misogyny. "Woman is like a slipper made to order; wear it if it fits you, throw it away if it does not." " You can never be safe from the cunning artifices of woman." " Woman is like a snake, charming as well as venomous." Hebrew literature breathes the same spirit, and the reading of the Bible often brings the color to the cheeks of a liberal-minded person of either sex. Arabian magic is even worse in this respect, and is so erotic that it is next to impossible to obtain an unexpurgated text of the Arabian Nights Entertainments, about 75 per cent of the matter being expunged from all current editions. The androcentric world view may almost be said to have its headquarters in India. The " Code of Manu " reflects it throughout. According to it " Woman depends during her childhood upon her father; during her youth upon her husband; in her widowhood upon her sons or her male relatives; in default of these, upon the sovereign." " She should always be in good humor and revere her husband, even though unfaithful, as a god." " If a widow she must not even pronounce the name of another man than her deceased husband." [1] The husband always addressed his wife as servant or slave, while she must address him as master or lord. The same code declares that " it is in the nature of the feminine sex to seek to corrupt men," and forbids any man to remain in any place alone with his sister, his mother, or his daughter. Even at the present day in India free choice, especially of the woman, has nothing to do with marriage, and parents and families arbitrarily dispose of the girls, often at a very tender age.

Modern countries differ somewhat in the prevailing ideas about women. No statement is more frequently repeated than that in any country the treatment of women is a true measure of the degree of civilization. It may now be added to this that the treatment of women is a true measure of the intensity of the androcentric senti- ment prevailing in any country. It might be invidious to attempt to classify modern nations on this basis, especially as individuals in any country differ so widely in this respect. It is a measure of civ- ilization or civility in individuals as well as in nations, and in every nation there are thoroughly liberal and fully civilized individuals. Neither can the nineteenth and twentieth centuries claim them all,

[1] "Code of Manu," Book V, Ordinances, Nos. 148, 154, 157.

as we have seen in the noble sayings of Condorcet, who was probably
the most civilized man of his time, far more so than Comte who
made him his spiritual father but did not share his liberality. In
placing Germany at the bottom of the scale in this basis of classification, therefore, numberless shining exceptions must be made, and
account taken only of the general spirit or public opinion relative to
women in that country. The German attitude toward women was
perhaps typified by the father of Frederick the Great, of whom it is
related as among his sterling qualities, that when he met a woman
in the street he would walk up to her with his cane raised, saying:
" Go back into the house! an honest woman should keep indoors."
Spencer says : —

Concerning the claims of women, as domestically associated with men,
I may add that here in England, and still more in America, the need for
urging them is not pressing. In some cases, indeed, there is a converse need.
But there are other civilized societies in which their claims are very inadequately recognized : instance Germany.

To which he appends the following footnote : —

With other reasons prompting this remark, is joined the remembrance of
a conversation between two Germans in which, with contemptuous laughter,
they were describing how, in England, they had often seen on a Sunday or
other holiday, an artizan relieving his wife by carrying the child they had
with them. Their sneers produced in me a feeling of shame — but not for
the artizan.[1]

Germans as a rule detest American women for their initiative and
boldness, daring to act and think independently of their husbands
and of men generally, and they apply to them the strongest term of
contempt that they have in their language in characterizing them
as *emancipirt*. Woman is much more respected in France, but under
Napoleon and his code there was a recoil toward barbarism. Napoleon said to the Council of State that " a husband should have absolute power over the actions of his wife." In the " Mémorial de
Sainte-Hélène " he is quoted to the following effect : —

Woman is given to man to bring forth children. Woman is our property ;
we are not hers; for she gives us children and man does not give any to her.
She is therefore his property, as the tree is that of the gardener. . . . A
single woman cannot suffice for a man for that purpose. She cannot be his
wife when she is sick. She ceases to be his wife when she can no longer

1 Justice ("Principles of Ethics," Vol. II), pp. 162–163 (§ 89).

give him children.   Man, whom nature does not arrest either by age or by any of these inconveniences, should therefore have several wives.[1]

Only a part of the oppressive laws of the code Napoleon have been repealed, but public opinion in France is far in advance of its laws, and judging from outward indications, I should be inclined to place that country, next to the United States, as the most highly civilized nation of the globe.   In this I am only uttering the view long ago put forth with large documentary support by Guizot.

Throughout the historic period woman has suffered from a consistent, systematic, and universal discrimination in the laws of all countries.   In all the early codes she was herself a hereditament, and when she ceased to be a chattel she was not allowed to inherit property, or was cut down to a very small share in the estate.   In this and many other ways her economic dependence has been made more or less complete.   Letourneau [2] has enumerated many of these discriminating laws, and we have only to turn the pages of the law books to find them everywhere.   When a student of law I scheduled scores of them, and could fill a dozen pages with a bare enumeration of such as still form part of the common law of England as taught to law classes even in the United States.   All this is simply the embodiment in the jurisprudence of nations of the universal androcentric world view, and it has been unquestioningly acquiesced in by all mankind, including the women themselves.

The Anglo-Saxon word *woman* reflects this world view, showing that it is older than the stock of languages from which this word is derived.   For although it is no longer believed by philologists that the first syllable of this word has anything to do with *womb*, still it is certain that the last syllable is the same as the German *Mann*, not *Mensch*, and that the rest signifies wife or female, as though man were the original and woman only a secondary creation.   As regards the Latin *femina*, while of course it has no connection with *faith* or *minus*, as stated in the " Witch Hammer," still the syllable *fe* is the hypothetical root from which *fecundity* comes, and the word signifies the fertile sex.   Primarily no such conceptions as beauty,

[1] "Mémorial de Sainte-Hélène," Journal de la vie privée et les conversations de l'Empereur Napoléon à Sainte-Hélène, par le Comte de Las Cases, Londres, 1823, Tome II, Quatrième partie, juin, 1816, pp. 117–118.
[2] " La Sociologie d'après l'Ethnographie," pp. 180 ff.

grace, delicacy, and attractiveness are associated with woman, and all notions of dignity, honor, and worth are equally wanting from the conception of the female sex. On the contrary, we find many terms of reproach, such as *wench*, *hag*, etc., for which there are no corresponding ones applicable to man.

Notwithstanding all this vast network of bonds that have been contrived for holding woman down, it is peculiar and significant that everywhere and always she has been tacitly credited with a certain mysterious power in which the world has, as it were, stood in awe and fear. While perpetually proclaiming her inferiority, insignificance, and weakness, it has by its precautions virtually recognized her potential importance and real strength. She is the cause of wars and race hostilities. There are always powerful female deities. Minerva is even made the goddess of wisdom. Ever and anon a great female personage, real or fictitious, appears, a Semiramis, a Cleopatra, a Joan of Arc, a Queen Elizabeth, or a Queen Victoria; Scheherazade with her thousand and one tales, Sibyls with their divinations and oracles, Furies, and Gorgons; and finally the witches with all their powers for evil. Although woman is usually pictured as bad, still there is no uncertainty about the supposed possession by her of some occult power, and the impression is constantly conveyed that she must be strenuously kept down, lest should she by any accident or remissness chance to "get loose," she would certainly do something dreadful.

One of the arguments most relied upon for the justification of the continued subjection of woman is that, in addition to being physically inferior to man, the differences between the sexes have been widening during past ages and are greater in civilized than in savage peoples. The investigations of Professor Le Bon have been widely quoted by all writers on the general subject. He found that the difference between the respective weight of the brain in man and woman constantly goes on increasing as we rise in the scale of civilization, so that as regards the mass of the brain, and consequently the intelligence, woman becomes more and more differentiated from man. The difference which exists between the mean of the crania of contemporary Parisian men and that of contemporary Parisian women is almost double the difference which existed in ancient Egypt. Topinard finds the same to be true of the fossil crania of prehistoric times. In certain South American tribes the

2 B

sexes scarcely differ except in sex itself.[1] According to Manouvrier, the cranial capacity of women has diminished from 1422 cubic centimeters in the stone age to 1338 cubic centimeters at the present day.[2]

Accepting these statements as in all probability correct, what is the lesson that should really be drawn from them? Letourneau argues that the difference between the life that women must lead in roving hordes and bands, doing most of the work to relieve the men for hunting and war, necessitated stronger bodies than modern civilized life requires for women. This is also doubtless true, and civilized woman would quickly succumb to such hardships. But is this an adequate explanation? I think not. We must remember how much nearer savage man is to the gynæcocratic stage, in which there is every reason to believe woman was nearly equal in strength to man. If the prehuman or animal stage saw the excessive development of the male, the earliest human stage found woman unchanged and in the full vigor of her natural strength, still choosing her mates and governing the life of the horde. But with the advent of the androcratic stage, while woman lost her power of selection, so that man could develop no farther, the abuses to which he subjected her soon began to tell upon her and produce degeneracy. In Chapter X we considered the effect of adverse conditions upon man in general, and saw how the status of a class might be lowered by insufficient nourishment and undue toil and exposure, which accounts for the superiority of the ruling and leisure classes. Now in the androcratic régime woman dropped into the condition of a subject class and was denied much that was necessary to maintain her normal existence. It is well known that savage women are usually underfed, that they are allowed no luxuries, made to subsist on the leavings of the men at whose table they are never permitted to sit, often have no meat or fish when the men have these articles, that they have little rest, must carry wood and water, drag lodge poles, and care for the children, besides preparing the meals for all, that they are insufficiently clothed in countries where clothing is needed, and that they are during their entire lives subjected to perpetual hardships and privations. Of course, as they bear the children all this reacts upon both sexes, but in the long run it affects the women more than the men

---

[1] References to the works and memoirs in which those statements occur, as well as numerous others to the same general effect, are given by Durkheim, " De la Division du Travail Social," Paris, 1893, pp. 58, 59.

[2] *Revue International de Sociologie*, 1899, p. 605.

who have ways of offsetting it, and in the course of generations it arrests female development and stunts the growth of women.

When we come to the historic period we have seen how universal and systematic has always been the suppression of woman and her legal and social exclusion and ostracism from everything that tends to build up either body or mind. When I reflect upon it the wonder to me is rather that woman has accomplished anything at all. The small amount that she has been allowed to use her mind has almost caused it to be atrophied. This alone is sufficient to account for all the facts enumerated above as supporting the androcentric theory, so far as the intellectual achievements of women are concerned. M. Jacques Lourbet in his " Problème des Sexes " (Paris, 1900) says : —

Let no one insist longer on the modest contribution of woman to the creative work of art and science. She suffers to this day from the ostracism of centuries that man has imposed upon her, from the network of exclusions and prohibitions of every kind in which she has been enveloped, and which have ended in producing that apparent inferiority, which is not natural but purely hereditary.

Professor Huxley in a letter to the *London Times* relative to the failure of a certain lady in her examination, remarked : —

Without seeing any reason to believe that women are, on the average, so strong physically, intellectually, or morally, as men, I cannot shut my eyes to the obvious fact that many women are much better endowed in all these respects than many men, and I am at a loss to understand on what grounds of justice or public policy a career which is open to the weakest and most foolish of the male sex should be forcibly closed to women of vigor and capacity. We have heard a great deal lately about the physical disabilities of women. Some of these alleged impediments, no doubt, are really inherent in their organization, but nine-tenths of them are artificial — the product of their mode of life. I believe that nothing would tend so effectually to get rid of these creations of idleness, weariness, and that " over-stimulation of the emotions," which, in plainer-spoken days, used to be called wantonness, than a fair share of healthy work, directed toward a definite object, combined with an equally fair share of healthy play, during the years of adolescence ; and those who are best acquainted with the acquirements of an average medical practitioner, will find it hardest to believe that the attempt to reach that standard is likely to prove exhausting to an ordinarily intelligent and well-educated young woman.[1]

It would seem that the treatment that woman has received and still receives under the operation of the androcentric world view is

[1] *Popular Science Monthly*, Vol. V, October, 1874, p. 764.

amply sufficient of itself to account for all the observed differences
between the sexes physically and mentally, and that the widening of
those differences during the historic period is abundantly accounted
for by the fact that the gynæcocratic stage persisted far into the
human period, during which women were the equals of men except
in respect of certain embellishments attending male efflorescence due
to prolonged female sexual selection or gyneclexis.   When this was
withdrawn man ceased to advance and woman began to decline
under the depressing effects of male abuse.   But there was another
element that contributed in the main to the same result.   This was
male sexual selection or andreclexis, which, as we have seen, was
confined to physical characters, and while it has given to woman all
the beauty and grace that she possesses, it tended rather to dwarf her
stature, sap her strength, contract her brain, and enfeeble her mind.
In these two principles, the first dating from the origin of the patriarchate during the protosocial stage, and the other dating from the
origin of the leisure class early in the metasocial stage, and both
therefore in operation at least twice as long, probably many times
as long, as the entire historic period, we certainly have a surplus of
influence bearing on the deterioration of woman, and a more than
adequate cause for all inferiority ever claimed or alleged by the
supporters of the androcentric theory.   Indeed, as we contemplate
these factors the wonder grows why woman did not sink still lower.
The only possible reason is that, despite all, she is and remains the
human race.

   The Future of Woman. — This topic does not of course properly
belong to pure sociology except in so far as it can be reduced to a
scientific prediction.   This can be made by any one, and no one
would care to venture into its details.   But such a survey as has
been made of the great field of sex development, biological, physiological, zoölogical, anthropological, and sociological, can scarcely
fail to suggest to the enlightened mind the prolongation of the connected series of processes that have taken place in the past and the
representation of the condition that is likely to ensue as the necessary result of such prolongation.   A single glance at the last two
centuries of the historic period compared with the centuries that
preceded them shows such an immense change in woman's condition
as to suggest that the vast downward curve has more than reached
the lowest point, and that the ordinates have begun to shorten.   We

find ourselves confronted by a great "ricorso," and the cyclic form already clearly impresses itself upon the mind. Not only this, but a closer scrutiny reveals the fact that the curve does not lie wholly in the same plane, and that the figure has three dimensions. In other words, it is not a cycle or circle, but a spiral, and the ends will never meet and restore a true gynæcocracy. With the completion of a revolution both man and woman will find themselves on a far higher plane, and in a stage that, for want of a better term, may be called *gynandrocratic*, a stage in which both man and woman shall be free to rule themselves.

But all this is after all an anticipation, since the rapid upward direction of the curve late in the historic period is wholly due to the influence of the sociogenetic forces to be considered in the next chapter, and the full nature of this influence cannot be clearly perceived until these forces have been studied and analyzed. We are here only concerned with the phylogenetic forces, and it is their influence that we have thus far sought to explain.

Recapitulation. — It may be advantageous briefly to recapitulate this necessarily prolonged survey of the gynæcocentric theory. Many of the heads are, it is true, sufficiently self-explaining, and a glance at them in their order will recall the steps in the chain of events, but others are more obscure, and a rapid survey of the whole field, though needless for some, will be useful to others.

First of all, it was found that all organisms, whether unicellular or multicellular, are capable not only of supplying the waste of their substance through nutrition proper, but also of that form of nutrition which goes beyond the individual (*ultra-nutrition*) and carries the process into another individual (*altro-nutrition*), and this is called *reproduction*.

In the second place, the manifest advantage of crossing strains and infusing into life elements that come from outside the organism, or even from a specialized organ of the same organism, was seized upon by natural selection, and a process was inaugurated that is called *fertilization*, first through an organ belonging to the organism itself (*hermaphroditism*), and then by the detachment of this organ and its erection into an independent, but miniature organism wholly unlike the primary one. This last was at first parasitic upon the primary organism, then complemental to it and carried about in a sac provided for the purpose. Its simplest form was a sac filled

with spermatozoa in a liquid or gelatinous medium. Later it was
endowed with an ephemeral independent existence, and so adjusted
that its contained sperm cells were at the proper time brought into
contact with the germ cells of the organism proper. This fertilizing
organ or miniature sperm sac was the primitive form of what subsequently developed into the male sex, the female sex being the
organism proper, which remained practically unchanged. The
remaining steps in the entire process consisted therefore in the subsequent modification and creation, as it were, of the male organism.

The development of a male organism out of this formless sperm
sac, or testicle, was accomplished through the continuous selection
by the organism proper, ultimately called the female, of such forms,
among many varying forms of the fertilizing agent as best conformed
to the tastes or vaguely-felt preferences of the organism, and the
exclusion of all other forms from any part in the process of fertilization. The peculiarities of form thus selected are transmitted by
heredity and, while they do not affect the female, they transform
the male in harmony with these preferences of the female or organism proper. As the male fertilizer is a product of reproduction by
the organism, it naturally inherits the general qualities of the
organism. The preferences of the organism are also likely to be
a form similar to itself. The organism, or female, therefore, literally creates the male in its own image, and from a shapeless sac it
gradually assumes a definite form agreeing in general characteristics
with that of the original organism. There is no other reason why
the male should in the least resemble the female, and but for these
causes a male animal might belong to an entirely different type from
the female. Even as it is the resemblance is often not close and the
sexes differ enormously.

The introduction of fertilization in connection with reproduction
was gradual and was not at first at all necessary to it. It came in
at the outset as an occasional resort for infusing new elements after
a long series of generations through normal reproduction. This
occasional fertilization is called the alternation of generations. It
is common to many of the lower organisms and to all plants, reproduction by buds being the normal form, and that by seeds being the
result of fertilization. So great was the advantage of fertilization
that in the animal kingdom it first came to accompany each separate
act of reproduction, and finally became a condition to reproduction

itself. From the fact that such is the case in all the higher animals, which are the ones best known to all, the error arose that fertilization is an essential part of reproduction, and that sex is necessary to reproduction, an error difficult to dislodge.

The male having been thus created at a comparatively late period in the history of organic life, it soon advanced under the influences described and began to assume more or less the form and character of the primary organism, which is then called the female. It lost its character of a formless mass of sperm cells and assumed definite shape. For a long time it did not exist for itself, but simply for its function, and was exceedingly small, frail, and ephemeral, often possessing no organs of nutrition or powers of self-preservation, and perishing as soon as it had performed its function, or without performing it, if not selected from among a multitude of males. This selection of the best examples and rejection of the inferior ones caused the male to rise in the scale and resemble more and more the primary organism, or female. But other qualities were also selected than those that the female possessed. This was due to the early development of the esthetic faculty in the female, and these qualities were in the nature of embellishments. The male, therefore, while approaching the form and stature of the female, began to differ from her in these esthetic qualities. The result was that in the two highest classes of animals, birds and mammals, the male became in many cases, but not in all, highly ornamental, and endowed with numerous peculiar organs, called secondary sexual characters. To further selection a plurality of males often occurred, and these became rivals for female favor. This led to battles among the males, which further developed the latter, especially in the direction of size, strength, weapons of offense, and general fighting capacity. These qualities were never used to force the female into submission, but always and solely to gain her favor and insure the selection of the successful rivals. In many birds and mammals these qualities thus became greatly over-developed, resulting in what I have called male efflorescence. To a considerable extent, but less than in many other species, the immediate ancestors of man possessed this over-development of the male, and in most primates the male is larger, stronger, and more highly ornamented than the female.

When the human race finally appeared through gradual emergence from the great simian stock, this difference in the sexes existed, and sexual selection was still going on. Primitive woman, though somewhat smaller, physically weaker, and esthetically plainer than man, still possessed the power of selection, and was mistress of the kinship group. Neither sex had any more idea of the connection between fertilization and reproduction than do animals, and therefore the mother alone claimed and cared for the offspring, as is done throughout the animal kingdom below man. So long as this state of things endured the race remained in the stage called gynæcocracy, or female rule. That this was a very long stage is attested by a great number of facts, many of which have been considered.

As it was brain development which alone made man out of an animal by enabling him to break over faunal barriers and overspread the globe, so it was brain development that finally suggested the causal nexus between fertilization and reproduction, and led to the recognition by man of his paternity and joint proprietorship with woman in the offspring of their loins. This produced a profound social revolution, overthrew the authority of woman, destroyed her power of selection, and finally reduced her to the condition of a mere slave of the stronger sex, although that strength had been conferred by her. The stage of gynæcocracy was succeeded by the stage of androcracy, and the subjection of woman was rendered complete.

The patriarchate, or patriarchal family, prevailed throughout the remainder of the protosocial stage, woman being reduced to a mere chattel, bought and sold, enslaved, and abused beyond any power of description. With the metasocial stage, brought about by the collision of primitive hordes and by a general system of wars and conquests resulting in race amalgamation, forms of marriage more or less ceremonial arose, which, though all in the nature of the transfer of women for a consideration, still somewhat mitigated the horrors of earlier periods, and resulted in a general state of polygyny among the upper classes. The powerful effect of this race mixture in hastening brain development, coupled with its other effect in creating a leisure class in which the physical wants, including the sexual, were fully supplied, resulted in a high esthetic sense in man, and led to a widespread system of male sexual selection, or andreclexis, through which the physical nature of woman began to be modified. Although this could affect only a comparatively small percentage of all women, it was sufficient to produce types of female beauty, and it is chiefly to this cause that woman has acquired the quality of a " fair sex," in so far as this term is applicable. The general effect of male sexual selection, however, was rather to diminish than to increase her real value, and to lower than to raise her general status. It increased her dependence upon man while at the same time reducing her power to labor or in any way protect or preserve herself.

Throughout all human history woman has been powerfully discriminated against and held down by custom, law, literature, and public opinion. All opportunity has been denied her to make any trial of her powers in any direction. In savagery she was underfed, overworked, unduly exposed, and mercilessly abused, so that in so far as these influences could be confined to one sex, they tended to stunt her physical and mental powers. During later ages her social ostracism has been so universal and complete that, whatever powers she may have had, it was impossible for her to make any use of them, and they have naturally atrophied and shriveled. Only during the last two centuries and in the most advanced nations, under the growing power of the sociogenetic energies of society, has some slight relief from her long thraldom been grudgingly and reluctantly vouchsafed. What a continued and increasing tendency in this direction will accomplish it is difficult to presage, but all signs are at present hopeful.

Classification of the Phylogenetic Forces

Just as the ontogenetic forces may be summed up in the word *hunger,* so the phylogenetic forces may be summed up in the word *love.* All social forces are appetites, and the two primary appetites are the appetite for food and the appetite for sex. We have seen how the latter originated. Reproduction, being only altro-nutrition, embodies no new principle until the stage of fertilization is reached, but in order to secure fertilization a new and special interest had to be developed strong enough to impel the active male element to seek the passive female organism. This interest constitutes the sexual appetite, primarily confined chiefly to the male, but finally common to both sexes, though always more intense and aggressive in the male. This appetite is properly called love, and is the original form of all love except such forms as, through pure ambiguity of language, belong to an entirely different class of psychic phenomena.

The classification of the phylogenetic forces must therefore consist in tracing the progress of this primary appetitive force and observing its differentiation and specialization, and after it has attained its fullest observed development, in comparing, analyzing, studying, and classifying its derivative branches. We have already followed out the principal events to which the phylogenetic forces gave rise in the animal world, in the ancestors of man, in primitive man, and to some extent in presocial, early social, and historic man, but our sketch closed almost before the origin of the principal branches of the main trunk had been given off, and some of the important early ramifications were only touched upon lightly in order to avoid breaking the main thread of the discussion. We shall now proceed more synthetically and look at the subject from above downward, taking man as we find him with the differentiation in its present advanced stage, and shall endeavor to recognize the creative products of the phylogenetic forces and arrange them in their logical rather than their serial order.

As a basis for their systematic treatment they may therefore be named and arranged, and each product or group of forces treated in the order adopted, so that nothing essential may be overlooked or omitted. As the phylogenetic forces must consist in different modes of manifestation of the one general force, love, the classification becomes that of the different kinds of love, in so far as that sentiment, or psychic unit, has undergone differentiation. Thus viewed, there are five kinds of love that are sufficiently distinct to be separately treated, but all of which are genetically connected, and all but one, or two at the most, are derivative. As they are all trunks or branches there can be no serial or lineal order of arrangement, and the order adopted is rather convenient than either genetic or chronological. The special reasons for preferring this order will appear as we proceed.

The sociologist recognizes the five following modes of manifestation of the phylogenetic forces, or forms of love : —

1. Natural love.	4. Maternal love.
2. Romantic love.	5. Consanguineal love.
3. Conjugal love.	

These will be treated in the above order.

Natural Love. — Natural love is the innate interest created by the principle of advantage and implanted, primarily in the male, to secure fertilization and the crossing of strains and thus to keep up a difference of potential in the organic world. It is therefore a typical dynamic principle, such as those dealt with in Chapter XI. It is the original form of all love, and all other forms are derivatives of it. It is the main trunk of which the rest are branches, a trunk that may be called monopodial (see *supra*, p. 72), since no one nor all the branches together tend to draw off appreciably from its vigor, and it is still found in full strength even in those individuals, races, and peoples who possess the derivative forms in their highest development. This is because the derivative forms alone are powerless to secure the primary ends of reproduction and variation, and however much a refined sentiment may deprecate the necessity it remains, and seems likely to remain, a necessity.

The fundamental reason why natural love is deprecated by developed minds is that it involves a mechanical adjustment. During the second or metaphysical stage of development of human thought matter was held to be vile and only the spiritual, including mind, was considered pure. This conception prevailed far into the positive stage; but science, which is the essence of the positive world view, teaches the spirituality of matter, and is fast dispelling the false metaphysical attitude with regard to it. It is therefore probable that the purity of natural love and of all the adjustments necessary to fertilization will ultimately be recognized by all enlightened minds.

Nevertheless, most philosophers have regarded it as a duty to condemn the only act by which the race can be preserved. Kant says, "In this act a man makes himself a thing; which contradicts the right of man to his own person."[1] Schopenhauer explains it by the assumption that when the "young, innocent, human intellect" first learned of this great secret of the universe it "shuddered at its enormity."[2] Tolstoi would have an end of all sexual relations and let the consequences take care of themselves! He insists with considerable truth that this is true Christian doctrine, and says:

[1] " In diesem Akt macht sich ein Mensch selbst zur Sache, welches dem Rechte der Menschheit an seiner eigenen Person widerstreitet," "Metaphysik der Sitten," Erster Theil, § 25. Sämmtliche Werke, Leipzig, 1838, neunter Theil, p. 91 ; 1868, Vol. VII, p. 77.

[2] "Die Welt als Wille und Vorstellung," 3d edition, Leipzig, 1859, Vol. II, p. 653.

Let us suppose that perfect chastity, that Christian ideal, be realized; what would happen? We should find ourselves simply in accord with religion, one of the dogmas of which is that the world is to have an end, and with science, which teaches that the sun is gradually losing its heat, which will in time accomplish the extinction of the human race.[1]

A modern American writer, Dr. George M. Gould, seems to take a somewhat similar view when he speaks of "the universal fig-leaf; the universal shame and secrecy; the silent contempt of *this* self for *that* self; the disgust of soul at sense; the commingled loathing and yet doing — such spontaneous emotions point to the fact that God also feels that way too." [2]

Comte, although the founder of the positive philosophy destined to dispel all these unnatural illusions relative to the essential turpitude of sex relations, had not himself sufficiently emerged from the metaphysical stage to free himself from their influence, and he proposed a solution of his own of the vexed problem. The Grand Être, Humanity, must not be rendered mortal by neglect of reproduction, but this must be accomplished in a manner consistent with perfect chastity. Hence his "bold hypothesis," [3] oftener called "utopia," [4] of the Virgin-Mother, according to which procreation is to become a function "exclusively feminine," a sort of voluntary parthenogenesis which will reconcile maternity with virginity. Notwithstanding the number of times he returns to the subject, not only in this volume, but also in his *Testament,* and the somewhat extended discussions of it, after reading it all with special care, I am still at a loss to understand the precise process that he proposes to adopt. It seems, however, to be primarily one of artificial self fertilization with the coöperation of man at least at first; but he seems to suppose that in the course of time, woman, by concentrating her attention upon it, may ultimately succeed in restoring the long-lost power possessed by the lower forms of life, not only of parthenogenesis, or *lucina sine concubitu,* but of complete asexual reproduction. Needless to say, Comte had no biological training for such a task, and the "utopia" is wholly wild and unscientific. Still less did he realize the effect that continuous self fertilization would have on human

1 " Des relations entre les sexes."   Plaisirs vicieux, p. 129.
2 " The Meaning and the Method of Life. A Search for Religion in Biology," by George M. Gould, New York and London, 1893, p. 169.
3 " Politique Positive," Vol. IV, p. 68.
4 *Ibid.*, pp. 241, 276, 304, etc.

progress. It would be a return to the protosocial if not to the
protozoan stage. Surely it is better to trust to the *natura naturans*
than to the erratic dreamings of philosophers who are guided by
pure reason. The deeper we penetrate the secrets of nature the
less do the mechanical, material, and physical processes seem to
differ from psychic and spiritual processes, and all will ultimately
prove to be the same.

The same metaphysical state of mind that has led to all these
absurd attempts to nullify the phylogenetic forces and to invent
artificial schemes to avoid nature's ways of securing the continuance
of the race, is responsible also for the general tendency to underrate and belittle sexual matters in society, to keep them perpetually
in the background, and to maintain the utmost possible ignorance
of them on the part of the youth of both sexes. The reason why
this method fails and leads to such unhappy results as it is now
known to do is that it puts forward a falsehood, viz., that such
matters are unimportant, when in fact they are the most vital of
all the subjects of human contemplation. As Schopenhauer says: —

When we consider the important rôle that sexual love in all its grades
and shades plays, not only in drama and fiction but also in the real world,
where, next to the love of life, it shows itself the most active of all impulses,
constantly absorbs half of the powers and thoughts of the more youthful
portion of mankind, is the final goal of almost every human effort, exerts a
fatal influence upon the most important events, interrupts the most serious
occupations at every hour, sometimes drives the greatest heads for a time
into delirium, does not hesitate to disturb the transactions of statesmen and
the investigations of savants by bringing in its love letters and locks of hair
and slipping them into ministerial portfolios and philosophical manuscripts,
plots daily the most involved and wicked intrigues, dissolves the most
worthy relations, rends the strongest bonds, sacrifices to itself sometimes
life or health, sometimes wealth, rank, and happiness, nay, even, makes the
honorable conscienceless, the faithful traitors, and becomes a fiendish demon
seeking to pervert, confound, and overthrow all things; — we are naturally
moved to cry out: Why all this fuss? What means this rush and roar,
this anguish and despair? The simple meaning is that every Jack has his
Jill. But why should such a trifle play so great a rôle and continually bring
disturbance and confusion into the well-regulated life of man? But to the
serious inquirer the mind gradually reveals the true answer: It is not a
trifle with which we are dealing here; it is a matter whose importance is
fully commensurate with the zeal and eagerness with which it is pursued.
The ultimate purpose of every love affair, whether it be played in sock or
buskin, is more important than any other purpose in human life, and

therefore altogether worthy of the profound seriousness with which it is prosecuted.[1]

The power of natural love can scarcely be exaggerated.

To taste amorous pleasures [says Letourneau] was the great preoccupation and the great joy of the islanders of Tahiti and the Society Isles. To vary their enjoyment they would often travel from one island to another, and they conceived the famous society of the Areoïs, of which a few words must now be said. Among the ancient Mexicans, the very ancient ones, those of the eleventh century, there existed a sect called the Ixcuinames, the members of which, in a country where the women were nevertheless required to eat apart, feasted and drank together without distinction of sex and lived in a state of promiscuity. The members of this sect constantly gave themselves up to orgies and obscene practices, mingling it all with religious ceremonies and sacrificing human victims. This is exactly what the Areoïs did, and this analogy is an argument to be invoked in favor of the American origin of a part of the Polynesians.

In Tahiti, in the Marquesas, etc., the association of the Areoïs had a religious color. In many countries and among many races man has thus placed his pleasures and his passions under the guardianship of heaven. The society of the Areois was a freemasonry at once mystic and lascivious (*lubrique*), under the patronage of the god Oro, son of Taaroa, the Polynesian Jehovah. No one was admitted into the fraternity without difficulty. After a long noviciate, the candidate, painted red and yellow, must first have, in the presence of his future colleagues, an attack of religious delirium. In a second trial, succeeding the first, after long months or even years, he would solemnly swear to put to death all the children that he should have. From this moment he belonged to the seventh and last class of the society; here he learned songs, dances, sacred mimics, which formed the ritual of the Areoïs. No one could rise through the grades of the fraternity except at the price of tests and new ceremonies, and a special mode of tattooing distinguished each grade of membership.

The object of the religious association of which we are speaking was the satisfaction, without rein or limit, of amorous wants, and for all the members infanticide was a duty. Among the members of the society, all the women being common to all the men, the cohabitation of each couple scarcely lasted more than two or three days. Life was thus spent in perpetual feasts. They celebrated, they wrestled, they sang; the women danced the amorous *Timorodie*. The first duty of every female member was to strangle her children at the moment of their birth; if, however, a new-born child should live even a half-hour, it was saved. To gain the right to keep her child a woman must find among the members a father of adoption; but she was driven out of the association and stigmatized with the name of " child-maker." [2]

---

[1] " Die Welt als Wille und Vorstellung," 3d ed., Leipzig, 1859, Vol. II, pp. 608–609.

[2] " La Sociologie," etc., pp. 56–58. Given chiefly on the authority of Moerenhaut, " Voyages aux Îles du Grand Océan," 1837, Vol. I, pp. 484–503. Letourneau omits certain important qualifications that Moerenhaut makes to the above.

There is no accounting for what the untutored reason of man will do if given free rein, and the above is an example of the complete triumph of feeling over function aided even by religious sanction. And although it has usually been the mission of religion to counteract such race-destroying tendencies, the Polynesians are by no means the only peoples whose religion has tended in the contrary direction. It is not necessary to go further than to mention the widespread institution of a celibate priesthood, which has robbed the world of a large share of the advantage that it would naturally derive from the existence of a leisure class. Although not confined to Christianity, that sect has extensively practiced this anti-social cult, and this at a time and place in the history of mankind when it produced its most pernicious effects. M. de Candolle,[1] and also Mr. Galton,[2] have sufficiently emphasized this truth.

Another indication of the power of the phylogenetic forces is the great prevalence among uncivilized peoples of the worship of the emblems of fecundity. Here natural love connects itself spontaneously with religion and forms an integral part of the great volume of religious feeling. This subject of phallic worship or phallicism, often extending to phalloktenism, has a voluminous literature, and in many parts of the world symbols in stone, in bronze, and even in gold, have been found, some of which have found their way into archæological museums. Japanese relics of this cult, now abandoned in that country, are very abundant, and Dr. Edmund Buckley not long since compiled a somewhat complete list of them and prepared a most interesting and instructive paper on the subject.[3] It is quite unnecessary to enter into this literature or to discuss the general subject here. It only concerns us to point out its significance as a normal fact in the history of the race.

It is difficult for civilized people to place themselves in a position to see how such a cult naturally arose. The irresistible tendency is to look at it as something abnormal. With most persons the abnormal is that which differs from existing and familiar things. But it should not require a very strong reasoning power to perceive that so powerful a motor as natural love in a race that had not yet ac-

---

[1] "Histoire des Sciences et des Savants," 2ᵉ éd., 1885, pp. 149 ff.

[2] "Hereditary Genius," pp. 343 ff.

[3] "Phallicism in Japan," a Dissertation presented to the Faculty of Arts, Literature, and Science, of the University of Chicago, by Edmund Buckley, Chicago, 1895. Printed by the University of Chicago Press.

quired any of the conventional ideas that now prevail with regard
to it, must result in institutions in some degree commensurate with
it in importance. What they would be might be hard to predict
a priori, but when we find an almost universal cult based on that fact
it is not more than we should naturally expect. At that stage everything tends to assume a religious form, and there is nothing more
natural than that this should do so. Neither is it just or correct to
call such a cult base and sensual. While feeling, no doubt, was a
prime mover, men had not yet learned to regard this particular form
of feeling as lower or less worthy than other forms. But all these
phallic cults must have arisen long after it had become universally
known that these organs are the seat of fecundity, and the group
consciousness of race preservation naturally and justly clothed them
with all the dignity that belongs to whatever preserves and strengthens
the race. We can imagine their ceremonies as largely reflecting this
high functional sentiment and as often wholly devoid of any other
feeling. In fact there are none of the more advanced religions that
do not embody survivals of primitive phallicism. Sex is in some
way always interwoven into all mythologies, theogonies, cosmogonies,
and religions. Where is there one without it ? It is now generally
admitted by scholars that in the Hebrew cosmogony the "fall of
man" simply typifies the sexual act, the "forbidden fruit." That
cosmogony was just above the point at which the sense of shame had
come to form a part of the psychic constitution of man. Adam and
Eve were naked and were not ashamed, but the partaking of the
forbidden fruit brought shame into the world.

Buddhistic and Christian asceticism, and, whether religious, philosophic,
or sensualistic, pessimism generally, has represented the beauty of woman and
sexual love as the baiting of the devil's hook. With unexampled clearness
and splendid analysis the great Schopenhauer has set forth this view, and if
he had but put God in the place of his diabolic will (blind, and yet, illogi-
cally enough, superbly, even fiendishly, cunning) the exposition would have
stood as a marvel of physiologico-philosophic reasoning and description.[1]

Haeckel, more rationally, and from the highest scientific standpoint, takes us entirely across the whole field of organic life and
eloquently shows that the sexual passion, everywhere and always,
has been the great life-tonic of the world, the sublimest and most
exalted as well as the purest and noblest of impulses : —

[1] " The Meaning and the Method of Life," by George M. Gould, 1893, p. 164.

If we once reflect what an extraordinarily important rôle the relation of
the two sexes has played everywhere in organic nature, in the kingdom of
plants, in animal and human life ; how that mutual affection and attraction
of both sexes, love, is the moving cause of the most manifold and remarkable processes, nay, one of the most important mechanical causes of the highest differentiation of life, we shall not be able too highly to appreciate this
reference of love to its original source, to the attractive power of two different cells.   Everywhere in living nature there flow the greatest effects from
this small cause.   Think only of the rôle that the flowers, the sexual organs
of flowering plants, play in nature ; or think of the array of wonderful phenomena that sexual selection produces in the animal world ; think, finally,
of the weighty significance that love possesses for human life : in every case
the single, original, impelling motive is the union of two cells ; everywhere
it is this simple process that is exerting so great an influence upon the development of the most manifold relations.   We may indeed assert that no other
organic process will bear the most remote comparison with this in the extent
and intensity of its differentiating effect.   For, is not the Semitic myth of
Eve, who tempted Adam to partake of "knowledge," and is not the old Greek
legend of Paris and Helen, and are not so many other classic fictions, merely
the poetic expressions of the immeasurable influence which love and sexual
selection, which depends upon it, have, since the differentiation of the two
sexes, exerted upon the course of the history of the world?   All other
passions that surge through the human breast are far less potent in their
combined effect than the passion of love which inflames the senses and
mocks the intellect.   On the one hand we should gratefully honor love as
the source of the most glorious works of art, the loftiest creations of poetry,
of sculpture, painting, and music ; we should recognize in it the most powerful factor in human morals, the basis of family life and of the development
of the state.   On the other hand we have to fear in it the devouring flame
which drives the unfortunate to destruction, and which has caused more sorrow, vice, and crime than all the other evils of the human race combined.
So wonderful is love and so infinitely important is its influence upon the
soul life, upon the most varied functions of the nervous system, that here,
more than anywhere else, the " supernatural " effects seem to baffle all natural explanation.   And yet, despite all, comparative biology and the history
of organic development clearly and unequivocally lead us back to the simplest source of love, to the *affinities of two different cells: sperm cell and
germ cell.*[1]

Commenting upon this remarkable passage in Haeckel's " Anthropogenie " at the time that the first German edition appeared, and
partially paraphrasing parts of it in a review of the work, I said : —

[1] "Anthropogenie, oder Entwickelungsgeschichte des Menschen," von Ernst
Haeckel Leipzig, 1874, pp. 656–657. Vierte, umgearbeitete und vermehrte Auflage,
Leipzig, 1891, pp. 792–793. Very slightly changed in the fourth edition. The last
lines in spaced letters here read, " *Wahlverwandtschaft zweier verschiedener ero-
tischer Zellen : Spermzelle und Eizelle (Erotishcher Chemotropismus).*"

2 C

From another point of view, this union and literal blending of the male and female principles is not only of the highest intellectual interest, but is calculated to awaken the most lively esthetic sentiments. Nothing more poetic or romantic has ever been presented to the human fancy by all the fictions of the world than the marvellous reality of this courtship of cells! The very fountain-head of love (*Urquelle der Liebe*) is reached in the affinities of two cells! The ruling passion of all ages has its ultimate basis in this new-found physiological fact. When the march of science shall have exposed the false basis upon which the present artificial code of social life rests, and when the fears of those who can imagine nothing better shall have been dispelled, then let the future Homer of science sing, not the illicit loves of Paris and Helen, which whelm great nations in untimely ruin, but the lawful wooings and the heroic sacrifices of the sperm-cell and the germ-cell as they rush into that embrace which annihilates both that a great and advancing race may not perish from the earth! And here there is no fiction, there is not even speculation. Both the plot and the details of this tale belong to the domain of established fact, and rest upon the most thorough scientific investigation.[1]

The purity and nobility of natural love have been perceived by all truly great minds, but few have had the courage to speak a word in favor of its redemption from the false and hypocritical odium that a pharisaical world seeks to cast upon it. All the more, then, should we prize such sentiments as the following from the noble soul of Condorcet: —

Would nature have lavished upon man so many charms, would she have enriched him with so many sources of delight, only to couple with them disgust, shame, and remorse? These desires which plunge us into a voluptuous intoxication, even while they agitate and torment us, are still pleasures to which those of no other senses can be compared; those enjoyments that infuse into all the organs of sense separately or all at once more and more delicious sensations, lead by degrees to that instant of delirium in which all our faculties are absorbed in one single faculty, that of tasting pleasure; those pleasures that often even exceed our physical powers of experiencing happiness, unite again in all that moral sensibility can create of delight in the union of two souls abandoned to each other, all whose movements are mutually communicated to each other, all sentiments blended and all joys doubled in being shared; finally, what seems to exceed all bounds of felicity, each enjoys, in addition to his own and her own happiness, the thought that the being loved is experiencing the same happiness, and

---

1 Haeckel's " Genesis of Man, or History of the Development of the Human Race," The *Penn Monthly*, Philadelphia, Vol. VIII, No. 88, April, 1877, pp. 266–284 ; No. 89, May, 1877, pp. 348–367 ; No. 91, July, 1877, pp. 528–548. Also revised, combined, and published under the same title as a pamphlet, with a preface, Philadelphia, 1879, 64 pages, 8°. The passage above quoted occurs on pp. 355–356 of the *Penn Monthly* for May, 1877, and on pp. 31–32 of the pamphlet referred to.

that this is his own and her own work! Thus nature has united for man, at one and the same instant, to the delirious pleasure of sense the enthusiasm of the delighted soul, and has lavished upon him at once all that the most diverse sources of enjoyment can yield that is most intimate, most sweet, and most rapturous.

But a calmer joy succeeds this delirium, mingles with all the feelings, with all ideas, and spreads over the entire life. A tender, sole, abandoned love, for which there can no longer exist a sacrifice, arises, feeds on the memory of moments of delight, on the hope of their renewal, on the sweet thought of mutually owing this happiness to each other, of being capable at any moment of being the cause the one for the other of pleasures continually renewed; a charm which no other form of bond is capable of calling forth.[1]

That such a tremendous power in society should require regulation goes without saying, but what are all marriage systems but modes of regulating this power? And here, more than anywhere else, is Bacon's aphorism true that " we can only conquer Nature by obeying her."[2] It can of course be controlled according to the principles set forth in Chapter IX, but cannot, any more than any other natural force, be destroyed or suppressed. It can only be directed. But it may be wrongly as well as rightly directed. It may be made to flow in dangerous as well as in safe channels. In general it may be said that man has succeeded fairly well in his attempts to direct the phylogenetic forces, chiefly through marriage systems, which have usually grown out of manifest necessities. But the higher flights of the reason, guided largely by the fact above noted that in the metaphysical stage the sexual act shocks the pure intellect, on account of its ignorance of the spiritual nature of matter, have chiefly aimed to direct these forces into injurious channels. All denials of their legitimate claims, and all schemes for eliminating them from society, all measures that tend to stigmatize them and render them criminal in human law, simply make them evil in their effects, while in and of themselves they are good.

The phylogenetic forces are somewhat exceptional in that they are to some extent subject to the individual will. Unlike the ontogenetic forces, their suppression in the case of any particular individual does not result in death. From this has arisen the false

---

[1] "Tableau," etc., pp. 363–364.

[2] " Neque natura aliter quam parendo vincitur." Novum Organum. Distributio Operis. " Works," Vol. I, New York, 1869, p. 227. " Natura . . . non nisi parendo vincitur." Aphorism III, ibid., p. 241. " Naturæ . . . non imperatur, nisi parendo." Ibid., Aphorism CXXIX, p. 337.

idea that they are capable of permanent suppression with impunity. All who are competent to speak upon this question agree that this is not the case. On this point Mr. Spencer remarks : —

Such part of the organization as is devoted to the production of offspring can scarcely be left inert and leave the rest of the organization unaffected. The not infrequent occurrence of hysteria and chlorosis shows that women, in whom the reproductive function bears a larger ratio to the totality of the functions than it does in men, are apt to suffer grave constitutional evils from that incompleteness of life which celibacy implies ; grave evils to which there probably correspond smaller and unperceived evils in numerous cases. . . . That the physiological effects of a completely celibate life on either sex are to some extent injurious, seems an almost necessary implication of the natural conditions.

But whether or not there be disagreement on this point, there can be none respecting the effects of a celibate life as mentally injurious. A large part of the nature — partly intellectual but chiefly emotional — finds its sphere of action in the marital relation, and afterwards in the parental relation ; and if this sphere be closed, some of the higher feelings must remain inactive and others but feebly active. Directly, to special elements of the mind, the relation established by marriage is the normal and needful stimulus, and indirectly to all its elements.[1]

Still more plainly speaks Dr. Maudsley : —

The sexual passion is one of the strongest passions in nature, and as soon as it comes into activity, it declares its influence on every pulse of the organic life, revolutionizing the entire nature, conscious and unconscious ; when, therefore, the means of its gratification entirely fail, and when there is no vicarious outlet for its energy, the whole system feels the effects, and exhibits them in restlessness and irritability, in a morbid self-feeling taking a variety of forms.[2]

The most common of these abnormal forms that the permanent suppression of the phylogenetic forces assumes is that of mysticism, which is a sort of disease due to sexual cerebration. Krafft-Ebing[3] and Tarnowsky[4] have studied this question and find that mystics habitually dream of a sort of sexual duality, with God as the male and the soul as the female element, or with Christ and the church

[1] "Principles of Ethics," Vol. I, pp. 534–535 (§ 231).

[2] "The Physiology and Pathology of the Mind," by Henry Maudsley, London, 1867, pp. 203–204.

[3] "Psychopathia sexualis," von R. v. Krafft-Ebing. I have only seen the English translation by Charles Gilbert Chaddock of the seventh German edition, Philadelphia and London, 1892. Of this cf. pp. 9 ff.

[4] "The Sexual Instinct and its Morbid Manifestations from the double standpoint of Medical Jurisprudence and Psychiatry," by B. Tarnowsky. Done into English now for the first time by W. C. Costello and Alfred Allinson, Paris.

similarly related, and that they continually emphasize these relations. Winiarsky sums up the conclusions of these authors and of his own studies of the same subject as follows : —

Sexual want unsatisfied and arrested is transformed into a whole series of psychic, often morbid phenomena, called love. This takes place not only among individuals, but in entire societies. An unhappy love affair in certain individuals is transformed into affection for their fellow-beings: thus it is that certain women become sisters of charity; in others it is transformed into poetry — it is thus that certain poets have revealed themselves; — in others, finally, it becomes mysticism : this the history of the saints attests.[1]

But whatever may be the power of particular individuals under the influence of religious or philosophical ideas to suppress by the exercise of the will the spontaneous demands of their nature, this must always be confined to a very small fraction of the human race, and for the great mass of mankind no such considerations can have weight or check the perennial flow of the great stream of passion that surges through society. As Schopenhauer says : —

From these considerations it is made clear why the sexual appetite has a character very different from every other; it is not only the strongest but also specifically of a more powerful class than all the rest. It is everywhere tacitly recognized as necessary and inevitable, and is not, like other desires, a matter of taste and of caprice. For it is the desire which itself constitutes the essence of man.[2]

We must therefore distinguish between individual necessity and *social necessity*. Sexual satisfaction is a social necessity. The individual may temporarily, or even for his entire life, by the power of his will under one or other delusion of the intellect, forego it, or he may be forcibly prevented for greater or less periods from experiencing it, but these are but eddies in an ocean whose waves sweep daily and forever from shore to shore. The phylogenetic forces are as irresistible as the winds that cause these waves or as the tides that periodically, perpetually, and irrepressibly wash the shores.

Not only is the sexual instinct the powerful social stimulus that has been described, but it is also an essentially social bond. The primary association is necessarily sexual. Society must begin with the propagating couple, and as this primary association necessarily increases the membership of the group, it is clear that the basis of

---

[1] Léon Winiarsky in *Revue Philosophique*, avril, 1898, p. 371.
[2] "Die Welt als Wille und Vorstellung," Leipzig, 1859, Vol. II, p. 585.

society must be sexual. It is therefore obvious that the sociologist cannot ignore such vital considerations, but must deal with sexual phenomena as with other social phenomena. It is not maintained that there has been any disposition on the part of sociologists to overlook the facts of primitive group life. These are the statical phenomena that always receive adequate attention. What has been overlooked, ignored, or even purposely avoided, is the dynamic side of the subject. Kinship groups, hordes, clans, gentes, tribes, states, and nations are simply effects. They should not absorb all attention to the exclusion of the causes that have produced them. These causes are the social forces, and the special causes of this class of effects are the phylogenetic forces that form the subject of this chapter. The origin and development in society according to natural laws that can be explained scientifically, of the sentiment called modesty, has led to the systematic avoidance of so vital a subject as this, and has consequently left the story of the world only half told. In fact, human history and sociology as they now exist are only expurgated editions, stale and lifeless from the omission of the main springs that have ever impelled the machinery of society.

Romantic Love. — All social forces are psychic, and in that sense spiritual. The application to any of them of the term *physical*, is therefore not strictly correct, but if it is done not to stigmatize them, but for the sake of distinguishing some from others, it may be justified and even useful. All feeling is psychic, but feelings differ in many ways, and among others in a certain greater or less remoteness from their physical seat, or vagueness and indefiniteness with regard to the location of the nerve plexuses, by the molecular activities within which the feelings are occasioned. Another difference consists in the degree in which the feeling is external or internal, and still another is that of the relative intensity and durability of feelings. All these differences are more or less correlated, and in general those feelings which are most vague and least definitely located in the body, those that are most internal, and those that are least intense and most durable, are classed as more spiritual, more elevated, and more refined. And in fact, there can be no doubt of the general correctness of this popular view, and, as has already been said, the true reason why this latter class of feelings is regarded as superior is that they yield a larger aggregate amount of satisfaction. Though lower from the standpoint of *necessity*, since they are not essential to life, they are higher from the standpoint of *utility*, i.e., they are *worth more* — more *worthy*.

But these feelings are derivative, and are the consequences of a qualitative development of the physical organization of man. For it is not the brain of man alone that has developed. The brain is only one of the many nerve plexuses of the body, and there is no reason to suppose that it is the only one that has undergone structural refinement. The brain has now been studied and the chief causes of mental superiority have been discovered. Primarily brain mass is the cause of intelligence, and until the process of cephalization had far advanced and the relatively large hemispheres had been superposed upon the original ganglionic nucleus, there could be no advance sufficient to constitute rational beings. And this attained, other things equal, increase of brain mass represents increased intelligence. But this is far from being the whole. There took place qualitative changes, and brains came to differ in kind as well as in size. Since the period of social assimilation this has undoubtedly been the principal advance that has been made. The cross fertilization of cultures worked directly upon these qualitative characters, rendering the most thoroughly mixed races, like the Greeks and the English, highly intelligent. The physiological or histological cause of this improved brain structure is now known in its general aspects. Brain superiority is measured chiefly, first, by the number of neurons in a cubic millimeter of the brain substance, and second, by the degree of extension and ramification of the plumose panicles that proceed from the summit of these pyramidal cells, and by the character of the axis cylinder at their bases.

Now, while there can be no doubt that this higher brain development vitally influences all the other nerve plexuses of the body, since every conscious feeling must be referred to the brain, it is altogether probable that a process of qualitative improvement has also and at the same time been taking place in the entire nervous system, and especially in the great centers of emotion, and if the serious study of these plexuses could be prosecuted, as has been that of the brain, differences would in all probability be detected capable of being described, as this has been done for the brain. In other words, the development of the human race has not consisted exclusively in brain development, but has been a general advance in all the great centers of spiritual activity.

It is this psycho-physiological progress going on in all races that have undergone repeated and compound social assimilation that has laid the foundation for the appearance in the most advanced races of a derivative form of natural love which is known as romantic love. It is a comparatively modern product, and is not universal among highly assimilated races. In fact, I am convinced that it is practically confined to what is generally understood as the Aryan race, or, at most, to the so-called Europeans, whether actually in Europe or whether in Australia, America, India, or any other part of the globe. Further, it did not appear in a perceptible form even in that ethnic stock until some time during the Middle Ages. Although I have held this opinion much longer, I first expressed it in 1896.[1] It is curious that since that time two books have appeared devoted in whole or in part to sustaining this view.[2] There is certainly no sign of the derivative sentiment among savages. Monteiro, speaking of the polygamous peoples of Western Africa, says: —

The negro knows not love, affection, or jealousy. . . . In all the long years I have been in Africa I have never seen a negro manifest the least tenderness for or to a negress. . . . I have never seen a negro put his arm round a woman's waist, or give or receive any caress whatever that would indicate the slightest loving regard or affection on either side. They have no words or expressions in their language indicative of affection or love.[3]

Lichtenstein[4] says of the Koossas: "To the feeling of a chaste tender passion, founded on reciprocal esteem, and an union of heart and sentiment, they seem entire strangers." Eyre reports the same general condition of things among the natives of Australia,[5] and it would not be difficult to find statements to the same effect relative to savage and barbaric races in all countries where they have been made the subject of critical study. Certainly all the romances of such races that have been written do but reflect the sentiments of their writers, and are worthless from any scientific point of view. This is probably also the case for stories whose plot is laid in Asia,

[1] *International Journal of Ethics,* Vol. VI, July, 1896, p. 453.

[2] " Antimachus of Colophon and the Position of Women in Greek Poetry," by E. F. M. Benecke, London, 1896. "Primitive Love and Love Stories," by Henry T. Finck, New York, 1899.

[3] "Angola and the River Congo," by Joachim John Monteiro. In two volumes. London, 1875, Vol. I, pp. 242–243.

[4] "Travels in Southern Africa," in the years 1803, 1804, 1805, and 1806, by Henry Lichtenstein, English translation, Dublin, 1812, p. 261.

[5] *Journals,* etc., Vol. II, p. 321.

even in India, and the Chinese and Japanese seem to have none of the romantic ideas of the West; otherwise female virtue would not be a relative term, as it is in those countries. This much will probably be admitted by all who understand what I mean by romantic love. The point of dispute is therefore apparently narrowed down to the question whether the Ancient Greeks and Romans had developed this sentiment. I would maintain the negative of this question. If I have read my Homer, Æschylus, Virgil, and Horace to any purpose they do not reveal the existence in Ancient Greece and Rome of the sentiment of romantic love. If it be said that they contain the rudiments of it and foreshadow it to some extent I shall not dispute this, but natural love everywhere does this, and that is therefore not the question. The only place where one finds clear indications of the sentiment is in such books as "Quo Vadis," which cannot free themselves from such anachronisms. I would therefore adhere to the statement made in 1896, when I said, "Brilliant as were the intellectual achievements of the Greeks and Romans, and refined as were many of their moral and esthetic perceptions, nothing in their literature conclusively proves that love with them meant more than the natural demands of the sexual instinct under the control of strong character and high intelligence. The romantic element of man's nature had not yet been developed."

The Greeks, of course, distinguished several kinds of love, and by different words (ἔρως, ἀγάπη, φιλία), but only one of these is sexual at all. For ἔρως they often used Ἀφροδίτη. They also expressed certain degrees and qualities in these by adjectives, e.g., πάνδημος. Some modern writers place the adjective οὐράνιος over against πάνδημος, as indicating that they recognized a sublimated, heavenly, or spiritual form of sexual love, but I have not found this in classic Greek. Neither do I find any other to the Latin Venus vulgivaga. But whether such softened expressions are really to be found in classic Greek and Latin authors or not, the fact that they are so rare sufficiently indicates that the conceptions they convey could not have been current in the Greek and Roman mind, and must have been confined to a few rare natures.

Romantic love is therefore not only confined to the historic races, those mentioned in Chapter III as representing the accumulated energies of all the past and the highest human achievement, but it is limited to the last nine or ten centuries of the history of those races. It began to manifest itself some time in the eleventh century of the Christian era, and was closely connected with the origin of chivalry under the feudal system. Guizot has given us perhaps the best presentation of that institution,[1] and from this it is easy to see how the conditions favored its development. In the first place the constant and prolonged absenteeism of the lords and knights, often with most of their retainers, from the castle left the women practically in charge of affairs and conferred upon them a power and dignity never before possessed. In the second place the separation of most of the men for such long periods, coupled with the sense of honor that their knighthood and military career gave rise to, caused them to assume the rôle of applicants for the favor of the women, which they could not always immediately attain as when women were forcibly seized by any one that chanced to find them. These conditions produced a mutual sense on the part of both sexes of the need of each other, coupled with prolonged deprivation on the part of both of that satisfaction. The men, thus seeking the women, naturally became chivalrous toward them. The solitary life of women of high rank made them somewhat a prey to the lusts of men of low degree, and the knights assumed the rôle of protecting them from all dangers. Moral and Christian sentiments also played a part, and we find among the provisions of the oath that every chevalier must make the following solemn vows: —

To maintain the just rights of the weak, as of widows, orphans, and young women.

If called upon to conduct a lady or a girl to any place, to wait upon her, to protect her, and to save her from all danger and every offense, or perish in the attempt.

Never to do violence to ladies or young women, even though won by their arms, without their will and consent.

Such an oath, made a universal point of honor, any breach of which would be an everlasting disgrace, and be punished severely by the order of knighthood to which they belonged, could not fail to produce a powerful civilizing effect upon the semi-barbaric men of that age. The whole proceeding must have also given to women a far greater independence and higher standing than they had ever before enjoyed since the days of gynæcocracy in the protosocial

---

[1] " Histoire de la Civilisation en France depuis la chute de l'Empire Romain," par M. Guizot, 3ᵉ éd., Vol. III, Paris, 1840, Sixième Leçon, pp. 351-382.

stage. Out of this condition of things there arose a special class of poets who wrote lyrics wholly different from the erotic songs of antiquity that go by that name. These poets were called troubadours, and some of them wandered from place to place singing the praises of the great court ladies, and still further inflaming the new passion, which was relatively pure, and contented itself with an association of men with women while conserving the honor and virtue of the latter. This, of course, was a passing phase and somewhat local, being mainly confined to southern France and parts of Spain. It degenerated, as did the whole institution of chivalry, and by the end of the thirteenth century nothing was left of either but the ridiculous nonsense that Cervantes found surviving into his time, and which he so happily portrayed in Don Quixote. But chivalry had left its impress upon the world, and while Condorcet and Comte exaggerated certain aspects of it, no one has pointed out its greatest service in grafting romantic love upon natural love, which until then had been supreme.

But it would be easy to ascribe too great a rôle, even here, to chivalry. The truth is not all told until chivalry is understood as an effect as well as a cause. Whatever may be said of the Middle Ages as tending to suppress the natural flow of intellectual activities, there can be no doubt that they were highly favorable to the development of emotional life. The intense religious fervor that burned in its cloisters for so many centuries served to create centers of feeling, and to increase the sensibility of all those nerve plexuses that constitute the true organs of emotion. Whatever may be the physiological changes necessary to intensify the inner feelings, corresponding to the multiplication and diversification of the neurons of the brain by which the intellect is perfected, such changes went on, until the men and women of the eleventh century found themselves endowed with far higher moral organizations than those of the ancient Greeks and Romans. They had been all this time *using* their emotional faculties as they never had been used before, and the Lamarckian principle of increase through use is as true of those faculties as it is of external muscles and organs. It is true of the brain, too, and when educationalists wake up to this truth the only solid basis for scientific education will have been discovered. But without a preparation in this latent growth of the emotional faculties neither chivalry nor romantic love could have made its appearance. The crusades, contemporary to a great extent with chivalry, and due also to the surplus emotion, taking here a religious course, became also a joint cause in the development not only of romantic love but also of many other lofty attributes, both ethical and intellectual. They failed to save the holy city, but they gained a far greater victory than that would have been in rationalizing, moralizing, and socializing Europe. Any one who thinks they were a failure has only to read Guizot's masterly summing up of their influence.[1]

Romantic love was due primarily to the greater equality and independence of woman. She reacquired to some extent her long-lost power of selection, and began to apply to men certain tests of fitness. Romantic love therefore marks the first step toward the resumption by woman of her natural scepter which she yielded to the superior physical force of man at the beginning of the androcratic period. It involves a certain degree of female selection or gyneclexis, and no longer permitted man to seize but compelled him to sue. But it went much farther than this. It did not complete a cycle and restore female selection as it exists in the animal world. It also did away with the pure male selection that prevailed throughout the androcratic régime. The great physiological superiority of the new régime cannot be too strongly emphasized. Its value to the race is incalculable. Female selection, or gyneclexis, as we saw, created a fantastic and extravagant male efflorescence. Male selection, or andreclexis, produced a female etiolation, diminutive stature, beauty without utility. Both these unnatural effects were due to lack of mutuality. Romantic love is mutual. The selection is done simultaneously by man and woman. It may be called *ampheclexis*. Its most striking characteristic consists in the phenomenon called "falling in love." It is not commonly supposed that this so-called "tender passion" is capable of cold scientific analysis. It is treated as something trivial, and any allusion to it creates a smile. Yet libraries are filled with books devoted exclusively to it, and these are as eagerly devoured by philosophers and sages as by schoolgirls.

Such books, of course, are not scientific. They are fictions, romances, lyrics. Yet many of them are classic. Such always contain much truth, and this is almost the only way in which truth of

---

[1] "Histoire générale de la Civilisation en Europe depuis la chute de l'Empire Romain," par M. Guizot, 4e éd., Paris, 1840, Huitième Leçon, pp. 231-257.

this class is attainable. Serious writers fight shy of the subject.
This emphasizes the idea that the subject is not serious. But as it
is the most serious of all subjects this naturally creates an almost
universal hypocrisy. My favorite way of illustrating this hypocrisy
is by contrasting the attitude of society toward a couple, say on the
day before and the day after their marriage. To heighten the contrast let us suppose first that one of the two dies on the first of
these days. The other is not even a mourner at the funeral. Next
that one dies on the latter of these days. The other is then the
chief mourner! Yet what real or natural difference is there between the relations of the two on the two days? Evidently none
whatever. The only differences in their relations at the two dates
are purely artificial and conventional.

Over and over again in the course of our studies into the origin
and nature of life, mind, man, and society we have encountered the
mysterious but silent power that unconsciously compasses ends not
dreamed of by the agents involved, the unheard voice of nature, the
unseen hand, the *natura naturans*, the future in the act of being
born. But nowhere has there been found a more typical or more
instructive example of this than that which is furnished by romantic
love. The end is nothing less than perfectionment of the human
race. Whatever individuals may desire, the demand of nature is
unmistakable. Primarily the object is to put an end to all tendencies toward extremes and one-sided development. It has been said
that this mutual selection tends toward mediocrity. This is not
strictly true, but there can be no doubt that it tends toward the
establishment of a mean. That mean may be regarded as an ideal.
It is not an ideal in the sense of exceptional beauty, unusual size,
excessive strength, or any other extraordinary quality. It is an
ideal in the sense of a normal development of all qualities, a symmetrical rounding out of the whole physical organism. In this of
course certain qualities that are considered most valuable fall considerably below the level attained in certain individuals, and this is
why it has been supposed to aim at mediocrity. But it is certainly
more important to have a symmetrical race than to have a one-sided,
topheavy race, even though some of the overdeveloped qualities are
qualities of a high order.

When a man and a woman fall in love it means that the man has
qualities that are wanting in the woman which she covets and wishes

to transmit to her offspring, and also that the woman has qualities not possessed by the man, but which he regards as better than his own and desires to hand on to posterity. By this is not meant that either the man or the woman is conscious of any of these things. They are both utterly unconscious of them. All they know is that they love each other. Of the reasons why they love each other they are profoundly ignorant. It is almost proverbial that tall men choose short wives, and the union of tall women with short men is only a little less common. Thin men and plump girls fall in love, as do fat men and slender women. Blonds and brunettes rush irresistibly together. But besides these more visible qualities there are numberless invisible ones that the subtle agencies of love alone know how to detect. All such unconscious preferences, often appearing absurd or ridiculous to disinterested spectators, work in the direction of righting up the race and bringing about an ideal mean.[1]

The principle works in the same way on mental and moral qualities, which are at bottom only the expression of internal instead of external differences in the anatomy of the body. For a bright mind is the result of the number and development of the brain cells, and all the manifold differences in character are ultimately based on the different ways in which the brain, the nervous system, and the entire machinery of the body is organized and adjusted. Generally speaking persons of opposite " temperaments," whatever these may be, attract each other, and the effect is a gradual crossing and mutual neutralizing of temperaments. The less pronounced these so-called temperaments the better for the race. They are in the nature of extremes, idiosyncracies, peculiarities, often amounting to intolerable and anti-social caprices, and producing in their exaggerated forms paranoiacs, mattoids, and monomaniacs. Love alone can " find the way " to eliminate these and all other mental, moral, and physical defects.

---

[1] The reverse is of course also true, and a decided aversion between a man and a woman means that their union would result in some prominent defect or imperfection in the offspring. The extent to which the great number of misfits in society, of people who are out of harmony with the social environment, of which criminals only represent the comparatively rare extreme cases, are due to conventional and compulsory marriages, which ought never to have been contracted, and which ought to be annulled as soon as they are found to be wrong, is little reflected upon, and society and the church continue to denounce divorces, when the very desire for divorce proves that such marriages are violations of nature and foes of social order and race perfection.

Romantic love is therefore a great agent in perfecting and balancing up the human race. It follows as matter of simple logic that it should be given full sway as completely as comports with the safety and stability of society. All attempts to interfere with its natural operation tend to check the progress of perfecting the race. Under the androcratic régime, during which woman had no voice in the selecting process, and under the patriarchal system generally where the marrying is done by the patriarch and neither party is consulted, nature's beneficent aims were thwarted, races grew this way and that, and mankind acquired all manner of physical and mental peculiarities. There were of course counteracting influences, and natural love, especially in the middle classes, helped to maintain an equilibrium, but male selection dwarfed woman and slavery dwarfed both sexes. The races of men with all their marked differences have doubtless been in large part due to the want of mutuality in selection for purposes of propagation.

This mutual selection under romantic love can be trusted not to work the extermination of the race from over-fastidiousness. It operates always under the higher law of reproduction at all events. This is proved by the universal influence of propinquity. " Great is Love, and Propinquity is her high priest." If there be but one man and one woman on any given circumscribed area they may be depended upon to love and to procreate. Very bashful persons who shun the opposite sex usually in the end marry the ones with whom circumstances forcibly bring them into more or less prolonged contact. The constant enforced separation of the sexes in the supposed interest of morality causes the sexual natures of those thus cut off from the other sex to become so hypertrophied that there is little chance for selection, and unions, too often illicit, take place with little concern for preferred or complementary qualities. Contrary to the views of moral theorists who advocate such enforced separation, marriages are fewer and occur later in life in societies where the sexes freely commingle and where there is the least restraint. It is also in such societies that the closest discrimination takes place and that the finest types of men are produced.

Where a reasonable degree of freedom of the sexes exists and there is no scarcity of men or of women, this passion of love becomes from a biological, from an anthropological, and from a sociological point of view, the highest of all sanctions. It is the voice of nature commanding in unmistakable tones, not only the continuance, but also the improvement and perfectionment of the race. In cases where arbitrary acts or social convention in violation of this command produce conjugal infelicity and despair, one might even indorse the following statement of Chamfort: —

When a man and a woman have a violent passion for each other, it always seems to me that, whatever may be the obstacles that separate them, husband, parents, etc., the two lovers belong to each other by Nature and by divine right in spite of human laws and conventions.

It is a curious fact that there is always a touch of the illicit in all the romances of great geniuses — Abelard and Héloïse, Dante and Beatrice, Petrarch and Laura, Tasso and Eleonora, Goethe and Charlotte von Stein, Wilhelm von Humboldt and Charlotte Diede, Comte and Clotilde de Vaux — and the romantic literature of the world has for one of its chief objects to emphasize the fact that love is a higher law that will and should prevail over the laws of men and the conventions of society. In this it is in harmony with the teachings of biology and with those of a sound sociology.

With regard to the essential difference between romantic love and natural love, it consists chiefly in the fact that the passion is satisfied by the *presence* instead of the *possession* of the one toward whom it goes out. It seems to consist of a continuous series of ever repeated nervous thrills which are connected if the object is near, but interrupted and arrested if the object is absent. These thrills, though exceedingly intense, do not have an organic function, but exist, as it were, for their own sake. That they are physical is obvious, and they are intensified by various physical acts, such as kissing, embracing, caressing, etc. In fact it is known that sexuality is not by any means confined to the organs of sex, but is diffused throughout the body. Not only are there nerves of sex in many regions, but there is actually erectile tissue at various points and notably in the lips. Romantic love gives free rein to all these innocent excitements and finds its full satisfaction as romantic love in these. Anything beyond this is a return to natural love, but it is known that such a return is not absolutely necessary to complete and permanent happiness. This is the great superiority of romantic love, that it endures while at the same time remaining intense. It is probably this quality to which Comte alludes in the passage first introduced into his dedication of the " Positive Polity " to Clotilde de Vaux, and then put as an epigraph at the head of the first chapter: "One tires of thinking and even of acting, but one never tires of loving."[1]

But "true love never runs smooth," and herein lies the chief interest of romantic love for sociology and its main influence on human progress. Besides its effect thus far pointed out in perfecting the physical organization of man, it has an even greater effect in perfecting his social organization. The particular dynamic principle upon which it seizes is that which was described in Chapter XI under the name of conation. It was there shown that the efficiency of this principle is measured by the distance in both space and time that separates a desire from its satisfaction. It is the special quality of romantic love to increase this distance. Under sexual selection proper, or gyneclexis, male desire was indeed long separated from its satisfaction, and the interval was filled by intense activities which produced their normal effects according to the Lamarckian law. But these effects, due to male rivalry, were purely biological and only showed themselves in modifications in organic structure. They produced secondary sexual characters and male efflorescence. This, as we have seen, must have lasted far into the human period. During the long period of androcracy that followed this stage, there was no selection, but only seizure, capture, rape, the subjection, enslavement, and barter of woman. There was no interval between the experience and the satisfaction of desire on the part of men, and very little effort was put forth to obtain women for this purpose. Hence during the whole of this period neither the Lamarckian principle nor the principle of conation could produce any effect. For the great majority of mankind this condition prevailed over the whole world, with greater or less completeness, down to the date of the appearance of romantic love. It still prevails within certain restrictions and under various forms and degrees, in all but the historic races. Under male sexual selection, or andreclexis, so far as its influence extended, there was no interval between desire and satisfaction, no effort, no conation. Its effects were confined to physical modifications, primarily in woman, due to inheritance of the qualities selected by men.

With the advent of romantic love, or ampheclexis, all this was changed. So far as physical modification is concerned the effect

---

[1] "On se lasse de penser, et même d'agir; jamais on ne se lasse d'aimer," "Politique Positive," Vol. I, Dédicace, p. viii; Discours préliminaire, p. 1.

2 D

was doubled by its application to both sexes alike, and instead of producing anomalies and monstrosities it worked, as already shown, for equilibration, symmetry, and normal average qualities or ideals. But here we also enter the field of social dynamics, and the principle of conation finds full expression. Schopenhauer [1] has acutely pointed out that the true romance never deals with happiness attained, but only with the prolonged struggle for happiness, with the troubles, disappointments, labors, and efforts of all kinds in search of happiness. It leads its heroes through a thousand difficulties and dangers, and the moment the end is reached the curtain falls! Tarde well says [2] that love is essentially a "rupture of equilibrium." The entire course of a romantic love is a heroic struggle for the restoration of disturbed equilibrium. What does all this mean? It means intense activity on the part of great numbers of the human race at the age of greatest efficiency. All this activity is expended upon the immediate environment and every throe of the struggle transforms the environment in some degree. The greater part of this transformation is useful and contributes to its full extent to social progress. In the early days and in the upper classes the demands of woman may have been somewhat trivial. Man must do something heroic, must prove his worthiness by acts of prowess, and such acts may even be opposed to true progress. But they at least develop manhood, courage, honor, and under the code of chivalry they must have a moral element, must defend the right, protect the weak, avenge dishonor, and uphold virtue. But in the lower ranks even then, and everywhere since the fall of the feudal system, woman demanded support and the comforts of life, luxuries where possible, and more and more leisure and accomplishment. To-day she demands a home, social position, ease, and economic freedom. More and more, too, she requires of men that they possess industry, thrift, virtue, honesty, and intelligence. Man must work for all this, and this struggle for excellence, as woman understands that quality, is an extraordinary stimulus, and leads to all forms of achievement.

But man also selects. Romantic love is mutual. Woman has as much to lose as man if it results in failure. And man sets ideals before woman. She must be worthy of him and she gently and naturally bows to his will and follows the course that he gives her

[1] "Die Welt als Wille und Vorstellung," Vol. I, pp. 377–378.
[2] "La Logique sociale," par G. Tarde, Paris, 1895, p. 426.

to understand is most grateful to him. Thus she develops herself in the direction of his ideals and both are elevated. She may also to some extent transform the environment, if it be no more than the inner circle of the family. The combined effect, even in an individual case, is considerable, and when we remember that in any given community, town, city, state, or country, the majority of men and women pass at least once, sometimes twice or several times, through the phase of life known as being in love, waiting and working for the longed-for day when they are to possess each other, struggling to prepare themselves for each other and for that happy event, we can readily believe that such a stimulus must work great social results. The history of the world is full of great examples, but the volume of achievement thus wrought is made up of thousands, nay, millions of small increments in all lands and all shades and grades of life, building ever higher and broader the coral reef of civilization.

Conjugal Love. — The love of a man for his wife or of a woman for her husband is an entirely different sentiment from that last considered. In a certain way it grows out of it, but it retains none of it, and it has other elements that are wanting in romantic love. Lovers imagine that after marriage they will continue to experience the thrills of love the same as before, the joys of perpetual presence and those of possession added. In this they are certainly mistaken; I will not say disappointed, because, if all is as it should be, what they get is really a far better article than that which they must give in exchange for it. For what, after all, is this beautiful thing called love *par excellence* but a wild, violent, tumultuous passion that completely absorbs their being, excludes all other sentiments and interests, stirs up their inmost depths, and unfits them for the normal pursuits of life? They are incapable while under its spell of enjoying anything else but each the other's presence. The man is unfitted for business, the woman for social life, and both for intellectual pursuits. The only spur that can make either party pursue other things is the sense of doing something that the other desires. It is then done not from any intrinsic interest in the work itself, but from the pleasure of pleasing the other. All the achievement wrought through romantic love, and the quantity is immense, proceeds, at least at first, from this motive, and not from the spontaneous love of work. Its great sociological advantage arises from the fact that this spur impels to activities that without it would never be put forth. Once thus started on the road to achievement an intrinsic interest usually arises and supplements the primary motive.

Romantic love has another drawback, that if anything interrupts it, which constantly happens, joy is turned to grief and even to despair, and so violent is the passion, that these disturbances constantly cause suicide or homicide or both. It is a precarious condition and is never an entirely settled and final state. In other words, it is at best a transient and ephemeral phase, an episode in life, during which it is not felt that this is the end. It is a state of hope, hope for another, an ulterior, a final and settled state to be attained through marriage. Marriage takes place. What follows? The tumultuous billows of romantic love are quickly calmed; the confused and undistinguishable but all-absorbing hopes and fears vanish never to return; the longings, yearnings, cravings of temporary separation disappear; but neither is that leaping, throbbing, exultant joy at meeting any longer felt as such. The prolonged warring of passion is over and peace supervenes. The pair are lovers no longer. James Whitcomb Riley's "Lost Lover" is a "touch of nature," and lovers who marry must say "good-by" as lovers. "Of the old embrace and the kiss I loved there lives no trace."

The philosophy of all this consists in the fact that love is desire and the satisfaction of desire terminates it. All desire is pain, and that love is pain is easily proved by simply imagining it wholly unrequited and unsatisfied. The joy, the pleasure, is not in the love, but in the act of satisfying it, and when that act ceases and satisfaction is fully attained, both the love and the joy, both the pain and the pleasure, end. Of these there remains nothing, and unless something else, something different from either of these, arises to take their place, the soul finds itself in some such a dead calm as vessels experience when they get into the very center of a great storm at sea, where sails and rudders are useless and they can only lie helpless on the bosom of the swell and drift at its mercy. There are unphilosophical natures for which this state becomes intolerable. For such there is nothing but the pall of ennui, and, it may be said in passing that this constitutes one of the most common causes of conjugal infelicity. Such natures have accustomed themselves to feed on passion, and when they find passion irretrievably gone they experience sore disappointment and rebel against fate.

But there is a still more unfortunate aspect of the subject. This is a natural consequence of the history of man as we have been tracing it. The romantic and the conjugal sentiments are both derivative and modern. They are the result of different causes and are wholly different. They are so different that both are capable of existing in the same individual at the same time. But they cannot both go out toward the same individual except during the early stages of the latter, where they may be likened to dissolving views. At least, if they do both go out toward the same individual, this is a most happy effect and is highly beneficial to society. I wish to speak here only of those cases, and they are of constant occurrence, in which these two sentiments coexist in the same individual but go out toward different individuals. Moralists are prone to deny the possibility of such a thing, but here, as in many other cases, fiction is more true to nature than social theory, since it is based on social facts. But fiction only gives us more or less idealized illustrations. For the naked facts we must look to social life itself. Here such facts exist in vast numbers and constitute the most difficult problem with which society has to contend.

This obstinate social fact has for its scientific basis a conflict between the biological imperative and the social imperative.[1] The former has been asserting itself during countless ages. The latter has only just come forward in the civilized state of man. Romantic love, as we have seen, as soon as allowed to develop through the emancipation of woman, became a powerful aid to the biological imperative in righting up the race that was growing awry under the influence of that extra-normal system which I have called androcracy. The essence of the biological impera-

[1] The expression "social imperative" was first introduced by Dr. Ludwig Stein of the University of Bern under circumstances which I have described in another place (*American Journal of Sociology*, Vol. VII, May, 1901, p. 757). It is applicable to all stages of social development. Dr. Stein, so far as I am aware, has employed it only in dealing with the later stages. But I am satisfied that it has its root in that same primordial, homogeneous, undifferentiated psychic plasm which I have called the "group sentiment of safety" (see *supra*, p. 134), out of which the most important human institutions have developed. Indeed, I regard this as the original form of the social imperative itself, and I have so characterized it (*supra*, p. 187).

tive is change, variety, the constant crossing of strains. It is a
dynamic principle and works for race vigor and race symmetry.
Romantic love favors it and leaves nothing to be desired from
this point of view. But that mutual choosing (ampheclexis) of
which romantic love consists does not go so far as to claim that
unions which it renders advantageous will remain permanently
advantageous. Ages of promiscuity that preceded the origin of
romantic love left their indelible impress on the race, and but
for the counter-principle of conjugal love, monogamy would have
been practicably impossible. Those who expect that such a deep-
seated race characteristic will wholly disappear in a few centuries
of superficial culture find the facts wholly opposed to their ideals.
Most of the moralists are utterly ignorant of this real human
history, and know no better than to condemn and denounce all
manifestations of the biological imperative which do not harmonize
with the categorical imperative as taught in their ethical philosophy.
But the former principle is infinitely older and far more basic, not
to say more reliable as a guide to human conduct.

It is these facts that occasion most of the sexual irregularity in
society, and social evils of this class are chiefly due to the failure of
men to recognize such fundamental truths, due in turn in the main
to their ignorance of the course of human and social evolution, and
of the real history of man and society.

Monogamic life, to be successful, requires a certain amount of
philosophy. At least it requires character. It calls for qualities of
heart and head that lie deep and that come out in their natural
purity and vigor as soon as the storm of passion that has kept them
in abeyance passes away and permits them to reassert themselves.
Then, freed from the thrall of passion, the cleared-up mind can begin to relish other pursuits and gain satisfactions of other and more
solid and useful kinds. But in all properly constituted minds there
remains at least a memory of the tender emotion which predis-
poses to the appreciation of mutual companionship not hitherto
enjoyed, and this sentiment, planted in natural soil, grows rapidly,
and soon begins to overshadow all others. Herein is found the
most typical exemplification of both the kindred principles already
alluded to (*supra*, p. 209), and called respectively *propinquity* and *the
sanctity of the second person*. It was shown that one of the happiest
traits of human nature consists in the fact that, where there are no

repugnant elements, the mere personal proximity of individuals leads to attachments that cannot be otherwise explained and have no other basis; to a degree of appreciation and mutual valuation that is wholly disproportionate to real worth. But, as in so many other of man's vaunted qualities, this one goes back far into the animal world : —

> A mastiff dog
> May love a puppy cur for no more reason
> Than that the twain have been tied up together.[1]

Nay, such natural enemies as cats and dogs become fast friends and affectionate companions when raised together.

Descriptions of conjugal love are hard to find, because, as Schopenhauer says, in all fiction and poetry, where romance ends there ends the tale, and the marriage, which is the goal of it all, if mentioned at all, is curtly disposed of in the last line or two that precede the "FINIS." It is therefore not in fiction that we are to look for a portrayal of conjugal love, but rather in works of philosophy, where attempts are made to find all the social factors. Schopenhauer himself disposes of it in the following words : —

> However, for the consolation of tender and loving natures, let it be added that sometimes to the passion of romantic love [*Geschlechtsliebe;* he never recognizes the distinction] there is associated another of wholly different origin, viz., true friendship founded on harmony of temperament, which, however, for the most part only makes its appearance when love proper has been quenched by satisfaction.[2]

Condorcet, who believed in the utmost freedom of divorce with a view to the ultimate attainment of the most complete harmony and mutuality, has pictured this final state of emotional equilibrium in the concluding part of the passage above quoted (pp. 386–387), and in the eloquent page that follows, but he does not characterize it as conjugal love. Comte, who taught that marriage should be indissoluble, essayed on several occasions to portray its perfect state : —

> This second epoch of moral education begins with conjugal affection, the most fundamental of all, in which the mutuality and the indissolubility of the bond insure complete devotion. Supreme type of all sympathetic instincts, its name is the only one that requires no qualification.[3]

---

1 Tennyson, " Queen Mary," Act I, Scene 4.
2 Die Welt," etc., Vol. II, pp. 638–639.
3 " Politique Positive," Vol. I, p. 95.

Again he says: —

The first and principal of these bonds consists in conjugal union, the most powerful of all domestic affections. Its preëminence is too well recognized, even in the midst of the existing anarchy, to call for any other special effort than a better analysis founded on a true knowledge of human nature, and calculated to dispel irrevocably all disturbing sophistry. The excellence of this bond consists first of all in the fact that it develops at once the three social instincts, cultivated too much apart in the three other domestic relations, no one of which, however, affords as great a stimulus as true marriage can do. More tender than brotherly love, conjugal union inspires a purer and more lively veneration than filial respect, as a more active and devoted sentiment than paternal protection.[1]

He sets forth very clearly the relations of natural love to conjugal love in the following passage: —

I confine myself here to recalling the fact that the sexual impulse, however indispensable it may usually be, especially to males, can do no more than heighten the conjugal affection, which it would be incapable of doing in default of a direct inclination. The carnal instinct only arouses relations which often lead man to truly appreciate woman. But when the attachment has thus been formed it persists and grows by its own charm, independently of any animal satisfaction, according to the common law of such cerebral reactions. It even becomes at once more intense and more permanent when it results from relations that are always pure, although the sexual impulse still remains perceptible.[2]

Dr. Shailer Mathews, writing under a strong religious bias, remarks : —

Between man and wife here is to be a union in spirit that springs from a love that is not mere passion, but is volitional and moral. When physical surroundings have passed away, then will the spiritual union, which must have accompanied the physical, survive, and the completed family become even more apparently like the completed society, a psychical union.[3]

There can of course be no doubt that conjugal love is a step more "psychical" and "spiritual" than romantic love, just as the latter is a step more so than natural love, and in precisely the same sense and no other, as set forth at the beginning of the last section, and without implying, any more than in that case, a generic or qualitative distinction. It is in this sense, too, that I have characterized it as "a better article" — more durable, possessing greater volume, greater utility, more real worth, and hence more worthy.

---

[1] "*Politique Positive*," Vol. II, pp. 186–187.   [2] *Op. cit.*, p. 188.
[3] *American Journal of Sociology*, Chicago, Vol. I, January, 1896, p. 459.

Thus far we have assumed only the result of a typical monogamic union following naturally upon romantic love. It may be said that such cases, though ideal, are really rare in fact. The widespread existence of conjugal infelicity seems to favor this view, and many deduce from it the conclusion that " marriage is a failure." But I think the statistics of marriage from this point of view, could they be obtained, which they obviously never can be because few are willing to declare their unhappiness in a public way, would show a slight preponderance of happy over unhappy marriages in enlightened monogamic countries. The problem of pure sociology is to explain the causes of unhappy marriages, while that of applied sociology is to show how they can be removed. With the latter we have here nothing to do. As to the former I venture to offer the following suggestions: —

It must be obvious that conjugal love as here portrayed cannot exist under polygamy. It is therefore even more unknown to all the ages during which polygamy prevailed than is romantic love. It cannot then be older than romantic love and must be confined to the same races and peoples. The forms of monogamy that preceded that epoch were chiefly economic in their purpose. They were based on the conception of natural love and its satisfaction as an economic commodity, and grew out of the increasing equality in power of individuals. Polygamy is essentially a monopoly of that commodity, and as fast as the spirit of liberty gave power to more and more men in society they revolted against that monopoly and secured as far as possible an equal distribution of property in women. Owing to the substantial numerical equality of the sexes this could only be attained by limiting every man to one wife. Every man who laid claim to more than one woman deprived another man of his claim to a woman. Although it is difficult to find any direct announcement of this principle as the basis of monogamy, still it is one of those spontaneous, self-executing laws that operate silently and perpetually until they work out the inevitable solution, and the transformed society accepts the result without knowing why and crystallizes it into an institution (monogamy), which is first generally accepted, then surrounded with a legal and religious sanction, and finally defended as something existing in the nature of things or as " ordained of God," or both.

As the property idea gradually disappeared and woman came to be looked upon, not as a possession, a chattel, a slave, but as a human being, a new adjustment became necessary. So long as a wife was only the property of her husband there could be no conjugal infelicity. Between them there existed such a social chasm that no more friction could arise than between a man and his horse. If she displeased him or became recalcitrant she was beaten into submission and shown her place as a simple contributor to his wants and pleasures. But when woman came to be regarded as a human being, if not the equal of man, at least a coagent with man in carrying on the operations of society, all this was changed, and there arose the possibility of a conflict of wills. Both conjugal love and conjugal infelicity are products of mutuality. The recognition of a certain degree of equality is an essential condition to both. The respect and friendly feeling, growing in part out of the memories of requited romantic love and satisfied natural love, as Condorcet has portrayed these sentiments, and in part out of propinquity and the enjoyment of things to which men become accustomed, work upon certain natures in the direction of forming and more and more closely knitting the fibers of conjugal love, and making the parties more and more indispensable and " dear " to each other, until this bond becomes exceedingly close, even indissoluble. On the other hand, the conflict of wills may tend more and more to separate and estrange, and ultimately result either in complete repugnance and separation, or in one or other of the innumerable family jars that make up domestic infelicity.

The careful and impartial student will, I think, admit that taking into account the past history and present condition of those peoples among whom romantic and conjugal love exist at all, both sentiments, but especially the latter, are on the increase, and that the human race is growing more and more monogamic. Monogamy involves an enormous moral strain. It is a severe discipline in requiring the constant habit of mutually yielding the one to the other in the exercise of the will. The race is developing in this direction and it becomes from age to age more easy to surrender the will to another with whom everything in life is so closely bound up. There are all degrees of difference in the distance to which different individuals have advanced in this direction, and the present status of marriage simply reflects these differences. To some monogamy is still intolerable, to others it is barely endurable, to still others it is generally satisfactory as the best condition attainable, while to a considerable number it is an ideal condition whose improvement even cannot be conceived of. Finally, as the extreme of development in this line, we have the uxorious, for whom their partners represent perfection, even more complete after marriage than before. Such persons are absolutely blind to all defects, and see each other in an entirely different light from that in which others see them. It is rather common for a man to greatly overestimate even the intellectual powers of his wife. Everybody knows such cases, and we have at least one example among truly eminent men; I refer to the case of John Stuart Mill. Uxoriousness, however, is often one-sided and confined to one of the parties. In such cases it is usually accompanied by more or less jealousy, and often causes unhappiness by restricting the natural liberty of the overrated consort. But uxoriousness is itself a proof of the possibility of ultimately attaining a state of complete monogamy.

All these degrees in the progress of man toward a monogamic state constitute so many examples of the artificial and derivative character of civilization, and show that man is constantly but slowly advancing toward complete sociability. Not naturally social, he is becoming social. If we could imagine uxoriousness to become first mutual and then universal, the problem of marriage would at least be solved. But mutual exaggeration is not desirable, and the perfect state would only be attained by universal mutual attachment coupled with just appreciation.

Conjugal love constitutes a third step in the ethical and esthetic development of the race. We may compare the effects of natural love, romantic love, and conjugal love with the somewhat similar series of steps, described in Chapter XIII, that were taken by man in the progress of the development of the ontogenetic forces. At each step the sum total of enjoyment is increased and civilization advanced. In the ideal state of conjugal love we seem to reach a condition of felicity, which, so far as it alone can contribute, admits of no improvement. It is full and strong; it is enduring, only ending with life; and it is calm and subdued, so as in no way to interfere with the other normal operations of life.

It remains only to point out that conjugal love is a social force even more efficient than either of the forms of love thus far considered. The principal stimulus is that of providing for the family that naturally grows out of this relation. For the man this is unquestionably the most productive of all stimuli. It is sufficiently intense to cause sustained effort, and instead of being only an episode of a few months' or at most years' duration, it is permanent, and continues from the date of the marriage until death to impel to deeds, if not of glory and renown, at least of usefulness and social value. Instead of having only the incentive of the desire to please another, it has added to this the incentive of work for its own sake. Freed from the distractions arising out of doubt, uncertainty, and the fear of not attaining the great end, he for whom that end is already attained can work for other ends and aim at even worthier ideals. In a word, the mental conditions attending conjugal love are the best possible for human achievement, and, as we have seen, this is the supreme test of social efficiency. Of all the phylogenetic forces, then, conjugal love seems to be the one that has contributed the greatest volume of human achievement, and it is therefore not to be wondered at that it is in the European race and during the past three or four centuries that the greatest achievements have been wrought by man.

Maternal Love. — It is not parental love with which we now have to deal, but with maternal love which is one of those attributes, like natural love, that is commonly, but erroneously, called an "instinct." The intention in using this term is to imply that it is something organic and inherent in the physical constitution, and in so far this view is correct. Maternal love is something that differs *toto cœlo* from paternal love and parental affection as distinguished from the maternal emotion. Yet these are constantly confounded by all popular writers, and even philosophers, still dominated by the androcentric world view, usually keep up, and never clear up, the confusion. Thus we find even so close a reasoner as Herbert Spencer saying: —

After this quantitative mental distinction there come the qualitative mental distinctions consequent on the relations of men and women to their children and to one another. Though the parental instinct, which, considered in its essential nature, is a love of the helpless, is common to the two, yet it is obviously not identical in the two. That the particular form of it which responds to infantile helplessness is more dominant in women than in men, cannot be questioned. In man the instinct is not so habitually excited by the very helpless, but has a more generalized relation to all the relatively weak who are dependent upon him.[1]

[1] " Study of Sociology," pp. 374–375.

Now this is, to my mind, a complete confusion of two, or even three, entirely distinct things, viz., maternal love, parental (consanguineal) love, and sympathy. Neither maternal love nor consanguineal love is based on sympathy, or if sympathy enters into them it is as a distinct and added element and has nothing to do with them primarily. Sympathy is the basis of man's moral nature, a product of a high rational power, capable of not only representing to self the painful states of others, but of experiencing the reflex of such representation in self as a form of pain. Maternal and consanguineal love are faculties planted in the nature of man through the laws of survival and advantage as conditions to the preservation and continuance of the race. I wholly reject his theory that they consist essentially or primarily in the love of the helpless. This latter can only be experienced by a highly rational being, while maternal love, at least, is shared alike by man and most of the animals with which most men are chiefly familiar.

This last-mentioned fact does not detract from the beauty, purity, or worth of maternal love as a human attribute. It is one of the characteristic attributes of the great class of animals called mammals to which man belongs and is directly connected with the leading function that distinguishes that class from all others, viz., the suckling of the young. The entire mammary system in this great class of animals is a part of the sexual system, and maternal love is primarily a sexual attribute. Thus Dr. Ely Van de Warker remarks : —

Through all the females of the Mammalia there exists a feeling toward their young called the *maternal instinct*. There is no necessity here of going into the question of instinct among animals, as to whether it partakes of the nature of an intellectual process. Whatever be its nature, it is evidently a part of generation, and as such is eminently sexual in its origin.[1]

Here instinct proper is confounded with one of those organic feelings developed in animals for the protection of offspring. This is a much less serious slip than to confound the latter with sympathy, which is often not advantageous at all, was not developed for any such purpose nor in any such way, and is not found in animals except in certain more or less doubtful rudimentary forms.

As the mammary glands are provided with nerves of sexual feeling, these are excited by the suckling of the young, and the mother

---

[1] *Popular Science Monthly*, Vol. VII, July, 1875, p. 292.

experiences a strong sexual pleasure in this act, which in animals must be a valuable motive for permitting it to be done, and thus calculated to preserve the lives of the young. Maternal love is intimately associated with this sexual feeling and grew directly out of it. It is in the mammal therefore that the sentiment of maternal love arose and this sentiment is not only common to all mammals, but is confined to that class of animals. What vague substitutes for it may exist among lower vertebrates is little known, but there may be such. It is probable, however, that the care for the young in these classes, including birds, is secured by true instincts, such as those by which eggs are hatched. The principle in the two cases is generically distinct.

The scientific importance as well as the poetic beauty of maternal love is thus portrayed by Haeckel: —

Only in this class [the Mammalia] is universally found that remarkable mode of caring for the young through the nourishing of the new-born child with the milk of the mother. Herein lies the physiological source of that highest form of *maternal love*, which has exerted such a momentous influence upon the family life of the various mammals, as well as upon the higher spiritual life of man. Of it truly sings the poet Chamisso: —

> "Nur eine Mutter, die da liebt
> Das Kind, dem sie die Nahrung giebt,
> Nur eine Mutter weiss allein,
> Was lieben heisst und glücklich sein."

If the Madonna is to us the loftiest and purest type of this human mother-love, we see on the other hand in ape-love (*Affenliebe*), in the extraordinary tenderness of the ape-mother, the counterpart of one and the same maternal instinct.[1]

Maternal love is an essentially conservative principle, but such principles are as useful to society as are the active and constructive ones. Hitherto its effects have been chiefly biological in protecting and preserving the race. As a social force it has only operated in a more or less negative way. Sometimes, however, it shows its immense power, and as a human passion it has been made the theme of many tragedies. No author has portrayed this power more accurately or more forcibly than Victor Hugo, and nowhere has he done this better than in his "Quatre-vingt Treize" and the rescue of the

---

[1] "Ueber unsere gegenwärtige Kenntniss vom Ursprung des Menschen," Vortrag gehalten auf dem Vierten Internationalen Zoologen-Congress in Cambridge, am 26. August, 1898, von Ernst Haeckel. Mit erläuternden Anmerkungen und Tabellen. Bonn, 1898, p. 23.

children from the Tourgue: "Maternity raises no issue: one cannot discuss with it. What makes a mother sublime is that she is a sort of beast. The maternal instinct is divinely animal. The mother is no longer a woman, she is simply female."

And it is true. The highest flights of this passion are those that most assimulate that animal stage when the female was the supreme guardian of her own, the stage of pure gynæcocracy. Then the female was not only the race, but did all the work of the race and chose the male besides. It was through this long discipline that not only maternal love but maternal courage and maternal efficiency were developed, and notwithstanding the trials to which woman was so long subjected, she is still capable of rising to the occasion, and without hesitation or deliberation, of defending her children in the face of the greatest dangers. Under this powerful spur her acts often seem almost miraculous.

With the advent of a stage of complete equality of the sexes this power is destined, it would seem, to play a much more important rôle than it has ever done in the past or than it plays in the present state of even the most advanced societies, and if women ultimately become the equals of men in the art of portraying events it is from them that we must expect this passion to be embellished and brought out in the literature of the future.

Consanguineal Love. — The love of kindred is probably an exclusively human attribute. It is, however, in all probability, not generically distinct from the consciousness of kind in general, but is such a special form of it that it may be regarded as distinct. It is generically distinct from maternal love, although it is felt by the mother in addition to that sentiment. It is the whole of paternal love as such, and also of filial and fraternal love. In the horde there naturally exists a sentiment of attachment on the part of each member of the kinship group for all the rest. Under the matriarchate all consider themselves as brothers and sisters, since the father is unknown, and in all races where there exists uncertainty as to the father, all the members of the clan are brothers.

The social value of this sentiment consists in the fact that it comes to constitute the blood bond, or feeling of attachment that exists among all the members of an ethnic group, and this bond, as is well known, is exceedingly strong. Properly to discuss it, however, it is necessary to look specially at its negative side, since it is here that

lies its dynamic quality.   In fact, it would have been possible and
proper to have treated all the forms of love from their negative or
correlative aspects.   For to every *love* there is a correlative *hate*,
and the force of repulsion is sometimes even more powerful than the
force of attraction.   The hate corresponding to natural love, romantic love, and conjugal love takes the form of *jealousy*.   In the animal
world, and to some extent in man, jealousy is a powerful dynamic
principle, but its action is chiefly biological.   It is the motive to all
male rivalry, and it is through this that were developed many of the
most striking secondary sexual characters, especially the formidable
weapons for fighting, but also strength of frame, muscle and sinew.
But so far as jealousy produces effects upon social structures, they
are chiefly destructive, so that jealousy is in the main an antisocial
force.   In passages cited from Schopenhauer, Haeckel, and others
these negative effects were sufficiently pointed out, and it was
scarcely necessary to treat them specially.   The form of hate corresponding to maternal love is quite different.   It is mingled with fear,
and consists in general hostility to all dangerous or threatening influences.   Any person, animal, or thing that stands, or is thought
to stand, in that attitude is hated and combated.

When it comes to consanguineal love, especially in that generalized
form constituting the blood bond, the corresponding hate becomes
race hatred.   Everybody has some idea of what race hatred means,
for it is not confined to savages, but exists between the most civilized
peoples.   It was at the beginning and has always remained the
principal cause of war.   To the sociologist it is one of the prime
factors of social progress, since without it there could never have
been that series of social phenomena described in the tenth and
eleventh chapters, resulting, first, in the most important social structures — law, the state, the people, the nation, — and second, in the
most important social advances due to the cross fertilization of cultures.   As these have already been treated in those chapters, and
from the economic side in Chapter XIII, it is only necessary here
to point out their genetic connection with this class of phylogenetic
forces, and thus bind all together into a single great group of social
phenomena, illustrating the law of sociological generalization.

CHAPTER XV

THE SOCIOGENETIC FORCES

THE sociogenetic forces, as shown in Chapter XII, are the socializing and civilizing impulses of mankind. In dealing with the ontogenetic and phylogenetic forces in the last two chapters we have been practically compelled to stop at the point in the historic development of the race where the sociogenetic forces began to make themselves felt, because the series of phenomena that subsequently took place is so greatly influenced by them that no adequate account of them could be given until their special nature had been pointed out. For, although derived from the others and deeply rooted in the physical nature of man, the sociogenetic forces as active agents in the world are relatively modern, and are the genetic products of the complicated series of events brought about by the action of primary social energy. These civilizing energies are so recent and so feebly seated that even in the most advanced races they form as yet only a thin veneering over the fabric thus wrought. Letourneau well says : —

Looking beneath the glittering surface of our so-called (*prétendues*) civilized societies the beast largely prevails over the angel, and taking existing humanity as a whole it may be said that the higher class of emotional and intellectual wants only constitute an epiphenomenon.[1]

In a general way it may be said that the sociogenetic forces are "life-mitigating," in the sense that they constitute the means of making life tolerable to a being capable of contemplating it. Without them it would be intolerable, because it would represent a pain economy, and life in a pain economy is only tolerable to a being unconscious of its condition and living under the optimistic illusion furnished by the primal impulse of self-preservation.

The sociogenetic forces naturally fall into three large groups, moral, esthetic, and intellectual, and considerable has already been said relative to the best order in which to treat these groups, and the

[1] "La Sociologie," etc., p. 37.

reasons therefor have been discussed. No linear or chronological order is possible, as all three originated, or rather made themselves distinctly felt, at nearly the same stage in human development. The classification according to relative nobility or worthiness is scarcely legitimate, as no two would perhaps agree upon it. That arrangement which seeks to determine the relative developmental grade of the three classes seems the most in harmony with biological and evolutionary treatment, but as they are distinct branches and no one is developed out of another, this is practicable only to a limited extent. If we ask which one has contributed most to the general end of them all — civilization — we may get varying answers. Most writers put the moral sentiments last in a climactic arrangement, as the highest from this point of view — the true, the beautiful, the good — but I would myself question this, and would award the claim to the true. Perhaps upon the whole the best ground for an arrangement of the sociogenetic forces is their immediate derivation from the essential forces, and especially from the phylogenetic group, placing that class first which seems to emerge most immediately out of the latter. This would at once dispose of the intellectual forces as most remote from this point of view, and narrow the question down to the moral and esthetic forces. Here there seems to be little room for a preference. The intimate association of all ideas of beauty with the reproductive process may be evenly paired with that widespread system of animal altruism which is based on the necessity of continuing the race. There are other considerations that cannot well be entered into here, but which will be fully set forth in connection with the moral forces, which turn the scale here in my mind in favor of giving this class the first place, and the order of treatment will therefore be, as already given, viz., 1, the moral forces; 2, the esthetic forces; 3, the intellectual forces.

THE MORAL FORCES

Considered from the standpoint of its origin, morality is of two kinds: *race morality* and *individual morality*. The roots of both of these classes penetrate very deeply. Both of them, as I view the subject, are exclusively human attributes, but both have their strict homologues in the animal world. As the passage from animality to humanity was wholly the result of brain development and consequent dawn of intelligence, so both kinds of morality were the products of the rational faculty, and the difference between them and their animal homologues is the difference between conscious and unconscious acts that subserve the same ends. The animal homologue of race morality is *instinct*, and that of individual morality is animal, or, as it may also be called, *reproductive altruism*. In one sense they all aim at race preservation, but the last couple reach the race through the individual.

Race Morality. — Under the head of "Restraints to Feeling," in Chapter VII, attention was called to the "instinct of race safety" that arose under the influence of the collective or group reason to offset the tendency to waywardness that individual reason had so greatly increased, and which instinct no longer prevented. This was characterized (p. 187) as the social imperative, or primordial plasma out of which were subsequently differentiated nearly all important human institutions — religion, law, government, custom, etc. It was certainly the beginning of race morality, the primary factor of which was the *mos*, from which term the word *moral* is derived. This form of morality operates entirely in the interest of function and against the claims of feeling. It seems therefore to be precisely the opposite of the currently accepted morality, which, as has been shown (*supra*, p. 131), is based wholly on feeling. For however much it may be necessary to restrain feeling, the moral quality can only arise in connection with feeling creatures. But race morality is no more concerned with the feelings of the individual than nature seems to be when everything is sacrificed to the safety of the race. In fact, in race morality man simply assists nature, or becomes an integral part of the natural forces that make for race preservation. The group puts its sanction upon everything that has this tendency. It is the "ultra-rational sanction" of Benjamin Kidd.

Race morality, therefore, consists essentially in custom, and if the customs of the world are all scrutinized the majority of them will be found to consist in restraints to conduct inimical to race safety. At least such was their primitive purpose, but many have of course departed widely from that purpose, which may now be difficult to trace. Here it becomes difficult to distinguish morals from religion. The latter is little more than the addition of supernatural penalties for the violation of the laws of race safety. This is probably the basis for the widespread belief that religion is essentially moral.

The current moral teaching, moral philosophy, or as it is some-times ostentatiously and erroneously called, "moral science," con-sists essentially in a morality of restraint, and is undoubtedly a survival of primitive race morality, although its teachers do not know this. Most of its precepts are negative or prohibitory. It is based on the deep-seated sense of the danger of over-indulging the passions. It is commonly supposed that it is the injury that "wrong" actions do either to the agent himself or to others that is embodied in its moral prohibition. This is a mistake, and explains why no amount of proof that an act contrary to the accepted moral code really does no harm to any one is accepted as a justification of such an act. He who so argues, no matter how cogently, is told that the act is wrong, not on account of its effects, but simply be-cause it is wrong; that there is an abstract right and an abstract wrong, irrespective of the effects in any particular case. Kant's rule of conduct: "Always act on a principle that you would like to see erected into a universal law," is quoted at him, and he is told that there exists a "pure morals" or "absolute ethics." A few may try to explain that the case in question is an exception, and that it will not do to allow any one to be a judge for himself of the effects of his actions. Or they may deny the possibility that any one can foresee all the effects of an action, and say that it is unsafe to trust present indications in this respect. But the majority decline to discuss the question at all, since this might be construed into an admission that exceptions were possible, and stand firmly on the ground of the infallibility of the moral code.

All this difficulty is caused by the failure to distinguish between race morality and individual morality, and to recognize the fact that the prevailing morality of restraint is simply a survival of the former. The effect of the action upon individuals has nothing whatever to do with its rightness or wrongness. The bottom of it all is the effect on the safety of the human race. "Duty" is simply conduct favorable to race safety. Virtue is an attitude of life and character consistent with the preservation and continuance of man on earth. Vice is the reverse of this, and is felt as an attack upon the race. These sentiments are difficult to analyze, and the moral reformer seldom or never knows that this is what he feels when he preaches morality. Usually theological in his make-up, he thinks that moral conduct is pleasing to God, and regards this as the real sanction, regardless of its effects. Here is where morals and religion most closely approach each other, for at the beginning all religion was race perception (*Gattungsempfindung*), and the creation of gods whose supposed will is thwarted by conduct dangerous to the race was simply a means of enabling the feeble mind of the individual to distinguish right from wrong conduct.

Mr. Spencer argued valiantly in " Social Statics " (1850) for an absolute ethics, but after studying the moral codes of uncivilized races and finding that there were no standards of right and wrong, he repudiated his early views and edited them all out of the revised edition of that work. This was inconsistent, which is no disparagement to a great mind, it is true; but it was not logical. He should have learned in all his investigations that the ethics of all uncivilized races is chiefly race ethics. From this point of view no amount of incongruity in ethical conceptions could affect their ethical character. If we can get rid entirely of the idea that " good " and " evil " have any connection whatever with benefit or injury to the individual or to any sentient being, and clearly grasp the truth that they relate exclusively to race safety and race danger, we can see that the quality of actions approved or disapproved has nothing to do with the pleasure or pain they may cause, but relates solely to their effect upon the race which is not a sentient thing. The idea of the race, however, narrows as we descend in the scale of civilization, and with the savage it is limited to his own race, tribe, clan, or horde. It is said that theft and murder are regarded as moral acts among some savages. This is probably not true within the horde, clan, tribe, etc., which places such acts in a different class from that now under consideration, a class soon to be considered. But even if true, these and many other acts sanctioned by the codes of savages which are severely condemned by our own, may be regarded as safe, may indeed be safe for such peoples from the standpoint of race preservation, which is the only standpoint in race morality.

The view that the morality of restraint is a survival of primitive race morality is the only one consistent with its defense, for most of it tends to diminish the amount of enjoyment instead of tending to increase it, as the opposite view would require. Whether it actually does secure race safety is another question. It may be only a social vestige, and as such have a somewhat pathologic character.

Individual Morality. — Individual morality is based on altruism. This term is not synonymous with sympathy if we extend it to animals. Animal altruism is a true instinct, and however beautiful it may be painted, it is not sympathy or compassion that prompts the "nurse" to allow herself to be devoured by the brood of cercariæ within her in order that they may live, or that causes the male spider or mantis to sacrifice his life in fecundating the female for the good of the species. The sociologist may therefore content himself with the mention of this animal homologue of human altruism as one of those great tap-roots that sociology sends far down into biology. Human altruism, in so far as it is not biological, *is* based on sympathy, and this is also the basis of all morality except race morality. If we except this and animal altruism we have left the popular avowed notion of morality, although, as already remarked, race morality is almost everywhere deeply but unconsciously felt by civilized man.

A great many attempts have been made to work out the genesis of the moral sense. These have all had two fatal vices, first its objectivation, and second its divorce from psychology. Of the first of these it need only be said that there is no moral sense as anything distinct from other psychic attributes, as a something apart, existing in and for itself, and constituting a distinct field of its own. If there were it could have no genesis. As to the second vice in trying to arrive at the origin of the moral sense, it is certain that it cannot be considered apart from the mind of man. In so far as it is anything at all it is a part of mind. Moreover, it is a complex psychic product and depends upon the coöperation and combination of both the subjective and the objective faculties. Its treatment from the genetic standpoint must therefore involve a slight anticipation of the discussion to be found in the next chapter and in Part III generally. At present, however, we are considering it only as a social force, and shall presuppose a knowledge of the human mind to that extent.

First of all then, be it said, morality is a product of brain development. It is true that everything else exclusively human is also a product of brain development, and that in real truth if the being called man had had every other attribute that he has and had not had a very much greater brain development than any other animal he would have been no more than any other animal of the same taxonomic rank. But the "moral sense," the conscious altruism, the ability to feel with other feeling beings, was not an early psychic attribute, but required a relatively high degree of brain development. As has been said before, it consists in a power of *representing* the psychic states of others to self, and the nerve adjustment necessary to produce a reflex vibration of the kind called a sensation when such states are thus represented. It is only the *intensive* sensations that are thus represented, which consist, as defined in Chapter VII, exclusively of pleasurable and painful states. But these states, as much as any other states of consciousness, are to another consciousness, "ejects," [1] in the sense given to that term by Professor Clifford. Notwithstanding the amount of pedantic refinement and copious dilution that this word has suffered at the hands of smaller men, it still has some value as an expression of a truth that is somewhat difficult to grasp, and one that is broader even than Clifford himself supposed. There is no reason why it should not extend to intensive feelings as well as to indifferent ones. The power of representation is the distinguishing characteristic of the growing intellect, but it is twofold, or takes two different directions, producing two distinct psychic faculties, the one subjective, the other objective. The subjective faculty produced by representation is sympathy, the objective one is imagination. We have only to do with the first of these here.

That sympathy is a rational faculty admits of no doubt. The syllogism of sympathy is this : A given influence produces pain (or pleasure) in me ; you are like me ; therefore the same influence will produce pain (or pleasure) in you. But this reasoning in and of itself is feelingless. To constitute a motive to action, *i.e.*, a force, there must be developed in the nervous system a reflex responsiveness such that the previously experienced sensations of pain or pleasure caused by the influence shall be remembered and revived,

---

1 " The inferred existence of your feelings, of objective groupings among them similar to those among my feelings, and of a subjective order in many respects analogous to my own, — these inferred existences are in the very act of inference *thrown out* of my consciousness, recognized as outside of it, as *not* being a part of me. I propose, accordingly, to call these inferred existences *ejects*, things thrown out of my consciousness, to distinguish them from *objects*, things presented in my consciousness, phenomena." — " On the Nature of Things in Themselves," by William Kingdon Clifford. *Mind*, a Quarterly Review of Psychology and Philosophy, London, Vol. III, No. 9, January, 1878, pp. 57–67. Passage quoted occurs on p. 58. Also in " Essays by the Late William Kingdon Clifford," edited by Leslie Stephen and Frederick Pollock. Second edition, London, 1886, pp. 274–286. Passage quoted occurs on p. 275.

that is, repeated as part of the "faint series" corresponding to the "vivid series" of sensations that were caused by the influence itself. It requires a considerable number of words to express this idea, but the idea itself is not so complex. It is simply that no one ever analyzes it, and therefore there are no special terms by which it can be briefly expressed. Nevertheless, all developed human beings constantly experience it. It might be an idle speculation to try to ascertain the absolute beginning of sympathy. It may be the reverse of Spencer's idea that it grew out of "love of the helpless." It is, indeed, probable that this was about the earliest manifestation of sympathy. It may also be that it first appeared in woman as a mother with her strong native love of her offspring, which, though in itself an entirely different faculty, early blended with, or helped to create, the derivative reason-born faculty of altruism.

The faint series of psychic phenomena is as strictly subjective as is the vivid series. It resides in the person's self or ego, and is in this only true sense egoistic. Altruism thus has an egoistic basis, or more properly, is a form of egoism. It might be called *reflex egoism*. The subjective ejects — other people's feelings — act upon the ego and produce similar but usually less intense feelings. Altruism or sympathy would not be a force, it could not be a motive, if it did not reside in the agent, *i.e.*, if it were not egoistic. All motives are necessarily egoistic. To condemn a motive because egoistic is therefore to condemn all motives. But the origin of subjective reflex motives marked an epoch in the history of man. From the standpoint of sociology and of human progress generally, this was the most important of all the steps the race has taken. The egoistic reason unaided by the altruistic reason could only work such results as the subjection of woman and the aggrandizement of the strong. These, if continued long enough and not counteracted, would become highly antisocial. They might even bring about the destruction of the race.

Altruism is therefore an essentially socializing force, *i.e.*, it is sociogenetic. Its name alone reveals its social character. Although itself egoistic it always expends itself on another. There can be no altruism without an *alter*. Altruism is not strictly synonymous with sympathy. The latter, though not necessarily negative, is usually so used. It is representative pain; scarcely representative pleasure. Altruism applies equally to both. Neither is

altruism synonymous with benevolence, still less with beneficence.
On this point Mr. Spencer remarks: —

I gladly adopt this word, for which we are indebted to M. Comte. Not
long since some critic, condemning it as new-fangled, asked why we should
not be content with such good old-fashioned words as benevolent and beneficent. There is quite sufficient reason. Altruism and altruistic, suggesting
by their forms as well as by their meanings the antitheses of egoism and
egoistic, bring quickly and clearly into thought the opposition, in a way that
benevolence or beneficence and its derivatives do not, because the antitheses
are not directly implied by them. This superior suggestiveness greatly
facilitates the communication of ethical ideas.[1]

There are of course those who criticise the form of the word as
derived directly from the French *autrui*, but retaining the *l* of the
Latin *alter*,[2] but *altrism* would be far less euphonious, and *autruism*
would be barbarous. The objection is captious. Comte worked up
to the use of the word in a wholly spontaneous way. Elaborating
his favorite aphorism: "vivre pour autrui," he found himself in
need of an adjective for the oposite of egoistic, and he used altruistic
(*altruiste*[3]), and needing a noun for the opposite of egoism, he used
altruism (*altruisme*[4]). Nothing more natural.

But altruism differs from sympathy in another respect. Sympathy is not necessarily a desire. It is simply a feeling. True, it
naturally suggests action. Being a pain, like other pains that are
not desires, it naturally, but not necessarily, gives rise to a desire
to act in such a way as to cause relief from the pain. This involves an intellectual operation, a knowledge of how to act to
attain the end. There are many pains which the sufferer does
not know how to relieve, and therefore does not act. Sympathy
may sometimes be such a pain. Altruism is a complex conception.
It is sympathy plus the desire to act. Or it may be representative
enjoyment plus the desire to increase the enjoyment observed
and represented. It is not merely a feeling, it is also a motive. If
that motive psychologically be the desire to diminish pain or increase pleasure in self, it has the unique quality that what it does to
self it must do to another in a degree as much greater as presenta-

[1] "Principles of Psychology," Vol. II, New York, 1873, p. 607, footnote to Altruistic Sentiments, title of Chapter VIII.

[2] Paul Barth, "Die Philosophie der Geschichte als Sociologie," Leipzig, 1897,
p. 25.

[3] "Politique Positive," Vol. III (1853), p. 700.

[4] *Ibid.*, p 727.

tive sensations are stronger than representative ones. All action, therefore, produced by this motive necessarily benefits others more than it benefits self, and it cannot injure either unless accidentally misguided.

Finally, the necessity that in all altruistic action at least two individuals be affected renders it *essentially social.* Its primary quality is *sociability.* Altruism and sociability are indissolubly connected. Ethnologists find it difficult to distinguish the two conceptions. It is preëminently a collective sentiment. This is the proof at once of the sociogenetic character of altruism and of the sociological character of ethics. Sociability arises as a natural and necessary consequence of altruism, and without a certain amount of sociability there could be no proper society. Altruism thus takes the form of *love.* Though not identical with any of the forms considered in the last chapter, and not in any correct sense phylogenetic or sexual, yet, as a still later derivative form of love than any of those, it belongs to the same great line of development of the affective sentiments of mankind, and has grown out of one or other of the properly phylogenetic forms. Its far deeper unconscious root in the altruism of animal reproduction has already been noted. After suffering a complete eclipse through all the higher grades of animal iife and through the earlier periods of human life, it was rebaptized by the dawning reason of man and came forth anew in a higher purified form as the first great socializing agent of the world.

Ethical Dualism. — Already on more than one occasion it has been found necessary to allude to the well-known but long nameless fact which Dr. Edward A. Ross has so appropriately called ethical dualism (see *supra,* p. 187). Whatever further needs to be said, including all discussion of its origin and true nature, belongs here. But the fact itself is too familiar to require any elaborate treatment. When we speak of altruism a very different idea arises in the mind from that which it is necessary to form of the altruism of primitive man. The difference is not so much in the nature of the sentiment as in its object or range. It was said that altruism primarily grew out of the phylogenetic affections or forms of love. We have now to determine from which one of these forms it was derived. It was stated that the arrangement of those forms in the last chapter was not or could not be linear or chronological, for maternal love is quite as old as natural love and far older than romantic love. It might have been pointed out that natural love and maternal love each begins a series of its own, and that there are thus two great trunk lines of phylogenetic motives. Consanguineal love is obviously derived from, or intimately bound up with maternal love, and whether it should be classed as phylogenetic may be open to question. However this may be, there can be no doubt that altruism, or *other-love*, in its rudimentary form is a direct offshoot from consanguineal love. It begins with the nearest of kin and is very slow to emerge from that condition. We actually carried consanguineal love far enough to include the primitive blood bond, and if that ends with the blood bond, altruism begins with the blood bond. In the horde and even in the clan there exists a certain attachment, amounting in the end to an affection, on the part of every member, to and for every other member of the group. This is the extent of primitive altruism, and beyond the group, as was pointed out, in place of love or affection there is hate or detestation.

From this point on there is an ever widening circle within which this altruistic affection goes out. It may be compared to a circular wave on the surface of a pool produced by a stone dropped into its center. At each wave the area of the circle increases, but at the same time the intensity of the force and influence diminishes. Maternal love is the most intense of all affections, but it is also the most restricted. Parental love is an increase in the amplitude with a diminution of the intensity. The more general forms of consanguineal love repeat the process in the same way and when the kinship group becomes large the same absolute quantity of force may be regarded as distributing itself to all the members. At last the personal element is lost sight of and we have simple race attachment. As the hordes combine to form clans the process is simply extended, and the same is true for the more composite groups. As the protosocial period draws to a close and social differentiation is succeeded by social integration through the encroachment of tribe upon tribe, through consequent increased race hatred, constant collision, and the resultant war and conquest of the weaker by the stronger, new complications arise. Race antipathy continues long after fertilization, but gradually subsides in rhythmic oscillations during the process of social karyokinesis and final amalgamation, as described in Chapter X. But at last, when the stage is reached at which a new people and a nation are formed, the altruistic principle reappears in a new form. The amalgamated mass becomes a unit and the original blood bond has its counterpart in what is vaguely called *love of country*, in which conception the people are included along with the land and physical environment. Patriotism, which was analyzed in Chapter XIII, is therefore a form of mutual attachment among all the members of a people. It is at once altruism and sociability. Notwithstanding the entire difference of origin it still greatly resembles the primitive blood bond and is dual in the same sense. There is still the correlative race hatred, or as it may now be called, national antipathy. This in turn results in wars and conquests on a higher plane, and these are followed by the same prolonged train of events as in simple assimilation. The effect is to widen the circle, and after numerous repetitions of the process the great nations of the world are ultimately produced. But that high national sentiment that we here find does not differ essentially from the lower type. It conforms, moreover, to the law above stated, diminishing in intensity with increasing amplitude. If any one is disposed to question this as to the positive form, he will certainly admit it for the negative form. If patriotism is not waning national antipathy certainly is. But a careful study of advanced nations shows a marked growth of the cosmopolitan spirit, which necessarily involves less relative attachment for the people and country of one's birth.

At any stage, however, it is easy to see that man's moral nature has always been dual. The sacred books of the Hebrew race show conclusively that morality was one thing for the Jew and another for the Gentile. With the Greeks all outside of Greece were "οἱ βάρβαροι." It was not otherwise in Rome, and it has always been so for all peoples and nations. Persons who may be very sympathetic as regards others of their own race are often utterly indifferent to those of another race. The Irish immigrants and settlers in America are intensely sensitive to the real or supposed sufferings of their own race in Ireland, but few of them would care how much an Englishman might suffer. One of the worst massacres of the Chinese in the west was perpetrated by Irishmen who were as recent arrivals in the country as the Chinese, and who in butchering them denounced them as "bloodie furriners"—a typical example of ethical dualism.

It is only with the highest types of men in enlightened nations that the widest circles of ethical influence are produced. Here we find a few individuals who are called philanthropists, and whose altruism is less or not at all limited by considerations of race or nationality. Sympathy here often outruns the judgment and involves inconsistencies and wasted effort. The greatest danger is in ignoring the law of parsimony and creating parasitic degenerates (see *supra*, p. 61). A curious fact in connection with this is that the great conquering races are the most philanthropic, the most altruistic. Neither are they always the most scientific in conducting charitable operations.

Humanitarianism may be distinguished from philanthropy as a still further step in the same direction, in which benevolent sentiments are placed more under the control of reason and philosophy. Properly it has nothing to do with dispensing charity, but seeks rather to reorganize society so that the minimum pain and the maximum enjoyment may be insured. Its aim is *meliorism*. In its most advanced form it eschews measures and devotes itself to the propagation of ideas, and especially to the diffusion of those forms of knowledge which, universally shared, will spontaneously and automatically work all needed and all possible reform.

The love of animals, which might be called *philozoism*, may be regarded as still another step in the spread of altruistic sentiments, including now all sentient beings in its wide embrace. If this were really added on to humanitarianism, such would be the case, but it must be carefully distinguished from various erratic forms of the sentiment which may exist without the coexistence of any of the other forms. Such are the cases of inconsistent sympathy lacking all rational basis and all true perspective and producing such social anomalies as, for example, the antivivisection movement. It may also be due to the absurdities of a cult, such as that of holding sacred the venomous cobra and dangerous leopard. Even vermin are held sacred by some races and allowed to generate filth and disease. A true, rational, and consistent love of animals and man because they are all feeling creatures is a noble impulse and marks the highest point in purely ethical development.

Here we should probably stop, but there is another step that seems to be in the same direction, although it transcends the bounds of the ethical world and hence can scarcely be called a form of altruism. I refer to the *love of nature*. It is not love in the sense of possible sympathy or of any conceivable benefit that can be done, and yet it still is love. It is the connecting link between the moral and the esthetic, and yet it is not wholly a sense of pleasure in the contemplation of the beautiful or the sublime. It is perhaps rather a religious sentiment, and is probably the last and final stopping place of religion. But still it is a feeling — *das Naturgefühl* — and when fully analyzed and understood it will, I think, be found to be the most elevated of all sentiments. It is the most disinterested, since there is no possible way in which man can contribute anything to nature. It is also wholly free from all expectation of material benefit from nature. In its highest expressions it even goes beyond admiration, because wonder is a mark of the undeveloped mind. It is not curiosity to know more of nature, although this, or at least an ardent desire to do so, necessarily accompanies it. Reduced to its simplest terms it is nothing more than an *appreciation* of nature. But when we reflect on what is implied in nature this is seen to be a lofty sentiment. For nature is *infinite*, and the serious contemplation of nature brings the mind into relations with the infinite. It is this which gives both dignity and charm to the sentiment, and connects it with religion, which, as Ratzenhofer says, is at bottom the striving of the finite mind after the infinite.

Such is ethical dualism, but the point to which we have traced it lies beyond the limits that are embraced by that expression. The amplitude becomes equal to infinity and the intensity equal to zero. It is no longer a dualism, it is a monism. In *ethical monism*, while there is no longer any love in the proper sense, so also there is no hate. If it could become universal there would be no need of any altruism. Human beings and animals would no more need sympathy than do mountains and clouds. If all producible happiness were actually produced and all preventable suffering were actually prevented there would not only be no "science" of ethics, but there would be no ethics, no moral conduct, no conduct at all as distinguished from natural activity. The world would become "amoral" or anethical. Ethics, which Spencer erects into a great science coördinate with and higher than sociology, would be eliminated from the world through the normal operation of its own laws.

But we are constantly told that what is generally understood as human progress or civilization does not increase the general sum of human happiness, or at least not the algebraic sum of happiness and misery, but rather that it diminishes it. To this it can only be answered that neither those who so assert nor those who would take the opposite view have any means of demonstrating their propositions, there being no unit of measurement of pleasure and pain. The truth must be arrived at in some other way, if at all. In the last two chapters I have endeavored to show that in both the ontogenetic and the phylogenetic development of mankind there has been a series of upward steps, and that at each step in both the means of enjoyment of the natural faculties has been increased. Moreover, it has been shown that entirely new, albeit derivative, faculties have been developed capable of yielding, and actually yielding enjoyments not previously experienced. I have now shown that the moral faculties are all new and have been added to all these. With all these increments to the primitive faculties man has certainly acquired enormously increased capacity for enjoyment. Those who deny that the absolute sum of enjoyment has not been increased must show how this is so. The burden of proof rests on them. I am not insensible to the force of their claims, nor do I deny that the greatly perfected organization of man through the influences I have enumerated augments his susceptibility to pain in the same degree as it does that to enjoyment. Nor do I deny that defective social organization results in immense suffering which a coarser organization would scarcely feel. But here the question transcends the limits of pure sociology. That science only deals with what has been attained and is likely to be attained through the continued operation of known agencies. Anything beyond this belongs to applied sociology, which deals with artificial means of accelerating the spontaneous processes of nature.

THE ESTHETIC FORCES

The esthetic faculty does not seem to be traceable quite as far back as is animal altruism, which is found in some asexual forms and perhaps in Protozoa, but when it is found it is always conscious. All sexual selection (gyneclexis) is based on it, and we saw how early this began to transform the male element, to mold it into forms and to adorn it with hues that charmed the female. We traced these transformations up through the successively higher types till they culminated in such glorious objects as the male bird of paradise, the lyre bird, the peacock's tail, and the pheasant's plumes. It cropped out in the insect world in quite another way, more directly connected with the ontogenetic forces, led to the cross fertilization of flowers, and gave to the world its floral beauties. Similarly it has been well-nigh demonstrated that many of the large and luscious showy fruits have resulted from the advantage that their attractiveness to birds gave them in securing the wider distribution of such forms and their consequent survival in the struggle for existence. Thus long anterior to the advent of man the esthetic faculty, as a necessary concomitant of nerve (we can scarcely say brain) development, was embellishing the earth with products that the highest human tastes unanimously agree to call beautiful.

But the esthetic faculty has passed through three stages, each a step higher than the preceding. These may be called respectively the receptive, the imaginative, and the creative. The first of these is passive while the other two are active in different ways. Between the passive stage and the imaginative stage there intervenes another psychic faculty which is not generally connected with the esthetic, but which can be shown to be the natural and necessary prelude and condition to imagination. This latter is a comparatively high stage in esthetic development and does not probably appear as an animal attribute at all, but only as an exclusively human attribute. The animal faculty corresponding to it and directly leading into it is *imitation*. Imitation is itself a very high animal attribute. It probably has its germs in some of the lower vertebrates, possibly in insects, but makes its first marked appearance in birds, notably in parrots, mocking birds, and birds related to these. It is faint or wanting in many mammals, but comes forth in its fullest developments in the apes. So marked is this quality in this family that the name of the ape in many languages is the same as that of a mimic.[1] Even in the developed languages in which the name has a different derivation, as the German and Anglo-Saxon, the same word is used as a verb, meaning to imitate or mimic, *e.g.*, to *ape* another. The French also have a verb *singer* in that sense, although *singe* is derived from *simia*. All this only shows that everywhere

----

[1] Lat., *simia*, from *similis, simulo;* Gr. πίθηκος, from πείθω, which sometimes has this meaning ; also most languages of native races where apes or monkeys are indigenous.

the most prominent psychic attribute of the ape is admitted to be the power of mimicry or imitation.

But the bird, the ape, the animal, gets no farther than this. If any animal has the rudiments of imagination it does not and cannot express them so that man can recognize that faculty. In fact, imagination is another mode of *representation* and stands in the same relation to objects that sympathy does to feelings. If we call sympathy subjective representation, as was done in the last section, we may call imagination *objective representation*. The one is the foundation of ethics, the other of esthetics. The ape imitates that which it sees. It never puts two things together to form a third thing which has no objective existence. This would be imagination. Imagination is essentially creative, and by calling the third stage creative it was not intended to deny this. Imagination can only work with the materials in consciousness, but it can dispose these at will and is not restricted to dealing with them in the form in which it finds them. It makes ideals out of these reals by a grouping of its own. It thus creates. But these creations are not real. They are not presented by the senses. They are reflexes. They may be called ejects, *i.e.*, *objective ejects*. Not being real, their cognition belongs to the faint series, the same as represented pains and pleasures.

The creative stage in the development of the esthetic faculty is that in which ideals are embodied in visible form so as to be cognizable by others besides the one who imagines them. It is *art*. This is a much later stage, but until it is reached the esthetic faculty as a transforming agent is chiefly a biotic force and works through selection and heredity. Now it becomes a social force and begins to exert its influence upon social structures. Ideals are realized and become esthetic creations. Such creations are among the most important of human achievements. Of the nature of esthetic creation enough was said in Chapter V, where it was used as an illustration or aid in studying the much less familiar phenomenon, genetic creation. This ground need not be gone over again.

We have seen that imitation preceded imagination, and imagination preceded creation. Now the earliest art was the most creative and the least imitative, and progress in art has, in a certain sense, been in the direction of a return to imitation. In the beginning the artificial creations of man differed *in toto* from anything real. There

2 F

was only the rudest attempt to imitate nature. Egyptian and Assyrian art and the old Chinese and Japanese art are all conventionalized, and do not closely resemble the objects they are intended to represent. They only symbolize them. Why this is may be difficult to explain. I venture the following tentative explanation: The earliest artists possessed very limited powers of delineation, perhaps in part due to defective powers of representation and imagination, and certainly in part to defective skill. Still they were the only artists and their rude representations were far above the minds of their contemporaries. They were regarded as next to perfect and were employed in connection with religious ceremonies and rites. These objects of art thus became sacred, and from this time no one dared vary them. They might be copied, but they could not be altered or improved. If this be taken as the basis of the whole, and all possible minor modifications due to varying conditions be allowed for, we have a rational explanation of the general and almost universal fact called the conservatism of art.

There must, however, necessarily be a limit to this slavish imitation of the artificial, and this was accompanied by a corresponding tendency toward the imitation of the natural, until at last in Grecian art we have works of art that are, although still ideals, nevertheless "true to nature," in the sense that every part brought together to form a whole has its counterpart in nature, was, indeed, in most cases, copied from nature. The whole, however, was unlike any whole in nature, and consisted of the *best* parts of many wholes combined to form an ideal whole.

But there was still another step, or series of steps, chiefly in the same direction. The sense of the beautiful seems at first to have been limited to what may in general be called symmetrical forms. The more geometrically perfect they were the more they attracted the primitive esthetic sense. Hence we find that savages are most attracted by artificial objects, such as beads, buttons, canes, umbrellas, and other mechanically wrought products. The natural objects first to appeal to man's esthetic faculties were the sun and moon, which present a shining circular disk, the rainbow, etc. A very distant and symmetrical mountain might also appeal to them. Next to these objects came animals and trees, also flowers, and finally the human body, especially the female form, smoothed off and perfected by the prolonged operation of andreclexis, came to be counted beautiful. Art had scarcely gone farther than this with the ancient Greeks, and little advance was made down to the renaissance. Landscape painting was scarcely known, and there is no evidence that nature at large was even admired by man. The present love of " scenery " is very modern and it is not probable that even the Greeks could have appreciated Switzerland. As Humboldt says, and as I have fully shown in a previous chapter, early man did not love, he only feared nature (*supra*, p. 109).

Now the modern idea of the beautiful, as most fully expressed in the heterogeneous reduced to order by perspective and rational synthesis, was an added faculty, not possessed by early man nor by existing savages, and the development of this faculty produced a complete revolution in art, immensely increasing its power to produce human enjoyment and stimulate activity. It also tended toward the imitation of nature, somewhat at the expense of the creative faculty, although this latter still has a wide field for its exercise. But nature in the large — scenery, landscape, wood, meadow, stream, hill, mountain, lake, sky, cloud, and sea — is so intrinsically beautiful that it is the highest aim of the artist to represent it exactly as it presents itself. So true is this that even photographic views, which, notwithstanding what they lack in color effects, are exact reproductions of all that the sensitized film is capable of recording, are considered beautiful, and these are so easily reproduced as to be within the reach of most of those whose tastes are sufficiently developed to appreciate them.

It has been said that art is non-progressive, that it serves no useful purpose in the world, that it does not raise the moral tone of society, that it adds no new truth to man's stock of knowledge, that it makes man no more comfortable, no better, and no wiser. This might almost be true without constituting an argument against the cultivation of the esthetic faculty. Love of the beautiful and its pursuit do not claim to constitute either an ontogenetic or a phylogenetic force in society. They constitute a typical sociogenetic force. Art is a socializing agency. It is an agency of civilization as distinguished from preservation and perpetuation. It is not a necessity. Shall we call it a luxury ? It is much more. In a pain economy it may be a luxury, but above that it becomes a utility. It finally becomes a *spiritual necessity*. As soon as the class of wants which may be distinguished as *needs* are satisfied this spiritual want, which, as we have seen, is planted deep in the animal nature, at once asserts itself, and the satisfaction of a spiritual want is as important as that of a material want. It serves to swell the volume of life. Men have esthetic interests as well as economic interests, and their claims are as legitimate.

In a word, the esthetic sentiment is an end in itself. Its satisfaction becomes one of the ends of the feeling being. The very word esthetic means feeling. The enjoyment of life consists in satisfying feelings. So long as feelings can be satisfied the more and the stronger they are the greater the volume of enjoyment. So long as desires are innocent, *i.e.*, do no injury to the individual or to others, it is a gain even to create them. The peculiarity of art is that it *creates desire in order to satisfy it.* This is as true of other arts as it is of music, but it is so obviously true of music that Schopenhauer made that an art entirely distinct from all the rest, the purpose of which, he claimed, is to typify and represent all the passions of the soul. It represents the will, which is ever striving, and when its end is attained, striving anew, and so on forever. So a melody is a constant wandering and deviation from the keynote, sometimes above, sometimes below, up and down, over all the tones, thirds, fifths, and octaves, and occasionally back to whence it started, and where it ultimately must end, otherwise the ear is wholly unsatisfied.[1] In all this there is a perpetual creation followed by satisfaction of desire, and in this consists all the beauty and all the charm of music.

There is much truth in this, and Schopenhauer's only mistake was in imagining that in this music differed from all other arts. It is the same in all, and the only difference consists in the ease with which it can be observed in music. In arts that appeal to the eye instead of the ear the process is practically instantaneous, as much more rapid and unseizable as the velocity of light is greater than that of sound. Yet music in the proper sense, melody and harmony, is another very modern art. Of course it began away back, along with poetry, in the primitive terpsichorean ceremony, as action and rhythmic noise, still, what we understand by music scarcely existed in antiquity and scarcely exists in any but the modern historical races. When we reflect how much richer human life is for this one art, we can form some idea of the sociogenetic value of art as a

[1] "Die Welt als Wille und Vorstellung," 3e éd., Leipzig, 1859, Vol. I, p. 307.

whole. With the extraordinary development of music during the
nineteenth century through the three stages, monophony (Bach),
symphony (Beethoven), and polyphony (Wagner), and at the hands
of such an array of composers, with the perfection of musical instruments and skill in performing upon them, it almost seems as if the
world was living and feasting on the musical art.

But a glance through the great galleries of the world is calculated
to impress one even more deeply with the quantity of achievement
in those far older arts, notably sculpture, while for architecture one
needs only to remain outside and admire the monumental piles that
adorn all the great capitals of the world and are copied again and
again even in the New World and in Australia. The older buildings
may sometime crumble and decay, but the different styles of architecture are imperishable and constitute the real achievements.

Literature is properly to be regarded as an art. It was action
before it was words, poetry before it was prose, rhythm before it
was rhyme, and esthetic before it was practical. In fact it is only
during the nineteenth century that its function as an esthetic end
was to any considerable extent subordinated to its function as a
means of conveying thought.

There is a reciprocal tendency for the esthetic and the practical to
shade off into each other. We saw how both the ontogenetic and
the phylogenetic activities tended to become more and more esthetic,
and now we see how the sociogenetic activities tend to become esthetic. In the great future the distinctions will be for the most
part removed.

THE INTELLECTUAL FORCES

In studying the moral and esthetic forces we have had no difficulty in finding points of contact with the phylogenetic and even
with the ontogenetic forces. But although these sociogenetic forces
have been the result of brain development, still it is difficult to connect the intellectual forces as such with any of these earlier and
more physical attributes. If it be true, as Professor Edinger points
out,[1] that the brain cortex was primarily a center of taste, this may
serve in a way to connect the appetite for food with the appetite for
knowledge, but the analogy would have no real significance. That

[1] "Die Entwickelung der Gehirnbahnen in der Thierreihe," von L. Edinger,
Allgemeine Medicinische Central Zeitung, LXV. Jahrg., Berlin, 1896, No. 79, pp.
949–951 ; No. 80, pp. 961–964.

the brain is an appetitive center, however, admits of no question, and there certainly is a resemblance between brain craving and other bodily cravings. It is only with this appetite as a true force that we here have to do, and not with the nature of mind in general.

Throughout the long series of psychic phenomena that are produced by the dynamic agent we have thus far been dealing only with those psychic faculties which may be classed under the head of emotions or affections, although in the esthetic faculty we saw that imagination partakes decidedly of the nature of an intellectual faculty, and also that sympathy was only possible through the exercise of true reason. Still sympathy itself is wholly feeling, and the love of the beautiful is also a feeling. We now rise a step higher toward a true intellectual operation and have to deal with an affection that resides in the organ of thought itself. But just as sympathy and esthetic taste must be distinguished from the rational processes by which they are alone made possible, so the intellectual affection, emotion, or appetite must be distinguished from thought itself. The truth is that the mind, or, if any one prefers, the brain, has an *interest* in its own operations, and the exercise of the intellectual faculty is attended with a satisfaction or pleasure, as definite and real as the satisfaction or pleasure attending the exercise of any other faculty. We are therefore still dealing with feeling, and there is no generic distinction between intellectual feeling and other forms of feeling. The mind enjoys the work it does, and often undertakes work that it can only do imperfectly, merely because it is " hard," and requires greater effort, being impelled by the satisfaction yielded by this effort. This accounts for the familiar fact that persons having great talents in a given direction often prefer to do something for which they have only medium or even inferior talents. Work in the field for which nature has specially endowed them is too easy to be enjoyable. The result is that they accomplish far less than if they had only labored in their natural field.

The mind has an interest chiefly in three things : 1, to acquire knowledge; 2, to discover truth; 3, to impart information. The interest in the acquisition of knowledge is perhaps the most intense, and partakes more exactly of the nature of a true appetite than either of the others. It is most prominent in the young, but may continue through life. Many young persons at a certain stage in their mental and physical development, usually for some years after the age of puberty, become literally hungry for knowledge, and devour everything that comes in their way. At first they are almost omnivorous, and are bent on storing their minds with everything that they did not know before. They will learn anything, and have small powers of discrimination. This fact is the strongest reason for placing such persons where everything they learn will form a useful contribution to their stock of knowledge, and not be mere trash and dross that can never be of any future service to them. Later on they begin to discriminate for themselves, and many almost self-educated men have succeeded in organizing their knowledge to good advantage. But this is exceptional, and systematic guidance is almost essential to any real success.

After the mind has become thus stored with knowledge the time at length arrives when it begins to work upon its own materials. The psychologists tell us how this is done.[1] This is a strictly creative process. By ransacking, as it were, every corner of the brain certain likenesses are discovered between images impressed upon different areas, or cells, or what not, and these are confronted and scrutinized, and their relations discovered. Something *new* results, something different from any of the separate items of intelligence that had been acquired during the receptive period. It may have no resemblance to any of them, yet it results from them. It is a *relation* subsisting between two or more of them, but it is real and definite, and constitutes a *tertium quid*, created by the brain's own activities. The mind *knows* it, so that it is an additional item of knowledge, but it did not come directly from the external senses ; only its elements thus came.

There are only two fundamental relations, those of agreement and disagreement. All other relations are derivatives of these. The variety is chiefly the result of degrees in agreement, which again must mean agreement in some of the parts of a complex whole and not in others. This is the distinction between *similarity* and *identity*, and similarity may be defined as *identity of parts*. So the mind searches out these identities of parts of its stored impressions and predicates them, forming a whole new and added stock of a different kind or class of knowledge. If the original knowledge acquired directly through the senses, including that kind of indirect acquisi-

---

[1] " The Principles of Psychology," by William James, Vol. I, pp. 284 ff.

tion that comes from reading and listening to others, be called *fact*, the new kind of knowledge created out of this by the mind itself in the manner described, may be called *truth*.

This creative process of the mind is attended, like the receptive process, with a strong interest and an intense satisfaction, and constitutes the second step in the act of generating intellectual energy. It bears less resemblance to a true appetite than does the first process, but the interest, zeal, and enjoyment are scarcely less.   Indeed, there is a certain depth and volume to the satisfaction attending the discovery of truth that has no parallel in the mere acquisition of knowledge.   Knowledge that is acquired is simply taken from the common stock and appropriated by the individual.   It was already possessed by others, perhaps by thousands or millions of men.   But a truth excogitated out of the knowledge thus acquired may not be known to any one else.   In the majority of cases, of course, the same truth has been evolved by other minds from similar materials, but the discoverer does not usually know this, and at least imagines that he is creating something wholly new.   This interest in the priority of discovery is exceedingly strong and fascinating and becomes the chief spur to original thought.

But facts are not the only materials received by the mind from without.   In advanced stages of civilization there are innumerable books, the purpose of writing which has been to express the author's thoughts.   Thoughts thus expressed are acquired by reading as well as statements of fact.   Many such thoughts are so simple that their mere statement shows that they are true, although the reader may never have evolved the same truth from the materials in his own mind.   The more obscure or profound truths expressed in books require to be thought out independently by the reader.   If the materials out of which they are constructed are not in his consciousness he is incapable of actually perceiving such truths.   They are to him only forms of words and not ideas.   This is why the world demands abundant evidence of every statement that is not of itself apparent, *i.e.*, self-evident.   No great theory can gain many adherents that is not supported by a vast array of facts.   Each separate mind must be put in possession of sufficient data to work out the conclusion for itself.   When a theory or hypothesis, such as that of natural selection, is thus supported it needs no advocates, because the facts combine to establish it in any mind that contains them.

The mind of a well-informed person contains a large store of facts and an equally large store of truths, *i.e.*, logical conclusions from facts. It uses the facts to increase the number of truths derived from both within and without. But it does not stop here. The combining of truths to form new truths is as legitimate a process of the mind as the combining of facts to form truths. Truths derived from the combination of other truths become truths of a higher order. The fundamental method of creative nature, as explained in Chapter V, applies to the operations of mind as well as to those of matter. This, as we saw, is the method of creating units of higher out of those of lower order and then using the latter as new units for still higher creations. This process of recompounding, or compound aggregation, which underlies all creative synthesis, when it reaches the intellectual plane is called *generalization*. This may be carried as far as the quality of the mind will permit, and the power of generalization (not of abstract reasoning, as is so often said) constitutes the best measure of intellectual power.

Generalization is inspiration. A new truth evolved from the stored facts and truths of the mind, often appears to come suddenly to view. Some of the greatest generalizations have seemed to burst upon the minds of their discoverers at a definite moment. They are often only subconscious, and consciousness seems to be occupied with other things at the time, so that the discoverers can relate the precise external circumstances, wholly disconnected from the discovery, under which the truth first dawned. On Oct. 15, 1858, Sir William Rowan Hamilton wrote: —

To-morrow will be the fifteenth birthday of the Quaternions. They started into life, or light, full-grown, on the 16th of October, 1843, as I was walking with Lady Hamilton to Dublin, and came up to Brougham Bridge, which my boys have since called Quaternion Bridge. That is to say, I then and there felt the galvanic circuit of thought *close;* and the sparks which fell from it were the *fundamental equations between i, j, k ; exactly such* as I have used them ever since. I pulled out, on the spot, a pocketbook which still exists, and made an entry, on which, *at the very moment*, I felt that it might be worth my while to expend the labor of at least ten (or it might be fifteen) years to come. But then, it is fair to say that this was because I felt a *problem* to have been at that moment *solved*, — an intellectual *want relieved* — which had *haunted* me for at least *fifteen years before*.[1]

[1] *North British Review*, Vol. XLV (N.S., Vol. VI), September–December, 1866, p. 57. Extract from a letter dated Oct. 15, 1858, giving an account of the discovery; in an article on Sir William Rowan Hamilton.

Emerson says : " Generalization is always a new influx of divinity into the mind. Hence the thrill that attends it ; " and Professor James remarks : " This victorious assimilation of the new is in fact the type of all intellectual pleasure." [1]   Galton says that men who have gained great reputations are men whom their " biographies show to be haunted and driven by an incessant instinctive craving for intellectual work." [2]   Nor is this a very modern passion, for both Plato [3] and Aristotle [4] considered the pleasures of the intellect, in its philosophical exercise, the highest of all enjoyments ; and Professor Le Conte, speaking of the idea of Plato, says : " All who have ever experienced the supreme joy of the discovery of new truth — I do not mean a new *fact*, but a new *idea* or a new *law* — know that it comes suddenly like a birth, like a revelation ; like a reminiscence." [5]

Galton also says that " sudden inspirations and those flashings out of results which cost a great deal of conscious effort to ordinary people, but are the natural outcome of what is known as genius, are undoubted products of unconscious cerebration." [6]   I can readily believe this from facts in my own experience, for although I have never made any great discovery, I have often been long haunted by a nascent idea which I could not formulate or clearly grasp, until at last it has opened out full on my consciousness at a time when I was making no effort to seize it. Once clearly presented, it grows in clearness and especially in importance, until I find myself compelled to drop other things and proceed to give it a definite form. Not to mention many other cases, I remember that this was the history of the idea embodied in my essay on " The Essential Nature of Religion," as late as 1897, the circumstances attending which, though not interesting, are as vivid in my memory as were those attending the discovery of quaternions. It has also been my almost daily experience for the greater part of my mature life to have thoughts flit into my mind and out again to disappear perhaps forever, unless I seize them at once and fix them by some process so that I can call them up at will. The approved method, of course, is to jot them down

[1] " Principles of Psychology," by William James, New York, 1890, Vol. II, p. 110.
[2] " Hereditary Genius," London, 1892, p. 36.
[3] " Republic," Book IX.
[4] " Nicomachean Ethics," Book X, Chapter VII.
[5] " Plato's Doctrine of the Soul, an Argument for Immortality, in Comparison with the Doctrine and Argument derived from the Study of Nature," by Joseph Le Conte. University of California. Philosophical Union, Bulletin No. 8, p. 4.
[6] *Nineteenth Century*, Vol. V, March, 1879, p. 433.

then and there, but they have a provoking way of coming at times and under circumstances when this is next to impossible; as in the middle of the night, or when I am with other persons to whom I should have to explain an apparent mental aberration, or when out in a storm where it would be difficult to make a memorandum. I have even had such thoughts when climbing a crag, and holding on with difficulty by the aid of both hands. Despite all the excitement and perhaps geological interest of such an experience, ideas totally foreign to it all will thus intrude. The most effective way I have found to save such evanescent thought waves is to select some one key word that if recalled will bring back the whole train of thought, and concentrate my effort on fixing that word in my mind until I get where I can make the necessary record. I find that I am not the only one who is troubled by fleeting ideas, for Dr. Carpenter mentions the same fact when he says: —

It is within the experience of most persons of active minds, that they can distinctly remember being struck by some particular " happy thought," which has afterwards entirely escaped them through not having been noted down at the time; it is a prudent system, therefore, to have a memorandum-book always at hand, for the registration of all noteworthy ideas.[1]

These transient thoughts, however, have another singular quality, that besides being almost instantaneous, they do not impress the mind with their importance, or rather, they seem so natural and simple that one is inclined to think it almost a matter of course that they can be recalled and used at will. This quality is highly seductive and tempts one to neglect them, so that only after repeated experiences of the fact that when gone they are gone forever, does one realize the necessity of seizing them before they take their flight.

Such is the constructive quality of the intellect, the most important of all the faculties, and probably, when comprehended in all its length and breadth, the one that has achieved the most, and contributed the largest additions to the general fact which is commonly understood as civilization.

We have now dealt with the receptive or acquisitive interest or appetite of the mind, and with its creative or constructive interest. It remains to consider what may be called its transitive or reproduc-

[1] " Principles of Mental Physiology," etc., by William B. Carpenter, New York, 1875, p. 536.

tive aspect, viz., the interest it has in conveying its acquisitions and constructions to other minds. It might be supposed that this would be very slight, but such is not the case. The developed human intellect is essentially altruistic. It delights in sharing its possessions with others. This is largely the case with simple knowledge, but it is still more true of ideas, I do not say truth, but what it considers to be truth. I shall not deal here with beliefs, though it might perhaps be shown that between ideas, *i.e.*, conceptions regarded as true, and beliefs there are all shades of resemblance. If beliefs were included it would be clear that the mind has an intense interest in their propagation. But beliefs are associated with so many other interests of an entirely different character that it would be next to impossible to keep these latter out of the way and deal with the beliefs as simply intellectual interests.

It is otherwise with simple ideas, whether these have been received from without and made to square with the data of consciousness, or created by the mind itself out of its own stock of materials. The intellect is intensely interested in both these classes of ideas, especially in the latter, and is rarely content to keep them wholly to itself. If we take the case of a really well-stored and active mind we find that it has been satisfied for a certain time simply to acquire, to accumulate and store up facts and to receive, compare, verify, and accept ideas based on facts that others (parents, teachers, associates, also books) may communicate to it. At the end of a certain period, usually continuing some time after puberty, sometimes till the age of twenty or later, during which the mind becomes stored with a large amount of information, a desire gradually springs up to communicate a portion of this information to others who, from their youth or from defective opportunities, are clearly seen to be wanting in most of it. This desire takes various forms. All that can be done by converse with others is accomplished in this way. Systematic instruction is often volunteered and gratuitously offered. The teacher's profession may be chosen, or a professional chair in some institution may be sought and obtained. More rarely public lecturing is resorted to. But when all these means fail there always remains one other, viz., authorship. The history of ideas, of science, and of human achievement in general, shows that the greatest sacrifices have been continually made in order to propagate thought, to diffuse knowledge, to promulgate truth, and to advance science.

Such employments are rarely remunerative, they are often made avocations in the enforced leisure of busy professional life. They are sometimes pursued in the face of poverty and want. This intellectual altruism is thus preëminently social and the results are socializing and sociogenetic.

The intellectual forces constitute the latest manifestation of the dynamic agent. No one of the three forms of interest that we have considered exists in the mind of the savage. He has no appetite for knowledge. The earliest aspect of this is curiosity or wonder, and it has been repeatedly observed by travelers that savages evince no curiosity even at what must be to them the strangest phenomena.[1] De Candolle[2] says that "the principle of all discoveries is curiosity." James calls it the lust for the new, and says that "the relation of the new to the old, before the assimilation is performed, is wonder."[3] The true explanation of the absence of curiosity, wonder, and all interest in or desire for knowledge among savages and inferior races generally, is that their brains have not developed to the receptive or acquisitive point. Its cells are comparatively coarse. If the neurons could be examined and compared with those of a highly civilized person there is no doubt that great differences would be found. But even if this brain structure is too fine for these differences to be detected by the most advanced appliances, still such differences exist and are the true cause of the intellectual differences. In this as in so many other respects savages and children at a certain stage of ontogenetic development agree, and in old age many men return to a second childhood in the matter of curiosity and interest as in other matters.[4]

This brings us to the question of the genesis of the higher attributes of the mind. That the brain has been developing throughout all the early stages of man's history is altogether probable, since it must have developed during the prehuman stage until, as shown in Chapter X, that particular creature ceased to be an animal confined to a definite area like other animals, and acquired sufficient control

---

[1] Captain Cook found this to be true of the Fuegians, Australians, Tasmanians, and other savages. See his several Voyages and compare: Darwin, "Journal of Researches," New York, 1871, pp. 227–228; Spencer, "Principles of Sociology," Vol. I, New York, 1877, pp. 97–99 (§§ 45, 46) ; Appendix B, pp. t. u.

[2] " Histoire des Sciences et des Savants," 2e éd., 1885, p. 320.

[3] "Principles of Psychology," Vol. II, p. 110.

[4] James, op. cit., Vol. II, pp. 401, 402.

over his environment to adapt it to his needs. What was called
social differentiation began here. The various phases described
were passed through, the patriarchate was established, and finally
the era of social integration was reached. There were probably
gains all through, but an entirely new impulse was given to brain
development with the advent of social amalgamation through conquest, subjugation, and the prolonged equilibration that followed.
Of all the social structures wrought by this process the one that
counted most effectively in accelerating brain development and intellectual refinement was the establishment of a system of caste. For
with caste came the leisure class, and without a leisure class it
would seem next to impossible at that stage of human history for
any considerable intellectual advance to have been made. In the
leisure class the struggle for existence is eliminated. The so-called
physical wants are supplied, and there remains necessarily a large
surplus of psychic energy demanding an opportunity to expend
itself. Much of this energy, indeed, by far the greater part of it,
was of course wasted — misdirected, erroneously applied, even per-
versely employed — but a certain percentage of it, if only by accident, must be turned to useful purposes. In fact, a perverse and
socially injurious exercise of surplus mental energy is not wholly
without beneficial effects, for if it do nothing else it will strengthen
the brain and lay the foundation for a future advantageous use of it
when the thus strengthened faculties are transmitted to descendants
more favorably situated for improving them.

With each successive assimilation fresh vigor is infused into society, the qualities acquired through leisure are diffused at least
through the privileged classes, and ultimately filter down into the
less favored ranks and leaven the whole. The ruling class, the
priesthood, the nobility, and ultimately a growing bourgeoisie, all
free themselves from the thralls of want and join the forces of civilization. At the expense, it is true, of the "toiling millions" these
favored ones develop physically and mentally. They are well
nourished and not overworked, exercising all their faculties more
or less in the way and degree that nature prescribes, and under
such conditions of existence their bodies grow freely and symmetrically, and surpass those of the lower classes in size and regularity of form, until they become readily distinguished from the
reduced, stunted, and more or less deformed bodies of the underfed,

overworked, and unduly exposed proletariat. But, other things equal, not only will a sound body contain a sane mind, but, under these circumstances, the mind will develop more rapidly than the body, and there will ultimately be much greater mental than physical difference between the upper and the lower classes.

Unjust and almost diabolical as this method seems, it is the method of nature the world over, in the organic as well as in the social world. In pure science we have only to recognize the fact and endeavor through it to explain the results attained. With the rise of industrialism and in the multitudinous vicissitudes of human history, but chiefly, after all, in consequence of the enlightenment brought about through the intellectual activities of the favored classes, a great leveling up of mankind began in the historic races some eight centuries ago which has continued to the present time, greatly accelerated during the last two centuries and becoming almost universal during the last half of the nineteenth century, whereby class distinctions have been in great part broken down and the qualities, both physical and mental, of the higher types of men have been transfused throughout all classes. It is costing the world something to assimilate such a mass, and to some there may seem to be a lowering of the tone of former days; but what is lost in diffusion is more than made up in the wider field offered for selection, so that it is even doubtful whether the maximum result has suffered any reduction.

I explain this on the principle enunciated by Helvetius,[1] which is in brief that (we will say, in the historic races) all men are intellectually equal in the sense that, in persons taken at random from different social classes the chances for talent or ability are the same for each class. The ones taken from the proletariat are as likely to prove talented as those from the ruling class, and so for all classes. This seems to contradict the facts above stated that the leisure class and the favored classes in general actually acquired, through the exercise of their privileges, a marked physical and mental superiority. The Helvetian doctrine must therefore be understood to refer only to the *capacity for development*, and not to the actual state of development at any given time. It would not be true now, and

---

[1] "De l'Homme, de ses Facultés intellectuelles et de son Éducation." Ouvrage Posthume de M. Helvetius, Londres, 1773, Vol. I, *passim*, but see especially Section II, the title of which reads, "Tous les hommes communément bien organisés ont une égale aptitude à l'esprit."

still less was it true when Helvetius wrote nearly a century and a half ago. But thus qualified I would accept it, and it is then only necessary for society to do for the less favored classes what nature long ago did for the more favored ones — give them *opportunity* for development. This leaves all the natural differences among men untouched, and deals only with the artificial differences due to social inequalities. Such considerations lead to the extreme verge of pure sociology with a strong temptation to transgress its limits and enter the field of applied sociology. We must therefore be content to have shown that the spontaneous processes going on in society, although by the application of the same uneconomical, prodigal, and inequitable method that characterizes all nature's processes, have actually brought about the present relatively high state of intellectual development, and raised the intellect of man to the position of a powerful agent of civilization.

THE SOCIOLOGICAL PERSPECTIVE

The somewhat extended treatment of social genesis that makes up Part II of this work may be properly closed by taking a backward glance over the ground covered, not with a view to recapitulating or summarizing the account given, but merely to gaining as true a conception as possible of the relations of the principal stages to one another and to the present state of the world. There are those who see so little beyond what lies in their immediate field of view that they lose sight of these relations and arrive at entirely false conclusions. It is proverbial that not even the wisest of men can see their own age as it will be seen in the light of history. It is another example of "the illusion of the near" (see *supra*, p. 49). It thus happens that many consider their own age degenerate. The little things that now chiefly absorb their vision have been eliminated from the history of the past and only the great things stand out, and they perpetually compare the current trifles, which seem to them so important and so deplorable, with the really important and universally approved steps that the world has taken in the past. They do not see that similar steps are being slowly taken at all times, and that the gains will ultimately emerge from the chaos and confusion of the present.

This illustration from history, which is the basis for the saying that "history is past politics," applies with increased force to the great train of events that constitutes the evolution of man and of society. As we have seen, it does not stop with man, but reaches back to the origin of life. Social evolution is only a continuation of organic evolution, and there is quite as much proof of the former as of the latter. The biologist is not rendered skeptical as to the fact of organic evolution because he finds along with the most highly developed forms others that seem to be almost at the base of the scale. He has various ways of explaining this fact, and few consider it necessary to assume a polyphyletic scale. But the existence of very low races of men contemporary with the highest types is a stumbling-block to many anthropologists and even sociologists, and shakes their faith in social evolution. I think it has been sufficiently shown why and how this is, but it is also true that there seems to be no race of men very near the base of the scale. There are very few in the gynæcocratic stage, nearly all have reached the patriarchate, and the greater number are wholly out of the proto-social stage and have undergone more or less social assimilation or race amalgamation. Along a number of distinct lines there has been a forward movement, until most of the black races, and preëminently the white races, have reached very advanced positions in social development. This has been accomplished by the several unconscious dynamic influences that have been described, and only to a very slight extent in the later stages of the last-named group of races has any conscious desire for change or improvement exerted any influence.

It may be willingly admitted that the most advanced state that has been reached even by the highest social types is still far from ideal, still, indeed, low, compared with what liberal minds are capable of conceiving, but this is not to the point in pure sociology. The question here is: Has there been social evolution? When we remember that only a few centuries ago the same races that have produced Laplace, Goethe, Newton, and Linnæus, occupying nearly the same territory, were warlike barbarians living in tents and fighting with bows and arrows and spears, there seems small warrant for questioning social evolution in these races. On this point Galton, in defense of a false proposition, still truly says: —

Man was barbarous but yesterday, and therefore it is not to be expected that the natural aptitudes of his race should already have become moulded into accordance with his very recent advance. We, men of the present cen-

2 G

turies, are like animals suddenly transplanted among new conditions of
climate and of food : our instincts fail us under the altered circumstances. . . .
My view is corroborated by the conclusion reached at the end of each of the
many independent lines of ethnological research — that the human race
were utter savages in the beginning; and that, after myriads of years of barbarism, man has but very recently found his way into the paths of morality
and civilization.[1]

To practically the same effect Letourneau says : —

Can it be said, with respect to benevolent and humanitarian sentiments,
that man has not progressed since primitive times ? It would be folly so to
maintain. At the outset man was scarcely to be distinguished from the
other higher mammals. His benevolent sentiments were feeble, intermittent,
easily set aside by his instincts and egoistic wants; but little by little, as
the pressure of hunger was relieved, his egoism became less fierce. At first
men only loved their children and this only for a brief period after the manner of animals, then they took more or less care of the aged and infirm.
For a long time kindness was only shown to members of the family, of the
tribe. But in modern times and among civilized nations, except in the case
of war, men have reached the point where they concede rights in certain
matters. Without too great optimism we may be allowed to believe that
humanitarian sentiments are destined to spread much farther. But this
noble side of the ethical man has developed very slowly in the human mind,
as we find exceptional traces of it even among the lower human types, who,
in this respect as in many others, indicate the successive steps taken by the
higher specimens of humanity. Thus it will not be without interest to study
in various races the manifestations of altruistic sentiments and the gradual
transition from the animal conscience to the human conscience.[2]

But most of the computations of human progress have been made
from a much smaller sociological parallax, viz., that which human
history presents. I do not see how any one can read history without
seeing this. Scarcely any of the shocking acts that blacken almost
every page of the history of every country would be even possible
to-day in any country. Kings did not hesitate to chop off the heads
or put out the eyes of their own sons whom they feared might seek
to usurp the throne. At every political revolution all the leaders of
the unsuccessful party were promptly put to death. Even as late
as the Medicis and " Bloody Mary " systematic massacres of all who
opposed the existing régime were ordered and carried out. Often in

[1] " Hereditary Genius," London, 1892, p. 337.
[2] " La Sociologie," etc., pp. 159-160. The chapter which follows this passage
undertakes to trace the growth of benevolent sentiments, but the treatment is brief.
The author felt this, and soon after, devoted an entire volume to the subject : L'Evolution de la Morale, Paris, 1894.

war no quarter was given, and that holy race, the Hebrews, who have given the civilized world its moral and religious standards, when they attacked a weaker people for the purpose of seizing and possessing their lands, usually, as their own inspired chronicles record, slew every man, woman, and child and left no soul to breathe. Children of the present day who are made to read such atrocities rarely have any conception of their meaning, their comprehension being mostly blurred and dazed by the "sacred" style of the Bible, which is simply the kind of English that everybody wrote in the time of King James. To-day there is a code of "civilized warfare," and any race or nation that violates it is considered uncivilized. Not only this, but in fighting uncivilized races civilized nations must conform to this code. Even as I write (April, 1902) there is a great moral uproar about the application to the insurgent Filipinos of a certain "water-cure" test that these same Filipinos have taught to the American soldiers, a test which from all accounts is much less severe than many of the "hazing" tests that are applied in our leading universities, for the crime of being a Freshman.

Mr. Spencer has gone over much of this ground [1] more at length than seems necessary here. A keen and sympathetic writer, Mr. Robert Blatchford, states the same truth in the following form : —

There was a time when women were tortured for witchcraft; when prisoners were tortured into the confession of crimes of which they were innocent; when good men and women were burnt alive for being unable to believe the dogmas of other men's religion; when authors had their ears cut off for telling the truth; when English children were worked to death in the factories ; when starving workmen were hanged for stealing a little food; when boards of capitalists and landlords fixed the workers' wages; when Trades Unionism was conspiracy, and only rich men had votes. Those days are gone; those crimes are impossible; those wrongs are abolished. And for these changes we have to thank the agitators.[2]

I quote the last sentence of this paragraph because it is suggestive. It raises the question: What is the cause of this change? Many will not agree with Mr. Blatchford that it is wholly or chiefly due to agitation. Others will make agitation in part an effect as well as a cause. At most the agitator is only a proxi-

---

[1] "Principles of Ethics," Vol. I, New York, 1892, pp. 293 ff. (Appendix to Part I. — The Conciliation). See also p. 408 (§ 160).

[2] "Merrie England," People's Edition, London, 1894, p. 193.

mate cause. I have no disposition to underrate or disparage the agitator. I undertook in Chapter V to analyze his social status, and found him to be essentially a social idealist or social artist. But there must be deeper causes that not only create the agitator and the reformer but that also created the quality of the moral and mental soil in which the seeds they sow will take root and grow. It is these deeper causes that we are seeking. They are many, but may for the most part be reduced to one, viz., the growth of sympathy in the human breast. For although sympathy cannot be depended upon as an economic force, still, without it moral reform would be impossible. By this I mean something definite and not a vague generality. I mean that those who suffer wrong and oppression could never have acquired the power to wrest justice from their oppressors without the aid of a widespread sympathy in their cause on the part of others than themselves, I had almost said, on the part of their oppressors. This recalls the paradox that I formulated fourteen years ago, viz., that "reforms are chiefly advocated by those who have no personal interest in them." [1] This taken in connection with the other paradox stated on the same page, viz., that "discontent increases with the improvement of the social condition," [2] furnishes the basis for arriving at a comprehension of some of the most subtle, and at the same time, some of the most potent causes of the moral advancement of the world. But into such questions we cannot now enter.

To any one who has read history it really is superfluous to enumerate examples of the superiority of modern to former civilization, even a few centuries back, but there are some kinds of evidence that lie deep and are known to but few. I will mention only one, and this on the authority of a Russian criminologist as set forth in a work that has not yet been translated into the better-known languages. This is a work on "Capital Punishment," by Wladimir Solieff, a chapter from which he has contributed to the *Revue Internationale de Sociologie* for March, 1898. From this I take the following extract : —

---

[1] *The American Anthropologist*," Vol. II, Washington, April, 1889, p. 123.

[2] To the illustrations supplied in that paper should be added that of the Reformation, which did not break out until many of the concessions demanded had been granted and the abuses had greatly diminished. This is forcibly shown by Guizot in the twelfth lecture of his course on the general history of civilization in Europe (4th edition, Paris, 1840, pp. 354–355).

Besides the constantly increasing legislative restrictions of the death penalty, progress is manifested still more directly by the extraordinary diminution in death sentences, and especially in sentences that have been carried out. In the last century, notwithstanding the comparatively less density of population, the number punished with death in the different states of Europe were counted by the tens of thousands. Thus in England, during the last fourteen years of the reign of Henry the Eighth, 72,000 persons were put to death, or an average of 5000 per annum. Under the reign of Elizabeth they count 89,000 executions, or about 2000 per annum. At the beginning of the nineteenth century, in spite of the notably increased population, we see in place of these thousands of annual executions, some dozens or hundreds at most; in the interval of the first twenty years (1806–1825) 1615 delinquents suffered death, that is, about 80 per annum. During the reign of Queen Victoria the number thus punished annually fluctuates between 10 and 38. In France during the twenties the annual number condemned to death still amounted to 72, while during the thirties it was only 30, during the forties, 39, during the fifties, 28, during the sixties, 11, during the seventies, also 11, during the eighties, only 5. In Austria the average number during the sixties was 7, and during the seventies it went down to 2.[1]

If statistics could be obtained for all countries now civilized and for, say, a thousand years, they would probably show a similar gradual decline in the death penalty throughout the world and for all this time. It may be taken not merely as a rude measure of the moral progress of the world, but more specifically of the increasing valuation of life, and this could then be projected backward to the time when at the death of a king thousands were sacrificed on his tomb, and many voluntarily gave up their lives for what seems to us such a trivial cause.

The subject might be looked at from a great number of distinct points of view and everywhere it would be found that human life has been in process of mitigation for a long period. The gradual emancipation of woman would prove one of the most fruitful of these lines, but perhaps enough has already been said on this point, especially under the heads of romantic love and conjugal love. Under ethical dualism the general progress of altruism was traced in ever expanding cycles. In art progress has gone on, but some arts have declined as others rose, notably sculpture and the purely literary art in favor of nature representation and scientific delineation. Music seems to be on the decline, but this may be only apparent, while the seeming decline of painting may be

[1] *Revue Internationale de Sociologie*, sixième année, mars, 1898, pp. 183–184.

due to the fact that the conservatism of art is so slow in yielding due meed to new schools, as was the case of the school of Millet; and then there is probably something in the doctrine of "peasantism," which seeks to rescue art from the exclusive control of the leisure class and place it at the disposal of the humblest of mankind. Progress may be quantitative rather than qualitative.

As regards intellectual progress, there surely is no call for defending it. It is the characteristic mark of all modern civilization, and even those who deny its influence in bettering mankind never question the enormous strides that knowledge, science, and the practical arts have made. I shall not reargue here the proposition I have so often defended that material civilization is essentially moralizing, but will close this chapter with the words of James Bryce, who, after descanting upon the triumphs of modern science, says : —

Still greater has been the influence of a quickened moral sensitiveness and philanthropic sympathy. The sight of preventible evil is painful, and is felt as a reproach. He who preaches patience and reliance upon natural progress is thought callous. The sense of sin may, as theologians tell us, be declining; but the dislike to degrading and brutalizing vice is increasing : there is a warmer recognition of the responsibility of each man for his neighbor, and a more earnest zeal in works of moral reform.[1]

[1] *The American Commonwealth*, London and New York, 1888, Vol. II, p. 407 (3d ed., 1895, Vol. II, p. 539).

PART III

TELESIS

CHAPTER XVI

THE DIRECTIVE AGENT

The intellectual forces, treated in the last section of the last chapter devoted to the dynamic agent, might seem to form a natural and easy transition to the treatment of the intellect or directive agent. This arrangement is certainly logical, but when we come to realize what the intellect really is, it will become apparent that there is no transition possible from feeling to thought or from intellect as a seat of emotion, appetite, and motive power to intellect as the organ or source of thought and ideas. The distinction is generic and there are no intermediate stages or gradations from the one to the other. They are phenomena of entirely different orders and do not admit of comparison. The attempt to reduce one to the other would be like attempting to reduce feet to pounds. Indeed, they are more unlike than any two different measurable units, since while one is in a sense measurable, being a force, the other is wholly incommensurable, being a relation. This absolute distinction is not in the least affected by the admission that I would myself freely make, that thought is a consequence of feeling, *i.e.*, a relation between feelings, for the thought is neither of the terms between which the relation subsists, but only the relation itself.

THE OBJECTIVE FACULTIES

The dynamic agent resides entirely in the subjective faculties of mind, and thus far attention has been wholly concentrated on those faculties. The directive agent resides exclusively in the objective faculties, and we have now to concentrate our attention on these faculties and to search after their true nature. It was shown in the sixth and seventh chapters that mind was of dual nature, subjective and objective, but its objective side could not be treated there. The science of subjective psychic phenomena ought to be called *esthetics*, and was so called by Kant in his "Transcendental Æsthetics." That of objective psychic phenomena is properly called

457

noetics, and this term was used, at least as an adjective, by Aristotle,[1] though in a somewhat different sense. Sir William Hamilton revived it and defined it as embracing "all those cognitions that originate in the mind itself."[2] The noun noetics would then become a new and useful term, while noetic would be nearly synonymous with intellectual. We might also have the corresponding word *noology*, which would not be synonymous with noetics, but would differ from it as all words thus formed differ from each other.

In the present chapter we can only give a brief *logical* treatment of objective psychic phenomena, leaving their historical or genetic treatment for the next chapter. This can be brief, because it is the only kind of treatment that is to be found in works on "intellectual philosophy," which until recently constituted the only treatment of the mind that any one thought worth offering. It cannot be said that this department has been slighted, and there remains scarcely anything to be said that can be called new. The sociologist does not need all that exists relating to this subject, and for our present purpose a small part of it is sufficient. We can well spare the reader any extended survey of the nature of the senses as the original sources of the materials of the mind, and confine ourselves to the principal steps in the psychologic process leading up to thought. We cannot, however, ignore the phenomena of sensation which lie at the foundation of both the subjective and the objective operations of the mind.

The classification of sensations is the most fundamental of all considerations relative to mental phenomena. The duality begins here, and the two great trunks that diverge from this point never again approach each other but always remain distinct. The two kinds of sensation, which I distinguish as *intensive sensation* and *indifferent sensation*, form the two primary roots of the mind, the subjective root and the objective root, and from this origin the two trunks rise as if separate and independent trees. By intensive sensation, as I have explained in Chapter VII, we must understand that form of sensation which constitutes an *interest* for the organ-

---

[1] "Nichomachean Ethics," VI, 2, 6. "Νοητικῶν μορίων" is here usually translated "intellectual parts," whereby the word *noetic* has been lost to modern languages.

[2] "Lectures on Metaphysics," by Sir William Hamilton, edited by H. L. Mansel and John Veitch, Edinburgh and London, 1859, Vol. II, pp. 349–350 (Lecture XXXVIII).

ism, and which must therefore be, to however slight a degree, agreeable or the reverse, and thus calculated to prompt action. This is the root of the subjective faculties as worked out in that chapter, the biologic origin of which was set forth at length. Out of this grew the whole affective and motor side of mind constituting the dynamic agent.

We have now to do with the other kind of sensation called indifferent, and we shall find that out of this has grown the entire objective, intellectual, or noetic department of mind. It was Reid[1] who first and most clearly explained and illustrated indifferent sensation, and distinguished it from intensive sensation, although of course he did not employ these terms. True, it need only be stated to be perceived by all that the sense of touch is so constituted that it is often possible to experience very distinct and vivid sensations that are neither pleasurable nor painful in the slightest degree. Probably every point on the surface of the body is capable of such sensations, but some parts are far more susceptible to them than others, as for example, the ends or "balls" of the fingers as compared with the back of the hand or even the corresponding parts of the toes. Everybody always knew this, but the meaning of it had never been reflected upon. Reid did not of course grasp its full meaning, but he drew special attention to the fact. Most persons who ever think of it at all probably look upon it as a question of degree, and would say that a painful sensation might be gradually diminished until it became an indifferent one. This is probably not the case at all, and the two kinds of sensations not only belong to two distinct orders, but are probably conveyed by different sets of nerves, as distinct as are the gustatory nerves of the tongue and palate from the monitory or pain nerves of the same organs. But Reid did not merely point out the distinction, he also showed that it was through these sensations that are neither pleasurable nor painful that the mind is able to distinguish objects, *i.e.*, that it gains its notions of the different properties of bodies. This is the important fact. Intensive sensations do not convey such notions. In fact it is through indifferent sensations and through these alone that sen-

[1] The Works of Thomas Reid, D.D., now fully collected with selections from his unpublished letters. Preface, notes, and supplementary dissertations by Sir William Hamilton. Prefixed, Stewart's account of the life and writings of Reid. Sixth edition, Edinburgh, 1863, Vol. I. A. "Inquiry into the Human Mind," Chapter V, Section II, p. 118.

tient beings acquire all their knowledge of the properties of bodies, and thus acquaint themselves with the nature of the external world. It is through them that we are enabled to gain a knowledge of the environment, and thereby to adapt ourselves to it. Indifferent sensation constitutes the primary source of all *knowledge ; i.e.*, knowledge of properties as distinguished from qualities.

The names given by different psychologists to the several steps in the objective psychologic process differ, and there has been a great amount of vague discussion indicating much confusion of thought. Without going into the subject with a view to clearing up the confusion I will indicate by simple terms what seem to be the principal steps in the process, and if any one prefers different terms it is of no moment, provided the process is understood. The first psychologic fact is the indifferent sensation, but this is produced by an object, so that the contact of an object with the nerves of sense is the initial step. This may be called an *impression*, employed in such a special sense as to exclude the sensation. It is thus the simple fact that an object comes into contact with the part of the body that is to experience and convey the sensation. The second fact or step is the *sensation*. I shall not attempt to follow the neurosis of the process, but shall adhere as closely as possible to the phenomena of psychosis. We have already seen what an indifferent sensation is. It is a distinct awareness, but unattended by any intensive, we might almost say, moral, quality. It arouses no *interest*, and therefore prompts no action. This stage, however, is certainly subjective — it is a feeling. In an intensive sensation, which is psychologically coördinate with indifferent sensation, the next step is a disposition to act. But in an indifferent sensation there is no such disposition. It is exactly here that the two great departments of mind diverge. Although indifferent in the sense of not arousing a subjective interest, the kind of sensation we are now considering does give rise to a series of psychologic steps, but they are objective, in that they all relate to the object that has impressed the sense. The sensation conveys to the mind a *notion* of the object. Some *property*, if it be only that of resistance, is made known to the mind. Every property that really causes a sensation is reported at once to the mind and recorded there. What shall this fact be called ? For it I prefer the old and well-known term, *perception*.

Perception, then, is the first objective step in the psychologic process, and from this fact it seems appropriate to call the objective faculties of the mind *perceptive,* and to use this term as the antithesis to the term *affective* applicable to the subjective faculties. Then, without inventing a new term we can use the same word perception in the passive sense for the record of a property conveyed to the mind through perception in the active sense, but it is better in purely scientific and technical language to use the shorter form *percept* for the *state* of consciousness, if I may be allowed to use that somewhat obsolete term, reserving the fuller form perception for the *act* of consciousness of conveying a notion of a property to the mind. The external world consists of objects, and these are constantly appealing to all the senses. It would seem that a single day in any ordinary environment would be sufficient to fill the mind with percepts so that no more could be added. But the psychologists have explained that the mind almost immediately learns to sift its materials, so that wholly useless percepts are not only not retained in consciousness, but are not allowed to occupy it. They are virtually excluded from it, and the result is the same as if only percepts of some supposed value were received.

Every object is a complex of properties, and if all the properties of an object be supposed to have been perceived there exist in the mind a large number of percepts. The next step is to unite these percepts into one, so that there shall be a state of consciousness corresponding to the whole object. The process by which this is done is called *conception,* and the product is a conception of the object, or a *concept.* Objects are not necessarily material, though there must be an ultimate material basis for all perceptions and conceptions. A property is a force of some kind residing in an object, and all the immaterial objects, such as love, justice, position, direction, distance, etc., are *relations* growing out of material things, and, though not properties, are perceivable and conceivable things, and are capable of generating percepts and concepts.

The next step in the psychologic process is to compare percepts and concepts and detect likenesses and differences. This process is sometimes called *judgment,* and the mental state corresponding to the act is a judgment. Here we are troubled to avoid using the same word in two senses, for we want to say that the mind *perceives* these likenesses and unlikenesses. This would make judgment another kind of perception. Considerable was said in the last chapter

relative to this process of mental exploration for identities, because
this act of mind is highly pleasurable and constitutes one of the
most effective of the sociogenetic forces. We are now concerned
only with the psychologic process, which is a different aspect of the
same general fact. Judgment in this restricted sense is the simplest
form of this mental exploration, and the more complex forms more
properly receive the name of *ideation*, the products being ideas,
which are creations of the mind in a very proper sense of the word
creation. This form of creation, however, is to be distinguished from
the form called *imagination*, in which the products are not real, *i.e.*,
they are not discovered truths, but created fictions. In both cases
they are creations in the sense that they are new-made things not
previously existing in the mind, but in the one case they have a
corresponding objective reality, while in the other there is no real
condition to which they correspond.

Reasoning is simply a more complex form of ideation, and the
ratiocination or ergotism of the logicians is only one kind of reasoning and one little used by the ordinary mind. The highest form of
reasoning is generalization, whereby the larger conceptions and the
conclusions or deductions from the widest inductions are grouped
into still higher laws and truths and the maximum unity is attained
in the operations of mind.

Such is a brief sketch of the nature of the directive agent with a
view solely to distinguishing it clearly from the dynamic agent.

Control of the Dynamic Agent

The two great agents or agencies of society are the dynamic and
the directive. To the former of these ten chapters were devoted.
It has been a prolonged search for the underlying forces of society,
and most readers will probably admit that the search has not been
in vain. We have dealt solely with the propelling force of society,
comparable to the wind that fills the sails or the steam power that
turns the screw of a vessel at sea. We have found an abundance of
this power, and we have seen what results it has accomplished. But
the social forces are natural forces and obey mechanical laws. They
are blind impulses. This is as true of the spiritual as of the physical forces. Natural or genetic restraints there certainly are, and we
have analyzed these and shown in what ways they take the place
of rational control and permit social evolution to go on. But thus

far the influence of ideas has been kept as completely out of view as possible, at least as a controlling agency.

But an agency need not necessarily be a force. The directive agent is not such, and yet its influence is immense. The dynamic agent seeks its end directly, but the essential characteristic of the directive agent is indirection. It seeks its end through means. It is a guiding agency. It is to be compared to the helm of a ship, or rather to the man at the helm, or to a pilot. Clearly to see that this is not a force we have only to imagine the ship becalmed. It matters not how skillful the helmsman, he is powerless without the propelling agent. And so society would instantly stop in its whole career should the dynamic agent — the wants and passions of men — fail for any cause, and cease to propel the social bark. Nevertheless, social evolution must always remain on a comparatively low plane unless raised to a higher level and guided to better things by the directive agent — the rational faculty of man. It is profitless to compare the respective values of two agencies both of which are absolutely essential to any high development.

As we have seen, the restraint and control of social energy is the only condition to social evolution. All true forces are in themselves essentially centrifugal and destructive. There are two ways in which the social energy has been controlled, the one an unconscious process comparable to that of organic evolution, and indeed to that of inorganic evolution in the formation of world systems, the other conscious, and wholly unlike the first. The unconscious method was fully set forth in Chapter X, and is that by which all social structures have been formed. The conscious method remains to be considered. It is the telic method or social telesis. Through the unconscious or genetic method — social genesis — all the fundamental social structures or human institutions were formed or constructed, and under the operations of the several dynamic principles considered in Chapter XI, these structures were enabled to change and social progress was made possible. Moreover, through the several sociogenetic forces, though still genetic, a certain degree of socialization was achieved and civilization was carried forward to a certain stage. It only required the addition of the telic or directive agent to make possible all the higher steps that have been taken practically in the same direction.

It was sufficiently difficult, in considering the ontogenetic and

phylogenetic forces, to leave out of view the more or less simultaneous and constantly increasing sociogenetic factors, but most embar-
rassing of all has been, all through our analysis of the strictly
genetic influences at work in society, to keep in the background the
effects of the telic agent, which, though theoretically later in origin,
has still been constantly on the scene since the dawn of manhood,
and was, indeed, as it has been necessary repeatedly to insist, the
distinguishing characteristic of man, and the condition precedent to
every event that typifies the human race and makes man other than
a simple constituent of the animal fauna of the globe. But in the
next chapter it will be shown that throughout all the earlier stages
of man's prehistoric, and even of his early historic career, this telic
faculty was so exclusively egoistic, and so completely an adjunct to
and servant of the dynamic agent or human will that it accomplished
little more than to heighten and strengthen man's fierce passions,
and sometimes, as in the subjection of woman, its effect was positively retrogressive, at least for a time. The egoistic reason is
normally centrifugal. When it is employed exclusively in guiding
its possessor to the more complete attainment of the satisfaction of
desire it vastly increases the waywardness of men in their tendencies
to make feeling an end at the expense of function. All through
man's early history, therefore, and to a large extent throughout his
later history and in the most advanced stages of society, the group
reason has been compelled to counteract these effects, and has constructed vast systems of religion to this end. But even these have
often overshot their mark by imagining hostile powers and leading
men into the most extravagant follies and shocking practices that
largely neutralize their beneficial influence upon society. For error
is itself the offspring of reason.

That primitive reasoning and early philosophy are anthropomorphic is now well understood by all, but it has escaped observation that the refined speculations of the philosophers of antiquity,
medieval times, and largely of more modern times, are also anthropomorphic. These philosophers have specially studied the human
mind, by which they always mean the objective, never the subjective, faculties. They early discovered the telic principle, but they
did not find it in the human mind. They only found it, or rather,
implanted it, in the mind of a divine being of their own creation,
and did not discover that they had taken the materials for it from

their own minds. As far back as Plato we find the germs of a doctrine that afterwards took the name of *teleology*, but this doctrine would be better called *theoteleology*, since it simply postulates a power outside of nature directing it toward some end. A careful scrutiny of the fundamental character of the rational faculty, or intellect, reveals the fact that it always operates on the telic or teleological principle. This principle may therefore be called *anthropoteleology*, although if any other being, whether lower or higher than man, can be shown to possess an intellect it must necessarily employ the same method.

If, then, we take a comprehensive view of all the phenomena of society we will see that they fall under two radically distinct classes, and we shall have the purely spontaneous or natural phenomena of society, on the one hand, produced by the dynamic agent, and the phenomena that result from intention or design, on the other hand, which are the products of the directive agent in the sense that but for the directive agent they would not have taken place. An iceberg breaks loose from its Arctic moorings and drifts across the Atlantic. It is sighted by an ocean steamer on its way from Liverpool to New York. The iceberg drifts on under the influence of wind and current, strikes the Gulf Stream and is borne away toward the coast of Norway, having pursued a very irregular, zigzag path, and ultimately melts away. The steamer pursues the definite course marked out for it on the charts and finally is brought by a pilot through the windings of New York harbor and is safely moored at the dock. The phenomena presented by the iceberg are strictly genetic, those presented by the ocean liner are mainly telic, although in both cases the forces of propulsion are nothing but dynamic forces producing motion in a straight line in the direction in which they act. The irregularities in the course of the iceberg are due to a plurality of genetic forces and represent their resultant direction. The bendings and windings executed by the vessel are due to externally imposed forces of direction from the intelligence of man, and are telic, or anthropoteleological.

Telic phenomena may also be called artificial, as distinguished from natural in the sense of genetic. For all art is telic. The distinction is sometimes said to be that between growth and manufacture, for growth is the type of the genetic process in organic nature, while manufacture is the final stage in art and results in wholly

2 H

artificial products. Social phenomena frequently illustrate this distinction on a large scale, as in the two classes of cities and towns,
those which have merely grown up spontaneously along certain
ancient lines, as along the paths that the cows originally followed in
coming home to be fed (said to be the origin of the streets of Boston),
and those, like Washington, that have been laid out on paper by an
engineer before there was any population, and the plan adhered to as
the city grew. In every case the forces of nature are directed and
controlled by the intellect. In the last case the dynamic agent of
society is thus directed, and in sociology the problem always ultimately becomes that of controlling the social forces. Left to themselves they blindly impel or propel mankind, and the world drifts
as aimlessly as the iceberg. The mission of the directive agent is
to guide society through no matter how tortuous a channel to the
safe harbor of social prosperity.

THE FINAL CAUSE

The directive agent is a final cause. Genetic phenomena are produced by efficient causes only. In an efficient cause a force acts
upon a body and impels it in the direction in which the force acts.
This is the simplest form, but most examples are compound. There
is a plurality of forces having different intensities and acting in
different directions. The body impressed has a motion of its own
and reacts upon the impinging bodies. Any degree of complication
may be imagined, but the principle is not affected and the general
effect will always be the exact resultant or algebraic sum of all the
forces involved. All natural, spontaneous, or genetic phenomena
conform to this law. There must be contact, impact, collision, pressure, always a *vis a tergo*. If we call the effect the end, then,
in genetic phenomena the effect is always in immediate contact
with the cause. This is as true of cell growth, or of the action
of the neurons of the brain in generating a thought, as it is of
two billiard balls. There is no "*actio in distans*," and the phrase
simply expresses our ignorance of the nature of certain media and
forces.

In contradistinction to this definition of an efficient cause, a final
cause is always more or less remote from its effect or end. This is
implied in the term *final*. We are now to inquire how this can be.
It has been repeatedly said that the directive agent is not a force.

It may now be equally said that a final cause is not a force. It is not, however, a simple, but a complex conception. No less than three things are embraced in the idea of a final cause. The end is *seen, i.e.,* known, by the mind. Some natural property or force is also known to exist and its action upon the material things to be moved is understood. This force or property is a means to the end, and it is only necessary to adjust the body to be moved in such a manner that the known natural force will impel it to the perceived end. This adjustment is usually accomplished by the exercise of muscular force of the agent in obedience to his will. Both the natural force and the muscular force are efficient causes, and all the motion is the result of these two forces. The final cause therefore consists essentially in the *knowledge* of the telic agent of the nature of the natural force and the relations subsisting between the subject, the object, the force, and the end.

This again is the simplest case, but no matter how complex the case may be it may be reduced to this simple form. As we saw in the case of the ship, natural forces alone propel. The helmsman exerts a slight muscular force at the wheel, but it is his knowledge of the effect of turning the wheel this way or that and so much, that constitutes his direction of the ship. The captain may simply command the man at the wheel, and thus, so far as he is concerned, reduce the muscular effort to that of speaking. The three steps are: knowledge, adjustment, natural force. The last is what " does the work." Without the knowledge the adjustment would be impossible, and without the adjustment the force would be ineffectual. The force and the adjustment are really both means, but in common language the latter is neglected, and it may then be said that a final cause is the rational employment of the means to an end. The means is always an efficient cause, so that final causes consist in the intelligent command or utilization of efficient causes or the forces of nature. This approaches very close to the formula used as a definition of civilization: " the utilization of the materials and forces of nature," and when closely viewed it is seen that civilization chiefly consists in the exercise of the telic faculty. If we regard all the forces of nature, including even the social forces, as so many means to the ends of man and society, telesis becomes the adjustment of means to ends, and all human effort is expended upon the means. There is a suggestive analogy here between intelligence and instinct, which latter, as we saw in Chapter VII, consists in the development of a desire for a means, brought about by natural selection to secure the ends of function. And now here on the higher human plane we find mankind in full pursuit of a great variety of means through which alone the attainment of cherished ends becomes possible.

In efficient causes the effect is always exactly equal to the cause. In final causes the effect is usually wholly out of proportion to the cause, if by cause we here mean the personal effort put forth. The cause and effect are really not commensurable, since the effort is not directed to the end at all. But speaking loosely the effect may be said to be in normal cases much greater than the cause, and in certain cases it is enormously greater. The adjustment may require very small outlay of energy, while the force into whose way the object may be thus placed may be exceedingly powerful. This is well exemplified in electric motors where the powerful circuits are cut and restored by a mere touch of the button. As a rule effort and intelligence are inversely proportional, so that the disproportion between cause and effect increases with man's knowledge of natural forces. This has been the constant tendency of science, which is nothing else than the grasp of natural laws and processes, so that the control and utilization of the powers of nature have kept pace with the growth of the telic faculty.

A final cause may therefore represent any amount of natural force that the intellect of man can reduce to his service. It is practically unlimited. The intellect has it in its power to subjugate all nature and to reduce all the forces of nature to the condition of contributors to man's needs. How far this process can be carried it is certainly too early to predict, especially in the light of what has been accomplished in the last two centuries, chiefly in the last one century. When we consider how little was done in this direction in all the ages that preceded the era of science, how little all the races of the world, outside of the one race that leads the movement, have ever done, and compare this with the achievements of that one race during this brief space of time, we dare not attempt to peer into the future. And when we realize that all this is the result of thought set in the right direction and devoted to things, which are, as we have seen, essentially dynamic, we may truly say that thought is the sum of all forces.

THE METHOD OF MIND

The method of mind is the precise opposite of the method of nature. The method of nature with unlimited resources is to produce an enormously redundant supply and trust the environment to select the best. This survival of the fittest involves a sacrifice of a great majority. It is therefore in a high degree wasteful. The number rejected is far greater than the number selected, and therefore all the energy expended in producing the ones that are rejected is wasted energy. It is a method of trial and error. Nature aims only at success, and success is secured through the indefinite multiplication of chances.[1] The alleged economy of nature is reduced to the fact that in the nature of things the genetic method can only evolve products adapted to the conditions of existence and therefore potentially successful. The failure of the greater number is due to the physical impossibility that all shall survive, and competition decides the fate of the less adapted. All genetic processes are characterized by this same prodigality. Everything accomplished by nature is uneconomical. If we can apply that term to inorganic nature it is the same there. Nature's operations are characterized by irregularity. Nothing is perfect. This aspect was considered in Chapter V, and this it is which the modern mind regards as beautiful. It is the shapelessness of natural objects, such as a cloud, a landscape, a coast line, or a mountain range that we admire. It is true that there is order in it if we can grasp a large enough mass and overlook the details, but seen in its entirety the world of nature is amorphous. This heterogeneity is chiefly caused by the two laws of the instability of the homogeneous and the multiplication of effects, or better perhaps, the exaggeration of effects. Change in a given direction, instead of tending to right itself, tends to produce greater change in the same direction, until all symmetry is lost. This will go on until some other influence

---

[1] I formulated the law of biologic economics in 1892 in my address to the Section of Economic Science and Statistics of the American Association for the advancement of Science at its Rochester Meeting. See the *Proceedings*, Vol. XLI, pp. 301–321; also published in a somewhat condensed form in the *Annals of the American Academy of Political and Social Science*, Vol. III, January, 1893, pp. 464–482. In a much expanded form this general discussion constitutes Chapter XXXIII of the " Psychic Factors of Civilization," 1893. Professor Huxley in his " Prolegomena " (1894) to " Evolution and Ethics " (Romanes Lecture, 1893) struck the same note, and his conclusions are the same as mine. In fact the discussion here follows the same lines as my address and differs chiefly in the illustrations. See " Collected Essays," Vol. IX.

unrelated to the first puts a check upon it. This usually produces a different kind of irregularity and complicates the process. There are certain great laws that must be conformed to. For example, water from a higher level must ultimately find a lower level and eventually the lowest possible level, but the course it will pursue in doing this will have the utmost irregularity. Hence the sinuous course of rivers, in which every drop of water usually travels at least twice, often many times as far as the actual distance from the source to the mouth of the river. Every deviation from a straight course increases the tendency to deviate still further, and this goes on until some insurmountable obstacle is encountered, when some other oblique course is taken and the same effects are repeated, and so on to the end.

Organic phenomena obey the same uneconomical laws, and thus all the strange and hideous denizens of the earth are thrust into existence — vermin of all horrid shapes, toads, lizards, Jurassic dragons (Dinosaurs), the monsters of the sea and of the land, even the huge ungainly mastodons, elephants, walruses, and whales, along of course with more shapely and many truly beautiful creatures. All these are only a few "favored" forms wrought at enormous expense and involving infinite sacrifice of life and energy. But it matters nothing, as the resources of nature are infinite. Such is the economy of nature, which is simply the absence of all economy.

The only true economy is telic. Only mind knows how to economize. Economy is only possible through prevision. Mind sees the end and pursues it. Still it must not be supposed that it pursues it directly, or in a straight line. Indirection, as we have seen, is its essence. But it pursues it effectively. Only the irrational seek their ends directly, but they fail to attain them. True economy harnesses the forces of nature and simply guides them to the foreseen end. "*Science, d'où prévoyance; prévoyance, d'où action.*" [1] Knowledge gives foresight, and foresight dictates the proper steps. In telic action there is no waste, or at least the waste is reduced to the minimum for the given state of any science, with the prospect of progressive reduction as the science and skill advance. Artificial watercourses are straight, or as nearly so as comports with the maximum economy. Schiaparelli rightly maintained that the rectilinear form of the "canals" on the surface of the planet Mars,

---

[1] Auguste Comte, "Philosophie Positive," Vol. I, p. 51.

indicate à *priori* the work of intelligent beings. It is only their great size and the extraordinary labor involved in their construction that staggers the observer. But Mars may have been inhabited by beings as advanced as the leading races of our planet for half a million years, and when we consider the transformations that man has made on the surface of the earth in a few thousand years, for the most part during two or three centuries, we can only imagine what he will do in the next ten thousand or hundred thousand years. We are utterly incapable of grasping such possibilities.

Noetic phenomena are far more rapid than genetic. We need not go back to the lifeless world building and rock building of the inorganic world, but compare the development of a floral organ or of a fin, a foot, or a wing. Take the paleontological record of any well-known line, even one as modern as the horse. It has taken at least five million years to unite the five digits of Eohippus into the one solid digit or hoof of the horse. It requires millions of years to produce an organic structure. Social structures, even the purely genetic ones, grow, evolve, and change far more rapidly than organic structures. But telic structures are comparatively of mushroom growth. How brief is the life of the factory, the steamship, the railway, the telegraph, the telephone, the bicycle (already in its dotage), the automobile! Yet most of these are giants, and if they do not stay it will be because a superior substitute will take their places. The law of telic phenomena seems to be a geometrical progression, every new structure breeding a brood of younger and better ones.

Such is the method of mind, and in its upward reaches it attains enormous complexity. It is said that intellectual operations cannot be predicted. Still they are subject to a few of the most general laws. But they have in the later stages of social evolution come to constitute so large a factor that they have wholly frustrated the plans of the political economists who refused to reckon with them. Sociology must not make this mistake, and all systems that ignore the directive agent are doomed to the same failure that has attended the political economy that was based on the " economic man." Both economics and sociology have a psychologic basis, but that basis is as broad as mind itself. Not only must all the interests of men, including their cerebral interests, be recognized, but the faculties upon which the highest types of men chiefly rely for the certain

success of those interests — the objective faculties — must be equally
recognized and thoroughly understood.

IDEA FORCES

Well and wisely did Bacon say that "truth is more easily extri-
cated from error than from confusion." It has ever been the bane
of the science of mind that mental phenomena that are generically
distinct and not even commensurable have been perpetually and inextricably jumbled together. This has been especially the case with
subjective and objective phenomena, which as we have seen belong
to two totally different orders of things. The expression idea forces
(*idées-forces*) represents one of these psychological jumbles, and is
equivalent to the expression *rudder-propulsion.* The human mind
sees certain effects of compound and combined forces and agencies,
and without even attempting to analyze the complex conditions
ascribes these effects to some one of the conditions. In this expression this is what is done, and it happens that the particular condition
to which the effects are attributed is not even a dynamic agency,
motor principle, or force in any sense of the word. This lack of
analysis has always characterized the philosophy of mind, and
modern psychology is far from being free from it. The logicians of
all men, like Hegel and Hamilton, are the ones who have introduced
the most illogical elements and caused the greatest confusion; as,
for example, such an expression as "the thinking will," when in fact
the will cannot think, and the faculty of thought cannot will.

What then can idea forces be? What do the authors who use the
expression mean by it? Nearly all aphoristic or epigrammatic expressions are literally incorrect. They usually involve an ellipsis,
and will not bear strict analysis. We should not be too critical of
them and pedantically exact. Bacon's saying that " knowledge itself
is a power,"[1] now a proverb, and in fact found in Proverbs (xxiv. 5),
is such an elliptical expression, as is also that other proverb that

---

[1] "Meditationes sacræ: Of Heresies." "Works," Philadelphia, 1844, Vol. I, p. 71.
Edmond About puts the same idea in the following form : "The history of civilization may be summarized in nine words : the more one knows, the more one can
perform," "Handbook of Social Economy, or, the Worker's A B C," by Edmond About (translated from the last French edition), New York, 1873, p. 29. The
original French is still more brief and epigrammatic : "L'histoire de la civilisation
peut se résumer en six mots : plus on sait, plus on peut," "A B C du Travailleur,"
par Edmond About, deuxième édition, Paris, 1869, p. 39.

"ideas rule the world." [1]   Johnson ventured a correction of Bacon's aphorism when he said that " knowledge is more than equivalent to force," [2] which brings it into line with the phrase that I have used, metaphorically, in this chapter, that "thought is the sum of all forces," but which I long ago more accurately framed in saying that "the final cause is not itself a cause, it is the appropriation of all causes." [3]   I have therefore no objection to the use of these comprehensive metaphors, even in scientific discussions, if only it does not result in the confusion of ideas.

Let us have idea forces, then, but let us explain their psychological significance.   Besides the general fact already brought out in dealing with final causes, that ideas do really appropriate and utilize for man all the forces of nature that he thoroughly understands, there is a more specific ground for the claim to the existence of idea forces.   The social forces, as I have so constantly insisted and so thoroughly demonstrated in Part II, consist of the whole volume of man's affective nature, but man, who even at the outset was a rational being, and who has steadily grown more rational during the whole course of his history, differs from animals in possessing two sources of feeling.   This could not be set forth in the treatment of the dynamic agent without anticipating considerations that belong here and could only be properly urged in connection with the directive agent.   All sentient beings have internal as well as external feelings, and the emotions, which are essentially internal, constitute everywhere the more powerful motives to action.   But in a rational being, and especially in a being that has acquired a store of ideas in the manner described in the early part of this chapter, there is a large class of feelings, indeed by far the larger part of the most important feelings that inspire action, which arise from ideas and not from external sense impressions, and to which no sense impressions could directly give rise.   Suppose a man receives a telegram announcing the death by accident of a child of his in another state or another country.   He does not see the child.   All he sees is a bit of paper with some markings on it.   But his soul is stirred to its very depths and he instantly acts according to the circumstances.   Such actions, and the life of every enlightened person is

[1] Cf. Comte, "Philosophie Positive," Vol. I, p. 40.
[2] Samuel Johnson, "The History of Rasselas," **Chapter XIII.**
[3] *The Monist*, Vol. V, January, 1895, p. 263.

chiefly made up of them, are called *ideo-motor* actions. It is not that the true force is not a feeling. Such feelings are the most intense and powerful of all, but they arise from *knowledge* in the mind, which is not feeling, but which arouses feeling. Such feelings are idea forces, and with this simple explanation the term ceases to be objectionable, and is in fact upon the whole useful.

It is thus that mind in the restricted sense of the intellect or rational faculty, although not a force in any scientific sense of the word, becomes a *factor*, and this is what I have had in mind in speaking of "mind as a social factor."[1] It has been working through all the ages and at all the stages of culture that were passed in review in Part II, and now we have only to go over all this long career of mankind and supply this factor at each stage and estimate its probable influence. This influence at length began to make itself strongly felt, and as we have seen, intellectual phenomena advance by a geometrical progression, so that it is the latest stages that show their impress in the most marked degree. This factor of direction, quite as much as the factor of propulsion, deserves to be accounted for, and to this task we shall next turn our attention.

[1] "Mind as a Social Factor," *Mind*, a Quarterly Journal of Psychology and Philosophy, London, Vol. IX, No. 36, October, 1884, pp. 563–573.

CHAPTER XVII

BIOLOGIC ORIGIN OF THE OBJECTIVE FACULTIES

THE thesis of this chapter is that the intellect is primarily an advantageous faculty and came into existence through the action of natural selection or the survival of the fittest in the struggle for existence. If so it is of biologic origin. The biologic origin of the feeling side of mind was the subject of Chapter VII. It was there shown that a few authors had recognized this, but no one had thoroughly analyzed the process. Thus far, however, no one to my knowledge has admitted the biologic origin of the thought side of mind or attempted to account for the intellect on natural principles. My own essay in this direction, constituting Part II of the "Psychic Factors of Civilization" and occupying more than a hundred pages, or about one-third of the work, after an interval of ten years still remains unique. The present chapter can be scarcely more than a condensation of that essay into much smaller space. I certainly have not changed my attitude on the subject, and the complete absence of discussion or even criticism has prevented me from advancing much beyond the point where I left it. I scarcely need insist that until the objective faculties are accounted for on natural principles there is no such thing as a science of psychology. Those who fail thus to account for them and still talk of the "science of mind" are wholly inconsistent. There is no science of what is unaccountable. They might as well talk of the science of ghosts or of witchcraft as of the science of mind unless mind be recognized as a natural reality, and demonology is as good a science as psychology so long as the object of the latter is as much a phantom as that of the former.

GENESIS OF MIND

In the last chapter the nature of objective mind was considered from a logical standpoint with a view to understanding the psychologic process in the individual mind. That form of treatment might also be called ontogenetic. We are now to consider it from a chronological, historical, or genetic standpoint, which may be looked upon as phylogenetic. The ontogenetic process or life history of a thought recapitulates in some sense the history of development of thought, though the connection between the two processes should not probably be insisted upon as causal. I have frequently spoken of the subjective and objective faculties as constituting the two great branches of mind in its full sense. It would have been better, and even more scientifically correct, to regard the objective faculties as a branch of the subjective considered as the main trunk. This is what Schopenhauer did, typifying the latter as the will, which we saw in Chapter VIII to be entirely permissible. For the intellect, as he maintained, is a relatively modern product, and he was also right in asserting that the will produced the intellect.[1] The objective faculties grew out of the subjective. He was right again in saying that the intellect was secondary in point of importance as well as of time. It was at first only ancillary, a servant of the will, a means to the attainment of the end of the feeling being. Its purpose was not to restrain and curb desire but to lead it to success. It was one of those extra-normal and unintended products, of which we have already met with so many, having no true place in the scheme of nature, which is organized solely in the interest of function. The intellect is therefore a typical epiphenomenon.

Notwithstanding, therefore, the extraordinary rôle that the study of mind in this sense has played in the history of philosophy, it has all been about a sort of "accident" that came into the world at a late and comparatively modern date, was not wanted nor welcomed, and for the greater part of its career held the position of vassal to that feudal lord, the will, which it not only served in abject submission, but, as we shall see, did not hesitate to stoop to acts of the meanest class and do the henchman's work of dark deeds and sinister practices. In short, it ministered to those very passions which the panegyrists of mind have always held too base to deserve a place in any scheme of philosophy. The reason why these philosophers did not see this is that they never studied the true intellect, the trunk and *souche* of the mind, but only certain of its later derivative branches that had lost most of the character of the parent faculty and formed a sort of excrescence or efflorescence whose brilliancy and ostentatious charms attracted and monopolized their attention, completely obscuring its true origin.

---

[1] "Ueber den Willen in der Natur," 4th edition, Leipzig, 1878, p. 39 (footnote).

Indifferent Sensation. — In the last chapter the importance of the two kinds of sensation, intensive and indifferent, was insisted upon, and it was pointed out that the latter is generically distinct from the former and is probably the effect of the existence of a separate class of nerves specialized exclusively for the purpose of conveying to the mind notions of the properties of objects. It now requires to be noted that this specialization constitutes the initial step in the genesis of the objective faculties. The lowest sentient beings are destitute of it and really have no need of any but intensive sensations, leading them to what is good for them and driving them away from what is injurious, *i.e.*, they only need to know the *qualities* of objects. But very early it becomes advantageous to a creature, independently of pleasure or pain, to gain a notion of the *properties* of certain leading constituents of its environment. Purely aquatic beings have less need of this because their medium is nearly homogeneous, but even life on the bottom of the sea, lake, or river, presents a certain degree of heterogeneity, and although the irregularities there met with may not tend to injure them, still success in procuring food and escaping enemies will be increased by a slight acquaintance with the nature of their environment. This advantage is seized upon by the principle of natural selection and those forms that acquire the power of discrimination among the objects with which they come in contact have their chances of survival increased and ultimately survive while the other class die out. Now it is clear that mere intensive sensation would not accomplish this object. It would not enable them to avoid danger by making a detour or to seek food by pursuing an irregular course. In fact, under the influence of intensive sensation alone there could be no interval between the organism and the source of pleasure or pain, between the body and its food or its enemy. Causation here would be of the strictly genetic type, in which, as we saw, cause and effect must be in immediate contact. It is so with the plant, with the polyp, sea-lily, sponge, and other fixed animals, and also with Protozoans that simply absorb nutriment from their media.

Intuition. — The simple power of beholding objects, I do not mean necessarily through an organ of sight, it may be only tactual, I call intuition, and hold it to be the primordial advantageous substrate of the objective mind. Its importance is shown by the fact that organs for this purpose are developed in so many very low organisms. They are not eyes at first, but sensitized areas, or specialized ends of tentacles, both of which ultimately become eyes. With the initial development of objective feeling — feeling that is neither good nor evil, but simply acquaints — the creature begins to explore its environment. Life becomes a series of more or less random trials. It is the stage of exploration or tentative stage. This initial faculty might be called *tentation*. The sea is the mother of all life, and no one knows how long there was life in the sea before the appearance of land animals. Paleontology teaches the long priority of marine life. In the Lower Silurian, and still more in the Cambrian, the waters were probably much warmer than they have ever been since, even in the tropics, and the internal heat of the earth doubtless contributed largely to this increased temperature. But long before any of the forms were developed that possessed parts capable of preservation in a fossil state there must have been myriads of soft, jelly-like organisms, protozoan in structure, and probably for the most part microscopic or very minute. There may have been colonies of such, polyzoans, and even true metazoans having such perishable structures, no trace of whose existence is preserved. One of the strongest arguments for the absolutely monophyletic character of all life is the probability that life originated under higher temperatures than anywhere prevail at the present time. This was in the sea where all the chemical conditions of life are found together, and as this was true for nearly the whole of the earth's surface, the continents having as yet scarcely been formed, we may well conceive that somewhere there would exist all the conditions for the origin of life.

Even in the Cambrian creatures as high as Trilobites were developed, and before the close of the Devonian the seas swarmed with fishes; *i.e.*, the vertebrate type had been fully formed. But land animals soon came on, and here higher psychic powers were needed. Still, throughout all geologic ages, and in the existing condition of the earth, there have always been humble aquatic creatures, both marine and fresh water, whose lives are spent practically in the groping, exploring, tentative stage of activity. The only rudiment of a rational faculty that they possess is this faculty of tentation, or the somewhat more developed power of intuition, by which they distinguish good from evil, food from enemies, and which at least guides their movements in the direction toward the former and from the latter. It is not the highly developed intuition of the old philosophers, much less the *Anschauung* of Kant, but the simplest of all forms of awareness applied to the most practical of objects.

Perception. — We have already seen that objective feeling leads to perception. This is the only source of a knowledge of properties, while subjective feeling reveals only qualities. But the primordial mind did not analyze the properties of objects. It used this faculty solely for practical purposes, and the properties possessed by the irregularities of the sea-bottom or of the surface of the land in case of terrestrial beings only concerned such beings in so far as they facilitated or obstructed the pursuit of food and mates. The properties, if we may call them such, that contributed to these ends were existence, *i.e.*, presence, magnitude, position, distance, direction, number, etc., all of which were determinants of the ability of the organism to attain its ends and to escape destruction. Most of these properties are simply relations, but they are relations among material objects having permanence, hardness, resistance, impenetrability, and for such creatures immovability. They must be avoided, surmounted, circumnavigated, or got around in some way, and the action or movements necessary to accomplish this could not be performed without the power of perceiving these relations and adjusting activities accordingly. Hence the primitive advantageous form of perception was the *perception of relations,* and the faculty of perception was developed through the elimination of those that failed thus to " take in " their situation and the survival of those that succeeded in taking it in.

This form of perception may be distinguished as intuitive perception. It is strictly egoistic, and although an objective faculty, it is intimately connected with subjective needs. In fact, it exists only for its subjective value in better preparing its possessor to attain its subjective ends. It is a clear example both of the impossibility of any faculty coming into existence unless it be thus advantageous, and also of how the most exalted attributes may have a humble and a simple origin. Intuitive perception does not differ essentially from the perception of the psychologists, and it contains all the elements in their germ.

Reason. — Like every other faculty, reason began as an advantageous faculty. Otherwise it could not have begun. But the primordial reason was not the *Vernunft* of Kant any more than the primordial intuition was his *Anschauung.* Neither of the latter is advantageous in the biological sense. It may sound like a contradiction of terms to say that while animals have reason they are not rational beings. Yet the popular use of the words reason and rational is such as to make the statement correct. Animal reasoning is intuitive, *i.e.,* it is synthetic. It is not an analysis, a syllogism, an enthymeme. It is, as it were, seeing or intuiting a conclusion. Its elements are simple. They are the perceptions that were last enumerated. Having perceived the properties and relations they now see, behold, or intuit what follows from a comparison or putting together of several of them. This they do when it concerns some interest and only then. Intuitive reason is egocentric. It is only exercised when useful, when it secures some end, when it leads to the satisfaction of desire or to the avoidance of danger. It is not deliberative. It is instantaneous. Of course it is only the higher animals that manifest this faculty in any marked degree. In most of them it is intimately connected with instinct, which for those that cannot reason at all serves the same purpose but stops at a much lower point. This close relation of instinct with reason is the basis for the prevailing idea that instinct has its foundations in reason. This is a complex question. Natural selection doubtless creates many instincts by seizing upon fortuitous variations in the advantageous direction, but it may also happen that a faint ray of reason may furnish a slight impetus to variation in such a direction rather than in another. This would make reason in part the basis of instinct. Most of the evidence for reasoning in animals is anecdotal and worthless. It proves too much and proves nothing. I have often heard highly intelligent qualities ascribed to horses, when it was evident that they were all in the " breaking." The intelligence was in the men who " broke " the horses. All claims to rational actions on the part of animals that cannot be shown to be the result of hereditary intuitive reasoning in the interest of the survival of the species are to be discredited. But reasoning of this kind, in such animals, for example, as the fox, is often exceedingly acute. In matters of interest animals may be almost unerring in their conclusions. Even in men it has been universally observed that reasoning is much more accurate when interests are involved than in indifferent cases. Dealers rarely make mistakes against themselves. An illiterate person who knows nothing of arithmetic will know it if underpaid for work. This is intuitive reasoning sharpened by the spur of interest. All reasoning was originally of this kind and the more developed forms and refinements of the rational faculty and reasoning process have grown out of this primordial trunk, ignored by the schools.

Intuitive reason is essentially active and aggressive, and hence dynamic and progressive. It seeks change, improvement, and a state of things better and higher than the actual state. But there is a form of mental operation which may be called reason, and which certainly is intuitive, apparently the reverse of this. It is passive and defensive, and does not seek change or betterment, but simply the maintenance of the existing status. It is the conservative element of mind. I called it "intuitive judgment," but it is not judgment in the psychologic sense of the mere recognition of the agreement or disagreement of registered percepts and concepts. If called judgment the word must be taken in something like its popular sense. This faculty is quite as necessary as the active reason, since any being is usually in a state at which it can subsist, and it is often more important to "let well enough alone" than to disturb existing conditions in the hope of securing something better. If reason be called positive this faculty must be called negative. It is the steering apparatus of the negative or protective social forces treated in Chapters XII and XIII, just as reason is the steering apparatus of the positive social forces. Reason discovers a free channel or current through which the dynamic agent can proceed, while judgment in this sense discovers a safe harbor where dangerous winds cannot destroy the frail craft of existence. The two faculties are respectively typical of the male and female natures, and although both sexes use both, still women make far more use relatively of the second than men, and what is called "woman's intuition"[1] is nothing else. We thus seem to have two great coördinate psychic trunks, the positive, initiative, aggressive, and dynamic, male trunk, and the negative, passive, defensive, and protective, female trunk — reason and judgment.

Indirection. — We have seen that the directive agent is a final

---

[1] The subject of woman's intuition has been so abundantly discussed that it seems needless to refer to the literature. Grant Allen's article so entitled and my reply to it were referred to in Chapter XIV (see *supra*, p. 298).

cause and that a final cause is the utilization of means to an end. We have now to note that this always involves indirection. This would follow from the definition of a final cause, since in no case does the agent act in the direction of the force he is to utilize. Usually his action is in an entirely different direction, often in the opposite direction, and it never has the least relation or resemblance to the action of the force. The intuitive reason goes out in all directions. Its earliest manifestations must have been in connection with the environment in overcoming obstacles to the pursuit of food and mates and the accomplishment of the ends of nature, nutrition and reproduction, *i.e.*, in the preservation and continuance of the species. For all organisms that derive their subsistence wholly from vegetation this practically holds throughout the series, but as many even very low animals are predatory and depend mainly or wholly on other animals for subsistence, a radical difference arises in the nature of the objects of pursuit and in the properties and forces that the directive agent must utilize in securing the ends of the organism. As all organisms are supposed to have feeling and to suffer pain in being seized and devoured by other creatures, there arises in the case of predatory subsistence what may be called a moral element. The animals preyed upon seek to escape from their natural enemies and the difficulty in procuring subsistence on the part of the predatory species is increased. In the animal of course there is no moral sense and no sympathy with suffering, and the act of preying can only be classed among those having attached to them a moral quality by expanding the ethical conception to embrace all sentient creatures. But if ethics is to be made a science this must be done, since the line between beings having a moral sense and beings destitute of any such sense could never be found. It may therefore be said that the directive agent applied to sentient beings in utilizing and exploiting them to the advantage of the one and to the injury of the other organism, is essentially *immoral*.

There is a difficulty here in the selection of terms. It will naturally be objected that so necessary and widespread a fact as the preying of animals upon one another, a practice that man is as guilty of as other animals, and that among the most morally advanced of men is considered almost necessary to life, cannot properly be called immoral. Only vegetarians so regard it, and these are commonly classed as morbidly sympathetic, and as examples of the inconsistency of sympathy to which reference was made in Chapter XV. I have myself shown[1] that if life is to be regarded as a good there is a sufficient justification of man's general treatment of the brute creation; that a larger amount of animal life exists under man's influence than could exist without it; that he creates more life than he destroys; that his methods of destruction are less painful than those of nature; that it is to his interest to treat animals well, to supply them with abundant food, and relieve them from those constant fears, both of enemies and of want, which characterize their condition in a wild state; and that when life is taken, it is done quickly and as painlessly as possible; that the reverse of all this is the case in nature, and hence a great amount of human sympathy is wasted on the creatures under man's control in consequence of ignorance of a few facts and principles.

Even in the wild state it might be maintained that, under the laws of multiplication as set forth by Malthus for the human race and extended to the whole animal world by Darwin, if the excess were not destroyed by predatory animals it would be removed by famine, and that the former method, bad as it is, results in less suffering upon the whole than the latter.

The word *moral* is so commonly employed as the opposite of immoral and in the sense of *right*, that any other use of it is likely to be misunderstood. Yet this is not its primary sense. This is: pertaining to the *mos*, custom or right. That is, any action which relates in any way to compliance with or violation of the customs or accepted code of action or conduct, is a moral action. Still more fundamental would be the definition of a moral act as one in any way involving pleasure or pain in sentient beings. Moral is then opposed, not to *immoral*, but to *unmoral*, non-moral, amoral, or anethical.[2] *Ethical* has primarily nearly the same meaning, but seems to be even more difficult to detach from other implications. I propose therefore to use the term *moral* for the form of indirection that affects feeling beings, and which is in the broad sense at the same time immoral.

Moral Indirection. — The form of action primarily relied upon by

[1] In a paper on the " Animal Population of the Globe," read before the Philosophical Society of Washington on Oct. 23, 1880. See abstract in the Bulletin of the Society, Vol. IV, pp. 27-29. The paper was a general discussion of an article I had prepared on the statistics of farm animals of the world, which appeared in full in the *Chicago Times* for Dec. 18, 1880, pp. 8-9.

[2] I used this word in 1896 (*American Journ. of Sociology*, Vol. II, September, 1896, p. 250) as an etymologically correct substitute for the bad form "amoral" used by French writers (Roberty, Bernès, Durkheim, etc.).

predatory animals is the *ruse*. The creatures preyed upon seek by every means in their power to escape. Having developed under these conditions they have acquired through natural selection the means of doing this in the majority of cases — fleetness, powers of flight, burrowing instincts, various means of concealment — and if their natural enemies had to depend upon direct pursuit they would usually fail and could not maintain a predatory subsistence. In the means of offense and defense there is a close analogy between nations and animal species. The two have in both cases grown up together. As weapons of war improve so do the forms of armor. It is a perpetual see-saw, but results in more terrible engines on the one hand and more inexpugnable battlements on the other. In the animal world the means of attack and the means of escape have also kept pace, but here the predatory species have not so much relied upon fleetness and strength as upon cunning, not so much upon physical as upon mental qualities. The analogy holds here also, for, as is well known, the victory is not to the strong but to the inventive nation. Mind in every case is the chief element of strength, and this strength is always proportioned to the degree to which telic methods are employed and the power acquired to call nature to the aid of muscle and sinew. Notwithstanding the enormous difference between the two planes of telic activity here compared there is absolutely no difference in the principle involved.

The ruse is the simplest form of deception, and this brings out the vital truth that in so far as mind deals with sentient beings deception is its essential nature. It might be supposed that the utilization of psychic forces involved in the deceiving and catching of other living things would require a higher order of intelligence than that required in utilizing physical forces and inanimate objects. Up to a certain point this doubtless is true, and, as we have seen, the first exercise of the rational faculty, the primordial tentation and intuition, was in connection with the physical environment. But this could only deal with the simplest and most obvious properties and relations, while, as we shall soon see, all other physical phenomena are too obscure to be thus utilized. Paradoxical as it may sound, biotic phenomena and laws are far more simple and intelligible than physical phenomena. Animals obey psychic forces, which, as we saw in Chapter VI and especially in Chapter VII, are true natural forces that may, in their simpler manifestations, be readily calculated in advance and implicitly relied upon. The ruse and deception in general do not call for specially high intellectual powers. As Mr. Havelock Ellis says: "The method of attaining results by ruses (common among all the weaker lower animals) is so habitual among women that, as Lombrose and Ferrero remark, in women deception is 'almost physiological.'"[1] And as much might have been said for children, mere babies habitually resorting to it, as every parent knows. It is therefore not surprising that predatory animals, depending for their very existence upon other simple-minded species with specialized means of escape in case of open attack, should soon develop the telic faculty in the particular direction and special form of deceiving and entrapping their prey. Instinct went a long way on this road, as in the spider's toils, and the cunning of the higher animals is so highly specialized and limited that it becomes half instinct.

Man, although not probably developed out of a predatory animal, found himself at his origin endowed with ample powers of deception to lay the animal world under tribute to him, and the two great primitive stages of his history, the venary and the pastoral stages, testify to the extent to which he made use of this simplest telic attribute. But he did not stop with the control and utilization of psychic forces as manifested in the animal world. The more cunning men and those more favorably situated early began the control and utilization of the less cunning and less favorably situated. Thus was begun the era of *exploitation* treated in Chapter XII. Mr. Veblen, with remarkable penetration, applies the term "predatory"[2] to the leisure class and points out that the methods of the "pecuniary occupations" even to-day are at least "quasi-predatory." All these methods involve deception and demonstrate that the intellectual method applied to psychic beings rests upon one fundamental principle, the principle of deception. The universality of deception in all mankind has been so generally recognized and so often illustrated that it is not necessary to treat it in detail. It will be sufficient to make a rough analysis of its principal forms arranged as nearly as practicable in the ascending order of intellectual development.

[1] "Man and Woman," by Havelock Ellis, Third Edition, London, 1902, p. 174.
[2] "The Theory of the Leisure Class," by Thorstein Veblen, New York, 1899, pp. 209, 336.

The cunning displayed by man in outwitting and circumventing animals is only a step higher than the ruse by which predatory animals deceive and catch their prey. The purpose is primarily the same, and hunting, fishing, etc., are simple forms of predation among animals of different powers of mind, man being in so far a predatory carnivorous animal. But when the idea arises, which does not always occur at the same relative historic stage of culture, of taking animals alive and compelling them to serve their captors in any of the various ways in which domestic animals are made useful to man, a slightly higher form of telic action is resorted to. The animals must be tamed. But a full-grown wild animal cannot be tamed. It will not eat in captivity and will destroy itself in its fright and frantic efforts to free itself. Animals must be taken while young, must be left unharmed and supplied with food. In this way, at least after a few generations, they become docile. They may then be induced to breed freely and be multiplied at will. All this requires considerable intelligence.

In exploiting men a still higher exercise of telic power is requisite, but perhaps not so much higher as might be supposed. No doubt slavery was as much due to cunning as to force. The lowest types of men are only just above the plane of animals and many slaves are scarcely more than domestic animals. In the metasocial state after the formation of caste, the inequalities among men were greatly increased and it was easy for a few of the higher class to keep the mass of mankind in subjection. This was accomplished primarily of course by force, but forms of deception were also constantly resorted to. The idea of the essential inferiority of the subject class must be steadily kept in the minds of that class. The least suspicion that this was not true would greatly disturb the social state. It was therefore a settled policy to enforce this idea, and a great variety of subterfuges were adopted to this end. At later stages, and even at the present time, those artificial social inequalities which enable the prosperous classes to thrive at the expense of the proletariat, and of the less favored classes where no true proletariat exists, are chiefly maintained through the systematic deception of the latter, and the inculcation through religious beliefs, when not otherwise possible, of the doctrine that the existing social condition is not only natural and necessary but divinely ordained. In fact from the first religion has always been the most potent of all the means of egoistic exploitation, for while it does not seem to favor any individual or class, it engenders a universal optimism and resignation which are highly favorable to all forms of exploitation.

Deception may almost be called the foundation of business. It is true that if all business men would altogether discard it matters would probably be far better even for them than they are, but taking the human character as it is, it is frankly avowed by business men themselves that no business could succeed for a single year if it were to attempt single-handed and alone to adopt such an innovation. The particular form of deception characteristic of business is called *shrewdness,* and is universally considered proper and upright. There is a sort of code that fixes the limit beyond which this form of deception must not be carried, and those who exceed that limit are looked upon somewhat as is a pugilist who "hits below the belt." But within those limits every one expects every other to suggest the false and suppress the true, while *caveat emptor* is lord of all, and "the devil take the hindmost."

In politics the practice of deception does not differ as much as is generally supposed from that of business. While principle is loudly proclaimed from the stump, interest lies behind it all. Another superficial view is that it is the "politicians" who are making a business of politics and leading the masses to do their bidding. There is only a basis of truth for this but it is not important. Back of the politician and demagogue lie the "vested interests," and these it is that are "making public opinion." It is customary in these days to laud the newspaper, but, except for the little news that it contains, which is to its managers a secondary consideration, the newspaper is simply an organ of deception. Every prominent newspaper is the defender of some interest and everything it says is directly or indirectly (and most effective when indirect) in support of that interest. There is no such thing at the present time as a newspaper that defends a principle. In 1895 Mr. John Swinton, a well-known and life-long newspaper man, in response to a toast: "The Independent Press," at a banquet of the New York Press Association, said: —

There is no such thing in America as an independent press unless it is in the country towns. You know it, and I know it. There is not one of you who dare express an honest opinion. If you express it, you know before-hand that it would never appear in print. I am paid $150 per week for keep-ing my honest opinions out of the paper I am connected with. Others of you are paid similar salaries for doing similar things. If I should permit honest opinions to be printed in one issue of my paper, like Othello, before twenty-four hours my occupation would be gone. The man who would be so foolish as to write honest opinions would be out on the street hunting for another job. The business of the New York journalist is to distort the truth, to lie outright, to pervert, to vilify, to fawn at the feet of Mammon, and to sell his country and race for his daily bread; or for what is about the same thing, his salary. You know this, and I know it; and what fool-ery to be toasting an "independent press." We are tools, and the vassals of rich men behind the scenes. We are jumping-jacks. They pull the string and we dance. Our time, our talents, our lives, our possibilities, all are the property of other men. We are intellectual prostitutes.

We might take up the legal profession and we would there find the same general fact — systematic deception. I used to smile when I heard good and simple country dames say that lawyers lived by lying, and I "studied law," acquired that profession, and was duly admitted to the bar. But long before the end I had learned that the good country dames were right and I was wrong. I was openly taught by the senior professor that my business was to gain my case, and that I was not to be the judge of the justice of the case. That was matter for the judge. I need scarcely add that I have never pleaded a case.

The form of deception used in warfare is called *strategy*, and the kind that nations practice is known as *diplomacy*. There is collec-tive deception as well as individual deception. There is deception in the home and deception in the church. The average sermon is a more or less clumsy, more or less artful piece of sophistry. A mo-ment's conversation with a stranger will usually reveal the fact that he is trying to deceive you about something, and if you do not dis-cover this it is generally because he has succeeded. Fashionable society consists wholly in sham, quackery reigns in the professions and charlatanism in scientific bodies; falsehood permeates business, and as you look out a car window, the rocks and trees are placarded all over with lies.[1]

[1] Most advertisements other than mere announcements for public information, such as those of governments, are in the nature of intentional deceptions. The superlatives, as "the best," the strong words, as "superior," and the word "only," almost always occurring in them, are simply falsehoods, and society would be justi-fied in forbidding their use as devices for "obtaining money under false pretenses."

Material Indirection. — It must not be supposed that there is any malicious intent in the universal deception and exploitation that characterize the application of telic methods to sentient things. Neither animals nor men cause others pain for the mere love of it. It is only that creatures susceptible to pain get in the way of irresistible natural forces and suffer accordingly. The lava that rolls down the sides of a Vesuvius or a Mont Pelée is not deterred by the presence at the base of a Pompeii or a St. Pierre. It is about the same with the vital and psychic forces that impel living beings. The end is the sole consideration. If that can be attained without causing pain it is the same to the agent. There is no particular reason why the telic method should be applied to feeling beings rather than to insentient and inanimate things. If such an exercise

The philosophy of advertising is interesting and has never to my knowledge been written. The economists know of course that the cost of advertising is added to the price, and that it belongs among the facts of "aggressive competition," which increases instead of diminishing prices. But this is by no means all. It really affects the quality more than the price. It is the price relative to the quality that it increases. If it greatly raised the price it would not "pay." Extensively advertised articles are not usually higher, but are rather lower in price than those only moderately advertised. The cost of advertising must therefore mainly come out of the quality. In general it may be safely assumed that an article that is placarded on the streets and along the railroads, and to which much space is given in the newspapers by means of striking advertisements, is, relatively to its price, a poor article. Connoisseurs of tobacco, for example, know this to be the case with cigars, and avoid these brands. But here is where the principles of human nature enter into the philosophy of advertising. The business success of advertising rests upon the feeble reasoning powers and the extraordinary gullibility of mankind in general. Whatever is constantly thrust before their eyes is sure to entrap a certain percentage, and therefore the absolute number caught will be proportional to the number baited. Two other principles of human nature work in favor of the advertiser. When a victim finds himself deceived he thereafter avoids that particular snare. The widely advertised article is therefore only bought once by the same person, and depends for its success upon the number of these temporary customers. It might be supposed that so many disappointed individuals would ruin the sale by their general condemnation. Not so. They have no motive for denouncing the article in question to others, while on the other hand they have the strong motive of self-esteem for not letting it be known that they have been so foolish as to allow themselves to be deceived. A good article is its own advertisement. The user who finds it excellent is eager to recommend it to others. This principle is very strong, and is closely allied to, if not identical with, the proselyting spirit in religion. Broadly stated it is that what one enjoys one wishes others to enjoy. But he who suffers naturally conceals the fact. The negative side of feeling, call it pain, disappointment, regret, chagrin, or what you will, is kept in the background. It is a mark of weakness, and no one will confess to weakness, physical or mental. This is the chief ground for the success of falsifying advertisements, but it is complicated by the strangely uncritical character of most people, by the fact that the articles generally have some merits, by the diversity of human tastes, and by the reservation that one may after all be mistaken.

of mind promises the same results it will be adopted. But the exploitation of other living things is simple and about the first thing to suggest itself.

The exploitation, we might almost say deception, of inanimate nature requires a higher development of the telic faculty. Material things do not move of themselves. Their properties are hidden and must be searched for. Physical forces are invisible and intangible, and when they cause motion, primitive man imputes to the objects moved life and intelligence. The egoistic utilization of the psychic forces residing in living things is common to animals and men, but the utilization of physical forces and the subtler properties of material bodies is an exclusively human power. Animals, as shown in Chapter XV, only reach the stage of imitation. They do not attain to that of imagination. In that chapter imagination was only connected with creative or esthetic art. We are now prepared to look deeper into the faculty of imagination, and to see that it constitutes the common parent of both creation and invention. It is the basis of and condition to both the great institutions that we call art — fine art and useful art.

The exercise of the telic faculty upon material things and physical forces, though not psychologically different from its exercise upon living things, is no longer called deception, and none of the terms employed in describing the different forms of deception — ruse, cunning, sagacity, tact, shrewdness, strategy, diplomacy — are applicable to it. The identically same psychic process is now called *ingenuity*, and the more involved forms of ingenuity result in invention. Ingenuity is the faculty while invention is the act, and the term is also used for the thing invented. Ingenuity and inventiveness are nearly synonymous. But ingenuity was not at its inception a disinterested faculty. Man was seeking to utilize everything whether animate or inanimate that could serve his ends. Some material objects were nutritious and he could appropriate them directly, others must be altered or modified and the nutrient elements extracted by processes varying in complication and calling forth greater or less exercise of the telic power. At a certain stage it was discovered that material objects might be made serviceable as aids in the capture of animals and as a protection from the elements. Thus weapons of the chase, traps and snares of simple design, and various devices were contrived to render the quest for food more easy and certain. A dead animal becomes brute matter, and while its flesh serves for food its skin is used as a means of protection. Even its bones and claws may serve some useful purpose. Reeds and bamboos, palm leaves and sticks from the jungle finally contribute to comfort and safety, and from such beginnings clothing and shelter must have been evolved. When the art of making fire was discovered another great step was taken, and thus little by little the human animal emancipated himself from the purely animal condition and assumed the rôle of man.

The most important result of this early exercise of the directive agent upon the inanimate world was the control thereby gained of the environment whereby that strictly animal characteristic was outgrown which restricts every species to its own particular habitat, to which it has become adapted, and beyond which it cannot range without encountering such hostile elements as to destroy it. Animals are *adscripti glebæ* in a far more absolute sense than the serfs of feudal ages. No degree of intensity in the dynamic agent, no amount of skill in capturing prey, could free the race of this natural serfdom. Only through the exercise of the telic faculty upon the inanimate world through ingenuity and invention could this great step be taken. The importance of this step may be appreciated when we remember that it rendered indefinite migration possible, and inaugurated the stage characterized in Chapter X as the stage of social differentiation. It was in fact the beginning of human society. The subsequent steps were there traced and we need only now supply the telic factor at each stage in order better to grasp the sum total of the influences at work in achieving the results described. This factor was always present and it increased in force more rapidly in the later than in the earlier stages.

We are concerned here with material indirection only as a phase of the genesis of mind. We have seen that it was intuitive, synthetic, and egocentric. Throughout the earlier stages of society it doubtless chiefly remained so, and the end to be attained through any ingenious device was constantly before the mind of the inventor to the practical exclusion of all other sentiments. But a time at length arrived when the mental exercise involved in invention began to constitute a satisfaction of its own. It was shown in Chapter XV that the discovery of truth yields a satisfaction that can scarcely be compared with any other. Nothing was there said of invention, but it is clear that it differs psychologically from the discovery of truth considered as the simple working over of the materials already in the mind and the extraction therefrom of new truths and higher generalizations. The inventor is dealing with material objects and with physical forces manifesting themselves through such objects. Invention takes advantage of the principle mentioned in Chapter V, that while matter can be neither created nor destroyed nor the sum total of its activities increased or diminished, its mode of motion may be varied in any desired way. Invention consists then essentially in varying the mode of motion of matter. But as this may be done at will, the particular way in which the inventor wills to vary it is that which will result in some advantage, primarily to the inventor, but ultimately to mankind in general. The inventive power consists therefore in the ability to see what variations in the mode of motion of the material objects under examination will result in advantage to man. This advantage to man constitutes utility, and therefore what the inventor is seeking is utility. Utility is a relation, and the perception of relations is one of the earliest manifestations of the telic faculty. But utilities are highly complex relations. Invention may then be defined as the *perception of utilities.* The complete oneness of the whole telic faculty from simple intuition to human invention is thus clearly brought out.

I have now cursorily passed in review all the strictly advantageous faculties in the scientific use of that term, and I think it can be safely said that not one of them has ever received attention in any of the myriad contributions to the philosophy of mind. Some of the names have been used, but in entirely different senses. I do not say that passages do not occur here and there in the literature of psychology that hint at the idea of a true natural genesis of mind. I have collected a considerable number of such, but none of them are sufficiently definite to make sure that this is the real idea. There are probably others that I have not met with. It seems certain that no systematic attempt has been made to account for the rational faculty as something that was called into existence and developed according to the general laws of organic evolution.

CHAPTER XVIII

THE NON-ADVANTAGEOUS FACULTIES

WHAT has been called "the mind" by those who have written on it consists almost entirely of the non-advantageous faculties of the human intellect. Not being advantageous to their possessors they could not be accounted for on the principle of advantage. Wallace, who independently discovered the principle of natural selection, admits this, abandons the attempt, and has recourse to the doctrine of spiritualism. By advantageous is of course meant that which fits a being to survive. It must in some way contribute to better nutrition, to physical protection, or to more certain propagation. All the faculties considered in the last chapter directly and conspicuously serve the first two of these ends, and it was seen in Chapter XIV that brain became at length a secondary sexual character and thus contributed to the phylogenetic development of the higher animal types and of man.

ORIGIN OF GENIUS

The non-advantageous faculties may all be included under the comprehensive term *genius,* taken in somewhat the same sense in which Galton uses it. The distinguishing characteristic of genius is that it does not have preservation or reproduction for its end, but is, as we may say, an end in itself. This does not mean that it is devoid of motive, for if it were it would be incapable of producing action. It only means that its motive is not an ontogenetic or a phylogenetic force, but is a sociogenetic force. It may be a moral force, and it is to some extent an esthetic force, but it is chiefly an intellectual force. When we reach the stage of genius the brain has become an emotional center, and as we saw in Chapter XV, the appetites, wants, and feelings of the intellect constitute motives of great strength. This alone accounts for the non-advantageous faculties in a thoroughly scientific manner, and there is no need of descanting on the "mystery of mind." It is no more mysterious than other things. Everything in nature becomes unexplainable if we

493

trace it far enough back. This was the method of the old philosophy, but it becomes a sort of " fool's puzzle," and is entirely abandoned by positive science, the progress of which has not been in the
least impeded by abandoning it.[1]

But there is still another way of accounting for the non-advantageous faculties. They are to be regarded as *derivative*, and as
having naturally grown out of the advantageous faculties. This
took place along three somewhat different lines. The first of these
lines was that of invention, the second that of esthetic creation, and
the third that of general intellectual exercise or philosophy. These
may be treated in this order.

Inventive Genius. — Invention in its later stages becomes subjective and takes the form of genius. As remarked in the last chapter,
the perception of utilities, at first simply as such, *i.e.*, as means of
attaining personal ends, often succeeding admirably in accomplishing this, soon began to constitute an independent stimulus, and the
search for utilities became a pleasurable occupation. This double
motive led to renewed application and heightened zeal, and there
arose on the part of the inventor a tendency to lose sight, temporarily
at least, of the practical end and to yield wholly to the spur of an-
ticipated success residing in his own mind. When invention reaches
this stage it becomes genius, and henceforth it exists for its own
sake. It becomes a passion and is pursued often at a sacrifice of
other pleasures and satisfactions and even of positive wants. This
accounts for the fact that many of the greatest inventors have been in
indigent circumstances and almost forgetful of their personal necessities. It is the same motive that actuates the unsuccessful inventor
and the deluded persons who vainly strive for years, or it may be
for a lifetime, to apply a false principle, such as " perpetual motion."

In modern times there is a very large number of almost professional inventors employed for the most part by manufacturing
establishments, and who are thus able to subsist by this alone. The
fact that such persons can always be found and that they have
sufficient inventive ability to enable such establishments to keep
abreast of the times and vie with one another in the constant production of improved appliances of all kinds, seems to prove that the

---

[1] I dealt at considerable length on this aspect in an address entitled : " Status of
the Mind Problem," delivered under the auspices of the Anthropological Society of
Washington on April 8, 1893, and published as Special Paper No. 1, of the Society,
Washington, 1894, pp. 18, 8°.

inventive power of man is widely diffused and capable of being "developed," *i.e.*, stimulated into activity by suitable opportunity. The surprising thing is that in all the best equipped universities and polytechnic institutes there seems to be no recognition of invention as a discipline apart from the regular professions of engineering, surveying, and manufacture. The manual training schools do, no doubt, encourage originality in the methods of work, but usually set patterns are closely followed and there is little play afforded for the inventive powers. There is no text-book, so far as I am aware, on invention in general, its fundamental principles and methods. It would seem that if invention could be recognized as a science or as a profession and thoroughly taught as such, the perception of utilities would be much more general among the educated public, and the awkward mechanical conditions under which society labors would be greatly improved. When we remember how vast have been the results that have been achieved through invention pursued in a purely spontaneous and unsystematized way, we naturally wonder what might be the effect of its reduction to scientific method and its inculcation through systematic courses of training and instruction.

Whatever may be said of other non-advantageous faculties it is at least clear that inventive genius is a direct outgrowth of the original egoistic faculty of invention. It is granted that no one would have ever designed an implement if it had not been seen that such implement would serve some other purpose than the mere pleasure of designing it; but the inventor, having designed one implement and found it to serve its purpose, takes a new interest in the second, and still more in the third, until at last his interest in the mere designing comes to prevail over his interest in its purpose. A sufficient prominence in this secondary interest constitutes inventive genius.

Creative Genius. — Although esthetic art is one of the best recognized fields for the display of genius, it is perhaps more difficult to account for creative than for inventive genius, but it has been seen that the esthetic faculty reaches far back into the animal world. By this is meant a certain pleasure in the sight, sound, or even the "feel" of certain things. Things that yield such pleasure are, to those who experience the pleasure, beautiful. In animals no higher stage is reached than that of appreciating beauty when it presents itself to their faculties, but man at a very early stage acquired the faculty at least of subjective creation, as imagination may be called, and of enjoying such subjective creations. The next step was to put together objects and parts of objects that imagination showed to be beautiful and thus to forms ideals, *i.e.*, representations of things that did not exist, but of which only the parts or elements had objective reality. Such ideals are creations, and their production constitutes creative genius.

I am unable to see why this is not a natural process. It is true that the interest subserved is not one of the primary wants of existence. It is, however, a want, and a somewhat imperative one even with primitive man. The religious sentiment, so universal in early man, was favorable to the development of creative art. "Ecclesiastical institutions," in Spencer's broad sense, gave rise to a demand for temples, decorations, and a variety of art products, which might have given an egoistic bent to creative art. There would then be a certain utility in creative products and they would be in the same position as early inventive products. The transition from the objective to the subjective here is as easy as there, and art is much better recognized as a passion than invention. It becomes, as its whole history attests, a consuming passion, and its development from this point on follows as a matter of course. The only difficulty is to account for its origin, and this, I think, has been done.

Philosophic Genius. — We come now to the faculty *par excellence* that has engaged the attention of the students of mind. The inventive faculty has been practically overlooked and the creative faculty has been taken as a matter of course, but the faculty or power of "abstract reasoning," as it is called, this is the great, the worthy, the noble attribute that exalts man above all nature and renders him divine. "On earth there is nothing great but man, in man there is nothing great but mind." [1]

---

[1] Sir William Hamilton was very fond of this aphorism and placed it on the fly-leaf of all the volumes of his lectures on metaphysics and logic and also on that of Reid's works in the edition edited by him. It is therefore commonly credited to him. But he did not himself claim this credit, and in his second lecture on metaphysics (see the edition of Mansel and Veitch, Edinburgh and London, 1859, p. 24) he repeats it and attributes it to " an ancient philosopher." The editors here explain in a footnote that the "ancient philosopher" was Phavorinus, and that the phrase is quoted from him by Joannes Picus Mirandula in his treatise, "In Astrologiam," Book III, Basil, p. 351. This treatise is contained in the " Opera Omnia Ioannis Pici Mirandulæ," Basileæ, 1557, and I find the passage in Lib. III, but on p. 519, *not* 351. The Latin text runs : " Nihil magnum in terra præter hominem, nihil magnum in homine præter mentem & animum." I learn that there is an earlier edition — Venice, 1498 — in which the passage also occurs.

I have not hesitated to admit that these faculties are non-advantageous, and, as developed faculties, cannot be accounted for on the
principle of natural selection. In so far I am in accord with Dr.
Alfred Russel Wallace who carefully set forth the main considerations as far back as 1870. Among such faculties he enumerates " the
capacity to form ideal conceptions of space and time, of eternity and
infinity — the capacity for intense artistic feelings of pleasure in form,
color, and composition — and for those abstract notions of form and
number which render geometry and arithmetic possible." And he adds :

> How were all or any of these faculties first developed, when they could
> have been of no possible use to man in his early stages of barbarism? How
> could " natural selection," or survival of the fittest in the struggle for exist-
> ence, at all favor the development of mental powers so entirely removed
> from the material necessities of savage men, and which even now, with our
> comparatively high civilization, are, in their farthest developments, in
> advance of the age, and appear to have relation rather to the future of the
> race than to its actual status? [1]

In the last chapter of his " Darwinism " he returns to this subject
and discusses the origin of the mathematical, musical, and artistic
faculties, and says that it is impossible to trace any connection
between their possession and survival in the struggle for existence,
because, as he says :

> The law of natural selection or the survival of the fittest is as its name
> implies, a rigid law, which acts by the life or death of the individuals sub-
> mitted to its action. From its very nature it can act only on useful and
> hurtful characteristics, eliminating the latter and keeping up the former to
> a fairly general level of efficiency. Hence it necessarily follows that the
> characters developed by its means will be present in all the individuals of
> a species, and, though varying, will not vary very widely from a common
> standard.[2]

This is a clear statement, and I fully agree with its author that
not only the faculties he enumerates but many others, some of
which remain to be mentioned, are non-advantageous in this sense,
and cannot be accounted for on the principle of natural selection.
But I insist that the original telic faculty in all its primary aspects
as set forth in the last chapter, answers to all the counts in the
above indictment, and not only might have been, but actually was

---

[1] "Contributions to the Theory of Natural Selection," a series of Essays, by
Alfred Russel Wallace, London, Macmillan and Co., 1870, pp. 351–352.

[2] "Darwinism. An Exposition of the Theory of Natural Selection with some of
its Applications," by Alfred Russel Wallace, London, 1889, p. 469.

2 K

brought into existence through the operation of this principle, and
that its development proceeded in this manner up to the point
where it was left in that chapter. The faculties we are here considering grew out of this, not through natural selection, but by more
or less exceptional overdevelopment in a comparatively small number.

It would be strange indeed if natural selection was the only principle on which anything could be accounted for. In Chapter XI
I enumerated three great dynamic principles: Difference of Potential (cross fertilization), Innovation, and Conation. I account for
the non-advantageous faculties chiefly on the first two of these.
But primarily they are to be looked upon as the result of continuous brain development, due to these and other causes, and the
developed brain, having an interest in its own operations, proceeds
to work out various results, to elaborate the materials stored up in
it, and to invent, create, and cogitate everything that it has the
capacity for. Weismann truly says that genius is not primarily
nor necessarily specialized, but takes whatever direction the particular circumstances happen to favor.

Gauss was not the son of a mathematician; Handel's father was a
surgeon, of whose musical powers nothing is known; Titian was the son
and also the nephew of a lawyer, while he and his brother, Francesco
Vecellio, were the first painters in a family which produced a succession of
seven other artists with diminishing talents. . . . At present, it is of course
impossible to understand the physiological conditions which render the
origin of such combinations possible, but it is very probable that the crossing of the mental dispositions of the parents plays a great part in it. . . .
The combination of talents frequently found in one individual, and the
appearance of different remarkable talents in the various branches of
one and the same family, indicate that talents are only special combinations
of certain highly developed mental dispositions which are found in every
brain. Many painters have been admirable musicians, and we very frequently find both these talents developed to a slighter extent in a single
individual. In the Feuerbach family we find a distinguished jurist, a
remarkable philosopher, and a highly talented artist; and among the
Mendelssohns a philosopher as well as a musician. . . . From all these
examples I wish to show that, in my opinion, talents do not appear to
depend upon the improvement of any special mental quality by continued
practice, but they are the expression, and to a certain extent the bye-product,
of the human mind, which is so highly developed in all directions.[1]

[1] " Essays upon Heredity and Kindred Biological Problems," by August Weismann.
Authorised translation edited by Edward B. Poulton, Selmar Schönland, and Arthur
E. Shipley, Oxford, 1889, pp. 96-98.

To most of this I heartily assent, and although I have omitted a number of his illustrations, there are others that he does not give which would sustain his position quite as well; for example the brothers Humboldt, one the man of all science, the other a great philologist. I believe that this illustrates an important law, which might be called the law of mutual repulsion in talented families, the very fact that one brother takes one direction being the reason why the rest take other directions, and the " black sheep " who does nothing may be due to the same principle and not to any lack of ability. But Weismann brings forward these facts in support of a false proposition which they do not sustain, viz., that the exercise of these faculties has no influence on their development.

It is usually considered that the origin and variation of instincts are also dependent on the exercise of certain groups of muscles and nerves during a single lifetime; and that the gradual improvement which is thus caused by practice, is accumulated by hereditary transmission. I believe that this is an entirely erroneous view, and I hold that all instinct is entirely due to the operation of natural selection, and has its foundation, not upon inherited experiences, but upon the variations of the germ. . . . In my opinion there is absolutely no trustworthy proof that talents have been improved by their exercise through the course of a long series of generations.[1]

Mr. Spencer in his " Factors of Organic Evolution " and in his several answers and rejoinders to Weismann's subsequent articles and addresses has sufficiently answered this point, and we may be spared from entering into the endless and hopeless discussion of the question of the transmission of acquired characters.[2] It only needs to be pointed out that his argument is a *reductio ad absurdum*, because he has just said that these faculties cannot be due to natural selection. If they are beyond the reach of natural selection and are not the result of exercising the parts of brain that cause them, then they are inexplicable from any point of view that Weismann has presented. Of course there remains the mutation theory of de Vries, but Weismann had not then heard of that. That theory is the same that I have called " innovation " and " fortuitous variation." This

---

[1] *Ibid.*, pp. 91, 95–96.

[2] Should any care to know my own notions on this question they will find them in the following papers: " Neo-Darwinism and Neo-Lamarkism," Annual Address of the President of the Biological Society of Washington, delivered January 24, 1891, *Proceedings of the Biological Society of Washington*, Vol. VI, pp. 11–71; " The Transmission of Culture," *The Forum*, Vol. XI, May, 1891, pp. 312–319; " Weismann's Concessions," *Popular Science Monthly*, Vol. XLV, June, 1894, pp. 175–184.

theory explains short steps, but it can scarcely explain Galileos, Newtons, and Shakespeares. That talents are so rarely perpetuated through many generations Weismann has himself explained through *panmixia*, but Galton has made a heroic effort to show that genius is hereditary, panmixia to the contrary notwithstanding. The fact is that all talent, ability, and superiority of every kind have been "acquired" by somebody by exercising the appropriate faculties, but about half of the gain is usually lost by the first cross, which, under the laws of mutual selection (*ampheclexis*), explained in Chapter XIV, joins the person of a special talent to another in which it is totally wanting, to prevent one-sidedness in the race. But the principle of *atavism* comes to the rescue, and the special talent of some more or less remote ancestor is added to the same talent in a parent, so that the effect appears to be sudden and uncaused. The gains are therefore not wholly lost; perhaps scarcely anything gained is ever lost. There is a certain cumulative effect in the long run, although, for the reasons stated, it appears to be spasmodic. Most of the cases of towering genius are probably to be ascribed to this special concentration in some particular descendant of the accumulated qualities of a long line of ancestors.

The defenders of natural selection have greatly retarded its universal acceptance by claiming too much for it. The "Neo-Darwinians" in particular, by ignoring or belittling the Lamarckian principle of exercise and the Darwinian principle of sexual selection, have forfeited their claim to be called Darwinians at all. The neglect of the factor of fortuitous variation, also recognized by Darwin, still further narrows the field and causes natural selection to be questioned by the skeptical. And now I shall propose another limitation to natural selection which, so far as I now remember, has thus far been overlooked, but which, it seems to me, needs only to be stated to be accepted by all unbiased minds. I will formulate it in two propositions: —

1. No organic or social structure can *originate* unless it is advantageous, or at least not *dis*advantageous.

2. Having originated, any structure may *vary* in a *non*-advantageous direction, but not greatly in a *dis*advantageous one.

An intellectual quality, talent, or faculty is a psychic structure based upon an organic structure of the brain. It must be advantageous at the start and common to all the members of a species to

insure its original creation. Such were all the advantageous intellectual faculties whose biologic origin was treated in the last chapter. But once in existence, any and all of these faculties may vary
in any given direction and grow into wholly non-advantageous
faculties, provided they do not become positively disadvantageous
in the sense of endangering the existence of the race. I thus
account for the non-advantageous intellectual faculties now under
discussion. Just how and why they thus varied has already been
shown.

We are not without analogies among organic structures and they
are also found among social structures. Of the former the more
extravagant secondary sexual characters, such as the antlers of an
elk which so greatly impede his movement through the dense forest,
are among the best examples. But we only need to look for them
to find them everywhere. The idea that everything organic must
necessarily be useful in the struggle for existence is one of those
extremes to which the doctrine of natural selection at first led
naturalists, and which has had to be combated with a large amount
of evidence. It may be said to be fairly exploded now, though still
defended by some. But a mere glance at the organic world as
a whole is sufficient to show that the precise forms it presents are
largely indifferent. Almost any other form would have done about
as well in most cases, and the actual forms are practically fortuitous.
I showed this for the genus Eupatorium (see *supra*, p. 241), a very
simple case but specially appropriate and instructive. The different
forms, which constitute the several species, doubtless resulted from
fortuitous variation or " mutation." There was no reason why such
forms should *not* exist. The variations, though non-advantageous,
were not *dis*advantageous, and there was therefore nothing to prevent them from taking place. Any genus of plants or animals
would serve the same purpose.

Among social structures the best examples of this law are to be
found among religions. Religion must have been primarily an
advantageous social structure, otherwise it could not have come into
existence. I have pointed out in what religion essentially consists
as such an advantageous social structure. The existence of the
human race seems at a certain stage to have depended upon the
group sentiment of safety and the means of enforcing it against
the wayward tendencies of a rapidly developing egoistic intellect,

destitute of all knowledge as to the consequences of the acts prompted by it. This constitutes an adequate explanation of the origin of religion. But religion once established, it soon began to vary, until now there are more religions than there are races of men. Many of these variations were wholly non-advantageous. Some of them were doubtless disadvantageous. A considerable amount of disadvantageous variation may take place, only it must not go to the length of endangering the race. Probably most religions are now somewhat disadvantageous. Certainly the adherents of any religion would admit this of all the rest, and even exaggerate their disadvantageousness.

Returning to the intellectual faculties, we find the same to have been true. The relief from physical want which the system of caste and the formation of a leisure class, both sacerdotal and political, during the early metasocial period, afforded, set free a large volume of intellectual energy hitherto expended in the struggle for existence, and it took a variety of directions. It was shown in Chapter V that the growth force, or primary bathmism of nature, pushes out in all conceivable directions, as from the center of a sphere. It may be added that the intellectual impulse does the same, and unless it meets with insuperable obstacles it will compass every field of nature. Its own innate interest constitutes its abundant motive power. The exercise of the intellectual faculties in the struggle for existence during countless ages had developed them to a very high degree, and, according to Weismann's theory above quoted, if the volume is present, the direction the impulse will take depends on circumstances. Freed now from egoistic exercise, this accumulated intellectual capital is liberally invested in disinterested, or non-advantageous projects. It is no longer held by the principle of advantage to any fixed course, and it goes off on strange lines and does unheard-of things. It may be compared to the erratic variations in color that animals and birds undergo in domestication. In the wild state the color is definitely fixed for each species. Protective imitation, sexual selection, and a variety of influences have finally combined to give each species its fixed color within certain limits of variation, which are also fixed. But no sooner is the bird or animal fully domesticated, so that all these influences are removed, than it begins to take on different colors. Birds become pied and animals striped and spotted. Doubtless these variations are ancestral and atavistic, but they could not appear in the wild state. Neither can this be explained by the mixing of breeds, for it is true of the turkey, which has no other wild species or variety with which it could be crossed under domestication.

There is another and very different comparison that might be made. The conditions of existence in human society, even in what we call advanced societies, closely resemble those which nature presents in wild animals. Men are restricted to certain kinds of action that are practically fixed, like the colors of animal species. Any one who does anything that does not come within the scope of these prescribed forms of action is not considered sane, although the act may be entirely harmless. All the permissible acts are what are called " practical." They tend in one form or another to preserve existence. No matter how wealthy a man may be, if he does anything that does not tend to acquiring more wealth, he is suspected of becoming unbalanced in his mind. This social tyranny is more marked in rural and backward districts and is slightly relieved in cities, and especially in educational centers, watering places, and health and pleasure resorts, but it is nowhere entirely absent. One cannot do anything which promises no gain, is not connected with some fashionable game or practice, and differs markedly from what a considerable number habitually do, without being set down at least as a " crank," if not as a suspicious character or insane person.[1]

Now the real élite of mankind, not the wealthy nor the influential, but those who use their reason most and who possess the largest stock of both knowledge and ideas, will not slavishly follow the herd, but are erratic and do just such things as lead the mass of mankind to look upon them with suspicion. They rise above both gain and fashion, and persistently violate the code of social action

---

[1] In Washington the warm weather often holds on through October and into November, the thermometer often reaching 80° or 85° Fahr. Once in such a season I started out for a ramble in the early days of November, and with a view to comfort I donned the straw hat that I had worn all summer. There was nothing in the weather to oppose such a proceeding, as it was a very warm day. As I passed along the streets I soon noticed that I was attracting attention. Men and women looked at me as much as to say, " You are out of fashion " ; " There goes a crank." But the boys, who, like savages, are much more bound by convention than grown people, mocked me openly, crying out : " What are you doing with that straw hat ? This ain't summer ; this is November," etc. This example shows how completely independent this social coercion is of all considerations of utility and of all intrinsic reasonableness growing out of the nature of things.

and rules of propriety. This typifies the emancipated intellect everywhere, and although the leisure class was a ruling class and not under the influence of the rest of mankind, still it found itself emancipated from all forms of restraint, and those members, always of course relatively few in number, who took pleasure in intellectual exercise could freely follow the lines of least resistance and greatest attraction, and could follow these lines fully out to their extreme logical conclusions.

Philosophy began as speculation. Facts or supposed facts of course lay at the bottom of it. Perceptions, conceptions, and ideas were in the minds of those early speculators, but they were little controlled, and imagination was scarcely differentiated from observation. Although thought took many directions, often wild and fantastic, the body of primitive speculation was confined to two great fields, which may be called respectively *cosmology* and *noology*. Neither of these can probably be said to have had priority over the other, but certainly the phenomena of mind claimed the attention of man as early as did those of the external world.[1]

This extremely early study of mind is a sort of anthropomorphism. Just as primitive men understood life because they possessed it, and ascribed all movement to living beings like themselves, so the first thinkers understood mind because they possessed it, and not only projected their own intelligence into all nature, but proceeded to speculate upon mind before they did upon matter. This form of speculation was practically sterile, but it was fascinating, and had the subjective advantage of cultivating and refining the thinking powers in a way that nothing else could do. Philosophers never abandoned this field and are still tilling it, almost as fruitlessly as at first. It never yielded any valuable results until it was cross fertilized by the germs of objective science and metaphysics was transformed into psychology. Nevertheless an enormous amount of sublimated intellectual energy has been expended on mind, and only extreme Weismannians will deny that mind has been thereby exalted.

The study of the Cosmos, on the other hand, which must have

---

[1] Professor Breasted thinks that the word " heart " in the inscription on the stone taken from the temple of Ptah at Memphis, signifies *mind*, and the context, so far as he was able to decipher it, seems to bear out this interpretation. He refers the inscription to the eighteenth dynasty, or about the sixteenth century before Christ. See his article in the *Monist* for April, 1902, Vol. XII, pp. 321–326.

begun at about the same time, was fertile from the start, and all that we know of the universe, including mind, has resulted from it. This is why it is beginning to be seen that the true Greek philosophers were not Socrates and Plato, but Thales and Pythagoras, and especially their talented contemporaries and followers, Anaximander, Anaximenes, Heraclitus, Empedocles, Anaxagoras, and Democritus. These may all be called cosmologists, although their theories differed greatly, and some of them combined the study of mind with that of nature. The form of speculation that seems to lie between thought and things and bind them together is mathematics, or as the Greeks chiefly understood it, geometry. This presented a peculiarly attractive field, since it was free from the encumbrance of concrete objects, and dealt with relations, or, popularly speaking, abstract ideas. Geometry was taught by Thales and Pythagoras and it was a favorite study of Plato. It harmonized well with speculations about mind, but it proved fruitful of results, and at the hands of Euclid it has come to constitute the basis of all knowledge of quantity. The various forms of calculus, as also our convenient " Arabic " notation, were probably excogitated from the brains of Brahminic priests contemporary with or earlier than the Greek philosophers named.

At that date, when so little was known of the concrete facts of nature, mathematical study and abstract speculation were more profitable than reasoning about material facts, because all theories of the universe that could be formed from such imperfect data must be extremely vague and largely false. Yet when we remember that not only the true nature of the solar system, but also the atomic theory of chemistry and the doctrine of evolution, were all formulated by the Greek cosmologists so that they can be readily recognized by modern science, we are in position to form an estimate of the power of the thinking faculty to comprehend nature. These conclusions were reached not by " abstract reasoning," but by *generalization*. With any considerable number of concrete facts to reason from, generalization is a far more important process than abstraction. It leads to *truth* in the proper sense, *i.e.*, the relation of agreement or disagreement of conceptions, ideas, and groups or clusters of these. It classifies phenomena and coördinates facts, phenomena and ideas, establishing comprehensive laws. This is true philosophy, and so long as error can be avoided every exercise

of mind in this direction increases man's acquaintance with his
environment and with the world at large.

Error is of course primarily due to insufficient knowledge, but an
even more prolific source of error has in fact been supplied by false
cosmogonies.   In one sense these false cosmogonies may be regarded
as the excogitations of the human mind, but they have not usually
been the work of philosophers striving to explain the universe.
They have been invented by the priesthood in support of the ecclesiastical power as a means of more easily and effectively enforcing the
group sentiment of race safety and checking wayward tendencies.
In short the false cosmogonies that have most impeded the progress
of truth have formed an integral part of the various religious systems of the world.   Thus they effectually prevented the general
acceptance of all except the mathematical truth arrived at by the
Greek philosophers, and when after nearly two thousand years these
truths were rediscovered and scientifically demonstrated, these false
cosmogonies reacted powerfully against their propagation and general
acceptance.

But observation as well as speculation has always gone on.   Many
minds are not specially constituted for abstraction and generalization,
but take pleasure in observation, and when freed from want and ex-
empted from the struggle for existence such minds amuse themselves
by exploring their surroundings, noting and perhaps recording rare
and peculiar facts and phenomena, accumulating "curiosities" in
private museums, and in many ways, perhaps unintentionally,
increasing human knowledge.   Many of the Greeks belonged to
this class, especially during the later centuries, and Aristotle
possessed the observational attribute in a high degree, while
Theophrastus and Dioscorides might almost be called naturalists.
The Alexandrian school supplied other observers, notably the Ptolo-
mies, and among the Romans the Plinies were not alone.   The
spirit of both speculation and observation smoldered through the
Middle Ages, but broke out anew at their close in a form that
could not again be smothered.

All know the history of science, and it is only necessary to
point out the fact that scientific discovery, as it has gone on during
the last five centuries, and especially the last two centuries, is nothing else than a revival of the philosophic genius of antiquity, this
time applied to an enormously increased volume of facts.   The

spirit of observation and accumulation was never suppressed, and the world was in possession of a large supply of data for thinking even in the time of Copernicus, which continued to increase and has never ceased to accumulate. It is often forgotten that science, which seems to have burst upon the world in the eighteenth century, had been incubating during the previous five hundred years, and could not have come forward in the manner it did but for that prolonged preparation. No matter what branch we study we are always carried back at least to the fifteenth century, and if we look critically into it we find that the chief reason why we cannot go back still farther is that it was in that century that printing was invented, and the greater part of the record prior to that event is lost from the inability to preserve manuscripts. Still a few names, such as those of Galen, Avicenna, Albertus Magnus, and Roger Bacon, stand out and afford a hint as to the intellectual activity of those earlier ages. As soon as the invention of printing made possible the permanent record of this activity the historical perspective shows a great galaxy of names of men whose labors laid the foundations for every branch of science. Even in so relatively obscure a branch as paleontology we find during the sixteenth century works bearing upon the subject by Alexander ab Alexandro, Agricola, Matthiolus, Gesner, Libavius, Kentmann, Balthasar Klein, Imperatus, and many others, and there were perhaps a hundred museums at that date containing fossils and other "curiosities." Geologists, zoologists, botanists, all find that their sciences were extensively cultivated all through the Middle Ages, and the pre-Linnæan literature of natural history cannot be ignored. In chemistry, all liberal-minded persons acknowledge their debt to the alchemists who are found scattered all through the same period down to Roger Bacon. Mathematics was always cultivated and astronomy was revived with Copernicus, Tycho Brahe, Kepler, Galileo, and Newton. Medicine, anatomy, and physiology were not wholly neglected between Galen and Vesalius. And so it was with all forms of knowledge, the materials for its scientific elaboration were accumulating during all these ages, and the solid character which the later study of nature took on was mainly due to the increased volume of facts.

The philosophic spirit also continued to exist, and with these enlarged resources it came forward in great force at about the same time as the scientific awakening. Mathematicians like Newton, Descartes, and Leibnitz, did not hesitate to philosophize. Leonardo da Vinci and Sir Thomas More stand out conspicuously in the fifteenth century, Giordano Bruno and Francis Bacon in the sixteenth, Spinoza, Locke, and Hobbes in the seventeenth. The early sociologists should also be mentioned, beginning with Ibn Khaldûn in the fourteenth century. Hobbes should be reckoned among these, and must be classed with Vico in the seventeenth century. But it was the eighteenth century that produced the largest crop of this class of philosophers, and most of these were enumerated in Chapter IV (supra, p. 56). Our present purpose is simply to show that the great scientific era was not suddenly inaugurated, but that it had a long and ample preparation in antecedent ages, without which it could not have begun.

I have not made a fourth division of the non-advantageous faculties, and called this application of thought to things scientific genius, because, as we have seen, it is not generically distinct from philosophic genius, especially from that branch of it which took the direction of cosmology. The only difference is in the increased data involving a more exact and systematic method. I have already several times insisted that science proper consists in reasoning about facts and not in the accumulation of facts, but the ability to reason soundly depends upon the possession of the facts about which to reason. Neither the facts without the reasoning nor the reasoning without the facts can lead to scientific truth. Science is mainly interpretation, and interpretation is a special kind of reasoning, it may be called a posteriori. Huxley happily characterized it as " the method of Zadig."[1] He also calls it

[1] " The Method of Zadig: Retrospective Prophesy as a Function of Science," by Thomas H. Huxley, Nineteenth Century, Vol. VII, No. 40, June, 1880, pp. 929–940.

Professor Huxley placed at the head of his article the remark made by Cuvier in his " Ossemens Fossiles " (4th ed., Vol. I, p. 185) relative to the significance of the tracks of cloven-footed animals: " C'est une marque plus sûre que toutes celles de Zadig." This was undoubtedly the first time that an application of the familiar stories of Zadig had been made to the scientific method, and that Cuvier had grasped their full force is clear when one reads what precedes, which is as follows: —

" Quelqu'un qui voit seulement la piste d'un pied fourchu, peut en conclure que l'animal qui a laissé cette empreinte ruminait ; et cette conclusion est tout aussi certaine qu'aucune autre en physique ou en morale. Cette seule piste donne donc à celui qui l'observe, et la forme des dents, et la forme des mâchoires, et la forme des vertèbres, et la forme de tous les os des jambes, des cuisses, des épaules et du bassin de l'animal qui vient de passer: c'est une marque plus sûre que toutes celles de Zadig " (pp. 184–185).

"retrospective prophesy," but it is not prophecy at all, it is simply inference from induction, which always involves deduction. It is the method of all observational science, specially characteristic of geology, but true also of all the physical and biological sciences. In physics and chemistry the difference consists chiefly in the artificial production of many of the facts through experimentation, but after the phenomena are produced the method is the same.

We have thus rapidly passed in review the non-advantageous faculties of man. The term *non-advantageous* has been sufficiently defined so that no one need stumble over the obvious fact that these faculties are the most advantageous of all to mankind at large. The distinction may be characterized as that between *individual* and *social* advantage. Individual advantage is biological, and the non-advantageous faculties can only be said to have a biologic origin in that they are genetically derived from the advantageous faculties under

A year earlier than Professor Huxley's article Mr. Andrew Wilson in an article entitled: "Clues and Traces in Natural History," contributed to the *Gentleman's Magazine* for March, 1879 (Vol. CCXLIV, pp. 292–309), notes Cuvier's expression and translates it into English (" is a surer mark than all those of Zadig ").

Professor Huxley's resources for information relative to Zadig seem to have been confined to what he gleaned from the romance of Voltaire so entitled ("Zadig ou la Destinée." Histoire Orientale. Œuvres Complètes de Voltaire, Paris, 1784, Vol. XLIV, Romans, Vol. I, pp. 1-100), and he gives the same story as Voltaire, viz., "Le chien et le cheval" (Chapter III). But there is another story, viz., the story of the lost camel, not mentioned by Voltaire or Huxley, which is much more familiar to most persons, and embodies the same lesson. Voltaire's authority from the historical point of view, is, as Huxley intimates, valueless, but he professes to date it from the year 837 of the Hegira. That all these stories go much farther back is certain. A thorough investigation shows that the story of the camel occurs in the Synhedrin (fol. 104a–104b), and is thus a part of the Talmud. I personally remember that this story occurred in one of the school "readers" used in America during my youth; it was therefore familiar to me.

For the above information and the loan of an extensive literature of the subject, to which justice cannot be done in a footnote, I wish to acknowledge my indebtedness to Dr. Cyrus Adler, Librarian of the Smithsonian Institution, a well-known Hebrew scholar and acknowledged authority on Semitic and other Oriental literature. Among the works consulted should, however, be mentioned the rare volume entitled: "A Group of Eastern Romances and Stories from the Persian, Tamil, and Urdu," with Introduction, Notes, and Appendix, by W. A. Clouston, privately printed, 1879 (see pp. 194 ff, 511); and the new annotated edition of the Talmud with German and Hebrew in parallel columns, now being published but not completed, the last fascicle of which to appear chanced to contain the story of the lost camel (Der Babylonische Talmud. Herausgegeben nach der editio princeps, Venedig, 1520–23, nebst varianten der spaeteren von S Lorja und J Berlin redivirten Ausgaben und der Muenchener Handschrift, nach Rabb. VL, moeglichst wortgetreu uebersetzt und mit kurzen Erklaerungen versehen von Lazarus Goldschmidt. Band VII, Civil- und Strafrecht. Zweite Lieferung: "Des Traktats Synhedrin" Zweite Haelfte, p. 461. Synhedrin XI, i ij. Fol. 104a–104b).

the influence of other principles than natural selection. These principles have been fully explained, and it has been shown that they are not confined to psychic and social phenomena, but are in full operation in the organic world and probably account for the origin of more species than are produced by natural selection. The principles of cross fertilization, of atavism, of innovation, of "mutation," are everywhere at work supplementing natural selection. But in the social world we have the added influence of the artificial emancipation of a part of mankind from the restraints of the environment, analogous to domestication, which liberates the psychic energy and permits a large surplus to expend itself in biologically non-advantageous ways, some of which have proved sociologically advantageous, resulting in the general condition described in Chapter III under the name of achievement.

CHAPTER XIX

THE CONQUEST OF NATURE

EQUIPPED with the directive agent as a guide to the dynamic agent, that "favored race" of beings called man set out on a career for the conquest of nature. Throughout his prehuman stage, like the rest of the animal world, this being had always been the slave of nature. The iron law of competition had held him in its grasp as it holds all organic beings. His was a struggle for existence like the rest, but he proved himself the fittest to survive and he survived. By a series of accidents, some of which have been recorded in this work, cephalization found in him its highest expression and brain became a factor in this struggle. *Facile princeps,* it soon gained the lead, and from that time on, this being, thus rendered human, distanced all competitors. He early saw the advantage of association and secured the added benefit of the law of the survival of the social. He passed through all the stages described in Chapters X to XV, and emerged into the stage of compound social assimilation with a military régime of exploitation, a sacerdotal caste, an intermediate and independent free business element, and a subordinate slave population. All except the last were under the influence of one or more of the dynamic principles enumerated in Chapter XI, and even the slaves felt the effect of the cross fertilization, especially in the form characterized as social chemistry. The whole mass was rising, but parts rose with special rapidity, the business element through the exercise of its advantageous, and the leisure class of its non-advantageous mental faculties.

What I have called a paradox, viz., that "the artificial is superior to the natural," was nevertheless freely acted upon as a truth in the earliest stages of civilization, and no progressive race has ever been content with the natural. Everywhere and always the environment, although it embodies all the elements of existence, has obstructed human progress, has withheld the necessary supplies, has doled out its resources in a niggardly way, and has starved to death by far the greater number of all the creatures that have been born. It began

511

thus with the human race, but with its intuitive, egoistic reason, with its inventive faculty, with its intellectual prevision and telic power, that race began its struggle against the law of nature. There are philosophers who cry: *laissez faire!* but every step that man has taken in advance, every invention he has made, all art, all applied science, all achievement, all material civilization, has been the result of his persistent refusal to let things alone, and of his determination to conquer the dominion of nature, to emancipate himself from his bondage to nature, and to become master of nature and of nature's powers. The *laissez faire* school of that early day was the priesthood, who looked upon every attempt to control the powers of nature and subject them to the will of man as an attack upon the divine order. Such anathemas continued to be hurled at impious inventors and blasphemous discoverers of scientific truth far down into the modern era. This ecclesiastical *laissez faire* policy, often with great power behind it, certainly retarded the march of the conquering host of science and art, but nothing could repress it, and it went on with its succession of triumphs that have placed the historic races where we find them to-day.

It was found that under the law already formulated that while the quantity of matter and motion in the universe is unchangeable, the mode of motion is capable of indefinite change, the phenomena of nature are susceptible of unlimited modification, and the environment may be transformed to any required extent. The transformation of the environment in the direction of utility, *i.e.*, of human advantage, is no more difficult than in any other direction. It was therefore simply a question of knowing how to accomplish this, and knowledge of this kind is that which underlies invention. It was also discovered that when the requisite knowledge is possessed, useful transformations are easy, in other words, that nature is easily managed by intelligence. The earliest operations of this class were what are called empirical. Empiricism may be distinguished from science as being the result of intuition instead of investigation. The utilities are sufficiently simple to be seen without special research, and do not have to be discovered in the scientific sense. It is said that art precedes science, and all the simpler arts of uncivilized races have been created without what is understood by scientific investigation. But it must not be supposed that art could exist without any exercise of intellectual faculties. For it there must exist in the mind a considerable amount of knowledge of the properties of bodies.

Empirical art consists chiefly in making useful things. It is what I characterized in Chapter V by the term *poesis*. It deals mostly with different substances found in the region inhabited by the artisan. It has mainly to do with properties as distinguished from forces. These known properties are perceived to contain utilities, and by the appropriate transformation of the substances these utilities are realized. One of the most universal of these substances is clay, and the potter's art, which is very early and widespread, is a typical empirical art. All arts are attended with labor, which is chiefly expended in multiplying the products of a single art, often with slavish adherence to a fixed pattern. But a certain degree of satisfaction attends the making of an artificial thing, and Mr. Veblen's "instinct of workmanship" sustains many a weary hour of toil. But the making of tools and weapons contributed much more to the conquest of nature than did the culinary and domestic arts, and this form of art was much more frequently intrusted to men, women being the principal primitive potters. Tools, first of rough, then of polished stone, then of copper (usually, but probably erroneously called bronze by archæologists), and at last of iron after the art of extracting iron from its ores had been acquired, have been the marks, and their quality the measures of culture in the progress of the race.

At length in some of the later stages of compound assimilation man began to see utilities in certain of the forces of nature, primarily those of water and wind. The animal ancestor of man, like the creatures that most closely approach him anatomically, was probably frugivorous, but his large size rendered an arboreal existence difficult, and doubtless compelled him to lead a chiefly terrestrial life. Here his diet must take a wider range, and it is well known how readily herbivorous animals adopt carnivorous habit. That man began his career as a practically omnivorous animal is highly probable, his taste for flesh and fish must necessarily increase. Both probably began with the consumption of invertebrates. The extent to which savages now live on shellfish points to this, and many eat large larvæ and even insects. To catch fish and mammals required a higher form of cunning than man first possessed, and birds were still more difficult to obtain.

2 L

HUMAN INVENTION

I use the adjective *human* because there is a widespread belief that animals invent. I have taken considerable pains to examine the evidence on this point, and I do not hesitate to reject it all without exception. The most of it consists of mere stories told by persons without the scientific habit of mind. The rest is for the most part due to the inability even of scientific minds to prevent projecting their own intelligence into animals and ascribing to their acts mental conceptions to which they are entirely incapable of attaining. All the accounts I have seen of apes " throwing stones " and " pelting with cocoanuts " are unsupported by any such evidence as such seductively anthropomorphic ideas as these require before they can be accepted as actual facts. I grant that they may sometimes loosen stones and let them roll down a steep hill or drop from a crag, and that they may detach cocoanuts and cause them to drop, mentally realizing that in both cases these acts may kill or drive off enemies including men. But that they attempt to direct these objects as missiles intended to hit their enemies is thus far lacking in adequate proof, and must be scientifically observed and carefully recorded with all the attendant circumstances before it can be accepted. With regard to their supposed use of the club as a weapon of attack and defense, I have seen nothing during the past ten years to change the result arrived at in the " Psychic Factors of Civilization " (pp. 254, 255), and I consider all such statements as equally unproved.

That the keen imitative powers and sharp intuitive cunning of apes and other animals comes very near to intelligence may be freely admitted, and I for one would certainly withhold nothing from them that they actually possess, but science admonishes us to adhere under all circumstances to the established truth. It is only a step from this grade of cunning to that which could arrange a pitfall for an unwary animal or a rude snare for a fish. The earliest man, driven by the necessities of existence, took this step, and it was devices such as these that constituted the first inventions. Nothing could be more interesting than a list of the truly primitive inventions. This of course can never be drawn up, because there are no absolutely primitive races, and archæology begins much too high in the series. But there have been some tolerably satisfactory approaches toward the preparation of such a list. The art of making fire is usually regarded as among the earliest, but when we remember that the human race almost certainly first emerged from the animal state at some point within the tropics we may well believe that there were other things more important than fire. Topinard says : —

> The making of tools or of means of defense against wild animals was without doubt the first step taken by man in the domain of intellect. I take it that the discovery of the means of obtaining fire was not made until some time later : among the lowest savages with whom we are acquainted, we find legends relating to this discovery, but none concerning the origin of the simplest weapons.[1]

As to what these primitive tools and weapons were Spencer says : —

> As aids to teeth and hands, the primitive man had nothing beyond such natural products as lay around him — bowlders, shells collected on the beach, bones, horns, and teeth from the animals he had killed or found dead, branches torn from trees by storms. Roughly speaking, sticks and stones were his tools, and the sticks were necessarily unshapen ; for he had nothing wherewith to cut their ends or smooth their surfaces. As alleged by General Pitt-Rivers, and shown by his collection, the stick was the parent of a group of implements — diggers, clubs, spears, boomerangs, throwing-sticks, shields, paddles ; and only in courses of ages did the unimaginative savage produce these derived forms.[2]

And he proceeds to show the necessary steps in the further development of these arts, as it would be appropriate to do here had it not been so often done by others. Almost the same was said much earlier by Letourneau,[3] but he dwells more especially on the early invention of the bow and the sling. At a later date this author makes the following just but significant remark : —

> There is one especially striking fact in primitive industry, viz., the essential similarity of the first instruments, tools, or arms, invented by all races throughout the whole world. In every place similarity of materials, wants, and organs has produced almost identical results.[4]

Professor Emil Du Bois-Reymond was dealing with a much more extended period and one coming farther down in the history of man-

---

[1] " Science and Faith, or Man as an Animal and Man as a Member of Society," by Paul Topinard ; translated by Thomas J. McCormack, Chicago, 1899, p. 145.

[2] " Principles of Sociology," Vol. III, New York, 1897, p. 328 (§ 723).

[3] " La Sociologie," etc., p. 564.

[4] *Revue Internationale de Sociologie*, IXᵉ Année, octobre, 1901, p. 722.

kind, when, in his address before the Scientific Lectures Association
of Cologne in 1878, speaking of the "first tools," he said: —

These were invented, not by one man, nor at one spot upon the earth, but
by many, and at points very distant from one another. Thus originated
levers, rollers, wedges, and axes; clubs and spears; slings, *sarbacands*, las-
sos; bows and arrows; oars, sails, and rudders; fishing nets, lines, and
hooks; finally, the use of fire, by which, as by speech, man is best distinguished from animals, and which even anatomically stamps him with the
character of a soot-stained lung. Man, therefore, at an early period was
unquestionably entitled to the epithet bestowed upon him by Benjamin
Franklin of "the tool-making animal."[1]

Pottery, as already remarked, was a primitive art, but could not
have antedated the art of making fire. Professor Ernst Mach thus
describes its hypothetical invention, wrongly ascribing it to accident: —

A small hole in the ground with fire kindled in it constituted the primitive stove. The flesh of the quarry, wrapped with water in its skin, was
boiled by contact with heated stones. Cooking by stones was also performed
in wooden vessels. Hollow gourds were protected from the fire by coats of
clay. Thus, from the burned clay accidentally originated the enveloping
pot, which rendered the gourd superfluous, although for a long time thereafter the clay was still spread over the gourd, or pressed into woven wicker-
work, before the potter's art assumed its final independence. Even then
the wicker-work ornament was retained, as a sort of attest of its origin.[2]

If such cases are to be classed as accidental then have all invention
and discovery been accidental. Nothing is more certain than that
all inventions are growths due to the successive additions of small
improvements naturally suggesting themselves in the manufacture
of the products. The Patent Office makes two classes: inventions
and improvements, and I am told by the examiners that it rarely
happens to grant a patent for an "invention," almost everything,
after comparison with earlier patents, coming properly under the
head of an "improvement." The art of pottery was therefore simply
an improvement, or a series of improvements upon the primitive use
of clay in cooking.

Mr. George Iles[3] has also ventured a sketch of the origin of pottery, which agrees well with that of Mach. It is as early as the

[1] *Popular Science Monthly*, Vol. XIII, July, 1878, p. 258.

[2] *The Monist*, Vol. VI, January, 1896, p. 164.

[3] "Flame, Electricity and the Camera: Man's Progress from the First Kindling
of Fire to the Wireless Telegraph and the Photography of Color," New York, 1900,
pp. 27–28.

sacred books of Sanchoniatho,[1] who ascribes it to the eighth generation of men.　Letourneau says: —

The art of pottery has almost everywhere been disdainfully abandoned
to women, which is undoubtedly due to the fact that this essentially primitive industry was invented during a social phase in which the chase and
war were the manly occupations, at a time also when the care of the kitchen
was left entirely to the weaker sex.[2]

Many think that the art is practically the invention of women,
and Professor Mason[3] and Dr. A. de Neuville[4] have shown that
many of the most useful inventions have been made by women.　It
is nevertheless probably true and certainly quite natural, as Havelock Ellis maintains,[5] that the inventions and arts created by women
are of a severely practical character and do not in their hands tend to
become ornamental or esthetic.

Glass seems to have been the natural outgrowth of pottery and is
very old, being found in Egyptian sarcophagi.　A large bead of glass
was found at Thebes upon which was inscribed the name of a monarch who reigned 1500 years before Christ, and their ancient monuments represent the glass-blowers of Egypt as a flourishing guild.
But they did not apparently understand the process of annealing
glass.　That was a modern discovery.　The Phenicians manufactured it for export.　What uses it was put to is difficult to say.
Probably it was chiefly ornamental, but Layard found a crystal lens
in the ruins of Nineveh, and we have seen that the Egyptians wrote
inscriptions on glass.　Socrates accused the sophists of wasting their
time experimenting with burning glasses, but neither the Greeks
nor Romans employed it in architecture, and windows in the modern
sense were unknown to the ancients, at least down to the close of
classic times.　At the time Pompeii was buried it had begun to
come into use, as certain fragments exhumed seem to attest.　Hallam
in his "Middle Ages," says : —

The two most essential improvements in architecture during this period,
one of which had been missed by the sagacity of Greece and Rome, were

[1] See Lubbock, "Origin of Civilization," New York, 1871, p. 120.
[2] "La Sociologie," etc., p. 568.
[3] "Woman's Share in Primitive Culture," by Otis Tufton Mason, New York,
1894.
[4] "Le Génie de l'Invention chez les femmes," *Revue des Revues*, Vol. XXXII, January, 1900, pp. 182–190.
[5] "Man and Woman," 3d ed.. London, 1902, pp. 316–317.

chimneys and glass windows.   Nothing apparently can be more simple than the former; yet the wisdom of ancient times had been content to let the smoke escape by an aperture in the center of the roof.[1]

The bow and arrow was a primitive weapon, being found in the hands of most of the lowest savages, and also among the relics of the lake dwellers of Robenhausen.   The arrow was probably a modification of the javelin and the bow the result of a series of steps in contriving means of hurling it with greater force and accuracy.

The plow grew out of the digger, and the primitive plow had no mold-board, did not throw a furrow to one side, but merely scratched the ground.   A wooden mold-board was introduced much later, but the iron plowshare was not invented until the end of the eighteenth century.

All the early pre-Chaldean arts are now known to have migrated northward from Southern Asia, and the archæology of Middle and Northern Asia, which has only recently been studied, is throwing great light upon the direction taken by the streams of primitive migration.   If it can be completed it will probably fill all the gaps between Asiatic and American civilizations.   In the primary social differentiation the small stream that penetrated Kamchatka and poured across Bering Strait, thus ultimately peopling America, was so nearly cut off from the great mass of mankind that only very few of the cultural advances were preserved, and American civilization had to begin almost at the foot of the ladder and take all the steps anew.   As a consequence much time was lost, and when Columbus discovered America he found the western hemisphere far behind the eastern in nearly everything that relates to human civilization. Nevertheless, the steps that had been taken were practically the same as those taken in the Old World so long before, and there can be little doubt that with sufficient time the New World would have substantially repeated the history of the Old.   But the conjuncture of the much more advanced eastern with the relatively backward western races has rendered this impossible, and now the latter are doomed to absorption by the former.

Most of the Greek art in the time of Homer was either Egyptian or Chaldean, both being introduced by the Phenicians.   Such were

[1] " View of the State of Europe during the Middle Ages," by Henry Hallam, in two volumes, Ninth Edition, London, 1846, Vol. II, p. 414.

the arts of metal working (chiefly bronze and iron), weaving, the construction of boats and war chariots, also of tripods, which constituted their chairs, and of such houses as they had. Espinas [1] says that they "were acquainted with the spindle and distaff, the sail boat, the bit, the bellows, the plow, the war chariot, the carriage, the hinge, the lock, the auger, the bow, the turning lathe, the potter's wheel, the balance." From the Phenicians they imported "prepared fabrics, wines, oil, and intoxicants; papyrus articles, linen (an exceedingly important product), ointments, prepared spices, incense, embalming-mixtures, perfumes, dyes, and drugs from Egypt, and the various products of metal work, ornaments and weapons of a superior quality." [2] But prior to the Trojan war the Greeks were an almost exclusively pastoral people, consisting of nomads from the east who had conquered the original less aggressive inhabitants and reduced them to slavery, becoming themselves partially fixed, and subsisting chiefly upon their oxen and sheep and a rude agriculture. Nevertheless they did not know the use of cows' milk and had not learned to make butter or cheese. Eggs are not mentioned in the "Iliad" or "Odyssey," and only the inhabitants of the maritime districts used salt, although, according to Sanchoniatho it was discovered in the eleventh generation of men. They reckoned by the decimal system, counting their fingers like other barbarians. They had no alphabet, but received later that of the Phenicians derived chiefly from Egypt, so that until that time those great epics must have been simply traditions whose preservation was intrusted to priests or other specially appointed guardians to hold in memory and transmit to their successors. An alphabet and the art of writing on papyrus or something more manageable than stone, glass, and metal, must therefore be set down as one of the great steps in civilization. Down to the time when Ctesibius of Alexandria invented the clepsydra, time was kept by the sun-dial, invented by the Babylonians and mentioned in the Bible (Isaiah xxxviii, 8). The power of steam was known and the principle embodied in Hero's engine, but no practical use was made by the ancients of so important a discovery. The extensive public works of the Romans prove that some of the most important principles of engineering,

---

[1] "Les Origines de la Technologie," par Alfred Espinas, Paris, 1897, p. 45 (chiefly on the authority of Hultsch and Blümner).

[2] "Homeric Society," by A. G. Keller, New York, 1902, p. 19.

including those of the arch and the catenary, had been worked out and applied.

It thus appears that the stream of human thought, intelligence, and inventive power moved westward from Southern Asia to Chaldea, Egypt, and Asia Minor, thence to Greece and Italy, and that from the Mediterranean shores it slowly spread to Western and Northern Europe.[1] In these regions had been formed all the most highly assimilated races, and here were slowly worked out, on the principles set forth in Chapter X, all the great historic nations through which had been maintained that continuity of the social plasm by which nothing was lost and every increment to civilization represented a gain and an advance beyond all that had been accomplished before. The movement that took place along more northern lines, from Central Asia to Northern Europe, had a different character. Although the ethnic elements were practically the same — rather more of the Aryan and less of the Semitic, but somewhat of a Turanian composition — they represented more of a peripheral and penumbral population lying originally on the margin of the primary nucleus and hence less thoroughly assimilated, socialized, and civilized. Even these had been preceded ages before by still less cemented peoples whom they found occupying all Europe, and whom it was necessary to subjugate and incorporate. Compared therefore with the Mediterranean elements these northern peoples during the ascendency of Rome were " barbarians," and with the aggressive attempts of the Romans to conquer them and add them to the empire, followed by the nemesis of barbarian invasion of Rome, there resulted the necessity of assimilating the entire mass, which caused an apparent retrograde movement and seemed to lower the status of civilization in the Mediterranean region. This was further complicated by the vast religious revolution attendant upon the substitution of Christianity not only for the pagan cults but also for all the barbaric cults. The consequence was nearly fifteen hundred years of apparent intellectual stagnation. Yet even this long period was not wholly fruitless. Here and there a flicker of inventive genius flashed up, as when the Saracen, Ebn Junis, at the end of the tenth century invented the pendulum; when the compass, perhaps invented by the Chinese, and certainly used by them in traveling overland, found its way to Europe and was applied to water

---

[1] Cf. Humboldt, " Cosmos," Vol. II, B, I; Bagehot, " Physics and Politics," p. 52.

navigation; when gunpowder, likewise of Asiatic origin, but hitherto only used for pyrotechnic display, was applied to projectiles and became an engine of war; or when the Saracens invented a process of making paper from linen rags and cotton. Even the great art of printing, whose invention broke the spell, had been independently invented in China and was actually brought to Europe by Venetian navigators.

The middle of the fifteenth century marks the beginning of the modern era. The invention and practical application of the art of printing was the turning point, but a long train of other, often apparently independent inventions and discoveries quickly followed. Oil painting came forward, completely superseding the wax painting of the ancients, and leading the way to the Renaissance. Engraving on copper, invented in 1460, gave birth to a new art and helped to swell the stream. The sixteenth century stands out most prominently, because it required half a century for the art of printing to begin to bear fruit. Leonardo da Vinci lived into the sixteenth century; Giordano Bruno just lived it out, as did Tycho Brahe; Galileo, Descartes, Francis Bacon, and Harvey did much of their work in it, but continued it far into the seventeenth. The sixteenth century produced the telescope and the microscope, at least in their rudiments, also the thermometer and the camera obscura. The vernier and proportional dividers were useful accessories to scientific work. Clocks and watches came forward run by weights, but it took another century to evolve the spring. Mills for grinding grain were invented in the fifth century and were driven by water power, but the flour was unbolted and the bran and hulls were all ground together. Now a bolting machine was invented and thenceforth men might have white flour. Heretofore they had always eaten with their fingers, for chop-sticks were unknown in the West. Now some unknown genius invented forks. Such are a few of the sixteenth-century inventions, but it would require pages merely to enumerate them all. Indeed there are always many the date of which cannot be ascertained, and still more that are so completely the products of natural evolution by minute accretions that they can scarcely be said to have had an origin.

The steam engine in the modern sense was preëminently the child of the seventeenth century, although it required the entire century to invent it. Beginning with Giambattista Porta's advance upon

Hero's engine, made in the first year of the century, and passing through the successive improvements of Caus, 1615, Branca, 1629, Worcester, 1650, Papin, 1690, it culminated in Savery's practically working machine not brought into complete existence until 1689. But Denys Papin was the true inventor of the piston, involving the most fundamental principle in the steam engine. This growth, however, had then only begun, and it lasted through the eighteenth, and, we may truly say, through the nineteenth centuries, and still continues. There can be no doubt that the invention of the steam engine constitutes the most important economic and industrial step the world has thus far taken, and it can only be compared to the invention of printing, the greatest intellectual step in the history of civilization. With the latter began the era of thought, with the former, the era of machinery.

Among other inventions of the seventeenth century may be mentioned as typical the air-pump by Hooke and Otto Guericke (more or less independently), and the barometer by Torricelli. Nor should we forget as among the most peculiar, the wheelbarrow by Pascal, a religious ascetic, but also a mathematician and philosopher.

As following upon the maturing of the steam engine it seems natural that the great inventions of the eighteenth century should be the loom and the spinning jenny, as it is these three that practically constitute the factory, and although a great many other industries, each the result of a series of preparatory inventions, sprang up in response to the new demand, still it was the factory, and the extensive production of spun and woven goods by machinery, that characterized this age. It was the beginning of what by a contradiction of terms is known as manufacture by machinery, and which M. Tarde has so happily and also so correctly renamed *machinofacture*.

When we come to the nineteenth century we find the inventions simply innumerable. It is difficult to characterize it by any single one, and it seems necessary to name at least two, but better still, three or four. If we mention the telegraph, there at once arise in the mind the colossal figures of the railway and the steamship. There also arise the other great applications of electricity. It may be called the age of electricity. But if we look to function rather than structure, it may be called the age of communication, for all these structures serve that end. The eighteenth century may then be called the age of production and the nineteenth that of distribution in the economic sense. In analogy to organic functions the eighteenth may be regarded as an age of social alimentation or digestion, while the nineteenth was one of circulation. This circulation, however, includes both nutritive and neural, the telegraph and telephone constituting an internuncial system. But in all this it is not meant to imply that the organs of production developed during the eighteenth century were not active during the nineteenth. The productivity of man has steadily increased throughout all this time. It is only that to this great alimentary system there was added the system of circulation both of things, including men, and of ideas.

The telegraph as a human invention stands in a somewhat similar relation to the nineteenth century that the steam engine did to the seventeenth. Started by Volta in 1800 it underwent all the successive improvements by Sömmering, 1809, Oersted, 1820, Henry, 1831, Weber, 1833, Steinheil, 1837, Morse and Vail (who devised the alphabet), 1837, Cooke, 1842, and emerged in 1845 as a practical business enterprise earning as high as one dollar per day !

The railway, hatched under ground, came to the surface in 1804, substituted iron for wooden rails in 1805, and equipped with Stephenson's improved locomotive in 1829, carried the first passengers from Liverpool to Manchester in 1830. The first steamboat dates from 1802 and the screw propeller from 1838.

As a few typical nineteenth-century inventions, given as nearly as practicable in the order of dates, may be mentioned: illuminating gas, 1804; electric lighting (Davy), 1810, (Moleyn, incandescent), 1841; photography (Daguerre and Nièpce), 1829; matches (John Walker), 1827 ; [1] India rubber or caoutchouc, 1839; gun-cotton, 1841 ;

[1] The following item appeared in the *Scientific American* for March 22, 1902, Vol. LXXXVI, No. 12, New York, p. 209 : —

INVENTOR OF THE LUCIFER MATCH

"There have been many claimants to the honor of being the maker of the first lucifer match. But a recent discovery of some old account books at Stockton-on-Tees, England, affords documentary evidence which proves beyond question that one John Walker, a Durham chemist, was the original inventor and maker of the match. According to a diary, in which Walker carefully noted all his business transactions, the first box of matches was sold for thirty-five cents in April, 1827. It appears that they at once became popular, and people traveled from the adjacent towns to purchase them. Walker employed the poor of Stockton to split the wood, but dipped them in the phosphorus mixture himself to insure their perfection. The inventor was pressed by his friends to patent the process ; he refused, however, affirming that he had ample means to satisfy his simple wants."

the Bunsen burner, 1845; the sewing machine, 1847. Of the last half of the century it is unnecessary to speak. All know the history of the ocean cable, of the telephone, of the bicycle, of the automobile, of the X-rays, of wireless telegraphy, etc.

In the conquest of nature by man unquestionably the first place must be given to invention, to the perception of utilities and the utilization of properties and forces locked up except to the key of intelligence in the apparently dead and lifeless material objects, or invisible and intangible in the subtle forces of nature. Still, as has already been said, the principle does not essentially differ from that employed in utilizing the psychic properties of animals, either through the ruse in capturing them for food or through those higher powers of cunning and calculation by which animals are domesticated and made to serve man. M. Tarde has recognized this and has also eloquently portrayed the effects of invention on civilization in the following characteristic passage from one of his recent works : —

The first savage who caused a spark to fly from two stones struck together did not suspect that from this would spring the religion of the hearth. The first savage who, having captured young lambs or calves alive, observed the ease with which they could be tamed, the advantage of fattening them rather than of killing them immediately, did not suspect that he was inaugurating a new era, the pastoral era, and a new political régime, the patriarchal family, the organized clan and tribe out of which would arise the nobility and the hereditary aristocracy. The first savage who conceived the idea, instead of simply gathering seeds and fruits, of sowing them and cultivating grains of wheat, and of planting fruit trees, did not divine that, from this simple idea there would be born the city, a wholly new form of government, and that from the patriarch, from the chief of the tribe or the clan, the power would pass, wholly transformed, to municipal magistrates. . . . The first man or the first woman who had the idea of a loom and of manufacturing cloth to sell outside, while before that every family made all the clothes they needed by the hands of its women or its slaves, this person introduced for the cities of the future, such as Florence with its " arts of wool," the microbe of industry and commerce, which, through the accumulation and liberation of capital, has democratized the world.[1]

Thus has invention not only satisfied a thousand wants but it has created many thousand more; and not only has it satisfied old wants and created new ones but it has also satisfied these latter

[1] "Les Transformations du Pouvoir," par G. Tarde, Paris, 1899, pp. 188–189.

and thereby contributed in an incalculable degree to the fullness of life or volume of existence, which alone constitutes social progress.

Scientific Discovery

Invention and discovery are reciprocal. Invention leads to discovery and discovery leads to invention. Without the arts necessary in the construction of a seaworthy ship and the invention of the compass the discovery of remote parts of the earth, including the New World, would have been impossible. Without the discovery of the power of steam and the nature of electricity the invention of the steam engine and the telegraph would have been equally impossible. If invention seems to come before discovery it is because throughout the long empirical stage of art the intuitive reason passed immediately from the perception of utility to practical application, and there was no preliminary stage of scientific research. But in this way only the more simple and obvious relations could be perceived. The deeper and more occult laws and principles which have been as much more fertile of results as they were more difficult to understand, could only be discovered after ages of thought, study, and investigation. This is what is distinguished as science, and all the later and greater inventions had to wait for this prolonged preparation.

Just as the chief mission of invention in its broadest sense is to counteract and so far as possible nullify the uneconomical and wasteful genetic method of nature and substitute for it the economical and fruitful telic method of mind, so it was the chief mission of science in its broadest sense to dispel the illusions of nature and the errors of the primitive reason based on these illusions, and to substitute for them the truths that lie hidden beneath the superficial appearances and the laws of nature that only reveal themselves to prolonged observation, experimentation, and reflection. The most fundamental of all nature's laws is the law of causation, and this is precisely the one that the primitive mind least understands. Du Bois-Reymond, in the address already referred to (*supra*, p. 516), says : —

Among men in a low grade of culture, the instinct of causality is satisfied with reasons for things that hardly deserve the name of *reasons*. Nothing, we are told by Charles Martins, strikes one so forcibly in conversing with the inhabitants of the Sahara as their lack of development in this respect. These people have no idea of "cause" or of "law" as we understand those terms. For them it is the *natural*, and not the *supernatural*, that has no existence. The French officer of engineers who sinks through the gypsum crust of the desert an artesian well, thus procuring for them the blessing of a new date-grove, is, in their eyes, not a man of superior acquirement whose eye penetrates to the interior of the earth, and who knows how to discover what there is hid, but a miracle-worker, who, albeit an infidel, is on better terms with Allah than themselves, and who, like Moses of old, strikes water from the rock.

The stage of empiricism overlapped far upon the scientific stage and cannot be said even now to have wholly passed away, but after social amalgamation had reached a certain point and social cleavage had become complete the leisure class, freed from the goad of want, began to employ its surplus energies in the greater and greater exercise of its non-advantageous faculties. *Primum vivere, deinde philosophari.* This explains the fact to which Comte called attention that the sciences were cultivated in the inverse order of their value to man. The non-advantageous faculties had no reason for searching for utilities, and they expended themselves chiefly in the search for things that had no apparent utility whatever. Much of this early research, if it can be dignified by that name, had in fact no utility beyond that of exercising and thus developing the faculties themselves. Such were the greater part of all the studies made of the mind itself, of the relations supposed to subsist between the human mind and the divine mind, of the nature of the supposed intelligences existing in nature outside of the human mind, of logic and dialectics, of ideas, of being, and of the soul. None of these lines of reflection have yielded anything whatever that has advanced or benefited the world. That these were the earliest lines followed is evidenced by the fact that they still prevail in Oriental philosophy, *i.e.*, in the philosophy of those parts of the world in which social amalgamation first took place and civilization began. The sterility of this form of philosophy is sufficiently attested by the nature of Oriental civilization, which, although so much older than Occidental civilization, has made scarcely any advance in science and the civilizing effects of science. The reason for this is perhaps partly racial, but is doubtless chiefly social, *i.e.*, it lies in the intense conservatism of those ancient peoples, which has prevented for ages any marked disturbance of the social equilibrium and the setting up of a difference of potential. But this is not the place to discuss this aspect of the subject.

Comte also pointed out the three principal methods of scientific discovery, viz., observation, experimentation, and comparison, and this is at once the order corresponding to that in which the sciences stand in his hierarchy and that in which, to a great extent, they have been studied. It is at least true that the earliest scientific study consisted chiefly in observation. The considerable advances which it is known that the Chaldeans, the Chinese, and the Egyptians made in astronomy were reached by this method. It is true that much of this relates to the fixed stars and has not yielded very important results, but the Babylonians knew full well the difference between fixed stars and planets, and were able actually to calculate eclipses. They determined the length of the year with considerable accuracy, and even understood the fact at least of the precession of the equinoxes. Thus Dr. Draper says : —

Ptolemy, the Egyptian astronomer, possessed a Babylonian record of eclipses, going back 747 years before our era. Long-continued and close observations were necessary, before some of these astronomical results that have reached our times could have been ascertained. Thus the Babylonians had fixed the length of a tropical year within twenty-five seconds of the truth ; their estimate of the sidereal year was barely two minutes in excess. They had detected the precession of the equinoxes. They knew the causes of eclipses, and, by the aid of their cycle called Saros, could predict them. Their estimate of the value of that cycle, which is more than 6585 days, was within nineteen and a half minutes of the truth. Such facts furnish incontrovertible proof of the patience and skill with which astronomy had been cultivated in Mesopotamia, and that, with very inadequate instrumental means, it had reached no inconsiderable perfection. These old observers had made a catalogue of the stars, had divided the zodiac into twelve signs ; they had parted the day into twelve hours, the night into twelve. They had, as Aristotle says, for a long time devoted themselves to observations of star-occultations by the moon. They had correct views of the structure of the solar system, and knew the order of emplacement of the planets. They constructed sun-dials, clepsydras, astrolabes, and gnomons.[1]

That these ancient astronomers were priests, and that this early study of nature was due to the establishment of a priesthood wholly exempt from the struggle for existence is evident from the fact that

---

[1] "History of the Conflict between Religion and Science," by John William Draper, fifth edition, New York, 1875, pp. 13–14. Cf. Laplace, "Exposition du Système du Monde," 6ᵉ édition, Paris, 1835, pp. 371 ff.

the results were regularly used in religious ceremonies. On this
point Laplace (*loc. cit.*, p. 374) remarks : —

Astronomical knowledge appears to have been the basis of all theogonies
whose origin is thus explained in the simplest manner.   In Chaldea and in
ancient Egypt astronomy was only cultivated in temples by priests who
founded upon it the superstitions of which they were the ministers.

India, which is perhaps theoretically nearer to the primordial
center of dispersion, does not show the same antiquity in observational science as Chaldea.   In the latter country the record reaches
back nearly two thousand years before the Christian era, while in
the former it is only certain for somewhat less than fifteen hundred
years.   There is, however, an Indian record covering over three
thousand years, but the authenticity of this has been called in
question.   Still, the record is really no just criterion of antiquity,
since there are so many ways in which it might be destroyed or lost.
That in both these countries observations had been regularly made
ages before any permanent mode of recording them had been invented, is next to certain.[1]

While speaking of India we should not omit to note that it was
here that originated the decimal system of notation, or so-called
" Arabic numerals," the influence of which on human life and social
evolution has been incalculable.   The fact that the Greeks and
Romans did not possess it makes it possible to conceive of the
world's having had to do without it altogether had it not been
evolved from some fertile Indian brain.   Whether it could have
been evolved from the clumsy Roman system may be an open question, although Humboldt, as already shown in Chapter III, has
worked out such a natural evolution of the value of position.
Draper claims (*loc. cit.*, p. 14) that the Babylonians had all the digits
except the zero, but they may have acquired their system from
India.

In China astronomical records go back quite as far as in Chaldea,
viz., to the reign of the emperor Yao, more than two thousand years
before our era.   There was in the charge of the priesthood a tri-
bunal of mathematics which prepared a calendar of eclipses (announced in advance) and of other celestial phenomena.   They had
the solstitial gnomon which marked the midday sun and the midnight stars; they measured time by clepsydras; they determined

[1] Laplace, *loc. cit.*, p. 376.

the position of the moon relative to the stars in eclipses; they constructed instruments for measuring the angular distances of the stars; they calculated the length of the year at 365¼ days. They made the angle of the plane of the earth's orbit to that of the ecliptic 23° 54', which, as Humboldt says,[1] is twenty-seven minutes greater than it was in 1850. Especially valuable are the ancient Chinese records relating to comets. In this connection Humboldt remarks: —

> While the so-called classic peoples of the West, the Greeks and Romans, did indeed sometimes note the spot where a comet was first seen in the heavens, never a word as to its apparent path, the rich literature of the nature-observing, all-recording Chinese give circumstantial accounts of the constellations through which every comet passed.[2]

Unfortunately the emperor Chi-hoang-ti, in the year 213 B.C., ordered most of the books containing astronomical records to be burned, whereby their mode of calculating eclipses and many important observations have been lost.

The ancient Egyptians must have cultivated astronomy, but about the only records they have left are to be found in the construction of the pyramids, the exactness of which presupposes considerable advance in mathematics, engineering, and mechanical skill. Their orientation with the points of the compass shows that the calculations were primarily astronomical. Professor Piazzi Smyth took great pains to examine, measure, and describe the pyramids. Basing his remarks on Professor Smyth's results, Dr. Alfred Russel Wallace in his opening address as President of the Biological Section of the British Association for the Advancement of Science at its meeting in Glasgow in 1876, and confining himself to the great Pyramid of Cheops, thus sums up the evidence: —

> The results arrived at are: —
> 1. That the pyramid is truly square, the sides being equal and the angles right angles.
> 2. That the four sockets on which the first four stones of the corners rested are truly on the same level.
> 3. That the directions of the sides are accurately to the four cardinal points.
> 4. That the vertical height of the pyramid bears the same proportion to its circumference at the base as the radius of a circle does to its circumference.
> Now all these measures, angles, and levels are accurate, not as an ordinary surveyor or builder could make them, but to such a degree as requires

---

[1] Cosmos, Vol. III, p. 302.
[2] Op. cit., Vol. I, p. 67; cf. also p. 236.

the very best modern instruments and all the refinements of geodetical
science to discover any error at all. In addition to this we have the wonderful perfection of the workmanship in the interior of the pyramid, the passages and chambers being lined with huge blocks of stones fitted with the
utmost accuracy, while every part of the building exhibits the highest
structural science.[1]

The date of the construction of this pyramid, the most ancient
human structure on the globe, is usually placed at about four thousand years before the commencement of our era, but Ranke thinks it
much older.[2]

All over Europe are to be found the remains of structures in
stone erected by the prehistoric races that lived there ages before
the present peoples invaded Europe from the east. The most remarkable of these is Stonehenge in Wiltshire, England. Since I had
the satisfaction of gazing upon that somber and impressive monument in 1900, Sir E. Antrobus, on whose estate it stands, has had
excavations made and caused the great leaning-stone to be set erect
before it should fall and perhaps break or damage other stones.
This work was superintended by Mr. Detmar Blow and Dr. Gow-
land in October, 1901, and the former of these gentlemen presented a paper on Jan. 21, 1902, to the Royal Institute of British
Architects, on " The Recent Discoveries at Stonehenge." The general conclusion was that Stonehenge belongs to the Palæolithic age
of human development, that the structure represents a temple for
observing the length of the year by the rising of the sun on the
longest day of the year, in order that the people should be able
to fix the time for performing agricultural operations. He gave a
number of astronomical data in support of the view that Stonehenge was a solar temple for observation in the height of summer,
and came to the conclusion that the avenue which was associated
with the Sarsen stones was laid down about the year 1680 B.C. His
conclusions were corroborated by Sir Norman Lockyer. Of course
it is to be understood that the civilization of a region so far from the
center of dispersion must be far behind such comparatively central
regions as India, Chaldea, and Egypt, but it is clear that it was
marching in the same direction, and but for the Indo-Germanic inva-

[1] British Association Report, Glasgow Meeting, 1876, London, 1877, Part II,
Notices and Abstracts, p. 117.
[2] " Weltgeschichte," von Leopold von Ranke, Zweite Auflage, Leipzig, 1881,
Vol. I, p. 8.

sion the old primitive civilization of Western Europe would have eventually worked up toward the present state, though, without those fruitful cross fertilizations, it would have taken vast ages longer to reach the same point.

The want of a written language and the general character of sacerdotal observation and thought have kept the world in general ignorance of who the men were that performed these intellectual achievements, and we can only vaguely ascribe them to the races that inhabited the areas on which their monuments are found. But when at last we approach the new, and at first comparatively backward civilization of Greece and the regions that surround it, we are near enough to the date of the invention of a symbolic alphabet and to records made on papyrus sheets or parchment to begin to learn what was transpiring in the world of thought. Beginning with Thales, Anaximander, Pythagoras, and Anaximenes in the seventh and sixth centuries, and continuing with Heraclitus, Empedocles, Anaxagoras, in the fifth, and Democritus, Aristotle, Epicurus, and Euclid, in the fourth, followed by Archimedes and the Alexandrian school in the third and second centuries before our era, we have a great mass of cosmological ideas, which seen thus in perspective, towers up into gigantic proportions. These men were not priests, but all belonged to the privileged class who possessed leisure and opportunity for observation and meditation, and while the earlier of them could only teach their doctrines to their disciples, these latter found ways at last of preserving and transmitting these thoughts, until they could ultimately be recorded and handed down as imperishable achievements of the human mind.

If all that these men and their contemporaries, too numerous to mention, actually taught the world could have been accepted and seized upon it would almost seem that we moderns would have had nothing to learn. About all that we of the past five centuries have accomplished has been to prove and " establish " the truths that they taught. I shall not undertake a systematic enumeration of them, but may be permitted to mention: the atomic theory, taught by Leucippus, Democritus, and Epicurus; the heliocentric system, taught by Pythagoras and Aristarchus of Samos; the conservation of energy, distinctly perceived by Epicurus; the nature of electricity, dimly foreshadowed by Thales; the fact of a universal struggle for existence, epigrammatically stated by Heraclitus and taught by

Lucretius; the discovery of the power of steam, demonstrated experimentally by Hero; the whole science of geometry, taught by all
the Greek philosophers and reduced to theorems by Euclid that
it has been found difficult to improve even in point of phraseology;
the law of specific gravity, discovered by Archimedes; the principle
of the lever and fulcrum, also worked out by Archimedes; the foundations of natural history, laid by Aristotle and built upon by Theophrastus; and finally the fundamental principles of psychology and
sociology, taught by Aristotle as well as by some of the sophists
and stoics.

I have said nothing of the wonderful development of art, especially of sculpture, but almost equally in poetry and drama, although
these too are imperishable achievements, because we are here dealing
with the progress of the human intellect in compassing the conquest
of nature. The unreflective mind might question whether the scientific principles here enumerated have really contributed to this end,
but any one who is at all familiar with the character of modern
science cannot fail to see that it is these and other great principles
of nature that really lie at the foundation of all scientific progress,
and that it is the general acceptance of these that paves the way for
all those practical applications of science that constitute the march
of civilization. The more serious objection, however, can scarcely be
waived, that all this volume of truth taught and revealed by the
Greek mind produced no appreciable effect in their day upon mankind and did not tend toward the better control of natural forces in
the interest of man. This is in the main, though not wholly true.
Much of it was taught as merely hypothesis, some of it only esoteri-
cally, as, for example, the heliocentric system by Pythagoras, who is
said to have taught the opposite openly. The world was not ripe
for such truths and did not get ripe for another fifteen hundred
years. But this detracts nothing from their real importance, since
this early announcement of them was merely sowing the seed, and
unless the seed be sown there can obviously be no crop, no ripening,
and no harvest.

As in the case of invention, so in that of scientific discovery, and
in fact of about everything but church history, scholasticism, and
religious casuistry, the first fourteen centuries of the Christian era
offer almost nothing worth recording. It is also a fact generally
overlooked, that during practically this same period Asia was passing

through a phase of its history similar to that through which Europe had to pass. Just as Christianity supplanted paganism in the West, so Buddhism first supplanted the older Indian cults, and then Mohammedanism swept over the whole eastern world from the Mediterranean to the Pacific. It also invaded Egypt and Northern Africa and strove to penetrate the continent of Europe, which it might perhaps have accomplished had it not been stopped and turned back by the hammer of Charles Martel on the plains of Tours in the year 732. But in Asia there has been no renaissance, except the recent awakening of Japan.

In Europe the Middle Ages were to some extent a period of gestation. The barbarian and Mohammedan invasions and the Crusades had a powerful awakening influence and repeatedly disturbed the social equilibrium, infusing fresh, but as yet coarse, unassimilated mental and physical elements, and requiring long periods for their refinement and complete readjustment. Only a few such names as those of Galen, the true founder of human anatomy, in the second century; Avicenna (an Arabian, but whose works became known in Europe), who lived in the tenth century and was familiar with all the sciences then known; Averrhoës, the Spanish Saracen and universal scholar; Ebn Junis in the tenth century, who discovered the principle of the pendulum six centuries before Huyghens; Albertus Magnus and Roger Bacon in the thirteenth century, both of whom made considerable advances in various sciences, especially in physiology and chemistry, are worth enumerating among those who contributed anything during the Middle Ages to the advancement of man's dominion over nature.

The very first of these great cosmic truths of antiquity to be revived at the dawn of the new era was the heliocentric system, worked out by Copernicus, but foreshadowed by a German cardinal, Nicolaus de Cusa, in 1444, or nearly a century before the appearance of the "De Revolutionibus." Humboldt quotes the passage which establishes his claim to priority to the doctrine that the earth moves: "Jam nobis manifestum est terram in veritate moveri. Terra non potest esse fixa, sed movetur ut aliæ stellæ."[1] Copernicus could

---

[1] "De docta Ignorantia," Lib. II, Cap. XII. This fragment, found in the Hospital at Cues by Clemens, in 1843, and another paper of Cardinal Cusa entitled "De Venatione Sapientiæ" (Cap. 28), set forth his theory, which was that both earth and sun revolve about a constantly changing pole of the universe. He therefore missed the essential truth. Cf. Humboldt, "Cosmos," Vol. II, pp. 71, 324; Vol. III, p. 271.

have known nothing of these tracts, which appear not to have been published, and Cusa does not seem to connect his system with the teachings of the ancients. But Copernicus was well grounded in the astronomical literature of antiquity and made frequent reference to it in the first edition of his work which appeared in 1543, or the year of his death.

The great work of Vesalius, by which the modern science of anatomy was created, appeared also in 1543. William Gilbert's investigations into the true properties of magnets were completed before the end of the sixteenth century. Sanctorius (1612) and Huyghens (1656) established the laws of the pendulum and made it a scientific and practical instrument. Descartes, in the first half of the seventeenth century, created the science of analytical geometry. From 1619 to 1628 Harvey discovered the circulation of the blood and elaborated the principles on which it takes place. Galileo's great scientific achievements all fell within this period and his death occurred in 1642. One of the most important of these, and one that is rarely mentioned in connection with him, was the discovery of the true nature of force, especially as exemplified in gravitation, the discovery of which is not usually ascribed to him. Of Galileo's results in this field of experimentation Lagrange said : " It forms to-day the most permanent and essential part of the glory of this great man. His discoveries of the satellites of Jupiter, of the phases of Venus, of sun spots, etc., required telescopes and application only ; but it was a mark of extraordinary genius to detect the laws of nature in the midst of phenomena which men always had before their eyes, but whose explanation had nevertheless always escaped the scrutiny of philosophers." [1]

We are to-day in position to speak of the discovery of the interstellar ether. It is no longer a hypothesis, although we are still lacking in information as to its true nature and essence. This was also a seventeenth century discovery, but whether to ascribe it to Bacon,[2] to Descartes, or to Hooke, may be open to question. The credit is usually given to Descartes. There was a similar conception in India, but to show its vagueness and unscientific character it

---

[1] " Mécanique Analytique," par J. L. Lagrange, nouvelle édition, revue et augmentée par l'auteur, Paris, 1811, Vol. I, pp. 221-222 (somewhat modified from the edition of 1788, p. 159).

[2] " Æther purus et interstellaris," Novum Organum, Pt. II, Aph. L. (" Works," Vol. I, 1869, p. 531).

is only necessary to point out that it was supposed to be the peculiar vehicle of *life* and of *sound*.[1]

Closely connected with the recognition of a universal ether as the medium of the radiant forces was the discovery by Huyghens and Hooke of the undulatory theory of light, as also that of the nature of heat in so far as Newton was able to understand it, and the full establishment by Newton of the law of gravitation, the data for which had been accumulating at the hands of Copernicus, Kepler, Hooke, Cassini, and even Simplicius in the sixth century. Now for the first time was the nature of planetary motions understood, and from this time we may correctly date all exact knowledge of the solar system and of the laws of the universe. Newton's three fundamental laws of motion connected astronomy and physics, heaven and earth, into a single grand monistic scheme, and placed all the sciences on a mathematical basis.

Reference was made in the last section to the invention of the air-pump by Torricelli, but this involved the great scientific discovery of the pressure of the atmosphere, and ultimately that of the behavior of gases in general. These discoveries were perfected by Boyle and Mariotte in the seventeenth century, and were destined to bear still greater fruit in the eighteenth and nineteenth at the hands of Charles, Avogadro, Ampère, and Clausius. For the most part must we also refer to the seventeenth century that astonishing genius Leibnitz. A recent reviewer has justly said : —

What a marvellously gifted man Leibniz was! The king of Prussia truly said of him, " He represents in himself a whole Academy "; and George I of England was quite justified in saying, " I count myself happy in possessing two kingdoms, in one of which I have the honor of reckoning a Leibniz, and in the other a Newton, among my subjects." A brilliant mathematician, contesting with Newton the honor of discovering the Calculus ; a gifted psychologist and epistemologist, equaling and surpassing in his *New Essays*, Locke's famous *Essay ;* a profound theologian, writing the most famous book on *Theodicy* which has ever been printed; a learned historian, producing a history of the House of Brunswick commended by Gibbon himself ; a far-sighted statesman and diplomatist, honored at several of the most powerful courts of Europe ; a great philosopher, founder of modern German speculative philosophy and worthy to be named with Kant himself; and, withal, an eminent scientist, " a man of science, in the modern sense, of the first rank," as Professor Huxley calls him, — these are a few of his claims to consideration.[2]

---

[1] Wilson, Sanskrit Dictionary, Art. *Âkâ'sa*.
[2] George Martin Duncan in the *Monist*, Vol. XII, April, 1902, p. 459.

The greatest discoveries of the eighteenth century grew out of seventeenth century conceptions of ether and gravitation. They relate to heat, light, and electricity. It is known that Bacon declared that heat is nothing but motion,[1] and Locke [2] held a similar view, while Newton regarded the propagation of heat as a succession of shocks in the radiant substance. Huyghens and Hooke also closely approached the modern view, but Boyle in 1744 seems to have been the first to make a clear statement of the law.[3] Nevertheless, none of these authors had got beyond a sort of material emanation, which so taxed the credulity of Count Rumford that in 1797 he essayed a new explanation and advanced the whole subject to the dynamic stage.[4] It was now ready for Davy, Joule, and Mayer in the century that followed to subject it to experimental demonstration and reduce it to exact mathematical form.

With regard to light, the two most important advances made during the eighteenth century were those of Euler in demonstrating the undulatory theory, discovered by Huyghens, and of Bradley in establishing the fact and the principles of aberration.

In the account given in the last section of the invention of the telegraph it was shown that the nineteenth century was preëminently the age of electricity, but some of the most important discoveries leading to these applications were made during the eighteenth century, and notably the celebrated experiments of Galvani on frogs' legs, supplemented by those of Volta, who, although he wrongly interpreted the phenomena, greatly increased the stock of knowledge, and was led to the invention of the pile known by his name. To this epoch also belongs the work of Franklin.

But the eighteenth century was scarcely less prolific in other great discoveries. In astronomy we have through Kant and Laplace clear statements of the nebular hypothesis, vaguely conceived by Anaximander and partially formulated by Tycho Brahe. In chemistry we have the discovery of oxygen, doubtless first by Priestley, but inde-

---

[1] "Sed quod ipsissimus Calor, sive *quid ipsum* Caloris, sit Motus et nihil aliud," Novum Organum, II, Aph. XX (" Works," Vol. I, p. 391).

[2] "Conduct of Human Understanding, Elements of Natural Philosophy," Chapter XI, "Works," London, 1801, Vol. III, pp. 297–299.

[3] "On the Mechanical Origin of Heat and Cold," by Robert Boyle, "Works," Vol. IV, London, 1772, pp. 236–259. See especially Experiment VI on pp. 249–250.

[4] "Inquiry concerning the Source of the Heat which is excited by Friction," by Benjamin Count Rumford, *Philosophical Transactions*, Vol. LXXXVIII, 1798, pp. 80–102.

pendently the same year (1774), though somewhat later, by Scheele, and also, as it is claimed, independently in 1775 by Lavoisier and Trudaine, all of which shows that the world was ripe for it. Nitrogen was certainly discovered by Scheele but Cavendish a little later placed its existence on a firm basis. The discovery of sodium and potassium by Davy and of iodine by Gay-Lussac soon followed, and the chemical elements began to be known. But perhaps the most signal of all the chemical advances of that period was the discovery by Lavoisier of the true nature of combustion and the overthrow of the metaphysical doctrine of phlogiston. Man had known fire as long as he had known water and much longer than he had known air, but never before did he know in what fire essentially consists. A committee of the French Academy successfully repeated Lavoisier's experiments in 1790, a congratulatory meeting was held in Paris, and in the presence of the assembled savants Madame Lavoisier, attired as a priestess of science, burned on an altar erected for the purpose the great work of Stahl: "Fundamenta Chemiæ Dogmaticæ et Experimentalis," embodying the exploded theory, while a band played a solemn requiem over its ashes!

In biology the eighteenth century was chiefly an age of accumulation and classification. Linnæus was wholly a child of it, as were Antoine and Bernard de Jussieu, while Laurent de Jussieu published his "Genera Plantarum" in 1789, from which the natural system of classification is usually counted. But the great principle of organic development through the struggle for existence, involving descent with modification, was distinctly enunciated by both Goethe and Erasmus Darwin before the close of that century. We may also add to its achievements the discovery of the nature of tissues, as well as of spermatozoa, by Louis Hamm, a student in the laboratory of Leeuwenhoek.

At the beginning of the nineteenth century all the great sciences were fairly established and the number of investigators was enormously increased. All the leading universities had long been in operation in Europe and several existed in America. These were turning their attention more and more to science and establishing well equipped laboratories for original research. All the great scientific academies had long been in existence and celebrated men were associated with them. In astronomy, in physics, in chemistry, in geology, in all branches of biology, and to some extent in anthropology, observations and experiments were being made, and every field of nature was being explored. Learned memoirs were published, the transactions of academies and societies were filled with contributions of all kinds recording the results of scientific work, and an immense monument was in process of erection to the industry and zeal of an awakened world. Thus began that " Wonderful Century " whose achievements Dr. Wallace has so ably summed up that it seems superfluous to attempt even an abridged enumeration of them. Nor is Wallace the only historian of nineteenth century science. For all that relates to the radiant forces Mr. Iles in " Flame, Electricity, and the Camera " has grandly summed it up and brought out its salient points, and there exists a considerable literature devoted to such historical surveys. One other work especially merits attention, as it emanates from a source to which no one would think of looking for such a treatise, viz., from a committee of more than thirty eminent French Catholic scholars headed by the rector of the Catholic University of Paris.[1] The work is not, as might have been surmised, a lamentation over the advance of materialism, but seems to breathe the spirit of the age. In the preamble, written by the Vicomte de Vogué, " the marvellous advance of scientific knowledge in the direction of subjugating the forces of nature, unifying the world, and transforming social life " are put down as the chief characteristics of the nineteenth century, and it is admitted that the grand results of the century had their origin in the cabinet of the savant, the laboratory of the naturalist, and the discoveries of the explorer.

It may, however, be profitable to dwell a moment on the general character of nineteenth century science, merely to appreciate its drift and to note the main channels into which all the antecedent streams of thought tended to converge. If we take up the different sciences in their natural order and give a moment's attention to each we shall soon see which ones came out most fully and received the largest contributions from the past. In other words we shall see what the world regarded as the most important directions for fresh activity resulting from the long, largely unconscious, and apparently aimless search for truth through earlier centuries. Beginning with mathematics, which for the Greeks was everything, which was the

---

[1] " Un Siècle. Mouvement du Monde de 1800 à 1900." Publié par les soins d'un comité sous la présidence de Monseigneur Péchenard, Paris, 1901.

only recognized science during the Middle Ages, and which down to Descartes and Leibnitz was the great respectable field of all intellectual exercise, we find the nineteenth century relegating it from the position of an end in itself to a means for the more thorough prosecution of the concrete sciences. Mathematicians themselves of course know many directions in which their noble science was advanced, but the non-mathematical world recognizes scarcely any great new principles that were brought forward. It is true that quarternions were discovered and an enormous literature grew up relative to non-Euclidean geometry and space of four dimensions, but only the most erudite mathematical specialists could take part in these speculations, and the concrete sciences have scarcely benefited by such discoveries.

In astronomy there was intense activity and a great series of instrumental appliances, especially telescopes, was brought to the aid of the science. Many important and a few truly signal discoveries were made, such as the measuring of distances of the fixed stars, inaugurated by Bessel in 1839, the discoveries of Chladni and others of the nature of meteoric streams, the discovery of the so-called canals on the surface of the planet Mars, and also of the satellites of that planet; still upon the whole, and relatively to some other sciences, it cannot be justly said that the nineteenth century was specially characterized by astronomical discovery. This, the most exact and positive of the concrete sciences, the most general and least complex in its laws and phenomena, and the one whose method of study is chiefly observation, passed its period of supremacy in the fifteenth and sixteenth centuries with Copernicus, Tycho Brahe, Kepler, Galileo, and Newton.

If we turn to physics, the science that stands next to astronomy in the characteristics enumerated, we see an immense difference. This had become a distinctively experimental science. Its phenomena relate chiefly to this world, and they are intimately connected with the welfare of man. Here was the great field to be conquered in the interest of the human race. The field was ripe and the tools were ready. There was comparatively little to do in barology, or that branch presided over by the law of gravitation. The pendulum, the balance, specific gravity, and atmospheric pressure were all known and their principles had been applied. But the great underlying principle of the conservation of energy, although dimly perceived from antiquity, required demonstration. It received it at the hands of Mayer, Helmholtz, and Joule, and physical science was placed upon a basis that can never be shaken. Intimately bound up with this grand discovery was the true nature of heat, which, as we have seen, had been fairly prophesied and almost proved, but which was now experimentally established by these same investigators. The nature of light still lacked that degree of demonstration that the scientific mind demands, and this it received through the researches of Young, Helmholtz, Tyndall, and Thomson (Lord Kelvin). Connected with this there arose an entirely new science, that of spectrum analysis. Not that Newton, Euler, and many others had not studied the solar spectrum. They did not found the science. This was reserved for Kirchhoff and Bunsen, Huggins and Lockyer, and a large corps of investigators chiefly in the second half of the nineteenth century. This new science has many arms and reaches out into so many of the other sciences that it becomes difficult to classify it. It constitutes a large part of that other new science, astrophysics, which, if regarded as a part of astronomy, should be excepted from the above remarks relative to that science. Spectrum analysis is in large part also chemistry, and furnishes all our knowledge of the chemistry of other worlds than ours. But upon the whole, we may perhaps best consider it a department of physics in the radiant group. Here too must be noted the X-rays and all the other ultraspectral and previously undiscovered rays with unpredictable properties and powers.

But great as were these advances in the domains of heat and light, those made in that of electricity were perhaps still greater. Here invention and discovery go hand in hand even more than in other experimental sciences. The great inventions were rapidly reviewed in the last section, but new apparatus was required at every step. There is no more perfect example of man persistently wresting the secrets from nature. Michael Faraday led the way, and we see successively towering up the names of Jacobi, Maxwell, Henry, Sturgeon, Davidson, Hertz, either working together or separately, and bringing forward one principle after another until the present edifice was successfully reared. One of the most remarkable results has been practically to identify the whole radiant group of forces and to demonstrate the intimate association of electricity, magnetism, light, and heat as interconvertible forms of cosmic energy.

In chemistry there were also great advances during the nineteenth century. The atomic theory was firmly established by Berzelius, Dalton, and others, and the most important relations subsisting among the chemical elements were worked out by Mendelejeff. Organic chemistry was founded and the different groups of organic compounds classified. The applications of chemistry to industry and domestic life were innumerable and their value incalculable. The social influence thus exerted, although less obvious and more quiet was probably quite as important as that due to physical discoveries.

If the greatest triumphs over nature in the interest of man took place in the domain of physics and chemistry, the deepest thought of the nineteenth century was concentrated upon the problem of life. In every science a philosophic period precedes the period of maximum utilization. In astronomy and physics this philosophic period began in the fifteenth century and lasted until the eighteenth. The nineteenth century was the philosophic period of biology. Darwin has often been called the Newton of biology and the comparison is just. But it is equally just to characterize Lamarck as the Copernicus of biology. For by philosophy we do not now mean speculation, or the propounding of theories based chiefly on meditation and reflection, such as were most of those, however exact, of the ancients. We now mean theories or hypotheses, it may be, but based on great accumulations of facts and worked out through the study and comparison of these facts. They are in reality generalizations and each step is established by a compilation and coördination of the facts. Such was the heliocentric theory as revived by Copernicus, such were Kepler's laws, such was the law of gravitation, and such was the atomic theory of chemistry.

The Greeks had stated many of the now recognized truths of biology, but their theories were only speculations, wonderful glimpses into natural truth, but wholly unsupported by scientific evidence. It must not be forgotten either that along with these just glimpses there went the wildest vagaries, and these latter greatly outnumbered the former. It is only after a great truth has been scientifically established that we go back and pick out the rare cases in which it had been as it were accidentally hit upon in the

midst of a great mass of erroneous ideas. These we leave behind
and forget, or excuse as due to the insufficiency of the data at the
command of those ancient philosophers. And we glean the few
grains that we now know to be golden, but which the finders may
have considered of little importance while imputing great value to
what we now know to have been dross. It is thus that the forerun-
ners of most great discoveries, instead of being neglected, as is usually supposed, often receive far more credit than they really deserve.

In biology, then known as natural history and divided into botany
and zoölogy, also including mineralogy, vast accumulations were made
during the four preceding centuries, and from the time of Linnæus, indeed for a century before his time, everything was described and classified, so that with the beginning of the nineteenth century the entire
known vegetable and animal kingdoms were represented in herbaria
and museums and all the species that could be distinguished were described and figured in large illustrated works. Any modern worker
knows that the literature goes back to the seventeenth and even to
the sixteenth century, although the binomial system of nomenclature
was introduced by Linnæus, and most of the codes endeavor to prevent
the use of names of earlier date than certain editions of his works.
But one has only to glance at those works to see that Linnæus himself derived the names from earlier authors. This was the period
of biological statics, and it was supposed by all these early naturalists
that species were absolutely fixed. Lamarck overthrew this doctrine
and inaugurated the period of biological dynamics. This new discovery of the mutability of species and the genealogical descent of
organic forms, perceived, as we have seen, by Goethe and Erasmus
Darwin, as a poetic idea, gave a wholly new impetus to biological
science. The comparison with the corresponding truth of astronomy
bears the closest inspection. In both sciences the discovery of a
general state of movement, making the science dynamic instead of
static as it had thus far been, inaugurated a new era and enormously
accelerated scientific activity. And when at last Darwin, just half
a century after the appearance of Lamarck's " Philosophie Zoölo-
gique " (1809), came out with his " Origin of Species " (1859), laden still
heavier with the facts of observation, and announcing the additional
principle of natural selection which explains *how* the transmutation
of species takes place, the whole world was electrified, and a vast
army of investigators plunged into the field of biology determined

to verify or disprove this bold yet fascinating hypothesis. The result, while it raised the hypothesis to a law of nature, also filled the world with knowledge of organic life and placed biology in the front rank of the advancing sciences.

Without attempting to enumerate the biological truths disclosed during the nineteenth century, the cellular theory may be mentioned as a type of them, as also the nature of tissues in the Metazoa, growing out of a knowledge of the cell. The cell is the biological unit and the whole science of biology (histology, morphology, physiology) rests upon it. But a deeper problem was attacked in the second half of the century, a problem which has not yet been solved, viz., that of the constitution of the cell and the ultimate unit of heredity. The solution of this problem will answer the question: What is life?

The law of evolution, in large part biological, but also cosmological, nay, also anthropological, psychological, and sociological, has been almost wholly the product of nineteenth century science. It is probably the most important of all the generalizations of the human intellect. It comes the nearest of all the truths that have been discovered to rendering man and society conscious of themselves. Self-consciousness consists in the state at which a being asks the questions: What? Whence? Whither? Evolution furnishes the first answer that science has ever made to these questions. In so far as its truths are known they dispel all the mystery that enshrouds the intellect. Not content with the conquest of nature and the subjection of its laws to human uses, man resolved to find out what he was, whence he came, and what was to be his destiny. He proceeded to interrogate nature at all points, and the thousand conflicting and commingled answers that he got, all rolled together, when closely listened to, were found to spell out the talismanic word: Evolution.

CHAPTER XX

SOCIALIZATION OF ACHIEVEMENT

IT was shown in Chapter III that the subject-matter of sociology is human achievement. The remaining sixteen chapters thus far written may be regarded as being devoted to the task of explaining what human achievement consists in and how it has been wrought. Not until the last chapter was reached was it possible to show the full significance of human achievement as the practical conquest of nature and the subjection of all the materials and forces of nature to the control and service of man. This has been accomplished mainly through the exercise of the directive agent in changing the mode of motion of physical bodies, so that by a sort of vortex action they are made to pour into the channels of human advantage instead of pursuing their natural courses and either running to waste or causing injury to human interests. Social evolution consists in this, and differs radically from organic evolution, since in the latter it is the environment that transforms the organism, while in the former man transforms the environment.

No one of course will question that all this belongs to sociology. In transforming the physical environment the entire social system is profoundly affected and society itself is transformed. Although this is accomplished wholly through telic activity, still there is a sense in which social evolution thus brought about may be regarded as genetic. What the economists call the law of supply and demand is a natural law. It is to be compared with the law by which air rushes into a vacuum, and which, before the nature of the atmosphere and of atmospheric pressure was discovered, could only be explained by saying that "nature abhors a vacuum." And it is the same law that governs the movement of the atmosphere over the whole globe and determines the direction and velocity of the winds. This economic, or rather, sociologic law is not affected by the fact that social demands are in large part supplied through the sagacious foresight of shrewd business men in a manner that is preëminently telic, although strictly individualistic. For example, as a modern city grows street railway lines are gradually extended farther and farther out into the suburbs to anticipate the increasing demands, and this will take place although the citizens of those sections make no special demand and take no steps to secure it. The corporations controlling the urban lines are ever on the alert to increase the volume of their business, and by the exercise of a strictly telic method forestall any such demand on the part of the citizens, who from inherent inertia, natural conservatism, personal indifference, and especially defective organization, would be extremely slow to move in such matters, and could scarcely be brought to the point of raising the funds necessary to construct such lines. Now although every step in social development of this kind is telic, still the development itself is genetic, and only goes on as fast as or a trifle faster than is necessary fully to supply the demand. Business shrewdness takes into account the future growth of the sections supplied and reaches a little farther out than the actual conditions of things require, so that perhaps for a short time the service may be attended with slight pecuniary loss, to be more than compensated by the increased volume of business in the near future, a considerable part of which, as is also foreseen, will be due to the superior attraction that such sections will possess as a consequence of the facilities thus supplied. Thus is social genesis secured through individual telesis.

If we look over the whole field of human achievement and social evolution we shall see that by far the greater part of it belongs to the class just described. The initiative is almost exclusively individual and the ends sought are egocentric in the widest sense, which must include the satisfaction of intellectual, moral, and even transcendental interests as well as those so-called physical wants that have to do with the functions of nutrition and reproduction. The social consequences, as was shown in Chapter XI, are unintended, and social evolution, however large the telic factor in it may be, is to all intents and purposes unconscious. In fact, so far as the phrase " social evolution " is concerned, I would restrict it wholly to this aspect, and would exclude from it any and all effects that can be shown to have been consciously produced. Such effects do not belong to *evolution*. They are products of social or collective telesis, and may be called *institution*.

2 N

SOCIALIZATION

The word *socialization,* now much used by certain writers, is as yet undifferentiated and has been given various shades of meaning, though all more or less connected with the ideas conveyed by the word *social.* As this is a popular and not a technical word, socialization naturally takes a wide range and would be of little use to sociology if it could not be limited to a single, definite meaning. The dictionaries only reflect the current vagueness, sometimes allying it to sociability and sometimes to socialism. There has been, however, of late a tendency on the part of careful writers to give to the verb *socialize* and the noun *socialization* a special meaning susceptible to exact definition. Thus, to socialize an industry, for example, means that society takes it under its charge and conducts it for its benefit. All industries are, at least thus far, initiated by individuals and conducted for their benefit. As all industries are in the nature of a supply to a public demand, in order to succeed even in benefiting the individual they must also benefit society, and it has been claimed with much show of truth that there is and must necessarily be a perfect adjustment between individual and social advantage in order that the industry be inaugurated and carried on. This was the standpoint of the old political economists. It is also the standpoint of some sociologists even now, as, for example, Mr. Herbert Spencer. But most modern economists and sociologists, while recognizing it as an important principle, decline to admit its universality. In this, however, they do but reflect the view of the great master, Adam Smith, who, like Darwin, and great masters generally, saw deeper than his professed disciples.[1]

It is not proposed to open up this large question here, which in fact belongs rather to applied sociology. We are only seeking a definition of socialization that shall be at once correct and definite in the sense that it shall always mean the same thing. This is not secured by including in it everything that has a social value or a social effect. It is almost impossible to conceive of a human achievement that does not answer this description. All individual action of any importance has a social bearing. Socialization must exclude all social effects that are only incidental. This sweeps

[1] Compare the much neglected paragraph with which he closed Book I of the "Wealth of Nations."

away at one stroke all that results from the principle of conation, explained in Chapter XI. These effects, though truly social, and though mighty and far-reaching, are wholly unconscious and unintended. As there shown, they are undesired even by the individual and unwelcome to society. They belong to the great unconscious means by which nature brings about changes in the types of social structure and consequent social evolution in the strictly genetic sense. Socialization is conscious, intentional, wished for, and welcomed telic action, not of the individual as such, but of those individuals into whose hands society, by whatever means, intrusts the conduct of its affairs.

Pure sociology can go no farther than to inquire what has actually been accomplished in this direction, although it would be legitimate to reason from this to what is likely to be accomplished in the future. But this latter is more or less hazardous, and it is better to confine ourselves, at least at the outset, to the past and the present. At first glance it might seem that very little would be found to reward such a search. When we survey human achievement through the conquest of nature, as this was sketched in the last chapter, the individual seems to be everything and society nothing but the passive beneficiary of all this gain as it leaks through the individual's hands and diffuses itself throughout the social mass. It is indeed true that society in its collective capacity makes few inventions or scientific discoveries, and it also, for the most part, leaves the practical application of these to social ends, to private enterprise and the keen business instincts of individuals, capitalists, and the various voluntary organizations devoted to the accumulation of wealth. For anything answering to our definition of socialization we have to look elsewhere, or at least we must place ourselves at a different point of view and consider the whole subject from a new angle of vision. To find such a view point we will need to go back almost as far as was done in Part II, and retrace some of the early steps there sketched, but in the fuller light of subsequent discussions.

Social Regulation

The classification of the functions of society into regulative and operative[1] is fundamental. We may give to both functions a wider

[1] Herbert Spencer, "The Principles of Sociology," Vol. I, New York, 1877, p. 459 (§ 210).

scope than is usually done, and, adapting it to the present discussion, we may say that while human achievement constitutes one at least of the most important operative functions of society, social regulation is that which makes it possible, is in fact a *sine qua non* of it. But the conception of achievement must now be widened, and made to include the regulative function itself. Examining this further we shall see that social regulation is no longer individual achievement but collective achievement, and we have here the condition itself to all achievement as a product, not of individual, but of social telesis. Let us look further into this.

It is generally recognized that many animals are only enabled to survive in the struggle for existence by dint of their gregarious or social habits. But none of these are able to migrate indefinitely and people the whole globe. This was the prerogative of man, but not until he had not only acquired the social habit but had developed the regulative function. Whether this was matriarchal or patriarchal, royal or sacerdotal, it was regulative, and had the power to check all wayward tendencies inimical to the race. In fact, long before there was anything that deserves the name of government there existed that group sentiment of the need of race preservation, which, call it religion, law, government, or whatever you choose, actually regulated the horde, clan, or social group, and permitted the operative functions to go on. Not merely the sentiment, but also the corresponding social structure existed, capable of enforcing the requirements of the group and punishing all antisocial violations of the group will. This was chiefly in the nature of " ceremonial government," but it was effective and all that was needed at that stage of social development. This group sentiment was at least dimly conscious. It was certainly intentional, and the results accomplished were desired and welcomed. It was a product of the group mind and had all the essential qualities of a telic phenomenon, but it was not egoistic except in the sense that the group constitutes an ego. This in fact it does, and all collective action must be regarded as the action of a unit or collective individual pursuing ends that are its own. All this becomes increasingly true through all the early stages of society until we arrive at the metasocial stage following upon the first race amalgamation due to conquest and subjugation.

Legal Regulation. — It was shown in Chapter X that the first step in the direction of the amalgamation of two races thus brought together was the gradual substitution of a form of general regulation for the crude special regulation of the military power, which ultimately became too onerous and annoying for the conquering race longer to tolerate. This took the form of primitive law and finally grew into a system of jurisprudence. It was the natural homologue at this stage of the primordial group regulation or ceremonial government, and no doubt many of the features of the former were retained as a basis for the latter. The power was still military, but the amount of energy that it was necessary to expend in enforcing general rules was far less than had been required to treat each case separately. Although primarily devoted to holding down the subject race, this system proved capable of being applied to other forms of regulation.

The State. — By far the most important consequence of this, as we also saw in Chapter X, was the constitution of the state. The discovery of the true origin and nature of the state might have been included among the scientific discoveries so rudely sketched in the last chapter. It has brushed away a greater amount of error than almost any other established truth in science. All the old ideas of the origin of the state are placed by it in the same list as the geocentric and Ptolemaic theories of astronomy, the doctrine of phlogiston in chemistry, and those of special creation and the immutability of species in biology. There is no longer any social compact, no divine right of kings or of "the powers that be," no abstract right. By a perfectly natural, evolutionary process society everywhere and always has worked out a regulative system which, while not an organism, may still be compared with the regulative system of the Metazoan body, and has precisely the same sanction as a positive fact. The state is a natural product, as much as an animal or a plant, or as man himself.

The basis of the state is law. It was the necessity for general regulation to take the place of the wasteful and difficult special regulation incident to conquest that gradually gave rise to a system of law, and it was the necessity for a social mechanism capable of enforcing law that the state grew up and took definite form. It was shown that until the state was formed there could be no property. Every one must keep his belongings on his person and defend them at every step. No matter how anything may have been acquired, every one has the same right to it and may seize it wherever found.

There is no such thing as right outside the state. If property cannot exist except under the protection of the state there can of course be no such thing as capital. There can be no industry in the economic sense. There is no use accumulating; the surplus cannot be retained. Wealth is only possible under the state. The more we reflect upon it the clearer we see that while the state itself achieves little, it is the condition to nearly all achievement. The state was primarily the mediator between conflicting races. Immediately following the conquest the conquered race had no status. It was completely under the dominion of the conquering race. Under the state as soon as formed the conquered race acquired rights and the members of the conquering race were assigned duties. The state thus becomes a powerful medium of social assimilation. The capable and meritorious of the subject race are given opportunity to exercise their faculties. The members of the superior race not belonging to the nobility or the priestly caste enter into business arrangements, become a mercantile or capitalist class, and control the finances of the people. These two classes blend and ultimately form the " third estate," which, on account of its activity and usefulness, is destined to increase in influence, as all history has shown. From it chiefly, too, are recruited all the inventors, artists, and finally the men of letters and of science. Even in Greece the priesthood had ceased to supply the brain of the race. After the revival of learning in Western Europe the nobility and the clergy fell almost entirely out of the ranks of those who were advancing the world. From that time social progress was intrusted to the middle class, the industrial and commercial class. Many eminent men of science, however, as de Candolle shows, have been sons or descendants of Protestant clergymen. The Catholic clergy, having no descendants, contributed next to nothing.

There is much less difference than appears at first sight between the function or mission of the state and that of the primordial regulative institution which secured the preservation of primitive society. It is the natural successor of that, only operating on a much higher plane. The social forces as such are, like the physical forces, centrifugal and destructive. The intuitive reason or egoistic intellect only renders them more so. There was absolute need at the outset of regulation and restraint to prevent the destruction of the race, and the first collective action was taken with this end in view. At the stage which produced the state this unrestrained individualism was as strong as ever and equally destructive of order. However natural the origin of the state may seem when we understand the conditions that called it forth, it was, in the last analysis, the result of a social necessity for checking and curbing this individualism and of holding the social forces within a certain orbit where they could interact without injury and where they could do constructive work. Without such restraint the competition in society knows no bounds. It is the law of the strongest and would ultimately restrict the human race to limited areas and conditions. The law of the multiplication or exaggeration of effects is in full force here as in the inorganic and the organic world. The first important consequence of this law is, as in the rest of nature, to put an end to competition and pass on to the next stage which is monopoly. Just as one strong plant or weed may invade a virgin flora and drive out every indigenous plant, covering vast tracts to the exclusion of everything else, so in society without a regulative apparatus, only the strong will remain, and all the more delicate elements that give variety to existence and render culture, art, and science possible will be ruthlessly crushed out. The state was the semi-unconscious product of a sort of group sense of this, organizing the machinery for the protection of the physically weaker, but socially better elements calculated to enrich, embellish, and ultimately to solidify and advance social conditions.

The state was therefore the most important step taken by man in the direction of controlling the social forces. The only possible object in doing this was the good of society as a whole. In part it was no doubt a sentiment of safety. The greatest good possible would be its salvation. But this ethical sentiment was something more than mere race ethics. There was mingled with it some idea of actual social benefit. This went still farther and embraced some vague conception of amelioration and of social progress. Ratzenhofer says : —

Thus the state becomes an instrument of morality as the ethical effect of the social process; out of the construction of society there results the conscious sacrifice of the individual in behalf of the community.[1]

It is fashionable in certain circles to attack and abuse the state, but most of this is done by individuals whose personal ends have

[1] "Die Sociologische Erkenntnis," p. 167.

been thwarted in the interest of the people, or by unthinking persons who merely repeat such statements which they find current. But nearly everybody, and especially the weaker, who also constitute much the larger classes of society, instinctively feel that the state means well for them and is always doing all that the influential classes will allow it to do for the benefit of society at large. Thus, says Simmel : —

> The highest wish of the Spartan and Thessalian slaves was to become slaves of the state rather than of individuals. In Prussia before the emancipation of the serfs the peasants attached to the state domains had a much preferable lot to that of those upon private estates. The situation of India under British administration is far better than under the sway of the East India Company and its private interests.[1]

The old maxim of the common law that "the king can do no wrong" merely reflects this truth. The state can only err. It cannot commit crime or do a wrong act. It has no malice or enmity, at least toward its own citizens. Their good is all it knows or aims at. Gumplowicz even goes further : —

> The social struggle consists in executing and realizing the institutions which constitute, at the expense of other circles, the power of the circle to which any one belongs. A *society*, whatever may be the errors of individuals, never errs when it is a question of utilizing these means, of appropriating them, and of setting them to work. . . . The individual often goes about listening to doctrines and becoming inspired by sentiments; society moves straight forward on its own road, which is the right road. Why? Because instead of reflecting and choosing, it obeys, *by virtue of a law of nature, the powerful impulse which its interests exert upon it*.[2]

Gumplowicz may here mean that while individuals may, in pursuing their own ends, do injury to others on account of the conflict of interests necessary to a plurality of individuals, the state, standing as it does alone, can safely pursue its ends, there being no possibility of conflict. If we could imagine one individual, person, or human being, wholly isolated, having no relations with any other, and acting strictly in his own interest, the moral element would be removed and he could do no wrong. It is the same with the state considered in the abstract, *i.e.*, without reference to other states.

But there is a still more important consideration. The state, although essentially an instrument of restraint to its members, is in

---

[1] *American Journal of Sociology*, Vol. II, September, 1896, p. 179.

[2] "Précis de Sociologie," par Louis Gumplowicz, Paris, 1896, p. 248. Compare also pp. 295, 296.

fact a means of making them free. Ratzenhofer has clearly seized this truth. Using the term *society* in the sense of the members of society, or at least, of small social groups, in contradistinction to the state, he sets forth the principle as follows: —

The state with its historically developed social structure finds itself in a continual struggle with fractions of social groups, whereby there is brought about at any given stage of culture a regulative effect between the policy of the state and that of society. Society, with its states and the social groups attached to both, develops into a social organization in which the social need is expressed by a mutual process of constraint and liberation. Since we must regard the social process as unconditioned, the opposition of state and society is not a hostile one in which the state is striving to check the social process, or society as the protector of collective interests is seeking to dissolve the states, but this antithesis is socially advantageous (*förderlich*). State and society mutually complete each other and maintain the social process in its path of general advantageous operation. The active reconciliation of dominant interests in these two complex individualities, state and society, is seen primarily in the fact that in their principal aspects the interests of each are the same. In the state individual interests must give way to collective interests, so that there results a harmonizing of interests, *i.e.*, a relative freeing of all individual interests from a constraint that lies outside of the social need; the state is thus a power whose end is liberation.[1]

De Greef, to much the same effect, remarks: —

Thus the theoretical debate between the individual and the state resolves itself into a transformation of the state for the greatest good of individuals, and the intervention of the collective power expands and justifies itself by the constant reduction, it is true, of despotic forms of this intervention, but also by the actual growth of this latter by means of superior forms of self-government in the interest of individual liberty.[2]

Those who attack the state either do not know, or else they temporarily forget that it is a product of evolution. It would be quite as rational to attack the solar system or the vertebrate type of structure. Comte in one of his early papers remarks: —

These various views are evidently conformable to the laws of human nature, and alone permit us to explain political phenomena in a satisfactory manner. Thus, in the last analysis, instead of seeing in the past a tissue of monstrosities, we should be able in a general way to regard society as having been most frequently as well directed in all respects as the nature of things permitted.[3]

[1] Ratzenhofer, *ibid.*, pp. 235–236.
[2] "Les Lois Sociologiques," par Guillaume De Greef, 2e éd., Paris, 1896, p. 151.
[3] "Plan des travaux scientifiques nécessaires pour réorganiser la société." Première série des travaux. Appendix to Vol. IV of the "Système de Politique Positive," p. 116.

De Greef states the fact as follows : —

In reality, society always governs itself, only it does it in a more or less conscious and contractual way; the alleged despots are only social agents, and often fulfill their office ignorant of the force that impels them and draws them on. Social bonds being at the outset naturally loose, it was necessary that this bond be as far as possible maintained by force; despotism was a societary development (*formation*) as natural at that time as charters, constitutions, deliberative assemblies, and the various more or less perfected forms by which society to-day tends to conduct itself from its own collective impulse resulting from the free assent of each of its members.[1]

Mr. Spencer is one of those who knows all this perfectly well, but often temporarily forgets it and follows what seems to have been an early acquired bias against the state, due no doubt, as are most prejudices, to what I have called "the illusion of the near." This was notably the case with the series of papers published by him in 1884.[2] These represent Herbert Spencer the impatient critic of contemporary local politics. But let us listen to Herbert Spencer the philosopher in 1860 when he had just completed the organization of his "Synthetic Philosophy" : —

We all know that the enactments of representative governments ultimately depend on the national will : they may for a time be out of harmony with it, but eventually they must conform to it. And to say that the national will finally determines them is to say that they result from the average of individual desires ; or in other words, from the average of individual natures. A law so initiated, therefore, really grows out of the popular character.

In the case of a government representing a dominant class, the same thing holds, though not so manifestly. For the very existence of a class monopolizing all power is due to certain sentiments in the community. But for the feeling of loyalty on the part of retainers, a feudal system could not exist. We see in the protest of the Highlanders against the abolition of hereditable jurisdictions, that they preferred that kind of local rule. And if to the popular nature must thus be ascribed the growth of an irresponsible ruling class, then to the popular nature must be ascribed the social arrangements which that class creates in the pursuit of its own ends. Even where the government is despotic, the doctrine still holds. The character of the people is, as before, the original source of this political form ; and, as we have abundant proof, other forms suddenly created will not act,

---

[1] "Introduction à la Sociologie," Première Partie, par Guillaume De Greef, Bruxelles, Paris, 1886, pp. 205-206.
[2] "The New Toryism," "The Coming Slavery," "The Sins of Legislators," "The Great Political Superstition," *Contemporary Review*, February to July, 1884. Appended to "Social Statics," abridged and revised, New York, 1892, under the general title, "The Man *versus* the State."

but rapidly retrograde to the old form. Moreover, such regulations as a despot makes, if really operative, are so because of their fitness to the social state. His acts being very much swayed by general opinion — by precedent, by the feeling of his nobles, his priesthood, his army — are in part immediate results of the national character; and when they are out of harmony with the national character they are soon practically abrogated.

The failure of Cromwell permanently to establish a new social condition, and the rapid revival of suppressed institutions and practices after his death, show how powerless is a monarch to change the type of the society he governs. He may disturb, he may retard, or he may aid the natural process of organization; but the general course of this process is beyond his control.[1]

We thus see that the state, though genetic in its origin, is telic in its method; that it has but one purpose, function, or mission, that of securing the welfare of society; that its mode of operation is that of preventing the antisocial actions of individuals; that in doing this it increases the freedom of human action so long as it is not antisocial; that the state is therefore essentially moral or ethical; that its own acts must necessarily be ethical; that being a natural product it must in a large sense be representative; that in point of fact it always is as good as society will permit it to be; that while thus far in the history of society the state has rarely performed acts that tend to advance mankind, it has been the condition to all achievement, making possible all the social, industrial, artistic, literary, and scientific activities that go on within the state and under its protection. There is no other human institution with which the state can be compared, and yet, in view of all this, it is the most important of all human institutions.

Collective Achievement

It has been said that the state achieves little. It would have been better to say that society in its collective capacity does not take a direct part in the operations that have been described under the head of achievement. The greater part of these belong to the general movement that has resulted in the conquest of nature. This, as we saw, consists chiefly in the mastery of the physical forces through invention and scientific discovery. This was preëminently the work of the individual. In contradistinction to this, the achievements of

---

[1] "The Social Organism," by Herbert Spencer, *Westminster Review*, New Series, Vol. XVIII, Jan. 1, 1860, pp. 92–93. "Essays, Scientific, Political, and Speculative," New York, 1891, pp. 267–268.

society, if we can call them so, have related to a certain conquest of
man. This has consisted in gaining a greater and greater mastery
of the social forces, primarily of the antisocial effects of the social
forces in the interest of social safety. It has been maintained from
the first that man is not by nature a social being in the full sense
of that expression. He was from the beginning and has always
remained an exceedingly quarrelsome and willful animal. It has
been noted that predaceous animals are not usually gregarious. Man
early became carnivorous, or rather omnivorous, and cannibalism is
one of the phases through which he has everywhere passed. If this
was chiefly confined to the eating of enemies it was because the
blood bond and other social influences partially protected his immediate kin. The enslavement of the captured, which gradually succeeded and ultimately supplanted cannibalism, was a matter of
policy and the rational calculation of the greatest gain. Exploitation, as depicted in Chapter XIII, worked no diminution in the
predatory and ferocious nature of man. His whole career has been
marked by belligerency, internecine strife, and universal rapacity.
The slow growth of sympathy and the moral sentiments somewhat
mitigated this, but less than is commonly supposed, and but for the
beneficent power of the state, seen by all to be in their interest,
society would have been impossible. Wherever this is even temporarily and locally withdrawn a state of things invariably results
which is not only intolerable but utterly incompatible with any form
of human achievement. It is well known that the state was very
slow in taking the punishment of crime out of the hands of private
individuals, and the great prevalence of family feuds under those
conditions is well described by Mr. Billson. He says: —

The large place occupied by blood-feuds in ancient Semitic societies and
the dark shadow which they cast over social life have been vividly portrayed
by Michaelis in his work on the Mosaic laws. The notoriously blightful
prevalence of such feuds among the American Indians is such as to prepare
us for Schoolcraft's account of a tribe to the south of Lake Superior, which
he found almost extinct through intestine feuds. Indeed, such instances are
by no means uncommon. A passage in which Mr. Bellew describes the
condition of the feud-ridden Berdurani, or northeastern Afghan tribes, so
forcibly illustrates the demoralization ensuing from feuds as to justify its
quotation at length: "Indeed," he says, "the quarrelsome character of this
people and the constant strife that they lead are declared by a mere glance at
their villages and fields, which bristle in all directions with round towers.

These are constantly occupied by men at enmity with their neighbors in the same or adjoining villages, who, perched up in their little shooting-boxes, watch the opportunity of putting a bullet into each other's body with the most persevering patience. The fields, even, are studded with these round towers, and the men holding them most jealously guard their lands from any one with whom they are at feud. Nothing belonging to their enemies is safe from their vengeance. If even a fowl strays from its owner into the grounds of another, it is sure to receive a bullet from the adversary's tower. So constant are their feuds that it is a well-known fact that the village children are taught never to walk in the center of the road, but always from the force of early habit walk stealthily along under cover of the wall nearest to any tower." These, it must be conceded, are extreme cases; yet they are a perfectly logical outgrowth of unaided and unhampered private retaliation.[1]

They are extreme cases only because in one form or another society has taken steps to prevent this state of things. But for collective action in some form this would be the normal condition of human society, or rather of the human animal, for there could be no society. In other cases where collective regulation is weak and ineffective we have a general state of brigandage. Such has been the condition of Southern Europe during long periods, and such, as it seems, is still the condition of parts of it, as witness the recent abduction of Miss Stone, and the powerlessness or indifference of the states in which it took place to secure the brigands or suppress the practice. On the frontier of a new country in process of settlement the form that this same fact assumes is the presence of lawless desperadoes traveling from place to place to rob and murder innocent settlers.

It was with such conditions as these that society had primarily to grapple, and no one can say that it has not upon the whole successfully accomplished its task. From the standpoint of achievement such action is to be compared to all that part of the conquest of nature which relates to the mastery of hostile forces. The averting of evil naturally precedes the extracting of good from the raw elements of nature, and we do not deny to the invention of clothing and shelter the title to be called achievements while awarding that title to the invention of a mortar for grinding corn. Society has always been rent by conflicting interests, and the great problem that presented itself to collectivity was that, not of harmonizing, but of reconciling such conflicting interests. The

[1] "The Origin of Criminal Law," by William W. Billson, *Popular Science Monthly*, Vol. XVI, February, 1880, p. 438.

means were law and the state, and the result was the substitution of civil justice for natural justice. Society exists because the rational mind was capable of perceiving the mutual advantageousness of submitting to authority. The process is one of adaptation, and law, state, society, and civilization are products of creative synthesis as this was defined in Chapter V.

Growth of Collectivism. — The domain of purely social action was at first very limited. As all know, the punishment of crime against individuals was not made a duty of society until after the fall of the feudal régime. The only crimes considered by the state were crimes against the state. But this is by no means the only function now considered necessarily collective that was once not so considered. Revenues were extensively farmed out to private parties and the finances of nations were largely in the hands of individual financiers. As the growth of collectivism has been nearly the same in all the countries of Europe it is as well illustrated by England as by any other country. Mr. Sidney Webb has given clear expression to the general facts in that country. He says : —

Representative government has taught the people how to gain collectively that power which they could never again individually possess. The present century has accordingly witnessed a growing demand for the legal regulation of the conditions of industry which represents a marked advance on previous conceptions of the sphere of legislation. It has also seen a progress in the public management of industrial undertakings which represents an equal advance in the field of government administration. Such an extension of collective action is, it may safely be asserted, an inevitable result of political democracy. When the Commons of England had secured the right to vote supplies, it must have seemed an unwarrantable extension that they should claim also to redress grievances. When they passed from legislation to the exercise of control over the executive, the constitutional jurists were aghast at the presumption. The attempt of Parliament to seize the command of the military forces led to a civil war. Its control over foreign policy is scarcely two hundred years old. Every one of these developments of the collective authority of the nation over the conditions of its own life was denounced as an illegitimate usurpation foredoomed to failure. Every one of them is still being resisted in countries less advanced in political development. . . .

The captains of war have been reduced to the position of salaried officers acting for public ends under public control; and the art of war has not decayed. In a similar way the captains of industry are gradually being deposed from their independent commands, and turned into salaried servants of the public.   Nearly all the railways of the world, outside of America and the United Kingdom, are managed in this way.   The Belgian Government works its own line of passenger steamers.   The Paris Municipal Council opens public bakeries.   The Glasgow Town Council runs its own common lodging houses, Plymouth its own tramways.   Everywhere, schools, water-works, gas-works, dwellings for the people, and many other forms of capital, are passing from individual into collective control.   And there is no contrary movement.   No community which has once "municipalized" any public service ever retraces its steps or reverses its action.[1]

We are here considering only the facts and the drift.   Mr. Webb is of course an interested witness, but that he has not exaggerated the facts may be learned from another witness whose bias in the opposite direction is much more strong, viz., Herbert Spencer.   In one of the articles that have already been mentioned, entitled, "The Coming Slavery," he thus deplores the tendencies of the times : —

Then, again, comes State-ownership of railways.   Already this exists to a large extent on the Continent.   Already we have had here a few years ago loud advocacy of it.   And now the cry, which was raised by sundry politicians and publicists, is taken up afresh by the Democratic Federation ; which proposes "State-appropriation of railways, with or without compensation." Evidently pressure from above joined by pressure from below, is likely to effect this change dictated by the policy everywhere spreading; and with it must come many attendant changes.   For railway-proprietors, at first owners and workers of railways only, have become masters of numerous businesses directly or indirectly connected with railways; and these will have to be purchased by Government when the railways are purchased.   Already exclusive letter-carrier, exclusive transmitter of telegrams, and on the way to become exclusive carrier of parcels, the State will not only be exclusive carrier of passengers, goods, and minerals, but will add to its present various trades many other trades.   Even now, besides erecting its naval and military establishments and building harbors, docks, breakwaters, etc., it does the work of ship-builder, cannon-founder, small-arms maker, manufacturer of ammunition, army-clothier and boot-maker; and when the railways have been appropriated, "with or without compensation," as the Democratic Federationists say, it will have to become locomotive-engine-builder, carriage-maker, tarpaulin and grease manufacturer, passenger-vessel owner, coal-miner, stone-quarrier, omnibus proprietor, etc.   Meanwhile its local lieutenants, the municipal governments, already in many places suppliers of water, gas-makers, owners and workers of tramways, proprietors of baths, will doubtless have undertaken various other businesses.   And when the State, directly or by proxy, has thus come into possession of, or has established, numerous concerns for wholesale production and for wholesale distribution, there will be good precedents for extending its function to retail

[1] "Fabian Tract," No. 69, London, 1896, pp. 14–15.

distribution : following such an example, say, as is offered by the French Government, which has long been a retail tobacconist.

In other places Mr. Spencer has turned aside from his philosophical writings to compile lists of these so-called socialistic laws for the purpose of condemning them, and when he finds that a considerable number of them have been repealed, as not accomplishing the purpose for which they were enacted, he seems to suppose that he has found an unanswerable argument against all measures looking to the enlargement of state functions. The socialists themselves have also carefully worked out the history of this movement, and there have been a few entirely judicial historians of it. Of these latter Mr. Lecky is perhaps the most conspicuous, and in several of his works, particularly his "Democracy and Liberty" and his "Map of Life, Conduct, and Character," he has endeavored to give an impartial summary of the growth of collectivism. Of the former of these works Professor Giddings says : —

Even the hardened reader of individualistic tracts will experience a new sensation as he turns Mr. Lecky's pages and follows through one continuous narrative the astonishing story of modern legislation against gambling, liquor-selling, cigarette-smoking and other modes of vice, and of the yet more elaborate legislation in behalf of " labor," consisting of laws limiting the hours of employment, regulating the internal affairs of the factory and the workshop, fixing the times and modes of wage payments, prescribing the details of tenement-house construction and management, forbidding the competitive employment of convict labor by the state, and even fixing a minimum wage for municipal laborers.[1]

In the later work mentioned, while sounding a warning voice against the fact that the English race are "contentedly submitting great departments of their lives to a web of regulations restricting and encircling them," Mr. Lecky nevertheless says that "the triumphs of sanitary reform as well as of medical science are perhaps the brightest page in the history of our century." [2]

Not less impartial and judicial in his views is Mr. James Bryce, and in grappling squarely with the doctrine of *laissez faire* he says : —

Modern civilization in becoming more complex and refined has become more exacting. It discovers more benefits which the organized power of

[1] *Political Science Quarterly*, Vol. XI, December, 1896, p. 724.
[2] " The Map of Life, Conduct, and Character," by William **Hartpole Lecky**, New York, 1899, pp. 14–15.

government can secure, and grows more anxious to attain them. Men live fast, and are impatient of the slow working of natural laws. The triumphs of physical science have enlarged their desires for comfort, and shown them how many things may be accomplished by the application of collective skill and large funds which are beyond the reach of individual effort.[1]

Ever and anon the steady march of collectivism receives a temporary check. In 1900 Parliament appointed a joint committee of both Houses to investigate it, of which the Earl of Crewe was chairman and Lord Avebury a member. The latter drew up a serious challenge which he published in the *Contemporary Review* for July of that year under the title of "Municipal Trading." His arguments need not be considered here, and upon the whole the effect of the investigation has been wholesome, since there is always the possibility that such a movement will go too far and bring on a reaction. The real advance can only take place as fast as it is advantageous, and any step that works more hardship than it relieves will be and should be prevented.

It is generally believed that collectivism is more pronounced on the Continent than it is in England, and in certain respects this is true, particularly with regard to railroads, but there seems to have been a greater amount of factory and other forms of moral legislation in England. In the United States there is no settled principle, and it is a question of majorities and political influence. But the less favored classes are beginning to learn the power of their ballots and are casting them in increasing numbers for collectivism. But the country which has taken the longest strides in this direction is Australia, for it seems to be true of all the colonies, but is more marked in some than in others. New Zealand leads, but South Australia is not far behind. Mr. Henry D. Lloyd has fully described the movement in New Zealand.[2] It is difficult to find entirely disinterested accounts of this movement in those once far-off countries, but the following extracts from the remarks of Dr. John A. Cockburn, Agent General of South Australia, made at the meeting of the American Academy of Political and Social Science on Oct. 25, 1899, on "The Extension of the Sphere of State

---

[1] "The American Commonwealth," by James Bryce, in two volumes, London and New York, 1888, Vol. II, p. 407.

[2] "Newest England. Notes of a Democratic Traveller in New Zealand, with some Australian Comparisons," by Henry Demarest Lloyd, New York, 1900. See also Fabian Tract, No. 74, London, 1896.

2 o

Activity in South Australia," show that the people of that colony are acting wholly in their own interests and not from the influence of theory. He said : —

I believe the majority of our people oppose the extension of the sphere of state activity, but when practical men are brought face to face with the actual necessities in relation to the settlement of a new country, they throw their theory to the winds and grapple with the actual requirements of the case, for dogma rigidly adhered to is an inveterate foe to progress. . . . There has been one railway in private hands in South Australia, but that within the last few months has been purchased by the state. We find that the railways are nowadays what the main roads were in the past. We find it to the interest of the community to work the railways, and in connection with working the railways, of course there are supplementary avenues of activity which have to be introduced. We have of course extensive workshops in connection with the railways. In these workshops we manufacture all our own locomotives. Whether we shall always continue to manufacture our own locomotives remains to be seen. Of course we want above all things to choose the method attended with the best practical results. We have recently made a batch of locomotives in the state workshops with a view to ascertaining whether the economy of production and the efficiency of the best service is in the hands of the state or in the hands of private individuals. Then, of course, the state is with us an express company which delivers parcels. We do not wait for manufacturers, as is the case in other parts of the world, yet one of the drawbacks in state enterprise is this, that every citizen has a right to know about government business, and if they are not served by the state in what they consider the best possible manner they are apt to ask some very awkward questions of the administration. Therefore, the functions of the state with us have been undertaken with the greatest possible solicitude for the approval of the people.

We have undertaken government workshops and manufacture all our own water pipes. In a dry country like Australia the water supply and irrigation are very important items. A very high grade of pipes is required. We have manufactured these for ourselves. Then, of course, the state owns all telegraphs and telephones, and in connection with the post-office we have a parcels post, which was introduced thirteen or fourteen years ago, and which has worked exceedingly well with us. The water-works are also owned by the state. The government also acts as public trustee, and we are very proud of our public trustee's department. It has been of benefit in many ways. Any one who wishes to leave his estate in unimpeachable hands has only to appoint the public trustee to take charge of it. Most of our hospitals and most of our charitable institutions are also state organizations and under state control.

It is chiefly in our agriculture that the sphere of state activity has been developed. The success of the community and our national welfare depend on the prosperity of the farmer, and, therefore, we adapt our institutions to make his occupation as profitable as possible. If the farmer does well the whole community is prosperous, the doctor gets his fees, the pastor gets his stipend raised, and everybody shares in the general prosperity. So the farmer is, as it were, that part of the community whose welfare we watch with the greatest possible interest. The state, in order to enable the farmer to get the greatest possible return for his labor, inaugurated what is known as the Government Produce Export Depot. We have also established a receiving depot. We take from the farmer and from the fruit grower his produce and send it to the world's markets. Before the state moved in this direction the small farmer or fruit grower was practically unable to reach the markets of the world, even though there was a great demand for his produce, by reason of the high rates for freights and insurance, which would be so high on small parcels that practically they were excluded. So the state stepped in, and by grouping together the little rivulets of produce into one shipment, sends them forward at the lowest possible charges for necessary expenses of transit. The state in this way has been able to bring the world's markets within the reach of the farmer and fruit grower.

The state in undertaking this function is able to insist upon a certain grade of quality. There is nothing more dangerous or more ruinous to those who send produce to a market than to have good produce accompanied by articles of inferior quality. The presence of articles of inferior quality deteriorates the value of the whole shipment. If articles are inferior we have nothing to do with them. No produce is sent unless it receives the government's stamp of approval. After the goods have been received and forwarded by the state, they are received in London by the receiving depot there. The government does not undertake their sale, but it selects corn and cotton brokers and auctioneers of recognized ability, who can be depended upon to make the best possible terms for the consignor and for the seller of the produce. Now, in South Australia, all the farmer has to do when he wishes to send a box of butter, honey, or some sheep abroad, is to write to the Agricultural Department, and if they are approved and forwarded the consignor has nothing more to do but to sit at home and await returns by check. . . .

The government in South Australia is the land owner. The lands belong to the state. We have lately held that it is much better for the state to lease than to sell land. We are now instituting a form of perpetual lease. The state purchases lands for the purpose of placing farmers upon them. The Department of Agriculture also issues a journal, which is called the *Journal of Agriculture and Industry*. This journal is now recognized as a very valuable guide and assistance to all farmers and has a considerable circulation.

I do not think that any government could stand by and witness a number of men out of employment, idly standing all day in the market places because no man will hire them, with hungry wives and children ; so we take the idle men and place them upon the idle lands and assist them in every way to make a settlement. We make advances to them, and it is rather an interesting experiment from the point of view of coöperative settlements. They hold their lands in common. The settlements have turned out very well. Idle hands are idle no longer, but are able to support families.

Of course no farmer can pay a high rate of interest, so we have established a state bank, which lends money to the farmer at 4 per cent interest, whereas previously he had to pay as high as 8, 9, 10, 25, sometimes 50, and even 70 per cent interest. We consider that the farmer should be able to get the money required for making improvements and purchasing machinery, and that he should be placed in a position in which he can keep his farm in good condition; so we have instituted this state bank, which is managed by a board of trustees, who are not responsible to the government, who cannot be removed from office except by very difficult steps, and who, therefore, act independently, and who are to carry on the bank for strict commercial interests. Many farmers are prospering to-day in consequence of this accommodation. The bank has been effective in reducing the rate of interest on mortgages and private loans.

In undertaking these various functions the state has been anxious not in any way to sap private enterprise, on which the prosperity of the community depends. The state has never been accused of interfering in private interests. We have always endeavored to place our toilers in a position in which they can get the best possible reward for their labors. If you bring hope into the life of the farmer, and make him sure of his reward, that his profits will not be taken away from him, then you make him more efficient. Instead of sapping private enterprise we are assisting private enterprise. We are not anxious to organize patriarchal institutions but fraternal ones, wherein men shall be banded together for mutual benefit and by coöperation become a brotherhood through the help of each man in his own particular way, following his own knowledge in the best possible way and receiving aid and guidance from the state." [1]

I have introduced so large a part of Dr. Cockburn's remarks not because they are at all striking or startling, but because they constitute a plain, unbiased statement of the condition of things in South Australia, not intended to defend or advocate the policy pursued, but simply to set it forth as it is. New Zealand would show a still longer step in the same direction, and all the Australian colonies are moving along the same line of the extension of state functions.

Now this universal growth of collectivism *pari passu* with the growth of intelligence is simply the natural and normal integration of functions with the development of social structure. The biological analogy at least holds to that extent. The only instructive analogies are those that relate to the coördination of functions. The state may

[1] Bulletin of the American Academy of Political and Social Science, New Series, No. 10., Philadelphia, Nov. 14, 1899; Publications of the Academy, No. 264, pp. 7–10.

be fairly regarded as the homologue of the brain. The brain represents an almost absolute central control of the bodily functions, at least of its conscious ones. Organic progress has consisted in the steady increase of this control, of the gradual transfer of unconscious functions to the list of conscious ones, until in all the higher animals the cerebral hegemony is complete. Society stands at a much lower stage in this process of development, viz., at that represented by certain animals considered very low in the scale; but the first forms of headship represent the earliest steps in the development of a ganglionic center, while the full-fledged state represents the brain of animals of a somewhat higher type. But the most complete functional integration thus far attained, as, for example, that of New Zealand or Switzerland, still falls far short of the degree of integration of the nervous system of the lowest vertebrates. It is surprising that Herbert Spencer, who of all social philosophers has most fully and ably pointed out these analogies, and who is practically the discoverer of the law of simultaneous differentiation and integration in the organic world, should fail to see that the same law holds in society. He indeed admits the process of differentiation, but virtually denies that of integration. Perhaps it would be more correct to say that he regards social differentiation as the true analogue of organic differentiation, and as something perfectly natural, normal, and proper, while looking upon social integration in this sense as something artificial, pathological, and improper; something to be deplored, combated, and antagonized to the utmost.

If the analogy were, indeed, exact, and if we had to look forward to a future state of social integration as complete as the organic integration of the highest mammals including man, we might take the alarm and either dread the consequences or console ourselves with the reflection that we as individuals will never be permitted to witness it. But aside from the folly of borrowing trouble from such a remote future, there is really no cause for alarm even for our descendants. Spencer has well pointed out the fundamental defect in the analogy, viz., that whereas in the organism it is the whole that is conscious and sentient while the parts are unconscious and insentient, in society it is the parts that are conscious and sentient while the whole is unconscious and insentient. This antithesis reverses the whole process and makes social development consist in steps looking to the benefit of the parts, whereas organic development consists in steps looking to the benefit of the whole. Development everywhere and necessarily results from pressure toward an advantageous end, and it cannot be conceived as moving toward a disadvantageous end. We have already seen that the legitimate effect of the state is to set the individual free, and every step through which we have traced the growth of collectivism has been in the direction of the greater and greater liberation of the individual from all the powers of nature that, left to themselves, tend to enchain him. In the organic process development may be metaphorically said to be in the direction of enslaving the parts, *i.e.*, of subordinating them to the whole for the good of the whole. This works no hardship, for what matter if the unconscious organs, vessels, tissues, and cells are enslaved ? But in the social process the result is the reverse of this. The parts (individuals) that were primarily enslaved are now set free, and every step is in the direction of greater freedom in the exercise of all their faculties.

It is to be observed that the growth of collectivism here sketched has been from the first a struggle with the forces of individualism which was supreme at the outset, and a gradual conquest of this field, much as the individual mind has conquered the field of physical nature, where the primitive forces were originally acting each for itself the same as the unrestrained social forces. It must not therefore be confounded with the various forms of communism that prevail in undeveloped societies, such as the village communities described by Sir Henry Sumner Maine and the North American tribes portrayed by Mr Lewis H. Morgan. Individualists, in resisting this movement, are fond of insisting that instead of social progress it represents a retrograde process toward the stage of primitive communism. This is the same argument used by royalists and monarchists against modern democracy, who used to predict the certain fall of the latter similar to the fall of the Greek and Roman republics. This latter argument has no force now because everybody knows that between modern democracies, which include the monarchies as well as the republics by name, and the ancient republics no comparison is possible and no essential resemblance exists. And yet they are quite as much alike as are the collective systems of the present and communal life of savage and barbaric tribes. There is no . doubt that the latter grew out of the impossibility at that stage of social development of maintaining social existence on the individualistic plan, and signify the triumph of the group sense of self-preservation. This brought into action the Gossenian [1] law, which, under such simple social conditions was easily made to prevail over the Jevonian [2] law, which had scarcely as yet taken an economic form, and was little more than the biologic law of struggle for existence working the destruction of the group and the restriction of the species to a circumscribed habitat.

This Jevonian law came into full force as an economic and sociological principle with the stage of conquest and race amalgamation, the sharp scission of society into classes or castes, the partition of the lands to influential individuals, and the establishment of latifundia and all other forms of private property. It was under this system that all the important arts, industries, and commercial enterprises arose. A strictly business class was formed out of the mesoderm of the metasocial tissues, and under the joint action of all these social classes the development sketched in the last chapter took place. The formation of the state supported by general laws was the first step taken by the collective mind. It checked rapacity but furthered activity. If the Gossenian law governed the collective movement (and this is for the sociological mathematicians to determine) the Jevonian law certainly continued to govern the thus liberated individual activities. It has never ceased to do so even in countries farthest advanced in collectivism. The freer the individual activity the more fully will this law act, and the whole movement may almost be described as the growth of individualism. Collectivism is not therefore the opposite of individualism. It is the failure to see this that makes English collectivism, and Anglo-Saxon collectivism in general, such a paradox. That it should prove that the great Anglo-Saxon race, the embodiment of the principle of free individual initiative, has made the longest strides in the direction of social initiative and social achievement is the marvel of those who ascribe Anglo-Saxon supremacy to this individualistic attribute. These writers, among whom we find Frenchmen such as Demolins, only see half of the truth. The whole truth is that Anglo-Saxon supremacy is due to the ability of that race to see and act upon the

---

[1] " Entwickelung der Gesetze des menschlichen Verkehrs, und der daraus fliessenden Regeln für menschliches Handeln," von Hermann Heinrich Gossen, Braunschweig, 1854, pp. 83–85.

[2] " Theory of Political Economy," by W. Stanley Jevons, London & New York, 1871, Chapters III, IV (see especially pp. 61–69).

principle that while individual initiative can alone accomplish great results, it *must be free,* and that, under the influence of the normal and natural forces of society, and taking the whole of human nature into the account, it cannot be free unless the avenues for its activity be kept open by the power of society at large.   Even the economists are beginning to see that " free competition " in business is a myth unless it be protected from the universal tendency of all competition in nature speedily and surely to end in monopoly.

Social Invention

We have seen that society has already gone far beyond its primitive rôle of mere regulation with a view to antagonizing the natural competitive influences that choke individual activity, exaggerate inequalities, and restrict liberty.   It has achieved in much the same sense that the individual achieves, the chief difference being that it has had to deal with the far more complex and inscrutable social forces.   We have now to note another parallel between individual achievement and social achievement.   We saw in the last chapter that most individual achievement had been due to invention and scientific discovery in the domain of the physical forces.   The parallel consists in the fact that social achievement consists in invention and discovery in the domain of the social forces.   It is still further completed by the circumstance that in both fields all the earlier achievements were empirical.   The social art, upon which Condorcet so frequently lays stress, is thus far mainly an empirical art, and, like the art of pottery, for example, has been the result of a series of separately discovered improvements upon the original invention.   In other words, it has been a growth due to long and repeated experiences, failures, and successes, under the influence of a slowly developing collective consciousness.

As legitimate conclusions from facts furnished by the past and the present belong properly to pure sociology, we may profitably dwell for a few moments upon the principles underlying collective action.   And first of all must it be again insisted that the social forces do not differ from other natural forces except in their complexity and consequent obscurity.   The difficulty in their comprehension due to these causes explains the long empirical stage in the social science.   Until within a few years there has been no investigation in social science such as that which led to the scientific era

in the other departments. The study of society is to-day where
that of physics and chemistry were in the fifteenth century. There
are still those in high seats of learning who deny that there are
social laws in the scientific sense. Those whose business it is to
deal practically and directly with the social forces, legislators, ad-
ministrators, judges, have rarely ever opened a book on sociology.
Is there, indeed, on sociology a book from which they could gather
any useful principles to guide them in the performance of their
duties ? There certainly should be text-books plainly setting forth
these practical principles, and the science should be taught to all
who are at all likely ever to be called upon to perform any of these
high functions.

If we carefully analyze an invention we shall find that it consists
first in recognizing a property or force and secondly in making
material adjustments calculated to cause that property or force to
act in the manner desired by the inventor, presumably to his advantage. He recognizes the property or force as always operative.
The only difference he makes in it is to cause it to act in a certain
way different from the way in which it was acting before he made
his adjustments. If he wishes air or gas of a certain kind to go
into an inclosed space he pumps out the air or gas already there,
establishes a passage, and the other fluid rushes in of itself. We
may say metaphorically that he *induces* it to go where he wants it.
In dealing with animals, while they are often driven and compelled
through fear to go where they are wanted, it is usually found easier
and cheaper in energy expended to induce or attract them by appealing to some want that is easily satisfied, as by showing them a
lump of salt.

Now the desires and wants of men constitute the forces of society,
complicated, as they are in the higher stages, by the directive agent
in all its manifold aspects. Social invention consists in making
such adjustments as will induce men to act in the manner most
advantageous to society. It is possible, as with animals, to drive
them, to force them, to coerce and compel them, but considering the
sensitive organization of the human animal, the knowledge that he
has of the motives of others, the keen sense of justice with which
he is endowed, and the influence which his intelligence gives him to
react upon harsh measures and bring the coercive power into disrepute, if not to cause its overthrow, it is far better, safer, and more

economical, whenever possible, to secure the end through some form of persuasion or inducement. The law of parsimony, as has been pointed out, is a universal law, and can be implicitly relied upon. The social inventor has only to make sure what will constitute a greater gain or marginal advantage and to devise measures that will harmonize this with the social good in order to secure with unerring certainty such a course of action on the part of all affected by the measures as will secure the end sought.

If in the framing of human laws this principle were always carefully studied it would soon be discovered that man is as easily managed by intelligence as, in the last chapter, nature was shown to be. It would be found that mandatory and prohibitory, and indeed penal legislation generally is for the most part unnecessary. That form of legislation, always heretofore and still the predominant type, is very expensive in many ways, but chiefly in causing irritation and reaction, and thus weakening the authority of the state. The day will undoubtedly come when it will be held to be intolerable. It restricts human liberty, of course presumably by liberating other assumed innocent parties whose liberty had been abridged by the offender. But the contention is that only the most obdurate offenders require to have their liberty restricted, since they, too, have wants, and the social inventor should devise means by which such wants shall be spontaneously satisfied through wholly innocuous or even socially beneficial action. This is the principle which I have called "attractive legislation,"[1] and upon which I have sufficiently insisted from a theoretical point of view in other works. I have also shown that it has been acted upon by enlightened states, though only to a limited extent. Most of the examples relate to the collection of revenues, which, from its paramount necessity, is the field in which the keenest collective thinking has been done. As an example in another field may be mentioned the act of Parliament introduced by Sir James Graham in 1843, reducing the working hours of children in factories to half time and requiring that the other half of the day be spent at school. Of this law Mr. Gunton says: —

The attendance of children at school being made an indispensable condition of their employment, tended to secure the aid of parents to enforce the

---

[1] "Dynamic Sociology" (see passages cited in the index); "The Psychic Factors of Civilization," p. 306.

school law. Even those parents who were the most ignorant and indifferent to the education of their children now became very eager to keep them constant in their school attendance, because it was the only means of securing their meager earnings.[1]

Moral purposes are also sometimes secured through the application of this principle, as where commodities regarded as socially injurious are excluded by duties so high as to become prohibitive, or where businesses, such as lotteries, considered immoral, are forbidden to send advertisements through the mails.

One of the features of the South Australian policy outlined by Dr. Cockburn, as quoted above, properly belongs to this class, and special attention should be called to it as belonging to a department in which collective action can secure the most important results. I refer to the " Government Produce Export Depot." It is not so much production as distribution that calls for intelligent collective action. Science and invention under purely individual initiative have rendered production practically unlimited. It is limited only by the difficulties in the way of distribution. By this I mean Social Distribution, as defined in Chapter XIII, and as distinguished from economic distribution. This is an exclusively social problem and can only be solved by social action. It is to-day the most important of all social problems, because its complete solution would accomplish nothing less than the abolition of poverty and want from society. The South Australian government has taken one short step in the direction of the solution of this problem.

Thus one by one are the great achievements of the individual intellect becoming socialized through collective action. The question is being seriously asked why society as a whole, and all mankind from the highest to the lowest, should not profit by the brilliant achievements of the élite of mankind. Inventors and scientific discoverers are generous, and if they could dictate the policy of the world the results would be freely distributed and completely socialized. All they would ask would be a modest competency for themselves and their families and a decent legacy for their heirs. Alas ! many of them never obtain even this. The results are taken up by the great economic world, as, indeed, they should be and must be, if they are ever realized, and society only secures so much as

---

[1] " Wealth and Progress, a Critical Examination of the Labor Problem," by George Gunton, New York, 1887, p. 299.

cannot be prevented from filtering through the economic sieve which is often very fine. The great world movement of socialization is nothing else than the gradual recognition of this by society in its collective capacity, and the tardy, often fitful, inconsistent, and uneven, but yet sure and steady determination ultimately to claim and to have its full share in the achievement of the human race.

SOCIAL APPROPRIATION

It was shown in Chapter III, and more fully in Chapter XIX, that human achievement consists essentially in knowledge — knowledge of what and of how, of things and of ways — which constitutes from the time of its acquisition a perpetual source of all material and spiritual blessings. The products perish, are consumed and enjoyed, but the knowledge insures their unlimited reproduction and multiplication. It is therefore of the utmost importance that this knowledge be preserved. What specially characterizes the historical races is that they have preserved the knowledge bequeathed to them by their predecessors and constantly added to it making the result cumulative. This has also caused progress in these races to go by ratios instead of by increments. It is this knowledge that constitutes the social germ-plasm, and it is its preservation that forms the sociological analogue of the continuity of the germ-plasm. As Weismann says, the germ-plasm is immortal. In much the same sense we may say that in the great trunk line of descent of civilization the social germ-plasm is immortal.

But Weismann is careful to explain that by immortality he only means that the germ-plasm that actually passes on from generation to generation thereby becomes immortal, which imputes no attribute of indestructibility or charmed existence to the germ-plasm itself. In fact it is among the frailest of beings, and not only succumbs quickly to any hostile power, but in the nature of things possesses an ephemeral existence unless it chance to be selected to the great function of continuing life. For every germ thus selected millions necessarily perish. It is much the same with the social germ-plasm, though the analogy here fails as to the principle involved. While the biological germ-plasm is the very bearer of heredity from generation to generation, knowledge, the social germ-plasm, is incapable of hereditary transmission. The apparent failure in the parallel here, however, is due to the tendency to cross the two fields and to apply biological principles to sociology. Organic and social heredity are not the same and cannot be interchanged.

Social heredity consists in the social transmission of this plasm from generation to generation, and this is not a vital but a social process. It consists in planting knowledge into individual minds after they are born. The only way that the social germ-plasm can be continued is by infusing it into the individual. No one is born with the least rudiment of it inherent in his mental constitution. Every one must *acquire* every item of it during life. Cut off any portion of mankind from the main stream of thought and it loses at once all that has been bequeathed to the civilized world at such enormous cost. This knowledge, wrought by toil and struggle, by patience and thought, by genius and skill, and heaped up little by little through ages of time, is the Promethean fire that must never be allowed to go out. There has always been a vague consciousness of this awful responsibility, and this consciousness has grown constantly clearer with time.

The supreme duty of civilized man is therefore obviously to maintain the continuity of the social germ-plasm. It is social self-preservation and is as imperative from the standpoint of society as is life from the standpoint of the individual. It is the life of society. Density of population, the press, means of travel and intercommunication, and the needs of commerce and industry, suffice to insure the general economic and material results of achievement, and to make the knowledge of which it consists generally available in society. But this is not complete social appropriation. This cannot be attained until the mass of mankind shall possess not merely the benefits of achievement but the knowledge itself. This, as any one can see, it never has possessed. Only a very limited number have an idea even of the history of achievement, and as to the knowledge, it is confined to a mere handful. There is, in fact, no one who possesses it all, and there is no need that any one do this. It is so vast that the best informed can have only general acquaintance with it as a whole. But by a careful classification it is possible to reduce it to a scheme that shall not only practically embrace it all but shall be fairly within the power of the ordinary mind to grasp and hold it if presented in the proper way.

The vague social consciousness of which I have spoken of the necessity for the social appropriation of human achievement has worked itself out into a variety of different systems of public *educa-tion*, but so differently have educationalists conceived the problem, and so false have been the greater part of the ideas of mankind as to what constitutes education, that the whole educational movement of the world has consisted in empirically staggering at a confused ideal only dimly and variously formed. While many individuals have formed such ideals and founded institutions for their realiza-tion, and while the church has always conducted educational enter-prises according to its own ideas of what education means, it is after all the state, or society in its collective capacity, that has made the most important advances in this direction. Whatever it has done has been of a more practical character than the efforts of individuals or ecclesiastical bodies. While it cannot be said to have clearly seen that education should consist in the social appropriation of the knowledge that has civilized the world, it has taken long steps toward the realization of this truth. Above all it has acted more than any other interest on the assumption that education is for all, that it is a social need, that its benefits are proportional to its gener-ality. It is now, in the leading countries of the world, extending it to the masses. In France, in Germany, and in the United States, it now reaches the great majority of the members of society. It is true that for the greater number of these the amount of instruction is very small. It does not include any knowledge at all except as incidentally acquired, but it usually puts into the hands of the learner the *tools* with which he may, if so disposed, obtain knowl-edge for himself. The so-called rudiments of an education are this and nothing more. Surely this must always be the first step, but unfortunately it is too often the only one. But in the great cities of the world many other steps are taken, until, in America, for example, the "High Schools" are almost turning out scholars, and certificates from many of them place the holders on the thres-hold of the higher institutions. Then the several American States are rapidly establishing what they call State Universities, some of which already take rank with the older endowed universities. The future of these institutions is hard to predict. It begins to look as if they might ultimately supersede the former. It is certain that they are freer and more democratic than endowed institutions, and while a few of the lesser ones are sometimes somewhat affected by political issues, they are never suspected of being organized for the purpose of creating public opinion on questions supposed to affect vested interests.

In France and Germany nearly all higher education is now socialized, and the state regards public instruction as one of its great functions. England and other countries are slowly working up toward this ideal, and there can be little doubt that the twentieth century will see the complete socialization of education throughout the civilized world. This is as it should be, for it is society that is chiefly interested in the result. It is the recipient of the principal benefits. Moreover, education is the one kind of human enterprise that cannot be brought under the action of the economic law of supply and demand. It cannot be conducted on " business principles." There is no " demand " for education in the economic sense. The child knows nothing of its value, and the parent rarely desires it. Society is the only interest that can be said to demand it, and society must supply its own demand. Those who found educational institutions or promote educational enterprises put themselves in the place of society and assume to speak and act for society, and not for any economic interest.

The action of society in inaugurating and carrying on a great educational system, however defective we may consider that system to be, is undoubtedly the most promising form thus far taken by collective achievement. It means much even now, but for the future it means nothing less than the complete social appropriation of individual achievement which has civilized the world. It is the crowning act in the long list of acts that we have only partially and imperfectly considered, constituting the socialization of achievement.

INDEX

[Figures in heavy type refer to heads.]

Outlines of Sociology

By LESTER F. WARD

Author of " Dynamic Sociology," etc., etc.

Cloth   12mo   **$2.00**

" The work is just what has been needed by the students of social science and by that larger army of those who desire a clear general knowledge of the topic without being obliged to go through massive compendiums of facts, generalizations, and principles. The work has had the rare advantage of being put through the crucible of public delivery and discussion." — *Mail and Express*, New York.

" Among the best of its kind, and sure to be accounted a notable contribution to the great discussion now going on over social subjects." — *Los Angeles Herald.*

" Mr. Ward makes a clear and logical presentation of his subject, and one full of suggestion and broad thought. To the student in search of a guide to the principles of sociology, the book must prove valuable." *Detroit Free Press.*

" This most recent work is marked by the same profound, continuous, and persistent thought, often from an original and somewhat individualized standpoint, yet absolutely scientific and dispassionate, and the same force and terseness of style which mark the pages of the author's first great work ' Dynamic Sociology.' " — *Public Opinion.*

THE MACMILLAN COMPANY

66 FIFTH AVENUE, NEW YORK

The Principles of Sociology

An Analysis of Phenomena of Association and of Social Organization

By FRANKLIN HENRY GIDDINGS, M.A.

Professor of Sociology in Columbia University

Cloth	8vo	$3.00 net

"It is a treatise which will confirm the highest expectations of those who have expected much from this alert observer and virile thinker. Beyond a reasonable doubt, the volume is the ablest and most thoroughly satisfactory treatise on the subject in the English language." — *Literary World.*

"The distinctive merit of the work is that it is neither economics nor history. . . . He has found a new field and devoted his energies to its exploration. . . . The chapters on Social Population and on Social Constitution are among the best in the book. It is here that the method of Professor Giddings shows itself to the best advantage. The problems of anthropology and ethnology are also fully and ably handled. Of the other parts I like best of all the discussion of tradition and of social choices; on these topics he shows the greatest originality. I have not the space to take up these or other doctrines in detail, nor would such work be of much value. A useful book must be read to be understood."
— Professor SIMON N. PATTEN, in *Science.*

The Elements of Sociology

A Text-book for Colleges and Schools

By FRANKLIN HENRY GIDDINGS, M.A.

Professor of Sociology in Columbia University

Cloth	8vo	$1.10 net

"It is thoroughly intelligent, independent, suggestive, and manifests an unaffected enthusiasm for social progress, and on the whole a just and sober apprehension of the conditions and essential features of such progress."
— Professor H. SIDGWICK in *The Economic Journal.*

"Of its extreme interest, its suggestiveness, its helpfulness to readers to whom social questions are important, but who have not time or inclination for special study, we can bear sincere and grateful testimony." — *New York Times.*

"Professor Giddings impresses the reader equally by his independence of judgment and by his thorough mastery of every subject that comes into his view." — *The Churchman.*

THE MACMILLAN COMPANY

66 FIFTH AVENUE, NEW YORK